Blackstone's

Police Opera

Blackstone's

Police Operational Handbook 2016

Police National Legal Database

Editor: Ian Bridges

Consultant Editor: Fraser Sampson

OXFORD
UNIVERSITY PRESS

OXFORD
UNIVERSITY PRESS

Great Clarendon Street, Oxford, OX2 6DP,
United Kingdom

Oxford University Press is a department of the University of Oxford.
It furthers the University's objective of excellence in research, scholarship,
and education by publishing worldwide. Oxford is a registered trade mark of
Oxford University Press in the UK and in certain other countries

First Edition published in 2006
Tenth Edition published in 2015

Impression: 1

Published in the United States of America by Oxford University Press
198 Madison Avenue, New York, NY 10016, United States of America

British Library Cataloguing in Publication Data
Data available

Library of Congress Control Number: 2015943758

ISBN 978–0–19–874340–8

Printed in Great Britain by
Ashford Colour Press Ltd, Gosport, Hampshire

Preface

This is the tenth edition of the *Blackstone's Police Operational Handbook*, which has been specifically designed to meet the needs of the operational police officer, police community support officer, special constable, or other practitioner who has to interpret and apply the criminal law within our community.

Due to the phenomenal success of previous editions and the positive comments that we have received it is apparent that the format and contents of the handbook are meeting the needs of our readers and proving to be an invaluable addition to the police officer's 'tool kit'.

Formulated and written by staff from the Police National Legal Database (PNLD) <http://www.pnld.co.uk>, the book covers a wide range of offences, and clearly explains and interprets the relevant legislation. It follows the style of the database by providing the wording of the offences, points to prove, meanings, explanatory notes, relevant cases, and practical considerations. In order to assist the officer further, the law/guidance notes are all presented in a 'bullet point', easy-to-understand format; thus at a glance, a quick and informed decision can be made in a host of everyday policing situations.

Although every effort has been made to include as many 'commonly dealt with offences' as possible, the size of the handbook dictates how many offences can be included. However, the number and variety of offences given within the areas of crime, assaults, drugs, sexual offences, public disorder, football, firearms, road traffic, licensing, and PACE powers and procedures, together with the guidance chapters and useful appendices, should be more than sufficient to cover most eventualities.

The handbook is fully up to date as of 1 June 2015 and includes the many changes made to the criminal law from: the Criminal Justice and Courts Act 2015, which gave new offences involving disqualified drivers by including causing death or serious injury while driving on a road, making 'revenge porn' an offence by disclosing private sexual photographs/films with intent to cause distress, amending the law on: meeting a child following sexual grooming now only requiring one or more occasions, possessing extreme pornographic images (increased type of images), malicious communication offences are now either way offences, and a three-year prosecutions time limit for the s 127 communications offence; the Serious Crime Act 2015 now makes it an offence to possess a paedophile manual, it adds 'drugs related activity' to gang injunctions, creates warrant search and seizure powers for drug cutting agents, includes 'psychological' injury to the child cruelty and 'prohibited drug' to the suffocation of infant offences, makes the loiter or solicit for prostitution offence now only applicable to those aged 18 or over, the child prostitution or pornography offences now relate to 'sexual exploitation of a child'; the Deregulation Act 2015 amends road traffic law regarding: insurance certificates, exemptions that apply to vehicles used in emergency for NHS, speed limits and off-road motoring events, drink/drug driving procedures, and repeals most offences under the 1847 Act, s 28; the Anti-social Behaviour, Crime and Policing Act 2014 creates new laws on: injunctions to prevent nuisance and annoyance, criminal behaviour orders, dispersal powers, community protection notices, public spaces protection orders, and further increases PCSO powers, and repeals: ASBOs, drink banning orders, closure of premises (drugs or disorder/nuisance), dispersal of groups and directions to persons (disorder); the Finance Act 2014 omits displaying of vehicle excise or trade licence disc offences; the Immigration Act 2014 amends 'relevant duty of care' for corporate manslaughter; the Children and Families Act 2014 amends the child abduction offence; the Crime and Courts Act 2013 creates the new offences of driving or in charge of a motor vehicle with concentration of specified controlled drugs being above specified limit; the Legal Aid, Sentencing and Punishment of Offenders Act 2012 removed the limit on 'Level 5' or 'statutory maximum' fines at a magistrates' court; together with other legislative changes, including PACE Code A, case updates, and new HO/MOJ Circulars guidance.

Officers are required to know what offences are indictable or either way for their search or arrest powers—the mode of trial icons (within each offence) provided in the book give this important information.

Whilst every care has been taken to ensure that the contents of this handbook are accurate, neither the publisher nor the authors can accept any responsibility for any action taken, or not taken, on the basis of the information contained within this handbook.

Please email <police.uk@oup.com> with any comments or queries.

Ian Bridges

Editor

June 2015

Acknowledgements

The Police National Legal Database (PNLD) (<http://www.pnld.co.uk>) is a Charitable Incorporated Organisation (CIO)—registered charity No 1159767. PNLD CIO is subscribed to and well known by all police forces in England and Wales, the Crown Prosecution Service, and other recognised organisations from within the criminal justice system.

The handbook, which is a natural development from our premier electronic database, would not have been created without the foresight and determination of Heather Croft (former Business Director), the hard work of Ian Bridges (Legal Adviser), and the support and guidance from staff at the Oxford University Press and Fraser Sampson (Consultant Editor).

Thanks are also extended to the PNLD legal advisers who have contributed to the production of the *Blackstone's Police Operational Handbook*.

Acknowledgement

Contents

Contents

Contents

Contents

Contents

Contents

Tables of Cases

Tables of Cases

Tables of Cases

Tables of Cases

Tables of Cases

Tables of Cases

European Court of Human Rights

Tables of Statutes

Tables of Statutes

Tables of Statutes

Statutory Instruments

Tables of Statutes

Table of Conventions

Abbreviations

A-G	Attorney-General
ACPO	Association of Chief Police Officers (see **NPCC**)
ANPR	Automatic Number Plate Recognition (system/camera)
AOABH	Assault Occasioning Actual Bodily Harm
ASBO	Anti-Social Behaviour Order
BB gun	Ball Bearing gun
BS	British Standard
BTP	British Transport Police
CBO	Criminal Behaviour Order
CC	Chief Constable or County Court
CCTV	Closed-circuit television
CED	Conducted Energy Device
CEO	Chief Executive Officer
CEOP	Child Exploitation and On-line Protection Centre
CIE	Continuous Insurance Enforcement
CJ	Criminal Justice
CJA	Criminal Justice Act
COP	Code of Practice
CPC	Certificate of Professional Competence
CPN	Community Protection Notice
CPR	Cardiopulmonary Resuscitation
CPS	Crown Prosecution Service
CRB	Criminal Records Bureau
CSE	Child Sexual Exploitation
CS spray	Named after the initials of the inventors—Corson and Staughton
CSO	*see* PCSO
DBO	Drink Banning Order
DBS	Disclosure and Barring Service (formerly ISA)
DC	Divisional Court
DEFRA	Department for Environment, Food and Rural Affairs
DNA	Deoxyribonucleic acid
DPP	Director of Public Prosecutions
DSA	Driving Standards Agency (now DVSA)
DVLA	Driver and Vehicle Licensing Agency
DVPN	Domestic Violence Protection Notice

Abbreviations

DVSA	Driver and Vehicle Standards Agency
ECHR	European Convention on Human Rights
ECtHR	European Court of Human Rights
EEA	European Economic Area
EPO	Emergency Protection Order
EU	European Union
FA	Football Association
FMU	Forced Marriage Unit
FPN	Fixed Penalty Notice
GB	Great Britain
GBH	Grievous Bodily Harm
GHB	Gamma-hydroxybutrate
GV	Goods Vehicle
HGV	Heavy Goods Vehicle
HIV	Human Immunodeficiency Virus
HL	House of Lords
HMCTS	Her Majesty's Courts and Tribunal Service
HMRC	Her Majesty's Revenue & Customs
HOC	Home Office Circular
HSE	Health and Safety Executive
IPCC	Independent Police Complaints Commission
ISA	Independent Safeguarding Authority (now DBS – above)
LA	Local Authority
MAPPA	Multi-Agency Public Protection Agreements
MASH	Multi-Agency Safeguarding Hubs
MC	Magistrates' Court
MCA	Magistrates' Courts Act
MIB	Motor Insurers' Bureau
MOD	Ministry of Defence
MOJ	Ministry of Justice
NAFIS	National Automated Fingerprint Identification System
NCA	National Crime Agency
NDNAD	National DNA Database
NHS	National Health Service
NIP	Notice of Intended Prosecution
NPCC	National Police Chiefs' Council (formerly **ACPO**)
NPS	New Psychoactive Substances

NPT	Neighbourhood Policing Team
OAPA	Offences Against the Person Act 1861
OFCOM	Office of Communications
OPL	Over the Prescribed Limit
PACE	Police and Criminal Evidence Act 1984
PCSO	Police Community Support Officer
PCV	Passenger Carrying Vehicle
PNC	Police National Computer
PND	Penalty Notices for Disorder/Police National Database
PND-E	Penalty Notices for Disorder—Education option
POA	Public Order Act 1986
PSPO	Public Spaces Protection Order
PSV	Public Service Vehicle
QBD	Queens Bench Division
RNID	Royal National Institute for Deaf People
RTC	Road Traffic Collision
SC	Supreme Court
SCGC	Self-Contained Gas Cartridge system
SI	Statutory Instrument
SIO	Senior Investigating Officer
SORN	Statutory Off Road Notification
TFPN	Traffic Fixed Penalty Notice
TW	Traffic Warden
TWOC	Taking a Conveyance without Owner's Consent
UK	United Kingdom
UKBA	UK Border Agency
UKMPB	UK Missing Persons Bureau
UKSC	United Kingdom Supreme Court
VDRS	Vehicle Defect Rectification Scheme
VEL	Vehicle Excise Licence
VED	Vehicle Excise Duty
VIPER	Video Identification Parade Electronic Recording
VOSA	Vehicle and Operator Services Agency (now DVSA)
VPS	Victim Personal Statement
YOI	Young Offenders' Institution
YOT	Youth Offending Team

Icons List

SSS   **Stop, search, and seize powers** under the Police and Criminal Evidence Act 1984, s 1 **or** stop, search, and seize powers under a statutory authority given within that chapter.

E&S   **Entry and search powers** under the Police and Criminal Evidence Act 1984, ss 17, 18, and 32.

PND   **Penalty Notices for Disorder offences** under the Criminal Justice and Police Act 2001, s 1.

TFPN   **Traffic Fixed Penalty Notices** under the Road Traffic Offenders Act 1988.

RRA   **Racially or Religiously Aggravated offences** under the Crime and Disorder Act 1998, ss 28–32.

CHAR   **Offences where evidence of bad character can be introduced** under the Criminal Justice Act 2003, s 103.

TRIG   **Trigger offences**—when police can test (request to take samples) for presence of Class A drugs, under the Criminal Justice and Court Services Act 2000, Sch 6.

PCSO   **Instances/offences when PCSOs can use their standard powers** (or discretionary power(s) if Chief Constable of the force concerned has designated the power(s) in question to PCSOs), under the Police Reform Act 2002.

Mode of trial
Indictable, either way, or summary.

Prosecution time limit
The time limit allowed for submission of the file (laying of the information).

Penalty
Maximum sentence allowed by law.

Chapter 1

Introduction

1.1 **Human Rights**

The Human Rights Act 1998 affects operational policing, legislation, court decisions and encompasses the fundamental rights and freedoms contained in the ECHR; this is illustrated in the following summarised sections relating to the police and criminal justice system:

Section 2

Requires a court to take account of the opinions/decisions of the ECtHR, the Commission, or Committee of Ministers when determining a question relating to a **Convention right**.

Section 3

Demands that all UK legislation must be construed and given effect in such a way as to be compatible with Convention rights.

Section 4

Permits the Supreme Court, High Court, or Court of Appeal to make a declaration of incompatibility on any question of UK law.

Section 6

Makes it unlawful for a **public authority** to act in a way incompatible with a Convention right. This includes a failure to act.

Section 7

Provides for an aggrieved party to take proceedings where a public authority has breached (or proposes to breach) s 6, but only if that person is (or would be) a victim of the unlawful act.

Section 8

Empowers a court to grant such remedy or **relief** within its powers as it considers just and appropriate.

Section 11

Preserves any other right or freedom enjoyed under UK law.

Meanings

Convention Right

Means the following rights and freedoms given in **Schedule 1**:
- Articles 2 to 12 and 14 of the **Convention**;
- Articles 1 to 3 of the First **Protocol**;
- Article 1 of the Thirteenth Protocol.

Public authority

This includes:
- a court or tribunal;
- any person (eg a police officer) whose functions are of a public nature.

Relief

Includes an award of damages or payment of compensation given through the civil courts, such as the county court or the High Court.

Convention

Means the Convention for the Protection of Human Rights and Fundamental Freedoms, agreed by the Council of Europe at Rome on 4 November 1950 as it has effect for the time being in relation to the UK.

Protocol

Means a protocol to the Convention which the UK has ratified or has signed with a view to ratification.

Schedule 1—Articles/Protocols

Article 2—Right to life

This right shall be protected by law. No one shall be deprived of life intentionally. Deprivation of life shall not be regarded as being in contravention of this Article if force is used, being no more than absolutely necessary, in order to—
- defend from unlawful violence;
- effect a lawful arrest;
- prevent the escape of a person lawfully detained;
- perform a lawful action to quell a riot or insurrection.

Article 3—Prohibition of torture

No one shall be subjected to torture or to inhuman or degrading treatment or punishment.

Article 4—Prohibition of slavery and forced labour

No one shall be held in slavery or servitude or be required to perform forced or compulsory labour.

Article 5—Right to liberty and security

No one shall be deprived of these rights save in the following cases and in accordance with a procedure prescribed by law—
- lawful detention (after conviction) by a competent court;

- lawful arrest or detention for failing to comply with the lawful order of a court or in order to secure the fulfilment of any obligation prescribed by law;
- lawful arrest or detention for the purpose of bringing the person before the competent legal authority on reasonable suspicion of having committed an offence or when it is reasonably considered necessary to prevent committing an offence or fleeing after having done so;
- detention of a minor by lawful order for the purpose of educational supervision or lawful detention for the purpose of bringing before the competent legal authority;
- lawful detention for the prevention of the spreading of infectious diseases, of persons of unsound mind, alcoholics or drug addicts, or vagrants;
- lawful arrest or detention to prevent unauthorised entry into the country or with a view to deportation or extradition.

Article 5 also deals with:
- promptly being informed as to the reason for arrest/charge;
- entitlement to trial within a reasonable time or release pending trial;
- entitlement to take proceedings for unlawful detention and the right to compensation in these instances.

Article 6—Right to a fair trial

Everyone is entitled to a fair and public hearing within a reasonable time by an independent and impartial tribunal established by law. Protection shall be given against publicity (for all or part of the trial) in the interests of: morals, public order, national security, juveniles, the private lives of the parties, or if it would prejudice the interests of justice.

Furthermore, everyone charged with a criminal offence shall—
- be presumed innocent until proved guilty according to law;
- be informed promptly, in a language which they understand, of the detail, nature, and cause of the accusation against them;
- have adequate time and facilities for the preparation of their defence;
- be allowed to defend themselves in person or through legal assistance of their choosing or be provided with free legal assistance (if insufficient funds) when the interests of justice so require;
- be allowed to produce/examine witnesses for/against them;
- have the free assistance of an interpreter if they cannot understand or speak the language used in court.

Article 7—No punishment without law

No one shall be found guilty of a criminal offence arising out of actions which at the time were not criminal, neither shall a heavier penalty be imposed.

Article 8—Right to respect private/family life

Everyone has the right to respect for their private and family life, home, and correspondence, except where a public authority acts in accordance with the law and it is necessary in a democratic society in the interests of national security, public safety, or the economic well-being of the country, for the prevention of disorder or crime, for the protection of health or morals, or for the protection of the rights and freedoms of others.

Article 9—Freedom of thought, conscience, and religion

Everyone has this right, including the freedom to change their religion or belief. These rights can be limited in certain circumstances.

Article 10—Freedom of expression

Everyone has the right to hold opinions and express their views either on their own or in a group without interference by a public authority. These rights can only be restricted in specified circumstances.

Article 11—Freedom of assembly and association

Everyone has the right to assemble with other people in a peaceful way, to associate with other people, including the right to form and join trade unions for the protection of their interests.

These rights may be restricted, but only in specified circumstances.

Article 12—Right to marry

Men and women of marriageable age have the right to marry and to found a family, according to the national laws governing the exercise of this right.

Article 14—Prohibition of discrimination

The enjoyment of the rights and freedoms set forth in this Convention shall be secured without discrimination on any ground such as sex, race, colour, language, religion, political or other opinion, national or social origin, association with a national minority, property, birth, or other status.

1st Protocol—Article 1 Protection of property, entitled to peaceful enjoyment of possessions

1st Protocol—Article 2 Right to education

1st Protocol—Article 3 Right to free elections

13th Protocol—Article 1 Abolition of the death penalty

Explanatory notes

- Examples of public authorities include: central and local government, the police, including police and crime commissioners, UK Border Agency, prisons, courts, tribunals, and the core public activities of private utilities companies that were once publicly owned.
- Section 7(8) stipulates that nothing in the 1998 Act creates a criminal offence.
- A criminal trial judge does not have the power to award damages for an alleged breach of a Convention right.
- Infringement of an individual's human rights will be open to examination in every criminal trial, civil or care proceedings, and tribunals.

Related cases

Austin v UK [2012] Crim LR 544, ECtHR Detaining people during a demonstration was not necessarily a breach of Art 5 (see **2.6.1** for details).

R (on the application of Saunders) v IPCC [2008] EWHC 2372 (Admin), QBD Article 2 imposes a duty to investigate adequately a death resulting from the actions of police officers. The IPCC were investigating a fatal shooting by the police and no steps were taken to prevent officers conferring prior to giving their first accounts. Held: that collaboration during the production of witness statements did not breach the Art 2 duty. However, this practice was criticised, particularly since the defence provided by s 3 Criminal Law Act 1967 (see **1.2.1**) is personal to the individual officer as to what they honestly believed at the time.

Osman v UK [1998] 29 EHRR 245, ECtHR The court must be satisfied that the authorities knew, or ought to have been aware, of the existence of a real and immediate risk to the life of an identified individual, from the criminal acts of a third party. Failure to take action within the ambit of their powers which reasonably might be expected to avoid the risk meant the positive obligation under Art 2 would be violated.

R (on the application of Bennett) v HM Coroner for Inner South London [2006] EWHC 196 (Admin), QBD If a police officer reasonably decides to use lethal force within the law of self-defence or s 3 (see **1.2.1**), then the reasonableness has to be decided on the facts which the user of the force honestly believed to exist and an objective test as to whether they had reasonable grounds for that belief.

Practical considerations

- Section 6, makes it unlawful for police officers to act in a way which is incompatible with a Convention right. In order to ensure compliance with this requirement, officers should make themselves familiar with these 'rights' which have been incorporated into this legislation.
- The proportionality and necessity test asks 'were the measures taken **necessary** in a democratic society and in **proportion** to the ultimate objective?'. This test should always be borne in mind by a police officer when dealing with an incident, members of the public, or an individual (eg is the force being used proportionate and necessary to prevent disorder, protect life/property, or deal with offenders).
- This test is reflected in the statutory power of arrest (see **12.2**)—unless an officer can show that arrest was **necessary** (eg there was no alternative) then the arrest power cannot be used.
- Before using their powers a police officer should consider this test in their decision-making process and ask themselves—
  - ✦ What is the objective to be achieved?
  - ✦ Is it urgent or (if desirable) could it be delayed?
  - ✦ If action is needed now what are the alternative means of dealing with this incident/individual?

+ Is the proposed action proportionate to the intended aim and the means to be used?
+ Can the least intrusive means be deployed?
+ If not, does a lawful power exist?

- The use of force must always be justified and reasonable otherwise an assault will be committed and any action taken could be rendered unlawful (see **1.2.1**).
- Where excessive force is used there is the possibility of a breach of Art 3 (inhuman or degrading treatment).
- If force is used disproportionately, this may amount to a breach of Art 8, as this Art guarantees not just the right to privacy, but also the right to physical integrity—the right not to be hurt in an arbitrary or unjustifiable way.
- There must be some objective justification for the decision or action taken.
- An important point, often overlooked, is the need to strike a proper balance between the interests and rights of the community at large as well as considering the rights of the individual.
- Lawful interference with an individual's human rights, especially depriving them of these rights, must be necessary and proportionate to the aim required to be achieved (eg lawful arrest/detention of a suspect meets the legitimate aim for the prevention and detection of crime).
- Always consider whether the aim can be met with minimal impact on the rights of the suspect and any other person likely to be affected.
- Article 15 allows governments to 'derogate' from the Convention in time of war or other public emergency threatening the life of the nation.

Links to alternative subjects and offences

1.2 Lawful Authorities—Use of Force

If a police officer uses force, this must be justified and reasonable and be based on a lawful authority—otherwise it will be an assault and would therefore become an unlawful act.

Statute, common law, and human rights set out the circumstances in which the use of force will be lawful, but each case will be decided upon its own peculiar facts.

Statute

Criminal Law Act 1967

(1) A person may use such **force** as is **reasonable** in the circumstances in the prevention of **crime**, or in effecting or assisting in the lawful arrest of offenders or suspected offenders or of persons unlawfully at large.

(2) Subsection (1) above shall replace the rules of the common law on the question when force used for a purpose mentioned in the subsection is justified by that purpose.

Criminal Law Act 1967, s 3

Police and Criminal Evidence Act 1984

Where any provision of this Act—

(a) confers a **power** on a **constable**; and

(b) does not provide that the power may only be exercised with the consent of some person, other than a police officer,

the officer may use **reasonable force**, if necessary, in the exercise of the power.

Police and Criminal Evidence Act 1984, s 117

Criminal Justice and Immigration Act 2008

(1) This section applies where in proceedings for an offence—

(a) an issue arises as to whether a person charged with the offence ('D') is entitled to rely on a defence within subsection (2), and

(b) the question arises whether the **degree of force used** by D against a person ('V') was reasonable in the circumstances.

(2) The defences are—

(a) the common law defence of **self-defence**;

(aa) the common law defence of defence of property; and

(b) the defences provided by section 3(1) of the Criminal Law Act 1967 (use of force in prevention of crime or making arrest).

(3) The question whether the degree of force used by D was reasonable in the circumstances is to be decided by reference to the circumstances as D believed them to be, and subsections (4) to (8) also apply in connection with deciding that question.

(4) If D claims to have held a particular belief as regards the existence of any circumstances—
   (a) the reasonableness or otherwise of that belief is relevant to the question whether D genuinely held it; but
   (b) if it is determined that D did genuinely hold it, D is entitled to rely on it for the purposes of subsection (3), whether or not—
      (i) it was mistaken, or
      (ii) (if it was mistaken) the mistake was a reasonable one to have made.

(5) But subsection (4)(b) does not enable D to rely on any mistaken belief attributable to intoxication that was voluntarily induced.

(5A) In a **householder case**, the degree of force used by D is not to be regarded as having been reasonable in the circumstances as D believed them to be if it was grossly disproportionate in those circumstances.

(6) In a case other than a householder case, the degree of force used by D is not to be regarded as having been reasonable in the circumstances as D believed them to be if it was disproportionate in those circumstances.

(6A) In deciding the question mentioned in subsection (3), a possibility that D could have retreated is to be considered (so far as relevant) as a factor to be taken into account, rather than as giving rise to a duty to retreat.

(7) In deciding the question mentioned in subsection (3) the following considerations are to be taken into account (so far as relevant in the circumstances of the case)—
   (a) that a person acting for a **legitimate purpose** may not be able to weigh to a nicety the exact measure of any necessary action; and
   (b) that evidence of a person's having only done what the person honestly and instinctively thought was necessary for a legitimate purpose constitutes strong evidence that only reasonable action was taken by that person for that purpose.

(8) Subsections (6A) and (7) are not to be read as preventing other matters from being taken into account where they are relevant to deciding the question mentioned in subsection (3).

(8A) For the purposes of this section a **householder case** is a case where—
   (a) the defence concerned is the common law defence of self-defence;
   (b) the force concerned is force used by D while in or partly in a **building**, or part of a building, that is a dwelling or is forces accommodation (or is both);
   (c) D is not a trespasser at the time the force is used; and
   (d) at that time D believed V to be in, or entering, the building or part as a trespasser.

(8B) Where—
   (a) a part of a building is a dwelling where D dwells;
   (b) another part of the building is a place of work for D or another person who dwells in the first part; and
   (c) that other part is internally accessible from the first part,

that other part, and any internal means of access between the two parts, are each treated for the purposes of subsection (8A) as a part of a building that is a dwelling.

(8C) [*Relates to 'forces accommodation' under Armed Forces Act 2006, s 96.*]

(8D) Subsections (4) and (5) apply for the purposes of subsection (8A)(d) as they apply for the purposes of subsection (3).

(8E) The fact that a person derives title from a trespasser, or has the permission of a trespasser, does not prevent the person from being a trespasser for the purposes of subsection (8A).

(8F) In subsections (8A) to (8C) **building** includes a vehicle or vessel.

(9) This section, except so far as making different provision for householder cases, is intended to clarify the operation of the existing defences mentioned in subsection (2).

(10) In this section—
  (a) '**legitimate purpose**' means—
      (i) the purpose of **self-defence** under the common law,
     (ia) the purpose of defence of property under the common law, or
     (ii) the prevention of crime or effecting or assisting in the lawful arrest of persons mentioned in the provisions referred to in subsection (2)(b);
  (b) references to **self-defence** include acting in defence of another person; and
  (c) references to the **degree of force used** are to the type and amount of force used.

Criminal Justice and Immigration Act 2008, s 76

Explanatory notes

- The Criminal Law Act 1967, s 3 allows the use of reasonable force in the prevention of crime or making a lawful arrest, and applies to any person. It also provides a defence when the force is used against an innocent third party, to prevent crime by another (*R v Hichens* [2011] EWCA Crim 1626). '**Crime**' does not cover crimes recognised as against international law; it only refers to crimes committed against domestic law either by statute or judicial decision (*R v Jones and others; Ayliffe & others v DPP, Swain v DPP* [2006] UKHL 16) (see **4.4**).
- Whereas s 117 of PACE relates to the use of **reasonable force** by a police officer whilst exercising their PACE powers (see **Chapter 12**).
- The Criminal Justice Act 2008, s 76 provides a statutory test as to using reasonable force for self-defence and defence of property at common law, preventing crime, or making an arrest. This does not alter common law and is not a complete statement of the law, but it does set out the basic principles (*R v Keane and McGrath* [2010] EWCA Crim 2514, CA). MOJ Circular 2/2013 deals with the use of force in self defence against intruders in a person's home.

Common Law

- Whether force used in defence of self or property, preventing crime, or in making an arrest is reasonable or excessive will be determined by the court taking into account all the circumstances. Consider the words of Lord Morris in *Palmer v R* [1971] AC 814, HL which emphasise the difficulties faced by a person confronted by an intruder or in taking any defensive action against attack:

'If there has been an attack so that defence is reasonably necessary, it will be recognised that a person defending himself cannot weigh to a nicety the exact measure of his defensive action. If the jury thought that in a moment of unexpected anguish a person attacked had only done what he honestly and instinctively thought necessary, that would be the most potent evidence that only reasonable defensive action had been taken.'

- Although this area of law is addressed by statute (above), the wider issues of self-defence under common law may still be relevant (see **2.1.2**).

Human rights

- In addition, under the provisions of the ECHR (see **1.1**), a further dimension in respect of the necessity and proportionality must be considered alongside the common law or statutory powers.
- Apart from using no more force than is absolutely necessary, considering proportionality will bring other factors into the equation, such as whether the force used is—
  - ♦ proportionate to the wrong that it seeks to avoid or the harm it seeks to prevent;
  - ♦ the least intrusive or damaging option available at the time.
- Striking a fair balance between the rights of the individual and the interests/rights of the community at large must be carefully considered.
- Any limited breaching of an individual's human rights must be both necessary and proportionate to the legitimate aim to be pursued (eg the lawful arrest or detention of that person is to pursue the legitimate aim of the prevention and detection of crime). Note, however, that certain Articles such as Art 3 cannot be lawfully breached.
- Therefore, any use of powers to cause inhuman or degrading treatment may amount to a breach—words alone may contribute to the demeaning treatment (eg of prisoners), and under extreme circumstances the use of words alone may suffice.
- If force is not used proportionately, then this may amount to a breach of various Articles of the ECHR (see **1.1** for details)—
  - ♦ Article 2: Use of lethal force, unless the level of force used was strictly proportionate to the lawful aim pursued;
  - ♦ Article 3: If excessive force is used—inhuman or degrading treatment;
  - ♦ Article 8: Guarantees not only the right to privacy/family life, but also the right not to be hurt in an arbitrary or unjustifiable way.

Practical considerations

- Police officers should choose the most reasonable, proportionate option available to them after taking the person(s)/group behaviour, circumstances, and other factors into account.
- Force used by an officer at an incident must be justified. When preparing your evidence state what the situation was like upon your arrival, the attitude of the individual(s)/group when they were approached, and what means were used (or attempted) to control the situation.
- Consider the ACPO (now NPCC) 2010 Manual of Guidance on Keeping the Peace which provides updated guidance on public order policing, planning and deployment, structure of command, communication, and tactical options.
- Some matters to consider when dealing with a public order situation would be the gathering of information and intelligence, in order to make a more effective threat assessment, then decide on the response options that are available, before deployment, in order to deal with the incident.

Links to alternative subjects and offences

1.3 **Managing Crime Scenes**

Anybody asked to protect/guard a crime scene must ensure that they are fully briefed about the circumstances of the offence being investigated.

The primary role (and responsibility) of managing a crime scene is to—
• protect the scene from contamination by others; and
• preserve the integrity of everything which could be used as evidence.

Protecting the crime scene

The extent of the scene—
• needs to be established; with the perimeter clearly marked with tape—denoting that it is a crime scene (remembering that is always easier to reduce the size than expand it later);
• the area needs to be secure and effectively cordoned off;
• if the scene is insecure and problems arise in trying to maintain a sterile scene, then assistance should be provided from the enquiry team.

Explanatory notes

Cordon off a crime scene

• When investigating crime, the police do not have a right to restrict movement on private land. However, in the circumstances of one case (wounding in a private shopping mall), the police were held to have been entitled to assume consent to cordon off the crime scene (*DPP v Morrison* [2003] EWHC 683, HC).
• Sections 33–36 of the Terrorism Act 2000 relates to police powers to cordon off an area for a terrorist investigation—for example to carry out a meticulous search for evidence in the wake of a bomb blast.

Maintaining a scene log

An accurate log must be contemporaneously recorded providing—
• a chronological report of any matters of note;
• full details of all authorised people attending, including time/date entering or leaving the scene;
• details/description of any person taking an unusual interest in the area of the crime (together with any vehicle used);
• any suspicious activities in or around the scene should be brought to the attention of the enquiry team as soon as possible.

Managing the scene

A person performing this role must be briefed as to—
• preventing any unauthorised access;
• preventing access to people who are not wearing protective suits;
• updating the SIO or scene manager with any significant matters or developments;
• what can and cannot be said to people.

Dealing with the media

Anyone protecting the scene of a crime must—

- be aware that the media deploys aerial drones to film crime scenes and police activity; drones can also pick up and record conversations. The Civil Aviation Authority prohibits the flying of remote-controlled drones within 150m of a built-up area or 50m of a person, vehicle or structure;
- be mindful of their appearance or comments made as they may be filmed or quoted by the media;
- avoid being seen smoking, chewing gum, laughing or other behaviour that might be regarded as inappropriate;
- prevent journalists from breaching the cordon;
- avoid restricting journalists from taking pictures of the scene or talking to members of the public who may be present as long as they remain outside the cordon (the editor will be responsible for determining which pictures are used and details included);
- not offer opinions or views to members of the press. Any enquiries should be directed to the press office.

Preserving the integrity of exhibits

Preservation of a crime scene is of paramount importance in order to ensure that evidence is recovered and its integrity maintained.

Consideration should always be given to—

- weather conditions;
- type of surface;
- visible evidence (eg fingerprints, blood, shoe marks, property);
- other matters (eg Have repairs been carried out? Will the forensic evidence be of any value?).

Any evidential prints/marks or objects that are found outside must be covered in order to protect them from the elements.

Make sure a contact telephone number for the victim is included with the details for the 'scenes of crime officer'.

Fingerprints

- Smooth, clean, and dry surfaces provide the best opportunity for finding and recovering fingerprints. Ensure such items/areas are preserved for examination by the 'scenes of crime officer'.
- Recover removable items found outside and place them against an internal wall to dry. Wet items should not be placed against radiators.
- Any pieces of paper, envelopes, or bin liners left by the offender(s) are often a good source of fingerprints.
- Fingerprints from scenes of crime can now be searched nationally on the National Automated Fingerprint Identification System (NAFIS).
- Details of any genuine suspects should be given to either the attending 'scenes of crime officer' or to the Fingerprint Bureau (eg suspect's name, date of birth, and CRB details, if known).

DNA

- DNA can be present in bloodstains and in saliva. Consequently police officers should be mindful that this can be present in discarded chewing gum, drink cans or bottles, and cigarette ends.
- DNA can also be recovered from saliva, hair, and skin (dandruff) left in masks or balaclavas, or from the handles of tools. Also, semen or other body fluids in sexual offences.
- The Home Office are the custodians of the national DNA Database (NDNAD) which collates two profile types of DNA that are—
  ✦ left at the scene of the crime by the offender—'Scene Samples';
  ✦ of people arrested and charged, or cautioned with a recordable offence—'CJ Samples' (PACE samples).
- Ensure that a DNA CJ sample is obtained from all people who are arrested for a 'recordable offence'.

Shoes

- Shoe marks found at the scene should be preserved (they must show some pattern detail to be of any evidential value). In this regard consider shoes worn by all burglary suspects.
- Surfaces where footwear marks might be present, but not immediately obvious (eg windowsills, linoleum, work surfaces), the mark may be revealed by techniques used by 'scenes of crime officers'.
- Some forces maintain a computerised database of shoes' marks and offenders' shoe impressions.

Glass

- Glass can rarely be of strong evidential value, but can be corroborative.
- Consider calling a 'scenes of crime officer' to serious crime scenes where a suspect is in custody, before glass is cleared away.
- Consider also combing a suspect's hair, and retaining clothing and shoes for traces of glass as soon as they arrive in custody.

Other items

- Fibres, paint, tool, and glove mark evidence can also connect an individual to a scene.

Forensic procedure

- Evidential items should be placed in brown paper bags, sealed, labelled, and continuity maintained.
- Remember special packaging requirements apply to certain categories of exhibits (eg bladed weapons and fire accelerants) for which specific advice may be obtained from your 'scenes of crime officers'.
- Further details regarding preserving the integrity of evidence in relation to accelerants can be found in arson (see **4.5.2**).

Prisoner handling

- In appropriate cases clothing should be taken from detainees at the earliest opportunity.
- Beware of contamination. Prisoners should be treated as a crime scene and dealt with by officers who have not been to the scene of the offence.
- If more than one prisoner is arrested, ensure they are transported in different vehicles.

Vehicle crime

- Stolen vehicles and vehicles used in crime invariably yield forensic evidence which may be linked to other crimes and provide a valuable source of intelligence.
- Depending on force procedure, where practicable, all stolen vehicles, or those used in crime, should be recovered to a suitable location where there is good lighting and the vehicle can be dried before examination.

Mobile phones

- If the mobile phone is switched on, record what is on the display.
- Do not push buttons other than to turn it off.
- Turn the mobile off.
- Seal in tamper-proof box, making sure buttons cannot be pressed.
- Submit to appropriate forensic supplier, with full details.
- Be aware that fingerprint powder can damage electronic equipment (seek advice).

Continuity

- Unfortunately, many cases are lost because police officers have failed to maintain evidential continuity of exhibits.
- You should be able to account for the exhibit's movements at every stage (point in time), between seizure and production in evidence.
- Ensure that this is maintained and reflected in the CJA witness statements, exhibit logs, and labels.
- Major investigations will have a trained exhibits officer appointed.

Links to alternative subjects and offences

1.3 Managing Crime Scenes

1.4 Identification Issues

The area of law dealing with physical identification is quite involved and cannot be dealt with in sufficient detail in this book. However, a brief overview of the subject can be given and the details provided are only meant to be a rough guide.

PACE Code of Practice D

Part 3 of Code D deals with identification by witnesses: making a record of first description and then detailing the various identification procedures where the suspect is known/not known.

Record of first description

- A record shall be made of the suspect's description as first given by a potential witness.
- This record of first description must—
  - ✦ be made and kept in a form which enables details of that description to be accurately produced from it, in a visible and legible form, that can be given to the suspect or the suspect's solicitor in accordance with this Code; and
  - ✦ unless otherwise specified, be made before the witness takes part in any identification procedures.
- A copy of the record shall where practicable, be given to the suspect or their solicitor before any identification procedures are carried out.
- A detailed description can be very important and should be obtained as soon as possible. If no formal identification of a suspect is made, a factual description may be given in evidence by a witness. This may, for example, be a distinctive tattoo which may help a jury decide if a defendant was responsible for the offence. Although a description is not classed by the courts as a form of identification (*R v Byron* The Times, 10 March 1999, CA).

Identity of suspect not known

- In these cases, a witness may be taken to a particular area to see whether they can identify the person they saw.
- Although the number, age, sex, race, general description, and style of clothing of other people present at the location (and the way in which any identification is made) cannot be controlled, the formal procedure principles shall be followed as far as practicable. Care must be taken not to direct the witness's attention to any individual unless, taking into account all the circumstances, this cannot be avoided.
- Another means of identification can be the showing of photographs, where the witness will be shown no fewer than 12 photographs at a time, which will, as far as possible, be of a similar likeness. An officer of sergeant rank or above shall be responsible for supervising and directing the showing of photographs. Ensure that the procedure for the showing of photographs as given in Code D, Annex E is complied with.

1.4 Identification Issues

- A witness must not be shown photographs, computerised or artist's composite likenesses, or similar likenesses, or pictures (including 'E-fit' images) if the identity of the suspect is known to the police and the suspect is available to take part in a video identification, an identification parade, or a group identification.

Identity of suspect known and available

If the suspect's identity is **known** to the police and they are **available**, the following identification procedures may be used—

- video identification (Code D, Annex A);
- identification parade (Code D, Annex B);
- group identification (Code D, Annex C).

Video identification

Where the witness is shown moving images of a known suspect, together with similar images of others who resemble the suspect, in certain circumstances still images may be used.

VIPER® (Video Identification Parade Electronic Recording) (see **Appendix 1**) is a video identification system provided by the National VIPER® Bureau and used by police forces throughout the UK, where accredited users can quickly create a bespoke video identification parade. There are also alternative versions available. The speed of the system potentially allows witnesses to view the video (DVD) compilation while the suspect is still in custody; it also provides far greater flexibility for witnesses, avoids any likelihood of confrontation with the suspect and increases the chances of an early guilty plea.

If identification is disputed or the suspect denies involvement, liaise with an inspector to authorise the procedure and serve the appropriate written notice (even if they refuse to take part). Act while the suspect is in custody/available to take the image capture—before they have the chance to change their appearance.

Identification parade

This is when the witness sees the suspect in a line of others who resemble the suspect.

Group identification

This is when the witness sees the suspect in an informal group of people.

Arranging identification procedures

- The arrangements for, and conduct of, the above identification procedures and circumstances in which an identification procedure must be held shall be the responsibility of an officer not below inspector rank who is not involved with the investigation: **'the identification officer'**.
- Generally, another officer or police support staff, can make arrangements for, and conduct, any of these identification procedures. Although the identification officer must be available to supervise effectively, intervene, or give advice.

- Officials involved with the investigation cannot take any part in these procedures or act as the identification officer (except where required by these procedures).
- This does not preclude the identification officer from consulting with the officer in charge of the investigation to determine what procedure to use.
- When an identification procedure is required, in the interest of fairness to suspects and witnesses, it must be held as soon as practicable.

When an identification procedure must be held

- This is whenever a witness—
  + has identified a suspect or purported to have identified them prior to any of the above identification procedures having been held; or
  + is available, who expresses an ability to identify the suspect, or where there is a reasonable chance of the witness being able to do so, and they have not been given an opportunity to identify the suspect in any of the above procedures, and the suspect disputes being the person the witness claims to have seen.
- An identification procedure shall then be held (Code D: 3.12) unless not practicable or would serve no useful purpose in proving or disproving whether the suspect was involved in the offence (eg when it is not disputed that the suspect is already well known to the witness claiming to have seen them commit the crime).
- Similarly an identification procedure may be held if the officer in charge of the investigation considers it would be useful.

Selecting the type of identification procedure

- If an identification procedure is to be held, the suspect shall initially be offered a video identification unless—
  + a video identification is not practicable; or
  + an identification parade is both practicable and more suitable than a video identification; or
  + a group identification is the more appropriate method.
- A group identification may initially be offered if the officer in charge of the investigation considers it is more suitable than a video identification or an identification parade and the identification officer considers it practicable to arrange.
- The identification officer and the officer in charge of the investigation shall consult with each other to determine which option is to be offered.
- An identification parade may not be practicable because of factors relating to the witnesses: their number, state of health, availability, and travelling requirements.
- A video identification would normally be more suitable if it could be arranged and completed sooner than an identification parade.
- A suspect who refuses the identification procedure first offered shall be asked to state their reason for refusing and may get advice from their solicitor and/or if present, their appropriate adult.

- The suspect, solicitor, and/or appropriate adult can make representations about why another procedure should be used.
- A record should be made of the reasons for refusal and representations made.
- After considering any reasons given, and representations made, the identification officer shall, if appropriate, arrange for the suspect to be offered an alternative which the officer considers suitable and practicable.
- If the officer decides it is not suitable and practicable to offer an alternative identification procedure, the reasons for that decision shall be recorded.

Notice to suspect

Prior to identification procedures being arranged, the following shall be explained to the suspect—

- the purposes of the identification procedures;
- their entitlement to free legal advice;
- the procedures for holding it, including their right to have a solicitor or friend present;
- that they do not have to consent to or co-operate in these identification procedures;
- if they do not consent to or co-operate in these identification procedures, their refusal may be given in evidence and police may proceed covertly without their consent or make other arrangements to test whether a witness can identify them;
- if appropriate, special arrangements for juveniles, mentally disordered, or mentally vulnerable people;
- if they significantly alter their appearance between being offered and any attempt to hold an identification procedure, this may be given in evidence and other forms of identification may be considered;
- a moving image or photograph may be taken of them when they attend any identification procedure;
- if, before their identity became known, the witness was shown photographs, a computerised or artist's composite likeness, or similar likeness, or image by the police;
- if they change their appearance before an identification parade, it may not be practicable to arrange another one and alternative methods of identification may be considered;
- that they or their solicitor will be provided with details of the first description of the suspect given by any witnesses who are to attend identification procedures.

This information must be in a written notice handed to the suspect, who should then be asked to sign a second copy and indicate if they are willing to take part or co-operate with the identification procedure.

Identity of suspect known but not available

- When the **known** suspect is not **available** or has ceased to be available, the identification officer may make arrangements for a video identification.

- If necessary, the identification officer may follow the video identification procedures but using still images.
- Any suitable moving or still images may be used and these may be obtained covertly if necessary. Alternatively, the identification officer may make arrangements for a group identification.
- The identification officer may arrange for the suspect to be **confronted** by the witness if none of the options referred to above are practicable. If this method of identification is used ensure compliance with Code D, Annex D.
- A **confrontation** does not require the suspect's consent.
- Requirements for information to be given to, or sought from, a suspect or for the suspect to be given an opportunity to view images before they are shown to a witness, do not apply if the suspect's lack of co-operation prevents this action.

Meanings

Known

Where there is sufficient information known to the police to justify the arrest of a particular person for suspected involvement in the offence.

Available

A suspect being immediately available or will be within a reasonably short time and willing to take an effective part in at least one of the identification procedures which it is practicable to arrange.

Confrontation

This is when the suspect is directly confronted by the witness.

Related cases

R v Najjar [2014] All ER (D) 87 (Apr), CA V had her phone stolen from a reception desk: this was captured on CCTV. V scanned the footage which showed N taking her phone and later recognised N when he walked into the reception area. Although no formal identification procedure had taken place as required by Code D, the footage provided the jury with a direct viewing of the incident and a full facial view of N; as a result the conviction could not be considered unsafe.

R v Deakin [2012] EWCA Crim 2637, CA Police officer knew suspect and viewed incident on CCTV. Breached Code D: 3.35 and Annex A as to video identification if the suspect is known.

R v Alexander and McGill [2012] EWCA Crim 2768, CA If a suspect is first identified through looking at pictures on Facebook (and subsequent VIPER® parade), the police should obtain a detailed statement as to the initial identification, and obtain the images that were looked at on Facebook.

R v Gojra and Dihr [2011] Crim LR 311, CA Offences committed against two complainants on the same occasion, but only one was asked to identify the offender at an ID parade. It was apparent that identity was an issue, so the police had breached Code D: 3.12.

1.4 Identification Issues

R v Turnbull (1976) 63 Cr App R 132, HL This case set out guidelines for dealing with a case involving disputed identification. The jury must examine the circumstances in which the identification was made, in particular—

A—Amount of time under observation.

D—Distance between witness and suspect.

V—Visibility at all times (in what light).

O—Observation impeded/obstructed in any way (traffic, objects, or people).

K—Known or seen before, how often, and in what circumstances.

A—Any reason to remember the suspect, if only seen occasionally and not well known.

T—Time lapse between observation and subsequent identification to police.

E—Error or material discrepancy between description given to police and actual appearance.

In every case where a witness describes a suspect, it is essential to consider these points, all of which should be included in any written statement.

R v Forbes (2001) 1 Cr App R 31, HL When identification is disputed by the suspect, an identification parade shall be held (if the suspect consents, unless unusual appearance, refusal, or other practical alternatives apply. A parade may also be held if the officer in charge of the investigation considers that it would be useful, and the suspect consents. Otherwise there will be a breach of Code D.

R v Chaney [2009] EWCA Crim 21, CA Code D provides safeguard procedures that also apply to police officer(s) when attempting to identify someone from a CCTV recording or image. When viewed by the officer a written record must be made as to: initial reactions, recognition, or doubt, words used, and factors relating to the image that caused that recognition to occur.

Practical considerations

- Where practicable, the 'first description' from the witness should be recorded in the police officer's pocket notebook, before asking the witness to make any identification.
- Do not assume that the description has been recorded elsewhere.
- Avoid using 'closed' questions (those which only need a 'yes' or 'no' answer) when obtaining description details.
- Care must be taken not to direct the witness's attention to any individual.
- However, this does not prevent a witness being asked to look in a particular direction, if this is necessary to—
  + make sure that the witness does not overlook a possible suspect simply because the witness is looking in the opposite direction; and
  + to enable the witness to make comparisons between any suspect and others who are in the area.
- Where there is more than one witness, every effort should be made to keep them separate.

- A written record should be made of any identification including—
  + date, time, and place when the witness saw the suspect;
  + whether any identification was made;
  + if so, how it was made and the conditions at the time;
  + if the witness's attention was drawn to the suspect (reason for this); and
  + anything said by the witness or the suspect about the identification or the conduct of the procedure.
- It is best practice, for any officer who recognises a suspect from either a 'still' photograph or CCTV image, to avoid being involved in the arrest of that individual, thereby ensuring they are available to take part in any forthcoming identification procedure, should the identification be disputed.

Links to alternative subjects and offences

Chapter 2

Assaults and Violence

2.1 Assault (Common/Actual Bodily Harm)

A common assault under s 39 of the Criminal Justice Act 1988 is in fact two separate matters: an assault and/or a battery. This area of law is dealt with first, before covering the more serious assault occasioning actual bodily harm (AOABH) under the Offences Against the Person Act 1861. Defences which may be available to assaults are then discussed.

2.1.1 Common assault—battery

> **Offence**
> Common **assault** and **battery** shall be summary offences
> Criminal Justice Act 1988, s 39

Points to prove

Assault
- ✓ unlawfully
- ✓ assaulted
- ✓ another person

Battery
- ✓ all points above
- ✓ application of unlawful force (eg by beating)

Meanings

Assault

Any act, which **intentionally** or **recklessly**, causes another person to apprehend immediate and **unlawful** personal violence (*Fagan v Metropolitan Police Commissioner* [1968] 3 All ER 442, QBD).

Battery

An act by which a person intentionally or recklessly applies force to the complainant.

Intent (see **4.1.2**)

Reckless (see **2.3.1**)

Unlawful (see **2.3.1**)

Explanatory notes

- There are two offences covered by this legislation: 'assault' and 'assault by beating' (battery).
- There is also a civil wrong of assault/battery.
- An 'assault' does not have to involve an actual application of force: it may just be threatening words used, although if violence is threatened, there must be the ability to carry out the threat at the time. A mere omission to act cannot be an assault.
- In both offences there has to be either an intentional causing of apprehension of immediate unlawful violence or subjective recklessness as to that apprehension.

Defences (see **2.1.2**)

Related cases

ZH v Metropolitan Police Commissioner [2012] EWHC 604 (Admin), QBD A police officer's failure to consider disabilities appropriately can result in liability for assault, false imprisonment, disability discrimination and breaches of human rights.

Wood v DPP [2008] EWHC 1056 (Admin), QBD A police officer grabbed a person's arm to stop them walking away, with no intention to arrest that person. This action amounted to an unlawful assault.

Haystead v CC Derbyshire Police [2000] 3 All ER 890, QBD A mother was punched by her boyfriend and as a result dropped and injured the baby she was carrying. The defendant was convicted of assault by battery directly on the mother, and indirectly on the baby.

Mepstead v DPP [1996] Crim LR 111, QBD Touching someone to attract their attention may be lawful.

Fagan v Metropolitan Police Commissioner [1968] 3 All ER 442, QBD It is irrelevant whether the battery is inflicted directly by the body of the offender, or with a weapon, or instrument such as a car.

Practical considerations

- If racially or religiously aggravated, consider the more serious racially/religiously aggravated offence (see **7.10**).

2.1.1 Common assault—battery

- An individual should be charged with either 'assault' or 'battery'—the inclusion of both in the same charge is bad for duplicity and could result in the charge being dismissed (*DPP v Little* (1994) 95 Cr App R 28, CA).
- Ensure that visible injuries are photographed.
- Include in your CJA witness statement evidence as to intent or recklessness.
- Ascertain whether any of the defences could apply.

Assault

- Unless extenuating circumstances apply, the police/CPS will invariably invite the aggrieved party to take their own action either by criminal prosecution or by civil action.
- Where a court decides that the assault or battery has not been proved or that it was justified, or so trifling as not to merit any punishment, they must dismiss the complaint and forthwith make out a certificate of dismissal. This certificate releases the defendant from any further proceedings (civil or criminal) (Offences Against the Person Act 1861, s 44).
- If the conduct involves threatening acts, words, gestures, or a combination of these, then consider alternative offences under the Public Order Act 1986, breach of the peace or harassment (see **7.7**).

Battery

- Ascertain the degree/severity of injury before charging.
- CPS guidelines specify the following injuries should normally be charged as battery: grazes, scratches, abrasions, minor bruising, swellings, reddening of the skin, superficial cuts, and a 'black eye'.
- Consider s 47, s 20, or s 18 of the Offences Against the Person Act 1861 for more serious injuries.

 Summary   6 months

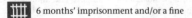 6 months' imprisonment and/or a fine

2.1.2 Assault occasioning actual bodily harm (AOABH)/Defences to assaults

Offences

Whosoever shall be convicted upon an indictment of any assault **occasioning actual bodily harm** shall be guilty of an offence.

Offences Against the Person Act 1861, s 47

Points to prove

✓ unlawfully
✓ assaulted
✓ another person
✓ occasioning him/her
✓ actual bodily harm

Meaning of actual bodily harm

Actual bodily harm has been defined as 'any hurt which interferes with health or comfort but not to a considerable degree'.

Explanatory notes

- Bodily harm has its ordinary meaning and is that which is calculated to interfere with the health or comfort of the victim, but must be more than transient or trifling.
- Examples of 'actual bodily harm' physical/mental injuries are given in **Practical considerations**.
- A conviction can be obtained if actual bodily harm is caused to the victim by some action which is the natural and reasonably foreseeable result of what the defendant said or did.

Defences to assault

Accident (as long as malice is not present)

Consent

- This can be expressly given to an application of force (such as tattooing or an operation), providing the activity is not illegal itself (injection of illegal drugs); or it can be implied (by getting into a crowded train where contact is unavoidable).
- An honestly held belief that consent had been given (or would have been given—emergency surgery to save life).

2.1.2 (AOABH)/Defences to assaults

- Submitting to an assault is not consent. Similarly, consent is negated if given due to duress or fraud (a trick), but the burden of proof is on the prosecution to prove that this was how consent was obtained.
- Consent cannot be given by a child or young person if they fail to understand the true nature of the act (what is involved).
- A teacher at a school with children who had behavioural problems, did not impliedly consent to being assaulted by the children (*H v CPS* [2010] EWHC 1374, QBD).
- Consent cannot be given to an assault that inflicts substantial bodily harm, such as in sadomasochism (*R v Brown & others* [1994] 1 AC 212, HL). Although some body mutilation in limited and non-aggressive circumstances may be acceptable (*R v Wilson* [1996] 2 Cr App R 241, CA).

Lawful sport

- Properly conducted lawful sports are considered to be for the public good and injuries received during the course of an event kept within the rules are generally accepted.
- Players are taken to have consented to any injuries which they might reasonably expect to suffer during the course of the match or contest.
- Criminal charges and proceedings should only be instigated in situations where the player acted outside the rules of the sport and the conduct was sufficiently serious as to be properly regarded as criminal.

Lawful correction

The Children Act 2004, s 58 ensures that parents no longer have the right to use force in the course of reasonable chastisement of their child that would go beyond a s 39 'common assault'.

Section 58 states that in relation to the following offences under—
- section 18 or s 20 (wounding and causing grievous bodily harm);
- section 47 (assault occasioning actual bodily harm);
- section 1 of the Children and Young Persons Act 1933 (cruelty under 16);
the battery of a child cannot be justified on the ground that it constituted reasonable punishment.

Self-defence (case law)

'A jury must decide whether a defendant honestly believed that the circumstances were such as required him to use force to defend himself from an attack or threatened attack; the jury has then to decide whether the force used was reasonable in the circumstances' (*R v Owino* [1996] 2 Cr App R 128, CA and *DPP v Armstrong-Braun* (1999) 163 JP 271, CA).

Self-defence (statutory test—reasonable force)

Criminal Justice and Immigration Act 2008, s 76 (see **1.2**).

Statutory authorities—using reasonable force (see **1.2**)

Related cases

R v Burns [2010] EWCA 1023, CA Causing injuries whilst physically ejecting an invited passenger (prostitute) from a car was a s 47 assault. B had not acted in self/other's defence, to prevent a crime or in defence of his own property (see **1.2.1**).

R v Keane and McGrath [2010] EWCA Crim 2514, CA Self-defence could be available to an aggressor where the violence offered by the victim was so out of proportion that the roles were effectively reversed.

H v DPP [2007] EWHC 960, QBD Not necessary to identify which particular injury had been caused by which defendant provided that some injury resulting in actual bodily harm had been caused by the defendant.

DPP v Smith [2006] 1 WLR 1571, QBD Cutting hair, or applying some unpleasant substance that marked or damaged the hair was capable of being AOABH. Harm is not limited to injury and includes hurt or damage.

R v Barnes [2004] EWCA Crim 3246, CA Provides guidance on consent in contact sports (see '**Defences to assaults—Lawful sports**').

T v DPP [2003] EWHC 266 (Admin), QBD Actual bodily harm can include loss of consciousness (even if there is no other physical injury) as it involves an impairment of the victim's sensory functions.

R v Chan-Fook [1994] All ER 552, CA Actual bodily harm can include psychiatric injury, but does not include mere emotions such as fear, distress, or panic.

R v Brown & others [1994] 1 AC 212, HL Sado masochists engaged in torture with each other cannot give consent, even though the 'victims' were all willing participants.

Actual Bodily Harm can include causing—

- a psychiatric illness (*R v Ireland* [1998] AC 147, HL) (see **7.12.2**);
- psychiatric 'injury' (*R v Chan-Fook* [1994] 2 All ER 552, CA—above);
- shock (*R v Miller* (1953) 118 JP 340, Assize Court).

R v Savage [1992] 1 AC 699, HL and **DPP v Parmenter [1991] 3 WLR 914, HL** No need to prove any intent to cause injury for assault occasioning actual bodily harm.

Practical considerations

- If racially or religiously aggravated, consider the more serious racially/ religiously aggravated offence (see **7.10**).
- Ensure that visible injuries are photographed.
- Include in your CJA witness statement details of injuries, circumstances of the incident, and any evidence as to intent or recklessness.
- Obtain medical evidence (hospital or doctor).
- Could any of the defences apply or be used by the defendant?

2.1.2 (AOABH)/Defences to assaults

- CPS guidance gives examples of injuries which could amount to 'actual bodily harm'—
    - loss or breaking of a tooth or teeth;
    - temporary loss of sensory functions (includes loss of consciousness);
    - extensive or multiple bruising;
    - displaced broken nose;
    - minor fractures;
    - minor cuts (not superficial), may require stitches (medical treatment);
    - psychiatric injury (proved by appropriate expert evidence) which is more than fear, distress, or panic.
- Consider s 20 or s 18 of the Offences Against the Person Act 1861 for more serious injuries (see **2.3**).

 Either way   None

 Summary: 6 months' imprisonment and/or a fine
Indictment: 5 years' imprisonment

Links to alternative subjects and offences

2.2 Assault/Resist/Impersonate and Obstruct—Police or Designated/Accredited Person or Emergency Workers

This area of law concerns offences involving assault with intent to resist or prevent arrest; assault, resist, or wilfully obstruct a police constable, designated or accredited person in the execution of their duty; and obstruct or hinder emergency workers.

2.2.1 Assault with intent to resist or prevent lawful arrest

Section 38 of the Offences Against the Person Act 1861 creates the offence of 'assault with intent to resist or prevent lawful arrest'.

Offences

Whosoever shall **assault** any person with **intent** to **resist or prevent** the lawful apprehension or detainer of himself or of any other person for any offence shall be guilty of an offence.

Offences Against the Person Act 1861, s 38

Points to prove

✓ assaulted
✓ with intent to resist/prevent
✓ the lawful apprehension/detention of
✓ self/other person
✓ for the offence of (specify)

Meanings

assault (see **2.1.1**)

intent (see **4.1.2**)

resist or prevent

The *Oxford English Dictionary* offers the following meanings—
resist—'to strive against, oppose, try to impede or refuse to comply with';
prevent—'stop from happening or doing something; hinder; make impossible'.

2.2.1 Assault with intent to resist or prevent lawful arrest

Explanatory notes

- The assault itself need not be any more serious than a common assault (which could be considered as an alternative charge).
- The intention to resist the lawful arrest (either of themselves or another person) must be proved.

Defences to assault (see 2.1.2)

Related cases

R v Self (1992) 95 Cr App R 42, CA The resisted arrest/detention must have been a lawful one. This can be problematic where s 24A 'citizen's arrests' are made and the arresting person did not have any lawful power to arrest/detain.

R v Lee (2000) 150 NLJ 1491, CA It is not a defence to this offence to hold an honest belief that a mistake is being made by the arresting/detaining officers.

Practical considerations

- It must be proved that—
  + the arrest/detention was lawful and
  + the person concerned knew that an arrest was being made on himself or another.
- Intention (at the time of commission of the offence) can be proved by—
  + interviewing defendant—admissions made and explanations as to their state of mind, actions, and intentions and/or
  + inferences drawn from the circumstances of the offence, evidence from witnesses, property found on defendant or in their control, and any other incriminating evidence.
- If this offence is committed by the person initially being arrested, the power of arrest comes from the original offence. Otherwise consider assaulting a police officer in the execution of their duty or breach of the peace.
- Could any of the general assault defences apply?
- Consider CPS guidelines and charging standards for assault with intent to resist arrest.

 Either way   None

 Summary: 6 months' imprisonment and/or a fine
Indictment: 2 years' imprisonment

      SSS Stop, search and seize powers   E&S Entry and search powers   RRA Racially or religiously aggravated offence

2.2.2 Assault constable in execution of duty

The Police Act 1996, s 89(1) provides the offences of assaulting a constable or person assisting a constable acting in the execution of their duty.

Offences

Any person who **assaults** a constable in the **execution of** his **duty**, or a person assisting a constable in the execution of his duty, shall be guilty of an offence.

Police Act 1996, s 89(1)

Points to prove

✓ assaulted a constable **or** person assisting a constable
✓ in execution of their duty

Meanings

Assault (see 2.1.1)

Execution of duty

The officer must be acting lawfully and in the execution of their duty (see 'Related cases').

Explanatory notes

- The duties of a constable have not been defined by any statute (see 'Related cases').
- This offence also applies to police officers from Scotland or Northern Ireland (while in England or Wales) who are acting within statutory powers or executing a warrant.
- Section 30 of the Police Act 1996 defines the jurisdiction of a constable as being throughout England and Wales and the adjacent UK waters. Special constables have the same jurisdiction, powers, and privileges of a constable.

Defences to assault (see 2.1.2)

Related cases (see 2.1.1 and s 17 entry at 12.3.2 for more cases)

Walker v Commissioner of Police of the Metropolis [2014] EWCA Civ 97, CA A police officer attended a domestic incident and restricted the suspect's movements in a doorway while appraising the situation. A fight ensued and W was acquitted on the s 89(1) charge as the officer had unlawfully detained W without arresting him. CA determined that W had not been deprived of his liberty, albeit freedom of movement was restricted for a few seconds, but this did not amount to false imprisonment. The subsequent public order arrest had been lawful, but the common law power to detain, short of arrest, to prevent a breach of the peace (see **7.3**) can only apply if the officer had this power in mind at the relevant time.

DPP v Hawkins [1988] 1 WLR 1166, QBD An arrest was rendered unlawful by a failure to provide the reason for arrest as soon as practicable after arrest. The reason could not be given retrospectively.

Collins v Wilcock [1984] 3 All ER 374, QBD A police officer was assaulted after holding the arm of a prostitute in order to detain her just to answer some questions. This act went beyond acceptable lawful physical contact and so constituted a battery; as a result the officer had not been acting in the execution of their duty when assaulted by the prostitute.

Robson v Hallett [1967] 2 All ER 407, QBD An officer may be a trespasser (and therefore not acting in the execution of their duty) if permission to enter or remain on property is withdrawn, but reasonable time must be given to leave property.

Mepstead v DPP [1996] Crim LR 111, QBD Touching someone to attract their attention may be lawful.

DPP v L [1999] Crim LR 752, QBD An unlawful arrest does not mean that the custody staff subsequently act unlawfully in detaining the person.

Practical considerations

- It is vital to prove that the officer was acting lawfully in the execution of their duty at the time of the assault.
- Officers should ensure they are acting within their powers and following relevant requirements or procedures (eg information to be given prior to search or at time of arrest under s 2 and s 28 PACE (see **12.1.2** and **12.2.2**)), otherwise they may no longer be acting within the execution of their duty (*Sobczak v DPP* [2012] EWHC 1319 (Admin)).
- The offence does not require proof that the defendant knew or ought to have known that the victim was a constable or that they were acting in the execution of their duty.
- A plain clothes officer should produce identification, as a failure to do so could mean that the officer was acting outside the execution of their duty.
- Section 68 of the Railways and Transport Safety Act 2003 and s 68 of the Energy Act 2004, stipulates that the s 89(1) and s 89(2) (see **2.2.3**) offences also apply to BTP and members of the Civil Nuclear Constabulary
- Do any of the general assault defences apply?
- Consider CPS guidelines and 2012 revised charging standards for this offence relating to injuries received amounting to a battery (see **2.1.1**).
- If the injuries justify a s 47 charge (see **2.1.2**) for a member of the public, then this will also be the appropriate charge for a constable.

 Summary   6 months

 6 months' imprisonment and/or a fine

2.2.3 **Resist/obstruct constable in execution of duty**

Section 89(2) of the Police Act 1996 deals with the offences of resisting or wilfully obstructing a constable in the execution of their duty.

Offences

Any person who **resists** or **wilfully obstructs** a constable in the **execution** of his **duty**, or a person assisting a constable in the execution of his duty, shall be guilty of an offence.

Police Act 1996, s 89(2)

Points to prove

✓ resisted/wilfully obstructed a constable or person assisting
✓ in the execution of constable's duty

Meanings

Resists (see 2.2.1)

Wilful obstruction

In this context it has to be deliberate obstruction.

Execution of duty (see 2.2.2)

Explanatory notes

* Resists does not imply that any assault has taken place and where a person in the process of being lawfully arrested tears himself away from the constable or person assisting, this will constitute resistance.
* The obstruction must be some form of positive act which prevents or impedes the officer in carrying out their duty.
  For the constable's duty and jurisdiction, see **2.2.2**.
  It must be proved that the officer was acting in the execution of their duty.

Related cases

Marsden v CPS [2014] All ER (D) 199 (Oct), CA Police were invited into house by H (partner of M) to deal with a domestic dispute, but were unable to rouse M sleeping on the couch. The officer had to re-enter the property, after M had awoken and shouted 'Fuck off' to the officer, and a violent struggle then ensued while the officer was trying to arrest him. Held: As the consent given by H had been re-iterated, that consent had been enduring. M's words ('fuck off') did not 'revoke' the licence (permission) for the officer to remain on the property.

2.2.4 Impersonate constable or wear/possess article

Sekfali and others v DPP [2006] EWHC 894, QBD Citizens have no legal duty to assist the police, but most would accept that it is a moral and social one; however, running away and fleeing can amount to an obstruction.

Smith v DPP (2001) 165 JP 432, QBD An officer can take someone aside to aid entry to premises even if there is no obstruction being caused.

Moss & others v McLachlan (1985) 149 JP 167, QBD A constable is under a general duty to prevent a breach of the peace occurring.

Lewis v Cox [1984] Crim LR 756, QBD A wilful act has to be deliberate and prevent, or make it more difficult, for the constable to carry out their duty. It is sufficient for a defendant to be aware that their actions cause this.

Rice v Connolly [1966] 2 All ER 649, QBD A citizen is entitled to refuse to answer questions or assist/accompany a police officer where no lawful reason exists and therefore this conduct does not automatically amount to resistance/obstruction.

Practical considerations (see 2.2.2)

SSS	RRA

♿ Summary   🕒 6 months

⌸ 1 month imprisonment and/or a level 3 fine

2.2.4 Impersonate constable or wear/possess article of police uniform

Section 90 of the Police Act 1996 deals with the offences of impersonating a member of a police force or special constable, or wearing/being in possession of any article of police uniform.

> **Offences**
>
> (1) Any person who **with intent** to **deceive** impersonates a member of a police force or **special constable**, or makes any statement or does any act calculated falsely to suggest that he is such a member or constable, shall be guilty of an offence.
> (2) Any person who, not being a constable, wears any **article of police uniform** in circumstances where it gives him an appearance so nearly resembling that of a member of a police force as to be **calculated to deceive** shall be guilty of an offence.
> (3) Any person who, not being a member of a police force or special constable, has in his possession any article of police uniform shall,

> unless he proves that he obtained possession of that article lawfully
> and has possession of it for a lawful purpose, be guilty of an offence.
>
> Police Act 1996, s 90

Points to prove

s 90(1) offence

- ✓ impersonated
- ✓ special constable/member of police force
- ✓ with intent to deceive

or

- ✓ with intent to deceive
- ✓ made a statement/did an act
- ✓ which calculated falsely to suggest
- ✓ that you were a special constable/member of a police force

s 90(2) offence

- ✓ not being a constable
- ✓ wore article(s) of police uniform
- ✓ in circumstances which made you appear to resemble
- ✓ being a member of police force
- ✓ so as to be calculated to deceive

s 90(3) offence

- ✓ not being a special constable/member of police force
- ✓ possessed article(s) of police uniform

Meanings

With intent (see **4.1.2**)

Deceive

Means to induce a person to believe a thing to be true which is in fact
false: in this case that the person is a police officer.

Special constable

Has the same jurisdiction, powers, and privileges as a constable.

Article of police uniform

Means any article of uniform or any distinctive badge, or mark, or document of identification usually issued to members of police forces or special constables, or anything having the appearance of such an article, badge, mark, or document.

Explanatory notes

- Section 68 of the Railways and Transport Safety Act 2003 states that
  s 90 (impersonation of constable) applies to a constable/special
  constable of the BTP.

2.2.5 Assault/resist/obstruct designated or accredited person

- In s 90(2) 'calculated to deceive' has been held to mean 'likely to deceive' (*Turner v Shearer* [1973] 1 All ER 397), although this does not require the defendant to have a specific intent to deceive as with the more serious offence under s 90(1).

> **Defence**—applicable to s 90(3) only
>
> Proof that they obtained possession of the article of police **uniform lawfully** and possession of it was for a lawful purpose.

Practical considerations

- The burden of proof in relation to the defence of lawful possession under s 90(3) is on the defendant, to prove on the balance of probabilities.
- For the s 90(1) and s 90(2) offences it is not necessary to prove intent to deceive a specific individual, or to prove that the person obtained any form of benefit or advantage as a result of the deception.

 Summary   6 months

  s 90(1)—6 months' imprisonment and/or a fine
s 90(2)—Level 3 fine
s 90(3)—Level 1 fine

2.2.5 Assault/resist/obstruct designated or accredited person in execution of duty

Section 46 of the Police Reform Act 2002 refers to offences in respect of suitably designated and accredited people as follows—

> **Offences**
>
> (1) Any person who **assaults**—
>   (a) a **designated person** in the execution of his duty,
>   (b) an **accredited person** in the execution of his duty,
>   (ba) an **accredited inspector** in the execution of his duty, or
>   (c) a person assisting a designated or accredited person or an accredited inspector in the execution of his duty,
>   is guilty of an offence.
> (2) Any person who **resists or wilfully obstructs**—

(a) a designated person in the execution of his duty,
(b) an accredited person in the execution of his duty,
(ba) an accredited inspector in the execution of his duty, or
(c) a person assisting a designated or accredited person or an accredited inspector in the execution of his duty,

is guilty of an offence.

Police Reform Act 2002, s 46

Points to prove

✓ assaulted or resisted/wilfully obstructed
✓ a designated/accredited person/accredited inspector or person assisting
✓ while in the execution of their duty

Meanings

Assaults (see **2.1.1**)

Designated person

Means a person designated under s 38 or s 39.

Accredited person

Means a person accredited under s 41.

Accredited inspector

Means a weights and measures inspector accredited under s 41A.

Resists or wilfully obstructs (see **2.2.3**)

Explanatory notes

- References to the execution of their duties relate to exercising any power or performing any duty by virtue of their designation or accreditation.
- A designated person can be either: a PCSO (see **11.1**), investigating officer, detention officer, or escort officer employed by the local policing body and under the direction/control of the designating chief officer of that force (s 38); or employees of companies contracted to provide detention and escort services so designated by a chief officer (s 39).
- An accredited person is a person whose employer has entered into arrangements for carrying out a community safety function under a community safety accreditation scheme set up by the chief officer for that police area under s 40 and has been granted accreditation by the chief officer under s 41. It can also be a person contracted out under Pt 4 with powers under Sch 5 of the Police Reform Act 2002.
- Under s 41A a chief officer of police may grant accreditation to a weights and measures inspector who is an inspector of weights and measures appointed under s 72(1) of the Weights and Measures Act 1985.

Defences to assault (see 2.1.2)

Related cases (see also 2.2.2 and 2.2.3)

R v Forbes and Webb (1865) 10 Cox CC 362 It is not necessary that the offender knows the person is a designated or accredited person.

Practical considerations (see also 2.2.2 and 2.2.3)

- Given the extensive and detailed restrictions on the powers of these individuals, the precise activities that were involved at the time will be closely scrutinised by a court. It will be critical to establish that the person was acting within the lawful limits of their powers at the time.
- It is also an offence under s 46(3) for any person who, with intent to deceive, impersonates the above persons.
- It is a summary offence to intentionally obstruct a person acting lawfully as an enforcement agent (formerly certified bailiffs) under the Tribunals, Courts and Enforcement Act 2007, sch 12, para 68(1).

 Summary   6 months

 Assaulted/assaulted a person assisting and impersonation:

6 months' imprisonment and/or a fine

Resisted/wilfully obstructed or resisted/obstructed a person assisting:

1 month's imprisonment and/or a level 3 fine

2.2.6 **Obstruct/hinder emergency workers and persons assisting**

The Emergency Workers (Obstruction) Act 2006 creates offences of obstructing/hindering certain emergency workers responding to an emergency, and obstructing/hindering persons assisting such emergency workers.

Offences against emergency workers

A person who without reasonable excuse obstructs or hinders another while that other person is, in a **capacity** mentioned in subsection (2) below, **responding** to **emergency circumstances**, commits an offence.

Emergency Workers (Obstruction) Act 2006, s 1(1)

> **Points to prove**
> ✓ without reasonable excuse
> ✓ obstructed or hindered
> ✓ emergency worker as described in s 1(2) who is
> ✓ attending/dealing/preparing to deal
> ✓ with emergency circumstances as given in s 1(3) and s 1(4)

Meanings

Capacity (of emergency worker)

(2) The capacity referred to in subsection (1) above is—

    (a) that of a person employed by a fire and rescue authority in England and Wales;

    (b) in relation to England and Wales, that of a person (other than a person falling within paragraph (a)) whose duties as an employee or as a servant of the Crown involve—

        (i) extinguishing fires; or

        (ii) protecting life and property in the event of a fire;

    (c) that of a person employed by a **relevant NHS body** in the provision of ambulance services (including air ambulance services), or of a person providing such services pursuant to arrangements made by, or at the request of, a relevant NHS body;

    (d) that of a person providing services for the transport of organs, blood, equipment or personnel pursuant to arrangements made by, or at the request of, a relevant NHS body;

    (e) that of a member of Her Majesty's Coastguard;

    (f) that of a member of the crew of a vessel operated by—

        (i) the Royal National Lifeboat Institution, or

        (ii) any other person or organisation operating a vessel for the purpose of providing a rescue service,

or a person who musters the crew of such a vessel or attends to its launch or recovery.

Responding to emergency circumstances

(3) For the purposes of this section and section 2 of this Act, a person is **responding** to emergency circumstances if the person—

    (a) is going anywhere for the purpose of dealing with emergency circumstances occurring there; or

    (b) is dealing with emergency circumstances or preparing to do so.

(4) For the purposes of this Act, circumstances are '**emergency circumstances**' if they are present or imminent and—

    (a) are causing or are likely to cause—

        (i) serious injury to or the serious illness (including mental illness) of a person;

        (ii) serious harm to the environment (including the life and health of plants and animals);

      (iii) serious harm to any building or other property; or

      (iv) a worsening of any such injury, illness or harm; or

  (b) are likely to cause the death of a person.

Emergency Workers (Obstruction) Act 2006, s 1

Offences against person assisting

(1) A person who without reasonable excuse obstructs or hinders another in the circumstances described in subsection (2) below commits an offence.

(2) Those circumstances are where the person being obstructed or hindered is assisting another while that other person is, in a capacity mentioned in section 1(2) of this Act, responding to emergency circumstances.

Emergency Workers (Obstruction) Act 2006, s 2

Points to prove

- ✓ without reasonable excuse
- ✓ obstructed or hindered
- ✓ a person who was assisting
- ✓ an emergency worker as described in s 1(2) who was
- ✓ attending/dealing/preparing to deal
- ✓ with emergency circumstances as given in s 1(3) and s 1(4)

Explanatory notes

- In s 1(2) a '**relevant NHS body**' is an NHS foundation trust, NHS trust, Special Health Authority, a clinical commissioning group, or Local Health Board.
- A person may be convicted of the offence under s 1 or s 2 of this Act notwithstanding that it is effected by: means other than physical means; or action directed only at any vehicle, vessel, apparatus, equipment, or other thing, or any animal used, or to be used by a person referred to in that section.
- For the purposes of ss 1 and 2, circumstances to which a person is responding are to be taken to be emergency circumstances if the person believes and has reasonable grounds for believing they are or may be emergency circumstances.
- Further details on this 2006 Act are dealt with in HOC 3/2007.
- The 2006 Act does not include police or prison officers because obstruction of a police constable is an offence under the Police Act 1996 (see **2.2.3**). This 1996 Act also covers prison officers by virtue of s 8 of the Prisons Act 1952 which stipulates that prison officers, whilst acting as such, shall have all the powers, authority, protection, and privileges as a constable.
- See **2.2.5** for assault or resist/wilfully obstruct a suitably designated or accredited person.

Summary

 6 months

 Fine

Links to alternative subjects and offences

2.3 Wounding/Grievous Bodily Harm

2.3.1 Wounding or inflicting grievous bodily harm

Section 20 of the Offences Against the Person Act 1861 provides the offence of 'wounding or inflicting grievous bodily harm'.

> **Offences**
>
> Whosoever shall **unlawfully** and **maliciously wound** or **inflict** any **grievous bodily harm** upon any other person, either with or without any weapon or instrument shall be guilty of an offence.
>
> Offences Against the Person Act 1861, s 20

> **Points to prove**
> - ✓ unlawfully
> - ✓ maliciously
> - ✓ wounded **or** inflicted grievous bodily harm
> - ✓ upon another person

Meanings

Unlawfully

Means without excuse or justification at law.

Maliciously

- Means malice (ill-will or an evil motive) must be present.
- 'Maliciously requires either an actual intention to do the particular kind of harm that was done or **recklessness** whether any such harm should occur or not; it is neither limited to, nor does it require, any ill-will towards the person injured' (*R v Cunningham* [1957] 2 All ER 412, CA).

Recklessness

Defendant being aware of the existence of the risk but nonetheless had gone on and taken it (*R v Cunningham* [1957] 2 All ER 412, CA).

Wound

Means any break in the continuity of the whole skin.

Inflict

- Inflict does not have as wide a meaning as 'cause'—grievous bodily harm can be inflicted without there being an assault.
- 'Grievous bodily harm may be inflicted either by: directly and violently assaulting the victim; or something intentionally done which although in itself is not a direct application of force to the body of the victim, does directly result in force being applied to the body of the victim so that he suffers grievous bodily harm' (*R v Wilson and Jenkins* [1983] 3 All ER 448, HL).

Grievous bodily harm

- Means 'serious or really serious harm' (*R v Saunders* [1985] Crim LR 230, CA).
- Bodily harm can include inflicting/causing a psychiatric harm/illness (silent/heavy breathing/menacing telephone calls— *R v Ireland* [1998] AC 147, HL) or include psychiatric injury, in serious cases, as well as physical injury (stalking victim— *R v Burstow* [1997] 4 All ER 225, HL).

Explanatory notes

- If it appears that the target of the attack was not the actual victim, then the 'doctrine of transferred malice' provides that if a person mistakenly causes injury to a person other than the person whom he intended to attack, they will commit the same offence as if they had injured the intended victim. The doctrine only applies if the crime remains the same and the harm done must be of the same kind as the harm intended (*R v Latimer* (1886) 17 QBD 359, QBD).
- As wounding and grievous bodily harm are both different, the distinction as to which offence is appropriate should be made.

Defences

May be available to a s 20 offence (see **2.1.2**).

Related cases

R v Barnes [2004] EWCA Crim 3246, CA Conduct outside what a player might regard as having accepted when taking part in contact sports may fall outside defences to assaults. Apart from proving unlawful and malicious, consider the foresight of the risk of harm. Case examined the defences in contact sports (see **2.1.2**).

R v Wilson & Jenkins [1983] 3 All ER 448, HL Frightened by the defendant the victim jumps through a window and breaks a leg. Grievous bodily harm has been 'inflicted' by the offender by inducing substantial fear, even though there is no direct application of force.

2.3.1 Wounding or inflicting grievous bodily harm

R v Martin [1881–85] All ER 699, CA M extinguished the lights of a theatre, and placed a bar across the doorway. Panic was intended to be the natural consequences of his actions but, if in the ensuing panic, people suffered serious injuries the defendant will have 'inflicted GBH' on those people.

A-G's Reference (No 3 of 1994) [1997] Crim LR 829, HL Transferred malice doctrine was accepted where defendant stabbed his girlfriend knowing she was pregnant and the knife penetrated the foetus.

R v Cunningham [1957] 2 All ER 412, CA Meaning of 'maliciously' and recklessness test (above).

R v Savage [1992] 1 AC 699, HL and **DPP v Parmenter [1991] 3 WLR 914, HL** In s 20 wounding/GBH cases—
- A s 47 assault (AOABH) can be an alternative verdict if it includes implications of assault occasioning actual bodily harm.
- '*Cunningham* malice' will suffice. It is enough that the defendant should have foreseen that some physical harm might result—of whatever character.

R v Brown & others [1994] 1 AC 212, HL Consent cannot be given to an assault that inflicts bodily harm of a substantial nature such as in sado-masochism.

R v Wilson [1996] 2 Cr App R 241, CA Some body mutilation in limited and non-aggressive circumstances may be acceptable.

R v Dica [2005] EWCA Crim 2304, CA Inflicting grievous bodily harm by infecting the victim with HIV through unprotected consensual sexual intercourse.

R v Konzani [2005] EWCA Crim 706, CA For a valid defence, there has to be a willing and informed consent to the specific risk of contracting HIV—this cannot be inferred from consent to unprotected sexual intercourse.

Practical considerations

- Consider the more serious racially/religiously aggravated offence (see **7.10**).
- In cases of 'transferred malice' the charge must specify at whom the intent was aimed (eg 'A wounded C with intent to cause GBH to B').
- It is good practice to describe any weapon or instrument used in the actual charge, particularly if the article has been recovered for production at court.
- The distinction between 'wound' and 'GBH' must be identified and considered, as they do not have the same meaning.
- Where both a wound and grievous bodily harm have been inflicted, choose which part of s 20 reflects the true nature of the offence (*R v McCready* [1978] 1 WLR 1376, CA).
- The prosecution must prove under s 20 that either the defendant intended, or actually foresaw, that the act would cause harm. Similarly that s/he was aware of the existence of the risk but nonetheless went on to take it.

- The s 18 offence requires intent while s 20 is 'unlawfully and maliciously'.
- A s 47 assault can be an alternative verdict to s 20 if it includes implications of AOABH.
- Consider CPS advice and guidance for unlawful wounding or inflicting GBH—
  + The distinction between charges under s 18 and s 20 is one of **intent**. The gravity of the injury may provide some evidence of intent.
  + Wounding means the breaking of the continuity of the whole of the outer skin, or the inner skin within the cheek or lip. It does not include the rupturing of internal blood vessels.
  + Minor wounds, such as a small cut or laceration, should be charged under s 47. Section 20 should be reserved for those wounds considered to be serious (thus equating the offences with the infliction of grievous or serious bodily harm).
  + Grievous bodily harm means serious bodily harm, such as:
    - injury resulting in permanent disability or permanent loss of sensory function; injury which results in more than minor permanent, visible disfigurement;
    - broken or displaced limbs or bones, including fractured skull, compound fractures, broken cheekbone/jaw or ribs;
    - injuries which cause substantial loss of blood, usually necessitating a transfusion; or resulting in lengthy treatment or incapacity;
    - psychiatric injury (expert evidence is essential to prove the injury).
- Obtain medical evidence to prove extent of injury.
- Obtain photographs of victim's injuries.

 Either way

 None

Summary: 6 months' imprisonment and/or a fine
Indictment: 5 years' imprisonment

2.3.2 Wounding or grievous bodily harm—with intent

Section 18 of the Offences Against the Person Act 1861 creates the offences of 'wounding or causing grievous bodily harm with intent'.

2.3.2 Wounding or grievous bodily harm—with intent

Offences

Whosoever shall **unlawfully** and **maliciously** by **any means whatsoever wound** or **cause** any **grievous bodily harm** to any person with **intent** to do some grievous bodily harm to any person, or with intent to **resist or prevent** the lawful apprehension or detainer of any person, shall be guilty of an offence.

Offences Against the Person Act 1861, s 18

Points to prove

✓ unlawfully and maliciously
✓ caused grievous bodily harm or wounded a person
✓ with intent to
✓ do grievous bodily harm or resist/prevent lawful apprehension/ detention of self/another

Meanings

Unlawfully (see **2.3.1**)

Maliciously (see **2.3.1**)

Any means whatsoever

This is given its literal meaning. A connection between the means used and the harm caused must be proved.

Wound (see **2.3.1**)

Cause

Defined as 'anything that produces a result or effect'.

Grievous bodily harm (see **2.3.1**)

Intent (see **4.1.2**)

Resist or prevent (see **2.2.1**)

Explanatory notes

- Cause has a wider meaning than 'inflict'. All that needs to be proved is some connection between the action (the means used) and the injury (sometimes called the chain of causation). There does not need to be a direct application of force.
- The issue of causation is separate from the test for intent.
- If appropriate consider the 'causation test' (see *R v Roberts* (1972) 56 Cr App R 95, CA—below).
- Intent must be proved either from verbal admissions on interview and/or other incriminating evidence (eg subsequent actions).

- The statutory test under s 8 of the Criminal Justice Act 1967 must be considered (see **4.1.2**).
- In relation to the offence of wounding or causing GBH with intent to resist or prevent lawful arrest/detention it must be proved—
  - arrest/detention was lawful;
  - defendant must have known that arrest was being made on them/ another person.

Defences (see **2.1.2**)

Related cases

R v Belfon [1976] 3 All ER 46, CA For the offence of wounding with intent the prosecution must prove that the defendant—
- wounded the victim;
- being deliberate and unjustified;
- intending (subjective test) to cause really serious bodily harm.

R v Roberts (1972) 56 Cr App R 95, CA A victim of an ongoing sexual assault jumped out of a car to escape and was seriously injured in doing so. The court considered the 'chain of causation' and applied the 'causation test'—

- If the victim's actions are reasonable ones which could be foreseen and were acceptable under the circumstances, then the defendant will be liable for injuries resulting from them.
- If the harm/injury was caused by a voluntary act on the part of the victim, which could not reasonably be foreseen, then the chain of causation between the defendant's actions and the harm/injury received will be broken and the defendant will not be liable for them.

Practical considerations (see also **2.3.1**)

- Section 18 does not come under racially or religiously aggravated assaults (see **7.10.2**), although this will be considered when determining sentence.
- The distinction between charges under s 18 and s 20 is one of **intent**, either a specific intent to cause GBH/wounding or intent to resist arrest.
- Knowledge that GBH was a virtually certain consequence of their action will not amount to an intention, but it *will* be good evidence from which a court can infer such intention.
- Other factors which may indicate the specific intent include—
  - a repeated or planned attack;
  - deliberate selection of a weapon or adaptation of an article to cause injury, such as breaking a glass before an attack;
  - making prior threats;
  - using an offensive weapon against, or kicking, the victim's head.

2.3.2 Wounding or grievous bodily harm—with intent

- Proof is required that the wound/GBH was inflicted maliciously. This means that the defendant must have foreseen some harm—although not necessarily the specific type or gravity of injury suffered or inflicted.
- Generally an assault under this section may be—
  - ◆ wounding with intent to do GBH;
  - ◆ causing GBH, with intent to do GBH;
  - ◆ wounding with intent to resist or prevent the lawful arrest/detention of self/any person;
  - ◆ maliciously causing GBH with intent to resist or prevent the lawful arrest of self/any person.
- Where evidence of intent is absent, but a wound or grievous bodily harm is still caused, then both s 18 and s 20 should be included on the indictment.
- Consider CPS advice and guidance for wounding/causing GBH with intent.
- In cases involving GBH, remember that s 20 requires the infliction of harm, whereas s 18 requires the causing of harm, although this distinction has been greatly reduced by the decisions in *R v Ireland* [1998] AC 147, HL and *R v Burstow* [1997] 4 All ER 225, HL (see **2.3.1**).
- Section 18 is of assistance in more serious assaults upon police officers, where the evidence of an intention to prevent arrest is clear, but the evidence of intent to cause GBH is in doubt.
- Section 6(3) of the Criminal Law Act 1967 permits a conviction for s 20 (inflicting GBH) in respect of a count for s 18 (causing GBH with intent), as 'cause' includes 'inflict' (*R v Wilson and Jenkins* [1983] 3 All ER 448, HL).
- Obtain medical evidence to prove extent of injury.
- Obtain photographs of victim's injuries.

SSS   **E&S**

 Indictable only   None

Life imprisonment

Links to alternative subjects and offences

2.4 **Child Cruelty and Taking a Child into Police Protection**

2.4.1 **Child cruelty**

The Children and Young Persons Act 1933, s 1 creates offences regarding any child or young person below the age of 16 years being exposed to moral, physical, or psychological danger by persons with responsibility for them.

Offences

If any person who has attained the age of 16 years and has **responsibility** for any **child** or **young person** under that age, wilfully assaults, ill-treats (whether physically or otherwise), neglects, abandons, or exposes him, or causes or procures him to be assaulted, ill-treated (whether physically or otherwise), **neglected**, abandoned, or exposed, **in a manner likely to cause** him unnecessary suffering or **injury to health** (whether the suffering or injury is of a physical or a psychological nature), that person shall be guilty of an offence.

Children and Young Persons Act 1933, s 1(1)

Points to prove

- ✓ being a person 16 years or over
- ✓ having responsibility
- ✓ for a child/young person (under 16 years)
- ✓ did wilfully or caused/procured the child/young person to be
- ✓ assaulted/ill-treated (whether physical or otherwise)/neglected/ abandoned/exposed
- ✓ in manner likely
- ✓ to cause unnecessary suffering/injury (physical or psychological) to health

---

Meanings

Responsibility (s17)

- The following shall be presumed to have responsibility for a child or young person—
  - (a) any person who—
    - (i) has **parental responsibility** for the child/young person; or
    - (ii) is otherwise legally liable to maintain the child/young person; and

(b) any person who has care of the child/young person.

- A person who is presumed to be responsible for a child or young person by virtue of (a) shall not be taken to have ceased to be responsible by reason only that they do not have care of the child/young person.

Parental responsibility

Means all the rights, duties, powers, responsibilities, and authority which by law a parent of a child has in relation to that child and their property.

Child

Means a person under 14 years of age.

Young person

Person who has attained the age of 14 but is under the age of 18 years.

Neglect in a manner likely to cause injury to health

- A parent or other person legally liable to maintain a child or young person, or the **legal guardian** of such a person, is deemed to have neglected in a manner likely to cause injury (physical or psychological) to health if they have failed to provide adequate food, clothing, medical aid, or lodging, or if, having been unable to do so, they have failed to take steps to procure it to be provided under relevant enactments.
- A person may be convicted of this offence—
  + even though actual suffering or injury (physical or psychological) to health, or the likelihood of it, was prevented by the action of another person;
  + notwithstanding the death of the child or young person in question.

Legal guardian

Means a **guardian** of a child as defined in the Children Act 1989.

Guardian

Includes any person who, in the opinion of the court having cognisance of any case in relation to the child or young person, or has for the time being the care of the child or young person.

Explanatory notes

- The Serious Crime Act 2015, s 66 added 'whether physically or otherwise' and 'psychological' to the physical suffering or injury. See HOC 8/2015 for further details.
- The term 'ill-treated' is not specifically defined, but will include bullying, frightening, or any conduct causing unnecessary suffering or injury to physical or mental health.
- Battery of a child cannot be justified on the grounds of reasonable punishment (see **2.1.2 'Defences to assault'**).

Practical considerations

- Section 548 of the Education Act 1996 prevents teachers in any school from giving corporal punishment.

2.4.2 Taking a child at risk into police protection

- The prosecution must prove a deliberate or reckless act, or failure to act. The test is **subjective**, not based on the notion of a reasonable parent or person in charge.
- If there has been ill-treatment by one or both parents, but there is no evidence to suggest which one, it may be possible to consider them jointly responsible.
- Consider taking the child/young person into police protection (see **2.4.2**).

 Either way None

IIII **Summary**: 6 months' imprisonment and/or a fine
Indictment: 10 years' imprisonment and/or a fine

2.4.2 **Taking a child at risk into police protection**

The Children Act 1989, s 46 provides police powers to take children under 18 years old who are at risk of significant harm into police protection.

Powers

(1) Where a constable has reasonable cause to believe that a **child** would otherwise be likely to suffer significant harm, he may—
   (a) remove the child to suitable accommodation and keep him there; or
   (b) take such steps as are reasonable to ensure that the child's removal from any **hospital**, or other place, in which he is being accommodated is prevented.
(2) For the purposes of this Act, a child with respect to whom a constable has exercised his powers under this section is referred to as having been taken into **police protection**.
(3) As soon as is reasonably practicable after taking a child into police protection, the constable concerned shall—
   (a) inform the local authority within whose area the child was found of the steps that have been, and are proposed to be, taken with respect to the child under this section and the reasons for taking them;

    (b) give details to the authority within whose area the child is ordinarily resident ('the appropriate authority') of the place at which the child is being accommodated;

    (c) inform the child (if he appears capable of understanding)—
        (i) of the steps that have been taken with respect to him under this section and of the reasons for taking them; and
        (ii) of the further steps that may be taken with respect to him under this section;

    (d) take such steps as are reasonably practicable to discover the wishes and feelings of the child;

    (e) secure that the case is inquired into by an officer designated for the purposes of this section by the chief officer of the police area concerned; and

    (f) where the child was taken into police protection by being removed to accommodation which is not provided—
        (i) by or on behalf of a local authority; or
        (ii) as a refuge, in compliance with the requirements of section 51,
    secure that he is moved to accommodation which is so provided.

(4) As soon as is reasonably practicable after taking a child into police protection the constable concerned shall take such steps as are reasonably practicable to inform—
    (a) the child's parents;
    (b) every person who is not a parent of his but who has parental responsibility for him; and
    (c) any other person with whom the child was living immediately before being taken into police protection,
of the steps that he has taken under this section with respect to the child, the reasons for taking them and the further steps that may be taken with respect to him under this section.

(5) On completing any inquiry under subsection (3)(e), the officer conducting it shall release the child from police protection unless he considers that there is still reasonable cause for believing that the child would be likely to suffer significant harm if released.

(6) No child may be kept in police protection for more than 72 hours.

(7) While a child is being kept in police protection, the designated officer may apply on behalf of the appropriate authority for an emergency protection order to be made under s 44 with respect to the child.

(8) An application may be made under subsection (7) whether or not the authority know of it or agree to its being made.

(9) While a child is being kept in police protection—
    (a) neither the constable concerned nor the designated officer shall have parental responsibility for him; but
    (b) the designated officer shall do what is reasonable in all the circumstances of the case for the purpose of safeguarding or promoting the child's welfare (having regard in particular to the length of the period during which the child will be so protected).

2.4.2 Taking a child at risk into police protection

(10) Where a child has been taken into police protection, the designated officer shall allow—
  (a) the child's parents;
  (b) any person who is not a parent of the child but who has parental responsibility for him;
  (c) any person with whom the child was living immediately before he was taken into police protection;
  (d) any person named in a child arrangements order as a person with whom the child is to spend time or otherwise have contact;
  (e) any person who is allowed to have contact with the child by virtue of an order under s 34; and
  (f) any person acting on behalf of any of those persons,
to have such contact (if any) with the child as, in the opinion of the designated officer, is both reasonable and in the child's interests.

Children Act 1989, s 46

Meanings

Child

Means a person under the age of 18.

Hospital

Any health service hospital within the meaning of the NHS Act 2006; and any accommodation provided by a local authority and used as a hospital under that Act.

Explanatory notes

- The spirit of the legislation is that all the parties including the parents, the child, and the local authority are kept informed, and given reasons for any actions. The child's wishes must be listened to but do not have to be acted upon.
- The police have a duty to protect the child until more formal arrangements can be made. It is possible for a child to be in police protection without physically moving them. For example, if a child is in hospital having been battered, they may be taken into police protection while leaving the child in the hospital.
- This power is appropriate for detaining and returning children missing from home as long as they are at risk from significant harm.

Related cases

Langley and others v Liverpool City Council [2006] 1 WLR 375, CA If practicable removal should be authorised by an emergency protection court order under s 44 and carried out by the local authority. If such an order is in force the police should not exercise their s 46 powers, unless there are compelling reasons for doing so.

Practical considerations

- HOC 17/2008 provides guidance as follows—
  - ✦ The designated officer under s 46(3)(e) will usually be an officer of the rank of Inspector.
  - ✦ These powers should only be used when the child would be likely to suffer significant harm.
  - ✦ Except in exceptional circumstances (eg imminent threat to a child's welfare), no child is to be taken into police protection until the investigating officer has seen the child and assessed their circumstances.
  - ✦ Consider entry powers under s 17 PACE (see **12.3.2**) as no power of entry is provided under these police protection powers.
  - ✦ A police station is not suitable accommodation for these purposes, but may be used as a temporary or emergency measure until suitable accommodation is identified.
- The Children Act 1989 includes other powers to protect children—
  - ✦ s 43—Child assessment orders;
  - ✦ s 44—Emergency protection orders;
  - ✦ s 47—Duty of local authority to investigate welfare;
  - ✦ s 48—Warrant/powers to ascertain if child requires protection;
  - ✦ s 50—Recovery of abducted children.
- A Local Safeguarding Children Board for each area should protect children from abuse and neglect. This involves a range of parties providing children's services and the police liaising with each other, including an information database whereby information can be shared between all partners.

Links to alternative subjects and offences

2.5 **Threats to Kill**

Section 16 of the Offences Against the Person Act 1861 provides the offence of threats to kill.

Offences

A person who, without lawful excuse makes to another a threat **intending** that the other would fear it would be carried out, to kill that other or a third person shall be guilty of an offence.

Offences Against the Person Act 1861, s 16

Points to prove

✓ without lawful excuse
✓ made threat to kill
✓ intending to cause fear threat would be carried out

Meaning of intending (see 4.1.2)

Explanatory notes

- This is a serious offence, particularly given its potential effect on the victim.
- There is no need to show that the defendant intended to kill anyone. The relevant intent has to be that the person receiving the threat would fear the threat (to kill them or a third person) would be carried out.
- A threat to a pregnant woman to kill her unborn baby is not an offence under this section.

Defences

- Having a lawful excuse, such as the prevention of crime or self-defence.
- It must be reasonable in all the circumstances to make the threat.

Related cases

R v Rizwan Mawji [2003] EWCA Crim 3067, CA Where a threat to kill was made to a victim by email and they printed that email, it could be adduced in evidence after they had given oral evidence without offending the rules of hearsay.

R v Williams (1987) 84 Cr App R 299, CA Evidence of a previous assault is admissible by the judge as it tends to prove that the accused intended the victim to take the threats to kill seriously.

R v Cousins [1982] 2 All ER 115, CA A lawful excuse can exist if a threat to kill is made for the prevention of crime or for self-defence, provided that it is reasonable in the circumstances to make such a threat.

R v Tait [1990] 1 QB 290, CA An unborn child is not a third person as it is not distinct from its mother. Therefore, a threat to kill the child in the womb or cause a miscarriage will not be an offence. However, a threat to kill the baby at birth will be an offence.

Practical considerations

- Generally the threats to kill are often made during a heated argument or a moment of aggression and as a result the case usually fails to pass the evidential test required owing to lack of proof of the required intent.
- The onus is on the prosecution to prove that there was no lawful excuse for making a threat. The jury should be directed to any facts that could give rise to a defence of lawful excuse which was reasonable. It is for the jury to decide what is reasonable and what amounts to a threat.
- Consider hearsay and bad character admissibility under the Criminal Justice Act 2003.
- Proof of the mens rea ('guilty mind'), as to the intention that the other person would fear the threat would be carried out to kill that person or a third person, is required.
- Evidence of previous history between the parties is admissible as tending to prove that the defendant intended his words to be taken seriously.
- Detail in your file and CJA witness statements the following points—
  + nature of the threats made—exact words used and in what context, include any previous threats made;
  + the fact that the threat was **understood** by the person to whom it was made and that the person feared the threat would be carried out;
  + describe the full circumstances of the incident, antecedent history details of the relationship between the defendant and complainant.
- Consider whether or not there are any 'aggravating' circumstances such as racial or religious motivation or terrorism.

 Either way   None

 Summary: 6 months' imprisonment and/or a fine
Indictment: 10 years' imprisonment

Links to alternative subjects and offences

2.6 False Imprisonment, Kidnapping, and Child Abduction

Contained within this topic area are the common law offences of kidnapping, false imprisonment, and child abduction under the Child Abduction Act 1984. Officers should be familiar with this area of law when dealing with any violent domestic incidents, sexual offences, or where people are taken against their will.

2.6.1 False imprisonment

False imprisonment is an offence at common law.

Offences

The unlawful and total restraint of the personal liberty of another, whether by constraining them or compelling them to go to a particular place or by confining them in a prison or police station or private place or by detaining them against their will in a public place.

Common Law

Points to prove

✓ imprisoned, detained, or arrested
✓ another person
✓ against his/her will
✓ unlawfully

Explanatory notes

- The wrongful act ('actus reus') of false imprisonment is the act of placing an unlawful restriction on the victim's freedom in the absence of any legal right to do so.
- There must also have been an element of intent ('mens rea') to restrain, either deliberately or recklessly.
- There is no offence if the victim is not physically restrained, unless the offender detains/intends to detain them by use of fear/threats. Unlawfully locking someone in a vehicle may be sufficient for this offence.

Defences

That the taking or detaining was in the course of a lawful arrest or detention under PACE (see 12.2) or acting under another statutory or common law power.

2.6.1 False imprisonment

Related cases

Bird v Jones (1845) 7 QB 742, QBD Preventing a person from proceeding along a particular way is not false imprisonment.

R v James, The Times, 2 October 1997, CA The victim's fear that she was being restrained had to arise from the defendant's intentional or reckless act to frighten her into staying where she was. If the victim's lack of will to escape was simply a by-product of an assault then the offence of false imprisonment is not committed.

R v Rahman (1985) 81 Cr App R 349, CA False imprisonment consists of the unlawful or reckless restraint of a person's freedom of movement from a particular place. 'Unlawful' is not restricted to the contravention of a court order.

Austin v UK [2012] Crim LR 544, ECtHR The police had imposed a cordon to isolate and contain a large crowd of protestors in volatile and dangerous conditions to prevent serious injury or damage. Held: In the circumstances, an absolute cordon had been the least intrusive and most effective means to be applied. Those within the cordon had not been deprived of their liberty in breach of Art 5 (see **1.1**). The police were fulfilling their duty of maintaining order and protecting the public, as required under both national and Convention law.

R (on the application of McClure and Moos) v Commissioner of Police of the Metropolis [2012] EWCA Civ 12, CA Two large demonstrations, each one having about 4000 protestors, took place in London in protest against the G20 Summit. The police contained the first disorderly demonstration to avoid both camps joining forces, thus preventing widespread violence occurring. It was held that the police 'kettling' tactics used were, on this occasion, a lawful means of preventing imminent and serious breaches of the peace (**7.3**).

Practical considerations

- A parent has no right to imprison their own child, although a parent is allowed to detain a child for purposes of reasonable parental discipline. Whether it is reasonable in all the circumstances is for a jury to decide.
- A victim could bring a civil action for damages (invariably after unlawful arrest by the police). Consider kidnapping (**2.6.2**) or child abduction (**2.6.3**) as alternatives.

E&S

 Indictable   None

 Life imprisonment and/or a fine

2.6.2 **Kidnapping**

Kidnapping is another offence at common law.

Offences

The taking or carrying away of one person by another, by force or **fraud**, without the consent of the person so taken or carried away, and without lawful excuse.

Common Law

Points to prove

✓ without lawful excuse
✓ by force/fraud
✓ took/carried away
✓ another person
✓ without their consent

Meaning of fraud

Means deceit, guile or trick. It should not be confused with the narrower meaning given to it for the purposes of consent in sexual offences.

Explanatory notes

- The important points to prove are the deprivation of liberty and carrying away even where a short distance is involved—and the absence of consent.
- In the case of a child it is the child's consent that should be considered (rather than the parent/guardian) and in the case of a very young child, absence of consent may be inferred.

Defences

Consent or lawful excuse.

Related cases

R v Hendy-Freegard [2007] EWCA Crim 1236, CA The victim must have been deprived of their liberty by the kidnapper for the offence to be made out. Inducing a person by deception to move from one place to another unaccompanied by the 'kidnapper' could not constitute a taking and carrying away or deprivation of liberty.

R v Wellard [1978] 3 All ER 161, CA The defendant purported to be a police officer and escorted/placed a female victim into his car a short distance away. Ingredients for the offence of kidnapping are that the

2.6.3 Child abduction

victim was deprived of their liberty; and carried away from the place where they wanted to be without lawful excuse.

R v Cort [2003] 3 WLR 1300, CA The defendant went to bus stops telling lone women that the bus they were waiting for had broken down and offering/providing lifts in his vehicle. The fact that the defendant had lied about the absence of the bus meant that, although they had got into the car voluntarily, the women had not given true consent to the journey and the offences of kidnap (and attempts) were complete.

Practical considerations

- A man or woman may be guilty of this offence in relation to their spouse or partner.
- Under s 5 of the Child Abduction Act 1984, consent of the DPP is required to prosecute for an offence of kidnapping if it was committed—
  + against a child under 16;
  + by a person connected with the child under s 1 (see **2.6.3**).
- In all other cases the consent of the DPP is not required.

 Indictable   None

 Life imprisonment and/or a fine

2.6.3 Child abduction

The Child Abduction Act 1984 provides two distinct child abduction offences: s 1—person connected to child (parent/guardian) and s 2—committed by other persons.

Person connected with child

> **Offences**
>
> Subject to subsections (5) and (8) below, a **person connected** with a child under the age of 16 commits an offence if he **takes** or **sends** the child out of the United Kingdom without the **appropriate consent**.
>
> Child Abduction Act 1984, s 1(1)

Points to prove

✓ being a parent/person connected with
✓ a child under 16 years of age
✓ took/sent that child
✓ out of the United Kingdom
✓ without the appropriate consent

Meanings

Person connected (s 1(2))

A **person connected** with a child for the purposes of this section is—

(a)   a parent of the child; or
(b)   in the case of a child whose parents were not married to each other at the time of birth, there are reasonable grounds for believing that he is the father of the child; or
(c)   the guardian of the child; or
(ca) a special guardian of the child; or
(d)   a person named in a child arrangements order as a person with whom the child is to live; or
(e)   has custody of the child.

Takes

A person is regarded as **taking** a child if they cause or induce the child to accompany them, or any other person, or causes the child to be taken.

Sends

A person is regarded as **sending** a child if they cause the child to be sent.

Appropriate consent (s 1(3))

(a)   This means the consent of each of the following—
  (i)   the child's mother;
  (ii)   the child's father, if he has parental responsibility for him;
  (iii)   any guardian of the child;
  (iiia) any special guardian of the child;
  (iv)   any person named in a child arrangements order as a person with whom the child is to live;
  (v)   any person who has custody of the child; or
(b)   the leave of the court granted under or by virtue of any provision of Pt 2 of the Children Act 1989; or
(c)   if any person has custody of the child, the leave of the court which awarded custody to him.

Explanatory notes

A court could deal with a parent who had abducted his/her child in three ways. First, for contempt of court (flouting a court order); secondly, prosecution for an offence under the 1984 Act; and thirdly, prosecution for kidnapping, either on the basis of force, or fraud in

2.6.3 Child abduction

achieving the removal of the child from the other parent (*R v Kayani; R v Sollim* [2011] EWCA Crim 2871, CA).

- This offence can also be committed (subject to the statutory defences given below) when a child is in the care of a local authority, or voluntary organisation, or place of safety whilst subject to adoption proceedings.

Defences

(4) A person does not commit an offence under this section by taking or sending a child out of the United Kingdom without obtaining the appropriate consent if—

    (a) he is a person named in a child arrangements order as a person with whom the child is to live, and he takes or sends the child out of the United Kingdom for a period of less than one month; or

    (b) he is a special guardian of the child and he takes or sends the child out of the United Kingdom for a period of less than three months.

(4A) Subsection (4) above does not apply if the person taking or sending the child out of the United Kingdom does so in breach of an order under Pt 2 of the Children Act 1989.

(5) A person does not commit an offence under this section by doing anything without the consent of another person whose consent is required under the forgoing provisions if—

    (a) he does it in the belief that the other person—

        (i) has consented; or

        (ii) would consent if he was aware of all the relevant circumstances; or

    (b) he has taken all reasonable steps to communicate with the other person but has been unable to communicate with him; or

    (c) the other person has unreasonably refused to consent.

(5A) Subsection (5)(c) above does not apply if—

    (a) the person who refused to consent is a person—

        (i) named in a child arrangements order as a person with whom the child is to live; or

        (ia) who is a special guardian of the child; or

        (ii) who has custody of the child; or

    (b) the person taking or sending the child out of the United Kingdom is, by so acting, in breach of an order made by a court in the United Kingdom.

Child Abduction Act 1984, s 1

Abduction of child by other person

An offence in relation to the taking or detaining of a child where th offender is not connected with that child states:

Offences

Subject to subsection (3), a person other than one mentioned in subsection (2) below, commits an offence if, without lawful authority or reasonable excuse, he **takes** or **detains** a child under the age of 16—

(a) so as to **remove** him **from** the **lawful control** of any person having lawful control of the child; or

(b) so as to keep him out of the lawful control of any person entitled to lawful control of the child.

Child Abduction Act 1984, s 2(1)

Points to prove

✓ without lawful authority/reasonable excuse
✓ detained or took
✓ a child under 16 years of age
✓ so as to remove/keep him/her
✓ from/out of the lawful control
✓ of a person having/entitled to lawful control
✓ of that child

Meanings

Takes (see s 1(1))

Detains

A person is regarded as detaining a child if they cause the child to be detained or induces the child to remain with them or any other person.

Remove from lawful control

This can be satisfied if the child is induced to take some action that they would not normally have done.

Explanatory notes

- The offence is subject to a statutory defence of consent (s 2(3)—below).
- This offence does not apply to persons listed in s 2(2) namely—
  ◆ the child's father and mother—being married to each other at the time of the birth;
  ◆ the child's mother—where the father was not married to her at the time of the birth;
  ◆ any other person mentioned in s 1(2)(c) to (e) above.

2.6.3 Child abduction

Defences

It shall be a defence for that person to prove—

(a) where the father and mother of the child in question were not married to each other at the time of his birth—
   (i) that he is the child's father
   (ii) that, at the time of the alleged offence, he believed, on reasonable grounds, that he was the child's father, or
(b) that, at the time of the alleged offence, he believed that the child had attained the age of 16 years.

Child Abduction Act 1984, s 2(3)

Related cases

R v CS [2012] EWCA Crim 389, CA The defence of necessity is not available under s 1.

R v Mohammed [2006] EWCA Crim 1107, CA (see 6.7.2 'Related cases')

R v A (Child Abduction) [2000] 2 All ER 177, CA The jury has to be satisfied that the defendant caused the child to accompany them. However, they do not have to be the sole or even the main cause for the child going with them (though the actions must be more than a peripheral or inconsequential cause).

Foster and another v DPP [2005] 1 WLR 1400, QBD Section 2 has two separate offences and alternative charges cannot be made. The mens rea of s 2 is an intentional or reckless taking or detention. It is immaterial that the child consents to removal from lawful control, but the s 2(3)(b) defence is available if it is believed that the child was 16 or over.

R v Wakeman [2011] EWCA 1649, CA W took the hands of two children and walked them 30 metres across a park to show them something interesting, without the consent of the nearby parents. The prosecution need only prove an intentional or reckless taking, or detention, the consequence of which was removing a child from the control of any person having lawful control of that child.

Practical considerations

- Child Abduction Warning Notices (formerly known as Harbourers Warning Notices) have provided useful evidence in many prosecutions, including large-scale 'grooming cases'. They have no statutory basis but, if properly used, can help to safeguard vulnerable youngsters and provide supportive evidence for criminal or other proceedings.
- Consider the more serious offence of kidnapping, but be aware that consent from the DPP may be required under s 5 (see 2.6.2).
- The s 1 offence (person connected with child) can only be committed by those people listed in s 1(2) **and** they must take or send that child out of the UK; the prosecution must rebut the defence of consent.

- A Convention agreement exists between the UK and other countries regarding liaison between the different civil jurisdictions in those countries in order to recover the abducted child.
- Section 2 (other people not connected with the child) will cover the situation where an agent snatches a child for an estranged parent. The parent in such a case may commit the offence of aiding and abetting or the principal offence.

 Either way　　　　　　　 None

Summary: 6 months' imprisonment and/or a fine
Indictment: 7 years' imprisonment

Links to alternative subjects and offences

2.7 **Suspicious Deaths**

Police officers investigating sudden/suspicious deaths should have a basic knowledge of the relevant law and powers. Apart from informing supervision, following **force policies/procedures** and requesting the assistance of scenes of crime officers, be mindful of scene preservation and the obtaining of forensic evidence (see **1.3**).

Murder; manslaughter; corporate manslaughter; causing or allowing the death of or serious physical harm to a child/vulnerable adult; 'overlaying' of an infant; infanticide; child destruction; and concealment of birth are all dealt with in this section.

2.7.1 **Murder**

The offence of murder comes under the common law and is defined as—

Offences

Where a person of **sound mind and discretion** unlawfully kills any **reasonable creature in being** and **under the Queen's peace**, with **intent** to kill or **cause grievous bodily harm**.

Common Law

Points to prove

✓ unlawfully killed a human being
✓ with intent to kill or cause grievous bodily harm

Meanings

Sound mind and discretion

Every person of the age of discretion is presumed to be sane and accountable for his actions, unless the contrary is proved. This means anyone who is not insane or under 10 years old.

Unlawfully

Means without lawful authority, legal justification, or excuse.

Kills

This is 'the act' ('actus reus') which is the substantial cause of death (stabbed, shot, strangled, suffocated, poisoned, etc).

Reasonable creature in being

Any human being, including a baby born alive having an independent existence from its mother.

Under the Queen's peace

This is meant to exclude killing in the course of war. A British subject takes the Queen's peace with them everywhere in the world.

Intent

An intention to kill or to cause grievous bodily harm is the 'mens rea' of murder (see **4.1.2**).

Cause/causation

If there is an 'intervening factor' between the defendant's actions and the death of the victim, the jury will consider whether the defendant's act **contributed significantly** to the death.

Grievous bodily harm (see **2.3**)

Explanatory notes

- It shall be conclusively presumed that no child under the age of 10 years can be guilty of any offence (Children and Young Persons Act 1933, s 50).
- If a defendant wishes to plead **insanity**, they will be judged on the M'Naghten Rules from *M'Naghten's Case* (1843) 10 Cl & F 200. This examines the extent to which, at the time of the commission of the offence, the person was 'labouring under such defect of reason from disease of the mind that either: (a) the defendant did not know what they were doing, **or** (b) they did know what they were doing but did not know it was wrong'.
- The onus is on the prosecution to prove that the killing was unlawful.
- If a person intentionally causes GBH and the victim subsequently dies as a result, that person is guilty of murder.
- Traditionally it required 'malice aforethought', but practically it is the relevant intent that will determine whether an unlawful killing is murder or manslaughter.
- The jury will consider whether the defendant's act **contributed significantly** to the death by applying the 'substantial test' as set out in *R v Smith* [1959] 2 All ER 193, Court Martial CA.
- Whether the defendant intended or foresaw the results of their actions will be determined by a number of factors including the statutory test under the Criminal Justice Act 1967, s 8 (see **4.1.2**).

Defences to murder

Insanity

See the meaning of 'sound mind and discretion' and explanatory notes as to 'insanity'.

Lawful killing

Means with lawful authority; legal justification or excuse, including self-defence (see **1.2.1**).

2.7.1 Murder

At war

This is self explanatory, not being under the 'Queen's peace' (see 'Meanings').

Specific defences

Loss of control

Where a person ('D') kills or is a party to the killing of another ('V'), D is not to be convicted of murder if—

(a) D's acts and omissions in doing or being a party to the killing resulted from D's loss of self-control,
(b) the loss of self-control had a **qualifying trigger**, and
(c) a person of D's sex and age, with a normal degree of tolerance and self-restraint and in the circumstances of D, might have reacted in the same or in a similar way to D.

Coroners and Justice Act 2009, s 54(1)

Diminished responsibility

(1) A person ('D') who kills or is a party to the killing of another is not to be convicted of murder if D was suffering from an abnormality of mental functioning which—
  (a) arose from a recognised medical condition,
  (b) substantially impaired D's ability to do one or more of the things mentioned in subsection (1A), and
  (c) provides an explanation for D's acts and omissions in doing or being a party to the killing.
(1A) Those things are—
  (a) to understand the nature of D's conduct;
  (b) to form a rational judgment;
  (c) to exercise self-control.

Homicide Act 1957, s 2

Suicide pact

Means a common agreement between two or more persons having for its object the death of all of them, whether or not each is to take his own life, but nothing done by a person who enters into a suicide pact shall be treated as done by him in pursuance of the pact unless it is done while he has the settled intention of dying in pursuance of the pact.

Homicide Act 1957, s 4(3)

Related cases

R v Gnango [2011] UKSC 59, SC G had a gun fight with X in a public place, both had the intent to kill the other. During the shooting a shot from X killed a passerby. By virtue of transferred malice, both were guilty of the passerby's murder.

R v Clinton [2012] EWCA Crim 2, CA Lord Judge commented that under s 54 and s 55 of the Coroners and Justice Act 2009, sexual infidelity cannot 'on its own' act as a trigger for the partial defence to murder for 'loss of control', but added that to ignore sexual infidelity can carry the potential for injustice. In short, sexual infidelity is not subject to blanket exclusion when the loss of control defence is under consideration.

R v Rahman and others [2008] UKHL 45, HL Victim died from a stab wound to the back during an attack by a number of people all armed with various weapons, but the identity of the person who had inflicted the fatal wound was unknown. This was joint unlawful enterprise to inflict unlawful violence, where a principal killed with an intention to kill which was unexpected and unforeseen by the others. The case gave a test to be applied as to liability.

R v Hatton [2005] EWCA Crim 2951, CA Self-defence—not possible if mistake induced by intoxication.

R v Cheshire [1991] 1 WLR 844, CA Even though medical negligence was the primary cause of death, the shooting had been a major contributory factor and the wounds inflicted were a significant cause of death.

R v Smith [1959] 2 All ER 193, Court Martial CA Only if the second cause is so overwhelming as to make the original wound merely part of the history can it be said that the death does not flow from the wound.

R v Malcherek and R v Steel (1981) 73 Cr App R 173, CA A defendant (who causes injury) necessitating medical treatment could not argue that the sole cause of death was the doctor's action in switching the life support system off.

R v Moloney [1985] 1 All ER 1025, HL The jury has to decide whether the defendant **intended** to kill or cause grievous bodily harm.

Practical considerations

- The defendant's act must be the substantial cause of death.
- The killing must be causally related to the acts of the defendant and not through an intervening factor which breaks the chain of causation.
- If there is doubt whether death was caused by some supervening event (such as medical negligence when treated), the prosecution do not have to prove that the supervening event was not a significant cause of death.
- Intention—mens rea ('guilty mind')—has to be proved (see **4.1.2**).
- The date of the offence is the actual date of death.
- Consent of the A-G is required where—
  - ♦ the injury was sustained more than three years before death; **or**
  - ♦ the accused has been previously convicted of the offence alleged to be connected with the death.
- If a person is suffering from a terminal disease and receives a wound that hastens their death, this killing would (with the required intent) be murder or manslaughter.
- A murder or manslaughter committed by a British citizen outside the UK may be tried in this country as if it had been committed here.
- Motivation will form a key part of any prosecution and the availability of any defences should be considered.
- The meaning of '**qualifying trigger**' for the partial defence to murder is where the defendant lost self-control because—
  - ♦ of fear of serious violence against defendant or another person; **or**

- ◆ it was attributable to things done or said (or both) which constituted circumstances of an extremely grave character and caused the defendant to have a justifiable sense of being seriously wronged.
- Guidance and details regarding the partial defences to murder for loss of control, diminished responsibility and infanticide, made by the Coroners and Justice Act 2009, is given in MOJ Circular 13/2010.
- Offences Against the Person Act 1861, s 4 is the offence of soliciting to murder: 'Whosoever shall solicit, encourage, persuade, or endeavour to persuade, or shall propose to any person, to murder any other person, shall be guilty of an offence and liable to imprisonment for life'.
- Section 2(1) of the Suicide Act 1961 deals with encouraging or assisting suicide, whereby a person commits an offence if they do an act capable of encouraging or assisting suicide or attempted suicide of another person, and the act was intended to encourage or assist suicide or an attempt at suicide.
- MOJ Circular 3/2010 explains the above encourage or assist suicide offence, as replaced by the Coroners and Justice Act 2009. Consider the CPS policy in respect of this offence, which requires DPP consent before prosecution.

 Indictable None

Life imprisonment

2.7.2 **Manslaughter**

Offence

Manslaughter is the **unlawful killing** of another human being which can either be a **voluntary** or **involuntary manslaughter** offence.

Common Law

Points to prove
✓ unlawful act or gross negligence
✓ killed a human being

Meanings

Unlawful killing (see 2.7.1)

Voluntary manslaughter

When a murder charge is reduced to voluntary manslaughter by reason of one of the specific defences to murder (see **2.7.1**).

Involuntary manslaughter

Is an unlawful killing without an intention to kill or cause grievous bodily harm. Apart from the required intent, the elements of the offence are the same as for murder (see **2.7.1**).

Manslaughter can be caused by:
- **unlawful act** (not omission): the unlawful act must be unlawful in itself (eg another criminal offence such as an assault or a threat to kill) and must involve a risk that someone would be harmed by it;
- **gross negligence** (involving breach of duty): gross negligence manslaughter requires a breach of a duty of care owed by the defendant to the victim under circumstances where the defendant's conduct was serious enough to amount to a crime.

Related cases

R v Evans [2009] EWCA Crim 650, CA This case considered the duty required in gross negligence manslaughter. Where a person has contributed to a state of affairs which they knew or ought reasonably to have known had created a threat to life then a duty arose for them to act by taking all reasonable steps to save the life at risk.

R v Kennedy [2007] UKHL 38, HL This case considered deaths where the victim was a consenting adult who self-administered drugs of their own free will and also considered their actions in preparing or passing the drugs. In the case of a fully informed and responsible adult it was not possible to find someone guilty of manslaughter where they had been involved in the supply of a Class A drug, which was then freely and voluntarily self-administered by the victim causing their death.

A-G's Reference (No 3 of 1994) [1997] Crim LR 829, HL A baby was born prematurely after an intentional stabbing which penetrated and damaged the foetus. The baby only lived for 120 days. The doctrine of 'transferred malice' was not wide enough to encompass murder, but was sufficient for manslaughter.

R v Roberts, Day (I) and Day (M) [2001] Crim LR 984, CA Intention to cause GBH is murder but an intention only to do some lesser harm is manslaughter.

R v Adomako Sulman & others [1993] 4 All ER 935, HL Manslaughter by gross negligence requires—
- that the defendant owed a duty of care to the victim;
- a breach of that duty;
- which caused the victim's death; and in circumstances where
- the defendant's conduct was so bad as to amount to a criminal act.

R v Misra and Srivastava [2004] All ER (D) 150, CA Grossly negligent medical treatment, which exposes the patient to the risk of death and causes the death of the victim would be manslaughter.

2.7.3 Corporate manslaughter

Practical considerations (for further considerations see **2.7.1**)

- Consider corporate manslaughter (see **2.7.3**) in work-related deaths involving negligence by the company/organisation.
- Previous convictions or past behaviour of the defendant in homicide cases may well be relevant, both to the issue of mens rea/intent and also to sentence.
- The burden of proof in relation to claiming diminished responsibility or acting in pursuance of a suicide pact lies with the defendant.
- Section 2(1) of the Suicide Act 1961 gives an **offence** of encouraging or assisting suicide of another (see **2.7.1**).

 Indictable None

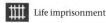 Life imprisonment

2.7.3 **Corporate manslaughter**

The Corporate Manslaughter and Corporate Homicide Act 2007 sets out the offence of corporate manslaughter for an organisation, where a gross failure in the way its activities were managed or organised resulted in a person's death.

Offences

(1) An **organisation to which this section applies** is guilty of an offence if the way in which its activities are managed or organised—
   (a) causes a person's death, and
   (b) amounts to a gross breach of a relevant duty of care owed by the organisation to the deceased.

Corporate Manslaughter and Corporate Homicide Act 2007, s 1

Points to prove

- ✓ being an organisation to which s 1 applies
- ✓ managed or organised its activities
- ✓ in a way that caused the death of a person
- ✓ by an act or omission
- ✓ which amounted to a gross breach of a relevant duty of care owed to that person

---

Meanings

Organisations to which s 1 applies—

- corporation;
- department or other body listed in **Sch 1**;
- police force;
- partnership, or a trade union or employers' association, that is an employer.

Schedule 1

This Schedule lists over 40 Government departments and other similar bodies, such as: CPS; DEFRA; Department for Transport; Department of Health; Foreign and Commonwealth Office; HMRC; Home Office; Ministry of Defence; and the Serious Fraud Office.

Explanatory notes

- An organisation will commit this offence if the way in which its activities are managed or organised causes a death and amounts to a gross breach of a duty of care owed to the deceased.
- The conduct must fall far below what would reasonably have been expected for it to be a gross breach. Any breaches of health and safety legislation will have to be taken into account—and how serious and dangerous those failures were.
- A duty of care exists for example in respect of the systems of work and equipment used by employees, the condition of worksites or premises occupied by the organisation, or to products or services supplied to customers. This Act does not create new duties, they are already owed in the civil law of negligence and the offence is based on these.

Practical considerations

- Officers dealing with fatal/potentially fatal work incidents that appear to involve negligence by the organisation should inform the HSE (see **Appendix 1**), as well as protecting the crime scene.
- Section 2 deals with the '**relevant duty of care**' owed by an organisation under the law of negligence to its employees or other persons working for them, as occupier of premises, or duty owed with the supply of goods or services, carrying out of any construction or maintenance operations or other commercial activity, or the use/ keeping of any plant, vehicle, or other thing.
- This Act applies to a police force, so making them liable for the corporate manslaughter offence if a person dies whilst detained in police custody. MOJ Circular 7/2011 gives guidance in relation to deaths of persons in police custody under s 2(2) who are owed a duty of care under the Act.
- Section 2(1)(d) states that a duty owed to a person, being a person within s 2(2), is someone for whose safety the organisation is responsible. Persons listed in s 2(2) are—
  + **detained** at a custodial institution, a **custody area at a court**, a **police station or customs premises (UK Border Agency)**;
  + detained in service custody premises (Army – MOD);

- detained at a removal centre, a short-term holding facility or in pre-departure accommodation;
- transported in a vehicle, or being held in any premises, in pursuance of prison escort arrangements or immigration escort arrangements;
- in secure accommodation in which they are placed (living);
- a detained patient.

- Juries will consider how the fatal activity was managed or organised throughout the organisation, including any systems and processes for managing safety and how these were operated in practice.
- A substantial part of the failure must have been at senior level, being people who make significant decisions about the organisation or substantial parts of it. This includes both centralised, headquarters functions as well as those in operational management roles.
- Directors, senior managers, or other individuals cannot be held liable for this offence, it will be the organisation that will be prosecuted. However, individuals can still be prosecuted for gross negligence manslaughter (*R v Winter* [2010] EWCA Crim 1474—see **2.7.2**) and for health and safety offences. Individuals will continue to be prosecuted where there is sufficient evidence and it is in the public interest to do so.
- Consent of the DPP is needed before a case of corporate manslaughter can be taken to court. Cases will be prosecuted by the CPS and Health and Safety charges will probably be dealt with at the same time.

 Indictment   None

An unlimited fine

2.7.4 Death or serious physical harm to a child/vulnerable adult

Section 5 of the Domestic Violence, Crime and Victims Act 2004 creates the offences of causing or allowing the death of or serious physical harm to a child or a vulnerable adult by means of an unlawful act.

Offences

A person ('D') is guilty of an offence if—
(a) a child or vulnerable adult ('V') dies or suffers serious physical harm as a result of the unlawful act of a person who—
  (i) was a member of the same household as V, and
  (ii) had frequent contact with him,
(b) D was such a person at the time of that act,

(c) at that time there was a significant risk of **serious physical harm** being caused to V by the unlawful act of such a person, and

(d) either D was the person whose act caused the death or serious physical harm or—

    (i) D was, or ought to have been, aware of the risk mentioned in paragraph (c),

    (ii) D failed to take such steps as he could reasonably have been expected to take to protect V from the risk, and

    (iii) the **act** occurred in circumstances of the kind that D foresaw or ought to have foreseen.

Domestic Violence, Crime and Victims Act 2004, s 5(1)

Points to prove

✓ being a member of the same household and having had frequent contact with a person who was at that time a child/vulnerable adult

✓ caused that person's death or

✓ caused that person to suffer serious physical harm or

✓ was, or ought to have been, aware that there was a significant risk of serious physical harm being caused to that person

✓ by the unlawful act of a member of their household

✓ which occurred in circumstances of the kind that the defendant foresaw or ought to have foreseen and

✓ the defendant failed to take such steps as they could reasonably have been expected to take to protect them from that risk

---

Meanings

Child

Means a person under the age of 16 years.

Vulnerable adult

Means a person aged 16 or over whose ability to protect themselves from violence, abuse, or neglect is significantly impaired through physical or mental disability or illness, through old age or otherwise.

Unlawful act (see 2.7.2)

Act

This includes a course of conduct and also includes omission.

Member of the same household

This includes people who do not live in that household, providing they visit often and for such periods of time that they are regarded as a member of it.

Serious physical harm

Means grievous bodily harm (see 2.3).

2.7.4 Death or serious physical harm to a child/vulnerable adult

Explanatory notes

The meaning of a **vulnerable adult** also includes a temporary vulnerability as well as one which is permanent.

Related cases

R v Khan and others [2009] EWCA Crim 2, CA This offence imposes a duty on members of the same household to protect children/vulnerable adults where their ability to protect themselves was impaired and vulnerability may be short or long-term. Furthermore, the defendant was aware of the risk of serious harm and foresaw or ought reasonably to have foreseen that an unlawful act or course of conduct would result in death, and failed to take reasonable steps to prevent the risk.

R v Stephens and Mujuru [2007] EWCA Crim 1249, CA S seriously assaulted M's daughter causing her serious injury, but neither S nor M sought medical intervention for her. Later S inflicted a severe blow to M's daughter's head resulting in her death. The question of M knowing that a significant risk of serious physical harm to her daughter existed was a matter of fact for the jury to decide and the term 'significant risk' is to be given its ordinary meaning.

Practical considerations

- If D was not the mother or father of V then they may not be charged with this offence if they were under the age of 16 at the time of the act that caused the death or serious harm. Similarly, they could not have been expected to take any such preventative steps to protect the victim before attaining that age.
- Charges can be brought against all members of a household who had responsibility for the death or serious harm of a child or vulnerable adult. This offence is not restricted to family members or carers; it also imposes a duty to protect the victim from harm. However, the question of who is a household member will be for the court to decide.
- If V dies, the death should still be thoroughly investigated to establish whether the person is responsible for murder or manslaughter. As the offence is limited to an unlawful act, it will not apply to accidental or cot deaths.
- Further details on allowing/causing the death is dealt with in HOC 9/2005, whereas MOJ Circular 3/2012 concerns the Domestic Violence, Crime and Victims (Amendment) Act 2012 which extended the original offence to now include serious physical harm.

 Indictable   None

 Causing/allowing death: 14 years' imprisonment and/or a fine
Causing/allowing serious physical harm: 10 years' imprisonment and/or a fine

2.7.5 **Over-laying/suffocation of infant under 3**

The Children and Young Persons Act 1933 provides for circumstances where a child has been suffocated while lying next to an adult.

Offences

Where it is proved that the death of an infant under three years of age was caused by suffocation (not being suffocation caused by disease or the presence of any foreign body in the throat or air passages of the infant) while the infant was **in bed** with some other person who has attained the age of sixteen years, that other person shall, if he was, when he **went to bed** or at any later time before the suffocation, under the influence of drink or a **prohibited drug**, be deemed to have neglected the infant in a manner likely to cause injury to its health.

Children and Young Persons Act 1933, s 1(2)(b)

Points to prove

✓ being a person 16 years or over
✓ caused the death of an infant under 3 years of age
✓ by suffocation
✓ while the infant was lying next to that person
✓ person under the influence of drink/prohibited drug
✓ when they went in to/on a bed/any furniture/surface for the purpose of sleeping

Meanings

In bed/went to bed

This includes a reference to the infant lying next to the adult in or on any kind of furniture or surface being used by the adult for the purpose of sleeping.

Prohibited drug

If possession of the drug immediately before taking it would be an offence under s 5(2) of the Misuse of Drugs Act 1971 (see **5.2.1**).

Explanatory notes

- The Serious Crime Act 2015, s 66 added a 'prohibited drug' to this offence and expanded on the infant being 'in bed' and when the adult 'went to bed'. HOC 8/2015 provides guidance on these changes.
- Consider a more serious charge, such as manslaughter (see **2.7.2**) or causing/allowing the death of a child (see **2.7.4**).
- Further details relating to s 1 are given at **2.4.1**.

Either way None

Summary: 6 months' imprisonment and/or a fine
Indictment: 10 years' imprisonment and/or a fine

2.7.6 Infanticide/child destruction/concealment of birth

This offence is committed by the mother of a child (under 12 months old), who by any wilful act or omission, causes the death of her child whilst mentally unbalanced (such as post-natal depression) due to child-birth or lactation.

Offences

Where a woman by any wilful act or omission causes the death of her child being a child under the age of twelve months, but at the time of the act or omission the balance of her mind was disturbed by reason of her not having fully recovered from the effect of giving birth to the child or by reason of the effect of lactation consequent upon the birth of the child, then, if the circumstances were such that but for this Act the offence would have amounted to murder or manslaughter, she shall be guilty of infanticide, and may for such offence be dealt with and punished as if she had been guilty of the offence of manslaughter of the child.

Infanticide Act 1938, s 1(1)

Points to prove

✓ a woman
✓ caused the death of her own child (being under 12 months of age)
✓ by wilful act/omission
✓ whilst balance of her mind disturbed

Practical considerations

- The date of offence will be the date death occurs.
- This offence reduces the act to manslaughter as the responsibility for her actions may have been reduced by the disturbance of her mind caused by childbirth.

- There is no reference to any intention to kill or cause serious bodily harm, only a wilful act or omission (*R v Gore* [2007] EWCA Crim 2789, HL).

Child destruction

- The Infant Life (Preservation) Act 1929, s 1(1) makes it an indictable offence for any person, by any wilful act, to intentionally destroy a child capable of being born alive, before it has an existence independent of its mother.
- Evidence that a woman had at any material time been pregnant for a period of 28 weeks or more shall be prima facie proof that she was at that time pregnant with a child capable of being born alive.
- It has been held that a foetus of between 18 and 21 weeks is not 'capable of being born alive' since it would be incapable of breathing even with the aid of a ventilator, and a termination of a pregnancy of that length is not an offence under this Act.

No person shall be found guilty of this offence if it is proved that the act was done in good faith for saving the life of the mother.

A registered medical practitioner does not commit this offence if the pregnancy is terminated in accordance with the provisions of the Abortion Act 1967, s 5(1).

Section 58 of the Offences Against the Person Act 1861 relates to administering drugs or using instruments to procure a miscarriage (abortion) at any time between conception and the birth of the child alive; whereas the 1929 Act prohibits the killing of any child capable of being born alive.

Concealment of birth

Under s 60 of the 1861 Act, if any woman delivers a child, every person who shall, by any *secret disposition* of the dead body of the said child, whether such child died before, at, or after its birth, endeavour to conceal the birth thereof, shall be guilty of an either way offence.

This offence relates to secret disposal, hiding of the dead body of a baby, where the baby has died before, at, or shortly after birth.

If the living body of a child is concealed, which then dies where it is concealed, clearly a more serious offence of homicide may be committed.

The offence is specific in that it must be a '**secret disposition**' *after the child has died*, the test being whether there is likelihood that the body would be found.

 Indictable None

 Life imprisonment

Links to alternative subjects and offences

Chapter 3

Crime: Dishonesty

3.1 Theft

The Theft Act 1968 provides for the offence of theft and other connected offences. Section 1 of the Act provides for the offence of theft, while s 11 covers the offence of removing articles from places open to the public and 23 concerns advertising rewards for the return of stolen or lost goods.

3.1.1 Theft (general)/theft of scrap metal

Theft is defined by s 1 of the Act, while ss 2–6 explain the elements contained within that definition.

Offences

A person is guilty of theft if he **dishonestly appropriates property belonging to another** with the **intention of permanently depriving** the other of it; and 'thief' and 'steal' shall be construed accordingly.

Theft Act 1968, s 1(1)

Points to prove

✓ dishonestly
✓ appropriated
✓ property
✓ belonging to another
✓ intention to permanently deprive the other of it

Meanings

Dishonestly

Section 2 defines what will not be considered as 'dishonest'.

3.1.1 Theft (general)/theft of scrap metal

- It is not considered dishonest if a person takes possession of property belonging to another, whether for themselves or a third person, believing that they have a legal right to deprive the other of it.
- It is not considered dishonest to take property belonging to another believing that, if the other had known about it and the circumstances they would have consented.
- It will not be dishonest if, not being a trustee or personal representative, a person takes possession of property believing that, by taking reasonable steps, the owner could not be discovered.
- It is for the court to decide if a person acted dishonestly (see **'Related cases'** R v Ghosh).
- Taking property belonging to another may be dishonest even if the perpetrator is willing to pay for it.

Appropriates

'Appropriates' is defined in s 3.

- If a person assumes the rights of an owner over property they are deemed to have appropriated it. This includes where they obtain the property without stealing and later assumes such rights by keeping or dealing with it as the owner.
- Where property (or a right or interest in it) is transferred to a person for its true value, any later assumption by the acquirer as to the rights of ownership will not amount to theft simply because the transferor had no right to transfer it.

Property

'Property' is defined by s 4.

- It includes money and all other property (real or personal) including 'things in action' and other intangible property. Unless expressly excluded by s 4, 'property' covers all property even if possession or control of it is prohibited or unlawful (eg drugs).
- Land, or things forming part of it, and taken from it by a person or on their instructions, can only be stolen if—
    + the person is a trustee or personal representative, or is authorised by power of attorney, as a company liquidator, or in some other way, to sell or dispose of land belonging to somebody else, and the appropriate it or anything forming part of it, by dealing with it in breach of the confidence entrusted in them; or
    + when the person is not in possession of the land, they appropriate anything forming part of it by severing it, causing it to be severed or after it has been severed; or
    + when, being in possession of the land under a tenancy, they appropriate all or part of a fixture or structure let for use with that land.
- Mushrooms (and other fungi), flowers, plants (including shrubs and trees), and fruit or foliage from a plant are all capable of being 'property' for the purposes of theft. Picking mushrooms, flowers, fruit, or foliage **growing wild** on land is not theft unless it is done for reward, sale, or other commercial purpose.

- Wild creatures, tamed or untamed, are regarded as property. However, a wild creature which is not tamed or normally kept in captivity (or the carcass of such animal) cannot be stolen unless it has been taken into possession by or on behalf of another, and such possession has not been lost or given up, or it is in the process of being taken into possession.

Belonging to another

'Belonging to another' is defined by s 5.
- Property belongs to any person having possession or control of it, or having a proprietary right or interest in it.
- Where property is subject to a trust, ownership includes the right to enforce that trust, and any intention to break it is regarded as intending to deprive a person having such right.
- Where a person receives property from or on account of another, and is under an obligation to the other to retain and deal with that property or its proceeds in a particular way, the property or proceeds shall be regarded (as against them) as belonging to the other.
- When a person obtains property because of another's mistake, and they are obliged to repay all or part of it, its proceeds or value then, to the extent of that obligation, the property or proceeds are regarded as belonging to the person entitled to restoration, and any intent not to repay it is an intention to deprive them of it.

Intention to permanently deprive

'Intention to permanently deprive' is defined by s 6.
- Appropriation of property belonging to another without meaning them permanently to lose it still has the intention of 'permanently depriving' them of it, if the appropriator intends to treat it as their own to dispose of regardless of the other's rights.
- Borrowing or lending the property may amount to treating it as their own if it is for a period and in circumstances equating to an outright taking or disposal.
- Where a person has possession or control of another's property, for their own purposes and without the other's permission, loans it to a third person with unachievable conditions for its return, they treat it as their own to dispose of regardless of the other's rights (eg pawning property belonging to another when not able to redeem it).

Explanatory notes

- It is immaterial whether the appropriation is made with a view to gain, or is made for the thief's own benefit.
- 'Things in action' include a cheque drawn to a payee, giving them an action (demand for payment), which they may enforce against the payer. It is, therefore, the property of the payee.
- 'Intangible property' includes patents, applications for patents, copyrights.
- 'Tenancy' means a tenancy for any period and includes a tenancy agreement, but a person who, when a tenancy ends, remains in

possession as statutory tenant or otherwise will be treated as having possession under the tenancy.

- Possession, in general terms, means having the right to use property as your own without having any legal title to it (eg hiring a car—you have possession while legal ownership remains with the hire company).
- Possession may be 'actual' (an item in your hand or pocket) or 'constructive' (an item at your home while you are elsewhere).
- Control means having the power to use or manage items without having legal title to them (eg a delivery service having control of letters and packages for delivery—it does not actually own any of them and may not even have 'possession' at all times).
- Proprietary right or interest means ownership or having legal title of property or similar rights.
- An obligation to make restoration of property belonging to another must be a legal obligation, not a moral or social one.
- Simple and genuine borrowing of property is insufficient to constitute theft because the necessary 'mens rea' is missing, unless the person intends to return the property in such a state that it loses its value or goodness (eg exam papers borrowed for copying would not be 'stolen' as they had not lessened in their intrinsic value).
- The theft or attempted theft of mail bags or postal packages, or their contents, whilst in transit between British postal areas is, even if it happens outside England and Wales, triable in England and Wales.

Related cases

R v Ghosh [1982] 2 All ER 689, QBD The court must decide what is dishonest according to the ordinary standards of reasonable and honest people, and whether that person realised that what they were doing was dishonest by those standards.

R v Smith and others [2011] EWCA Crim 66, CA S contacted V (known drug dealer) and arranged a meet for £50 worth of heroin. V handed the drugs over to avoid a further beating. Unless expressly excluded by s 4, 'property' covers all property even if possession or control of it is prohibited or unlawful (eg drugs).

R (on the application of Ricketts) v Basildon MC [2010] EWHC 2358 (Admin), QBD Taking bags of donated items left outside a charity shop or from its bins is still theft.

R v Hinks [2000] 4 All ER 833, HL H influenced, coerced, or encouraged the complainant who was naive, gullible, and of limited intelligence to hand over large sums of money. Receiving a valid gift is appropriation; if the circumstances surrounding the acceptance of the property would be considered dishonest (by a reasonable person), then that conduct becomes theft.

R v Skivington [1967] 1 All ER 483, CA It is not considered dishonest if a person believes they have the legal (as opposed to moral) right to deprive the other of the property.

Lawrence v Metropolitan Police [1972] 2 All ER 1253, HL It is not necessary for the prosecution to prove that the property was taken without the consent of the owner. If consent is shown it does not mean that there is no dishonesty if the consent was obtained without full knowledge of the circumstances.

R v McPherson [1973] Crim LR 191, CA It is an appropriation if, at the time the property is taken, there is an intent to steal.

DPP v Gomez (1993) 96 Cr App R 359, HL Goods taken with the consent of someone empowered to give it can nevertheless be an 'appropriation'. Consent to the removal of items that are obtained by fraud, deception, or false representation amounts to the dishonest appropriation of goods.

R v Ngan [1998] 1 Cr App R 331, CA Appropriation must take place in England and Wales.

R v Arnold [1997] 4 All ER 1, CA Where property is received from, or on account of, another and the recipient is under an obligation to retain and deal with it (or its proceeds) in a particular manner, the property (or proceeds) are regarded as belonging to the other.

National Employers MGIA Ltd v Jones [1987] 3 All ER 385, CA For a buyer to gain 'good title' to property that they buy, the seller must have a lawful right to it in the first place. Therefore someone who innocently buys goods that turn out to have been stolen does not become the lawful owner.

Practical considerations

- Consider stop, search and seizure powers under s 1 of PACE (see **12.1.1**).
- All five of the elements contained within the theft definition must be proved to obtain a conviction.
- In the absence of a reliable admission of dishonesty, this evidence will have to be proved by other evidence such as: Where was the property found? Had it been hidden? What were the subsequent actions of the defendant?
- Other matters that should be addressed include—
  - ◆ Evidence of who owns the property and/or that the defendant does not.
  - ◆ Does the offender have any claim on the property?
  - ◆ Does the offender own any similar property/have the means to have paid for it?
  - ◆ Any attempts to alter the property or change its appearance.
  - ◆ Proof that only some of the property was stolen is sufficient for a conviction.
  - ◆ The current location of the property.
  - ◆ The value of the property stolen/recovered.
- The fact that a man and woman are married or are civil partners, does not preclude one from stealing property belonging to the other.

+ A person is not exempt from answering questions in recovery proceedings on the grounds that to do so would incriminate them or their spouse or civil partner.
+ However, a statement or confession made in recovery proceedings is not admissible in proceedings for an offence under this Act as evidence against them or their spouse or civil partner.
- Consider issuing a PND for retail/commercial thefts under £100 (see **7.1.1**).
- Consider additional evidence (eg security video, CCTV footage).
- Low value shoplifting (value does not exceed £200) may be triable only summarily under the MCA 1980, s 22A; but it is still considered an 'indictable offence' for PACE purposes (see **12.2.4**).

Theft of scrap metal

- The Scrap Metal Dealers Act 2013 was passed in order to curb metal theft from a range of sectors—including the rail network, electric/ telecommunication distribution, memorials and street furniture.
- It is a summary offence under s 1 of the Act for a person to carry on business as a scrap metal dealer unless authorised by a licence under this Act.
- A person carries on business as a scrap metal dealer if the business—
  + consists wholly or partly in buying or selling scrap metal, whether or not the metal is sold in the form in which it was bought, or
  + carries on as a motor salvage operator.
- Scrap metal includes—
  + any old, waste or discarded metal or metallic material, and
  + any product, article or assembly which is made from or contains metal and is broken, worn out or regarded by its last holder as having reached the end of its useful life.
- But gold, silver or alloy which contains by weight 2% or more gold or silver, are not scrap metal.
- Section 12(1) of the Act stipulates that a scrap metal dealer must not pay for scrap metal except by a 'non transferable' cheque, or by an electronic transfer of funds (authorised by credit or debit card or otherwise). Payment cannot be made by cash or 'paying in kind' (with goods or services).
- Under s 12(4), if scrap metal is paid for in breach of s 12(1), the following commit a summary offence—
  + the scrap metal dealer;
  + the site manager (if payment on site);
  + any person who makes the payment acting for the dealer.
- It is a defence for the scrap metal dealer or site manager to prove that they—
  + made arrangements to ensure payment was not in breach of s 12(1), and
  + took all reasonable steps to ensure compliance with those arrangements.
- Section 15(6) makes it a summary offence if comprehensive records of receipt or disposal of scrap metal are not recorded as required by s 13 or s 14 or kept for 3 years from receipt or disposal. This ensures that the seller/purchaser of the scrap metal can be readily identified.

- Under s 16 of the Act a constable or local authority officer may—
  - ✦ enter and inspect a licensed site at any reasonable time on notice to the site manager, but are not entitled to use force to enter the site;
  - ✦ require production of and inspect any scrap metal kept on site or records kept under s 13 or s 14 for receipt/disposal of scrap metal; and make copies/extracts from such records;
- A justice of the peace may issue a warrant authorising entry onto premises to ensure compliance with the Act.
- It is a summary offence (s 16(13)) if a person: obstructs a right of entry or inspection, or fails to produce a record when so required, under the s 16 powers.

 Either way   None

 Summary: 6 months' imprisonment and/or a fine
Indictment: 7 years' imprisonment and/or a fine

3.1.2 Removal of articles from places open to the public

Section 11 of the Theft Act 1968 covers the offence of removing articles from places open to the public.

Offences

Subject to subsections (2) and (3) below, where the public have access to a building in order to view the building or part of it, or a **collection** or part of a **collection** housed in it, any person who without lawful authority removes from the building or its grounds the whole or part of any article displayed or kept for display to the public in the building or that part of it or in its grounds shall be guilty of an offence.

Theft Act 1968, s 11(1)

Points to prove

✓ without lawful authority
✓ removed from building/grounds of building
✓ to which public have access
✓ to view building/collection/part thereof
✓ the whole/part of article displayed/kept for display to public

---

SSS Stop, search and seize powers	**E&S** Entry and search powers	**PND** Penalty notice for disorder offences	**91**
CHAR Offences where bad character can be introduced	**TRIG** Trigger offences		

3.1.2 Removal of articles from places open to the public

Meaning of collection

This includes a collection got together for a temporary purpose, but references in this section to a collection do not apply to a collection made or exhibited for the purpose of effecting sales or other commercial dealings.

Explanatory notes

- Access to grounds alone is insufficient. The public must have access to a building to view it, part of it or a collection or part of it housed therein.
- Payment for the privilege of viewing the collection is irrelevant, as is whether such payment merely covers expenses or makes a profit.
- Articles displayed are not confined to works of art, the test being that the article, which may be priceless or valueless, is displayed or kept for public display.
- Note that this offence does not require any intent to permanently deprive the owner of the article taken.

Defences

A person does not commit an offence under this section if he believes that he has lawful authority for the removal of the thing in question or that he would have it if the person entitled to give it knew of the removal and the circumstances of it.

Theft Act 1968, s 11(3)

Defence notes

The burden is on the prosecution to prove the absence of genuine belief on the part of the defendant.

Related cases

R v Durkin [1973] 2 All ER 872, CA It has to be proved that the collection was intended to be permanently available for exhibition to the public. That intention was sufficiently manifested in this case by the local authority's practice of periodically displaying to the public at the gallery the pictures in their permanent collection.

Practical considerations

- Ascertain the dates on which the building/articles is/are on display.
- Public access to a building for other purposes (eg a shopping mall) when a collection is displayed as an incidental to the main purpose of access (shopping) is unlikely to fall into this section.
  - However, if the collection was displayed in a separate part of the building with access given purely to view it, it would fall into this section.
- Removal need not be during the times the public have access, it can occur even when the buildings/grounds are closed. However, per

s 11(2), if the display is temporary, removal must take place on a day
when the public have access to the buildings/grounds in order to view.
• Does the defendant have any claim on the property?
• Current location of the article(s).
• Value of property taken/recovered.
• Obtain CJA witness statements.
• Consider additional evidence (eg security video, CCTV footage).

 Either way   None

 Summary: 6 months' imprisonment and/or a fine
Indictment: 5 years' imprisonment and/or a fine

3.1.3 Advertising rewards for the return of stolen/lost goods

Section 23 of the Theft Act 1968 deals with the offence of advertising
rewards for the return of stolen or lost goods.

Offences

Where any public advertisement of a reward for the return of any goods
which have been stolen or lost uses any words to the effect that no
questions will be asked, or that the person producing the goods will be
safe from apprehension or inquiry, or that any money paid for the purchase
of the goods or advanced by way of loan on them will be repaid, the
person advertising the reward and any person who prints or publishes the
advertisement shall be guilty of an offence.

Theft Act 1968, s 23

Points to prove

✓ advertiser/printer/publisher
✓ publicly advertised
✓ offer of reward for return of lost/stolen goods
✓ used words implying
✓ no questions asked/producer safe from apprehension/enquiry or
any money paid will be repaid/loan repaid

3.1.3 Advertising rewards for the return of stolen/lost goods

Explanatory notes

- This is an offence of strict liability and does not require any specific mens rea.
- The offence applies not just to the person advertising the reward, but the person who prints or publishes the advertisements is also liable.
- A charge under this section may consist of any one or more of the elements contained in the section.

Related cases

Denham v Scott [1983] Crim LR 558, QBD A weekly paper published an advertisement offering reward for return of stolen goods and implying that no questions would be asked. This offence is one of strict liability and an employee of a company which publishes such an advertisement can also be guilty of the s 23 offence.

Practical considerations

- What inducement was included in the advertisement?
- Obtain a copy of the advertisement.
- Obtain evidence of origin of advertisement (eg invoice from printer).
- Any evidence of who placed the advert?
- Obtain CJA witness statement.

 Summary   6 months

 Level 3 fine

Links to alternative subjects and offences

3.2 **Robbery**

The Theft Act 1968 provides for the offence of theft and other connected offences. Section 8 provides for the offences of robbery and assault with intent to rob, whilst s 21 concerns the offence of blackmail.

3.2.1 **Robbery**

Offences

A person is guilty of robbery if he **steals**, and immediately before or at the time of doing so, and in order to do so, he uses **force** on any person or puts or seeks to put any person in fear of being then and there subjected to force.

Theft Act 1968, s 8(1)

Points to prove

✓ stole property
✓ immediately before/at the time of doing so
✓ and in order to do so
✓ used force on a person or put/sought to put person in fear of immediate force

Meanings

Steals (see **3.1.1**)

Force

Means the ordinary meaning and whether force has been used is a matter for the court to decide (*R v Dawson & James* (1976) 64 Cr App R 170, CA).

Explanatory notes

- The offence of theft must be proved before robbery can be substantiated.
- Section 8(2) deems that a person guilty of robbery is guilty of an offence.
- Force or the threat of force must be used immediately before or at the time of the theft.
- A threat to use force has to be made with the intention that something should happen immediately.
- The purpose of the use of force is to facilitate the theft; using force to escape is not robbery.
- If the offence is carried out by a number of assailants, but only one uses violence towards the victim, the others cannot be held responsible for the violence unless a prior agreement between them to use that degree of violence in order to achieve their objective is shown.

3.2.1 Robbery

- In order to seek to put somebody in fear, the state of mind of the offender is what is important (rather than that of the victim).
- If a person, while stealing or attempting to steal mailbags or postal packages, or their contents, whilst in transit between British postal areas, commits robbery or attempted robbery, the offence is triable in England and Wales, even if it is committed outside England and Wales.

> **Defences**
>
> If an honest belief that a legal claim of right to the property exists (*R v Skivington* [1967] 1 All ER 483, CA).

Related cases

R v DPP [2012] EWHC 1657 (Admin), QBD Snatching a cigarette did not constitute 'force' required for an offence of robbery to be made out.

R v Smith and others [2011] EWCA Crim 66, CA At an arranged meeting to sell heroin, a drug dealer was robbed of the drugs. Robbery includes stealing property (drugs) which it is unlawful to possess.

R v DPP [2007] EWHC 739 (Admin), QBD A large group surrounded the victim and took items from him. Although shocked, the victim did not feel scared, threatened, or put in fear. It is generally the intention of the perpetrator rather than the fortitude of the victim which dictates whether it is robbery. A threat of force can be from words, or implied by actions/conduct or both.

R v Hale (1979) 68 Cr App R 415, CA Appropriation is a continuing act and a defendant who takes items from a shop or a housekeeper and uses violence on the proprietor/owner during the course of the appropriation (eg when approached by the owner) may be guilty of robbery.

R v Clouden [1987] Crim LR 56, CA Very little force is required and a push or nudge to put the victim off balance to enable a theft to take place can be sufficient.

Smith v Desmond & Hall [1965] 1 All ER 976, HL The threat or use of force can be on any person, in order to make a set of circumstances arise, so that the theft can take place (eg threatening a signalman making him stop a train further down the track so that its contents can be stolen).

Corcoran v Anderton (1980) 71 Cr App R 104, CA Use of force applied indirectly (eg pulling at a handbag held by the victim) can under some circumstances amount to robbery as force is transferred to the person.

Practical considerations

- Ownership and value of any property stolen/recovered.
- The fear of being subjected to force must be genuine and can be proved in the victim's statement (although it is the defendant's intention to cause fear that is the key element).
- Specific words used by the defendant will be critical.
- It is not necessary to prove that somebody was actually put in fear, only that the accused sought to put somebody in fear of force.
- The force used must be to enable the theft to take place.
- The use of force after the theft is complete is not robbery.
- A threat of force can also be implied, as long as the victim believes that force will be used against them and therefore allows the theft to take place.
- An assault committed as an afterthought following a theft is not robbery, but it is assault and theft.
- Obtain CJA witness statements.
- Consider blackmail (see **3.2.3**) when the threats are for force to be used on a future occasion.
- Any additional evidence (eg security video, CCTV footage).

 Indictment None

 Life imprisonment

3.2.2 Assault with intent to rob

Offences

A person guilty of **robbery**, or of an assault with **intent** to rob, is guilty of an offence.

Theft Act 1968, s 8(2)

Points to prove

✓ assault
✓ intended to rob

| SSS | Stop, search and seize powers | E&S | Entry and search powers | CHAR | Offences where bad character can be introduced | 97 |

TRIG Trigger offences

3.2.2 Assault with intent to rob

Meanings

Robbery (see **3.2.1**)

Intent (see **4.1.2**)

Explanatory notes

- This offence is committed if a victim is assaulted in order to rob them, but the robbery is not completed because of interference or resistance, or it could not be completed because the assailant demanded property which the victim did not have.
- If a person, whilst stealing or attempting to steal mailbags, or postal packages, or their contents, whilst in transit between British postal areas, commits assault with intent to rob, the offence is triable in England and Wales, even if it is committed outside England and Wales.

Defences (see **3.2.1**)

Practical considerations

- What was the purpose of the assault?
- Was there an unsuccessful attempt to steal property from the victim?
- There is no need for actual violence, as an assault does not require it. However, where no force is actually used immediately before or at the time of the unsuccessful attempt to rob, consider attempted robbery (see **4.1.1**).
- If the assault occurs when the assailant has a firearm in their possession consider offences under the Firearms Act 1968 (see **8.3**).
- What was the degree of violence used towards the victim?
- Obtain CJA witness statements.
- Consider any additional evidence (eg security video, CCTV footage).
- If the defence to robbery is available, consider the assault in isolation.

 Indictment   None

 Life imprisonment

3.2.3 **Blackmail**

Section 21 of the Theft Act 1968 deals with the offence of blackmail.

Offences

A person is guilty of blackmail if, with a view to gain for himself or another or with **intent** to cause loss to another, he makes any unwarranted demand with menaces; and for this purpose a demand with **menaces** is unwarranted unless the person making it does so in the belief—
(a) that he has reasonable grounds for making the demands; **and**
(b) that the use of the menaces is a proper means of reinforcing the demands.

Theft Act 1968, s 21(1)

Points to prove

✓ with view to gain for self/another **or** intent to cause loss to another
✓ made unwarranted demand with menaces

Meanings

Intent (see **4.1.2**)

Menaces

The ordinary meaning of menaces applies (eg threats).

Explanatory notes

- The nature of the act or omission demanded is immaterial.
- It is also immaterial whether the menaces relate to action to be taken by the person making the demand or a third party.
- The words 'with a view to gain' and 'with intent to cause loss' are alternative, separate, and distinct phrases.
- The posting, making, or receipt of the threat must occur in this country.

Defences

In the belief that—
- they had reasonable grounds for making the demands; **and**
- the use of the menaces is a proper means of reinforcing the demands.

Defence notes

- Belief in both s 21(a) and (b) must be present for this defence. If only one is present the offence of blackmail will still be made out.

3.2.3 Blackmail

- The onus is on the defendant to prove the belief, but the prosecution must cover this defence in interview or by other means to negate it.

Related cases

R v Clear (1968) 52 Cr App R 58, CA Person threatened need not be frightened, but the menaces must be enough to unsettle the mind of an ordinary person when the threat and demand are made.

Treacy v DPP [1971] 1 All ER 110, HL A letter containing a demand with menaces posted in England and delivered abroad is sufficient for this offence.

R v Bevans [1988] Crim LR 237, CA Gain is not restricted to money; merely obtaining something they did not previously have will suffice.

R v Harvey [1981] Crim LR 104, CA Conduct including threats cannot be proper means of reinforcing a demand.

Practical considerations

- The menaces do not need to relate to action to be taken by the person making the demand.
- Cover the defence in interview or other means in order to negate it.
- Obtain CJA witness statement.
- If the evidence for 'gain' or 'loss' is vague, consider s 1 of the Malicious Communications Act 1988 (see **7.12**).
- Identify any evidence of contact/threats made to the complainant by the defendant (eg notes, letters, telephone or social media).
- Consider confiscation of cash and property as this blackmail offence is listed as a 'criminal lifestyle' offence under Sch 2 of the Proceeds of Crime Act 2002 (see **5.5** for details).

 E&S

 Indictment   None

Ⅲ 14 years' imprisonment

Links to alternative subjects and offences

3.3 **Burglary/Aggravated Burglary**

The Theft Act 1968 provides for the offence of theft and other connected offences. Section 9 creates the offence of burglary and s 10 aggravated burglary.

3.3.1 **Burglary**

Offences

(1) A person is guilty of burglary if—
  (a) he enters any **building** or part of a building as a **trespasser** and with **intent** to commit any such offence as is mentioned in subsection (2) below; or
  (b) having entered any building or part of a building as a trespasser he steals or attempts to **steal** anything in the building or that part of it or inflicts or attempts to inflict on any person therein any **grievous bodily harm**.

(2) The offences referred to in subsection (1)(a) above are offences of stealing anything in the building or part of a building in question, of inflicting on any person therein any grievous bodily harm or of doing unlawful **damage** to the building or anything therein.

Theft Act 1968, s 9

Points to prove

✓ entered a building/part of a building
✓ as a trespasser
✓ with intent
✓ to steal property therein/inflict grievous bodily harm on person therein/do unlawful damage to the building or anything therein

or

✓ having entered a building/part of a building
✓ as a trespasser
✓ stole or attempted to steal anything therein/inflicted or attempted to inflict grievous bodily harm on any person therein

Meanings

Building

'Building' includes an outhouse, a shed, an inhabited vehicle, or a vessel irrespective of whether the resident is there or not.

Trespasser

Trespass means to pass over a limit or boundary or to unlawfully enter another's building or land. An offender must either know or be reckless as to whether they are a trespasser. Entry gained by fraud is still trespass.

Intent (see **4.1.2**)

Steal (see **3.1**)

Grievous bodily harm (see **2.3.1**)

Unlawful damage (see **4.4**)

Explanatory notes

- There does not have to be a forced entry into the building, merely proof that the person has entered as a trespasser.
- Entry into a building may be an actual physical entry, by use of an instrument (eg a hook on a stick through an open window) or by an innocent agent (eg a child under 10 years old).
- The offence does not differentiate between different types of building—but the punishment does (see below).
- A person who has entered one part of a building legally and then enters into another part of the same building as a trespasser falls within this section.
- In s 9(1)(a) the original intention need not be completed—it is sufficient that the intention existed at the time of entry.
- In s 9(1)(b) no specific intention is required at the time of entry as the intruder commits one of the acts having entered as a trespasser.

Related cases

R v Saw and others [2009] EWCA Crim 1, CA Burglary of a home is a serious criminal offence. The court listed aggravating features in a burglary that should be included in the file so they can be addressed by the court when sentencing.

S v DPP [2003] EWHC 2717 (Admin), QBD S stood outside a building knowing that a burglary was ongoing. Watching and knowing a crime is being committed is not sufficient to establish joint enterprise/guilt. It should be considered whether S had encouraged the crime or had participated through joint enterprise (eg acted as lookout) but had not done so. Merely being present was not sufficient for burglary.

R v Brown [1985] Crim LR 212, CA The least degree of entry is sufficient to constitute this element of the offence, eg putting a hand or instrument through an open window or letterbox.

B & S v Leathley [1979] Crim LR 314, CC A freezer container may be a building under this section.

R v Walkington [1979] 2 All ER 716, CA A person who enters a building as a trespasser with the intention of committing a relevant offence therein, but gets caught before they manage to commit that offence, will still commit burglary.

3.3.1 Burglary

R v Wilson & Jenkins [1983] 3 All ER 448, HL If force is applied either directly or indirectly then harm is inflicted, eg a victim who is so intimidated by an intruder that they jump from a window thereby causing injury then harm has been caused although no actual force is used.

Practical considerations

- Consider stop, search and seizure powers under s 1 of PACE (see **12.1.1**).
- Ensure a degree of entry into the building can be proved; otherwise consider other offences relevant to the circumstances.
- If satisfied the offender entered the building gather evidence as to right to be there—CJA witness statements.
- A building may include structures made of wood, steel, or plastic, but it would not include a tent (inhabited or not), articulated trailer (on wheels), open-sided bus shelter, or carport.
- An inhabited caravan would be a building under this legislation.
- A static caravan permanently connected to mains water, sewers, and gas/electricity would probably be a building even when it was not occupied.
- A touring caravan parked in the driveway of a house is a vehicle. However, if it was no longer used for touring, and instead used for storage as a garden shed, it may well then be a building.
- A person who enters a shop legally and then goes into a store room may be a trespasser.
- A person who legally enters premises and later becomes a trespasser due to hostilities by them does not become a trespasser for burglary. They must have been a trespasser at the time of entry into that part of the building.
- A person acting as a lookout should be treated as a joint principal.
- Is there any other evidence available (eg security video, CCTV)?
- Is there any evidence of the intent for an offence under s 9(1)(a)? For theft this may be easy to prove (eg the possession of burgling tools), but it may be more difficult for GBH or damage.
- The type of building may affect the sentence.
- If any person in the dwelling was subjected to violence (or threat) then the case is triable on indictment only.
- If the defendant had a firearm/imitation firearm with them, then consider also s 17(2) of the Firearms Act 1968 (see **8.3.5**).

 Either way   None

 Summary: 6 months' imprisonment and/or a fine
Indictment: 10 years' imprisonment (dwelling—14 years' imprisonment)

 Stop, search and seize powers   Entry and search powers   Offences where bad character can be introduced
Trigger offences

3.3.2 **Aggravated burglary**

Section 10 of the Theft Act 1968 creates the offence of aggravated burglary, where the trespasser has with them, at the time of committing the burglary, one or more of the specified articles.

Offences

A person is guilty of aggravated burglary if he commits any **burglary** and at the time **has with him** any **firearm** or **imitation firearm**, any **weapon of offence**, or any **explosive**.

Theft Act 1968, s 10

Points to prove

✓ committed burglary
✓ had with them
✓ firearm/imitation firearm/weapon of offence/explosive

Meanings

Burglary (see **3.3.1**)

Has with him

This phrase has a narrower meaning than 'possession' (see **8.3.6**).

Firearm (see **8.1.1**)

Includes an airgun or air pistol (see **8.7.2**).

Imitation firearm

Anything which has the appearance of being a firearm, whether capable of being discharged or not.

Weapon of offence

Any article made or adapted for use for causing injury to or incapacitating a person, or intended by the person having it with him for such use.

Explosive

Means any article manufactured for the purpose of producing a practical effect by explosion, or intended by the person having it with him for that purpose.

Related cases

R v Daubney (2000) 164 JP 519, CA Defendant must know that they had the article with them.

3.3.2 Aggravated burglary

R v Kelly (1993) 97 Cr App R 245, CA A burglar who used a screwdriver to break into premises then, when challenged by the occupants, used that same screwdriver to threaten them, was held to have a weapon of offence with him at the time.

R v O'Leary (1986) 82 Cr App R 341, CA In a s 9(1)(a) burglary (enters with intent), if the burglar has with them an article (listed above), the offence is committed at the time of entry. However, under s 9(1)(b) (having entered), the point at which aggravated burglary is committed is when they commit the theft or grievous bodily harm with the article—not at the time of entry.

R v Klass [1998] 1 Cr App R 453, CA Entry into a building with a weapon is an essential element of this offence. Therefore, if there is only one weapon and it is with an accomplice who remains outside the building, neither of the offenders would commit aggravated burglary.

R v Stones [1989] 1 WLR 156, CA A burglar in possession of a knife for self-protection while carrying out a burglary may be tempted to use it if challenged and would therefore commit this offence.

Practical considerations

- Was the burglary committed under s 9(1)(a) or (b)? This affects the point in time at which the offence occurred.
- If there is more than one offender, is there evidence that somebody actually entered the building with the weapon? If not, charge with burglary or the relevant offence.
- What reason did the offender have for possessing the article?
- Where it is unclear whether the offender had the article with them at the relevant time, charge them with burglary and charge possession of the article separately.
- The offence may be committed where the offender takes possession of an article in one part of a building and then enters another part of the building with it.
- Obtain evidence of ownership and right of entry into building.
- Obtain CJA witness statements.
- Is there any other evidence (eg security video, CCTV footage)?

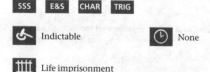

| SSS | E&S | CHAR | TRIG |

♿ Indictable   🕐 None

▦ Life imprisonment

SSS Stop, search and seize powers
E&S Entry and search powers
CHAR Offences where bad character can be introduced
TRIG Trigger offences

Links to alternative subjects and offences

3.4 **Dishonestly—Abstract Electricity/Retain a Wrongful Credit**

Further offences provided for by the Theft Act 1968 are dishonestly abstracting electricity under s 13 and dishonestly retaining a wrongful credit under s 24A.

3.4.1 **Dishonestly abstracting electricity**

Offences

A person who **dishonestly uses without due authority**, or dishonestly causes to be wasted or diverted, any electricity commits an offence.

Theft Act 1968, s 13

Points to prove

✓ dishonestly
✓ used without due authority or caused to be wasted/diverted
✓ electricity

Meanings

Dishonestly

This means a state of mind as opposed to the conduct (although the conduct will often be a feature from which dishonesty can and will be inferred) (*Boggeln v Williams* [1978] 2 All ER 1061, QBD).

Uses

Consumption of electricity that would not have occurred without an action by the accused.

Without due authority

Means without the proper authorisation.

Explanatory notes

• This section is made necessary by the fact that electricity does not fit into the definition of property under s 4 for theft (see **3.1.1**) and, therefore, it cannot be stolen. This also means that entering a building and abstracting electricity (or intending to) will not be burglary.

- A tramp who obtains warmth by an electric fire, which is already switched on, would not commit this offence, but if they switched the fire on they would commit this offence.
- Employees using their employer's electrically powered machinery for their own use would commit an offence under this section.
- It is not necessary for anybody to benefit from the wasted or diverted electricity. A person who, out of spite, switches on an electrical appliance before leaving a building would commit this offence.

Related cases

R v McCreadie & Tume [1992] Crim LR 872, CA It is sufficient for the prosecution to show that electricity was used without the authority of the electricity authority and that there was no intention to pay for it (eg squatters).

Boggeln v Williams [1978] 2 All ER 1061, QBD A householder who bypasses the electric meter after their supply has been disconnected dishonestly causes the electricity to be diverted.

Practical considerations

- Obtain evidence of dishonest use, waste, or diversion of electricity (eg note the state of the meter, cash box missing).
- The person using the electricity does not have to be the person who reconnects the supply (eg a person using electricity with no intention to pay for it after a disconnected supply has been unlawfully reconnected by a third person would commit this offence).
- Check for sign of break-in to the premises, which may negate or support the story of the householder.
- Utilities bill may assist to prove diversion to bypass the meter.
- There is no requirement for the electricity to be supplied through the mains (eg it may be supplied from a car battery). Thus a person who takes a pedestrian-controlled electric vehicle which is not classed as a conveyance (see **4.3.1**) may commit this offence.
- Obtain CJA witness statement from electricity supplier.

 E&S

 Either way

 None

Summary: 6 months' imprisonment and/or a fine
Indictment: 5 years' imprisonment

3.4.2 **Dishonestly retain a wrongful credit**

Offences

A person is guilty of an offence if—
(a) a **wrongful credit** has been made to an account kept by him or in respect of which he has any right or interest;
(b) he knows or believes that the credit is wrongful; and
(c) he dishonestly fails to take such steps as are reasonable in the circumstances to secure that the credit is cancelled.

Theft Act 1968, s 24A(1)

Points to prove

✓ knowing/believing
✓ wrongful credit made to account
✓ kept by them in which they had right or interest
✓ dishonestly
✓ failed to take reasonable steps to cancel the credit

Meanings

Wrongful credit

A **credit** to an account is wrongful to the extent that it derives from—
- theft (see **3.1.1**);
- blackmail (see **3.2.3**);
- fraud (see **3.8.1**); or
- stolen goods (see **3.5**).

Credit

Means a credit of an amount of money.

Explanatory notes

- In determining whether a credit to an account is wrongful, it is immaterial (in particular) whether the account is overdrawn before or after the credit is made.
- Any money dishonestly withdrawn from an account to which a wrongful credit has been made may be regarded as stolen goods.

Practical considerations

- Where did the credit originate?
- Obtain supplementary evidence (eg bank statements, cheque book).
- What steps could/have been taken to cancel the credit.
- Obtain CJA witness statement.

Either way   None

 Summary: 6 months' imprisonment and/or a fine
Indictment: 10 years' imprisonment

Links to alternative subjects and offences

3.5 **Handling Stolen Goods**

Section 22 of the Theft Act 1968 creates various combinations of offences of handling stolen goods knowing or believing them to be stolen.

Offences

A person handles **stolen goods** if (otherwise than in the course of the stealing) **knowing** or **believing** them to be **stolen goods** he dishonestly **receives** the goods, or dishonestly **undertakes** or assists in their **retention**, removal, disposal or **realisation** by or for the benefit of another person, or he **arranges to do so**.

Theft Act 1968, s 22(1)

Points to prove

- ✓ otherwise than in the course of stealing
- ✓ knowing/believing goods to be stolen
- ✓ dishonestly received them or
- ✓ dishonestly undertook/assisted
- ✓ in the retention/removal/disposal/realisation of them

or

- ✓ arranged to do so
- ✓ by/for the benefit of another

Meanings

Stolen goods (s 24(2))

References to stolen goods shall include, **in addition** to the **goods** originally stolen and parts of them (whether in their original state or not)— **any other goods** which directly or indirectly represent or have at any time represented the stolen goods in the hands of the thief or handler of the goods (or any part of them) as being the proceeds of any disposal or realisation of the whole or part of the goods stolen or stolen goods handled by him of goods so representing the stolen goods.

Goods

Includes money and every other description of property except land, and includes things severed from the land by stealing (see **3.1.1**).

Knowing

Means actually having been told by somebody having first-hand knowledge (eg the thief or burglar) that the goods had been stolen (*R v Hall* (1985) 81 Cr App R 260, CA).

Believing

Means the state of mind of a person who cannot be certain that goods are stolen, but where the circumstances indicate no other reasonable conclusion (*R v Elizabeth Forsyth* [1997] 2 Cr App R 299, CA).

Dishonestly

A court must decide what is dishonest according to the ordinary standards of reasonable **and** honest people, and whether that person knew that what they were doing was dishonest by those standards (*R v Ghosh* [1982] 2 All ER 689, QBD).

Receives

Means gaining **possession** or control of the goods.

Possession

Means either actual physical possession or constructive possession (storing the goods in premises belonging to them).

Undertakes

Includes where the person agrees to perform the act(s) that constitute the offence.

Retention

Means keeping possession of, not losing, continuing to have (*R v Pitchley* [1972] Crim LR 705, CA).

Realisation

Means the conversion of the goods, invariably into money (*R v Deakin* [1972] Crim LR 781, CA).

Arranges to do so

Means arranging to receive, retain, remove, dispose, or convert the stolen goods. This can be done without actually seeing or having had anything to do with the goods.

Explanatory notes

- Where a person is being proceeded against for handling stolen goods only, s 27(3)(a) provides for '**special evidence**' (eg their previous dealings with stolen goods within the 12 months prior to the current incident) to be introduced into the proceedings. No charge or conviction regarding the previous incident is necessary.
- Similarly, s 27(3)(b) allows the introduction of evidence of a previous conviction for theft or handling within 5 years of the present incident. In this case a notice must be served on the defence 7 days prior to use of the evidence in court.
- Where the only evidence on a charge of handling stolen goods is circumstantial in that an accused person is in possession of property recently stolen (doctrine of recent possession), a court may infer guilty knowledge if: (a) the accused offers no explanation to account for their possession, or (b) the court is satisfied that the explanation they offer is untrue.

- Any benefit to the receiver is irrelevant.
- Someone who handles stolen goods, whilst having no knowledge or reason to believe them to be stolen, will not commit this offence.
- Actions taken for the benefit of another are only relevant in the offence of handling stolen goods—they have no significance in relation to the receiving of such goods.

Related cases

R v Kousar [2009] EWCA Crim 139, CA A wife who knew her husband was storing stolen business merchandise in the matrimonial home, acquiesced in its being there, and did not demand its removal, was not in control or possession of the goods.

R v Duffus (1994) 158 JP 224, CA The 'special evidence' under s 27(3)(a) or (b) can only be introduced to assist in proving that the accused knew or believed that the goods were stolen.

R v Ghosh [1982] 2 All ER 689, QBD Case sets out a two-stage test (see 'Meanings—Dishonestly' above).

National Employers Mutual Ltd v Jones [1987] 3 All ER 385, CA Paying value for goods that subsequently turn out to be stolen does not transfer good title to the buyer.

R v Nicklin [1977] 2 All ER 444, CA Where a particular form of handling is specified in the charge the defendant cannot then be found guilty of another form with which they have not been charged.

R v Brown [1969] 3 All ER 198, CA 'Assists' includes permitting the storage of stolen goods in premises and denying knowledge of their whereabouts.

R v Figures [1976] Crim LR 744, CC Handling of goods stolen abroad is only an offence in this country if the handling takes place here. If the handling is complete before coming here there is no offence under this section.

R v Bloxham (1982) 74 Cr App R 279, HL A person who innocently buys goods for value and later discovers they were, in fact, stolen goods cannot commit the offence of assisting in their disposal by selling them as they benefited from their *purchase* not their sale.

Practical considerations

- Under s 24(3), **goods** are **not regarded** as **still being stolen** goods after return to the person from whom stolen or to other lawful possession or custody, or after that person and any other person having a claim to them ceases, as regards those goods, to have any right to restitution regarding the theft.
- Ownership of the goods and evidence of theft must be established.
- Check for any evidence of previous dealings with stolen goods within the previous 12 months.
- Check previous convictions for theft or handling within the previous 5 years.

- Check for communications between the handler, the thief or any potential buyers or distributors.
- Check for evidence of removal or alteration of identifying features.
- Obtain evidence of the true value of the goods.
- If the facts fit both theft and handling stolen goods, use the relevant alternate charges and let the court decide which offence, if any, is committed.
- Several people may be charged on one indictment, concerning the same theft, with handling all or some of the goods at the same or various times, and all such persons may be tried together. This does not apply to a summary trial.

   TRIG

 Either way None

Summary: 6 months' imprisonment and/or a fine
Indictment: 14 years' imprisonment

Links to alternative subjects and offences

3.6 **Going Equipped**

The Theft Act 1968 provides for several other key offences of which theft is a constituent part. Section 25 creates the offences of going equipped for any burglary or theft.

Offences

A person shall be guilty of an offence if, when not at his **place of abode**, he **has with him** any **article** for use in the course of or in connection with any **burglary** or **theft**.

Theft Act 1968, s 25(1)

Points to prove

✓ not at place of abode
✓ had with them
✓ article(s) for use in course of/in connection with
✓ a burglary/theft

Meanings

Place of abode

This normally means the place or site where someone lives. Using its natural meaning it normally includes the garage and garden of a house but it is ultimately a matter for the court or jury to decide.

Has with him

This phrase has a narrower meaning than 'possession' (see 8.3.6).

Article

This has a wide meaning. It may include a whole range of items and substances, from treacle and paper to assist in breaking a window quietly, a car jack for spreading bars, or pieces of spark plug ceramic for breaking car windows.

Burglary (see 3.3.1)

Theft (see 3.1.1)

Includes taking a conveyance without owner's consent (see 4.3.1).

Explanatory notes

- A direct connection between the article and a specific act of burglary or theft does not need to be proved.
- You do not need to prove that the person found with the article intended to use it themselves—intended use by another will suffice.

Related cases

R v Bundy [1977] 2 All ER 382, CA A 'place of abode' includes a person living rough in a car when on a site with the intention of abiding there. However, that same person in the same car would not be at their place of abode when travelling from one site to another.

R v Tosti & White [1997] Crim LR 746, CA A person charged with going equipped, when the offence of burglary or theft has not been completed, may also be charged with that offence or with attempting to commit it.

National Employers Mutual Ltd v Jones [1987] 3 All ER 385, CA For a buyer to gain a good title to property the person selling the property must have a lawful right to the property in the first instance. No such right could ever exist if the goods were originally stolen. In this case the insurance company was the true owner and entitled to the car.

Practical considerations

- What articles were with or available to the defendant?
- Where were the articles?
- What were their possible/intended uses?
- Did the defendant have a lawful purpose for having the article(s) in their possession at that particular time/place?
- Has the defendant used such articles in committing offence previously?
- Obtain CJA witness statements.
- This offence caters for some preparatory acts prior to the commission of one or more of the specified acts.
- This offence can only be committed before the intended burglary or theft, not afterwards.
- Possession of the article(s) after arrest is not sufficient for this offence.
- When two or more people are acting in concert the possession of housebreaking implements by one of them would be deemed to be possession by all of them.
- A person who has a relevant article with them, but has not yet decided whether to use the article, does not have the necessary intent to commit the offence.
- Taking a conveyance without the owner's consent is, for the purposes of this section, to be treated as theft.
- Once it has been proved that the defendant had a relevant article with them, the defendant will need to prove possession for a purpose other than burglary or theft.

3.6 Going Equipped

 Either way   🕐 None

Summary: 6 months' imprisonment and/or a fine
Indictment: 3 years' imprisonment

Links to alternative subjects and offences

3.7 **Making off without Payment**

The Theft Act 1978 creates specific offences relating to fraudulent conduct. Section 3 creates the offence of making off without payment (also known as 'bilking') when on-the-spot payment is required or expected for goods or a service and the perpetrator intends to avoid payment.

Offences

Subject to subsection (3) below, a person who, knowing that **payment on the spot** for any **goods** supplied or service done is required or expected from him, **dishonestly** makes off without having paid as required or expected and with **intent** to avoid payment of the amount due shall be guilty of an offence.

Theft Act 1978, s 3(1)

Points to prove

✓ knowing immediate payment is required/expected
✓ for goods supplied/service done
✓ dishonestly
✓ made off
✓ without having paid as required/expected
✓ with intent to avoid payment of amount due

Meanings

Payment on the spot

This includes payment at the time of collecting goods on which work has been done or in respect of which service has been provided.

Goods (see **3.5**)

Dishonestly (see **3.5**)

Intent (see **4.1.2**)

Explanatory notes

- The term '**goods supplied or service done**' will include making off without payment for fuel at a self-service petrol station, meals at restaurants, or hotel accommodation/services where the charge is levied after supplying the goods/service.
- If a motorist forgets to pay for petrol and drives off, but later remembers that they had not paid, and then returns to the filling station to pay, they may not commit the offence due to lacking the necessary intent.

3.7 Making off without Payment

- Where there is an agreement to defer payment, any such agreement would normally eliminate the expectation of payment on the spot.

Defences

Subsection (1) above shall not apply where the supply of the goods or the doing of the service is contrary to law, or where the service done is such that payment is not legally enforceable.

Theft Act 1978, s 3(3)

Defence notes

A payment not being legally enforceable may be where the service provider breaks a contract (eg a taxi driver who fails to complete a journey) or where the contract cannot be enforced through the courts.

Related cases

R v Brooks & Brooks (1983) 76 Cr App R 66, CA 'Making off' involves leaving the place or passing the point where payment is expected or required.

R v Vincent [2001] Crim LR 488, CA If an agreement to defer payment is obtained dishonestly it would not reinstate the expectation for payment on the spot.

Practical considerations

- What goods or services have been provided?
- The goods or services provided must be specified in the charge.
- It is important to prove that the person knew that 'payment on the spot' was required.
- Did the accused have money or means with which to pay the bill?
- Is the payment legally enforceable?
- There must be an intention to avoid payment completely and not merely intent to defer or delay it.
- Obtain CJA witness statement.
- Is there any further evidence (eg CCTV footage)?

 SSS   CHAR

 Either way   None

 Summary: 6 months' imprisonment and/or a fine
Indictment: 2 years' imprisonment

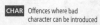

SSS Stop, search and seize powers   CHAR Offences where bad character can be introduced

Links to alternative subjects and offences

3.8 Fraud Offences

The Fraud Act 2006 ss 1 to 4 detail the three different ways of committing fraud, s 12 the liability of company officers, s 13 evidential matters relating to fraud, and ss 6, 7 possess/make articles for use in fraud.

3.8.1 Fraud offence

Section 1 creates the general offence of fraud, and ss 2 to 4 detail three different ways of committing fraud by false representation; failing to disclose information; or by abuse of position.

Offences

(1) A person is guilty of fraud if he is in breach of any of the sections listed in subsection (2) (which provide for different ways of committing the offence).

(2) The sections are—
   (a) section 2 (**fraud by false representation**),
   (b) section 3 (**fraud by failing to disclose information**), and
   (c) section 4 (**fraud by abuse of position**).

Fraud Act 2006, s 1

Points to prove

False representation

✓ dishonestly made a false representation
✓ intending to make a gain for yourself/another or
✓ intending to cause loss to another/expose another to a risk of loss

Failing to disclose information

✓ dishonestly failed to disclose to another
✓ information which you were under a legal duty to disclose
✓ intending, by that failure
✓ to make a gain for yourself/another or
✓ to cause loss to another/expose another to a risk of loss

Fraud by abuse of position

✓ occupying a position in which you were expected
✓ to safeguard, or not to act against, the financial interests of another
✓ dishonestly abused that position
✓ intending to make a gain for yourself/another or
✓ intending to cause loss to another/expose another to a risk of loss

---

Meanings

Fraud by false representation (see **3.8.2**)

Fraud by failing to disclose information (see **3.8.3**)

Fraud by abuse of position (see **3.8.4**)

Gain and loss

(1) The references to gain and loss in sections 2 to 4 are to be read in accordance with this section.

(2) 'Gain' and 'loss'—
   (a) extend only to gain or loss in money or other property;
   (b) include any such gain or loss whether temporary or permanent; and 'property' means any property whether real or personal (including things in action and other intangible property).

(3) 'Gain' includes a gain by keeping what one has, as well as a gain by getting what one does not have.

(4) 'Loss' includes a loss by not getting what one might get, as well as a loss by parting with what one has.

Fraud Act 2006, s 5

Dishonestly (see **3.5**)

Intention (see **4.1.2**)

Explanatory notes

Section 1 creates the general offence of fraud, and ss 2 to 4 detail three different ways of committing the fraud offence.

All three fraud offences require an intention to make a gain for oneself or another or cause loss to another/expose another to a risk of loss.

Similarly in all of these fraud offences intention must be proved (see **4.1.2**).

Property covers all forms of property, including intellectual property, although in practice this is rarely 'gained' or 'lost'.

If any offences are committed by a company, the company officers may also be liable under s 12 (see **3.8.5**).

Section 13 deals with evidential matters under this Act, conspiracy to defraud or any other offences involving any form of fraudulent conduct or purpose (see **3.8.6**).

3.8.2 Meaning of fraud by false representation

Meanings

Fraud by false representation

(1) A person is in breach of this section if he—

3.8.2 Meaning of fraud by false representation

    (a) **dishonestly** makes a false **representation**, and

    (b) **intends**, by making the representation—

        (i) to make a **gain** for himself or another, or

        (ii) to cause loss to another or to expose another to a risk of loss.

(2) A representation is false if—

    (a) it is untrue or misleading, and

    (b) the person making it knows that it is, or might be, untrue or misleading.

(3) '**Representation**' means any representation as to fact or law, including a representation as to the state of mind of—

    (a) the person making the representation, or

    (b) any other person.

(4) A representation may be express or implied.

(5) For the purposes of this section a representation may be regarded as made if it (or anything implying it) is submitted in any form to any system or device designed to receive, convey or respond to communications (with or without human intervention).

Fraud Act 2006, s ?

Gain and loss (see **3.8.1**)

Dishonestly (see **3.5**)

Intention (see **4.1.2**)

Explanatory notes

- The offence of fraud by false representation comes under fraud s 1 (see **3.8.1**) and **not** s 2.
- The gain or loss does not actually have to take place.
- There is no restriction on the way in which the representation may be expressed. It can be spoken, written (hardcopy or electronically), or communicated by conduct.
- An example of a representation by conduct is where a person dishonestly uses a credit card to pay for goods. By tendering the card, they are falsely representing that they have the authority to use it for that transaction. It is immaterial whether the retailer accepting the card is deceived by this representation.
- The practice of 'phishing' (eg sending an email purporting to come from a legitimate financial institution in order to obtain credit card and bank account details, so that the 'phisher' can access and fraudulently use those accounts) is another example of false representation.
- Subsection (5) is given in broad terms because it may be difficult to distinguish situations involving modern technology and/or human involvement. It could well be that the only recipient of the false statement is a machine or a piece of software, where a false statement is submitted to a system for dealing with electronic communications and not to a human being (eg postal or messenger systems). Another example of fraud by electronic means can be entering a number into a 'chip and pin' machine.

3.8.3 **Meaning of fraud by failing to disclose information**

Meanings

Fraud by failing to disclose information

A person is in breach of this section if he—

(a) **dishonestly** fails to disclose to another person information which he is under a **legal duty** to disclose, and

(b) **intends**, by failing to disclose the information—

  (i) to make a **gain** for himself or another, or

  (ii) to cause **loss** to another or to expose another to a risk of loss.

Fraud Act 2006, s 3

Gain and loss (see **3.8.1**)

Dishonestly (see **3.5**)

Intention (see **4.1.2**)

Explanatory notes

- The offence of fraud by failing to disclose information comes under fraud s 1 (see **3.8.1**) and **not** s 3.
- A legal duty to disclose information may include duties under both oral and/or written contracts.
- The concept of **'legal duty'** may derive from statute, a transaction that requires good faith (eg contract of insurance), express, or implied terms of a contract, custom of a particular trade/market, or a fiduciary relationship between the parties (eg between agent and principal). This legal duty to disclose information may be where the defendant's failure to disclose gives the victim a cause of action for damages, or the law gives the victim a right to set aside any change in their legal position to which they may consent as a result of the non-disclosure. An example of an offence under this section could be where a person intentionally failed to disclose information relating to their physical condition when making an application for life insurance.

3.8.4 **Meaning of fraud by abuse of position**

Meanings

Fraud by abuse of position

(1) A person is in breach of this section if he—

  (a) occupies a **position** in which he is expected to safeguard, or not to act against, the financial interests of another person,

  (b) **dishonestly** abuses that position, and

  (c) **intends**, by means of the abuse of that position—

    (i) to make a **gain** for himself or another, or

(ii) to cause **loss** to another or to expose another to a risk of loss.

(2) A person may be regarded as having **abused** his position even though his conduct consisted of an omission rather than an act.

Fraud Act 2006, s 4

Gain and loss (see **3.8.1**)

Dishonestly (see **3.5**)

Intention (see **4.1.2**)

Explanatory notes

- The offence of fraud by abuse of position comes under fraud s 1 (see **3.8.1**) and **not** s 4.
- The offence of committing fraud by dishonestly abusing their **position** applies in situations where they are in a privileged position, and by virtue of this position are expected to safeguard another's financial interests or not act against those interests.
- The necessary relationship could be between trustee and beneficiary, director and company, professional person and client, agent and principal, employee and employer, or even between partners. Generally this relationship will be recognised by the civil law as importing fiduciary duties. This relationship and existence of their duty can be ruled upon by the judge or be subject of directions to the jury.
- The term **'abuse'** is not defined because it is intended to cover a wide range of conduct. Furthermore, the offence can be committed by omission as well as by positive action.
- Examples of offences under this section are—
  - ♦ purposely failing to take up the chance of a crucial contract in order that an associate or rival company can take it up instead to the loss of their employer;
  - ♦ a software company employee uses their position to clone software products with the intention of selling the products to others;
  - ♦ where a carer for an elderly or disabled person has access to that person's bank account and abuses their position by transferring funds for their own gain.

3.8.5 Liability of company officers for offence by company

Liability

(1) Subsection (2) applies if an offence under this Act is committed by a body corporate.

(2) If the offence is proved to have been committed with the consent o connivance of—

(a) a director, manager, secretary or other similar officer of the body corporate, or

(b) a person who was purporting to act in any such capacity,

he (as well as the body corporate) is guilty of the offence and liable to be proceeded against and punished accordingly.

3) If the affairs of a body corporate are managed by its members, subsection (2) applies in relation to the acts and defaults of a member in connection with his functions of management as if he were a director of the body corporate.

Fraud Act 2006, s 12

Explanatory notes

This section provides that if people who have a specified corporate role are party to the commission of an offence under the Act by their body corporate, they will be liable to be charged for the offence as well as the corporation.

Liability for this offence applies to directors, managers, company secretaries, and other similar officers of companies and other bodies corporate.

Furthermore, if the body corporate is charged with an offence and the company is managed by its members, the members involved in management can be prosecuted too.

3.8.6 **Admissible evidence**

Evidence

) A person is not to be excused from—

(a) answering any question put to him in **proceedings relating to property**, or

(b) complying with any order made in proceedings relating to property,

on the ground that doing so may incriminate him or his spouse or civil partner of an offence under this Act or a related offence.

) But, in proceedings for an offence under this Act or a **related offence**, a statement or admission made by the person in—

(a) answering such a question, or

(b) complying with such an order,

is not admissible in evidence against him or (unless they married or became civil partners after the making of the statement or admission) his spouse or civil partner.

'Proceedings relating to property' means any proceedings for—

(a) the recovery or administration of any property,

(b) the execution of a trust, or

(c) an account of any property or dealings with property,

and **'property'** means money or other property whether real or personal (including things in action and other intangible property).

3.8.6 Admissible evidence

(4) 'Related offence' means—
    (a) conspiracy to defraud;
    (b) any other offence involving any form of fraudulent conduct or purpose.

Fraud Act 2006, s 13

Explanatory notes

- This means that during any proceedings for—
    + the recovery or administration of any property;
    + the execution of a trust; or
    + an account of any property or dealings with property;
  a person cannot be excused from answering any question or refuse to comply with any order made in those proceedings on the grounds of incrimination under this Act; conspiracy to defraud; or an offence involving any form of fraudulent conduct or purpose.
- However, any statement or admission made in answering such a question, or complying with such an order, is not admissible in evidence against them or their spouse or civil partner (unless they married or became civil partners after the making of such a statement or admission).
- Although this section is similar to s 31(1) of the Theft Act 1968 where a person/spouse/civil partner is protected from incrimination, while nonetheless being obliged to cooperate with certain civil proceedings relating to property, it goes beyond that section by removing privilege in relation to this Act, conspiracy to defraud and any other offence involving any form of fraudulent conduct or purpose.
- A civil partnership is a relationship between two people of the same sex ('civil partners') registered as civil partners under the Civil Partnerships Act 2004 and ends only on death, dissolution, or annulment.

Related cases

R v Minet [2009] All ER (D) 215, CA M was in financial difficulties with his plumbing business and made fraudulent transactions using his customers' card details. This was a clear breach of trust. M had been allowed into the victims' homes and been entrusted with their credit cards and details. He had clearly been under an obligation to deal honestly with them.

Kensington International Ltd v Congo and others [2007] EWCA C 1128, CA Case provides guidance relating to disclosure, evidence, and other aspects of s 13.

R v Ghosh [1982] 2 All ER 689, QBD A court/jury must decide whether according to the standards of reasonable and honest people, what was done was dishonest. If it was dishonest by those standards the court/jury must then decide whether the defendant realised that what they were doing was, by those standards, dishonest.

DPP v Gomez (1993) 96 Cr App R 359, HL If consent to take property is obtained by fraud then the property is obtained dishonestly and may fall into this offence or theft.

Practical considerations

- Consider stop, search and seizure powers under s 1 of PACE (see **12.1.1**).
- The words used may be spoken or written. Alternatively, there may be nothing done or said in circumstances where a reasonable and honest person would have expected something to be said/done (eg to correct a mistake).
- The fraud may be proved by admissions, the defendant's actions or a combination of both.
- Acts may be dishonest even if the perpetrator genuinely believed them to be morally justified.
- If committed by a body corporate with the consent or connivance of one of its officers they, as well as the body corporate, are liable to be proceeded against (see **3.8.5**).

  Either way   None

Summary: 6 months' imprisonment and/or a fine
Indictment: 10 years' imprisonment and/or a fine

3.8.7 Possess or control article for use in fraud

Section 6 deals with the offence of having in their possession or under their control an article for use in fraud.

Offences

A person is guilty of an offence if he has in his **possession** or under his control any **article** for use in the course of or in connection with any fraud.

Fraud Act 2006, s 6(1)

3.8.7 Possess or control article for use in fraud

Points to prove
✓ had in your possession/under your control
✓ an article
✓ for use in the course of/in connection with a fraud

Meanings

Possession (see **8.1.1**)

Article

Means an article—
- made or adapted for use in the course of or in connection with an offence of fraud; or
- **intended** by the person having it with them for such use by them or by some other person.

It also includes any program or data held in electronic form.

Fraud (see **3.8.1**)

Intention (see **4.1.2**)

Explanatory notes
- Having the article after the commission of the fraud is not sufficient for this offence.
- The prosecution must prove that the defendant was in possession of the article, and intended the article to be used in the course of or in connection with some future fraud. It is not necessary to prove that they intended it to be used in the course of or in connection with any specific fraud; it is enough to prove a general intention to use it for fraud.
- Similarly it will be sufficient to prove that they had it with them with the intention that it should be used by someone else.
- Examples of electronic programs or data which could be used in fraud are: a computer program that can generate credit card numbers; computer templates that can be used for producing blank utility bills; computer files containing lists of other people's credit card details or draft letters in connection with 'advance fee' frauds.

 Either way   None

 Summary: 6 months' imprisonment and/or a fine
Indictment: 5 years' imprisonment and/or a fine

SSS Stop, search and seize powers   **E&S** Entry and search powers   **TRIG** Trigger offences

3.8.8 Making or supplying article for use in fraud

Section 7 deals with the offences of making or supplying an article for use in fraud.

Offences

A person is guilty of an offence if he makes, adapts, supplies or offers to supply any **article**—

(a) knowing that it is designed or adapted for use in the course of or in connection with **fraud**, or

(b) **intending** it to be used to commit, or assist in the commission of, fraud.

Fraud Act 2006, s 7(1)

Points to prove

✓ made/adapted/supplied/offered to supply
✓ an article
✓ knowing that it was designed/adapted for use in the course of/in connection with fraud

or

✓ intending it to be used to commit/assist in the commission of fraud

Meanings

Article (see **3.8.7**)

Fraud (see **3.8.1**)

Intention (see **4.1.2**)

Explanatory notes

The offence is to make, adapt, supply, or offer to supply any article, knowing that it is designed or adapted for use in the course of or in connection with fraud, or intending it to be used to commit or facilitate fraud.

Such an example would be where a person makes devices which when attached to electricity meters cause the meter to malfunction. The actual amount of electricity used is concealed from the provider, who thus suffers a loss.

Practical considerations

A general intention to commit fraud will suffice rather than a specific offence in specific circumstances (eg credit card skimming equipment may provide evidence of such an intention).

3.8.8 Making or supplying article for use in fraud

- Proof is required that the defendant had the article for the purpose of or with the intention that it be used in the course of or in connection with fraud, and that a general intention to commit fraud will suffice.
- Consider s 12 (see **3.8.5**) as to liability of company officers for offences under this Act if they are committed by a body corporate. Similarly s 13 deals with evidential matters for offences under this Act.

 Either way None

 Summary: 12 months' imprisonment and/or a fine
Indictment: 10 years' imprisonment and/or a fine

Links to alternative subjects and offences

The Fraud Act 2006 provides for the offence of fraud and other fraudulent offences of which dishonesty is a constituent part. Section 11 makes it an offence for any person, by any dishonest act, to obtain services for which payment is required, with intent to avoid payment.

Offences

(1) A person is guilty of an offence under this section if he obtains services for himself or another—
   (a) by a **dishonest act**, and
   (b) in breach of subsection (2).
(2) A person obtains services in breach of this subsection if—
   (a) they are made available on the basis that payment has been, is being or will be made for or in respect of them,
   (b) he obtains them without any payment having been made for or in respect of them or without payment having been made in full, and
   (c) when he obtains them, he knows—
      (i) that they are being made available on the basis described in paragraph (a), or
      (ii) that they might be,
but **intends** that payment will not be made, or will not be made in full.

Fraud Act 2006, s 11

Points to prove

✓ obtained services for yourself/another by a dishonest act
✓ services were available on the basis that payment made for/in respect of them
✓ you obtained them without any payment/in full
✓ when you obtained them you knew that they were being/might be made available on the basis described above
✓ but you intended that payment would not be made/made in full

---

Meanings

Dishonest act (see 3.5)

Intention (see 4.1.2)

3.9 Obtaining Services Dishonestly

Explanatory notes

- This section makes it an offence for any person, by any dishonest act, to obtain services for which payment is required, with intent to avoid payment.
- This offence replaced the offence of obtaining services by deception in s 1 of the Theft Act 1978, although this offence contains no deception element.
- It is not possible to commit the offence by omission alone and it can be committed only where the dishonest act was done with the intent not to pay for the services as expected.

Practical considerations

- The person must know that the services are made available on the basis that they are chargeable, or that they might be.
- There is nothing to suggest that the services obtained need to be lawful for this offence to be committed (eg services of a prostitute).
- There must be some action or communication by the defendant rather than an error wholly initiated by the supplier of the service which is unaffected by behaviour on the part of the defendant.
- The offence is not inchoate, it requires the actual obtaining of the service, for example data or software that is only available on the internet once you have paid for access rights to that service.
- Examples of this offence would be where a person—
  + dishonestly uses false credit card details or other false personal information to obtain the service;
  + climbs over a wall and watches a sports event without paying the entrance fee—such a person is not deceiving the provider of the service directly, but is obtaining a service which is provided on the basis that people will pay for it;
  + attaches a decoder to a television set in order to view/have access to cable/satellite channels for which they have no intention of paying.
- Consider s 12 (see **3.8.5**) as to liability of company officers for offences under this Act if they are committed by a body corporate.

 E&S

 Either way   None

 Summary: 6 months' imprisonment and/or a fine
Indictment: 5 years' imprisonment and/or a fine

Links to alternative subjects and offences

Chapter 4

Crime: General

4.1 Criminal Attempts/Meaning of Intent/Encourage or Assist Crime

4.1.1 Criminal attempts

In certain circumstances where an offence is not actually committed, the **attempt** to do so is an offence in itself. The Criminal Attempts Act 1981 creates an offence of 'attempting' to commit certain crimes. It is imperative to prove intent (mens rea) for attempt offences, as well as other offences requiring intent. Intent is therefore discussed in detail.

Offence

(1) If, with intent to commit an offence to which this section applies, a person does an act which is more than merely preparatory to the commission of the offence, he is guilty of attempting to commit the offence.

(2) A person may be guilty of attempting to commit an offence to which this section applies even though the facts are such that the commission of the offence is impossible.

(3) In any case where—
  (a) apart from this subsection a person's intention would not be regarded as having amounted to an intent to commit an offence; but
  (b) if the facts of the case had been as he believed them to be, his intention would be so regarded

then, for the purposes of subsection (1) above, he shall be regarded as having had an intent to commit that offence.

Criminal Attempts Act 1981, s 1

Points to prove

✓ with intent
✓ attempted
✓ (wording of the offence attempted)

Meanings

Intent (see **4.1.2**)

Offence to which this section applies

▸ This section applies to any offence which if it were completed, would be triable as an indictable or an either way offence, **other than**—
  ♦ conspiracy (at common law or under s 1 of the Criminal Law Act 1977 or any other enactment);
  ♦ aiding, abetting, counselling, procuring, or suborning the commission of an offence;
  ♦ an offence under s 2(1) of the Suicide Act 1961 (encouraging or assisting suicide) (see **2.7.1**);
  ♦ offences under s 4(1) (assisting offenders) or s 5(1) (accepting or agreeing to accept consideration for not disclosing information about a relevant offence) of the Criminal Law Act 1967.

This section also applies to low-value shoplifting as defined by the Magistrates' Courts Act 1980, s 22A (see **12.2.4**).

More than merely preparatory (see 'Explanatory notes' below)

Explanatory notes

Therefore, a person may attempt an offence that is either indictable or triable either way. However, offences that are 'summary only' cannot be attempted, together with the above specific exclusions.

Whether an act is more than merely preparatory to the commission of an offence is ultimately for the jury/court to decide. However, two tests have been set out over the years and have been accepted by the higher courts. These are—

♦ The test set out in *R v Eagleton* (1855) Dears CC 515: whether there was any further act on the defendant's part remaining to be done before the completion of the intended crime.

♦ The decision in *Davey v Lee* (1967) 51 Cr App R 303: the offence of attempt is complete if the defendant does an act which is a step towards the commission of the specific crime, which is immediately (and not just remotely) connected with the commission of it, the doing of which cannot reasonably be regarded as having any other purpose than the commission of the specific crime.

Remember—a criminal attempt is not the same as having the intent to commit the offence. If an act is only preparatory (eg obtaining an insurance claim form to make a false claim), then it is not an attempt. There would have to be some other act such as actually filling the form out and posting it. Mere intent is not enough.

A typical example is *R v Geddes* [1996] Crim LR 894. Here G had hidden materials on school premises, which could be used for kidnapping a child. There was no evidence he had started to carry out his intended action. The Court of Appeal determined that his actions were merely preparatory to the offence and did not go far enough to amount to an attempt. Compare this case with *R v Tosti and White* [1997] EWCA Crim 222 in which examining a padlock was considered to be more than a preparatory act.

4.1.1 Criminal attempts

- Attempting the impossible can be sufficient for a criminal attempt, as illustrated in the case of *R v Shivpuri* [1986] UKHL 2 (below).

Related cases

R v Ilyas (1984) 78 Cr App R 17, CA When a criminal attempt begins, an act has to be more than merely preparatory.

R v Shivpuri [1986] UKHL 2, HL S was arrested by customs officers in possession of a suitcase in which S believed he had hidden heroin. The 'drugs' turned out to be harmless powder, but by receiving and hiding the powder in the suitcase, S had done an act that was more than merely preparatory to the commission of the import of heroin offence (even though it was harmless powder). S was guilty of attempting to import heroin—by attempting the impossible under s 1(2).

A-G's Reference (No 1 of 1992) [1993] 2 All ER 190, CA Attempted penetration not necessary for attempted rape.

R v Williams (1991) 92 Cr App R 158, CA No attempt needed for perverting the course of justice charge.

Practical considerations

- Criminal attempt offences can only occur where the principal offence is either an indictable offence or one that is triable either way.
- Even though damage under £5,000 can be dealt with at magistrates' court, a suspect can still be charged with attempting to damage property under £5,000, because the attempted damage offence is still an 'either way' offence. It is not a purely summary offence in the normal sense (*R v Bristol Justices, ex parte Edgar* [1998] 3 All ER 798).
- Where a person commits the full offence of aid, abet, counsel or procure, the offender should be charged as principal to the main offence where the offence is indictable or either way (Accessories and Abettors Act 1861, s 8).
- When investigating attempted murder consideration must be given to the CPS advice offered in the assault charging standards (see '**Assault**' 2.1 and '**Murder**' 2.7.1).
- Powers of arrest, search, mode of trial, penalty, and time limits are the same as those relating to the principal offence.
- Consider confiscation of cash and property for an offence of attempting, conspiring, or inciting the commission of a 'criminal lifestyle' offence under Sch 2 to the Proceeds of Crime Act 2002 (see **5.5** for details).

 E&S

 CHAR Where substantive theft/sexual offences apply

 TRIG Only in relation to attempt of the following offences—
- Theft—s 1 (see **3.1**)
- Robbery—s 8 (see **3.2**)

E&S Entry and search powers   **CHAR** Offences where bad character can be introduced   **TRIG** Trigger offences

- **Burglary**—s 9 (see **3.3.1**)
- **Handling stolen goods**—s 22 (see **3.5**)
- **Fraud**—s 1 (see **3.8.1**)

 As principal offence   As principal offence

 As principal offence

4.1.2 **Meaning of intent**

The mens rea, which is Latin for 'guilty mind', has to be proved—more so in 'attempts' than in any other offence.

Intent

This can be proved by drawing on various sources of information—
- admissions made by the defendant in interview which reveal their state of mind at the time of commission of the offence;
- answers given by the defendant to questions regarding their actions and intentions at the time of the offence;
- by inference from the circumstances of the offence;
- evidence from witnesses;
- actions of the defendant before, during and after the event, and property found on them or in their control (such as a vehicle for transporting property).

To prove intent, you need to take all of the above into account. However, the important thing is that you have to **prove** the defendant's **state of mind** at the time. A jury/magistrates' court must consider the circumstances and decide whether the defendant would have intended or foreseen the results which occurred by way of a subjective test.

Statutory test

A court or jury in determining whether a person has committed an offence—
(a) shall not be bound by law to infer that he intended or foresaw a result of his actions by reason only of its being a natural and probable consequence of those actions; **but**
(b) shall decide whether he did intend or foresee that result by reference to all the evidence, drawing such inferences from the evidence as appear proper in the circumstances.

Criminal Justice Act 1967, s 8

4.1.3 Encourage or assist crime

Subjective/objective tests

The difference between 'objective' and 'subjective' tests are important here. *Black's Law Dictionary* defines the terms as—

- **Objective**: 'Of, relating to, or based on externally verifiable phenomena, as opposed to an individual's perceptions, feelings, or intentions.' This is sometimes used in the context of the 'reasonable person' test—What would a reasonable man or woman perceive to be the rights or wrongs of the matter in question or the likely outcome?
- **Subjective**: 'Based on an individual's perceptions, feelings, or intentions, as opposed to externally verifiable phenomena.' In a legal context this is more or less the opposite of objective. Instead of the hypothetical reasonable person, subjectivity requires a court to establish whether the offender was in fact conscious of a risk or other factor.

Strict liability

For some rare criminal offences, 'strict liability' will be enough to secure a conviction. The liability for committing this type of offence does not depend on an intention (such as causing harm) or particular state of mind (eg recklessness), but is based on the breach of a duty. Beyond road traffic offences, the occasions where strict liability offences will be encountered by police officers are minimal.

4.1.3 **Encourage or assist crime**

Part 2 (ss 44–67) of the Serious Crime Act 2007 abolishes the common law offence of incitement and creates three encouraging or assisting crime offences. This area of law is far too wordy and involved to give full details, but sufficient law is provided to give an idea as to what is involved.

Offences

A person commits an offence if—

(a) he **does an act capable of encouraging or assisting the commission of an offence**; and

(b) he **intends** to encourage or assist its commission.

Serious Crime Act 2007, s 44(1)

Points to prove

✓ did an act which was capable of encouraging or assisting
✓ in the commission of an offence namely (*detail offence*)
✓ intending to
✓ encourage or assist in its commission

Meanings

Does an act

This includes a reference to a course of conduct.

Capable of encouraging or assisting

(1) A reference in this Part to a person's doing an act that is capable of encouraging the commission of an offence includes a reference to his doing so by threatening another person or otherwise putting pressure on another person to commit the offence.

(2) A reference in this Part to a person's doing an act that is capable of encouraging or assisting the commission of an offence includes a reference to his doing so by—
   (a) taking steps to reduce the possibility of criminal proceedings being brought in respect of that offence;
   (b) failing to take reasonable steps to discharge a duty.

(3) But a person is not to be regarded as doing an act that is capable of encouraging or assisting the commission of an offence merely because he fails to respond to a constable's request for assistance in preventing a breach of the peace.

Serious Crime Act 2007, s 65

Encouraging or assisting commission of an offence

Reference in Pt 2 to encouraging or assisting the commission of an offence is to be read in accordance with section 47.

Intends (see **4.1.2**)

Explanatory notes

- A person is not taken to have intended to encourage or assist the commission of an offence merely because such encouragement or assistance was a foreseeable consequence of that person's act.
- If a person (D1) arranges for a person (D2) to do an act that is capable of encouraging or assisting the commission of an offence, and D2 does the act, D1 is also to be treated for the purposes of this Part as having done it.
- **Section 47** provides further meanings, assumptions, and in particular sets out what is required to prove intent or belief and whether an act would amount to the commission of an offence.

Defences of acting reasonably

(1) A person is not guilty of an offence under this Part if he proves—
   (a) that he knew certain circumstances existed; and
   (b) that it was reasonable for him to act as he did in those circumstances.

(2) A person is not guilty of an offence under this Part if he proves—
   (a) that he believed certain circumstances to exist;
   (b) that his belief was reasonable; and

4.1.3 Encourage or assist crime

(c) that it was reasonable for him to act as he did in the circumstances as he believed them to be.
(3) Factors to be considered in determining whether it was reasonable for a person to act as he did include—
  (a) the seriousness of the anticipated offence (or, in the case of an offence under section 46, the offences specified in the indictment);
  (b) any purpose for which he claims to have been acting;
  (c) any authority by which he claims to have been acting.

Serious Crime Act 2007, s 50

Practical considerations

- Other sections worthy of note in Pt 2 of the Act are as follows—
  + s 45—Encouraging or assisting an offence believing it will be committed;
  + s 46—Encouraging or assisting offences believing one or more will be committed;
  + s 47—Proving an offence under Pt 2;
  + s 48—Further provision as to proving a s 46 offence;
  + s 49—Supplemental provisions;
  + s 51—Protective offences: victims not liable;
  + s 56—Persons who may be perpetrators or encouragers.
- A person may commit an offence under Pt 2 whether or not any offence capable of being encouraged or assisted by his act is committed. MOJ Circular 4/2008 provides further details and guidance on Pt 2 of the Act.
- Consider confiscation of cash and property for an offence under s 44, which is listed as a 'criminal lifestyle' offence under Sch 2 to the Proceeds of Crime Act 2002 (see **5.5** for details). Similarly aiding, abetting, counselling, or procuring the commission of the s 46 offence is also listed under Sch 2.
- For a s 46 offence, a defendant might believe that his conduct would assist in the commission of one or more different offences by another individual without necessarily knowing, or being able to identify, the precise offence or offences which the person to whom he offered encouragement or assistance intended to commit or would actually commit (*R v Sadique* [2013] EWCA Crim 1150, CA).

 s 46—Indictment   None

 s 44 or s 45—Per anticipated offence   Variable as to trial venue

 ss 44–46—Penalty per anticipated offence, subject to s 58

Links to alternative subjects and offences

4.2 Vehicle Interference and Tampering with a Motor Vehicle

The Criminal Attempts Act 1981 and the Road Traffic Act 1988 creates offences which protect motor vehicles such as vehicle interference and tampering with motor vehicles. Although a defendant may be trying to take a vehicle without the owner's consent, the 1981 Act does not allow 'criminal attempts' for purely summary offences.

4.2.1 Vehicle interference

Offences

(1) A person is guilty of the offence of vehicle interference if he interferes with a **motor vehicle** or **trailer** or with anything carried in or on a motor vehicle or trailer with the intention that an offence specified in subsection (2) below shall be committed by himself or some other person.

(2) The offences mentioned in subsection (1) above are—

    (a) theft of the motor vehicle or part of it;

    (b) theft of anything carried in or on the motor vehicle or trailer; and

    (c) an offence under section 12(1) of the Theft Act 1968 (taking a conveyance)

and if it is shown that a person accused of an offence under this section intended that one of those offences should be committed, it is immaterial that it cannot be shown which it was.

Criminal Attempts Act 1981, s 9

Points to prove

✓ interfere with a

✓ motor vehicle/trailer/part of/anything carried in/on it

✓ with intent that an offence of

✓ theft/taking and drive away without consent

✓ should be committed

Meanings

Interferes (see 'Related cases' below)

Motor vehicle

Means a mechanically propelled vehicle intended or adapted for use on a road (see **10.1.3**).

Trailer

Means a vehicle drawn by a motor vehicle (see **10.1.3**).

Intention (see **4.1.2**)

Explanatory notes

This offence 'fits' between the offence of going equipped (an offence which may be committed prior to any contact with a 'conveyance') and the offence of taking a conveyance without the owner's consent or theft (which is dependent on whether or not an intention to permanently deprive can be established).

Related cases

Reynolds and Warren v Metropolitan Police [1982] Crim LR 831, CC Interference has to be more than merely looking into vehicles and/or touching them.

Practical considerations

- Has the suspect possession of any implements for use in the offence that would not necessarily complete the offence of going equipped?
- Is there any CCTV evidence available?
- Check on the availability of witness evidence for CJA statements.

 Summary 6 months

 3 months' imprisonment and/or a level 4 fine

4.2.2 **Tampering with motor vehicles**

Offences

If while a **motor vehicle** is on a **road** or on a parking place provided by a local authority, a person—

(a) gets on to the **vehicle**, or

(b) **tampers** with the brake or **other part of its mechanism**

without lawful authority or reasonable cause he is guilty of an offence.

Road Traffic Act 1988, s 25(1)

4.2.2 Tampering with motor vehicles

Points to prove

✓ without lawful authority or reasonable cause
✓ got on to/tampered with
✓ the brakes/other mechanism of a motor vehicle
✓ on a road/parking place provided by local authority

Meanings

Motor vehicle/vehicle (see 10.1.3)

Road (see 10.1.1)

Tampers

Means improperly interfering with something.

Other part of its mechanism

Means any mechanical part and not just those of a similar type to the brake.

Explanatory notes

- The motor vehicle must be on a road (see **10.1.1**) and/or on a parking place provided by the local authority.
- It is for the prosecution to prove the above and that the accused got onto or tampered with the motor vehicle without lawful authority or reasonable cause.

Defences

People with lawful authority and reasonable cause will have a defence. Lawful authority might take the form of a police officer or firefighter releasing the brake of a vehicle to move it in an emergency.

Practical considerations

- Has the suspect possession of any implements for use in the offence that would not necessarily complete the offence of going equipped?
- Is there any CCTV evidence available?
- Check on the availability of witness evidence for CJA statements.

 Summary   ⏱ 6 months

 Level 3 fine

Links to alternative subjects and offences

4.3 **Taking a Conveyance without Owner's Consent**

The following topic covers three aspects: taking a conveyance without the owner's consent (TWOC), aggravated vehicle-taking, and the taking of pedal cycles. TWOC can also be known as unlawful taking of a motor vehicle (UTMV) or taking and driving away (TDA).

4.3.1 **Taking a conveyance without owner's consent**

Offences

Subject to subsections (5) and (6) below, a person shall be guilty of an offence if, without having the **consent of the owner** or other lawful authority, he **takes** any **conveyance** for his own or another's use or, knowing that any conveyance has been taken without such authority, drives it or **allows himself** to be carried in or on it.

Theft Act 1968, s 12(1)

Points to prove

There are several sets of circumstances depending on the role taken in the offence. Following relates to initial taker only:
✓ without the consent
✓ of the owner/other lawful authority
✓ took a conveyance
✓ for your own/another's use

Meanings

Owner

If the conveyance is subject to a hiring or hire purchase agreement means the person in possession of the conveyance under that agreement.

Takes

Some movement of the conveyance is essential (*R v Bogacki* [1973] 2 All ER 864).

Conveyance

Means any conveyance constructed or adapted for the carriage of a person or persons whether by land, water, or air, **except** that it **does not include** a conveyance constructed or adapted for use only under the control of a person not carried in or on it.

Explanatory notes

- An important point is that the conveyance must be capable of carrying a person. A machine such as a small domestic lawnmower is not a conveyance, but one upon which the operator sits would be.
- A horse is an animal and therefore not 'constructed or adapted', so it is not a 'conveyance'.
- Pedal cycles are catered for in s 12(5) (see **4.3.3**).
- You must prove the use or intended use as a means of transport. If the conveyance is not used in this way (eg pushing a car away from a drive entrance to remove an obstruction), then there is no 'taking'.
- If it is used to ride on while being pushed then there may be a taking (*R v Bow* [1977] Crim LR 176).
- A dinghy on a trailer that is to be used as a dinghy at some future time is still 'taken' for the taker's/another's own use. Use has been held to mean 'use as a conveyance' and future intended use is sufficient (*R v Marchant and McAllister* (1985) 80 Cr App R 361).
- The term 'carried in or on' requires some movement of the conveyance. In *R v Miller* [1976] Crim LR 147, a man found sitting in a boat that had been moored was found not guilty of the offence. The normal movement of the waves was deemed insufficient for the ingredients of the offence. However, the vertical movement of a hovercraft would be sufficient, because that is not a 'natural' movement taking place independently of the use of the conveyance.
- The term '**consent of the owner**' does not arise simply on occasions where specific permission has been given. Problems tend to arise where the owner has given some form of conditional consent; case law suggests that if the borrower of a car, for instance, makes a reasonable detour to their journey, then that detour will still be made 'with the consent of the owner'. However, using the conveyance for a wholly or substantially different purpose may well be an offence. This element is also relevant to one of the statutory defences (below).
- To prove the term '**allows himself**', it is necessary to show that the defendant knew that the conveyance had been taken without the consent of the owner or other lawful authority. The person may not know that when they get into the conveyance, but if they find out subsequently, they are expected to make some attempt to leave.
- The essential difference between this offence and the offence of theft is that in this offence there is an absence of any intention to permanently deprive the owner of their property.

Defences

A person does not commit an offence under this section by anything done in the belief that he has lawful authority to do it or that he would have the owner's consent if the owner knew of his doing it and the circumstances of it.

Theft Act 1968, s 12(6)

4.3.1 Taking a conveyance without owner's consent

Defence notes

- The prosecution must prove that the defendant did not believe that they had lawful authority (such as a police or local authority power of removal, or repossession by a finance company).
- Apart from the belief that the owner would have consented if they had known of the using of the conveyance, it must also be shown that they believed that the owner would have consented had they known of the circumstances of the taking and the using of it.

Related cases

R v Bogacki [1973] 2 All ER 864, CA 'Taking' must involve movement.

R v Pearce [1973] Crim LR 321, CA 'Taking' should be given its ordinary meaning.

R v Wibberley [1965] 3 All ER 718, CA Using a company vehicle outside working hours.

McKnight v Davies [1974] Crim LR 62, CA The taking is complete when consent is exceeded.

Whittaker v Campbell [1983] 3 All ER 582, QBD Consent of owner is valid even if obtained by fraud.

R v Peart [1970] 2 All ER 823, CA Misrepresentation must be fundamental to void consent.

R v Marchant and McAllister (1985) 80 Cr App R 361, CA Intended use sufficient.

Practical considerations

- Consider stop, search and seizure powers under s 1 of PACE (see **12.1.1**).
- If on the trial of an indictment for theft of a conveyance, the jury are not satisfied that the accused committed theft, they may find the accused guilty of the s 12(1) offence.
- As the offence is only summary, there is no such thing as an 'attempted taking of a conveyance' (see **4.1.1**).
- Consider the more serious offence of aggravated vehicle-taking (see **4.3.2**).
- In the interview, the situation where the person becomes aware that the conveyance has been taken after they had entered it should be covered along with any subsequent efforts to leave the conveyance.
- The Act allows for the extension of **prosecution time limits**, where proceedings shall not be commenced after the end of the period of 3 years beginning with the day on which the offence was committed. Subject to the 3-year maximum period, proceedings may be commenced at any time within the period of 6 months beginning with the **relevant day**.
- The '**relevant day**' means the day on which sufficient evidence is available to justify proceedings.

Summary

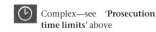 Complex—see **'Prosecution time limits'** above

 6 months' imprisonment and/or a fine. Discretionary disqualification.

4.3.2 **Aggravated vehicle-taking**

Section 12A of the Theft Act 1968 creates the various offences of 'aggravated vehicle-taking'.

Offences

(1) Subject to subsection (3) *[defence]* a person is guilty of aggravated taking of a vehicle if—

  (a) he commits an offence under section 12(1) (taking a conveyance without consent) (in this section referred to as the 'basic offence') in relation to a mechanically propelled vehicle, **and**

  (b) it is proved that, at any time after the vehicle was unlawfully taken (whether by him or another) and before it was recovered, the vehicle was driven or injury or damage was caused, in one or more of the circumstances set out in paragraphs (a) to (d) of subsection (2).

(2) The circumstances referred to in subsection (1)(b) are—

  (a) that the vehicle was driven **dangerously** on a road or other public place;

  (b) that, owing to the driving of the vehicle, an **accident** occurred by which injury was caused to any person;

  (c) that, owing to the driving of the vehicle, an accident occurred by which **damage** was caused to any property, other than the vehicle;

  (d) that damage was caused to the vehicle.

Theft Act 1968, s 12A

Points to prove

✓ without the consent
✓ of the owner/other lawful authority
✓ took (being the initial taker)
✓ a mechanically propelled vehicle for
✓ your own/another's use

(The 'basic offence')

4.3.2 Aggravated vehicle-taking

> **And** after it was taken and before it was recovered—
> ✓ the vehicle was driven dangerously on a road/public place **or**
> ✓ accident which caused injury to person(s), damage to any property or the vehicle

Meanings

Dangerously (see **10.7.1**)

A vehicle is driven dangerously if—
- it is driven in a way which falls far below what would be expected of a competent and careful driver; **and**
- it would be obvious to a competent and careful driver that driving the vehicle in that way would be dangerous.

Accident

Means 'any unintended occurrence which has an adverse physical result' and the legislation does not specify that it has to occur on a road or even in a public place.

Damage

Means any damage not just criminal damage.

Explanatory notes

- 'Owner' has the same meaning as s 12(1) (see **4.3.1**).
- Consider the offence of dangerous driving (see **10.7.1**).
- A vehicle is recovered when it is restored to its owner or to other lawful possession or custody.
- It would appear that a vehicle has been recovered once the police, owner, or some other person with the authority of the owner, takes responsibility for the vehicle. However, if the police have been informed of the location of a taken vehicle, it has yet to be decided whether 'recovered' is from the time of the call or the time the police arrive at the scene and take physical control.
- This offence only applies to mechanically propelled vehicles and not to all conveyances.
- Passengers in a vehicle involved in such an offence can also be liable to prosecution. Their culpability would be increased depending upon the extent or degree of encouragement they may have given to the driver.

Defences

A person is not guilty of an offence under this section if he proves that, as regards any such proven driving, injury or damage as is referred to in subsection (1)(b) (aggravating factors) above, either—
(a) the driving, accident or damage referred to above occurred before he committed the basic offence; or

(b) he was neither in, nor on, nor in the immediate vicinity of, the vehicle when that driving, accident or damage occurred.

Theft Act 1968, s 12A(3)

Related cases

Dawes v DPP [1995] 1 Cr App R 65, QBD Injury to a person or damage to property owing to driving or damage caused to the taken vehicle (whether by driving or not) needs to be proved.

R v Wheatley and another [2007] EWCA Crim 835, CA Passengers can also be liable and the degree of their culpability will depend upon the amount of encouragement they give the actual driver of the vehicle.

Practical considerations

- The fact that the person who originally took the vehicle is not the person who caused the accident resulting in personal injury is irrelevant—the initial taker can still be prosecuted for the aggravated offence. Nor is there any requirement that the driver of the 'taken vehicle' has to be at fault when a personal injury accident occurs (*R v Marsh* [1996] 8 CL 54).
- Always bear in mind the above defences when interviewing.
- The aggravated offence never becomes statute barred as it is an either way offence. Even if the damage caused is under £5,000 and the offence is triable only summarily, it is still an either way offence.
- By virtue of s 12A(5), a person who is found not guilty of this offence can still be found guilty of taking a vehicle without consent as an alternative.

 Either way   None

 Summary: 6 months' imprisonment and/or a fine

Indictment: 2 years' imprisonment, **but** where a person dies as a result of an accident involving the offence, 14 years' imprisonment

4.3.3 Take pedal cycle without owner's consent

Taking or riding a pedal cycle without the consent of the owner or other lawful authority is an offence.

4.3.3 Take pedal cycle without owner's consent

Offences

Taking a conveyance shall not apply in relation to pedal cycles; but, subject to subsection (6) below *[defences]*, a person who, without having the consent of the owner or other lawful authority takes a pedal cycle for his own or another's use, or rides a pedal cycle knowing it to have been taken without such authority, shall be guilty of an offence.

Theft Act 1968, s 12(5)

Points to prove

- ✓ without consent of the owner/lawful authority
- ✓ takes/rides
- ✓ pedal cycle
- ✓ for own or other's use

Explanatory notes

- A pedal cycle is neither propelled by mechanical power nor is it electrically assisted.
- There are many types of 'hybrid' vehicles, such as motorised scooters that may qualify as mechanically propelled vehicles or conveyances. Ultimately this is a question of fact for the court to decide.

Defences (see 4.3.1)

Related cases

Sturrock v DPP [1996] RTR 216, QBD Where it is admitted that no consent had been given there is no need for an owner to be identified or any statement taken. The court can infer that the bicycle has an owner.

Practical considerations

- The prosecution must prove that the accused did not have lawful authority, such as a police or local authority power of removal, or repossession by a finance company.
- As this is a summary offence, there is no offence of 'attempting to take a pedal cycle' (see **4.1.1**).

 Summary   6 months

 Level 3 fine

SSS Stop, search and seize powers   CHAR Offences where bad character can be introduced   TRIG Trigger offences

Links to alternative subjects and offences

4.4 **Criminal Damage**

The offence of criminal damage is designed to protect people's property from the unlawful actions of others. Section 1 of the Criminal Damage Act 1971 creates the offence of simple 'criminal damage'.

Offences

A person who without lawful excuse **destroys** or **damages** any **property belonging to another intending** to destroy or damage any such property or being **reckless** as to whether any such property would be destroyed or damaged shall be guilty of an offence.

Criminal Damage Act 1971, s 1(1)

Points to prove

- ✓ without lawful excuse
- ✓ destroyed/damaged
- ✓ property to value of
- ✓ intending to
- ✓ destroy/damage such property **or**
- ✓ being reckless whether it was destroyed/damaged

Meanings

Destroyed

Means property which is incapable of being repaired and can only be replaced.

Damaged

Means property that has suffered some physical harm, impairment, or deterioration.

Property (s 10(1))

Means property of a tangible nature, whether real or personal, including money and—

(a) including wild creatures which have been tamed or are ordinarily kept in captivity, and any other wild creatures or their carcasses if, but only if, they have been reduced into possession which has not been lost or abandoned or are in the course of being reduced into possession; but

(b) not including mushrooms growing wild on any land or flowers, fruit or foliage of a plant growing wild on any land.

Belonging to another

This is property that belongs to another person who has custody or control of it, or who has a right or an interest in it, or has a charge over it.

Intending (see **4.1.2**)

Reckless

The test set out in *R v G and R* [2003] UKHL 50 applies, which states that a person acts 'recklessly' for the purposes of s 1 with respect to—
• circumstances where that person is aware of a risk that exists or will exist;
• a result when they are aware of a risk that it will occur;
and it is, in the circumstances known to them, unreasonable to take the risk.

The **first part** provides for those existing or future circumstances known to the defendant which, in the circumstances as known to them, made it unreasonable to take the risk they took. An example would be a tramp taking shelter in a barn full of dry hay: aware of the risk they light a fire to boil water for a cup of tea, and set the barn alight.

The **second part** of the test applies if the person is aware that the result of their actions is a risk and, in the circumstances as known to them, it would be unreasonable to take that risk. An example would be an adult who lets off a large rocket and ignores instructions which state that the firework should be launched from a tube embedded in the ground and instead launches it from a bottle standing upright on the pavement. As a result the rocket goes through the window of a house opposite and causes a fire.

The case of *G and R* involved two children aged 11 and 12 who set fire to a shop when lighting newspapers in a yard at the back. It was argued in their defence that, although the act might have been an obvious risk to the average person, it might not be obvious to such young children. The House of Lords agreed and overturned the previous '**objective**' test in the case of *R v Caldwell* [1981] 1 All ER 961.

Explanatory notes

The important thing to prove or disprove (in addition to the damage itself) is the state of mind (intent) or that they were reckless in their actions, in destroying/damaging the property.

Defences

Lawful excuse

(1) This section applies to any offence under section 1(1) and any offence under section 2 or 3 other than one involving a threat by the person charged to destroy or damage property in a way which he knows is likely to endanger the life of another or involving an intent by the person charged to use or cause or permit the use of something in his custody or under his control so to destroy or damage property.

(2) A person charged with an offence to which this section applies shall, whether or not he would be treated for the purposes of this Act as having a lawful excuse apart from this subsection, be treated for those purposes as having a lawful excuse—

(a) if at the time of the act or acts alleged to constitute the offence he believed that the person or persons whom he believed to be entitled to consent to the destruction of or damage to the property in question had so consented, or would have so consented to it if he or they had known of the destruction or damage and its circumstances; **or**

(b) if he destroyed or damaged or threatened to destroy or damage the property in question or, in the case of a charge of an offence under section 3, intended to use or cause or permit the use of something to destroy or damage it, in order to protect property belonging to himself or another or a right or interest in property which was or which he believed to be vested in himself or another, and at the time of the act or acts alleged to constitute the offence he believed—

   (i) that the property, right or interest was in immediate need of protection; and

   (ii) that the means of protection adopted or proposed to be adopted were or would be reasonable having regard to all the circumstances.

(3) For the purposes of this section it is immaterial whether a belief is justified or not if it is honestly held.

Protect life or property

(4) For the purposes of subsection (2) above a right or interest in property includes any right or privilege in or over land, whether created by grant, licence or otherwise.

(5) This section shall not be construed as casting doubt on any defence recognised by law as a defence to criminal charges.

Criminal Damage Act 1971, s 5

Defence notes

Damage caused to protect life, prevent injury, or stop unlawful imprisonment of a person is also a valid defence (*R v Baker and Wilkins* [1997] Crim LR 497, CA).

Related cases

R v Jones and others; Ayliffe and others v DPP, Swain v DPP [2006] UKHL 16, HL Defendants took part in protests at military bases against the war in Iraq and damaged the perimeter fence and vehicles. Claimed damage done to prevent the international crime of aggression and so was a 'lawful excuse' under s 5. Held: The right of citizens to use force or cause damage on their own initiative is limited when not defending their own person or property and furthermore it does not cover customary international law.

Johnson v DPP [1994] Crim LR 673, QBD When lawful excuse is the defence, two questions need to be asked. The first is an objective question (eg whether the act of damage was done in order to protect property); and second, a subjective question (whether the defendant believed that the property was in immediate need of protection and the means of protection used were reasonable).

Chamberlain v Lindon [1998] 2 All ER 538, QBD Requirement of immediacy (under s 5(2)(b)(i) above) will still be satisfied if the threat to property (or rights in property) is already taking place. Here, the defendant was charged with criminal damage after destroying a wall erected by his neighbour which obstructed a right of access to his property. The defendant had a lawful excuse for his action because the obstruction to his rights had already happened and he believed rights would be further prejudiced if the wall remained in place.

Drake v DPP [1994] Crim LR 855, QBD Damage must affect the integrity of the object damaged.

'A' (a juvenile) v R [1978] Crim LR 689, CC Spitting on a police uniform did not constitute damage.

Hardman & others v CC of Avon & Somerset [1986] Crim LR 330, CC Cost of cleaning (here a pavement artist's water-soluble drawing on a street) may still amount to 'damage'.

Practical considerations

- Consider stop, search and seizure powers under s 1 of PACE (see **12.1.1**).
- If property has been destroyed, the value specified in the charge should reflect the full replacement cost.
- Charging that property was both 'destroyed' and 'damaged' is an unnecessary duplication, so wherever possible a choice should be made.
- Consider applying for a warrant (under s 6) to search for and seize anything in custody or control of suspect on their premises. Having reasonable cause to believe, has been used **or is intended for use** without lawful excuse to either: destroy or damage property— belonging to another or in a way likely to endanger the life of another.
- If the destruction or damage has been caused by fire, an offence of arson under s 1(3) should be charged (see **4.5.2**).
- Consider the more serious offence of racially or religiously aggravated criminal damage (see **7.10**).
- Consider issuing a PND if damage value is below £300 (see **7.1.1**).
- If the full offence is not committed consider attempt criminal damage (see **4.1**).
- The same incident may involve separate activities, some causing ordinary damage and some damage by fire (eg protestors break into a laboratory building, smash laboratory equipment, and set fire to some files). In such circumstances they are separate offences and best charged as such.
- There is a special offence of criminal damage to an ancient monument under the Ancient Monuments and Archaeological Areas Act 1979, s 28. The advantage of using this offence is that the owner can also be liable for damaging the protected monument which they own.
- Consider the offences of having an article with intent to commit damage (see **4.7**) or made threats to cause damage (see **4.6**).

4.4 Criminal Damage

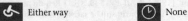

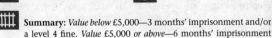

Summary: *Value below* £5,000—3 months' imprisonment and/or a level 4 fine. *Value* £5,000 *or above*—6 months' imprisonment and/or a fine

Indictment: 10 years' imprisonment

Links to alternative subjects and offences

4.5 Damage with Intent to Endanger Life and Arson

Damage with intent to endanger life is also known as aggravated damage. This and arson are serious offences because of their potential to have disastrous effects on other people's lives and the wider community.

This section is presented in two parts: damage with intent to endanger life and then arson.

4.5.1 Damage with intent to endanger life

Section 1(2) of the Criminal Damage Act 1971 creates the serious offence of destroying or damaging property intending that, or being reckless as to whether life would be endangered.

Offences

A person who without **lawful excuse, destroys** or **damages** any property, whether **belonging to** himself or **another**—

(a) **intending** to destroy or damage any property or being reckless as to whether any property would be destroyed or damaged; and
(b) intending by the destruction or damage to **endanger** the **life** of another or being **reckless** as to whether the life of another would be thereby endangered;

shall be guilty of an offence.

Criminal Damage Act 1971, s 1(2)

Points to prove

✓ without lawful excuse
✓ destroy/damage
✓ property
✓ whether belonging to self or another
✓ with intent destroy/damage or reckless destroy/damage **and**
✓ intending by destruction/damage to endanger life of another or
✓ being reckless as to whether such life would thereby be endangered

Meanings

Lawful excuse (see 'Defences' below)

Intent (see **4.1.2**)

4.5.1 Damage with intent to endanger life

Destroy (see **4.4**)

Damage (see **4.4**)

Property (see **4.4**)

Belonging to another (see **4.4**)

Endanger life

Does not require an attempt to kill or injury to occur. It is sufficient that life was endangered.

Reckless (see **4.4**)

Explanatory notes

- Consider attempt murder or manslaughter (see **4.1** and **2.7**).
- No actual injury need occur; all that is required is evidence that life was endangered. For example, if a jealous person cuts the brake pipe of his rival's car, no harm may actually come to the intended victim, but the potential for harm exists. Either intention to endanger the life of another or recklessness in that regard must be proved and the potential for harm to someone other than the defendant must be proved.
- The actual damage caused must also be the cause of the danger. For example, shooting at a person in a room (through a window) both endangers life and damages the window, but it is not the damage that endangers the life.

Defences

- Lawful excuse could be attempting to effect a rescue in order to save life, but in doing so it could endanger life.
- Statutory lawful excuse defence for damage given in s 5 (see **4.4**) specifically precludes damage with intent to endanger life and arson.

Related cases

R v Wenton [2010] EWCA Crim 2361, CA Any endangerment to life must directly arise from the act of damage/destruction. Therefore, the damage caused—not just *the act* of causing the damage/destruction—must give rise to the danger to life.

R v Webster & others [1995] 2 All ER 168, CA Two cases were considered. The first case involved a coping stone thrown from a bridge onto a moving railway carriage where no injury was caused. The defendant's intention was for the stone to injure the passengers, therefore the offence was 'recklessness causing damage which could endanger life' (eg the debris that flew around the carriage following the incident). In the second case, the defendants threw bricks at a police car from a stolen car, aiming for its windscreen. The windscreen broke, causing loss of vision to the officer. These circumstances would be sufficient for the offence of causing damage with intent to endanger life. Establishing intention is important, so ascertain in interview what the offender's intentions were or what the perceived outcome of their actions would be.

R v Merrick [1995] Crim LR 802, CA M cut an electric mains cable and left live cabling exposed for 6 minutes; was convicted of damaging property, being reckless as to whether life was endangered. On appeal, M argued that he had weighed up the work and decided there was no significant risk, therefore he was not 'reckless'. Conviction was upheld on the reasoning that if M had wanted to make sure that he was outside the definition of 'reckless', remedies to eliminate risk would have to be taken before starting the work. It was too late to take action once the risk had been created.

R v Hardie [1984] 3 All ER 848, CA Recklessness after the defendant has taken drugs is insufficient as the defendant could not form the necessary mens rea.

Practical considerations

- The same incident may involve separate activities, some causing ordinary damage and some damage by fire (eg protestors break into a laboratory building, smash laboratory equipment, and set fire to some files). In such circumstances they are separate offences and best charged as such.
- Damage by fire is arson (see **4.5.2**).

 Indictable   None

 Life imprisonment

4.5.2 **Arson**

Section 1(3) of the Criminal Damage Act 1971 creates the offence of 'arson'.

> **Offences**
>
> An offence committed under this section by **destroying** or **damaging**
> **property** by fire shall be charged as arson.
>
> Criminal Damage Act 1971, s 1(3)

 Stop, search and seize powers   **E&S** Entry and search powers   **RRA** Racially or religiously aggravated offence   **163**

PCSO Police community support officers

Points to prove

Arson

✓ without lawful excuse
✓ destroy/damage
✓ by fire
✓ property with intent to destroy/damage it **or**
✓ being reckless whether such property was destroyed/damaged

Arson—endanger life

✓ all points to prove for arson (above) and
✓ intending by destruction/damage to endanger life of another **or**
✓ being reckless as to whether such life would be endangered

Meanings

Destroy (see **4.4**)

Damage (see **4.4**)

Property (see **4.4**)

Explanatory notes

For the offence to be complete, some of the damage must be by fire; this does not include smoke damage. It is enough, however, that wood is charred (*R v Parker* [1839] 173 ER 733).

Defences

There is no specific defence for arson.

Related cases

R v Drayton [2005] EWCA Crim 2013, CA A charge of causing criminal damage by fire under s 1(3) still constitutes a charge of arson even if 'arson' is not specifically stated in the charge.

Practical considerations

- Intention or recklessness must be proved. A burglar who accidentally dropped a lighted match used for illumination could be reckless.
- The same incident may involve separate activities, some causing ordinary damage and some damage by fire. These are separate offences and should be so charged.
- Most arsons involve the use of **'accelerants'** such as petrol or lighter fuel to start the fire. If it is suspected that accelerants might have been used, special procedures need to be implemented in order to obtain forensic samples.
- An accelerant is used to increase the speed of a chemical reaction. For police purposes, this usually means something to speed up the spread

of a fire during an arson attack. Accelerants (such as petrol) are volatile and will evaporate if left in the open air. Do not confuse accelerants with oils and greases, which demand different treatment.

- Procedures for the careful preservation and packaging which must be carried out to enable the detection of accelerants can be divided into three basic areas—
  - ✦ clothing;
  - ✦ at the scene;
  - ✦ fragile items.
- Submit the control sample of the suspected accelerant in a clean metal container with a well-fitting cap, sealed inside a **nylon bag**. If no metal can is available, use a clean glass container but protect any rubber insert in the cap with a nylon film. For this purpose cut up part of one of the nylon bags, and use the rest as a control—see below. Isolate from all other samples.
- Control sample of nylon bag used to seal any sample: in a case where a nylon bag has been employed to seal a sample, a control nylon bag from the same batch as the one used to contain the samples should be submitted. This should be sealed but should only contain air.
- Important—never dry out items suspected of containing fire accelerants before packaging. Never store or transport items for examination for the presence of fire accelerant materials in close proximity to a control sample of fire accelerant or anything taken from the defendant. Even a suspicion of contamination will destroy the evidential value of the samples.

 Either way

 None

 Summary: 6 months' imprisonment and/or a fine
Indictment: Life imprisonment

Links to alternative subjects and offences

 SSS Stop, search and seize powers | **E&S** Entry and search powers | **RRA** Racially or religiously aggravated offence

PCSO Police community support officers

4.6 Threats to Destroy or Damage Property

Section 2 of the Criminal Damage Act 1971 creates specific offences relating to threats to destroy or damage property.

Offences

A person who without **lawful excuse** makes to another a threat, **intending** that the other would fear it would be carried out—
(a) to **destroy** or **damage** any **property** belonging to that other or a third person; or
(b) to destroy or damage his own property in a way which he knows is likely to **endanger** the **life** of that other or a third person
shall be guilty of an offence.

Criminal Damage Act 1971, s 2

Points to prove

✓ without lawful excuse
✓ threatened to destroy/damage property of a person
✓ intending
✓ a person would fear that the threat would be carried out

Threaten damage own property to endanger life

✓ without lawful excuse
✓ threatened to destroy/damage
✓ your own property
✓ in a way you knew
✓ was likely to endanger life of another
✓ intending a person would fear threat would be carried out

Meanings

Lawful excuse (see 'Defences' 4.4)

Intending (see 4.1.2)

Destroy (see 4.4)

Damage (see 4.4)

Property (see 4.4)

Endanger life (see 4.5.1)

Explanatory notes

- It is not necessary to show the other person is actually in fear that the threat will be carried out; what has to be proved is that the defendant intended the other to fear it will be carried out.
- It does not matter that the defendant may not actually intend to carry out the threats and/or the victim may not even believe them. The offender's **intention** to create such a fear is sufficient— and necessary—to complete the offence.
- The test for whether the action amounts to a threat is objective, ie 'would the reasonable person conclude that a threat had been made?' (*R v Cakmak and others* [2002] EWCA Crim 500). Only intention will do; unlike s 1 there is no mention of reckless in this section.
- The threat must be to another person, and can relate to a third party—such as 'I will smash up your son's car if you don't do what I say'—the threat is to one person about their or a third person's property.
- In s 2(b) above, the offender can threaten to damage their own property in a way that is likely to endanger the life of another, such as a landlord threatening to burn down a house he owns if a tenant will not leave.
- In relation to the meaning of 'threats in criminal damage', two points must be considered—
  + the type of conduct threatened; and
  + the threat itself.
- There is no specific requirement for the threatened act to be immediate and a threat to do damage to a property at some time in the future may well suffice; each case will depend on the circumstances surrounding it.

Defences

Having a lawful excuse will be a defence under s 5 (see **4.4**).

Related cases

R v Ankerson [2015] EWCA Crim 432, CA The intention of the defendant must have been to create a genuine fear that the threat might be carried out, even where the listener was not certain that the threat would be carried out. The critical word was fear. To fear that something would happen was not to be equated with a belief that it would happen.

 SSS   E&S

 Either way   None

 Summary: 6 months' imprisonment and/or a fine
Indictment: 10 years' imprisonment

Links to alternative subjects and offences

4.7 Custody/Control of Articles with Intent to Damage and Sale of Paint Aerosols to Persons under 16

Even when criminal damage has not been committed or threatened, there may be an offence of possessing articles with an intention to cause damage. An offence of selling paint aerosols to children is designed to curb criminal damage to property by way of graffiti.

4.7.1 Custody/control of articles with intent to damage

Section 3 of the Criminal Damage Act 1971 creates the offence of 'going equipped' intending to destroy or damage property.

Offences

A person who has **anything** in his **custody** or under his **control intending** without **lawful excuse** to use it or **cause** or **permit** another to use it—
(a) to **destroy** or **damage** any **property belonging** to some **other person** or
(b) to destroy or damage his own or the user's property in a way which he knows is likely to **endanger** the **life** of some other person;
shall be guilty of an offence.

Criminal Damage Act 1971, s 3

Points to prove

✓ had in custody/control
✓ an article/object/substance/anything at all
✓ intending
✓ without lawful excuse
✓ to destroy/damage or to cause/permit another to use the article etc
✓ property belonging to another/own or user's property knowing life of another is likely to be endangered

---

Meanings

Anything

Means its natural/everyday meaning and can range from explosives to a box of matches or a hammer.

4.7.1 Custody/control of articles with intent to damage

Custody or control

It must be proved that the defendant had custody or control of the article in question. This is a wider term than possession and could cover occasions where the defendant does not have the article with them.

Intent (see **4.1.2**)

Lawful excuse (see **4.4**)

Cause

Means some degree of dominance or control, or some express or positive authorisation, from the person who 'causes'.

Permit

Requires general or particular permission, as distinguished from authorisation, and the permission may be express (eg verbal/written) or implied (eg the person's actions). A person cannot permit unless they are in a position to forbid and no one can permit what they cannot control.

Destroy (see **4.4**)

Damage (see **4.4**)

Property (see **4.4**)

Belonging to another (see **4.4**)

Endanger life (see **4.5.1**)

Explanatory notes

- The offence is split into two parts, but certain elements are common to both. Intent to use/cause/permit must be proved in all cases, as must the element of having anything in the defendant's custody/control and the absence of lawful excuse.
- The act intended does not have to be immediate; it can be at some time in the future (eg someone storing bomb-making materials for future use).
- The only difference between s 3(a) and s 3(b) offences is that in (b) there is an element of knowledge of the likelihood of endangering the life of someone else and the offender's own property can be the object of the intended damage (eg a person carrying a can of petrol to set fire to their own house with their partner inside).

Defences

Having a lawful excuse (see **4.4**).

Related cases

R v Fancy [1980] Crim LR 171, CC The intention must be to commit some specific damage.

R v Buckingham (1976) 63 Cr App R 159, CC Intention for an 'immediate use' is not necessary; an intention to use some time in the future will suffice.

Either way   (🕐) None

  Summary: 6 months' imprisonment and/or a fine
Indictment: 10 years' imprisonment

4.7.2 **Sale of aerosol paints to children**

Section 54 of the Anti-social Behaviour Act 2003 makes it an offence to sell aerosol spray paints to persons under 16, in order to reduce the incidence of graffiti criminal damage caused by young persons.

Offences

A person commits an offence if he sells an aerosol paint container to a person under the age of sixteen.

Anti-social Behaviour Act 2003, s 54(1)

Points to prove

✓ sale
✓ an aerosol paint container
✓ to a person under the age of 16

Meaning of aerosol paint container

Means a device which contains paint stored under pressure, and is designed to permit the release of the paint as a spray.

Defences

(4) It is a defence for a person charged with an offence under this section in respect of a sale to prove that—
　(a) he took all reasonable steps to determine the purchaser's age, and
　(b) he reasonably believed that the purchaser was not under the age of sixteen.

4.7.2 Sale of aerosol paints to children

> (5) It is a defence for a person charged with an offence under this section in respect of a sale effected by another person to prove that he (the defendant) took all reasonable steps to avoid the commission of an offence under this section.
>
> Anti-social Behaviour Act 2003, s 54

Practical considerations

- You will need to show that the sale was concluded, rather than simply the advertising or negotiating.
- There is no need to prove any intention by the purchaser or any specific knowledge/suspicion of intended knowledge on the part of the seller.
- Age to be proved by birth certificate or valid ID card.

 Summary   6 months

 Level 4 fine

Links to alternative subjects and offences

4.8 Intimidation of a Witness/Juror and Perverting the Course of Justice

Witnesses and/or jurors involved in the investigation or trial of criminal offences are protected from intimidation and/or threat by s 51 of the Criminal Justice and Public Order Act 1994. This area of law is presented in two parts: intimidation of a witness/juror, and perverting the course of justice.

4.8.1 Intimidation of a witness/juror

Offences

Intimidation

(1) A person commits an offence if—
   (a) he does an **act** which intimidates, and is **intended to intimidate**, another person ('the victim'),
   (b) he does the act knowing or believing that the victim is assisting in the **investigation of an offence** or is a witness or potential witness or a juror or **potential juror** in proceedings for an offence; and
   (c) he does it **intending** thereby to cause the investigation or the course of justice to be obstructed, perverted or interfered with.

Threats

(2) A person commits an offence if—
   (a) he does an **act** which harms, and is **intended** to harm, another person or, intending to cause another person to fear harm, he **threatens** to do an act which would **harm** that other person,
   (b) he does or threatens to do the act knowing or believing that the person harmed or threatened to be harmed ('the victim'), or some other person, has assisted in an investigation into an offence or has given evidence or particular evidence in proceedings for an offence, or has acted as a juror or concurred in a particular verdict in proceedings for an offence; and
   (c) he does or threatens to do it because of that knowledge or belief.

Criminal Justice and Public Order Act 1994, s 51

Points to prove

Intimidate a witness/juror

✓ knew/believed person was

4.8.1 Intimidation of a witness/juror

> ✓ assisting investigation of offence or a witness/potential witness or juror/potential juror
> ✓ in proceedings for offence
> ✓ did an act which
> ✓ intimidated that person and was intended to do so
> ✓ intending to cause investigation/course of justice to be obstructed or perverted or interfered with
>
> *Harm/threaten a witness/juror*
>
> ✓ knew/believed person or another had assisted in investigation/given evidence in proceedings/acted as juror/concurred in particular verdict
> ✓ because of that knowledge/belief
> ✓ threatened/did an act which
> ✓ harmed/was intended to harm/would have harmed person

Meanings

Investigation into an offence

Means such an investigation by the police or other person charged with the duty of investigating offences or charging offenders.

Offence

Includes an alleged or suspected offence.

Potential juror

Means a person who has been summonsed for jury service at the court at which proceedings for the offence are pending.

Act intending to intimidate

If, in proceedings against a person for an **offence under subsection (1)** it is proved that he did an act falling within paragraph (a) with the knowledge or belief required by paragraph (b), he shall be presumed, unless the contrary is proved, to have done the act with the intention required by paragraph (c) of that subsection.

Criminal Justice and Public Order Act 1994, s 51(7)

Intended (see 4.1.2)

Act intending to threaten/harm

In proceedings against a person for an offence under subsection (2) (**threats**) if it can be proved by the prosecution that within the **relevant period** he did or threatened to do an act described by (a) above with the knowledge or belief of (b) above, then he shall be presumed, unless the contrary is proved, to have done the act (or threatened to do the act) with the motive required by (c) above.

Criminal Justice and Public Order Act 1994, s 51(8)

The relevant period

In this section 'the relevant period'—

(a) in relation to a witness or juror in any proceedings for an offence, means the period beginning with the **institution of the proceedings** and ending with the first anniversary of the conclusion of the trial or, if there is an appeal or a reference under s 9 or s 11 of the Criminal Appeal Act 1995, of the conclusion of the appeal;

(b) in relation to a person who has, or is believed by the accused to have, assisted in an investigation into an offence, but was not also a witness in proceedings for an offence, means the period of one year beginning with any act of his, or any act believed by the accused to be an act of his, assisting in the investigation; and

(c) in relation to a person who both has, or is believed by the accused to have, assisted in the investigation into an offence and was a witness in proceedings for the offence, means the period beginning with any act of his, or any act believed by the accused to be an act of his, assisting in the investigation and ending with the anniversary mentioned in paragraph (a) above.

Criminal Justice and Public Order Act 1994, s 51(9)

Institution of proceedings

For the purposes of the definition of the relevant period in subsection (9) above—

(a) proceedings for an offence are instituted at the earliest of the following times:

   (i)   when a justice of the peace issues a summons or warrant under s 1 of the Magistrates' Courts Act 1980 in respect of the offence;

   (ii) when a person is charged with the offence after being taken into custody without a warrant;

   (iii) when a bill of indictment is preferred by virtue of s 2(2)(b) of the Administration of Justice (Miscellaneous Provisions) Act 1933;

(b) proceedings at a trial of an offence are concluded with the occurrence of any of the following, the discontinuance of the prosecution, the discharge of the jury without a finding, the acquittal of the accused or the sentencing of or other dealing with the accused for the offence of which he was convicted; and

(c) proceedings on an appeal are concluded on the determination or abandonment of the appeal.

Criminal Justice and Public Order Act 1994, s 51(10)

Explanatory notes

- For equivalent offences in some civil proceedings see s 39 and s 40 of the Criminal Justice and Police Act 2001.
- In respect of the relevant period, this subsection means that the statutory presumption can only be used during the relevant period. It is still possible to bring a prosecution for this offence many years after that period, but the prosecution will not have the advantage of being able to use this presumption.

4.8.1 Intimidation of a witness/juror

- In relation to both offences, it will be immaterial whether or not the act is (or would be) done, or that the threat is made—
  - otherwise than in the presence of the victim or
  - to a person other than the victim.
- Two cases regarding the above provision have determined the following—
  - Relating to both offences, the person making the threats still commits an offence if they use a third party to convey them to the witness/juror. The 'messenger' could be an innocent agent (eg a victim's relative), who simply passes on a message without understanding its meaning or effect (*A-G's Reference (No 1 of 1999)* [2000] QB 365).
  - The threats can be made by telephone, letter, or by other means. It is not necessary for the offender and victim to be in the same place at the same time (*DPP v Mills* [1996] 3 WLR 1093).
- The harm done or threatened may be financial as well as physical (whether to the person or a person's property) and the same applies with regard to any intimidatory act that consists of threats.
- This offence is in addition to, and does not necessarily replace any offence which currently exists at common law (eg perversion of the course of justice, which is usually charged as an attempt, conspiracy, or incitement).

Related cases

R v ZN [2013] EWCA Crim 989, CA For witness intimidation the victim has to be intimidated. If the victim was not intimidated then consider an offence of attempting witness intimidation.

Van Colle and another v CC of Hertfordshire [2008] UKHL 50, HL In the absence of special circumstances, the police owed no common law duty of care to protect a witness from harm, unless a threat assessment found the need to warrant further action (*Osman v UK* (1998) 29 EHRR 245, for test in relation to Art 2 claim—see **1.1**).

R v Normanton [1998] Crim LR 220, CA Spitting, although a common assault, is not harm for the purposes of this legislation unless it causes some physical or mental injury, such as an infection.

R v Waters [1997] Crim LR 823, CA As the witness had threats made against him and his family, he was no longer willing to support the prosecution. Although giving oral evidence at trial, he claimed to be unable to identify his attackers. Accepted that he was prevented from giving oral evidence through fear so the original statement was admitted.

R v Singh (B), Singh (C) and Singh (J) [2000] Cr App R 31, CA There must be evidence that the investigation had started at the time of the intimidation.

Practical considerations

- *R v Davis* [2008] UKHL 26 concerned the use of anonymous witness evidence at trial. The House of Lords judgment placed a restriction on the court's ability to allow evidence to be given anonymously during criminal trials; as a result protection is now provided through the Coroners and Justice Act 2009 (see below).

- Sections 74 to 85 of the Coroners and Justice Act 2009 deal with anonymity in criminal investigations for murder/manslaughter where a firearm or knife was used, and the issue of investigation anonymity orders to prohibit disclosure of information in order to prevent identification of potential witnesses. MOJ Circular 6/2010 provides guidance on these orders.
- Sections 86 to 97 of the Coroners and Justice Act 2009 concern the anonymity of witnesses, and the issue, discharge, or variation of witness anonymity orders in order to protect a witness or prevent the identity of a witness in criminal proceedings being disclosed. MOJ Circular 8/2009 provides guidance on these witness anonymity provisions.

E&S

 Either way   None

 Summary: 6 months' imprisonment and/or a fine
Indictment: 5 years' imprisonment and/or a fine

4.8.2 Perverting the course of justice

Offences

Committed where a person or persons—

- acts or embarks upon a course of conduct
- which has a tendency to, and
- is intended to pervert,
- the course of public justice.

Common Law

Points to prove

✓ with intent to pervert
✓ the course of public justice
✓ do an act/series of acts
✓ tending to pervert course of public justice

Explanatory notes

- Examples where conduct is capable of amounting to this offence are—
  + making false allegations;
  + perjury;
  + concealing offences;
  + obstructing the police;
  + assisting others to evade arrest;
  + failing to prosecute;
  + procuring and indemnifying sureties;
  + interference with witnesses, evidence, and jurors;
  + publication of matters calculated to prejudice a fair trial.
- A positive act is required (eg failing to respond to a summons was insufficient to warrant a charge of perverting the course of justice).
- Any act or course of conduct that tends or is intended to interfere with the course of public justice can amount to an offence. In order to get a conviction, it is not sufficient to prove that the conduct actually did, or had a tendency to, pervert the course of justice. The evidence must prove that the offender intended that it would do so.
- It is not necessary for the offender's motives to be the procurement of a false verdict or the defeat of the ends of justice. Trying to introduce genuine evidence by unlawful means is perverting the course of justice (eg a witness takes incriminating photos but refuses to give evidence). Steps are then taken by the investigator to get another witness to introduce them as evidence (*A-G's Reference (No 1 of 2002)* [2002] EWCA Crim 2392).

Related cases

R v T [2011] EWCA Crim 729, CA T deleted child pornography files from a memory stick, intending to prevent a criminal investigation against her husband. Held that an act which might mislead the police or make their investigation more difficult, could pervert the course of justice.

R v Headley (1996) 160 JP 25, CA H was summonsed and convicted for a traffic offence (in his absence), after another person used his details, but H did nothing about it. Deliberate inaction is not perverting the course of justice.

R v Kiffin [1994] Crim LR 449, CA It is possible to pervert the course of justice even if no offence could be shown to have been committed. In this case, removing account books/records subject of PACE warrant application out of jurisdiction.

R v Toney [1993] 1 WLR 364, CA Perverting the course of justice need not be by improper means. T attempted to persuade a witness to alter his evidence at T's trial. There was no evidence of improper means, but T was still convicted of perverting the course of justice.

Practical considerations

- Putting the term 'attempting to pervert the course of justice' in a common law indictment was misleading because it is a substantive rather than an inchoate (incomplete) offence. It should be charged as 'doing acts tending and intended to pervert the course of justice' (*R v Williams* (1991) 92 Cr App R 158).

- Perverting the course of justice is usually charged as an attempt, conspiracy, or incitement.
- There has been comment by the courts where this offence has been used for relatively minor attempts to pervert the course of justice and it is charged alongside an offence that is serious enough to permit the offender's condut to be taken into account when sentencing for the main offence. In *R v Sookoo* [2002] EWCA Crim 800, a shoplifter had attempted to hide his identity and inevitably failed, the prosecutors should not include a specific count of perverting the course of justice. Such conduct may serve to aggravate the original offence and the judge may increase the sentence as a result. However, in *R v Pendlebury* [2003] EWCA Crim 3426, P gave a positive breath test but a false name to police and had four previous convictions for doing the same thing. He argued that he should not be charged with perverting the course of justice but it should simply be an aggravating factor. Held that P's conduct was not too trifling to amount to the offence because it was the third occasion on which he had given false particulars against a background of persistent and serious offending.
- A more appropriate use for this offence will be where a great deal of police time and resources are involved in putting the matter right, or there may be cases where innocent members of the public have their names given and they have been the subject of questioning and even detention.

E&S

 Indictment   None

Life imprisonment

Links to alternative subjects and offences

5.1 Produce/Supply a Controlled Drug and Supply of Articles

The Misuse of Drugs Act 1971 regulates certain drugs and designates which drugs are controlled by assigning them to certain categories (A, B, or C). If the drug is a controlled drug it will be unlawful, with exceptions, to import, export, produce, supply, or possess that drug. Section 4 deals with producing or supplying a controlled drug and s 9A supplying or offering articles for the purpose of administering or preparing controlled drugs.

5.1.1 Produce/supply a controlled drug

Section 4 of the Misuse of Drugs Act 1971 provides a prohibition on the production, supply, and offering to supply of controlled drugs, with offences for contravening such prohibitions.

Offences

(1) Subject to any **regulations under section 7** of this Act, or any provision made in a **temporary class drug order by** virtue of **section 7A** for the time being in force, it shall not be lawful for a person—
  (a) to **produce** a **controlled drug;** or
  (b) to supply or offer to **supply** a controlled drug to another.
(2) **Subject to section 28** of this Act, it is an offence for a person—
  (a) to produce a controlled drug in contravention of subsection (1) above; or
  (b) to be concerned in the production of such a drug in contravention of that subsection by another.
(3) Subject to section 28 of this Act, it is an offence for a person—
  (a) to supply or offer to supply a controlled drug to another in contravention of subsection (1) above; or

(b) to be concerned in the **supplying** of such a drug to another in contravention of that subsection; or

(c) to be concerned in the making to another in contravention of that subsection of an offer to supply such a drug.

Misuse of Drugs Act 1971, s 4

Points to prove

s 4(2)(a) offence

✓ produced
✓ controlled drug of Class A/B/C

s 4(2)(b) offence

✓ concerned in the production
✓ by another of
✓ controlled drug of Class A/B/C

s 4(3)(a) offence

✓ supply or offered to supply (type of drug)
✓ a controlled drug of Class A/B/C

s 4(3)(b) offence

✓ was concerned in
✓ supplying (type of drug)
✓ a controlled drug of Class A/B/C

s 4(3)(c) offence

✓ was concerned in making an offer
✓ to supply (type of drug)
✓ a controlled drug of Class A/B/C

Meanings

Regulations under section 7

Currently the Misuse of Drugs Regulations 2001—see '**Defences**' below.

Temporary class drug order by section 7A

Section 7A gives the power to make an order under s 2A and s 2B. This order then makes a substance or product a Class A, B or C controlled drug until it can be formally classified and added to Sch 2 to the Act.

Produce

Means producing by manufacture, cultivation, or any other method, and 'production' has a corresponding meaning. Stripping a cannabis plant of its leaves comes within the term 'any other method' for the purposes of production (*R v Harris & Cox* [1996] Crim LR 36).

Controlled drug

Means (per s 2) a substance or product that is classified under Class A, B, or C in Sch 2 to the Act; or a drug subject of a temporary class drug order.

5.1.1 Produce/supply a controlled drug

The PNLD website at <http://www.pnld.co.uk> lists the drugs according to the Class, chemical names and/or the 'trade name', including the 'street' or 'slang' names.

Supply

Furnishing or providing a person with something that person wants or requires for their purpose. Including where an offender is looking after drugs whether voluntarily or involuntarily if they intend returning them to the person for whom they were being 'minded' or even anyone else (*R v Maginnis* [1987] 1 All ER 907 (voluntary minding) and *R v Panton* [2001] EWCA Crim 611 (involuntary minding, eg after threats have been made against them)).

Subject to section 28 (see 'Defences' below)

Explanatory notes

- The offence of offering to supply a controlled drug is complete when the offer is made. It does not matter whether the defendant intended ever to follow the offer through (see *R v Goddard* [1992] Crim LR 588).
- Section 37 (interpretation) states that supplying includes distributing.
- In *R v Hunt* [1987] 1 All ER 1, HL it was made clear that the onus is on the prosecution to prove all elements, including the fact that the drug could not be lawfully possessed by the defendant in the circumstances, or that it was not in a lawful form (some classified drugs are chemically mixed into a form which can be bought over the counter as a remedy for simple ailments).
- *R v Maginnis* [1987] 1 All ER 907, HL involved possession of a packet of cannabis which was being kept for a friend (a drug trafficker). The return of the drugs to the trafficker was deemed to be **supply**.
- Undercover or 'test purchase' officers are trained to a National Standard and comply with NPCC guidelines. Where appropriate, authority is obtained under Pt 2 of the Regulation of Investigatory Powers Act 2000, before surveillance takes place.

Defences

Section 28 of the Misuse of Drugs Act 1971

This applies to offences under s 4(2) and (3), s 5(2) and (3), s 6(2) and s 9 of this Act and provides that it shall be a defence if the defendant proves that they—

- neither believed nor suspected nor had reason to suspect that the substance or product in question was a controlled drug; or
- believed the substance or product in question to be a controlled drug or a controlled drug of a description such that, if it had been that controlled drug or a controlled drug of that description, they would not at the material time have been committing any offence to which this section applies.

Regulation 5—Licences to produce, supply, possess

Where any person is authorised by a licence of the Secretary of State issued under this regulation and for the time being in force to produce, supply, offer to supply or have in his possession any controlled drug, it shall not by virtue of section 4(1) or 5(1) of the Act be unlawful for that person to produce, supply, offer to supply or have in his possession that drug in accordance with the terms of the licence and in compliance with any conditions attached to the licence.

Regulation 6—General authority to supply and possess

(1) Notwithstanding the provisions of section 4(1)(b) of the Act, any person who is lawfully in possession of a controlled drug may supply that drug to the person from whom he obtained it.

(2) Notwithstanding the provisions of section 4(1)(b) of the Act, any person who has in his possession a drug specified in Schedule 2, 3, 4 or 5 which has been supplied by or on the prescription of a practitioner, an extended formulary nurse prescriber, a registered nurse, a pharmacist independent prescriber, a supplementary prescriber or a person specified in Schedule 8 acting in accordance with a patient group direction for the treatment of that person, or of a person whom he represents, may supply that drug to any doctor, dentist or pharmacist for the purpose of destruction.

(3) Notwithstanding the provisions of section 4(1)(b) of the Act, any person who is lawfully in possession of a drug specified in Schedule 2, 3, 4 or 5 which has been supplied by or on the prescription of a veterinary practitioner or veterinary surgeon for the treatment of animals may supply that drug to any veterinary practitioner, veterinary surgeon or pharmacist for the purpose of destruction.

(4) It shall not by virtue of section 4(1)(b) or 5(1) of the Act be unlawful for any person in respect of whom a licence has been granted and is in force under section 16(1) of the Wildlife and Countryside Act 1981 to supply, offer to supply or have in his possession any drug specified in Schedule 2 or 3 for the purposes for which that licence was granted.

(5) Notwithstanding the provisions of section 4(1)(b) of the Act, any of the persons specified in paragraph (7) may supply any controlled drug to any person who may lawfully have that drug in his possession.

(6) Notwithstanding the provisions of section 5(1) of the Act, any of the persons so specified may have any controlled drug in his possession.

(7) The persons referred to in paragraphs (5) and (6) are—
   (a) a constable when acting in the course of his duty as such;
   (b) a person engaged in the business of a carrier when acting in the course of that business;
   (c) a person engaged in the business of a postal operator (within the meaning of the Postal Services Act 2000) when acting in the course of that business;
   (d) an officer of customs and excise when acting in the course of his duty as such;
   (e) a person engaged in the work of any laboratory to which the drug has been sent for forensic examination when acting in the course of his duty as a person so engaged;
   (f) a person engaged in conveying the drug to a person who may lawfully have that drug in his possession.

Misuse of Drugs Regulations 2001, regs 5 and 6

5.1.1 Produce/supply a controlled drug

Related cases

R v Dang and others [2014] EWCA Crim 348, CA The defendants ran a business making and supplying bespoke hydroponic equipment to cannabis farms throughout the UK. Held that they had been properly convicted of conspiracy to be concerned in the production of cannabis by another.

R v Marron [2011] EWCA Crim 792, CA M's luggage was searched at the airport by HMRC and found to contain 44kg of a fine white powder. M was convicted of conspiracy to supply cocaine, by importing a non-controlled drug (Phenacetin) that is used as a 'cutting agent' for cocaine.

R v Prior [2004] EWCA Crim 1147, CA An offer to supply can be related to an immediate or future supply no matter how unspecified the offer itself may be. It is immaterial who took the initiative (whether it is the offeror or offeree).

R v Hodgson [2001] EWCA Crim 2697, CA Evidence of the number of visitors, for short periods, to a property may be evidence from which drug dealing may be inferred.

R v Leeson [2000] 1 Cr App R 233, CA It does not matter whether a person thinks they are dealing in a specific type of controlled drug if they are in fact dealing in another. The wording of the dealing offence is such that the type of controlled drug does not matter.

R v Shivpuri [1986] 2 All ER 334, HL Attempting to supply something that in fact was not a controlled drug can nevertheless be a criminal attempt.

R v Russell [1992] Crim LR 362, CA Making crack from cocaine is 'producing'.

R v Gill (Simon Imran) (1993) 97 Cr App Rep 2, CA An 'offer to supply' fake drugs is an offence.

Practical considerations

- Consider offences under s 23 or s 24 of the Offences Against the Person Act 1861—
  - s 23—Whosoever unlawfully and maliciously administers to, or causes to be administered to, or taken by, any other person any poison or other destructive or noxious thing, so as to endanger the life of that person, or so as to inflict grievous bodily harm upon that person is guilty of an offence (Indictment—10 years' imprisonment);
  - s 24—Whosoever shall unlawfully and maliciously administer to or cause to be administered to or taken by any other person any poison or other destructive or noxious thing, with intent to injure, aggrieve, or annoy such person, shall be guilty of an offence (Indictment—5 years' imprisonment).
- Section 4A of the Misuse of Drugs Act 1971 aggravates the offence of supplying a controlled drug where the offender (drug dealer) uses a courier (under 18) in the vicinity of school premises (including school land).

- HOC 82/1980 recommends that cultivation of cannabis (see **5.3.1**) be charged under this section instead of s 6 of the Misuse of Drugs Act 1971 in view of s 37(1) of this Act which provides a definition of 'produce'. The term has a much wider meaning than just chemically making a drug.
- The specific power to search, detain a person or vehicle/vessel, and seize any drugs is given in s 23(2) (see **5.4.1**). Ensure that s 2 of PACE (see **12.1.2**) is complied with, because any breaches of s 2 will mean that the search is unlawful and may affect the admissibility of any evidence obtained.
- Section 110 of the Powers of Criminal Courts (Sentencing) Act 2000 provides for a minimum sentence of 7 years' imprisonment for a third successive conviction for an offence of trafficking in a Class A drug. Trafficking includes an offence under s 4(2) or (3) (production and supply of controlled drugs).
- Producing/cultivating magic mushrooms, being a Class A drug (see **5.3.2** for further details).
- Consider confiscation of cash and property for the s 4(2) and (3) offences of unlawful production/supply of controlled drugs; these are listed as 'criminal lifestyle' offences under Sch 2 to the Proceeds of Crime Act 2002 (see **5.5** for details).

 Either way   None

   Class A drug
Summary: 6 months' imprisonment and/or a fine
Indictment: Life imprisonment and/or a fine

Class B drug
Summary: 6 months' imprisonment and/or a fine
Indictment: 14 years' imprisonment and/or a fine

Class C drug
Summary: 3 months' imprisonment and/or a fine
Indictment: 14 years' imprisonment and/or a fine

5.1.2 Supply articles to administer or prepare drugs/drug-cutting agents

Section 9A of the Misuse of Drugs Act 1971 creates a prohibition on the supply or offering to supply articles for administering or preparing a controlled drug.

5.1.2 Supply articles to administer or prepare drugs

Offences

(1) A person who **supplies** or **offers** to supply any article which may be used or adapted to be used (whether by itself or in combination with another article or other articles) in the **administration** by any person of a **controlled drug** to himself or another, believing that the article (or the article as adapted) is to be so used in circumstances where the administration is unlawful, is guilty of an offence.

(3) A person who supplies or offers to supply any article which may be used to prepare a controlled drug for administration by any person to himself or another believing that the article is to be used in circumstances where the administration is unlawful is guilty of an offence.

Misuse of Drugs Act 1971, s 9A

Points to prove

✓ supplied/offered to supply article(s)
✓ which might be used/adapted
✓ for administration of a controlled drug
✓ to self/another
✓ believing article(s)
✓ was/were to be used
✓ in circumstances where administration unlawful

Meanings

Supplies (see **5.1.1**)

Offers (see 'Related cases' **5.1.1**)

Controlled drug (see **5.1.1**)

Administration

Includes administering it with the assistance of another.

Explanatory notes

The Misuse of Drugs Act 1971 generally penalises the possession or supply of a drug, rather than the administration. However, the administration of a drug will be unlawful for the purpose of this section when its possession is unlawful.

Defences

(2) It is not an offence under subsection (1) above to supply or offer to supply a hypodermic syringe, or any part of one.

(4) For the purposes of this section, any administration of a controlled drug is unlawful except—

(a) the administration by any person of a controlled drug to another in circumstances where the administration of the drug is not unlawful under section 4(1) of this Act,

(b) the administration by any person of a controlled drug, other than a temporary class drug, to himself in circumstances where having the controlled drug in his possession is not unlawful under section 5(1),

(c) the administration by any person of a temporary class drug to himself in circumstances where having the drug in his possession is to be treated as excepted possession for the purposes of this Act (see section 7A(2)(c)).

Misuse of Drugs Act 1971, s 9A

Practical considerations

The scope of the 'article(s)' is wide and includes, for example, plastic bottles which are intended to be used or adapted for smoking controlled drugs.

Specified healthcare professionals are exempted from s 9A regarding certain articles per reg 6A of the Misuse of Drugs Regulations 2001; this includes their supplying aluminium foil as part of a drug treatment plan; see HOC 14/2014 for further details.

It is not an offence to supply or offer to supply a hypodermic syringe, or any part of one.

Consider s 23 or s 24 of the Offences Against the Person Act 1861 for the offences of unlawfully and maliciously administering any poison or other noxious thing (see **5.1.1**).

Section 9 of the Misuse of Drugs Act 1971 deals with opium, and subject to s 28 (lack of knowledge defence) provides the following offences: smoke or use prepared opium; frequent a place used for opium smoking; have in their possession any pipes or other utensils made or adapted for use in connection with the smoking or preparation for smoking of opium, which have been used by them or with their knowledge and permission in that connection or which they intend to use or permit others to use in that connection.

Drug-cutting agents

Drug-cutting agents are substances added to drugs by dealers in order to increase the volume of a drug to maximise their profits. For example, benzocaine, lidocaine, and phenacetin are commonly added to cocaine without the user noticing as they have the appearance of cocaine and provide anaesthetic qualities, thus mimicking the effects of cocaine.

These substances are often not in themselves illegal, for example benzocaine and lidocaine are used in health and veterinary care, but using legal substances for illegal purposes to substantially increase criminal profits has become a serious problem.

Part 4 of the Serious Crime Act 2015 (ss 52 to 65) confers new powers on a constable, officer of the NCA, or HMRC customs officer to seize,

5.1.2 Supply articles to administer or prepare drugs

retain, and destroy substances intended to be used as cutting-agents for controlled drugs (as specified in sch 2 or subject to a temporary class drug order) under the Misuse of Drugs Act 1971 (see **5.1.1**).

- A drug-cutting agent is defined as a substance which is added to a controlled drug in connection with the unlawful supply or exportation of the drug. Therefore it can be any substance intended for use in this way
- The powers in Part 4 of the Act enable a police or customs officer to enter and search premises for suspected drug-cutting agents, pursuant to a search and seizure warrant under s 52, and to seize and retain these substances. The process for application and execution of the warrant mirrors that given in the 1971 Act. When lawfully on premises (for example, at a port) police and customs officers can seize substances under s 56, on reasonable grounds to suspect they are intended for use as drug-cutting agents.
- Section 54(4) makes it a summary offence for a person, without reasonable excuse, to obstruct a police or customs officer executing or seeking to execute a search and seizure warrant.
- Previously powers under PACE 1984 had to be used to seize drug-cutting agents as there was no specific power to do so. Consider the offence of conspiracy to supply class A drugs (*R v Marron* [2011] EWCA Crim 792, CA—see **5.1.1**) or assisting in the commission of an offence under the Serious Crime Act 2007 (see **4.1.3**).
- Further details and guidance are provided in 'Guidance on Part 4 of the Serious Crime Act 2015: The seizure and forfeiture of drug-cutting agents' (Home Office—April 2015), and HOC 8/2015.

 Summary   6 months

 6 months' imprisonment and/or a fine

Links to alternative subjects and offences

5.2 **Possession of/with Intent to Supply a Controlled Drug**

The Misuse of Drugs Act 1971 makes a distinction between people who are lawfully allowed to possess controlled drugs and people who are unlawfully in possession of such drugs. Possession (unless exempt) of a controlled drug is unlawful, as is possession of controlled drugs with intent to supply.

5.2.1 **Possessing a controlled drug**

Offences

(1) Subject to any **regulations under section 7** of this Act for the time being in force, it shall not be lawful for a person to have a **controlled drug** in his **possession**.

(2) Subject to **section 28** of this Act and to **subsection (4)** below, it is an offence for a person to have a controlled drug in his possession in contravention of subsection (1) above.

(2A) Subsections (1) and (2) do not apply in relation to a **temporary class drug**.

Misuse of Drugs Act 1971, s 5

Points to prove

✓ possess [name of drug]
✓ a controlled drug of Class A/B/C

Meanings

Regulations under section 7 (see **5.1.1**)

Controlled drug (see **5.1.1**)

Possession

Proof of unlawful possession requires the following three elements—

the drug must be in the custody or control (actual or **constructive**) of the defendant;

the defendant must know or suspect the existence of the drug in question;

the drug must be a controlled drug within the meaning of the Act.

Temporary class drug (see **5.1.1**)

5.2.1 Possessing a controlled drug

Explanatory notes

- Simple possession of a temporary class drug will not be an offence. However, all other offences will apply to temporary class drugs; see HOC 12/2011 for further details.
- **Constructive possession** is when the defendant does not have immediate physical possession of the drugs but has almost as much control over them. An example would be a person who leaves drugs in a 'left luggage' locker and retains the keys. Although they no longer have 'actual' custody of the drugs, they have a high degree of control over them which amounts to possession. If the defendant handed the keys to an innocent agent who holds them as a favour, the defendant still has constructive possession. Similarly, if that other person knows that drugs are in the locker then, by keeping the keys, they are also in constructive possession of the drugs.

Defences

Section 28 and Regulations under s 7 (see **'Defences' 5.1.1**)

Section 5(4)

In any proceedings for an offence under subsection (2) above in which it is proved that the accused had a controlled drug in his possession, it shall be a defence for him to prove—

(a) that, knowing or suspecting it to be a controlled drug, he took possession of it for the purpose of preventing another from committing or continuing to commit an offence in connection with that drug and that as soon as possible after taking possession of it he took all such steps as were reasonably open to him to destroy the drug or to deliver it into the custody of a person lawfully entitled to take custody of it; or

(b) that, knowing or suspecting it to be a controlled drug, he took possession of it for the purpose of delivering it into the custody of a person lawfully entitled to take custody of it and that as soon as possible after taking possession of it he took all such steps as were reasonably open to him to deliver it into the custody of such a person.

Misuse of Drugs Act 1971, s 5(4)

Defence notes

The defence under s 5(4) is to cater for situations such as—

- a parent discovers their child has a controlled drug, takes possession of it, and flushes it down the lavatory;
- a passerby discovers heroin lying on the pavement, takes possession of it, and then gives it to the police.

Related cases

R v Hunt [1987] 1 All ER 1, HL Prosecution must prove all elements of unlawful possession under Misuse of Drugs Regulations.

R v Altham [2006] EWCA Crim 7, CA Using cannabis to alleviate chronic pain was still unlawful possession.

Practical considerations

- For produce/supply a controlled drug (see **5.1.1**).
- The Misuse of Drugs Regulations 2001 allows a person to possess some drugs for certain legitimate reasons (eg medicinal, research) (see **5.1.1**). Regulation 4(2) deals with drugs in Pt 2 of Sch 4 (anabolic steroids and human growth hormones) and states that the importation or exportation of these drugs is to be carried out in person and only for that person's use. This prevents access to these drugs through postal, freight, or courier services. HOC 9/2012 provides further details.
- HOC 15/2012 states that substances suspected to be controlled drugs must be sent to a forensic science laboratory for analysis unless they are seizures of—
  - ✦ cannabis, including cannabis resin but excluding cannabis (hash) oil; or
  - ✦ a small quantity (for personal use only) of certain controlled drugs, which gave a positive result when tested with a Home Office approved kit (see **Annex A** below).

This is providing the case is dealt with at magistrates' court (some cases Crown Court), a trained law enforcement member confirms that it is that drug and the identification of the drug is not in dispute.

- **Annex A** of HOC 13/2014 lists the Home Office approved kits, derived from three types: marquis reagent kits that rely on colour change; immunoassay kits that provide a line indication; and electronic kits that produce a digital readout. These kits test and identify the following drugs for evidential purposes: heroin; morphine; amphetamine; cocaine; MDMA (ecstasy); ketamine (now a Class B drug—see HOC 8/2014 for details); and methylmethcathinone (including mephedrone).
- The specific power to search, detain a person or vehicle/vessel and seize any drugs is given in s 23(2) (see **5.4.1**). Ensure that s 2 of PACE (see **12.1.2**) is complied with, otherwise the search is unlawful and may affect the admissibility of any evidence obtained.
- Cannabis and its derivatives are a Class B controlled drug. HOC 1/2009 provides guidance on cannabis offences.
- Possession of cannabis under s 5(2) can be dealt with by PND for offenders 18 and over. ACPO guidance gives a three-stage escalation procedure (see **7.1.2**).
- For possession of magic mushrooms, which is a Class A drug, see **5.3.2**.

PND (Cannabis)	**SSS**	**E&S**	**TRIG**	**PCSO**

♿ Either way	🕐	None

5.2.2 Possession with intent to supply

Class A
Summary: 6 months' imprisonment and/or a fine
Indictment: 7 years' imprisonment and/or a fine

Class B
Summary: 3 months' imprisonment and/or a level 4 fine
Indictment: 5 years' imprisonment and/or a fine

Class C
Summary: 3 months' imprisonment and/or a level 3 fine
Indictment: 2 years' imprisonment and/or a fine

5.2.2 **Possession with intent to supply**

The Misuse of Drugs Act 1971 creates a specific offence of possessing a controlled drug with intent to supply it.

Offences

Subject to **section 28** of this Act, it is an offence for a person to have a **controlled drug** in his **possession**, whether lawfully or not, with **intent** to **supply** it to another in contravention of **section 4(1)** of this Act.

Misuse of Drugs Act 1971, s 5(3)

Points to prove

✓ possess
✓ [name of drug]/an unspecified controlled drug of class A/B/C
✓ with intent to supply

Meanings

Controlled drug (see 5.1.1)
Possession (see 5.2.1)
Intent (see 4.1.2)
Supply (see 5.1.1)
Section 4 (see 5.1.1)

Explanatory notes (see 5.1.1 and 5.2.1)

Defences

Section 28 (lack of knowledge defence)—see **5.1.1**.

Related cases (see also **5.1.1** and **5.2.1** cases)

R v Batt [1994] Crim LR 592, CA Cash found with drugs not evidence of intent to supply.

R v Kearley [1992] 2 All ER 345, HL Hearsay evidence alone will not prove intent.

R v Gordon [1995] Crim LR 142, CA Evidence must be relevant to the specific offence charged.

R v Maginnis [1987] 1 All ER 907, HL Giving drugs back to the owner can be 'supplying'.

R v Scott [1996] Crim LR 653, CA Lifestyle may prove possession, but not intent to supply.

R v Lambert [2001] UKHL 37, HL A judge must treat the s 28 defence as an evidential burden on the defendant rather than a legal requirement to be proved on the balance of probabilities.

Practical considerations (see also **5.1.1** and **5.2.1**)

- What is and what is not admissible evidence of 'possession' and 'intent to supply' is the subject of numerous cases. For example, in *R v Griffiths* [1998] Crim LR 567, the defendant was charged with 'possession with intent to supply' a huge amount of drugs which were found in his home. The court accepted that evidence of large sums of cash in the defendant's house along with the drugs may be used as part of the prosecution case to show that the defendant was in possession of those drugs with intent to supply.
- It would appear that lifestyle/paraphernalia can sometimes be used to help prove the 'possession' element but not the 'intent to supply' element where dealers are being prosecuted.
- Provided a controlled drug is involved, it does not matter that a dealer thought they were supplying another controlled drug.
- The specific power to search, detain a person or vehicle/vessel and seize any drugs is given in s 23(2) (see **5.4.1**). Ensure that s 2 of PACE (see **12.1.2**) is complied with, as any breaches will mean that the search is unlawful and may affect the admissibility of any evidence obtained.
- Consider confiscation of cash and property for the s 5(3) offence of possession of controlled drug with intent to supply; this is listed as a 'criminal lifestyle' offence under Sch 2 to the Proceeds of Crime Act 2002 (see **5.5** for details).

5.2.2 Possession with intent to supply

 Either way None

 Class A
Summary: 6 months' imprisonment and/or a fine
Indictment: Life imprisonment and/or a fine

Class B
Summary: 6 months' imprisonment and/or a fine
Indictment: 14 years' imprisonment and/or a fine

Class C
Summary: 3 months' imprisonment and/or a level 4 fine
Indictment: 14 years' imprisonment and/or a fine

Links to alternative subjects and offences

5.3 **Cultivate Cannabis, Possess Khat, 'Magic Mushrooms', and 'Legal Highs'**

This chapter deals with the offences of cultivating cannabis, possessing khat, possessing or producing 'magic mushrooms', and possessing or dealing in 'legal highs'.

5.3.1 **Cultivate cannabis/possess khat**

Section 6 of the Misuse of Drugs Act 1971 makes it an offence to cultivate cannabis plants.

Offences

(1) Subject to any **regulations under section 7** of this Act for the time being in force, it shall not be lawful for a person to cultivate any plant of the genus **cannabis**.

(2) **Subject to section 28** of this Act, it is an offence to cultivate any such plant in contravention of subsection (1) above.

Misuse of Drugs Act 1971, s 6

Points to prove

✓ cultivation of cannabis plant(s) being a Class B drug

Meanings

Regulations under section 7

Allow cultivation of the cannabis plant under licence (see '**Defences**' below).

Cannabis

This includes the whole plant.

Section 28 (see '**Defences**' below)

Explanatory notes

- The mere growing of the cannabis plant is regarded as an act of 'production'.
- It is necessary to prove that the defendant gave some attention to the plant in order to show 'cultivation'—watering, heating, and lighting would be common examples.

5.3.1 Cultivate cannabis/possess khat

Defences

Section 28 (lack of knowledge) (see **5.1.1**)

Regulations under section 7

Where any person is authorised by a licence of the Secretary of State issued under this regulation and for the time being in force to cultivate plants of the genus Cannabis, it shall not by virtue of section 6 of the Act be unlawful for that person to cultivate any such plant in accordance with the terms of the licence and in compliance with any conditions attached to the licence.

Misuse of Drugs Regulations 2001, reg 12

Defence notes

- Acting without a valid licence or failing to comply with the conditions of the licence is an offence under s 18 of the Misuse of Drugs Act 1971 (although other more serious offences may also have been committed).
- Certain people can lawfully possess/supply a controlled drug and/or can be licensed to do so (see **5.1.1**).
- There is no general defence of medical necessity to the offence of production/possession/supply of cannabis (*A-G's Reference (No 2 of 2004)* [2005] EWCA Crim 1415, CA).

Practical considerations

- HOC 82/1980 recommends that the cultivation of cannabis be charged under s 4(2) 'producing cannabis' or being 'concerned in the production of cannabis' (see **5.1.1**). This is because under s 37(1) the definition of 'produce' has a much wider meaning than just chemically making a drug and means: by manufacture, cultivation, or any other method. Stripping a cannabis plant of its leaves comes within the term 'any other method' for the purposes of production (*R v Harris and Cox* [1996] Crim LR 36).
- Any equipment used at 'cannabis farms', which usually consists of hydroponic equipment to provide the lighting and heating, electrical fans, air ventilation systems, transformers, and other equipment, can be seized under s 19 of PACE (see **12.3.4**).
- Instead of storing this bulky equipment, which has been seized as evidence, consider s 22 of PACE which states that photographs of the equipment will be sufficient evidence.
- Supplying hydroponic equipment could be an offence of conspiring to be concerned in the production of cannabis by another (*R v Dang and others* [2014] EWCA Crim 348, CA—see **5.1.1** for details).
- In order to ascertain whether a building is being used as a 'cannabis farm' consider the use of a thermal camera or heat-seeking equipment which can detect high infrared values; this is because the buildings emit a lot of heat due to the intensive use of heating and lighting equipment used for the growing environment.

- The use and cultivation of 'skunk', being a far stronger strain of cannabis, has greatly increased. Studies by the Home Office have found that 80 per cent of cannabis seized is of the skunk variety, which has been linked to causing mental health problems.
- Cannabis and its derivatives are classified as a Class B controlled drug. As regards possession under s 5(2) (see **5.2.1**), ACPO guidance gives a three-stage escalation procedure which involves issuing a PND for offenders 18 and over (see **7.1.2**).

Possess khat

- Khat is a herbal product from the leaves and shoots of the shrub Catha edulis, and is used socially in homes, parties, and khat cafes. When chewed for several hours it gives a mild stimulant effect, so providing an increase in energy levels, alertness, and self-esteem. Due to the risks and potential harm associated with khat it has been classified as a Class C controlled drug.
- Possession of khat is an offence under s 5(2) of the 1971 Act (see **5.2.1**) and can be dealt with by a £60 (lower tier) PND (see **7.1.1**), although with the bulky nature of khat and its reliance on international freight, law enforcement will also focus on UK borders.
- HOC 11/2014 provides further details and gives a three-stage escalation procedure for dealing with possession for personal use only—not for possession with intent to supply or other offences. This is similar to that used for possession of cannabis (see **7.1.2**): with a 'khat warning' for a first offence, PND for a second offence, and prosecution for a third offence.
- Annex B of HOC 11/2014 provides guidelines for identifying khat, being visual for khat warnings and PND issue, but in other cases done forensically.

 Either way

 None

Summary: 6 months' imprisonment and/or a fine
Indictment: 14 years' imprisonment and/or a fine

5.3.2 'Magic mushrooms'/'legal highs'

Fungus (of any kind) that contains psilocin or an ester of psilocin, commonly known as 'magic mushrooms', is in the Class A drugs schedule under the Misuse of Drugs Act 1971.

5.3.2 'Magic mushrooms'/'legal highs'

Offences

Possess

Possess a Class A **controlled drug** (see **5.2.1** for full wording)

Misuse of Drugs Act 1971, s 5(2)

Produce

Produce a Class A **controlled drug** (see **5.1.1** for full wording)

Misuse of Drugs Act 1971, s 4(2)(a)

Points to prove

Possess

- ✓ possess a fungus containing psilocin or an ester of psilocin (magic mushrooms)
- ✓ being a Class A controlled drug

Produce

- ✓ produce a fungus containing psilocin or an ester of psilocin (magic mushrooms)
- ✓ being a Class A controlled drug

Meanings

Possess (see **5.2.1**)

Controlled drug (see **5.1.1**)

Produce (see **5.1.1**)

Explanatory notes

- Section 21 of the Drugs Act 2005 has made 'magic mushrooms' a Class A drug.
- Regulation 4A of the Misuse of Drugs Regulations 2001 (see **'Defences'** below) provides four circumstances where a person could possess 'magic mushrooms' and would not be liable for committing a s 5(1) possession of a Class A controlled drug offence.

Defences

The Misuse of Drugs Act, s 5(1) defences (see **5.2.1**)

Regulation 4A

(1) Section 5(1) of the Act (which prohibits the possession of controlled drugs) shall not have effect in relation to a fungus (of any kind) which contains psilocin or an ester of psilocin where the fungus—

    (a) is growing uncultivated;

    (b) is picked by a person already in lawful possession of it for the purpose of delivering it as soon as is reasonably practicable into the custody of a person lawfully entitled to take custody of it and it remains in that person's possession for and in accordance with that purpose;

(c) is picked for either of the purposes specified in paragraph (2) and is held for and in accordance with the purpose specified in paragraph (2)(b), either by the person who picked it or by another person; or

(d) is picked for the purpose specified in paragraph (2)(b) and is held for and in accordance with the purpose in paragraph (2)(a), either by the person who picked it or by another person.

(2) The purposes specified for the purposes of this paragraph are—

(a) the purpose of delivering the fungus as soon as is reasonably practicable into the custody of a person lawfully entitled to take custody of it; and

(b) the purpose of destroying the fungus as soon as is reasonably practicable.

Misuse of Drugs Regulations 2001, reg 4A

Practical considerations

- The specific power to search, detain a person or vehicle/vessel, and seize any drugs is given in s 23(2) (see **5.4.1**). Ensure that s 2 of PACE (see **12.1.3**) is complied with, as a breach of s 2 will mean the search is unlawful and may affect the admissibility of any evidence obtained.
- Simple possession of magic mushroom spores is not illegal, owing to the fact that they do not contain psilocin (the 'controlled drug') until they are actually cultivated.

'Legal highs'

- New Psychoactive Substances (NPS), known as 'legal highs', are an emerging threat in the UK and worldwide; they are mainly produced in China and India and usually sold and consumed as either a white powder, pill, liquid, or smoking substance.
- Although these substances are not controlled by the Misuse of Drugs Act 1971, they are manufactured to mimic the effects of illegal drugs such as cocaine, ecstasy, cannabis, and other hallucinogenics. When the NPS becomes subject to a temporary class drug order under s 7A of the 1971 Act (see **5.1.1**), the manufacturers make a similar substance by altering its chemical composition so it still remains a 'legal high'.
- NPS are generally sold via the internet or from 'head shops'. Head shops are shops, market stalls, or other retail outlets which often sell NPS and drugs paraphernalia. For example: NPS purporting to be bath salts, incenses, room deodoriser, research chemicals, or other goods in small samples all at high prices; displays of paraphernalia for smoking, insufflating, or storing NPS or other drugs; or drug related designs or references displayed on goods.
- Head shops selling NPS are often vague and creative in descriptions given of their products and their purported uses, stating that the NPS are not sold for human consumption and give legal secondary uses for the drug paraphernalia/articles.

5.3.2 'Magic mushrooms'/'legal highs'

- There are no Home Office kits to identify NPS, with forensic testing being the only option. Similarly, there is no specific legislation to control NPS or head shops, so consider the offences of: selling/supplying controlled drugs (see **5.1.1**), drugs articles (see **5.1.2**), supplying intoxicating substances (see **11.5.1**), or breaching consumer protection legislation.
- Test purchases could establish if items sold as NPS contain or are controlled drugs (including temporary controlled drugs) by forensic testing, in which case a s 23(3) drugs warrant (see **5.4.1**) can be applied for. If a search warrant is executed it may be beneficial for trading standards officials to accompany the police to enforce consumer protection regulations.
- The General Product Safety Regulations 2005 prohibits the supply of any unsafe product. Trading standards have successfully challenged the disclaimer 'not approved for human consumption', as the supplier is aware that once sold they would be consumed. To comply with consumer law, the supplier must know what is contained in every product they sell and the risks associated with consumption.
- Consider approaching the local authority for them to issue a PSPO (see **7.15.2**), which could ban people using 'legal highs' in a public place, with a power to seize the NPS and if appropriate to issue a fixed penalty notice.

 Either way   None

 Possess—s 5(2) offence

Summary: 6 months' imprisonment and/or a fine
Indictment: 7 years' imprisonment and/or a fine

Produce—s 4(2)(a) offence

Summary: 6 months' imprisonment and/or a fine
Indictment: Life imprisonment and/or a fine

Links to alternative subjects and offences

 SSS Stop, search and seize powers   E&S Entry and search powers   TRIG Trigger offences

PCSO Police community support officers

5.4 Drug Search Powers/Permit Drug Use on Premises

5.4.1 Power to search, detain, and seize drugs

Search powers under s 23 or s 23A of the Misuse of Drugs Act 1971 confers powers on a constable to stop, detain, and search a person, vehicle, or vessel for controlled drugs and an obstruction offence for failing to comply.

Power to search, detain, and seize drugs

If a constable has **reasonable grounds** to suspect that any person is in possession of a **controlled drug** in contravention of this Act or of any regulations or orders made thereunder, the constable may—
(a) search that person, and detain him for the purpose of searching him;
(b) search any **vehicle** or **vessel** in which the constable suspects that the drug may be found, and for that purpose require the person in control of the vehicle or vessel to stop it;
(c) seize and detain, for the purposes of proceedings under this Act, anything found in the course of the search, which appears to the constable to be evidence of an offence under this Act.

Misuse of Drugs Act 1971, s 23(2)

Offences

A person commits an offence if he—
(a) **intentionally obstructs** a person in the exercise of his powers under this section.

Misuse of Drugs Act 1971, s 23(4)

Points to prove

✓ intentionally obstructed
✓ constable/authorised person in exercise of s 23 powers

5.4.1 Power to search, detain, and seize drugs

Meanings

Reasonable grounds (see **12.1**)

Controlled drug (see **5.1.1**)

Vehicle (see **10.1.3**)

Vessel

Includes a hovercraft within the meaning of the Hovercraft Act 1968.

Intentionally obstructs

Where a person deliberately does an act which, though not necessarily aimed at or hostile to the police, makes it more difficult for the police to carry out their duty and they intentionally do the act knowing that their conduct will have an obstructive effect *(Lewis v Cox* [1984] Crim LR 756, QBD).

Explanatory notes

- Section 23(1) gives a constable/authorised person power to enter premises relating to producing or supplying (eg chemists) any controlled drugs, in order to inspect the drug stocks or demand production and inspection of books or documents regarding dealings in such drugs.
- Where a person is acting under s 23(1), it is an offence (s 23(4)(b)–(c)) to conceal books, documents, stocks, or drugs; or when demanded, failing (without reasonable excuse) to produce the books or documents.
- Section 23A gives a constable power to search and detain a person (or vehicle or vessel) on reasonable grounds to suspect that the person is in possession of a temporary class drug (see **5.1.1**). Also to seize, detain, and dispose of such a drug. It is an offence under s 23A(6) to intentionally obstruct a constable exercising this power; guidance is provided in HOC 12/2011 regarding temporary class drug offences and powers.
- These powers are exercisable *anywhere* and must be conducted in accordance with the related COP and PACE (see **12.1**).

Related cases

Browne v Commissioner of Police for the Metropolis [2014] EWHC 3999, QBD Failure by the officer to comply with s 2 PACE (see **12.1.2**) and use of excessive force, rendered a search unlawful and led to damages being awarded for assault.

James v DPP [2012] EWHC 1317 (Admin), QBD The co-operation of the person to be searched must be sought in every case, even if the person initially objects to the search. Reasonable force may be used to conduct the search if the person is unwilling to co-operate or resists (see Code A, para 3.2).

R v Bristol [2007] EWCA Crim 3214, CA The officer failed to give his name and police station prior to a s 23 drug search, thus breaching s 2

PACE (see **12.1.2**) and, making the search unlawful. As a result the officer was not acting in the execution of his duty and the s 23(4) offence was not committed.

Practical considerations

Personal safety

- Contact with the blood or saliva of drug abusers (particularly those users who inject) carries a risk of infection with serious diseases such as AIDS, HIV, and Hepatitis.
- Every effort should be made to avoid such fluids entering your own body through cuts, eyes, or the mouth. Should such contact occur, the possibility of infection is minimised by the contact area being thoroughly washed immediately and medical advice sought as soon as practicable.

Searching of suspects

- Care should always be taken to avoid unguarded needles piercing the skin, if such an event does occur seek medical advice as soon as practicable.
- When conducting a search initially request the suspect/prisoner to turn out their own pockets, before patting the outside of pockets to detect the presence of a syringe.
- Drug abusers will go to extreme lengths to conceal drugs on or in their bodies. Drugs are commonly found in body orifices. Certain circumstances must prevail before an intimate search may be conducted.
- Search a person minutely: small amounts of drugs can be concealed, for example, in the lining of clothing, under plasters supposedly covering an abrasion, or stuck to the skull under the hairline.
- Searching inside a person's mouth does not constitute an intimate search.

Handling of drugs

- Certain drugs may be absorbed through the skin; it is therefore always advisable to wear gloves when handling drugs.
- **Never under any circumstances taste the drugs.**
- There will be occasions when the name of the drug seized is unknown and doubt as to whether it is controlled. Always seek advice and assistance from a supervisory officer or the drug squad.

Drug abusers' equipment

- Abusers use a wide range of paraphernalia to prepare and administer their drugs. The following list (which is not exhaustive) may provide evidence of that activity where premises are searched—
  - ✦ syringes and needles; scorched tinfoil and spoons; small mirrors, razors, and straws; tubes of tinfoil; ligatures; lemon juice or citric acid; cigarette papers and home-made cigarettes; bloodstained swabs; square folds of paper which may contain powder; cling film; small self-sealing bags; weighing scales; hookah pipes.

5.4.2 Occupier/manager permits drug use on premises

General

- Section 23(3) of the Misuse of Drugs Act 1971 allows a warrant to be issued for any constable to enter (if need be by force) premises named in the warrant and to search the premises and any persons found therein for evidence of offences relating to controlled drugs (see **12.4** for application procedures).
- Ensure all s 23(3) search powers are in the warrant; a warrant authorising premises search only does not give grounds to search people found therein (*CC of Thames Valley v Hepburn* [2002] EWCA Civ 1841). If the warrant authorises the search of premises and people it is reasonable to restrict their movement to conduct a proper search (*DPP v Meadon* [2003] EWHC 3005 (Admin)).
- Comply with PACE and the COP for the grounds for searching people, conduct of the search, and completion of a search record (see **12.1**); using reasonable force to detain and carry out the search (PACE, s 117) (see **1.2**).
- When using s 23 search powers, ensure that the s 2 PACE requirements are met (see **12.1.2**) (eg police officer fails to state name and police station), otherwise the search will be deemed unlawful and may affect the admissibility of any evidence obtained.
- Although s 23(2) authorises detention of a suspect for the purpose of searching, it does not give the officer a general right to question the suspect. However, they may ask questions incidental to exercising that power.
- Section 23(2)(b) does not give an officer the right to stop a vehicle or to search it simply because they suspect the vehicle (not the occupants) has been used in connection with a drug offence on a previous occasion (*R v Littleford* [1978] CLR 48).
- Nothing in s 23(2) prejudices any other powers available to a constable to search or seize/detain property.
- Consider road traffic law to stop the vehicle (see **10.2**).

E&S

 Either way   🕐 None

 Summary: 6 months' imprisonment and/or a fine
Indictment: 2 years' imprisonment and/or a fine

5.4.2 Occupier/manager permits drug use on premises

Section 8 of the Misuse of Drugs Act 1971 makes it an offence for occupiers and managers of premises to permit certain activities relating to drugs to take place on those premises.

Offences

A person commits an offence if, being the **occupier** or concerned in the **management** of any premises, he **knowingly permits** or **suffers** any of the following activities to take place on those premises, that is to say—

(a) **producing** or attempting to produce a **controlled drug** in contravention of **section 4(1)** of this Act;

(b) **supplying** or attempting to supply a controlled drug to another in contravention of section 4(1) of this Act, or offering to supply a controlled drug to another in contravention of section 4(1);

(c) preparing opium for smoking;

(d) smoking cannabis, cannabis resin or prepared opium.

Misuse of Drugs Act 1971, s 8

Points to prove

✓ being the occupier/concerned in managing of premises
✓ knowingly
✓ permitted/suffered to take place
✓ on premises
✓ the production/attempted production **or**
✓ supplying/attempted to supply/offering to supply to another
✓ Class A/B/C drug namely [if known] **or**
✓ preparing of opium for smoking **or**
✓ smoking of cannabis, cannabis resin, or prepared opium

Meanings

Occupier

Whether a person is in **lawful** occupation of premises has created some difficulty. In *R v Tao* [1976] 3 All ER 65, a college student who paid rent for a room on the campus was deemed to be the occupier of that room; Lord Justice Roskill commented that it would be 'somewhat astonishing' if a squatter could not be an 'occupier' under the Act. Similarly there may be different occupiers at different times or an occupier who only had that status for certain periods. The question was always one of fact (*R v Coid* [1998] Crim LR 199, CA).

Management

Implies a degree of control over the running of the affairs of the venture or business. If a person controls premises by running, planning, or organising them they will be managing. Sharing or assisting in the running of premises is sufficient for the purposes of 'being concerned in the management'.

Knowingly (see **9.1.3**)

Permits (see **10.14.1**)

Suffers

Means an unwillingness or failure to prevent.

5.4.2 Occupier/manager permits drug use on premises

Producing (see 5.1.1)

Controlled drug (see 5.1.1)

Section 4(1) (see 5.1.1)

Supplying (see 5.1.1)

Explanatory notes

- As long as the defendant is aware that the premises are being used to supply controlled drugs, it does not matter, for the purposes of establishing guilt, which type of drug is involved (*R v Bett* [1998] 1 All ER 600). However, there is a difference so far as the penalty is concerned as to which class of drugs were used.
- This offence is limited to the activities specified at (a) to (d). It is not committed, for example, by a landlord who knows that one of their tenants is in their room injecting themselves with amphetamines. They may commit the offence if, for example—
  - ◆ a drug is being supplied to others on the premises;
  - ◆ a controlled drug is being produced on the premises;
  - ◆ the occupants are smoking cannabis.
- The Misuse of Drugs Regulations 2001 allows a person to possess some drugs for certain legitimate reasons (eg medicinal, research) (see 'Defences' 5.1.1).

Related cases

R v McGee [2012] EWCA Crim 613, CA Where a person permits the supply of class A drugs to take place on their premises, the prosecution must prove that the supply took place 'on the premises' rather than 'from the premises'.

R v Lunn [2008] EWCA Crim 2082, CA It is more serious where the manager of a public house allows premises to be used for drugs compared to the owner of a private house; this is because it is drug taking in public, thus making it appear to be an acceptable activity and may encourage others to partake.

R v Auguste [2003] EWCA Crim 3929, CA During a police raid a block of cannabis resin and two reefers were found. Although several men were in the house, there was no smell of cannabis having been smoked. Held: Activity of actually smoking cannabis must be carried out before this offence is committed.

R v Brock and Wyner (2001) 2 Cr App R 3, CA The offence under s 8(b) has two elements: (i) knowingly permits—knowledge of the dealing, which could be actual knowledge or the defendant closing their eyes to the obvious; or (ii) suffers—unwillingness to prevent the dealing, which could be inferred from the failure to take reasonable steps to prevent it. A belief that they had taken reasonable steps does not provide them with a defence.

Practical considerations

- Whenever the decision to search premises can be planned in advance, a warrant should be obtained under the Misuse of Drugs Act 1971, s 23(3) (see **5.4.1** and **12.4**).
- The police have a power to close premises associated with nuisance or disorder by issuing a closure notice under the Anti-social Behaviour, Crime and Policing Act 2014, s 76 (see **7.13.5**).
- Consider confiscation of cash and property for premises relating to controlled drugs under s 8; as this is listed as a 'criminal lifestyle' offence under Sch 2 to the Proceeds of Crime Act 2002 (see **5.5** for details).

Class A/B

Summary: 6 months' imprisonment and/or a fine
Indictment: 14 years' imprisonment and/or a fine

Class C

Summary: 3 months' imprisonment and/or a fine
Indictment: 14 years' imprisonment and/or a fine

Links to alternative subjects and offences

5.5 **Proceeds of Crime**

The Proceeds of Crime Act 2002, s 75 sets out the criminal lifestyle criteria which could be subject to a confiscation order; this is to be read in conjunction with Sch 2 (lifestyle offences) and s 6 (confiscation order procedure).

Criminal lifestyle criteria

(1) A defendant has a **criminal lifestyle** if (and only if) the following condition is satisfied.
(2) The condition is that the offence (or any of the offences) concerned satisfies any of these tests:—
  (a) it is specified in **Schedule 2**;
  (b) it constitutes conduct forming part of a course of criminal activity;
  (c) it is an offence committed over a period of at least six months and the defendant has benefited from the conduct which constitutes the offence.
(3) Conduct forms part of a course of criminal activity if the defendant has benefited from the conduct and—
  (a) in the proceedings in which he was convicted he was convicted of three or more other offences, each of three or more of them constituting conduct from which he has benefited, or
  (b) in the period of six years ending with the day when those proceedings were started (or, if there is more than one such day, the earliest day) he was convicted on at least two separate occasions of an offence constituting conduct from which he has benefited.
(4) But an offence does not satisfy the test in subsection (2)(b) or (c) unless the defendant obtains **relevant benefit** of not less than £5000.
(5) **Relevant benefit** for the purposes of subsection (2)(b) is—
  (a) benefit from conduct which constitutes the offence;
  (b) benefit from any other conduct which forms part of the course of criminal activity and which constitutes an offence of which the defendant has been convicted;
  (c) benefit from conduct which constitutes an offence which has been or will be taken into consideration by the court in sentencing the defendant for an offence mentioned in paragraph (a) or (b).
(6) **Relevant benefit** for the purposes of subsection (2)(c) is—
  (a) benefit from conduct which constitutes the offence;
  (b) benefit from conduct which constitutes an offence which has been or will be taken into consideration by the court in sentencing the defendant for the offence mentioned in paragraph (a).

Proceeds of Crime Act 2002, s 75

Criminal lifestyle offences

Schedule 2 lists the criminal lifestyle offences—

Drug trafficking

Misuse of Drugs Act 1971

- s 4(2) or (3) (unlawful production/supply of controlled drugs) (see **5.1.1**);
- s 5(3) (possession of controlled drug with intent to supply) (see **5.2.2**);
- s 8 (premises relating to controlled drugs) (see **5.4.2**);
- s 20 (assisting/inducing offence outside UK).

Customs and Excise Management Act 1979: committed in breach
of import or export drug restriction

- s 50(2) or (3) (improper importation of goods);
- s 68(2) (exportation of prohibited or restricted goods);
- s 170 (fraudulent duty evasion).

Criminal Justice (International Co-operation) Act 1990

- s 12 (manufacture/supply substance used for drugs);
- s 19 (using a ship for illicit traffic in controlled drugs).

Money laundering

- s 327 (concealing etc criminal property);
- s 328 (assisting another to retain criminal property).

Directing terrorism

- Terrorism Act 2000, s 56 (directing the activities of a terrorist organisation).

People trafficking

- offence under s 25, 25A, or 25B of the Immigration Act 1971 (assisting unlawful immigration etc) (see **11.3**);
- offence under s 59A of the Sexual Offences Act 2003 (trafficking for sexual exploitation) (see **6.12.3**);
- offence under s 4 of the Asylum and Immigration (Treatment of Claimants, etc) Act 2004 (labour and other exploitation).

Arms trafficking

Customs and Excise Management Act 1979: in connection with a
firearm or ammunition—

- s 68(2) (exportation of prohibited goods);
- s 170 (fraudulent duty evasion).

Firearms Act 1968, s 3(1)

- dealing in firearms or ammunition by way of trade or business (see **8.1.2**).

Counterfeiting

Forgery and Counterfeiting Act 1981

- s 14 (making counterfeit notes or coins);
- s 15 (passing etc counterfeit notes or coins);
- s 16 (having counterfeit notes or coins);
- s 17 (make/possess materials or equipment for counterfeiting).

Intellectual property

Copyright, Designs and Patents Act 1988

- s 107(1) (make/deal in article which infringes copyright);
- s 107(2) (make/possess article designed or adapted to make copy of a copyright work);
- s 198(1) (making or dealing in an illicit recording);
- s 297A (making or dealing in unauthorised decoders).

Trade Marks Act 1994, s 92(1), (2), or (3)—

- unauthorised trade mark use.

Prostitution and child sex

Sexual Offences Act 1956, s 33 or 34: keeping or letting premises for use as a brothel.

Sexual Offences Act 2003

- s 14 (arranging or facilitating commission of a child sex offence) (see **6.5.3**);
- s 48 (causing or inciting sexual exploitation of a child);
- s 49 (controlling a child in relation to sexual exploitation);
- s 50 (arranging or facilitating sexual exploitation of a child);
- s 52 (causing or inciting prostitution for gain);
- s 53 (controlling prostitution for gain) (see **6.11.3**).

Blackmail

Theft Act 1968, s 21: blackmail (see **3.2.3**).

Gangmasters (Licensing) Act 2004, s 12(1) or (2): acting as a gangmaster without a licence, possession of false documents.

Inchoate offences

- offence of attempting, conspiring, or inciting the commission of an offence specified in this Schedule (see **4.1.1**);
- offence under s 44 of the Serious Crime Act 2007 of doing an act capable of encouraging or assisting the commission of an offence specified in this Schedule (see **4.1.3**).
- offence of aiding, abetting, counselling, or procuring the commission of such an offence.

Explanatory notes

- The criminal lifestyle tests are designed to identify individuals who may be living off crime and make them account for their assets, which are liable to be confiscated if the person is unable to account for their lawful origin.
- The first test is that s/he is convicted of an offence specified in Sch 2.
- The second test is that the defendant is convicted of an offence of any description, provided it was committed over a period of at least six months, and obtained not less than £5,000 from that offence and/or any others taken into consideration by the court on the same occasion.
- The third test is that the defendant is convicted of a combination of offences amounting to 'a course of criminal activity'.
- This third test is more complicated than the other two. The defendant satisfies it if s/he has been convicted in the current proceedings—
  - ♦ of four or more offences of any description from which s/he has benefitted; or
  - ♦ of any one such offence and has other convictions for any such offences on at least two separate occasions in the last six years.

  In addition, the total benefit from the offence(s) and/or any others taken into consideration by the court must be not less than £5,000.
- The purpose of confiscation proceedings under s 6 is to recover the financial benefit that the offender has obtained from his criminal conduct. Proceedings are conducted according to the civil standard of proof, being on the balance of probabilities.
- In certain circumstances the court is empowered to assume that the defendant's assets, and his income and expenditure during the period of six years before proceedings were brought, have been derived from criminal conduct and to calculate the confiscation order accordingly.
- Confiscation orders may be made in the Crown Court following conviction. Where the conviction takes place in the magistrates' court, a confiscation order can only be made if the defendant is either committed to the Crown Court for sentence or for sentence and confiscation under s 70.

Links to alternative subjects and offences

Chapter 6

Sexual Offences and Assaults

6.1 **Rape**

Rape and other sexual offences were consolidated by the Sexual Offences Act 2003.

6.1.1 **Rape**

The offence of rape is covered by ss 1 (rape) and 5 (rape of a child under 13) of the Sexual Offences Act 2003.

Offences

A person (A) commits an offence if—

(a) he **intentionally penetrates** the **vagina**, **anus** or **mouth** of another person (B) with his **penis**,

(b) B does not **consent** to penetration, and

(c) A does not **reasonably believe** that B consents.

Sexual Offences Act 2003, s 1(1)

Points to prove

✓ intentionally
✓ without consent
✓ penetrated anus/vagina/mouth
✓ of another person
✓ with the defendant's penis
✓ not reasonably believing that s/he had consented

Meanings

Intentionally (see also **4.1.2**)

This is the defendant's aim or purpose in pursuing a particular course of action. If the defendant intended to penetrate but was physically unable to do so or he admitted that it was his intent then the law states that he still had the necessary intent.

Penetration

Means a continuing act from entry to withdrawal.

Vagina

Includes vulva.

Consent

Both s 75 (evidential presumptions about consent) and s 76 (conclusive presumptions about consent) apply to this offence (see '**Defences**' below).

Reasonable belief

Whether a belief is reasonable is to be determined having regard to all the circumstances, including any steps A has taken to ascertain whether B consents.

Explanatory notes

- As the definition of vagina includes vulva, then full penetration is not essential to commit rape.
- The offence of rape includes not only penile penetration of the vagina and anus but also of the mouth as this act could be just as traumatising and damaging for the victim.
- As penetration can be proved by reference to scientific evidence (sperm, semen, bruising, etc), consent often becomes the major, if not only, issue.
- The offence of rape is gender specific in that only a male (over the age of 10) can commit the offence; the gender of the complainant is irrelevant. This section and s 5 (see **6.1.2**) are the only offences throughout the whole Act that are gender specific because they refer to penile penetration.

Defences

A critical issue in rape cases is **consent** and s 74 to s 76 deal specifically with these issues.

Consent

A person consents if he **agrees** by choice, and has the **freedom** and **capacity** to make that choice.

Sexual Offences Act 2003, s 74

Evidential presumptions about consent

(1) If in proceedings for an offence to which this section applies it is proved—
- (a) that the defendant did the **relevant act**,
- (b) that any of the circumstances specified in subsection (2) existed, and
- (c) that the defendant knew that those circumstances existed,

the complainant is to be taken not to have consented to the relevant act unless sufficient evidence is adduced to raise an issue as to whether he consented, and the defendant is to be taken not to have reasonably believed that the complainant consented unless sufficient evidence is adduced to raise an issue as to whether he reasonably believed it.

(2) The circumstances are that—
- (a) any person was, at the time of the relevant act or immediately before it began, using violence against the complainant or causing the complainant to fear that immediate violence would be used against him;
- (b) any person was, at the time of the relevant act or immediately before it began, causing the complainant to fear that violence was being used, or that immediate violence would be used, against another person;
- (c) the complainant was, and the defendant was not, unlawfully detained at the time of the relevant act;
- (d) the complainant was asleep or otherwise unconscious at the time of the relevant act;
- (e) because of the complainant's physical disability, the complainant would not have been able at the time of the relevant act to communicate to the defendant whether the complainant consented;
- (f) any person had administered to or caused to be taken by the complainant, without the complainant's consent, a **substance** which, having regard to when it was administered or taken, was capable of causing or enabling the complainant to be stupefied or overpowered at the time of the relevant act.

(3) In subsection (2)(a) and (b), the reference to the time immediately before the **relevant act** began is, in the case of an act that is one of a continuous series of sexual activities, a reference to the time immediately before the first sexual activity began.

Sexual Offences Act 2003, s 75

Conclusive presumptions about consent

(1) If in proceedings for an offence to which this section applies it is proved that the defendant did the relevant act and that any of the circumstances specified in subsection (2) existed, it is to be conclusively presumed—
- (a) that the complainant did not consent to the relevant act, and
- (b) that the defendant did not believe that the complainant consented to the relevant act.

(2) The circumstances are that—
- (a) the defendant intentionally deceived the complainant as to the nature or purpose of the relevant act;

(b) the defendant intentionally induced the complainant to consent to the relevant act by impersonating a person known personally to the complainant.

Sexual Offences Act 2003, s 76

Defence notes

Meaning of 'relevant act' (s 77)

References to the term 'relevant act' in ss 75 and 76 vary according to the offence committed and are where the defendant intentionally—

- Penetrates, with his penis, the vagina, anus or mouth of another person [*Rape (s 1)*].
- Penetrates, with a part of his body or anything else, the vagina or anus of another person, where the penetration is sexual [*Assault by penetration (s 2)*].
- Touches another person, where the touching is sexual [*Sexual assault (s 3)*].
- Causes another person to engage in a sexual activity [*Causing a person to engage in sexual activity without consent (s 4)*].

Consent (s 74)

The **freedom** to **agree** is intended to stress that a lack of protest, injury, or consent by the victim does not necessarily signify consent.

- Freedom is not defined in the Act so it must be a matter of fact as to whether the victim was free to agree or whether pressure or threats ruled out that agreement.
- A person might not have sufficient **capacity** if they suffer from a mental disorder, was incapacitated due to drink/drugs, or their age prevents them from being able to do so.
- Capacity is not defined so it will be for the court to decide from all the available evidence.

Evidential presumptions about consent (s 75)

- The term '**substance**' in s 75(2)(f) is not defined, so anything capable of stupefying or overpowering would be covered; this would include substances such as alcohol, GHB, or Rohypnol.
- Section 75(3) covers the situation where there have been a number of sexual acts, of which penetration is the culmination, and the defendant is being prosecuted for them and the threats occurred immediately before the first sexual act. In that case the presumption still applies.
- Where the prosecution proves that the defendant did a **relevant act** (in this case rape) and the situations described in s 75(2) existed and the defendant knew they existed, then the complainant will be presumed not to have consented and the defendant will be presumed not to have reasonably believed the complainant consented.

Conclusive presumptions about consent (s 76)

- Where the prosecution prove that the defendant did a **relevant act** and any of the circumstances described above existed then it is conclusively presumed that the complainant did not consent and the defendant did

not believe that the complainant consented to the relevant act. Therefore, evidence as to the existence of the intentional deception will be critical.
- Deceiving the complainant as to the nature or purpose of the act could be where the complainant is told that digital penetration of her vagina is necessary for medical reasons when in fact it is only for sexual gratification of the defendant.
- Impersonation would cover circumstances where the defendant deceives the complainant into believing that he is her partner causing the complainant to consent to the sexual act.

General

- If none of the situations described in ss 75 and 76 apply, then the prosecution must show that the circumstances of the offence were such that the defendant could not reasonably believe that the complainant consented.
- If the defendant states that he did reasonably believe that the complainant consented then it would be a matter for the jury to decide as to whether a reasonable person would come to the same belief having regard to all the circumstances. In interview he should be asked what assured him that the victim consented or that it was consensual.
- The circumstances will include the personal characteristics of the defendant. The defendant's age; general sexual experience; sexual experience with this complainant; learning disability; and any other factors that could have affected his ability to understand the nature and consequences of his actions which may be relevant depending on the circumstances of the particular case.
- The Act makes it clear there is an onus on parties involved in a relevant sexual activity to ensure that they have the true consent of the other person(s) and that they took reasonable steps to make sure true consent has been freely given prior to any sexual act taking place.

Related cases

R v Bree [2007] EWCA Crim 804, CA Temporary loss of capacity to choose whether to have sexual intercourse, through consumption of alcohol, means consent is not present. The issues of consent in s 74 with the 'capacity to make that choice' need to be addressed.

R v McAllister [1997] Crim LR 233, CA The circumstances of a possibly reluctant consent may be infinitely varied. On each occasion the jury has to decide whether an alleged agreement to a sexual act may properly be seen as a real consent or obtained by improper pressure which the complainant could not reasonably withstand from the defendant.

Practical considerations

- Ejaculation does not have to occur for the rape to be committed.
- All reports of rape must be treated as genuine and the victims treated with sensitivity. Only a suitably trained or qualified person should be used to take a statement or obtain evidence from the victim.
- The crime scene should be identified and preserved, ensuring that cross-contamination does not occur (see **1.3**).

- Evidence of the offence should be seized, including clothing and any articles used, such as condoms.
- Consider medical and forensic examination of the victim and offender.
- Consider DPP Guidance on consent in rape cases regarding capacity, steps taken to obtain consent and reasonable belief in the consent. In January 2015, CPS published a joint protocol setting out how the police and CPS will deal with all rape cases from the initial complaint through to end of trial.
- HOC 1/2015 gives guidance on the 'date rape' drug GHB, now under sch 2 to the Misuse of Drugs Regulations 2001, so ensuring stricter control to reduce the risks of diversion and misuse.
- Obtain evidence of first complaint if appropriate and available.
- Advise the victim not to shower, bathe, drink, or smoke, and to retain the clothing they were wearing at the time of the attack.
- Consider CCTV and other potential evidence from independent witnesses.

 Indictable   None

 Life imprisonment

6.1.2 **Rape of a child under 13**

This is covered by s 5 of the Sexual Offences Act 2003.

> **Offences**
>
> A person commits an offence if—
> (a) he **intentionally penetrates** the vagina, anus or mouth of another person with his penis, and
> (b) the other person is under 13.
>
> Sexual Offences Act 2003, s 5(1)

Points to prove

✓ intentionally
✓ penetrated the anus/vagina/mouth
✓ of a person under 13
✓ with the defendant's penis

6.1.2 Rape of a child under 13

Meanings

Intentionally (see **6.1.1**)

Penetrates (see **6.1.1**)

Vagina (see **6.1.1**)

Explanatory notes

- There is no issue of consent under this section. Whether the child consented or not is irrelevant making this almost an offence of 'strict liability'.
- This section also includes not only penetration of the vagina and anus but also penile penetration of the mouth as in s 1.
- This section replaces the offence of unlawful sexual intercourse with a girl under 13 in the Sexual Offences Act 1956, s 5.

Related cases

R v G [2008] UKHL 37, HL G, aged 15, had sex with a girl of 12 years old in his room with her full consent and at the time he believed her to be aged 15. Reasonable belief as to consent or age was irrelevant as the offence was absolute and imposed strict liability.

Practical considerations

- Full penetration does not have to occur and it is not necessary to prove any additional consequences (eg that the hymen was broken).
- Once it can be proved that penetration occurred, it will be very hard to show that it was anything other than intentional but it is still a necessary ingredient of the offence.
- Prove age of child. Only a suitably trained or qualified person should be used to take a statement or obtain evidence from the child/victim.
- Specific provisions for the police and other agencies to protect the welfare and safety of children are given in the Children Act 2004 (see **2.4.2**).
- Whilst offences between adults and children will always be viewed as serious, account should be taken of Art 8 (respect for private life) in relation to the criminalisation of consenting children.
- Consider CPS charging principles based on the Code for Crown Prosecutors.
- Consider all the evidential responsibilities highlighted as with the s 1 offence of rape.

 Indictable

 None

 Life imprisonment

Links to alternative subjects and offences

6.2 **Sexual Assault by Penetration**

These offences are covered by s 2 and s 6 (child under 13) of the Sexual Offences Act 2003.

6.2.1 **Assault by penetration of a person aged 13 or over**

Offences

A person (A) commits an offence if—
(a) he **intentionally penetrates** the **vagina** or anus of another person (B) with a **part of his body** or **anything else**,
(b) the penetration is **sexual**,
(c) B does not **consent** to the penetration, and
(d) A does not **reasonably believe** that B consents

Sexual Offences Act 2003, s 2(1)

Points to prove

✓ intentionally
✓ sexually penetrated
✓ the anus/vagina of another person aged 13 or over
✓ with a part of the body and/or a thing
✓ without consent
✓ not reasonably believing that s/he had consented

Meanings

Intentionally (see **6.1.1**)

Penetration (see **6.1.1**)

Vagina (see **6.1.1**)

Part of his body (see s 79(3))

References to a part of the body include references to a part surgically constructed (in particular, through gender reassignment surgery).

Anything else

This term has not been defined but it is an extremely wide category and will cover anything that can be used to penetrate the body of another.

Sexual

For the purposes of this Part (except section 71), penetration, touching or any other activity is sexual if a reasonable person would consider that—

(a) whatever its circumstances or any person's purpose in relation to it, it is because of its nature sexual, or

(b) because of its nature it may be sexual and because of its circumstances or the purpose of any person in relation to it (or both) it is sexual.

Sexual Offences Act 2003, s 78

Consent (see **6.1.1**)

Reasonable belief (see **6.1.1**)

Explanatory notes

- Section 79(3) takes into account surgically reconstructed genitalia. Medical examination could reveal that a person has undergone reconstructive surgery. A person can have their birth certificate changed to reflect their new gender under the Gender Recognition Act 2004.

- Once penetration has been proved, it will be difficult for the defendant to show that it was not their intention to do so. However, as partial penetration will suffice, there may be occasions (such as during a sporting or gymnastic contact) where the defendant claims inadvertent partial penetration by, say, a finger. It would then be for the prosecution to prove otherwise.

- If the defendant states that they reasonably believed that the complainant consented then it will be a matter for the jury to decide as to whether a reasonable person would come to the same belief having regard to all the circumstances.

- The circumstances include the personal characteristics of the defendant; the defendant's age; general sexual experience; sexual experience with this complainant; learning disability; and any other factor that could have affected their ability to understand the nature and consequences of their actions may be relevant depending on the circumstances of the particular case.

- The reasonableness test does not oblige the defendant to have taken any specific steps to ascertain consent, but any taken will be highly pertinent to the case.

- Parties to relevant sexual activity must ensure that they have the true consent of the other person(s) and that they took reasonable steps to make sure true consent had been freely given prior to any sexual act taking place.

- This offence was created in order to reflect the seriousness of assault by penetration, previously being indecent assault, which was perceived not to carry the appropriate penalties for such a serious offence. It carries the same penalty as rape (life imprisonment), thus reflecting its gravity.

- **Section 78 which defines 'sexual'** is a mixed test consisting of an objective test based on what a reasonable person would consider to be sexual and the purpose of the person involved—

6.2.1 Assault by penetration of a person aged 13 or over

+ subsection (a) where there is no doubt that the activity is sexual, such as oral sex or penetration by vibrator; and
+ subsection (b) where the activity could also have some other purpose, apart from a sexual one and also where the defendant's act was not sexually motivated. This would cover situations where the defendant penetrates his victim with an object with the sole intent of committing a violent act not a sexual one (eg penetration with the handle part of a knife to humiliate and assert their power over the victim).

- The defendant may not have intended the act to be sexual but from a reasonable person's point of view and because of its nature, a reasonable person would consider that it might be sexual.
- Medical examinations or intimate searches by the relevant authorities (such as police and customs) or such other treatment where penetration is involved but is not sexual (eg in colonic irrigation) will not normally be deemed sexual.
- Unlike rape, this offence can be committed by digital penetration and also penetration by any other part of the body, such as a fist, tongue, and toes.
- Full penetration is not essential to commit the offence.
- Items included in the term 'anything else' can be such objects as bottles, vibrators, and other similar objects and substances.

Defences

Sections 75 and 76 apply to this offence, see **6.1.1 'Defences'** for further details.

Practical considerations

- Any reports of serious sexual assault must be treated as genuine and the victims with sensitivity.
- Evidence of the offence should be seized and includes clothing, condoms, and articles used.
- Ensure cross-contamination does not occur.
- Obtain evidence of first complaint if appropriate and available.
- Advise the victim not to shower, bathe, drink, or smoke and to retain the clothing they were wearing at the time of the attack.
- Consider CCTV and other evidence from potential witnesses.

 Indictable   None

 Life imprisonment

6.2.2 **Assault by penetration of a child under 13**

This offence is the same as s 2 above, except the complainant is under 13 and there is no issue of consent.

Offences

A person commits an offence if—
(a) he **intentionally penetrates** the **vagina** or anus of another person with a **part of his body** or **anything else,**
(b) the penetration is **sexual**, and
(c) the other person is under 13.

Sexual Offences Act 2003, s 6

Points to prove

✓ intentionally
✓ sexually penetrated
✓ anus/vagina of a girl aged under 13
✓ anus of a boy aged under 13
✓ with a part of the body and/or a thing

Meanings

Intentionally (see **6.1.1**)

Penetrates (see **6.1.1**)

Vagina (see **6.1.1**)

Part of his body (see **6.2.1**)

Anything else (see **6.2.1**)

Sexual (see **6.2.1**)

Explanatory notes (see **6.2.1** notes)

Practical considerations (also see **6.2.1** considerations)

- This is an offence of strict liability (see **6.1.2**).
- It is not necessary for the victim to know or explain what they were penetrated with.
- The offence can be used in cases where the child does not possess the knowledge to identify the nature of what they had been penetrated with.

6.2.2 Assault by penetration of a child under 13

- Prove age of child. Only a suitably trained or qualified person should be used to take a statement or obtain evidence from the victim.
- The Children Act 2004 (see **2.4.2**) makes specific provisions for the police and other agencies to protect the welfare and safety of children.

 Indictable

 None

 Life imprisonment

Links to alternative subjects and offences

 SSS Stop, search and seize powers   **E&S** Entry and search powers

 CHAR Offences where bad character can be introduced

6.3 **Sexual Assault by Touching**

6.3.1 **Sexual assault by touching a person aged 13 or over**

This offence is covered by s 3 of the Sexual Offences Act 2003.

Offences

A person (A) commits an offence if—
(a) he **intentionally touches** another person (B),
(b) the touching is **sexual,**
(c) B does not **consent** to the touching, and
(d) A does not **reasonably believe** that B consents.

Sexual Offences Act 2003, s 3

Points to prove

✓ intentionally touched
✓ another person aged 13 or over
✓ by touching her/his body
✓ that touching was sexual
✓ not reasonably believing that s/he was consenting

Meanings

Intentionally (see **6.1.1**)

Touches

This includes touching—
• with any part of the body,
• with anything else,
• through anything,
and in particular includes touching amounting to penetration.

Sexual (see **6.2.1**)

Consent (see **6.1.1**)

Reasonable belief (see **6.1.1**)

Explanatory notes

• This section covers non-penetration sexual assaults of another person aged 13 or over. It will cover a wide spectrum of behaviour that would include the defendant rubbing up against the complainant's private parts through the person's clothes for their sexual gratification.

6.3.1 Sexual assault by touching a person aged 13 or over

- Touching includes touching through clothes, touching with anything, and touching that amounts to penetration. It does not have to involve using the hands and can involve any part of the body being used or touched or even an object such as a sex toy.
- The offence does not require that the defendant intended that the touching be sexual, only that the touching itself was intentional. The sexual aspect of the touching is a separate element.
- Whilst there could not be many examples of 'accidental' or inadvertent penetration, accidental touching occurs all the time. Jostling in a crowded street, travelling on a busy train or bus, and attending sports events can all lead to some form of contact with others.
- It will normally be apparent that the defendant intentionally touched the victim (because of the part of the body touched or used, or because of accompanying circumstances) but there will still be far more room for a defence of lack of intent than in penetration offences.
- In most cases of sexual assault the sexual element will be non-contentious. For example, where a man gropes a female's genitals, it would be hard to imagine a set of circumstances where this would not be sexual and in those cases s 78(a) (see **6.2.1**) will be relied on.
- If with regard to all the circumstances, the purpose and nature of the touching, a reasonable person would consider it sexual then it will be covered by s 78(b). However, it is not certain if the more obscure sexual fantasies would be covered at all by s 78. Would a reasonable person consider the removal of a shoe as sexual, looking at the purpose and nature of it? If not then this would not constitute 'sexual' touching even if the offender received sexual gratification from doing it. This reflects the former common law position with regard to such offences (see **'Explanatory notes'** under **6.2.1** for further details on 'sexual' and s 78).

Defences

Sections 75 and 76 apply—see **6.1.1 'Defences'** for further details.

Related cases

R v Ciccarelli [2011] EWCA Crim 2665, CA C claimed that, at a party, X had touched him between the legs and tried to kiss him. Later, while X was asleep, he touched her with his erect penis from behind, tried to pull her knickers down and climbed on top of her; she woke up and made C leave the room. C made no attempt to awaken X prior to his sexual advances and there was insufficient evidence for him to raise the issue of reasonable belief under s 75.

R v H [2005] 1 WLR 2005, CA A female was approached by a man who said to her 'Do you fancy a shag?' and then grabbed at her tracksuit bottoms, attempting to pull her towards him. By s 78(b) the touching of the clothing was sexual and so was a 'sexual assault by touching'.

R v Heard [2007] EWCA Crim 125, CA Police officers took H to hospital who was drunk, emotional, and injured. He was abusive, singing noisily, and danced suggestively towards one of the police officers (P). H punched P in the stomach and then took out his penis, rubbing it up and down P's thigh. The touching of P with his penis was intentional and was a sexual assault under s 3.

Practical considerations

- Reports of serious sexual assault must be treated as genuine and the victims treated with sensitivity.
- As with all serious sexual offences identify any scene, preserve it and seize any articles or associated items relevant to the offence for which the offender has been arrested.
- Prevent any potential for cross-contamination.
- Keep the offender and victim separate.
- Consider medical and forensic examination for victim and offender.

 Either way   None

Summary: 6 months' imprisonment and/or a fine
Indictment: 10 years' imprisonment

6.3.2 **Sexual assault by touching a child under 13**

This offence is covered by s 7 of the Sexual Offences Act 2003 and is the same as s 3 but there is no need to prove lack of consent by the child; any such consent is irrelevant.

Offences

A person commits an offence if—
(a) he **intentionally touches** another person,
(b) the touching is **sexual**, and
(c) the other person is under 13.

Sexual Offences Act 2003, s 7

6.3.2 Sexual assault by touching a child under 13

Points to prove
✓ intentionally touched
✓ a girl/boy under 13
✓ and the touching was sexual

Meanings

Intentionally (see **6.1.1**)

Touches (see **6.3.1**)

Sexual (see **6.2.1**)

Explanatory notes
- Consent is not an issue as this is an offence of strict liability (see **6.1.2**).
- Points raised in **6.3.1** relating to the touching and its sexual nature are still relevant to this offence.

Related cases

R v Weir [2005] EWCA Crim 2866, CA W was on trial for sexual assault by touching a 10-year-old girl. Despite not being the same offence category, a previous caution for taking an indecent photograph of a child was disclosed at court under s 103(2)(b) of CJA 2003. This was allowed as it showed a propensity to commit the s 7 offence.

Practical considerations
- Prove age of child. Only a suitably trained or qualified person should be used to take a statement or obtain evidence from the victim.
- The Children Act 2004 (see **2.4.2**) makes specific provisions for the police and other agencies to protect the welfare and safety of children.
- If possible identify and preserve a scene, and seize any articles suspected of being used in the offence. Always consider the potential for cross-contamination (see **1.3**).

 Either way   None

 Summary: 6 months' imprisonment and/or a fine
Indictment: 14 years' imprisonment

Links to alternative subjects and offences

6.4 **Sexual Activity with a Child**

This offence is covered by s 9 of the Sexual Offences Act 2003.

Offences

(1) A person aged 18 or over (A) commits an offence if—
   (a) he **intentionally** touches another person (B),
   (b) the **touching** is **sexual**, and
   (c) either—
      (i) B is under 16 and A does not **reasonably believe** that B is 16 or over, or
      (ii) B is under 13.
(2) A person is guilty of an offence under this section, if the touching involved—
   (a) penetration of B's anus or vagina with a part of A's body or anything else,
   (b) penetration of B's mouth with A's penis,
   (c) penetration of A's anus or vagina with a part of B's body, or
   (d) penetration of A's mouth with B's penis.

Sexual Offences Act 2003, s 9

Points to prove

Non-penetrative under 13

✓ defendant aged 18 or over
✓ intentionally touched
✓ a girl/boy under 13
✓ the touching was sexual

Penetrative under 13

✓ defendant aged 18 or over
✓ intentionally touched complainant sexually
✓ sexual touching involved penetration of—
   ♦ complainant's anus/vagina with part of D's body or thing or
   ♦ complainant's mouth with D's penis or
   ♦ D's anus/vagina with part of complainant's body or
   ♦ D's mouth with complainant's penis
✓ complainant being under 13

Penetrative between 13 and 15

✓ per points to prove of **'Penetrative under 13'** except
✓ complainant is aged 13/14/15
✓ not reasonably believing complainant was 16 or over

> ### *Non-penetrative aged between 13 and 15*
> ✓ defendant aged 18 or over
> ✓ intentionally touched a girl/boy aged 13/14/15
> ✓ not reasonably believing s/he was 16 or over
> ✓ the touching was sexual

Meanings

Intentionally (see **6.1.1**)

Touching (see **6.3.1**)

Sexual (see **6.2.1**)

Reasonable belief (see '**Defence**' below)

Explanatory notes

This offence is very similar to s 3 and s 7 (see **6.3**), but the defendant is aged 18 or over and touching involved in s 9(2) is specified in terms of what was used on/in what part of the body. Consent is not mentioned in s 9, but per s 7—if the complainant is under 13 then consent is irrelevant.

> #### Defences
> Proving a reasonable belief that the child was 16 or over at the time. This only applies if the victim is aged between 13 and 15. If under 13 the offence is one of strict liability.

Defence notes

- If the victim is aged between 13 and 15 the prosecution must provide evidence that the defendant's belief was not reasonable. For example, that the defendant knew that a girl attended school and had not yet taken her GCSE examinations.
- However, if the defendant and the complainant met for the first time over the internet, the complainant provided photographs of her in which she looked much older than she in fact was and if she told the defendant that she was 18 and looked 18, then the belief may be reasonable.
- If the prosecution can provide such evidence it is open to the defendant to rebut it, if he can show on the balance of probabilities his belief was reasonably held.

Practical considerations

- This offence is gender neutral.
- Consent is not an issue, but if complainant is under 13 consent is irrelevant as the offence will be one of strict liability.
- Identify and preserve any scene. Prevent cross-contamination.
- Seize any articles/clothing or associated equipment which is relevant.

6.4 Sexual Activity with a Child

- Consider charging principles in the Code for Crown Prosecutors.
- Consider factors which include the age and emotional maturity of the parties, whether they entered into the sexual relationship willingly, any coercion or corruption by a person, relationship between the parties and whether there was any existence of a duty of care or breach of trust.
- The discretion of the CPS not to charge where it is not in the public interest would be partially relevant where the two parties were close in age, for instance an 18-year-old and a 15-year-old, and had engaged in mutually agreed sexual activity.

s 9(1) offence

 Either way

 None

 Summary: 6 months' imprisonment and/or a fine
Indictment: 14 years' imprisonment

s 9(2) offence

 Indictment

None

14 years' imprisonment

Links to alternative subjects and offences

SSS Stop, search and seize powers **E&S** Entry and search powers **CHAR** Offences where bad character can be introduced

6.5 **Child Sexual Exploitation Offences**

6.5.1 **Cause/incite child under 16 to engage in sexual activity**

The offence of cause/incite a child under 16 to engage in sexual activity, where the offender is aged 18 or over is under the Sexual Offences Act 2003, s 10.

Offences

(1) A person aged 18 or over (A) commits an offence if—
  (a) he **intentionally causes** or **incites** another person (B) to engage in an activity,
  (b) the activity is **sexual**, and
  (c) either—
    (i) B is under 16 and A does not **reasonably believe** that B is 16 or over, or
    (ii) B is under 13.
(2) A person is guilty of an offence under this section, if the activity caused or incited involved—
  (a) penetration of B's anus or vagina,
  (b) penetration of B's mouth with a person's penis,
  (c) penetration of a person's anus or vagina with a part of B's body or by B with anything else, or
  (d) penetration of a person's mouth with B's penis.

Sexual Offences Act 2003, s 10

Points to prove

Non-penetration

✓ offender aged 18 or over
✓ intentionally
✓ caused/incited
✓ a girl or boy 13/14/15, not reasonably believing s/he was 16 or over or
✓ under 13
✓ to engage in sexual activity
✓ of a non-penetrative nature

> **Penetration**
> ✓ per first six points of '**Non-penetration**'
> ✓ involving the penetration of
> ✓ girl/boy's anus/vagina **or**
> ✓ girl/boy's mouth with another person's penis **or**
> ✓ a person's anus/vagina with part of girl/boy's body or by girl/boy with anything else **or**
> ✓ a person's mouth with the boy's penis

Meanings

Intentionally (see 6.1.1)

The defendant's aim or purpose in pursuing a particular course of action.

Causes

Defined by the *Concise Oxford Dictionary* as 'be the cause of, make happen'. This infers that the defendant must take some positive action rather than an omission to act. Examples could be the use of force, threats, deception, or intimidation.

Incites

Defined by the *Concise Oxford Dictionary* as 'encourage, stir up, urge or persuade'. Examples could be bribery, threats, or pressure.

Sexual (see 6.2.1)

Reasonably believe (see 6.4)

Explanatory notes

- The sexual activity that is caused or incited involves the victim being engaged in that sexual activity. This can be, for example, where the defendant causes or incites the child to sexually touch themselves or for the child to masturbate or strip for the defendant's sexual gratification.
- It may be with a third person (eg where the defendant causes or incites the child to have oral sex with the penis of another person).
- The incitement itself is an offence so the sexual activity does not have to take place for the offence to be committed.
- Section 10(2) replicates some of the other offences covered in the Act, such as rape, assault by penetration. This duplication is intended to cover every possible scenario that could be envisaged ensuring that offenders do not escape prosecution as a result of a loophole in the law.
- Examples of an adult causing or inciting a child to engage in sexual activity could be promising a reward, persuading the child that it is perfectly acceptable behaviour that other children engage in all the time and they would be abnormal not to agree, or saying that the activity was necessary to check the child's body for bruises, lice etc, or to try on clothes.

- Where the child is under 13, the offender should be charged with the s 8 offence (see **6.5.2**), especially if it involves penetration as it then carries life imprisonment. However, s 10 might be used where the offender is under 18 or the child is under 13 and it only became known during trial that the child was actually under 13. The extension of s 10 to under-13s now means that the trial could continue with the original charge where necessary, thus closing a potential loophole in the law.

Practical considerations

- Prove age of child. Only a suitably trained or qualified person should be used to take a statement or obtain evidence from the victim.
- It is not intended to cover health professionals, or anyone providing sex education, advice, or contraception to children.
- This offence could be considered where the offender and victim are very close in age (eg an offender of 18 and a victim of 15) and are in a relationship and both have entered into a sexual relationship willingly.
- Where the child is aged 13 or over, but under 16, the prosecution must prove that the defendant did not reasonably believe that s/he was 16 or over. If the child is under 13 the offence is one of strict liability.
- If possible identify and preserve crime scene, seize any articles and evidence relevant to the offence.

Child Sexual Exploitation (CSE) Offences

- It is an offence under the Sexual Offences Act 2003, s 47 to intentionally obtain for themselves the sexual services of a child aged under 18, where those services have been paid for or where payment has been promised.
- HOC 8/2015 provides guidance on child sexual exploitation offences (CSE) under s 47 (above) and ss 48 to 50 of the 2003 Act—
  - ✦ 48 Causing or inciting sexual exploitation of a child;
  - ✦ 49 Controlling a child in relation to sexual exploitation;
  - ✦ 50 Arranging or facilitating sexual exploitation of a child.
- The Serious Crime Act 2015, s 69 makes it an either way offence to be in possession of a paedophile manual, being an item (includes anything in which information of any description is recorded) that contains advice or guidance about abusing children sexually. This covers offences under Pt 1 (ss 1 to 79) of the 2003 Act or the Protection of Children Act 1978, s 1 (see **6.6.1**).
- Section 116 of the Anti-social Behaviour, Crime and Policing Act 2014 provides that a police officer (inspector or above) may issue a notice to the owner, operator, or manager of a hotel, on reasonable belief that the hotel has been or will be used for the purposes of CSE, or conduct preparatory to or connected with CSE.
- A constable may require a person issued with such a notice to provide the police with name and address details of guests staying at the

hotel. It is a summary offence under s 118(1) if a person fails without reasonable excuse to comply with this requirement.

s 10(1) offence

Either way

None

Summary: 6 months' imprisonment and/or a fine
Indictment: 14 years' imprisonment

s 10(2) offence

Indictment

None

14 years' imprisonment

6.5.2 Cause/incite child under 13 to engage in sexual activity

The offence of cause/incite a child under 13 to engage in sexual activity is covered by s 8 of the Sexual Offences Act 2003.

> **Offences**
>
> (1) A person commits an offence if—
>   (a) he **intentionally causes** or **incites** another person (B) to engage in an activity,
>   (b) the activity is **sexual**, and
>   (c) B is under 13.
> (2) A person is guilty of an offence under this section, if the activity caused or incited involved—
>   (a) penetration of B's anus or vagina,
>   (b) penetration of B's mouth with a person's penis,
>   (c) penetration of a person's anus or vagina with a part of B's body or by B with anything else, or
>   (d) penetration of a person's mouth with B's penis.
>
> Sexual Offences Act 2003, s 8

Points to prove

Non-penetration

✓ intentionally caused/incited
✓ a boy/girl under 13
✓ to engage in sexual activity
✓ of a non-penetrative nature

Penetration

✓ per first three points of '**Non-penetration**'
✓ involving the penetration of
✓ boy/girl's anus/vagina or
✓ boy/girl's mouth with another person's penis or
✓ a person's anus/vagina with a part of boy/girl's body or by boy/girl with anything else or
✓ a person's mouth with the boy's penis

Meanings

Intentionally (see **6.1.1**)

Cause (see **6.5.1**)

Incite (see **6.5.1**)

Sexual (see **6.2.1**)

Explanatory notes

- This offence is the same as the s 10 offence save that the defendant can be of any age and that the victim is under 13.
- In relation to sexual activity caused or incited, the offence covers the same situations as does the offence under s 4 except that, for this offence, consent is irrelevant.

Practical considerations

- Section 8 consists of four separate offences: causing or inciting, penetrative or non penetrative sexual activity, you must specify which offence it is. The sexual activity must be of the child (*R v Grout* [2011] EWCA Crim 299, CA).
- If possible, identify and preserve crime scene, seize any articles and documentation relevant to the offence.
- Prove age of child. Only a suitably trained or qualified person should be used to take a statement or obtain evidence from the victim.

 SSS   **E&S**   **CHAR**

s 8(1) offence

 Either way   🕐 None

Summary: 6 months' imprisonment and/or a fine
Indictment: 14 years' imprisonment

s 8(2) offence

 Indictment 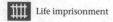 None

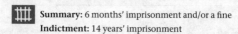 Life imprisonment

6.5.3 **Arrange/facilitate commission of a child sex offence**

This offence is covered by s 14 of the Sexual Offences Act 2003.

> **Offences**
>
> A person commits an offence if—
> (a) he **intentionally arranges** or **facilitates** something that he intends to do, intends another person to do, or believes that another person will do, in any part of the world, and
> (b) doing it will involve the commission of an offence under any of sections 9 to 13.
>
> *Sexual Offences Act 2003, s 14(1)*

Points to prove
- ✓ intentionally
- ✓ arranged/facilitated
- ✓ an act which the defendant
- ✓ intended to do or
- ✓ intended/believed another person would do
- ✓ in any part of the world
- ✓ and doing it will involve the commission of an offence
- ✓ under ss 9/10/11/12/13

Meanings

Intentionally (see 6.1.1)

Arranges

Organise or plan, reach agreement about an action or event in advance.

Facilitates

Make it happen, make it easier to achieve or promote.

Explanatory notes

- The defendant does not have to be the one who will commit the sexual offence; it will be enough if they intended/believed that they or another person will commit the relevant offence in any part of the world.
- The offence covers a situation where the defendant takes a person to a place where there is a child in the belief that the person is likely to engage in sexual activity with that child.
- It also caters for situations whereby the defendant arranges for them or another the procurement of a child with whom they propose to engage in sexual activity. For example, the defendant is going on holiday and plans to engage in sexual activity with children whilst there and so arranges through an agency to meet children.
- The sexual activity does not have to occur for the offence to be committed.
- The relevant offences are—
  - ✦ s 9—Sexual activity with a child;
  - ✦ s 10—Causing or inciting a child to engage in sexual activity;
  - ✦ s 11—Engaging in sexual activity in the presence of a child;
  - ✦ s 12—Causing a child to watch a sexual act;
  - ✦ s 13—Child sex offences committed by children or young persons.

Defences

(2) A person does not commit an offence under this section if—
   (a) he arranges or facilitates something that he believes another person will do, but that he does not intend to do or intend another person to do, and
   (b) any offence within subsection (1)(b) would be an offence against a child for whose **protection** he acts.
(3) For the purposes of subsection (2), a person acts for the **protection** of a child if he acts for the purposes of—
   (a) protecting the child from sexually transmitted infection,
   (b) protecting the physical safety of the child,
   (c) preventing the child from becoming pregnant, or
   (d) promoting the child's emotional well-being by the giving of advice,
   and not for the purpose of obtaining sexual gratification or for the purpose of causing or encouraging the activity constituting the offence within subsection (1)(b) or the child's participation in it.

Sexual Offences Act 2003, s 14

Defence notes

This is intended to protect those people such as healthcare workers who are aware that a person is having sex with a child under 16 and give them condoms as they believe that if they do not the child will have unprotected sex. It appears as if the healthcare worker must warn the person that what they are doing is illegal, but is allowed to give the condoms without committing an offence under this section.

Practical considerations

- The specified offence (under ss 9–13) does not have to take place. If it does occur or would have occurred if it were not for there being facts which made the commission of the offence impossible, then it may be easier to prove the above offence.
- Obtain any evidence which proves the links (eg advertisement, emails, and bookings for hotels).
- Seize mobile phone, computer hard drive, and any other physical evidence relevant to the offence.
- This offence is listed as a 'criminal lifestyle' offence under Sch 2 to the Proceeds of Crime Act 2002 (see **5.5** for details).
- The Child Sex Offender (CSO) disclosure scheme is operated by CEOP (see **Appendix 1**). For further guidance and details about this matter see HOC 7/2010.

 E&S   CHAR

 Either way None

 Summary: 6 months' imprisonment and/or a fine
Indictment: 14 years' imprisonment

6.5.4 **Meeting a child following sexual grooming**

This offence is covered by s 15 of the Sexual Offences Act 2003.

Offences

A person aged 18 or over (A) commits an offence if—
(a) A **has met or communicated** with another person (B) on one or more occasions and subsequently—
  (i) A **intentionally** meets B,
  (ii) A travels with the intention of meeting B in any part of the world or arranges to meet B in any part of the world, or
  (iii) B travels with the intention of meeting A in any part of the world,

(b) A intends to do anything to or in respect of B, during or after the meeting mentioned in paragraph (a)(i) to (iii) and in any part of the world, which if done will involve the commission by A of a **relevant offence**,

(c) B is under 16, and

(d) A does not **reasonably believe** that B is 16 or over.

Sexual Offences Act 2003, s 15(1)

Points to prove

✓ being a person 18 or over (A)

✓ has on one or more occasions met/communicated

✓ with a person under 16

✓ not reasonably believing that person to be 16 or over

✓ intentionally met or travelled intending to meet or arranged to meet that person or that person has travelled with the intention of meeting (A)

✓ in any part of the world

✓ intending to do anything to/in respect of that person

✓ during/after the meeting and in any part of the world

✓ which if done would involve commission by (A)

✓ of a relevant offence

Meanings

Has met or communicated

The reference to A having met or communicated with B is a reference to A having met B in any part of the world or having communicated with B by any means from, to or in any part of the world.

Intentionally (see **6.1.1**)

Relevant offence

Means an offence under Pt 1 (ss 1–79 inclusive) and anything done outside England and Wales being an offence within Pt 1.

Reasonably believe (see **'Defences'** below)

Explanatory notes

• A defendant must have communicated on one or more occasions or had one prior meeting with the person. The communication could be by telephone, texting, or email. These communications do not have to contain sexually explicit language or pornography but could, for example, be something as seemingly innocuous as the offender giving the victim swimming lessons or meeting them incidentally through a friend.

• Where person A has met or communicated with person B only once before the event mentioned in s 15(1)(a)(i) to (iii), an offence under s 15 is committed only if these events took place on or after 13 April

2015, when s 15 was amended by the Criminal Justice and Courts Act 2015, s 36. Prior to that date it would have to be 'on at least two occasions'. MOJ Circular 1/2015 provides further details.

- They must intentionally meet or travel with the intention of meeting or arrange to meet each other. This meeting can take place anywhere in the world as long as some part of the journey took place in England, Wales, or Northern Ireland.
- The meeting itself does not have to take place, arranging will suffice, although the intent to commit the relevant offence (in any part of the world) will have to be proved.
- This offence is intended to deal with predators who groom young children by gaining their trust, lying about their age, then arranging to meet them in order to sexually abuse them. This offence is preventative, in that the relevant sexual offence does not have to occur in order for the offence to be committed.

Defences

Reasonable belief that the victim is 16 or over (see **6.4 'Defence notes'**).

Related cases

R v G [2010] EWCA Crim 1693, CA There is no requirement that either communication be sexual in nature. A sexual intent must exist at the time of arranging the meeting, but the meeting does not have to take place.

R v Mohammed [2006] EWCA Crim 1107, CA M sent intimate text messages to a vulnerable 13-year-old girl, with severe learning difficulties and behavioural problems. Both found together 8 miles from her foster home. M confirmed she had visited his home; the abduction was short-lived, with the girl being willing and initiating contact, but no sexual act had taken place. M's motivation was sexual and he had blatantly taken her from the control of carers. Convicted of child abduction and s 15(1).

R v Mansfield [2005] EWCA Crim 927, CA 'The law is there to protect young girls against their own immature sexual experimentation and to punish older men who take advantage of them.'

Practical considerations

- Prove that the victim is under 16. Only a suitably trained or qualified person should be used to take a statement or obtain evidence from the victim.
- Any articles in the defendant's possession such as condoms, pornography, rope, and lubricant could help to prove intent.
- The Children Act 2004 (see **2.4.2**) makes specific provision for the police and other agencies to protect the welfare and safety of children.
- Offence applies to all offences in Pt 1 of the Act (ss 1–79).
- All evidence in relation to the grooming should be seized (eg any communications, bookings, or other documents which link the defendant and victim).

- Consider CCTV evidence.
- Seize any computer and mobile phone that could have been used.
- Section 72 allows sexual offences committed outside the UK to be dealt with in England and Wales, as if the person had committed the act in the UK provided certain conditions are met. The conditions are that the defendant is a UK national or resident who commits an act in a country outside the UK, and the act, if committed in England and Wales, would constitute a sexual offence given in Sch 2.

 E&S **CHAR**

 Either way   None

 Summary: 6 months' imprisonment and/or a fine
Indictment: 10 years' imprisonment

Links to alternative subjects and offences

6.6 Indecent Photographs/Images: Persons under 18/Disclose With Intent to Cause Distress

6.6.1 Take, distribute, publish indecent photographs of person under 18

This offence is covered by s 1 of the Protection of Children Act 1978.

Offences

Subject to sections 1A and 1B [**defences**], it is an offence for a person—
- (a) to take, or permit to be taken, or to **make**, any **indecent photograph** or **pseudo-photograph** of a child; or
- (b) to **distribute** or show such indecent photographs or pseudo-photographs; or
- (c) to have in his possession such indecent photographs or pseudo-photographs, with a view to their being distributed or **shown by himself** or others; or
- (d) to publish or cause to be published any advertisement likely to be understood as conveying that the advertiser distributes or shows such indecent photographs or pseudo-photographs or intends to do so.

Protection of Children Act 1978, s 1(1)

Points to prove

s 1(1)(a), (b)
- ✓ made/permitted to be taken/took/showed/distributed
- ✓ indecent photograph(s)/pseudo-photograph(s)
- ✓ of a child/children

s 1(1)(c)
- ✓ possessed
- ✓ indecent photograph(s)/pseudo-photograph(s)
- ✓ of child/children
- ✓ with a view to it (them) being distributed/shown to another

s 1(1)(d)
- ✓ published/caused to be published
- ✓ an advertisement which is likely to convey or be understood
- ✓ that the advertiser
- ✓ distributes/shows or intends to distribute/show
- ✓ indecent photograph(s)/pseudo-photograph(s)
- ✓ of child/children

Meanings

Make

Includes downloading images from the internet and storing or printing them (*R v Bowden* [2000] 1 WLR 1427).

Indecent photographs

- Includes indecent film, a copy of an indecent photograph or film, and an indecent photograph comprised in a film.
- Photographs (including those comprised in a **film**) shall, if they show children and are indecent, be treated for all purposes of this Act as indecent photographs of children and so as respects pseudo-photographs.

Photograph

References to a photograph include—

- the negative as well as the positive version; and
- data stored on a computer disc or by other electronic means which is capable of conversion into a photograph;
- a tracing or other image, whether made by electronic or other means (of whatever nature)—
  - ◆ which is not itself a photograph or pseudo-photograph; but
  - ◆ which is derived from the whole or part of a photograph or pseudo-photograph (or a combination of either or both); **and** data stored on a computer disc or by other electronic means which is capable of conversion into the above tracing or image.

Notes: If the impression conveyed by a pseudo-photograph is that of a child, the pseudo-photograph shall be treated as showing a child and so shall a pseudo-photograph where the predominant impression conveyed is that the person shown is a child notwithstanding that some of the physical characteristics shown are those of an adult.

Film

This includes any form of video recording.

Pseudo-photograph

Means an image, whether made by computer graphics or otherwise howsoever, which appears to be a photograph.

Indecent pseudo-photograph

This includes a copy of an indecent pseudo-photograph; and data stored on a computer disc or by other electronic means which is capable of conversion into an indecent pseudo-photograph.

Child

A person under the age of 18.

Distribute

Means to part with possession to another person, or exposes or offers for acquisition by another person.

6.6.1 Take, distribute, publish indecent photographs

Shown by himself

Means shown by the defendant to other people.

Explanatory notes

- The image does not have to be stored in a way that allows it to be retrieved. However, the image must be made deliberately. Innocently opening a file from the internet may not be an offence, see s 1(4)(b) in **'Defences'** below.
- The attendant circumstances of the way in which the images have been downloaded, stored, labelled, and filed will be important in demonstrating the extent to which the defendant was or should have been aware of their indecent nature. Other correspondence (by email or otherwise) with the defendant will also be useful here, as will any evidence of a general interest in paedophilia (*R v Mould* [2001] 2 Crim App R (S) 8).

Defences

1(4) Where a person is charged with an offence under subsection 1(b) or (c), it shall be a defence for him to prove—
   (a) that he had a legitimate reason for distributing or showing the photographs or pseudo-photographs or (as the case may be) having them in his possession; or
   (b) that he had not himself seen the photographs or pseudo-photographs and did not know, nor had any cause to suspect, them to be indecent.

Marriage and partnership

1A(1) This section applies where, in proceedings for an offence under s 1(1)(a) of taking or making an indecent photograph or pseudo-photograph of a child, or for an offence under s 1(1)(b) or (c) relating to an indecent photograph or pseudo-photograph of a child, the defendant proves that the photograph or pseudo-photograph was of the child aged 16 or over, and that at the time of the offence charged the child and he—
   (a) were married or civil partners of each other, or
   (b) lived together as partners in an enduring family relationship.

1A(2) Subsections (5) and (6) also apply where, in proceedings for an offence under s 1(1)(b) or (c) relating to an indecent photograph or pseudo-photograph of a child, the defendant proves that the photograph or pseudo-photograph was of the child aged 16 or over, and that at the time when he obtained it the child and he—
   (a) were married or civil partners of each other, or
   (b) lived together as partners in an enduring family relationship.

1A(3) This section applies whether the photograph or pseudo-photograph showed the child alone or with the defendant, but not if it showed any other person.

1A(4) In the case of an offence under s 1(1)(a), if sufficient evidence is adduced to raise an issue as to whether the child consented to the photograph or pseudo-photograph being taken or made, or as to whether the defendant reasonably believed that the child so consented, the defendant is not guilty of the offence unless it is proved that the child did not so consent and that the defendant did not reasonably believe that the child so consented.

1A(5) In the case of an offence under s 1(1)(b), the defendant is not guilty of the offence unless it is proved that the showing or distributing was to a person other than the child.

1A(6) In the case of an offence under s 1(1)(c), if sufficient evidence is adduced to raise an issue both—

(a) as to whether the child consented to the photograph or pseudo-photograph being in the defendant's possession, or as to whether the defendant reasonably believed that the child so consented, and

(b) as to whether the defendant had the photograph or pseudo-photograph in his possession with a view to its being distributed or shown to anyone other than the child,

the defendant is not guilty of the offence unless it is proved either that the child did not so consent and that the defendant did not reasonably believe that the child so consented, or that the defendant had the photograph or pseudo-photograph in his possession with a view to its being distributed or shown to a person other than the child.

Instances when defendant is not guilty of the offence

1B(1) In proceedings for an offence under s 1(1)(a) of making an indecent photograph or pseudo-photograph of a child, the defendant is not guilty of the offence if he proves that—

(a) it was necessary for him to make the photograph or pseudo-photograph for the purposes of the prevention, detection or investigation of crime, or for the purposes of criminal proceedings, in any part of the world,

(b) at the time of the offence charged he was a member of the Security Service or the Secret Intelligence Service, and it was necessary for him to make the photograph or pseudo-photograph for the exercise of any of the functions of that Service, or

(c) at the time of the offence charged he was a member of GCHQ, and it was necessary for him to make the photograph or pseudo-photograph for the exercise of any of the functions of GCHQ.

1B(2) In this section 'GCHQ' has the same meaning as in the Intelligence Services Act 1994.

Protection of Children Act 1978, ss 1(4), 1A, and 1B

6.6.1 Take, distribute, publish indecent photographs

Defence notes

- The defence given in s 1(4)(b) as to 'not seeing and did not know, nor had any cause to suspect, them to be indecent' would cover situations where an email attachment was opened innocently and not subsequently deleted owing to a genuine lack of IT skills (eg may still be in a 'deleted' directory, 'recycle bin', or other 'temporary' directory) or innocently downloading an image from the web, then immediately deleting the image without realising that it was also stored as a back-up copy in a temporary internet directory.
- In a Crown Court case the 'Trojan Horse' virus defence was successful. In short, expert evidence confirmed the likelihood of this virus being responsible for 14 depraved images saved on the defendant's personal computer. It was accepted that these could have been sent remotely, without the defendant's knowledge. Although this case is not binding on other courts, and each case will be determined according to its own particular facts, officers should be aware of the possibility of this defence being raised.

Related cases

R v Harrison [2007] EWCA Crim 2976, CA 'Pop-up' images are made by the computer user opening a web page and not the website designer.

R v Porter [2006] EWCA Crim 560, CA If a person cannot retrieve deleted images on a computer then they are no longer in possession, custody or control of those images.

R v Dooley [2005] EWCA Crim 3093, CA If downloaded material was accessible to all club members then it is downloaded with a view to its distribution or showing to others.

R v Smith and Jayson [2002] 1 Cr App R 13, CA Deliberately opening an indecent computer email attachment or downloading an indecent image from the internet, so it can be viewed on a screen, is making a photograph.

R v Bowden [2001] 1 WLR 1427, CA Downloading would come within s 1 'to make' as a file is created when the photograph is downloaded.

Practical considerations

- Problems arise when young people take and share indecent photos of themselves invariably on mobile phones known as 'sexting', and if prosecuted for the s 1 offence means that the young person would be placed on the sex offenders register.
- NPCC and CEOP considers that a safeguarding approach should apply to children and young people involved in 'sexting'. The Children Act 1989, s 1(1) states that with statutory intervention the welfare of the child is paramount; this is reinforced by the Children Act 2004, s 11, which places a duty on key persons and bodies to safeguard and promote the welfare of children.
- It is not an offence under this Act to possess photographs to show to yourself although this is an offence under s 160 of the Criminal Justice Act 1988 (see **6.6.2**).

- MOJ Circular 6/2010 provides guidelines about extending the 'marriage/other relationships' provisions to offences relating to indecent pseudo-photographs of persons under 18.
- Proceedings for this offence requires the consent of the DPP.
- Ascertain how the photographs or pseudo-photographs were made, discovered, and whether stored.
- Seize all computer equipment as evidence under s 20 of PACE (see **12.3.4**).
- The 1978 Act schedule permits forfeiture of indecent images of children and the devices that hold them without the involvement of a court, unless the owner or other person with an interest in the material gives notice of a legitimate claim to the property.
- There are some authoritative factors in deciding whether or not a defence may apply, depending on whether the person(s)—
  - ✦ acted reasonably in all the circumstances;
  - ✦ reported the photographs or pseudo-photographs as soon as was practicable and to the appropriate authority;
  - ✦ stored the photographs or pseudo-photographs in a secure and safe manner;
  - ✦ copied or distributed the photographs or pseudo-photographs unnecessarily.

 E&S **CHAR**

 Either way   None

 Summary: 6 months' imprisonment and/or a fine
Indictment: 10 years' imprisonment

6.6.2 Possession of indecent photograph(s) of person under 18

Section 160 of the Criminal Justice Act 1988 concerns the offence of simple possession of indecent photographs or pseudo-photographs of a person under 18.

Offences

Subject to **section 160A** it is an offence for a person to have any **indecent photograph** or **pseudo-photograph** of a **child** in his possession.

Criminal Justice Act 1988, s 160(1)

6.6.2 Possession of indecent photograph(s) of person under 18

Points to prove

✓ possessed
✓ indecent photo(s)/pseudo-photograph(s)
✓ of a child/children

Meanings

Section 160A (see '**Defences**' below).

Photographs (see **6.6.1**)

Indecent photograph (see **6.6.1**)

Pseudo-photograph (see **6.6.1**)

Child (see **6.6.1**)

Explanatory notes

Where there is evidence of intent to distribute or show then the offence under s 1 of the Protection of Children Act 1978 (see **6.6.1**) should be used.

Defences

160(2) Where a person is charged with an offence under subsection (1) above it shall be a defence for him to prove—
   (a) that he had a legitimate reason for having the photograph or pseudo-photograph in his possession; or
   (b) that he had not himself seen the photograph or pseudo-photograph and did not know, nor had any cause to suspect, it to be indecent; or
   (c) that the photograph or pseudo-photograph was sent to him without any prior request made by him or on his behalf and that he did not keep it for an unreasonable time.

160A(1) This section applies where, in proceedings for an offence under section 160 relating to an indecent photograph or pseudo-photograph of a child, the defendant proves that the photograph or pseudo-photograph was of the child aged 16 or over, and that at the time of the offence charged the child and he—
   (a) were married or civil partners of each other, or
   (b) lived together as partners in an enduring family relationship.

160A(2) This section also applies where, in proceedings for an offence under section 160 relating to an indecent photograph or pseudo-photograph of a child, the defendant proves that the photograph or pseudo-photograph was of the child aged 16 or over, and that at the time when he obtained it the child and he—
   (a) were married or civil partners of each other, or
   (b) lived together as partners in an enduring family relationship.

160A(3) This section applies whether the photograph or pseudo-photograph showed the child alone or with the defendant, but not if it showed any other person.

160A(4) If sufficient evidence is adduced to raise an issue as to whether the child consented to the photograph or pseudo-photograph being in the defendant's possession, or as to whether the defendant reasonably believed that the child so consented, the defendant is not guilty of the offence unless it is proved that the child did not so consent and that the defendant did not reasonably believe that the child so consented.

Criminal Justice Act 1988, ss 160 and 160A

Defence notes

The conditions for the defence are listed under s 160A(1)–(4). If any of these conditions are not satisfied, the prosecution need only prove the offence as set out in s 160. But if the three conditions are satisfied, the defendant is not guilty of the offence unless the prosecution proves that the child did not consent and that the defendant did not reasonably believe that the child consented.

Related cases

R v Porter [2006] EWCA Crim 560, CA The computer hard drives of P were found to contain deleted images which could only be retrieved using specialist software, which P did not have. If a person cannot access deleted images on a computer then he was no longer in custody, control or possession of those images. The jury must decide on this issue having regard to all the relevant circumstances and the defendant's knowledge at the time.

R v Matrix [1997] Crim LR 901, CA A shop assistant may possess indecent photographs as well as the shop owner.

Atkins v DPP and Goodland v DPP [2000] 2 All ER 425, QBD Atkins: images stored in a temporary directory unbeknown to the defendant did not amount to possession; knowledge was required.

Practical considerations

Ensure that the photographs or pseudo-photographs are seized.

Seize the computer or storage mechanism as evidence under s 20 of PACE (see **12.3.4**).

The schedule in the Protection of Children Act 1978 permits forfeiture of indecent images of children and the devices that hold them without the involvement of a court, unless the owner or some other person with an interest in the material gives notice of a legitimate claim to the property.

Check on the audit chain for the photograph and documents relating to them to ensure possession is the only suitable charge.

Consent of the DPP required.

6.6.3 Disclose indecent photographs

- MOJ Circular 6/2010 provides guidelines about extending the 'marriage/other relationships' provisions to offences relating to indecent pseudo-photographs of persons under 18.
- Section 62 of the Coroners and Justice Act 2009 gives the offence of possession of a prohibited **image** of a person under 18, being a non-photographic image which is pornographic and is grossly offensive, disgusting, or otherwise of an obscene character. MOJ Circular 6/2010 provides guidance on this matter. Any such image found in possession of a school pupil by a member of staff at the school can be given to a police constable (see **8.10.5**).
- Section 63 of the Criminal Justice and Immigration Act 2008 deals with the offence of possession of **extreme pornographic images**, being an image that portrays, in an explicit and realistic way, any of the following, being an act which involves—
  + threatening a person's life;
  + serious injury to a person's anus, breasts, or genitals;
  + sexual interference with a human corpse;
  + a person performing intercourse or oral sex with an animal (whether dead or alive),
  + rape of a person's vagina, anus or mouth by another with the other person's penis; or
  + rape of a person's vagina or anus by another with a part of the other person's body or anything else,

and a reasonable person looking at the image would think that any such person or animal was real.

Any such images found in possession of a school pupil by a member of staff at the school can be given to a police constable (see **8.10.5**).

 Either way   None

 Summary: 6 months' imprisonment and/or a fine
Indictment: 5 years' imprisonment and/or a fine

6.6.3 Disclose indecent photographs/films with intent to cause distress

This offence is dealt with by s 33 of the Criminal Justice and Courts Act 2015.

Offences

(1) It is an offence for a person to **disclose** a **private sexual photograph or film** if the disclosure is made—
   (a) without the **consent** of an individual who appears in the photograph or film, and
   (b) with the **intention** of causing that individual distress.
(2) But it is not an offence under this section for the purpose to disclose the photograph or film to the individual mentioned in subsection (1)(a) or (b).

Criminal Justice and Courts Act 2015, s 33

Points to prove

✓ disclose
✓ private sexual photograph(s)/film(s)
✓ without consent of person who appears in photograph(s)/film(s)
✓ intending to cause that person distress

Meanings

Disclose

By any means, s/he **gives** or **shows** it to a person or **makes it available** to a person.

Gives/shows/makes available

Something that is given, shown or made available to a person is disclosed whether or not it—
- is given, shown or made available for reward, and
- has previously been given, shown or made available to the person.

Private

If it shows something that is not of a kind ordinarily seen in public.

Sexual

A photograph or film is sexual if—
- it shows all or part of an individual's exposed genitals or pubic area,
- it shows something that a reasonable person would consider to be sexual because of its nature, or
- its content, taken as a whole, is such that a reasonable person would consider it to be sexual.

Photograph or film

Means a still or moving image in any form that—
- appears to consist of or include one or more **photographed or filmed images**, and
- in fact consists of or includes one or more **photographed or filmed images** (including images that have been altered in any way).

6.6.3 Disclose indecent photographs

Photographed or filmed image

Means a still or moving image that: was, or is part of, an image originally captured by photography or **filming**.

Filming

Means making a recording, on any medium, from which a moving image may be produced by any means.

Consent

Consent to a disclosure includes general consent covering the disclosure, as well as consent to the particular disclosure.

Intention (see **4.1.2**)

Explanatory notes

- This offence, otherwise known as 'revenge porn', will generally apply to a finished relationship where a partner publishes a photograph or film of a sexual nature to get back at their ex-partner.
- A person charged with this offence is not to be taken to have disclosed a photograph or film with the intention of causing distress merely because that was a natural and probable consequence of the disclosure.
- Further to the meaning of a 'photograph or film', this includes a negative version of an image, and data stored by any means which is capable of conversion into an image so described.

Defences

(3) It is a defence for a person charged with an offence under this section to prove that he or she reasonably believed that the **disclosure** was necessary for the purposes of preventing, detecting or investigating crime.

(4) It is a defence for a person charged with an offence under this section to show that—

    (a) the **disclosure** was made in the course of, or with a view to, the **publication of journalistic material**, and

    (b) he or she reasonably believed that, in the particular circumstances, the publication of the journalistic material was, or would be, in the public interest.

(5) It is a defence for a person charged with an offence under this section to show that—

    (a) he or she reasonably believed that the photograph or film had previously been disclosed for reward, whether by the individual mentioned in subsection (1)(a) and (b) or another person, and

    (b) he or she had no reason to believe that the previous disclosure for reward was made without the consent of the individual mentioned in subsection (1)(a) and (b).

Criminal Justice and Courts Act 2015, s 33

Defence notes

- A person is taken to have shown the matters mentioned in subsection (4) or (5) if—
  - ♦ sufficient evidence of the matters is adduced to raise an issue with respect to it, and
  - ♦ the contrary is not proved beyond reasonable doubt.
- For the purposes of subsections (1) to (5)—
  - ♦ **consent** to a **disclosure** includes general consent covering the disclosure, as well as consent to the particular disclosure, and
  - ♦ **publication of journalistic material** means **disclosure** to the public at large or to a section of the public.

Practical considerations

- This offence involves the sharing of private, sexual materials (either as photograph or film images) without the victim's consent and with the purpose/intention of causing them embarrassment or distress.
- The sexual material is not restricted to the genital/pubic area, but anything a reasonable person would consider to be sexual; for example, someone who is engaged in sexual behaviour or posing in a sexually provocative way.
- It concerns images shared electronically or in hardcopy, including uploading of images onto the internet, sharing by text/email or showing someone a physical or electronic image.
- This offence could apply to an image which appears to be originated from a film or photograph, even if the original has been altered in some way or where two or more images are combined.
- Photograph or film images that are completely computer generated, but made to look like an original photograph/film image, would not come under this offence because they are not a record of a real private event.
- Annex C in MOJ Circular 1/2015 provides further details and guidelines regarding this offence.

E&S   **CHAR**

  Either way   None

 Summary: 6 months' imprisonment and/or a fine
Indictment: 2 years' imprisonment and/or a fine

6.6.3 Disclose indecent photographs

Links to alternative subjects and offences

6.7 Indecent Exposure and Outraging Public Decency

6.7.1 Indecent exposure

This offence is covered by s 66 of the Sexual Offences Act 2003.

Offences

A person commits an offence if—
(a) he **intentionally** exposes his **genitals**, and
(b) he intends that someone will see them and be caused alarm or distress.

Sexual Offences Act 2003, s 66(1)

Points to prove

✓ intentionally
✓ exposed genitals
✓ intending
✓ someone would see them
✓ and be caused alarm/distress

Meanings

Intentionally (see **6.1.1**)

Genitals
Means male or female sexual organs.

Explanatory notes

- Offence would generally exclude naturists and streakers whose intention is not to cause alarm or distress.
- Exposure of the genitals must be intentional and not accidental.
- The offence applies to either sex. However, genitals do not include a female's breasts or the buttocks of either sex, so a female flashing her breasts or someone mooning (exposing their buttocks) will not be caught within this offence.
- Offence can be committed anywhere and is not restricted to public places.

Practical considerations

- CPS guidance in relation to naturists/nudity states that where there is no intention to cause alarm or distress and there is no sexual context then it would be appropriate to take no action. However, if people were caused harassment, alarm, and distress then consider the s 5 public order offence (see **7.8**), as 'disorderly' describes this behaviour as it does not conform to the normal standards of society which require people to be clothed in public.

- Proof of the relevant intent (both as to the genitals being seen and alarm or distress being caused thereby) will be critical to a successful prosecution.
- The precise location and the time of day could be important in showing a likely intention by the defendant.
- The accompanying words/conduct of the defendant will be relevant here, along with any preparatory or subsequent actions.
- Is this offence isolated or one of a series?

 Either way None

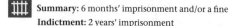 **Summary:** 6 months' imprisonment and/or a fine
Indictment: 2 years' imprisonment

6.7.2 **Outraging public decency**

This is an offence at common law.

Offences

It is an offence to commit an act of a **lewd, obscene**, and **disgusting** nature, which is capable of outraging public decency, in a **public place** where at least two members of the public who were actually present at the time could have witnessed it.

Common Law

Points to prove

✓ in a public place
✓ committed an act capable of being seen by two or more persons present
✓ of a lewd/obscene/disgusting nature thereby outraging public decency
✓ by behaving in indecent manner

E&S Entry and search powers   **CHAR** Offences where bad character can be introduced

Meanings

Lewd

Means lustful or indecent.

Obscene

Means morally repugnant or depraved.

Disgusting

Means repugnant or loathsome.

Public place

Means a place to which the public have access or a place which is visible to the public.

Explanatory notes

- Consider if statutory offences would be more suitable, such as the Sexual Offences Act 2003, or the Public Order Act 1986.
- Such conduct can also be an offence of public nuisance at common law (see **7.13.4**).

Related cases

R v F [2010] EWCA Crim 2243, CA The two-person rule applicable to outraging public decency had not been satisfied where, on the agreed evidence, F had stopped the act of masturbating in his car whenever other people came into the area, but continued once they had gone.

R v Hamilton [2007] EWCA Crim 2062, CA H admitted to 'upskirting' by positioning a camera at a certain angle to film up the skirts of women. Held that two elements must be satisfied. First, that the 'act' was so lewd, obscene, or disgusting in nature that public decency was outraged. Secondly the 'act' took place in public and was capable of being seen by two or more people actually present, even though no one actually sees the 'act' (filming).

Rose v DPP [2006] EWHC 852 (Admin), QBD A couple had oral sex in ATM area of bank captured on CCTV, foyer was well lit, and passers-by could see the act. More than one person must see the act for the offence of outraging public decency.

R v Walker [1996] 1 Cr App R 111, CA Defendant exposed himself and masturbated in front of two young girls in his living room. As public could not see into his living room then it was not a public place for this offence.

Smith v Hughes [1960] 1 WLR 830 The balcony of a private house visible to the public was a sufficiently public place for this offence.

R v Gibson [1990] 2 QB 619 The 'act' does not have to be a 'live' activity, nor does it have to be of a sexual nature. It may be the act of putting a disgusting object on public display, such as displaying a sculpted head with a real human foetus dangling from it in a public art gallery.

6.7.2 Outraging public decency

Practical considerations

- More than one person must be able to witness the lewd act.
- Conduct must grossly cross the boundaries of decency and be likely to seriously offend the reasonable person (rather than simply upsetting or even shocking).
- In sexual offences, this offence is reserved for offences where masturbation or sexual intercourse occurs (as with the current fad of 'dogging'). There is no requirement to prove that those persons who witnessed the act were actually disgusted or outraged by it. The test is an objective one based on whether a reasonable person would be disgusted.
- Where the circumstances are appropriate, positive evidence of disgust can be given by a police officer.

 E&S   **CHAR**

 Either way   None

 Summary: 6 months' imprisonment and/or a fine
Indictment: Imprisonment and/or a fine

Links to alternative subjects and offences

6.8 **Voyeurism**

This offence is created by s 67 of the Sexual Offences Act 2003.

Offences

(1) A person commits an offence if—
  (a) for the purpose of obtaining sexual gratification, he observes another person doing a **private act**, and
  (b) he knows that the other person does not **consent** to being observed for his **sexual gratification**.

(2) A person commits an offence if—
  (a) he operates equipment with the intention of enabling another person to observe, for the purpose of obtaining sexual gratification, a third person (B) doing a private act, and
  (b) he knows that B does not **consent** to his operating equipment with that intention.

(3) A person commits an offence if—
  (a) he records another person (B) doing a private act,
  (b) he does so with the intention that he or a third person will, for the purpose of obtaining sexual gratification, look at an image of B doing the act, and
  (c) he knows that B does not consent to his recording the act with that intention.

(4) A person commits an offence if he installs equipment, or constructs or adapts a **structure** or part of a structure, with the intention of enabling himself or another person to commit an offence under subsection (1).

Sexual Offences Act 2003, s 67

Points to prove

Observing (s 67(1))

✓ for purpose of obtaining sexual gratification
✓ observed another person
✓ doing a private act
✓ knowing that the person
✓ does not consent to being observed
✓ for defendant's sexual gratification

Operating equipment to observe (s 67(2))

✓ operated equipment
✓ with the intention of enabling another person
✓ for the purpose of obtaining sexual gratification
✓ to observe a third person doing a private act

✓ knowing that person does not consent
✓ to defendant operating equipment with that intention

Recording a private act (s 67(3))

✓ recorded another person doing a private act
✓ with intention that
✓ defendant or a third person
✓ would for the purpose of obtaining sexual gratification
✓ look at an image of that other person doing the act
✓ knowing that the other person does not consent
✓ to defendant recording the act with that intention

Install equipment/construct/adapt a structure (s 67(4))

✓ installed equipment **or**
✓ constructed/adapted a structure/part of a structure
✓ with intent
✓ to enable defendant or third person
✓ to commit an offence under s 67(1)

Meanings

Private act

A person is doing a private act if they are in a place where they could reasonably expect privacy and their genitals, breasts, or buttocks are exposed or covered only by underwear, they are using the toilet, or doing a sexual act that is not normally done in public.

Consent

Defendant must **know** that the person does not consent to being observed for **sexual gratification**. They may have consented to being observed for some other reason.

Sexual gratification

In s 67(1) the sexual gratification must be for the defendant, in the other subsections it could be for a third party's sexual gratification.

Structure

Includes a tent, vehicle, or vessel, or other temporary or movable structure.

Explanatory notes

- Previously it was not an offence to watch someone for sexual gratification. This will cater for such situations involving 'Peeping Toms'.
- For s 67(2)–(4), it is irrelevant whether or not any third parties knew that the person did not consent.
- Section 67(2) is aimed at those who install webcams or other recording equipment for their own gratification or for that of others. An image is defined as 'a moving or still image and includes an image

produced by any means and, where the context permits, a three-dimensional image'.

- Section 67(4) would cover a person who installed a two-way mirror or a spy-hole in a hotel room. The offender would commit the offence even if the peephole or mirror was discovered before it was ever used.

Related cases

R v Bassett [2008] EWCA Crim 1174, CA Whether a person had a reasonable expectation of privacy would depend on the facts in each case and would be closely related to the nature of the observation taking place. Some parts of the body are those which people would expect privacy for (eg female breasts as opposed to the bare male chest).

Practical considerations

- Any equipment used requires seizing.
- CCTV footage may be of use.
- Search for films made and evidence of equipment hire.
- Medium/equipment used for recording/storing image can be seized for examination and evidence.

 E&S   **CHAR**

 Either way   None

Summary: 6 months' imprisonment and/or a fine
Indictment: 2 years' imprisonment

Links to alternative subjects and offences

E&S Entry and search powers   **CHAR** Offences where bad character can be introduced

6.9 **Sexual Activity in a Public Lavatory**

This offence is covered by s 71 of the Sexual Offences Act 2003.

> **Offences**
>
> A person commits an offence if—
> (a) he is in a lavatory to which the public or a section of the public has or is permitted to have access, whether on payment or otherwise,
> (b) he **intentionally** engages in an activity, and,
> (c) the **activity is sexual**.
>
> Sexual Offences Act 2003, s 71(1)

> **Points to prove**
> ✓ being in a lavatory
> ✓ to which the public/a section of the public
> ✓ have/are permitted to have access
> ✓ whether on payment/otherwise
> ✓ intentionally
> ✓ engaged in a sexual activity

Meanings

Intentionally (see 6.1.1)

Sexual activity

An activity is sexual if a reasonable person would, in all the circumstances but regardless of any person's purpose, consider it to be sexual.

Explanatory notes

- Offence covers lavatories to which the public, or a section of the public, have access, whether or not payment is involved. This would include staff toilets in large/small premises where the public could have access.
- The sexual activity does not have to be specified, it would be enough to record details of what was seen or heard.
- There is no requirement to prove that anyone was alarmed or distressed by the activity.
- This offence replaced the former offence known as 'cottaging'.

Practical considerations

- Sexual in s 71 is different than used throughout the Act, in that it is what a reasonable person would consider sexual, regardless of the person's purpose.
- The offence is gender neutral, so the sexual activity could be committed by a male or female against a male or female.
- If possible obtain independent evidence.

 Summary   6 months

 6 months' imprisonment and/or a fine

Links to alternative subjects and offences

6.10 Trespass, Administer Substance and Commit an Offence—with Intent to Commit Sexual Offence

6.10.1 Trespass with intent to commit a sexual offence

This offence is covered by s 63 of the Sexual Offences Act 2003 which relates to being a trespasser on premises with intent to commit a relevant sexual offence on those premises.

Offences

A person commits an offence if—
(a) he is a **trespasser** on any **premises**,
(b) he **intends** to commit a **relevant sexual offence** on the premises, and
(c) he knows that, or is **reckless** as to whether, he is a trespasser.

Sexual Offences Act 2003, s 63

Points to prove

✓ knowingly/recklessly
✓ trespassed on premises
✓ with intent to
✓ commit a relevant sexual offence
✓ on those premises

Meanings

Trespasser (see **3.3.1**)

Premises

Include a structure or part of a structure. This would include premises, yard, garden, vehicle, tent, vessel, or other temporary or movable structure (eg caravans).

Intent (see **4.1.2**)

Relevant sexual offence

Means all the sexual offences included within Pt 1 of the Act (ss 1–79 inclusive), including an offence of aiding, abetting, counselling, or procuring such an offence.

Reckless

In these circumstances means that they were aware of the risk that they might be trespassing, but ignored that risk and continued with the course of action they were pursuing.

Explanatory notes

A person might enter premises without being a trespasser but become one later. For example, a person enters the public area of a shop but then goes into the stockroom. In such circumstances the person then becomes a trespasser because the implied permission granted by the shop owner to potential customers is to enter the shop and browse; they do not have the right to go into the stockroom.

Related cases

R v Cunningham [1957] 2 All ER 412 The test for 'subjective reckless-ness'. It is not sufficient to show that if the defendant had stopped to think, it would have been obvious to them that there was a risk. The pros-ecution had to prove that the defendant was aware of the existence of the risk but nonetheless had gone on and taken it.

Practical considerations

- The offence is not gender specific, so can be committed by a male intending to commit a sexual offence on a female or vice versa. Equally the victim and defendant could be of the same sex.
- The defendant does not have to commit the relevant sexual offence for this offence to be committed; it is sufficient to have the intent to commit a relevant sexual offence at any time while trespassing.
- Ensure evidence of trespass is obtained.
- Obtain CCTV evidence if available.
- Consider other offences (eg false imprisonment) if insufficient evidence available to prove this offence.

  Either way   None

Summary: 6 months' imprisonment and/or a fine
Indictment: 10 years' imprisonment

6.10.2 **Administer substance intending to commit sexual offence**

This offence is covered by s 61 of the Sexual Offences Act 2003.

Offences

A person commits an offence if he **intentionally administers** a substance to, or **causes** a substance **to be taken** by, another person (B)—
(a) knowing that B does not consent, and
(b) with the intention of stupefying or overpowering B, so as to enable any person to engage in a **sexual activity** that involves B.

Sexual Offences Act 2003, s 61(1)

Points to prove

- ✓ intentionally
- ✓ administered a substance to **or**
- ✓ caused a substance to be taken by
- ✓ another person
- ✓ knowing that s/he did not consent
- ✓ with intention of stupefying/overpowering
- ✓ so as to enable any person
- ✓ to engage in a sexual activity involving victim

Meanings

Intentionally (see 6.1.1)

Administer

In *R v Gillard* (1988) 87 Cr App Rep 189 held to include conduct that brings a substance into contact with the victim's body, directly or indirectly. For example, by injection or by holding a cloth soaked in the substance to the victim's face.

Causes to be taken

This would cover such conduct as slipping a date rape drug directly into a drink or deceiving the victim as to the nature of the substance (eg telling the victim it is a painkiller when in fact it is a sedative).

Sexual (see 6.2.1)

Explanatory notes

- This offence is intended to cover situations where so-called 'date rape' drugs (such as Rohypnol or GHB (gamma-hydroxybutrate)—see **6.1.1**) are given to a person in order to allow the defendant or someone else to engage in sexual activity with them. It also covers the spiking of a person's drink with alcohol when they believed they were drinking a soft drink.

• It does not matter how the substance is administered (eg by drink, injection). The offence has a very wide ambit in that it allows for one person to administer the substance or cause the substance to be taken and another to engage in the sexual activity (although no sexual activity need actually take place).

• The required consent refers to the taking/administering of the substance as opposed to the intended sexual activity. In s 76(2)(f) there is an evidential presumption that the victim does not consent to the sexual activity under s 1 (see **6.1.1**) where a substance which would stupefy or overpower has been administered.

Practical considerations

• The offence is committed whether or not there is any sexual activity as long as the substance was administered and there was the relevant intention.

If there was no sexual activity, it may be hard to prove this offence. However, consider offences under s 23 or s 24 of the Offences Against the Person Act 1861 as to administering a poison or other noxious thing (see **5.1.1**).

If there was sexual activity then consider other offences, not just this one.

Consider taking samples and medical examinations where appropriate.

Gather evidence by seizing any appropriate documentation.

Seize mobile phones where there is evidence of link between defendants and victims at the relevant time.

Consider CCTV footage.

 Either way   None

Summary: 6 months' imprisonment and/or a fine
Indictment: 10 years' imprisonment

6.10.3 **Commit an offence with intent to commit sexual offence**

This offence is covered by s 62 of the Sexual Offences Act 2003.

Offences

A person commits an offence under this section if he commits any offence with the **intention** of committing a **relevant sexual offence**.

Sexual Offences Act 2003, s 62(1)

Points to prove

✓ committed any offence
✓ with the intention of committing
✓ a relevant sexual offence

Meanings

Intention (see **6.1.1**)

Relevant sexual offence (see **6.10.1**)

Explanatory notes

- This offence involves the commission of **any** criminal offence, with the intention of the defendant carrying out a relevant sexual offence.
- *Any* offence will be covered (eg burglary, assault, kidnap, blackmail).
- This offence is intended to cater for such situations where the victim is kidnapped, assaulted, poisoned, or blackmailed in order that the defendant can thereby rape them or carry out some other sexual act that the victim would not otherwise consent to.
- The offence is committed whether or not the relevant sexual offence actually takes place, for example if the police find the kidnap victim prior to their being raped.

Practical considerations

- The first offence does not necessarily have to involve the intended victim of the ulterior sexual offence, for example where the defendant steals a car from one person in order to drive to the house of another person and rape them.
- If the sexual offence did take place then the defendant would be charged with that relevant sexual offence as well as this one.
- Obtain forensic evidence by identifying and preserving crime scene.
- Ensure there is no cross-contamination.
- Seize any evidence of defendant's knowledge of victim through previous text messages and emails, and if necessary seize phones and computers.

Either way

 None

 Summary: 6 months' imprisonment and/or a fine

Indictment: 10 years' imprisonment

Note: If kidnapping or false imprisonment—life imprisonment.

Links to alternative subjects and offences

6.11 Prostitution: Soliciting and Paying for Services of Prostitute (Subject Exploitation)

6.11.1 Persistently loitering/soliciting in street/public place for prostitution

This offence is contrary to s 1 of the Street Offences Act 1959.

Offences

It shall be an offence for a person aged 18 or over (whether male or female) **persistently** to **loiter** or **solicit** in a **street** or **public place** for the purpose of **prostitution**.

Street Offences Act 1959, s 1(1)

Points to prove

✓ person aged 18 or over
✓ persistently
✓ loitered or solicited
✓ in street/public place
✓ for purpose of prostitution

Meanings

Persistently

Conduct is persistent if it takes place on two or more occasions in any period of three months.

Prostitute

Means any person who offers sexual services for reward and includes a person acting as a 'clipper' (a person who offers a sexual service, but does not provide it themselves).

Loiter

Means to dawdle or linger idly about a place, proceeding with frequent pauses (see '**Related cases**' below).

Solicit

Means to accost and offer oneself.

Street

Includes any bridge, road, lane, footway, subway, square, court, alley or passage, whether a thoroughfare or not, which is for the time being open to the public; and the doorways and entrances of premises abutting on a street, and any ground adjoining and open to a street.

Public place

Any highway and any place to which at the material time the public has access, on payment or otherwise, as of right or by virtue of express or implied permission.

Explanatory notes

- Section 68(7) of the Serious Crime Act 2015 now makes this offence apply only to persons aged 18 and over, thus recognising that a person under 18 is a victim (child sexual exploitation). It is an offence to pay for the sexual services of a child under the Sexual Offences Act 2003, s 47 (see **6.5.1**). HOC 8/2015 provides guidance on this matter.
- Any reference to a person loitering or soliciting for the purposes of prostitution is a reference to a person loitering or soliciting for the purposes of offering services as a prostitute.
- Men or women aged 18 or over can be prostitutes.

Related cases

Williamson v Wright [1924] SC(J) 570 Implying the idea of lingering, slowing down on one particular occasion does not amount to loitering.

Horton v Mead [1913] All ER 954 An action unaccompanied by words and need not reach the mind of the person intended to be solicited.

Smith v Hughes [1960] 2 All ER 859 A prostitute soliciting from a balcony or window of a house adjoining a street is treated as being in the street for the purposes of this offence.

Behrendt v Burridge [1976] 3 All ER 285 A prostitute sitting on a stool in a window under a light is soliciting.

Weisz v Monahan [1962] 1 All ER 664 The placing of notices in windows offering the services of a prostitute has been held not to be soliciting.

Practical considerations

- A court can make an order requiring a person convicted of this offence to attend three meetings with a named supervisor or with such other person as the supervisor may direct. If such order is made, the court may not impose any other penalty for the offence.
- The purpose of this order is to assist the offender by addressing the cause, and finding ways to cease engaging in such conduct in the future.
- HOC 6/2010 provides guidance on the amendments to loitering for the purposes of prostitution.

6.11.2 Soliciting to obtain services of a prostitute

- Official guidelines for dealing with prostitution ensures that all the relevant agencies work in partnership to ensure that individuals do not become involved in prostitution in the first place or to create opportunities to leave prostitution.
- **Prostitution adverts:** s 46 of the Criminal Justice and Police Act 2001 makes it an offence to place on, or in the immediate vicinity of, a public telephone an advertisement relating to prostitution services, with the intention that the advertisement should come to the attention of any prospective customers.
- Consider seizing CCTV for evidential purposes.

 Summary   6 months

 Level 2 fine (after a previous conviction: level 3)

6.11.2 **Soliciting to obtain services of a prostitute**

This offence is covered by s 51A of the Sexual Offences Act 2003.

> **Offences**
>
> It is an offence for a person in a **street** or **public place** to **solicit** another (B) for the purpose of obtaining B's sexual services as a **prostitute**.
>
> Sexual Offences Act 2003, s 51A

Points to prove

✓ solicited
✓ another person (B)
✓ for purpose of obtaining
✓ B's sexual services as a prostitute

Meanings

Solicit (see **6.11.1**)

Prostitute

Means a person (B) who, on at least one occasion and whether or no
compelled to do so, offers or provides sexual services to another person in

---

return for payment or a promise of **payment** to B or a third person; and 'prostitution' is to be interpreted accordingly.

Payment

Means any financial advantage, including the discharge of an obligation to pay or the provision of goods or services (including sexual services) gratuitously or at a discount.

Street (see 6.11.1)

Public place (see 6.11.1)

Explanatory notes

The reference to a person in a street or public place includes a person in a vehicle in a street or public place.

Practical considerations

HOC 6/2010 provides guidance on this s 51A soliciting offence.

 Summary

 6 months

 Level 3 fine

6.11.3 Paying for sexual services of a prostitute subject to exploitation

Section 53A of the Sexual Offences Act 2003 makes it an offence for a person to pay or promise payment for sexual services of a prostitute who has been subject to exploitative conduct.

Offences

A person (A) commits an offence if—
(a) A makes or promises **payment** for the sexual services of a prostitute (B),
(b) a third person (C) has engaged in **exploitative conduct** of a kind likely to induce or encourage B to provide the sexual services for which A has made or promised payment, and
(c) C engaged in that conduct for or in the expectation of **gain** for C or another person (apart from A or B).

Sexual Offences Act 2003, s 53A(1)

6.11.3 Sexual services of a prostitute subject to exploitation

Points to prove

✓ (A) made or promised payment
✓ for sexual services of a prostitute (B)
✓ B subject to exploitative conduct of a kind likely to induce/encourage B to provide the sexual services
✓ third person (C) engaged in exploitative conduct
✓ for/expectation of gain for C or another person (apart from A or B)

Meanings

Payment (see 6.11.2)

Prostitute (see 6.11.2)

Exploitative conduct

Conduct which involves the use of: force; threats (whether or not relating to violence); any other form of coercion; or any form of deception.

Gain

Means any financial advantage, including the discharge of an obligation to pay or the provision of goods or services (including sexual services) gratuitously or at a discount; or the goodwill of any person which is or appears likely, in time, to bring financial advantage.

Explanatory notes

- It is irrelevant where in the world the sexual services are to be provided and whether those services are provided, and/or whether A is, or ought to be, aware that C has engaged in exploitative conduct.
- This is a strict liability offence which is committed if someone pays or promises payment for sexual services of a prostitute who has been subject to exploitative conduct.
- The person responsible for the exploitative conduct must have been acting for or in the expectation of gain for him/herself or another person, other than the payer or the prostitute.
- The use of threats is not restricted to threats of physical violence it could be 'psychological' threats, such as threatening to inform immigration/police, withdrawing accommodation or financial support, or to stop supplying drugs.

Practical considerations

- This offence is aimed at protecting vulnerable/exploited females by trying to reduce the demand for prostitution by placing the emphasis of the law onto the user, rather than the prostitute.
- HOC 6/2010 provides guidance on the Policing and Crime Act 2009 provisions relating to prostitution: paying for sexual services of a prostitute subject to exploitation; loitering for purposes of prostitution; soliciting; and closure notices/orders.

Section 53 of the Sexual Offences Act 2003 makes it an offence for a person to intentionally control another person's activities relating to prostitution, in any part of the world, where the defendant does so for, or in the expectation of, gain for him/herself or a third party.

Section 71 of the Coroners and Justice Act 2009 creates an offence of holding another person in slavery or servitude, or requiring a person to perform forced or compulsory labour (see Art 4, **1.1**). MOJ Circular 7/2010 provides guidance on this as it can be used where trafficking may not have taken place or cannot be proved.

Under ss 60A to 60C of the Sexual Offences Act 2003, a court can order forfeiture of a vehicle, ship, or aircraft used by a person convicted under s 59A regarding trafficking of people into/within/out of the UK or travel within or depart from another country for sexual exploitation.

Part 2A (ss 136A–136R) of the Sexual Offences Act 2003 deals with court orders and Closure Notices (issued by superintendent or above) for premises used for specified prostitution or pornography offences under s 136B or specified child sex offences under s 136BA.

 Summary   6 months

 Level 3 fine

.inks to alternative subjects and offences

7.1 **Penalty Notices for Disorder**

Penalty Notices for Disorder (PNDs) were established by s 1 of the Criminal Justice and Police Act 2001.

7.1.1 **Penalty notices for disorder offences**

A PND can no longer be issued to a person under 18. Offences for which a PND can be issued are as follows—

Upper tier

Penalty—£90 (18 and over)

Throwing fireworks in a thoroughfare

Explosives Act 1875, s 80 (see **8.8.6**).

Wasting police time or giving false report

Criminal Law Act 1967, s 5(2) (see **11.4.1**).

Disorderly behaviour while drunk in a public place

Criminal Justice Act 1967, s 91 (see **7.2.1**).

Theft (under £100 retail/commercial only) (see **7.1.2** 'Shoplifting and criminal damage' for guidance)

Theft Act 1968, ss 1–7 (see **3.1.1**).

Destroying or damaging property (under £300) (see **7.1.2** 'Shoplifting and criminal damage' for guidance)

Criminal Damage Act 1971, s 1(1) (see **4.4**).

Possess cannabis and its derivatives, being a Class B controlled drug (see **7.1.2** 'Cannabis possession' for guidance)

Misuse of Drugs Act 1971, s 5(2) (see **5.2.1**).

Behaviour likely to cause harassment, alarm, or distress

Public Order Act 1986, s 5 (see **7.7**).

Send offensive/false messages on public communications network

Communications Act 2003, s 127(2) (see **7.12.2**).

Breach Fireworks Regulations 2004 prohibitions: curfew/possess Category 4

Fireworks Act 2003, s 11 (see **8.8**).

Sale of alcohol anywhere to a person under 18

Licensing Act 2003, s 146(1) (see **9.1.2**).

Supply of alcohol by or on behalf of a club to a person aged under 18

Licensing Act 2003, s 146(3) (see **9.1.2**).

Buy or attempt to buy alcohol on behalf of a person under 18

Licensing Act 2003, s 149(3)(a) (see **9.1.4**).

Buy/attempt to buy alcohol for consumption by under 18 on relevant premises

Licensing Act 2003, s 149(4) (see **9.1.4**).

Sell or attempt to sell alcohol to a person who is drunk

Licensing Act 2003, s 141 (see **9.2.1**).

Deliver/allow delivery of alcohol to person under 18

Licensing Act 2003, s 151 (see **9.1.6**).

Knowingly give a false alarm of fire

Fire and Rescue Services Act 2004, s 49 (see **7.12.3**).

Lower tier

Penalty—£60 (18 and over)

Being drunk in a highway, public place, or licensed premises

Licensing Act 1872, s 12 (see **7.2.2**).

Trespassing on a railway

British Transport Commission Act 1949, s 55.

Throw stone, matter, or thing at a train/apparatus on railway

British Transport Commission Act 1949, s 56.

Possess khat or preparation/product containing khat, being a Class C controlled drug (see **7.1.2** 'Khat possession' for guidance)

Misuse of Drugs Act 1971, s 5(2) (see **5.3.1**).

Leave/deposit litter

Environmental Protection Act 1990, s 87(1) (see **7.16.2**)—issuing restrictions apply (see **7.16** and **11.1.1**).

Consume alcohol in a designated public place

Criminal Justice and Police Act 2001, s 12 (see **9.4**).

Allow person under 18 to consume alcohol on relevant licensed premises

Licensing Act 2003, s 150(2) (see **9.1.5**).

7.1.2 Police operational guidance for issuing PNDs

Police operational guidance on PNDs has been updated by the MOJ on 24 June 2014.

PND scheme

- The main aim of the PND scheme is to provide a quick and effective alternative disposal option for dealing with low-level, anti-social and nuisance offending. The PND is a type of fixed penalty notice for specified offences (see **7.1.1**). It does not prevent other means of disposal, and arrest should be considered where appropriate.
- A person has 21 days from issuing the PND to either pay the penalty or request a court hearing or (in some cases—see **'Educational course schemes'** below) attend an educational course. Failure to do this within that period will mean a fine of one and a half times the penalty being registered at court for fine enforcement.
- Payment of the penalty or completing the course is not an admission of guilt, and will discharge any liability to be convicted of the offence. A PND is not a criminal conviction, but for recordable offences a PNC entry may be made which may be disclosed under an enhanced DBS check.
- PNDs can be issued by constables (including special constables), and PCSOs, trading standards officers, or accredited persons for certain offences. No one can demand a PND; similarly, no one should be forced to accept a PND. Where a person is uncooperative consider an alternative disposal.
- PNDs are only available to a person aged 18 or over, providing they are suitable (see **'Persons'** below), and the evidential test in the Code for Crown Prosecutors is satisfied. The PND may be given either on the spot, at a police station or any other place at a later date.

Pre-conditions for issuing a PND

A PND may **only** be issued where—

- they have reason to believe a person has committed a PND offence and they have sufficient evidence to support a successful prosecution (interviews and questioning must be consistent with the practice and procedures established by PACE 1984, Code C);
- the offence is not too serious and is suitable for being dealt with by PND;
- the suspect is suitable, compliant, and able to understand what is going on;

- a second or subsequent offence, which is known, does not overlap with the PND offence (see **'Offences'** below);
- the offence(s) involve(s) no one below the age of 18;
- sufficient evidence as to the suspect's age, identity, and place of residence exists.

Offences

A PND will not be appropriate where—

- there has been any injury (or any realistic threat or risk of injury) to any person;
- there has been a substantial financial/material loss to the private property of an individual;
- a penalty offence is committed in association with another offence, including a penalty offence;
- the provisions of the Protection from Harassment Act 1997 might apply;
- the behaviour constitutes part of a pattern of intimidation;
- the offence involves domestic violence;
- it is a football-related offence;
- an offence has been committed jointly with a person under 18;
- any designated premises supervisor has committed an offence (but may be appropriate for bar staff when taking action against premises found or known to be serving alcohol to underage drinkers).

Shoplifting and criminal damage

- PND disposal for 'shoplifting' will only be appropriate where the value of goods does not exceed £100 and remains fit for sale, although in certain cases a PND can still be issued (eg consumed food/drink).
- Shop workers who steal from their employers will not be appropriate for a PND, as such behaviour is a breach of trust and needs to be dealt with by prosecution or other means.
- Label swapping can be dealt with by PND if they opt to deal with the offence as theft. A PND cannot be issued for the offence of making off without payment (see **3.7**).
- PND disposal may only be used for criminal damage up to a value of £300.
- The PND for shop theft can only be issued by a constable, whereas a PND for damage can be issued by constable and PCSO.
- PND disposal for shop theft/criminal damage will not be appropriate for substance misusers. The reason is that they may be better dealt with by court or conditional caution which can direct them to treatment.

Throwing fireworks

A PND may be appropriate where fireworks are thrown so as to cause annoyance and nuisance, but this will not be the case if it is part of a pattern of intimidation or there was intention to cause harm.

7.1.2 Police operational guidance for issuing PNDs

False reports

- When dealing with offences under the Communications Act 2003, s 127(2), Criminal Law Act 1967, s 5(2), and the Fire and Rescue Service Act 2004, s 49, a PND may be appropriate if the 999 service is misused or the person has made nuisance calls, but this will not be the case for serious misuse such as making a hoax bomb threat.
- A PND may be issued without DPP consent for wasting police time. Where the offender requests a hearing, a summons will be raised in the normal way and the CPS will give delegated DPP consent.

Possession of cannabis or khat

- A PND may be issued for possession of cannabis and its derivatives, or khat and any preparation or other product containing khat for personal use. A PND cannot be given for other drug offences or possession with intent to supply.
- ACPO guidance on cannabis possession and the national framework guidance on khat possession for personal use provides a three-stage escalation procedure where an offender will receive a cannabis or khat warning for a first offence, a PND for a second offence, and prosecution for a third or subsequent offence.

Associated with other offences

- If a PND offence is clearly associated with another offence, including a penalty offence, a PND should not be issued and the offences should be charged together (eg drunk and disorderly and damage, due to being drunk).
- A PND may be issued if a penalty offence does not 'overlap with' or is 'associated with' another offence—for example, a PND s 5 public order offence—then found in possession of stolen credit cards for which a charge is deemed appropriate.
- A PND may be issued in addition to dealing with a second or subsequent offence in another way, although ensure that a PND is not issued in addition to dealing with a very serious offence.
- Where a PND is issued for a penalty offence and it subsequently comes to light after the incident that a more serious or non-penalty offence was committed on the same occasion, officers may bring a charge for the subsequent offence. Payment of a penalty does not discharge liability to conviction for a more serious offence (*R v Gore* [2009] EWCA Crim 1424, CA). Ultimately, it will be for the CPS to determine, based on the facts of the case, whether a prosecution may be brought in respect of a subsequent or more serious offence.

Persons

A PND will not be appropriate where the suspect is—
- below the age of 18;
- unable to provide a satisfactory address for enforcement purposes;
- unable to understand the language, PND procedure, or what is being given to them;

- under the influence of drugs or alcohol, in which case consider arrest or issuing the PND at another time;
- a known Class A drug or substance misuser, then it would be better dealt with by court or a conditional caution which can direct a person to suitable substance treatment;
- uncooperative, non-compliant, or presents a considerable risk of not paying the penalty or completing the educational course;
- subject to: a custodial sentence, including home detention curfew, or a suspended sentence order; or a community penalty other than a fine, including an ASBO (under which the conduct may constitute a breach);
- known to have previous convictions for disorder offences, recently issued with a PND, or given a simple or conditional caution for such offences—but consideration could be given to issuing a PND, depending on the circumstances.

Jointly committed offences

Where a person under 18 and a person aged 18 or over jointly commit a penalty offence, then a PND will not be appropriate for the person aged 18 or over. In such cases other forms of disposal should be considered.

Identification

- Age, identity, and address checks must be rigorous. The PNC and PentiP must be thoroughly checked, including the disposals page. If doubt as to identity exists consider exercising s 24 PACE arrest powers.
- Fingerprints may be taken with consent under s 61 PACE and Part 4 of Code D; this will support identification for any PND issued for a penalty offence.

Victims

- Consider the seriousness of the offence and its effect on the victim. Consult with the victim about the potential issue of a PND and take their views into account before reaching a decision.
- Be mindful that PND disposal removes the possibility of a compensation order, although the victim can still seek redress through civil litigation. The victim should be made aware of this.

Educational course schemes

- The Criminal Justice and Police Act 2001 permits a chief officer of police to establish a PND educational course scheme in relation to one or more penalty offences, but this is not mandatory. It means a constable can give a person a PND with an education option (**PND-E**) where appropriate.

  A PND-E gives a person the opportunity to discharge their liability to be convicted of the penalty offence by paying for and completing an educational course that relates to the penalty offence (although a record of the PND-E will remain on PentiP and the PNC (if given for a recordable offence) as with a 'standard' PND). Alternatively, a person can opt to pay the penalty in full or request to be tried (as with a PND).

Links to alternative subjects and offences

7.2 **Drunkenness in Public Places**

Section 91 of the Criminal Justice Act 1967 and s 12 of the Licensing Act 1872 deal with offences to do with drunkenness in public places, namely those of being drunk and disorderly and of being drunk in a highway.

7.2.1 **Drunk and disorderly**

Offences

Any person who in any **public place** is guilty, while **drunk**, of **disorderly behaviour** shall be liable to a summary conviction.

Criminal Justice Act 1967, s 91(1)

Points to prove

✓ while in a public place
✓ whilst drunk
✓ guilty of disorderly behaviour

Meanings

Disorderly behaviour

Is defined by the *Oxford English Dictionary* as 'unruly or offensive behaviour'.

Public place

Includes any highway and other premises or place to which at the material time the public have or are permitted to have access, whether on payment or otherwise.

Drunk

Means the everyday meaning of 'drunk'. Defined by the *Collins* and *Oxford English Dictionaries* as: 'intoxicated with alcohol to the extent of losing control over normal physical and mental functions' and 'having drunk intoxicating liquor to an extent which affects steady self-control' *R v Tagg* [2001] EWCA Crim 1230, CA).

Explanatory notes

▶ It does not apply to a person who is disorderly as a result of **sniffing glue** or **using drugs**. The common meaning of 'drunk' does not cater for such conduct, as confirmed by *Neale v RMJE (a minor)* (1985) 80 Cr App R 20.

7.2.2 Drunk on a highway

- If the offender has taken liquor and drugs, the court must be satisfied that the loss of self-control was due to the liquor and not the drugs.
- Whether or not someone was in a state of drunkenness was a matter of fact for the court/jury to decide.
- A landing in a block of flats, to which access was gained by way of key, security code, tenant's intercom, or caretaker, has been held **not** to be a public place because only those admitted by or with the implied consent of the occupiers had access.

Related cases

Williams v DPP [1993] 3 All ER 365, QBD The landing in a block of flats, with access gained by a key code lock, was held **not** to have been a 'public place' because entry was restricted to residents, people admitted by residents, and trades people with knowledge of the code.

H v DPP [2005] EWHC 2459 (Admin), QBD Conduct must be disorderly whilst drunk to satisfy the offence. The offence is not committed if the defendant only becomes disorderly after the arrest.

Practical considerations

- This offence can be dealt with by PND (see **7.1.1**).
- Home Office guidance relates to issuing a PND for this offence (see **7.1.2**).
- Comply with CPS public order charging standards and guidance for drunk and disorderly.
- Consider applying for a criminal behaviour order (see **7.13.2**).

| PND | PCSO |

♿ Summary   ⏱ 6 months

┃ Level 3 fine

7.2.2 **Drunk on a highway**

Section 12 of the Licensing Act 1872 creates the offence of being 'drunk and incapable' in a highway, public place, or licensed premises, whilst in possession of a loaded firearm or being in charge of various conveyances or animals.

Offences

Every person found **drunk** in any **highway** or other **public place**, whether a building or not, or on any licensed premises, shall be liable to a penalty.

Every person who is drunk while in charge on any highway or other public place of any **carriage**, horse, **cattle**, or steam engine, or who is drunk when in possession of any loaded **firearms**, shall be liable to a penalty.

Licensing Act 1872, s 12

Points to prove

Drunk and incapable

✓ drunk and incapable
✓ highway/public place/licensed premises

Other drunk offences

✓ drunk
✓ whilst in charge of
✓ pedal cycle/carriage/horse/cattle/steam engine **or** when in possession of a loaded firearm
✓ on/in a highway/public place

Meanings

Drunk (see 7.2.1)

Highway/public place (see 7.2.1)

Incapable

Means 'incapable of looking after oneself and getting home safely'.

Carriage

Includes vehicles such as trailers and bicycles (whether being ridden or pushed).

Cattle

Includes sheep and pigs.

Firearm (see 8.1.1)

Explanatory notes

- A motor vehicle is a 'carriage'. However, it may be more appropriate to consider the offence of driving or being in charge while over the prescribed limit under s 4 of the Road Traffic Act 1988 (see **10.10**).
- Case law suggests that residents in licensed premises cannot be convicted of this offence outside the permitted hours when the premises are closed to the public. However, the duty of the licensee to prevent drunkenness on the premises is unaffected.

7.2.2 Drunk on a highway

- See also the related offences of drunk and disorderly in a public place (see **7.2.1**).
- Section 2 of the Licensing Act 1902 makes it an offence to be drunk in charge of a child who appears to be under the age of 7 years.

Practical considerations

- This offence can be dealt with by means of a PND (see **7.1.1**).
- If this offence involves a firearm consider s 19 of the Firearms Act 1968 which has a far greater penalty (see **8.5**).
- Officers should frequently assess the condition of drunks which can sometimes be life threatening (eg inhalation of vomit).
- Be aware that other medical conditions could give the impression that somebody is drunk (eg diabetic coma). It is best to convey the person to hospital if there are any doubts.
- Section 34 of the Criminal Justice Act 1972 provides a police constable with a power to take a drunken offender to a 'detoxification' or alcohol treatment centre. While a person is being so taken they shall be deemed to be in lawful custody.

 Summary   6 months

 Drunk and incapable
Level 1 fine

Drunk in charge of firearm/carriage/horse/steam engine
1 month's imprisonment or a level 1 fine

Links to alternative subjects and offences

7.3 **Breach of the Peace**

'Breach of the peace' is a common law concept which involves various powers in order to prevent a breach of the peace in both public and private places: these are arrest, intervene, or detain by force.

It is not a criminal offence, but a 'complaint', laid before the court with an application made for a person to be bound over to keep the peace.

Complaint

Breach of the peace

The power of a magistrates' court on the complaint of any person to adjudge any other person to enter into a recognizance, with or without sureties, to keep the peace or to be of good behaviour towards the complainant shall be exercised by order on complaint.

Magistrates' Courts Act 1980, s 115(1)

Points to prove

✓ behave in a manner
✓ whereby breach of the peace
✓ was occasioned/likely to be occasioned

Meaning of breach of the peace

A breach of the peace may occur where harm is done or is likely to be done to a person, or to their property in their presence, or they are in fear of being harmed through assault, affray, riot, or other disturbance (*R v Howell* [1982] QB 416, QBD).

Court powers

- Section 115 of the Magistrates' Courts Act 1980 provides magistrates' courts with the power to order a person to be 'bound over' to keep the peace and/or be of good behaviour towards a particular person.
- The power of a magistrates' court on the complaint of any person to adjudge any other person to enter into a recognizance, with or without sureties, to keep the peace or to be of good behaviour towards the complainant shall be exercised by order on complaint.
- If any person fails to comply with the order, the court may commit that person to custody for a period not exceeding 6 months or until they comply with the order.

7.3 Breach of the Peace

Explanatory notes

- The ECtHR in *Hashman and Harrup v UK* (2000) 29 EHRR 241, ECtHR found the notion of 'to be of good behaviour' was too vague and uncertain (see '**Related cases**' below). A later court 'practice direction' stated that any such order must specify the type of activity from which the offender must refrain.
- In the case of *Steel v UK* (1998) 28 EHRR 603, ECtHR it was held that the concept of breach of the peace had been clarified by the courts to the extent that it was sufficiently established that a breach of the peace was committed only when a person caused harm, or appeared likely to cause harm, to persons or property, or acted in a manner the natural consequence of which was to provoke others to violence. It was a procedure that came within the ambit of the ECHR and is lawful as long as the action taken is proportionate to the nature of the disturbance and also having regard to the values of freedom of expression and assembly.
- Notwithstanding that for some purposes proceedings under s 115 are treated as criminal proceedings, since the procedure is by way of complaint it is primarily a civil process. The jurisdiction of the justices does not depend on a summons being issued, nor does the absence of a complaint in the form prescribed invalidate the procedure.

Related cases

Wright v Commissioner of Police of the Metropolis [2013] EWHC 2739, QBD W was involved in a demonstration and moved into a protest pen. Held: The police 'kettling' tactics in this case had been minimal, necessary and proportionate. W had still been free to demonstrate, albeit not quite where he had wished to.

R (on the application of McClure and Moos) v Commissioner of Police of the Metropolis [2012] EWCA Civ 12, CA (see **2.6.1**).

Austin v UK [2012] Crim LR 544, ECtHR (see **2.6.1**).

Hashman and Harrup v UK (2000) 29 EHRR 241, ECtHR The defendants had not acted violently or threatened violence, but had behaved *contra bonos mores* (behaviour seen as 'wrong rather than right in the judgement of the majority of contemporary fellow citizens'). The ECtHR stated that the expression 'to be of good behaviour' was imprecise and did not give sufficiently clear guidance for their future behaviour. Held: That Art 10 (freedom of expression) had been violated, binding over for *contra bonos mores* behaviour was incompatible with the ECHR and rights such as freedom of expression or assembly.

R (on the application of Hawkes) v DPP [2005] EWHC 3046 (Admin) QBD Verbal abuse not enough to commit breach of the peace.

R (on the application of Laporte) v CC of Gloucestershire [2006] UKHL 55, HL Three coaches stopped and searched under a s 60 authority (see **8.11.3**) on intelligence that occupants would cause disorder at a RAF base were returned back to London. Although the police actions were based on a reasonable and honestly held belief in preventing an apprehended breach of the peace, they had acted unlawfully and disproportionately because a breach of the peace was not 'imminent' at the time the coaches were stopped; thus interfering with the protesters' rights under Arts 10 and 11 (see **1.1**).

McGrogan v CC of Cleveland Police [2002] EWCA Civ 86, CA If a person is detained for an actual or threatened breach of the peace, then continued detention is limited to circumstances where there is a real, rather than a fanciful, fear, based on all the circumstances, that if released the detained person would commit/renew a breach of the peace within a relatively short time. It cannot be justified on the ground that sooner or later the prisoner, if released, is likely to breach the peace. The officer must have an honest belief, based on objectively reasonable grounds, that further detention was necessary to prevent such a breach of the peace. Ensure compliance with PACE Codes (see **12.2.1**).

Practical considerations

- A breach of the peace is not an offence, so bail cannot be given.
- Breach of the peace can occur on private premises. If the police have genuine grounds to apprehend such a breach, they have a power of entry to deal with or prevent a breach of the peace (see s 17(6) of PACE, **12.3.2**). This right of entry is not absolute, but must be weighed against the degree of disturbance that is threatened.
- A police officer must not remain on private premises once a breach has finished (assuming it is not likely to re-occur), but as long as the officer is lawfully on the premises in the first instance, they are entitled to be given the opportunity to withdraw.
- Officers attending private premises with officials such as bailiffs may have to enter them to prevent a breach of the peace while a Court Order is being enforced.
- An individual arrested to prevent a breach of the peace does not have to be taken before a court. There is no power to continue the person's detention beyond the time where a recurrence or renewal of the breach of the peace is likely. If there is such danger they should be detained for court (see *McGrogan v CC of Cleveland Police* [2002] EWCA Civ 86, CA above).
- There is a continuing role for the common law power to detain short of arrest in order to prevent a breach of the peace, although in order for it to apply an officer would need to have it in mind at the relevant time (*Walker v Commissioner of Police of the Metropolis* [2014] EWCA Crim 897, CA—see **2.2.2**).
- Release may occur at any stage: at the scene, after they have been taken from the scene, or at the police station.

  Summary   6 months

  Breach of the order may result in up to 6 months' imprisonment

Links to alternative subjects and offences

7.4 **Riot and Violent Disorder**

The Public Order Act 1986 provides the statutory offences of riot and violent disorder.

7.4.1 **Riot**

Offences

Where twelve or more persons who are **present together** use or threaten unlawful **violence** for a **common purpose** and the conduct of them (taken together) is such as would cause a **person of reasonable firmness** present at the scene to fear for his personal safety, each of the persons using unlawful violence for the common purpose is guilty of riot.

Public Order Act 1986, s 1(1)

Points to prove

✓ 12 or more persons present together used/threatened unlawful violence for common purpose
✓ and conduct would cause fear for personal safety
✓ to a person of reasonable firmness

Meanings

Present together

Means that all the people concerned were actually present at the scene of the incident aiming for a common purpose.

Common purpose (s 1(3))

The common purpose may be inferred from conduct.

Violence

Includes violent conduct towards property as well as violent conduct towards persons. It is not restricted to conduct causing, or intended to cause, injury or damage, but includes any other violent conduct (eg throwing at or towards a person a missile of a kind capable of causing injury, which does not hit or falls short).

Person of reasonable firmness

This test is an objective one by which the court can judge the seriousness of the disturbance using a fixed standard—namely whether or not a person of reasonable firmness would be put in fear by the conduct.

7.4.1 Riot

Explanatory notes

- It is immaterial whether or not the 12 or more use or threaten unlawful violence simultaneously.
- No **person of reasonable firmness** need actually be, or be likely to be, present at the scene.
- A court will not consider this hypothetical person (of reasonable firmness) to be someone who is the target for the people who are involved in the disturbance, but someone who is a bystander to the incident (*R v Sanchez* [1996] Crim LR 572, CA).
- Riot may be committed in private as well as in public places.
- The common purpose can be either lawful or unlawful, and must be proved either by admission or as above by inference from conduct.

Defences

Intention

(1) A person is guilty of riot only if he intends to use violence or is aware that his conduct may be violent.

(2) A person is guilty of violent disorder or affray only if he intends to use or threaten violence or is aware that his conduct may be violent or threaten violence.

(7) Subsections (1) and (2) do not affect the determination for the purposes of riot or violent disorder of the number of persons who use or threaten violence.

Effect of intoxication

(5) For the purposes of this section a person whose awareness is impaired by **intoxication** shall be taken to be aware of that of which he would be aware if not intoxicated, unless he shows either that his intoxication was not self-induced or that it was caused solely by the taking or administration of a substance in the course of medical treatment.

(6) In subsection (5) **'intoxication'** means any intoxication, whether caused by drink, drugs or other means, or by a combination of means.

Public Order Act 1986, s 6

Defence notes

- Intent or awareness must be proved. Even if intent can only be proved against two people but they were part of a group of, say, 13 who can be shown to have used unlawful violence, the two can still be convicted of riot.
- The intoxication defence applies to the following offences—
  - s 1 riot—unlawful violence;
  - s 2 violent disorder—unlawful violence;
  - s 3 affray—unlawful violence;
  - s 4 threatening words or behaviour; and
  - s 5 harassment, alarm, or distress.

Practical considerations

- Refer to **8.11** for details of powers to stop and search when it is anticipated that serious violence may take place, and to remove masks.
- Consent of the DPP is required.
- Consider the CPS public order charging standards.
- A person who was feeling threatened does not actually have to be a 'person of reasonable firmness', but their evidence may support other evidence that will satisfy the court that such a person would have been in fear of their personal safety had they been present. This evidence could be provided by—
  - ✦ witnesses including police officers and bystanders (who may or may not be of reasonable firmness);
  - ✦ the types of injuries sustained;
  - ✦ damage to property;
  - ✦ security cameras;
  - ✦ news photographs or film footage.

 Indictable only None

 10 years' imprisonment

7.4.2 **Violent disorder**

Offences

Where three or more persons who are **present together** use or threaten unlawful **violence** and the conduct of them (taken together) is such as would cause a **person of reasonable firmness** present at the scene to fear for his personal safety, each of the persons using or threatening unlawful violence is guilty of violent disorder.

Public Order Act 1986, s 2(1)

Points to prove

- ✓ used/threatened unlawful violence
- ✓ 3 persons present together
- ✓ use/threaten unlawful violence and their conduct (taken together)
- ✓ would cause a person of reasonable firmness present at the scene
- ✓ to fear for their personal safety

7.4.2 Violent disorder

Meanings

Present together

Means no more than being in the same place at the same time.

Person of reasonable firmness (see **7.4.1**)

Violence (see **7.4.1**)

Explanatory notes

- It is immaterial whether or not the three or more use or threaten unlawful violence simultaneously.
- No **person of reasonable firmness** need actually be, or likely to be, present at the scene.
- Violent disorder may be committed in private as well as in public places.
- If three or more people had been present together and using violence, even if intent can only be proved against one person, then that person can be convicted—it is not necessary that 'three or more persons' be charged with the offence. Following *R v Mahroof* [1988] Crim LR 72, CA (see below) it is good practice to specify 'others' in the charge, even if their identity is not known and they were not arrested.

Defences

Intention (see s 6(2) and s 6(7) **7.4.1**)

Effect of intoxication (see **7.4.1**)

Defence notes

Intent

To use or threaten violence must, therefore, be proved for each individual. This means that even if only one person has the intent they can still be charged if it can be proved that at least two others were using or threatening violence and they were present together. Words alone may suffice for the threats.

Related cases

R v NW [2010] EWCA Crim 404, CA In s 2 the term 'present together' is intended to mean no more than being in the same place at the same time. Also there is no requirement for a common purpose among those using or threatening violence.

R v Mahroof [1988] Crim LR 72, CA There must be three people involved in the violence or threatened violence. In this case two of the three charged were acquitted and there had been others who had not been mentioned in the charge. If they had, M could have been convicted, but in the absence of three people M's appeal was allowed.

Practical considerations

- Refer to **8.11** for details of powers to stop and search when it is anticipated that serious violence may take place, and powers to remove masks.
- Consider CPS public order charging standards for violent disorder.
- Sections 34 to 49 of the Policing and Crime Act 2009 deal with injunctions to prevent gang-related violence. The Serious Crime Act 2015 substituted s 34 so it now includes drug-dealing activity as well. HOC 8/2015 provides guidance on this matter.

 Either way

 None

 Summary: 6 months' imprisonment and/or a fine
Indictment: 5 years' imprisonment and/or a fine

Links to alternative subjects and offences

7.5 **Affray**

The purpose of the offence of affray is to prevent incidents of public disorder and the fear of it. For the offence of affray to be committed, the threat of violence needs to be capable of affecting others.

Offences

A person is guilty of affray if he uses or **threatens** unlawful **violence** towards another and his **conduct** is such as would cause a person of **reasonable firmness** present at the scene to fear for his personal safety.

Public Order Act 1986, s 3(1)

Points to prove

✓ used/threatened unlawful violence
✓ towards another
✓ and your conduct was such as would cause
✓ a person of reasonable firmness to fear for personal safety

Meanings

Threatens

A threat cannot be made by the use of words alone.

Violence

See **7.4**, except affray **does not include** violent conduct towards property.

Conduct

Where two or more persons use or threaten the unlawful violence, it is the conduct of them taken together that must be considered for the purpose of the offence.

Reasonable firmness

No person of reasonable firmness need actually be, or be likely to be, present at the scene. The concept meets the same criteria as riot (see **7.4.1**).

Explanatory notes

- Affray may be committed in private as well as in public places.
- Notionally there are at least three parties involved in an affray—
  - the individual making threats;
  - the person subject of the threats;

+ the bystander of reasonable firmness who does not need to be physically present as long as evidence is available to prove that such a person would be affected.

Defences

Intent (see s 6(2) **7.4.1**)

Effects of intoxication (see '**Defences**' 7.4.1)

Defence notes (see 'Defence notes' 7.4.2)

Related cases

Leeson v DPP [2010] EWHC 994 (Admin), QBD A violent domestic in private, with no realistic prospect of anyone arriving who could be 'in fear of violence', was held not to be an affray. The purpose of this offence was to protect people who were near a violent altercation, from fear of unlawful violence being used on them.

R v Plavecz [2002] Crim LR 837, CA A doorman pushed a customer out of a nightclub doorway who then fell over. Defendant was charged with assault and affray, but the court stated that where the incident was basically '**one-on-one**' it was inappropriate to use the public order offence of affray.

I v DPP, M v DPP, H v DPP [2001] UKHL 10, HL About 40 young people were 'hanging around' with some carrying petrol bombs. None of them lit or waved a petrol bomb about in a threatening way and there was no actual disturbance. On police arrival the gang scattered and the three defendants threw away their petrol bombs as they ran off. Held: The mere possession of a weapon, without the threatening situation, would not be enough to constitute a threat of unlawful violence. Affray requires that the offender must be 'using/threatening unlawful violence towards another'; what amounted to such a threat was a question of fact in each case, but in this instance, there were no threats made and no violence was used.

Practical considerations

- Unlike riot and violent disorder, affray can be committed by one person acting alone. However, where two or more people are involved in the violence or threatened violence, it is the conduct of them taken together that will determine whether the offence is made out.
- Refer to **8.11.3** for details of powers to stop and search when it is anticipated that serious violence may take place and to remove masks.
- Consider CPS public order charging standards for affray.
- See **12.1.1** for powers to stop and search for knives and offensive weapons.

7.5 Affray

- The person feeling threatened does not have to be a 'person of reasonable firmness', but evidence may support other evidence that will satisfy the court that a 'person of reasonable firmness' would have been in fear of their personal safety (see **7.4.1** for 'other evidence' examples).

 Either way   None

 Summary: 6 months' imprisonment and/or a fine
Indictment: 3 years' imprisonment

Links to alternative subjects and offences

7.6 **Fear or Provocation of Violence**

The Public Order Act 1986 deals with offences and powers relating to public order. Section 4 creates the offence of causing fear or provocation of violence, often known as 'threatening behaviour'.

Offences

A person is guilty of an offence if he—

(a) uses towards another person **threatening, abusive or insulting** words or behaviour, or

(b) **distributes or displays** to another person any writing, sign or other visible representation which is threatening, abusive or insulting,

with **intent** to cause that person to believe that immediate unlawful violence will be used against him or another by any person, or to provoke the immediate use of unlawful violence by that person or another, or whereby that person is likely to believe that such violence will be used or it is likely that such violence will be provoked.

Public Order Act 1986, s 4(1)

Points to prove

s 4(1)(a) offence

✓ use towards another person
✓ threatening/abusive/insulting words or behaviour
✓ with intent to **either**
✓ cause that person to believe
✓ that immediate unlawful violence
✓ would be used against them or another
✓ by any person **or**
✓ provoke the immediate use of unlawful violence
✓ by that person/another **or**
✓ that person was likely to believe
✓ that such violence would be used **or**
✓ likely that such violence would be provoked

s 4(1)(b) offence

✓ distribute/display
✓ to another
✓ a writing/sign/visible representation
✓ which was threatening/abusive/insulting
✓ with intent to **either**
✓ (*continue from this point in above offence—to end*)

7.6 Fear or Provocation of Violence

Meanings

Threatening

Includes verbal and physical threats, and also violent conduct.

Abusive

Means using degrading or reviling language.

Insulting

Has been held to mean scorning, especially if insolent or contemptuous.

Intent (see 'Defences' 'Intent' below)

Distribute

Means spread or disperse.

Display

Means a visual presentation.

Explanatory notes

- An offence under this section may be committed in a public or a private place, except that no offence is committed where the words or behaviour are used, or the writing, sign, or other visible representation is distributed or displayed, by a person inside a **dwelling** and the other person is also inside that or another dwelling (s 4(2)).
- **Dwelling**—means any **structure** or part of a structure occupied as a person's home or as other living accommodation (whether the occupation is separate or shared with others) but does not include any part not so occupied, and for this purpose '**structure**' includes a tent, caravan, vehicle, vessel, or other temporary or movable structure.
- No offence will be committed if the display is inside a dwelling, if it is displayed only to people also inside, although if it is displayed from inside to people outside the dwelling, then an offence under s 4 may be committed.
- Whether behaviour is insulting or not is a question of fact for the justices/court to decide (*Brutus v Cozens* [1972] 2 All ER 1297, HL).

Defences

Intent

A person is guilty of an offence under s 4 only if he **intends** [see **4.1.2**] his words or behaviour, or the writing, sign or other visible representation, to be threatening, abusive or insulting, or is aware that it may be threatening, abusive or insulting.

Public Order Act 1986, s 6(3)

Intoxication (see 'Defences' '*Effect of intoxication*' **7.4.1**).

Related cases

Hughes v DPP [2012] EWHC 606 (Admin), QBD A blow delivered in such a way as to avoid giving the victim any advanced warning or perception that immediate unlawful violence was going to be used against them, could not constitute an offence under section 4(1).

DPP v Ramos [2000] Crim LR 768, QBD If the victim believes that the threatened violence will occur at any moment, this will be sufficient for the 'immediacy' requirement.

Swanston v DPP (1996) 161 JP 203, QBD A witness/officer present when the offence took place can give evidence to prove the threatening behaviour and intent, even if the victim does not give evidence.

Rukwira and Johnson v DPP [1993] Crim LR 882, QBD Dwelling does not include communal landings outside **self-contained** flats.

Atkin v DPP [1989] Crim LR 581, QBD The person threatened should be present. The threatening words must be addressed directly to another person who is present and either within earshot or aimed at someone thought to be in earshot.

Practical considerations

- Section 17(1)(c)(iii) of PACE gives a constable a specific power to enter and search premises for the purpose of arresting a person for an offence under s 4 (see **12.3.2**).
- If this offence is **racially or religiously aggravated** the more serious offence under s 31(1)(a) of the Crime and Disorder Act 1998 should be considered (see **7.10.4**). It is not open to the court to convict on both the simple and aggravated offences if they arise out of the same facts *(R (on the application of Dyer) v Watford MC* [2013] All ER (D) 88 (Jan)).
- Consider religious or racial hatred offences (see **7.9**).
- It is not duplicitous if the three alternatives 'threatening, abusive or insulting', are charged, though all three need not be present.
- Consider CPS public order charging standards.

RRA   **E&S**

 Summary   6 months

 6 months' imprisonment and/or a fine

RRA Racially or religiously aggravated offence   **E&S** Entry and search powers

Links to alternative subjects and offences

7.7 **Intentional Harassment, Alarm, or Distress**

Section 4A of the Public Order Act 1986 creates the offences of intentionally causing a person harassment, alarm, or distress by using threatening, abusive, insulting words or behaviour, or disorderly behaviour; or displaying any writing, sign, or other representation that is threatening, abusive, or insulting.

Offences

A person is guilty of an offence if, with **intent** to cause a person **harassment, alarm or distress**, he—

(a) uses **threatening**, **abusive** or **insulting** words or behaviour, or **disorderly behaviour**, or

(b) displays any writing, sign or other visible representation which is threatening, abusive or insulting,

thereby causing that or another person harassment, alarm or distress.

Public Order Act 1986, s 4A(1)

Points to prove

s 4A(1)(a) offence

✓ used threatening/abusive/insulting words/behaviour **or** used disorderly behaviour

✓ towards another person

✓ with intent to cause harassment/alarm/distress

✓ and caused that/another person

✓ harassment/alarm/distress

s 4A(1)(b) offence

✓ displayed threatening/abusive/insulting writing/sign/other visible representation

✓ with intent to cause a person harassment/alarm/distress

✓ and caused that/another person

✓ harassment/alarm/distress

Meanings

Harassment

Means to subject someone to constant and repeated physical and/or verbal persecution.

Alarm

Means a frightened anticipation of danger.

Distress

Means to cause trouble, pain, anguish, or hardship.

Intent (see **4.1.2**)

Threatening (see **7.6**)

Abusive (see **7.6**)

Insulting (see **7.6**)

Disorderly behaviour

The *Oxford English Dictionary* states 'unruly, unrestrained, turbulent or riotous behaviour'.

Explanatory notes

- This offence is similar to the s 5 offence (except 'insulting'—see **7.8**), but this offence requires proof of **intent** to cause alarm, harassment, or distress.
- An offence under this section may be committed in a public or private place, but no offence is committed if it takes place inside a dwelling and the affected person is also inside that or another dwelling.
- Although this offence can be committed on private premises there is no specific power of entry.

Defences

It is a defence for the accused to prove—
(a) that he was inside a dwelling and had no reason to believe that the words or behaviour used, or the writing, sign or other visible representation displayed, would be heard or seen by a person outside that or any other dwelling, or
(b) that his conduct was reasonable.

Public Order Act 1986, s 4A(3)

Related cases

S v CPS [2008] EWHC 438 (Admin), QBD When posting offensive material on the internet, S had the required intent and had taken the risk that the intended harm would be caused to C. The fact that C had not seen the material until being shown it by the police at a later date did not break the chain of causation for the purposes of this offence.

R (on the application of R) v DPP [2006] EWHC 1375 (Admin), QBD A 12-year-old boy gestured and shouted obscenities at the police and was arrested for a s 4A offence. Although maybe intending to insult and annoy there was no intention to cause the officer alarm or distress. For a police officer to be distressed evidence of real emotional disturbance or upset is required, showing more than is normally experienced during their course of duty.

Dehal v CPS [2005] EWHC 2154 (Admin), QBD D placed a poster on a noticeboard in a Sikh Temple which contained abusive and insulting comments regarding the teachings being an incorrect translation of the Holy Book. A defence under s 4A(3)(b) was submitted that this amounted to 'reasonable conduct'. Held: This prosecution breached Art 10 (freedom of expression) unless it was necessary to prevent public disorder. It is imperative that there is no restriction placed on a legitimate protest.

Lodge v DPP The Times, 26 October 1988, QBD It is not necessary that the person alarmed was concerned about physical danger to them, it could be alarm about an unconnected third party.

Practical considerations

- There must be evidence of intent to cause harassment, alarm, or distress and one of those forms of abuse must actually be caused to someone (not necessarily the person who was its original target).
- Consider s 5 (see **7.8**) where there is no evidence of intent.
- Where the extent of the behaviour results in the fear or realisation of violence consider s 4(1) (see **7.6**) or assault charges (see **2.1**, **2.2**, or **2.3**).
- If there is repeated harassment consider s 1 of the Protection from Harassment Act 1997 (see **7.11.1**).
- If a power of entry is required consider s 17 of PACE (see **12.3.2**), ongoing breach of the peace (see **7.3**), or s 4 (see **7.6**).
- Consider the behaviour in the context of the circumstances—behaviour that causes distress to an elderly woman may not be distressing to a young man.
- If other people, besides the police officer and the defendant, are present include that fact in your evidence.
- If this offence is racially and/or religiously aggravated consider the more serious offence under s 31 of the Crime and Disorder Act 1998 (see **7.10.4**) or ss 17 to 23 of the Public Order Act 1986 which relate to racial hatred offences (see **7.9**).

 RRA   **SSS**

 Summary   6 months

▦ Summary: 6 months' imprisonment and/or a fine

Links to alternative subjects and offences

7.7 Intentional Harassment, Alarm, or Distress

7.8 **Threatening/Abusive Words/ Behaviour**

Section 5 of the Public Order Act 1986 creates an offence of being threatening or abusive in a way which is likely to cause harassment, alarm, or distress.

Offences

A person is guilty of an offence if he—
(a) uses **threatening** or **abusive** words or behaviour, or **disorderly behaviour**, or
(b) displays any writing sign or other visible representation which is threatening or abusive,

within the hearing or sight of a person likely to be caused **harassment, alarm** or **distress** thereby.

Public Order Act 1986, s 5(1)

Points to prove

✓ used threatening/abusive words/behaviour or disorderly behaviour **or**
✓ displayed writing/sign/visible representation being
✓ threatening/abusive
✓ within hearing/sight of a person likely to be caused
✓ harassment/alarm/distress
✓ with intention/awareness that conduct/actions
✓ would have that effect

Meanings

Threatening or abusive (see 7.6)

Harassment, alarm, and distress (see 7.7)

Disorderly behaviour (see 7.7)

Explanatory notes

- The Crime and Courts Act 2013, s 57 removed the word 'insulting' from s 5 and s 6(4).
- What may distress an old woman of 75 years may not distress a young man of 20 years. The conduct has to be **likely to cause** distress. However, you can fear for the safety of someone else (particularly if you are a police officer), and it does not necessarily have to be for yourself (see *Lodge v DPP* at **7.7**).

- An offence under this section may be committed in a public or a private place except that no offence is committed when the words or behaviour are used, or the writing, sign, or other visible representation is displayed, by a person inside a dwelling and the other person is also inside that or another dwelling.

Defences

Specific

5(3) It is a defence for the accused to prove—

(a) that he had no reason to believe that there was any person within hearing or sight who was likely to be caused harassment, alarm or distress; or

(b) that he was inside a dwelling and had no reason to believe that the words or behaviour used, or the writing, sign or other visible representation displayed, would be heard or seen by a person outside that or any other dwelling; or

(c) that his conduct was reasonable.

Intent

6(4) A person is guilty of an offence under section 5 only if he intends his words or behaviour, or the writing, sign, or other visible representation, to be threatening, or abusive, or is aware that it may be threatening, or abusive, or (as the case may be) he intends his behaviour to be or is aware that it may be disorderly.

Public Order Act 1986, ss 5(3) and 6(4)

Intoxication (see **'Defences'** *'Effect of intoxication'* **7.4.1**)

Defence notes

Article 6 (right to a fair trial—see **1.1**) does not prohibit rules which transfer the burden of proof to the accused, provided it is only an 'evidential burden' where the defendant only needs to give believable evidence which justifies the defence and does not need to reach any specific standard of proof. Proving the guilt of the defendant still remains with the prosecution (eg s 28 of the Misuse of Drugs Act 1971—see **5.1.1**).

Intoxication (see 'Defence notes' **7.4.1**)

Related cases

Gough v DPP [2013] EWHC 3267 (Admin), QBD A conviction for walking naked through a town centre was proportionate, albeit G's right to freedom of expression under Art 10 had been engaged.

Harvey v DPP [2011] All ER (D) 143 (Admin), QBD Two police officers stopped a group of people in the public area of a block of flats. H objected to a cannabis drug search and said 'Fuck this man, I ain't been smoking nothing'. H was warned about swearing, but continued and was arrested for s 5. Police officers regularly hear this language so are unlikely to be affected by it. The swearing had not caused the officers, young people in the group or anyone in the area harassment, alarm, or distress.

Abdul and others v DPP [2011] EWHC 247 (Admin), QBD Group of Muslims hurled abuse and waved placards with offensive slogans such as 'Butchers of Basra' at soldiers marching through a town on return from Afghanistan. Freedom of expression under Art 10 (see **1.1**) was not an unqualified right; the focus on minority rights should not result in over-looking the rights of the majority.

Taylor v DPP [2006] EWHC 1202 (Admin), QBD The prosecution do not have to call evidence that the words were actually heard or behaviour seen.

R (on the application of DPP) v Humphrey [2005] EWHC 822 (Admin), QBD Threatening or abusive words or behaviour must be within the hearing or sight of a person **likely** to be caused harassment, alarm, or distress. Actual harassment, alarm, or distress does not have to occur. It is judged on the impact it would have had on the reasonable man or woman.

Norwood v DPP [2003] EWHC 1564 (Admin), QBD Defendant displayed a poster in his flat window, visible from the street, which said 'Islam out of Britain' and 'Protect the British People'. It bore a reproduction of one of the 'twin towers' in flames along with a Crescent and Star surrounded by a prohibition sign. Poster was deemed capable of causing harassment, alarm, or distress. The defence of reasonable conduct and the rights of freedom of expression under Art 10 carry a duty to avoid unreasonable or disproportionate interference with the rights of others; if they do interfere disproportionately the state has a duty to intervene.

Percy v DPP [2001] EWHC 1125 (Admin), QBD Defacing an American flag and stamping on it outside an American airbase was basically a peaceful protest. Held: That a criminal prosecution was not a proportionate response and breached an individual's right to freedom of expression under Art 10 (see **1.1**).

Practical considerations

- Ensure any possible defences raised are covered in interview or rebutted by other evidence.
- If this offence is racially or religiously aggravated (see **7.10**). Consider racial and religious hatred offences (see **7.9**).
- The s 5 offence should be distinguished from the similar s 4A offence, which requires specific intent (see **7.7**).
- Words or behaviour are alternatives and one or other should be specified in the charge, and must be proved.
- Consider issuing a PND for this offence (see **7.1**).
- It is not duplicitous if both alternatives are charged, 'threatening or abusive', though both need not be used.
- Consider CPS public order charging standards.

7.8 Threatening/Abusive Words/Behaviour

 Summary   6 months

 Level 3 fine

Links to alternative subjects and offences

7.9 **Racial, Religious, or Sexual Orientation Hatred Offences**

Sections 17 to 29 of the Public Order Act 1986 relate to racial hatred offences, whereas ss 29A to 29N refer to religious or sexual orientation hatred offences.

7.9.1 **Use of words/behaviour or display of written material (racial)**

Section 18 creates the offence of using words or behaviour, or displaying written material, intending or likely to stir up racial hatred.

Offences

A person who uses **threatening**, **abusive** or **insulting** words or behaviour, or **displays** any **written material** which is threatening, abusive or insulting, is guilty of an offence if—

(a) he **intends** thereby to stir up **racial hatred**, or
(b) having regard to all the circumstances racial hatred is likely to be stirred up thereby.

Public Order Act 1986, s 18(1)

Points to prove

✓ used/displayed threatening/abusive/insulting
✓ words/behaviour/written material
✓ intended/likely to stir up racial hatred

Meanings

Threatening, abusive, and insulting (see 7.6)

Display (see 7.6)

Written material

Includes any sign or other visible representation.

Intention (see 4.1.2)

Racial hatred

Means hatred against a group of persons defined by reference to colour, race, nationality (including citizenship), or ethnic or national origins.

7.9.1 Use of words/behaviour or display of written material (racial)

Explanatory notes

- Racial hatred can be directed against a racial or religious group outside Great Britain.
- Insulting does not mean behaviour which might give rise to irritation or resentment.
- Offence may be committed in a public or private place, but if committed inside a dwelling then the s 18(4) defence may apply—see below.
- An intention to stir up racial hatred must be proved, or if having regard to all the circumstances, racial hatred is likely to be stirred up.

Defences

(4) For the accused to prove that he was inside a **dwelling** and had no reason to believe that the words or behaviour used, or the written material displayed, would be heard or seen by a person outside that or another dwelling.

(5) A person who is not shown to have intended to stir up racial hatred is not guilty of an offence under this section if he did not intend his words or behaviour, or the written material, to be, and was not aware that it might be, threatening, abusive or insulting.

Public Order Act 1986, s 18

Defence notes

For meaning of '**Dwelling**', see **7.6** '**Explanatory notes**'.

Practical considerations

- If the s 18, s 19, s 21, or s 23 offence relates to the display of written racial hatred material, the court may order forfeiture of the material.
- The following applies to all racially aggravated offences—
  + every section from s 18 to s 23 creates a separate offence (see **7.9.2** list) and one or more such offences may be charged together;
  + if the offence is committed by a body corporate, with the consent or connivance of a director, manager, company secretary, or other similar officer or person acting as such, then under s 28, they as well as the company are guilty of the offence;
  + consider the CPS public order charging standards for racial hatred offence;
  + consent of Attorney-General/Solicitor-General required.

 Either way   None

Summary: 6 months' imprisonment and/or a fine
Indictment: 7 years' imprisonment and/or a fine

7.9.2 Publishing/distributing written material (racial)

Section 19 of the Public Order Act 1986 creates the offence of publishing or distributing written material intending or likely to stir up racial hatred.

Offences

A person who **publishes or distributes written material** which is **threatening, abusive or insulting** is guilty of an offence if—
(a) he **intends** thereby to stir up **racial hatred**, or
(b) having regard to all the circumstances racial hatred is likely to be stirred up thereby.

Public Order Act 1986, s 19(1)

Points to prove

✓ published/distributed
✓ threatening/abusive/insulting written material
✓ intended/likely to stir up racial hatred

Meanings

Publishes or distributes

Means its publication or distribution to the public or a section of the public.

Written material (see 7.9.1)

Threatening, abusive, or insulting (see 7.6)

Intends (see 4.1.2)

Racial hatred (see 7.9.1)

Defences

For accused who is not shown to have intended to stir up racial hatred to prove that he was not aware of the content of the material and did not suspect nor had reason to suspect, that it was threatening, abusive or insulting.

Public Order Act 1986, s 19(2)

7.9.3 Religious or sexual orientation hatred offences

Related cases

R v Sheppard [2010] EWCA Crim 65, CA S created and uploaded onto the internet written material which cast doubt on the holocaust and made disparaging racial remarks. Although taking place in the UK, the website was hosted by a server in California. The court had jurisdiction as a 'substantial measure' of these activities took place in the UK. Held: That written material includes articles in electronic form and it was also published/distributed over the internet for general access to the public.

Practical considerations (see 7.9.1)

- References to publication and distribution of written material are to its publication or distribution to the public or a section of the public.
- Other racial hatred offences under Pt 3A are—
  - ✦ public performance of play—s 20;
  - ✦ distributing, showing, or playing a recording—s 21;
  - ✦ broadcasting or including programme in programme service—s 22;
  - ✦ possession of racially inflammatory material—s 23.

 Either way   None

 Summary: 6 months' imprisonment and/or a fine
Indictment: 7 years' imprisonment and/or a fine

7.9.3 Religious or sexual orientation hatred offences

Section 29B creates the offence of using words or behaviour, or displaying written material, intending or likely to stir up religious or sexual orientation hatred.

> **Offences**
>
> A person who uses **threatening** words or behaviour, or **displays** any **written material** which is threatening, is guilty of an offence if he **intends** thereby to stir up **religious hatred** or **hatred on the grounds of sexual orientation**.
>
> Public Order Act 1986, s 29B(1)

Points to prove

✓ used threatening words or behaviour or displayed threatening written material

✓ intended to stir up religious or sexual orientation hatred

Meanings

Threatening (see 7.6)

Displays (see 7.6)

Written material (see 7.9.1)

Intention (see 4.1.2)

Religious hatred

Means hatred against a group of persons defined by reference to religious belief or lack of religious belief.

Hatred on the grounds of sexual orientation

Means hatred against a group of persons defined by reference to sexual orientation (whether towards persons of the same sex, the opposite sex, or both).

Explanatory notes

Racial or sexual orientation hatred may be committed in a public or a private place, but if committed inside a dwelling the s 29B(4) defence may apply.

Defences

For the accused to prove that he was inside a dwelling and had no reason to believe that the words or behaviour used, or the written material displayed, would be heard or seen by a person outside that or another dwelling.

Public Order Act 1986, s 29B(4)

Defence notes (see 7.9.1)

Practical considerations

- If the offence under s 29B relates to the display of written material, the court may, under s 29I, order forfeiture of the material. Forfeiture applies to publishing or distributing written material (s 29C), distributing/showing/playing a recording (s 29E), and possession of inflammatory material (s 29G).
- The following apply to religious or sexual orientation hatred offences—
  - ✦ every section from s 29B to s 29G creates a separate offence and one or more such offences may be charged together;

7.9.3 Religious or sexual orientation hatred offences

+ if the offence is committed by a body corporate with the consent or connivance of a director, manager, company secretary, or other similar officer or person acting as such, then under s 29M, they as well as the company are guilty of the offence;
+ consider CPS public order charging standards;
+ consent of the Attorney General is required.

• HOC 29/2007 introduced Pt 3A on religious hatred, stating that for each offence the words, behaviour, written material, recordings, or programmes must be threatening and intended to stir up religious hatred. Part 3A was created with the offences of stirring up hatred against persons on religious grounds because Jews and Sikhs have been deemed by courts to be racial groups, but Muslims and Christians are religious rather than racial groups.
• MOJ Circular 5/2010 gives some explanatory guidance to the offences of intentionally stirring up hatred on the grounds of sexual orientation which have been added to the Pt 3A religious hatred offences.

Protection for freedom of expression

Religious hatred

Section 29J states that nothing in Pt 3A shall be read or given effect in a way which prohibits or restricts discussion, criticism, or expressions of antipathy, dislike, ridicule, insult, or abuse of particular religions, or the beliefs or practices of their adherents, or of any other belief system, or the beliefs or practices of its adherents, or proselytising, or urging adherents of a different religion or belief system to cease practising their religion or belief system.

Sexual orientation

Section 29JA states that in Pt 3A, for the avoidance of doubt, the discussion or criticism of sexual conduct or practices, or the urging of persons to refrain from or modify such conduct or practices shall not be taken of itself to be threatening or intended to stir up hatred.

• Other religious or sexual orientation hatred offences under Pt 3A are—
  + publishing or distributing written material—s 29C;
  + public performance of play—s 29D;
  + distributing, showing or playing a recording—s 29E;
  + broadcasting or including programme in programme service—s 29F; and
  + possession of inflammatory material—s 29G.
They are all either way offences and carry the same penalty as s 29B offence.

 E&S   **RRA**   **PCSO**

 Either way   None

 Summary: 6 months' imprisonment and/or a fine
Indictment: 7 years' imprisonment and/or a fine

E&S Entry and search powers   **RRA** Racially or religiously aggravated offence   **PCSO** Police community support officers

Links to alternative subjects and offences

7.10 **Racially/Religiously Aggravated Offences**

Sections 28 to 32 of the Crime and Disorder Act 1998 relate to racially or religiously aggravated offences.

7.10.1 **Meaning of 'racially or religiously aggravated'**

Section 28 states when a specific offence is deemed 'racially or religiously aggravated'.

Definition

An offence is racially or religiously aggravated for the purposes of ss 29 to 32 below if—

(a) at the time of committing the offence, or immediately before or after doing so, the offender demonstrates towards the victim of the offence hostility based on the victim's **membership** (or **presumed** membership) of a **racial or religious group**; or

(b) the offence is motivated (wholly or partly) by hostility towards members of a racial or religious group based on the membership of that group.

Crime and Disorder Act 1998, s 28(1)

Meanings

Membership

In relation to a racial or religious group, includes association with members of that group.

Presumed

Means presumed by the defendant (even if it is a mistaken presumption).

Racial group

Means a group of people defined by reference to race, colour, nationality (including citizenship), or ethnic or national origins.

Religious group

Means a group of people defined by religious belief or lack of religious belief.

Explanatory notes

It is immaterial whether or not the offender's hostility is also based, to any extent, on any other factor not mentioned in s 28(1).

Related cases

Jones v DPP [2011] 1 WLR 833, QBD The motive does not have to be proved for each limb of s 28(1). No subjective intent is required for s 28(1)(a) as the test is objective, with just the need to show racial hostility. However, under s 28(1)(b) the motivation behind the behaviour has to be proved.

Taylor v DPP [2006] EWHC 1202 (Admin), QBD Guidance issued on racially aggravated offences.

R v Rogers [2007] UKHL 8, HL Defendant called three Spanish women 'bloody foreigners' and told them to 'go back to their own country' before pursuing them in an aggressive manner. Held: It is immaterial whether the hostility was based on factors other than simple racism or xenophobia. The denial of equal respect and dignity to people seen as different can be more deeply hurtful, damaging, and disrespectful than if it were based on a more specific racial characteristic.

DPP v M [2004] EWHC 1453 (Admin), QBD The defendant kept using the words 'bloody foreigners' before going outside and damaging the window of the kebab shop. The word 'foreigners' satisfied the meaning within s 28(3) and the word 'bloody' meant that the defendant had demonstrated some hostility towards a racial group.

Practical considerations

A police officer is just as entitled to protection under these provisions as anyone else (eg a person committing the offence of threatening behaviour by using racial taunts against the police could be prosecuted for the racially aggravated version of the offence).

7.10.2 **Racially or religiously aggravated assaults**

Section 29 relates to racially or religiously aggravated assault offences.

Offences

A person is guilty of an offence under this section if he commits—
(a) an offence under s 20 of the Offences Against the Person Act 1861 [see **2.3.1**]; or
(b) an offence under s 47 of that Act [see **2.1.2**]; or
(c) a common assault [see **2.1.1**],
which is **racially or religiously aggravated** for the purposes of this section.

Crime and Disorder Act 1998, s 29(1)

7.10.2 Racially or religiously aggravated assaults

> **Points to prove**
> ✓ committed offence under s 20 or s 47 of OAPA 1861; or s 39 of CJA 1988
> ✓ such offence was racially/religiously aggravated

Meaning of racially or religiously aggravated (see 7.10.1)

Explanatory notes

If, on the trial on indictment of a person charged with this offence, the jury find the defendant not guilty of the offence charged, they may find them guilty of the relevant 'basic' offence (eg s 20 or s 47 of the OAPA 1861; or s 39 of CJA 1988).

Related cases

DPP v Woods [2002] EWHC 85 (Admin), QBD On being refused entry to licensed premises, the doorman was called a 'black bastard' and assaulted. Although the words were used out of frustration, and the victim was unconcerned and did not consider the words racially offensive, the offence of racially aggravated common assault was still committed.

DPP v Pal [2000] Crim LR 256, QBD Asian caretaker asked four youths, two Asian and two white, to leave the premises. One Asian youth refused, pushed the caretaker against a bin, accused him of being a white man's lackey and a brown Englishman, then kicked him before leaving. Held: Not racially aggravated common assault as the caretaker was abused because of his job not his race. Therefore, this was **not** hostility based on the victim's membership of a racial group.

Practical considerations

Always charge the defendant with the relevant 'basic' offence, as there is no provision for an alternative verdict at a magistrates' court.

 Either way   None

 Offence under s 29(1)(a) or (b)
Summary: 6 months' imprisonment and/or a fine
Indictment: 7 years' imprisonment and/or a fine

Offence under s 29(1)(c)
Summary: 6 months' imprisonment and/or a fine
Indictment: 2 years' imprisonment and/or a fine

7.10.3 **Racially or religiously aggravated criminal damage**

Section 30 creates an offence of racially or religiously aggravated criminal damage.

Offences

A person is guilty of an offence under this section if he commits an offence under s 1(1) of the Criminal Damage Act 1971 (destroying or damaging property belonging to another) which is **racially or religiously aggravated** for the purposes of this section.

Crime and Disorder Act 1998, s 30(1)

Points to prove

✓ committed s 1(1) criminal damage offence (see **4.4**)
✓ offence was racially/religiously aggravated

Meaning of racially or religiously aggravated (see 7.10.1)

Explanatory notes

- For the purposes of this section, s 28(1)(a) (see **7.10.1**) has effect as if the person to whom the property belongs or is treated as belonging for the purposes of that Act was the victim of the offence.
- If, on the trial on indictment of a person charged with this offence, the jury find the defendant not guilty of the offence charged, they may find them guilty of the relevant 'basic' offence.

Practical considerations

- Where this offence is shown to be motivated by racial hostility under s 28(1)(b) (see **7.10.1**) there is no need to identify a specific victim (eg painting racist graffiti on a wall would be likely to constitute this offence).
- This offence is triable either way irrespective of the value of the damage caused (unlike the relevant 'basic' offence).

 Either way   None

 Summary: 6 months' imprisonment and/or a fine
Indictment: 14 years' imprisonment and/or a fine

7.10.4 Racially or religiously aggravated public order offences

Section 31 relates to racially or religiously aggravated public order offences.

Offences

A person is guilty of an offence under this section if he commits—
(a) an offence under s 4 of the Public Order Act 1986 (fear/provocation of violence) [see **7.6**]; or
(b) an offence under s 4A of that Act (intentional harassment, alarm, or distress) [see **7.7**]; or
(c) an offence under s 5 of that Act (harassment, alarm, distress) [see **7.8**],
which is **racially or religiously aggravated** for the purposes of this section.

Crime and Disorder Act, s 31(1)

Points to prove

✓ committed an offence
✓ under s 4 or s 4A or s 5 of the Public Order Act 1986
✓ such offence was racially/religiously aggravated

Meaning of racially or religiously aggravated (see 7.10.1)

Explanatory notes

- If, on the trial on indictment of a person charged with an offence under s 31(1)(a) or (b), the jury find him not guilty of the offence charged, they may find him guilty of the 'basic' offence.
- For the purposes of s 31(1)(c), s 28(1)(a) (see **7.10.1**) shall have effect as if the person likely to be caused harassment, alarm, or distress were the victim of the offence.

Related cases

DPP v McFarlane [2002] EWHC 485, QBD During an argument over a disabled parking bay a white person referred to a black person as a 'jungle bunny', a 'black bastard', and a 'wog' and was charged with racially aggravated threatening behaviour. Anger about another's inconsiderate behaviour is not an excuse for racial comments.

Norwood v DPP [2003] EWHC 1564 (Admin), QBD Displaying a racially insulting poster in a window where it could be seen by the public can constitute an offence. Its location and contents were capable of causing harassment, alarm, or distress to any right-minded member of society.

DPP v Ramos [2000] Crim LR 768, QBD After a serious bomb attack, threatening letters were sent to an organisation offering help and advice to the Asian community. Held: That it was the state of mind of the victim, not the likelihood of violence happening. If the wording of the letter suggested immediate violence would occur, it was for the magistrates to decide whether the victim believed, or was likely to believe, that violence could occur at some time. The sender had established an intention to cause the victim to believe that violence could occur at any time.

DPP v Woods [2002] EWHC 85 (Admin), QBD When abuse is racially aggravated, it is important to prove racial hostility towards the victim or racial motivation.

Practical considerations

If the defendant is found not guilty of the offence charged under s 31(1) (a) or (b) at magistrates' court there is no provision for an alternative verdict, therefore it is good practice to include the relevant 'basic' offence as an alternative charge.

Offence under s 31(1)(a) or (b)

 Either way   None

 Summary: 6 months' imprisonment and/or a fine
Indictment: 2 years' imprisonment and/or a fine

Offence under s 31(1)(c)

 Summary   6 months

 Level 4 fine

7.10.5 Racially or religiously aggravated harassment/stalking

Section 32 concerns the offences of harassment/stalking or putting a person in fear of violence or stalking involving fear of violence or serious harm or distress which is racially or religiously aggravated.

E&S Entry and search powers   **RRA** Racially or religiously aggravated offence   **PCSO** Police community support officers   325

7.10.5 Racially or religiously aggravated harassment/stalking

Offences

A person is guilty of an offence under this section if he commits—
(a) an offence under section 2 or 2A of the Protection from Harassment Act 1997 (offences of harassment and stalking); or
(b) an offence under section 4 or 4A of that Act (putting people in fear of violence and stalking involving fear of violence or serious alarm or distress),

which is **racially or religiously aggravated** for the purposes of this section.

Crime and Disorder Act 1998, s 32(1)

Points to prove

✓ committed an offence
✓ under s 2, s 2A, s 4, or s 4A of the Protection from Harassment Act 1997
✓ such offence was racially/religiously aggravated

Meaning of racially or religiously aggravated (see 7.10.1)

Explanatory notes

- Offences relating to the Protection from Harassment Act 1997 (above) are harassment (s 2 – see **7.11.1**), stalking (s 2A – see **7.11.3**), putting people in fear of violence (s 4 – see **7.11.2**) and stalking involving fear of violence or serious alarm or distress (s 4A – see **7.11.4**).
- If, on the trial on indictment of a person charged with an offence under s 32(1)(a), the jury find them not guilty of the offence charged, they may find them guilty of the basic offence. Similarly if found not guilty of an offence under s 32(1)(b), they may find them guilty of an offence under s 32(1)(a).
- If the matter is dealt with at magistrates' court (summary) for an offence under s 32(1)(a) and found not guilty, there is no provision for an alternative verdict so it is good practice to include the relevant basic offence as an alternative. Similarly for a s 32(1)(b) offence, include the s 32(1)(a) offence as an alternative.

Practical considerations

Section 5 of the Protection from Harassment Act 1997 provides a court with the power to make a restraining order (see **7.11.5**).

 E&S **RRA**

 Either way

 None

 E&S Entry and search powers

 RRA Racially or religiously aggravated offence

Offence under s 32(1)(a)

Summary: 6 months' imprisonment and/or a fine

Indictment: 2 years' imprisonment and/or a fine

Offence under s 32(1)(b)

Summary: 6 months' imprisonment and/or a fine

Indictment: 7 years' imprisonment and/or a fine

Links to alternative subjects and offences

7.11 **Harassment/Stalking**

The Protection from Harassment Act 1997 provides criminal and civil remedies to restrain conduct amounting to harassment or stalking. Sections 42 and 42A of the Criminal Justice and Police Act 2001 concern prevention of harassment of a person in their own home.

7.11.1 **Harassment—no violence**

Section 1 prohibits harassment, while s 2 creates the offence of harassment.

Offences

1(1) A person must not pursue a **course of conduct**—
    (a) which amounts to **harassment** of another, and
    (b) which he knows or ought to know amounts to harassment of the other.

1(1A) A person must not pursue a course of conduct—
    (a) which involves harassment of two or more persons, and
    (b) which he knows or ought to know amounts to harassment of those persons, and
    (c) by which he intends to persuade any person (whether or not one of those mentioned above)—
        (i) not to do something that he is entitled or required to do, or
        (ii) to do something that he is not under any obligation to do.

2(1) A person who pursues a course of conduct in breach of section 1(1) or (1A) is guilty of an offence.

Protection from Harassment Act 1997, ss 1(1), (1A), and 2(1)

Points to prove

✓ pursued a course of conduct
✓ on at least two occasions
✓ amounting to harassment
✓ which you knew/ought to have known amounted to harassment

Meanings

Course of conduct

- Must involve to a single person under s 1(1), conduct on at least two occasions in relation to that person, **or** to two or more persons under s 1(1A), conduct on at least one occasion in relation to each of those persons
- Conduct includes speech.

Harassment

Includes causing the person(s) alarm or distress.

Explanatory notes

- If a reasonable person in possession of the same information as the defendant would think the course of conduct amounted to harassment, then the offender should have realised this as well (*Kellett v DPP* [2001] EWHC 107 (Admin)).
- A person may be subjected to harassment by writing (eg emails or letters), orally (eg in person or by telephone), or by conduct.
- An offender does not have to act in a malicious, threatening, abusive, or insulting way. It could be that they may be infatuated with the victim and actually intend them no harm.
- The court can issue a 'restraining order' against the defendant. If required ask the CPS to apply for one (see **7.11.5**).

Defences

Section 1(1) or (1A) does not apply to a course of conduct if the person who pursued it shows—

(a) that it was pursued for the prevention or detection of crime,
(b) that it was pursued under any enactment or rule of law or to comply with any condition or requirement imposed by any person under any enactment, or
(c) that in the particular circumstances the pursuit of the course of conduct was reasonable.

Protection from Harassment Act 1997, s 1(3)

Defence notes

- These defences would apply to the police, customs, security services, including the private sector (eg private detective or store detective).
- A suspect suffering from some form of obsessive behaviour or schizophrenia cannot use their mental illness as a defence because of the 'reasonable person' test.

Related cases

Plavelil v DPP [2014] EWHC 736 (Admin), QBD The fact that repeated untrue malicious allegations might be easily rebutted did not mean that they were not oppressive harassment.

Kosar v Bank of Scotland [2011] EWHC 1050 (Admin), QBD A company was not precluded from being able to commit a criminal offence of harassment contrary to s 2(1) of the 1997 Act.

Hayes v Willoughby [2011] EWCA Civ 1541, CA If a defendant could not show that their course of conduct had been pursued for the purpose of preventing or detecting crime it was accordingly unlawful.

7.11.1 Harassment—no violence

Buckley, Smith v DPP [2008] EWHC 136 (Admin), QBD Case provides guidance on a continuing course of conduct over a period of time.

Daniels v Metropolitan Police Commissioner [2006] EWHC 1622, QBD In establishing vicarious liability for harassment there must be an established case of harassment by at least one employee who is shown on at least two occasions to have pursued a course of conduct amounting to harassment, or by more than one employee each acting on different occasions in furtherance of some joint design.

DPP v Baker [2004] EWHC 2782 (Admin), QBD Harassment may occur either continuously or intermittently over a period of time. Providing at least one of the incidents relied on by the prosecution occurred within the six-month limitation period.

Lau v DPP [2000] All ER 224, QBD During an argument Lau hit his girlfriend across her face. Four months later he threatened violence against her new boyfriend. Held: Lau had not 'pursued a course of conduct' because of the time between the two incidents and the conduct was against two different people.

Practical considerations

- Evidence of previous complaints of harassment to prove continuance of the harassment on at least two separate occasions.
- Two isolated incidents do not constitute a course of conduct.
- Consider serving a harassment warning notice on the suspect. Have any previous warning notices been served on the suspect?
- A campaign of collective harassment applies equally to two or more people as it does to one. Namely, conduct by one person shall also be taken, at the time it occurs, to be conduct by another if it is aided, abetted, counselled, or procured by that other person.
- Consider the intentional harassment, alarm, or distress offence under s 4A of the Public Order Act 1986 (see **7.7**).
- If it is racially or religiously aggravated harassment see **7.10.5**.
- Obtain CJA witness statements.
- Obtain all available evidence (eg other witnesses, CCTV camera footage, detailed telephone bills, entries in domestic violence registers, harassment notice).
- Could any of the defences apply?
- Consider the offence of stalking under s 2A (see **7.11.3**).

 RRA

 Summary   6 months

 6 months' imprisonment and/or a fine

7.11.2 **Harassment (fear of violence)**

Section 4 relates to a course of conduct, which, on at least two occasions, causes another to fear that violence will be used against them.

Offences

A person whose **course of conduct** causes another to fear, on at least two occasions, that violence will be used against him is guilty of an offence if he knows or ought to know that his course of conduct will cause the other so to fear on each of those occasions.

Protection from Harassment Act 1997, s 4(1)

Points to prove

✓ caused fear of violence
✓ by a course of conduct on at least two occasions
✓ which you knew/ought to have known
✓ would cause fear of violence on each occasion

Meaning of course of conduct (see 7.11.1)

Explanatory notes

* The person whose course of conduct is in question ought to know that it will cause another to fear that violence will be used against him on any occasion if a reasonable person with the same information would think it would cause the other so to fear on that occasion.
* A defendant found not guilty of this offence (at trial on indictment) may be convicted of s 2 harassment (see **7.11.1**) or s 2A stalking (see **7.11.3**).
* The court can issue a 'restraining order' against the defendant (see **7.11.5**).

Defences

It is a defence for a person charged with an offence under this section to show that—

(a) his course of conduct was pursued for the purpose of preventing or detecting crime,
(b) his course of conduct was pursued under any enactment or rule of law or to comply with any condition or requirement imposed by any person under any enactment, or
(c) the pursuit of his course of conduct was reasonable for the protection of himself or another or for the protection of his or another's property.

Protection from Harassment Act 1997, s 4(3)

Defence notes (see **7.11.1**)

Related cases

R v Widdows [2011] EWCA Crim 1500, CA A charge of harassment is not normally appropriate for use as a means of criminalising conduct during incidents in a long and predominantly affectionate relationship in which both parties persisted and wanted to continue.

R v Curtis [2010] EWCA Crim 123, CA Prosecution to establish that course of conduct amounts to harassment. The conduct has to be an oppressive, unreasonable, and unacceptable campaign, to a degree that would be a criminal matter.

R v Patel [2004] EWCA Crim 3284, CA Incidents must be so connected in type and context that they amount to a course of conduct.

Howard v DPP [2001] EWHC 17 (Admin), QBD A family suffered continual abuse from their neighbours. One of the many threats made by the defendant was to kill their dog. This was sufficient grounds for the family to fear violence being used against them.

Practical considerations (see also **7.11.1**)

- Offence could cover long-standing disputes where fear of violence is a possibility against one of the parties.
- Consider stalking involving fear of violence or serious alarm or distress (see **7.11.4**) or intentional harassment, alarm, or distress offence under s 4A of the Public Order Act 1986 (see **7.7**).

 Either way   None

 Summary: 6 months' imprisonment and/or a fine
Indictment: 5 years' imprisonment and/or a fine

7.11.3 **Stalking**

Section 2A creates the offence of stalking.

> **Offences**
>
> (1) A person is guilty of an offence if—
>   (a) the person pursues a course of conduct in **breach of section 1(1)**, and
>   (b) the **course of conduct** amounts to **stalking**.
> (2) For the purposes of subsection (1)(b) (and section 4A(1)(a)) a person's **course of conduct** amounts to **stalking** of another person if—

(a) it amounts to **harassment** of that person,
(b) the **acts or omissions** involved are ones associated with stalking, and
(c) the person whose course of conduct it is knows or ought to know that the course of conduct amounts to harassment of the other person.

Protection from Harassment Act 1997, s 2A

Points to prove

✓ pursued a course of conduct in breach of s 1(1)
✓ that conduct amounted to stalking
✓ which you knew/ought to have known
✓ amounted to harassment

Meanings

Breach of section 1(1) (see **7.11.1**)

Harassment (see **7.11.1**)

Includes causing the person(s) alarm or distress.

Acts or omissions (s 2A(3))

The following are examples which, in particular circumstances, are associated with stalking–

- following a person,
- contacting, or attempting to contact, a person by any means,
- publishing any statement or other material – relating or purporting to relate to a person, or purporting to originate from a person,
- monitoring the use by a person of the internet, email or any other form of electronic communication,
- loitering in any place (whether public or private),
- interfering with any property in the possession of a person,
- watching or spying on a person.

Explanatory notes

- Stalking is most often found where a person is fixated and/or obsessed with another. This can manifest itself in a pattern of persistent and repeated contact, or attempts to contact, the victim. Examples of behaviours associated with stalking are given in s 2A(3) (above).
- An offender does not have to act in a malicious, threatening, abusive, or insulting way. It could be that they may be infatuated with the victim and intend them no harm.
- The court can issue a 'restraining order' against the defendant (see **7.11.5**).

Practical considerations

- Refer the victim to relevant support agencies: National Stalking Helpline or Paladin, including victim support (see **Appendix 1**) and local domestic violence support groups. Ensure compliance with the Victim Code and that a VPS is taken (see **13.4**).

7.11.4 Stalking (fear of violence/serious alarm or distress)

- Section 2B allows a justice of the peace to issue a warrant, which authorises a constable to enter and search premises on reasonable grounds for believing that—
  + a stalking offence under s 2A has been, or is being, committed, and
  + there is material on the premises which is likely to be of substantial value (whether by itself or together with other material) to the investigation of the offence.
- Section 4A concerns the offence of stalking involving fear of violence or serious alarm or distress (see **7.11.4**).
- HOC 18/2012 provides further details concerning the s 2A and s 4A stalking offences and power of entry under s 2B.
- If it is racially or religiously aggravated stalking see **7.10.5**.
- Consider the offence of intentional harassment, alarm, or distress under s 4A of the Public Order Act 1986 (see **7.7**).

 Summary   6 months

 6 months' imprisonment and/or a fine

7.11.4 **Stalking (fear of violence/serious alarm or distress)**

Section 4A relates to stalking causing another to fear, on at least two occasions, that violence will be used against them or causes them serious alarm or distress which has a substantial adverse effect on their usual day-to-day activities.

> **Offences**
>
> A person (A) whose course of conduct—
> (a) amounts to **stalking**, and
> (b) either—
>   (i) causes another (B) to fear, on at least two occasions, that violence will be used against B, or
>   (ii) causes B serious alarm or distress which has a **substantial adverse effect** on B's usual day-to-day activities,
> is guilty of an offence if A knows or ought to know that A's course of conduct will cause B so to fear on each of those occasions or (as the case may be) will cause such alarm or distress.
>
> Protection from Harassment Act 1997, s 4A(1)

Points to prove

✓ course of conduct that amounted to stalking
✓ caused another to fear on at least two occasions that violence would be used **or**
✓ caused serious alarm/distress which had a substantial adverse effect on B's usual day-to-day activities
✓ which you knew/ought to have known
✓ would cause either fear of violence on each occasion **or** serious alarm/distress

Meaning of stalking (see 7.11.3)

Explanatory notes

- The phrase '**substantial adverse effect**' on the usual day-to-day activities' is not defined in section 4A. Although HOC 18/2012 states that evidence of a substantial adverse effect may include the victim—
  - ✦ changing their routes to work, work patterns, or employment;
  - ✦ arranging for friends or family to pick up children from school;
  - ✦ installing additional security in/around their home;
  - ✦ suffering from physical or mental ill-health;
  - ✦ suffering from stress due to deterioration in performance at work;
  - ✦ moving home; or
  - ✦ stopping /changing the way they socialise.
- If the victim continues with their existing routines in defiance of a stalker, they may still be able to evidence the substantial impact on their usual day-to-day activities.
- The person whose course of conduct is in question ought to know that it will cause another to fear that violence will be used against them on any occasion if a reasonable person in possession of the same information would think the course of conduct would cause the other to fear on that occasion.
- For the purposes of this section the person whose course of conduct is in question ought to know that their course of conduct will cause the victim serious alarm or distress which has a substantial adverse effect on the victim's usual day-to-day activities if a reasonable person in possession of the same information would think the course of conduct would cause the victim such alarm or distress.

Defences

It is a defence for A to show that—

(a) A's course of conduct was pursued for the purpose of preventing or detecting crime,

(b) A's course of conduct was pursued under any enactment or rule of law or to comply with any condition or requirement imposed by any person under any enactment, or

(c) the pursuit of A's course of conduct was reasonable for the protection
of A or another or for the protection of A's or another's property.

Protection from Harassment Act 1997, s 4A(4)

Defence notes (see 7.11.1)

Practical considerations (see also 7.11.3)

• If on the trial on indictment of a person charged with a s 4A offence,
the jury find that person not guilty, they may find the person guilty
of an offence under section 2 (see 7.11.1) or 2A (see 7.11.3).
• The court can issue a 'restraining order' against the defendant (see 7.11.5).
• If it is racially or religiously aggravated stalking see 7.10.5.
• Consider intentional harassment, alarm, or distress offence under
s 4A of the Public Order Act 1986 (see 7.7).

 Either way   None

 Summary: 6 months' imprisonment and/or a fine
Indictment: 5 years' imprisonment and/or a fine

7.11.5 **Restraining orders**

Restraining orders can be made against a person convicted of any offence
under s 5 or acquitted of an offence under s 5A.

Offences

If without reasonable excuse the defendant does anything which he is
prohibited from doing by an order under this section, he is guilty of an offence.

Protection from Harassment Act 1997, s 5(5)

Points to prove

✓ without reasonable excuse
✓ did something prohibited by a restraining order

Explanatory notes

- A court sentencing or otherwise dealing with a defendant convicted of **any offence** may, as well as sentencing or dealing with the defendant in any other way, make a restraining order under s 5 or s 5A. HOC 17/2009 provides guidelines on restraining orders to protect a person from harassment or violence.
- Under s 5A a court can make a restraining order on a person acquitted of an offence, if the court believes a restraining order is necessary to protect a person from harassment or stalking. It is also an offence to breach a s 5A restraining order, as s 5A(2) states that s 5(3) to (7) applies to an order under s 5A as they apply to an order under s 5.
- The order may prohibit the defendant from doing anything described in the order, for the purpose of protecting the victim(s), or any other person mentioned in the order, from further conduct which amounts to harassment, stalking or will cause fear of violence or serious alarm or distress.
- The order may last for a specified period or until a further order is made.
- The prosecutor, defendant, or any person named therein may apply for it to be varied or discharged by a further order.

Related cases

R v Buxton [2011] EWCA Crim 2923, CA A restraining order can be made to protect a company.

R v Major [2010] EWHC 3016, QBD If a court issues a restraining order on acquittal there must be clear evidence that the victim needs protection from harassment from the defendant.

R v Evans [2004] EWCA Crim 3102, CA The terms of a restraining order must be precise and capable of being understood by the offender.

Practical considerations

- Unlike the previous sections of this Act, one incident is sufficient to breach an order.
- These are criminal matters and should not be confused with civil injunctions.
- When an order is made it must identify the protected parties: so ensure the details are available.
- Include a copy of the original order in the file for CPS attention.
- If you require a further order you must request CPS apply for one.

E&S

 Either way   None

Summary: 6 months' imprisonment and/or a fine
Indictment: 5 years' imprisonment and/or a fine

7.11.6 **Civil remedies**

Section 3 provides a civil remedy for harassment, allowing the victim to obtain damages and/or an injunction. Section 3A provides for injunctions to protect persons from harassment within s 1(1A).

Offences

Where—
(a) the High Court or a county court grants an **injunction** for the purpose mentioned in **subsection (3)(a)**, and
(b) without **reasonable excuse** the defendant does anything which he is prohibited from doing by the injunction,
he is guilty of an offence.

Protection from Harassment Act 1997, s 3(6)

Points to prove

✓ without reasonable excuse
✓ pursued course of conduct prohibited by injunction
✓ granted by High Court/county court

Meanings

Injunction

An order or decree issued by a court for a person to do or not do that which is specified for a specified amount of time.

Subsection (3)(a)

In such proceedings the High Court or a county court grants an injunction for the purpose of restraining the defendant from pursuing any conduct which amounts to harassment.

Reasonable excuse (see 'Defence' below)

Explanatory notes

- An actual or perceived breach of s 1 may result in a claim in civil proceedings by the victim of the course of conduct in question.
- On such a claim, damages may be awarded for, among other things, any anxiety caused by, and financial loss resulting from, the harassment.
- Where, in such proceedings, the court grants an injunction restraining the defendant from pursuing any conduct amounting to harassment, and the plaintiff considers that the defendant has done anything prohibited by the injunction, they may apply to have a warrant issued for the arrest of the defendant.

- The warrant application must be made to the court that issued the injunction.
- Section 3A stipulates that where there is an actual or apprehended breach of s 1(1A) (see **7.11.1**) by the relevant person, then any person who is or may be—
  + a victim of the course of conduct in question; or
  + a person falling within section 1(1A)(c);

  may apply to the High Court or a county court for an injunction restraining the relevant person from pursuing any conduct which amounts to harassment in relation to any person or persons mentioned or described in the injunction.

Defences

The defence of reasonable excuse was meant for a **life-saving** situation such as a rescue from a burning house or something similar (*Huntingdon Life Sciences v Curtin* [1997] EWCA Civ 2486).

Related cases

Thomas v News Group Newspapers Ltd [2001] EWCA A national newspaper and journalists were sued for harassment under s 3 after publishing an article about police discipline which gave the complainant's name, place of work, and described them as 'a black clerk'. Held: It was not the conduct of the offender that created the offence or civil wrong of harassment, but the effect of that conduct.

DPP v Moseley [1999] All ER (D) 587, QBD A High Court injunction had been granted to prevent harassment of a mink farmer. The defendant took part in a peaceful protest within the area covered by the injunction and claimed this conduct was reasonable. Held: Only in serious circumstances could it be reasonable to flout a High Court injunction.

Practical considerations

If a person is convicted of a breach of an injunction under this section, their conduct is not punishable as a contempt of court, or vice versa.

 Either way   None

 Summary: 6 months' imprisonment and/or a fine
Indictment: 5 years' imprisonment and/or a fine

7.11.7 **Harassment of person in their home**

Sections 42 and 42A of the Criminal Justice and Police Act 2001 give the police power to direct a person to leave a dwelling to prevent harassment and an offence of harassing a person in their home.

Offences

42(7) Any person who knowingly fails to comply with a requirement in a **direction** given to him under this section (other than a requirement under subsection (4)(b)) shall be guilty of an offence.

42(7A) Any person to whom a constable has given a direction including a requirement under subsection (4)(b) commits an offence if he—
  (a) returns to the vicinity of the premises in question within the period specified in the direction beginning with the date on which the direction is given; and
  (b) does so for the purpose described in subsection (1)(b).

42A(1) A person commits an offence if—
  (a) that person is present outside or in the vicinity of any premises that are used by any individual ('the resident') as his **dwelling**;
  (b) that person is present there for the purpose (by his presence or otherwise) of representing to the resident or another individual (whether or not one who uses the premises as his dwelling), or of persuading the resident or such another individual—
    (i) that he should not do something that he is entitled or required to do; or
    (ii) that he should do something that he is not under any obligation to do;
  (c) that person—
    (i) intends his presence to amount to the **harassment** of, or to cause alarm or distress to, the resident, or
    (ii) knows or ought to know that his presence is likely to result in the harassment of, or to cause alarm or distress to, the resident; and
  (d) the presence of that person—
    (i) amounts to the harassment of, or causes alarm or distress to, any person falling within subsection (2); or
    (ii) is likely to result in the harassment of, or to cause alarm or distress to, any such person.

Criminal Justice and Police Act 2001, ss 42, 42A

Points to prove

s 42(7) offence

✓ outside/in vicinity of premises
✓ knowingly
✓ contravened the direction of a constable

s 42(7A) offence
- ✓ having been given a direction by a constable
- ✓ to leave the vicinity of premises
- ✓ not to return within a specified period
- ✓ returned there within that period
- ✓ to persuade the resident/another individual
- ✓ not to do something they are entitled to do/do something not obliged to do

s 42A(1) offence
- ✓ present outside/in vicinity of a dwelling
- ✓ to persuade resident/other individual
- ✓ not to do something entitled/required to do/to do something not obliged to do
- ✓ intended to harass/cause alarm/distress to the resident
- ✓ knew/ought to have known such presence was likely to do so
- ✓ and their presence amounted to harassment/caused alarm/distress/likely to do so

Meanings

Directions

(1) Subject to the following provisions of this section, a constable who is at the scene may give a **direction** under this section to any person if—

    (a) that person is present outside or in the vicinity of any premises that are used by any individual ('the resident') as his **dwelling**;

    (b) that constable believes, on reasonable grounds, that that person is present there for the purpose (by his presence or otherwise) of representing to the resident or another individual (whether or not one who uses the premises as his dwelling), or of persuading the resident or such another individual—

        (i) that he should not do something that he is entitled or required to do; or

        (ii) that he should do something that he is not under any obligation to do; and

    (c) that constable also believes, on reasonable grounds, that the presence of that person (either alone or together with that of any other persons who are also present)—

        (i) amounts to, or is likely to result in, the **harassment** of the resident; or

        (ii) is likely to cause alarm or distress to the resident.

(2) A direction under this section is a direction requiring the person to whom it is given to do all such things as the constable giving it may specify as the things he considers necessary to prevent one or both of the following—

    (a) the harassment of the resident; or

    (b) the causing of any alarm or distress to the resident.

7.11.7 Harassment of person in their home

(3) A direction under this section may be given orally; and where a constable is entitled to give a direction under this section to each of several persons outside, or in the vicinity of, any premises, he may give that direction to those persons by notifying them of his requirements either individually or all together.

(4) The requirements that may be imposed by a direction under this section include—

    (a) a requirement to leave the vicinity of the premises in question, and

    (b) a requirement to leave that vicinity and not to return to it within such period as the constable may specify, not being longer than 3 months;

and (in either case) the requirement to leave the vicinity may be to do so immediately or after a specified period of time.

(5) A direction under this section may make exceptions to any requirement imposed by the direction, and may make any such exception subject to such conditions as the constable giving the direction thinks fit; and those conditions may include—

    (a) conditions as to the distance from the premises in question at which, or otherwise as to the location where, persons who do not leave their vicinity must remain; and

    (b) conditions as to the number or identity of the persons who are authorised by the exception to remain in the vicinity of those premises.

(6) The power of a constable to give a direction under this section shall not include—

    (a) any power to give a direction at any time when there is a more **senior ranking** police officer at the scene; or

    (b) any power to direct a person to refrain from conduct that is lawful under section 220 of the Trade Union and Labour Relations (Consolidation) Act 1992 (right peacefully to picket a work place);

but it shall include power to vary or withdraw a direction previously given under this section.

Criminal Justice and Police Act 2001, s 42

Dwelling

Means any structure or part of a structure occupied as a person's home or as other living accommodation (whether the occupation is separate or shared with others) but does not include any part not so occupied, and for this purpose 'structure' includes a tent, caravan, vehicle, vessel, or other temporary or movable structure.

Harassment (see 7.11.1)

Explanatory notes

- A requirement in a direction under s 42(4)(b) means to leave that vicinity immediately or after a specified period of time and not to return within a specified period (no more than 3 months).

- Under the s 42A(1)(d)(i) offence a person falls within s 42A(2) if he is the resident, a person in the resident's dwelling, or a person in another dwelling in the vicinity of the resident's dwelling.
- Under s 42 a constable in attendance may give a direction to any person if that person is outside or in the vicinity of premises used by a resident as their dwelling, having reasonable grounds to believe that the person's presence amounts to harassment of the resident or is likely to cause them alarm or distress.
- Such a direction requires the person to whom it is given to do everything specified by the constable as necessary to prevent the harassment of and/or the causing of alarm or distress to, the resident.
- A direction under s 42 may include a requirement to leave—
  + the vicinity of the premises in question; and
  + not return to it within such period as the constable may specify, not being longer than 3 months.
- The references in s 42A(1)(c) and (d) to a person's presence refer to their presence either alone or together with any other person(s) also present.
- For s 42A offence a person ought to know that their presence is likely to result in the harassment of, or cause alarm or distress to, a resident if a reasonable person possessing the same information would think that their presence would likely have that effect.

Practical considerations

- Directions given under this section may be given orally, but it is important that the direction must be both heard and understood by the person concerned.
- If a direction is given to more than one person the constable may give it to them either individually or all together.
- The power of a constable to give a direction under s 42 does not include where there is a more **senior-ranking** officer present. If the senior officers are of the same rank, then the greater length of service in that rank determines who should give the direction.
- Similarly a constable cannot give a direction if the person(s) are exercising their right to peacefully picket a workplace.
- A constable may vary or withdraw any direction previously given.

 Summary   6 months

 Offence under s 42(7)

  3 months' imprisonment and/or a level 4 fine

  Offence under s 42(7A) or s 42A

  6 months' imprisonment and/or a level 4 fine

Links to alternative subjects and offences

7.12 **Offensive/False Messages**

The Malicious Communications Act 1988 concerns the sending and delivery of letters or other articles to cause distress or anxiety; the Communications Act 2003 regulates all types of media, including the sending of grossly offensive material via the public electronic communications network; whilst the offence of giving or causing to be given a false alarm of fire is dealt with by the Fire and Rescue Services Act 2004.

7.12.1 **Send letters etc intending to cause distress/anxiety**

Section 1 of the Malicious Communications Act 1988 creates offences relating to the sending of indecent, offensive, or threatening letters, electronic communications, or articles with intent to cause distress or anxiety to the recipient.

Offences

Any person who sends to another person—
(a) a letter, **electronic communication** or article of any description which conveys—
   (i) a message which is indecent or grossly offensive;
   (ii) a threat; **or**
   (iii) information which is false and known or believed to be false by the sender; or
(b) any article or electronic communication which is, in whole or part, of an indecent or **grossly offensive** nature,
is guilty of an offence if his purpose, or one of his purposes, in sending it is that it should, so far as falling within paragraph (a) or (b) above, cause distress or anxiety to the recipient or to any other person to whom he intends that it or its contents or nature should be communicated.

Malicious Communications Act 1988, s 1(1)

Points to prove

s 1(1)(a) offence

✓ sent a letter/an electronic communication/an article
✓ which conveys an indecent/grossly offensive message/threat/ false information which you knew/believed to be false
✓ for the purpose of causing distress/anxiety
✓ to the recipient/any other person
✓ to whom its contents/nature were intended to be communicated

---

7.12.1 Send letters etc intending to cause distress/anxiety

---

s 1(1)(b) offence

✓ sent to another person
✓ an article/an electronic communication
✓ wholly/partly of an indecent/grossly offensive nature
✓ for the purpose of causing distress/anxiety
✓ to the recipient/any other person
✓ to whom its contents/nature were intended to be communicated

---

Meanings

Electronic communication

Includes any—

• oral or other communication by means of an **electronic communications network**; and
• communication (however sent) that is in electronic form.

Electronic communications network

Means—

• a transmission system for the conveyance, by the use of electrical, magnetic, or electro-magnetic energy, of signals of any description; and
• such of the following as are used, by the person providing the system and in association with it, for the conveyance of the signals—
  ✦ apparatus comprised in the system;
  ✦ apparatus used for the switching or routing of the signals; and
  ✦ software and stored data.

Grossly offensive

This has to be judged by the standards of an open and just multi-racial society. Whether a message falls into this category depends not only on its content but on the circumstances in which the message has been sent (*DPP v Collins* [2005] EWHC 1308, HL).

Explanatory notes

• Sending includes delivering or transmitting and causing to be sent, delivered, or transmitted; 'sender' will be construed accordingly.
• Offence only requires that the communication be sent—not that the intended victim actually received it.

Defences

A person is not guilty of an offence by virtue of subsection (1)(a)(ii) above [threat] if he shows—

(a) that the threat was used to reinforce a demand made by him on reasonable grounds; and
(b) that he believed, and had reasonable grounds for believing, that the use of the threat was a proper means of reinforcing the demand.

Malicious Communications Act 1988, s 1(2)

Related cases

Connolly v DPP [2007] EWHC 237, QBD C telephoned chemist shops to ascertain whether they stocked the morning after pill, sending pictures of aborted foetuses to those that did. These pictures were indecent and grossly offensive with the purpose of causing distress or anxiety. Rights of expression under Art 9 or Art 10 (see **1.1**) did not excuse the distress and anxiety caused, and conviction was necessary in a democratic society. The words 'indecent' and 'grossly offensive' have their ordinary meaning.

Practical considerations

- As well as letters and telephone systems this offence would include emails, fax, text messages, facebook, twitter or other social media.
- What was the intended purpose of the defendant in sending the communication?
- If the intent is to cause the victim annoyance, inconvenience, or needless anxiety, then consider the offence under s 127 of the Communications Act 2003 (see **7.12.2**).
- If there has been more than one incident an offence under s 2 or s 2A of the Protection from Harassment Act 1997 may be appropriate (see **7.11.1** or **7.11.3**).
- If any threat used includes an unwarranted demand consider the more serious offence of blackmail (see **3.2.3**).
- Preserve the means or item that was used to deliver the message to the victim.
- The original message can be retrieved from phones or computers, the original letter or envelope can be fingerprinted or examined for DNA.

 Either way   None

 Summary: 6 months' imprisonment and/or a fine

Indictable: 2 years' imprisonment and/or a fine

7.12.2 Improper use of electronic public communications network

Section 127 of the Communications Act 2003 creates offences regarding improper use of a public electronic communications network.

7.12.2 Improper use of electronic public communications network

Offences

(1) A person is guilty of an offence if he—
   (a) sends by means of a **public electronic communications network** a message or other matter that is **grossly offensive** or of an indecent, obscene or **menacing** character; or
   (b) causes any such message or matter to be so sent.

(2) A person is guilty of an offence if, for the purpose of causing annoyance, inconvenience or needless anxiety to another, he—
   (a) sends by means of a public electronic communications network, a message that he knows to be false,
   (b) causes such a message to be sent, or
   (c) **persistently** makes use of a public electronic communications network.

Communications Act 2003, s 127

Points to prove

s 127(1) offence

✓ sent
✓ by means of a public electronic communications network
✓ a message/other matter
✓ being grossly offensive/indecent/obscene/menacing character
or
✓ caused such a message/matter to be so sent

s 127(2) offence

✓ to cause annoyance/inconvenience/needless anxiety to another
✓ sent by means of a public electronic communications network
✓ a message known to be false
or
✓ caused such a message to be sent
or
✓ persistently made use
✓ of a public electronic communications network

Meanings

Public electronic communications network

Means an **electronic communications network** provided wholly or mainly for the purpose of making electronic communications services available for use by members of the public.

Electronic communications network (see 7.12.1)

Grossly offensive (see 7.12.1)

Menacing

Means a message which conveys a threat; which seeks to create a fear in or through the recipient that something unpleasant is going to happen. Here the intended or likely effect on the recipient must ordinarily be a central factor (*DPP v Collins* [2005] EWHC 1308, HL).

Persistently

Includes any case in which the misuse is repeated on a sufficient number of occasions for it to be clear that the misuse represents a pattern of behaviour, or practice, or recklessness as to whether people suffer annoyance, inconvenience, or anxiety.

Explanatory notes

- 'Electronic communications network' covers current and future developments in communication technologies (eg telephone, computers (internet), satellites, mobile terrestrial networks, emails, text messages, fax, radio, and television broadcasting including cable TV networks).
- These offences do not apply to anything done in the course of providing a broadcasting service, such as a television programme; public teletext; digital television; radio programme; or sound provided by the BBC.
- Sections 128 to 130 empower OFCOM (Office of Communications) to enforce this Act to stop a person persistently misusing a public electronic communications network or services.

Related cases

R v Johnson [1996] 2 Cr App R 434, CA Making numerous obscene/offensive telephone calls can amount to a public nuisance (see **7.13.4**).

R v Ireland [1998] AC 147, HL and **R v Burstow [1997] 4 All ER 225, HL** Silent telephone calls which caused psychiatric injury to a victim was capable of being an AOABH (see **2.1**) or grievous bodily harm (see **2.3**) if they caused the victim to fear imminent violence on themselves. Expert evidence confirmed that the victims had suffered palpitations, breathing difficulties, cold sweats, anxiety, sleeplessness, dizziness, and stress.

Practical considerations

- These offences do not apply to a private/internal network. In these instances consider s 1 of the Malicious Communications Act 1988 (see **7.12.1**).
- Under subsection (1) there is no requirement to show any specific purpose or intent by the defendant.
- Consider s 1 of the Malicious Communications Act 1988 (see **7.12.1**) if the offence involves intent to cause the victim distress or anxiety.
- Also consider an offence under the Protection from Harassment Act 1997 (see **7.11**).

7.12.3 Giving/cause to be given false alarm of fire

- If threats or information relate to bombs, noxious substances, or the placing of dangerous articles, consider offences under the Anti-terrorism, Crime and Security Act 2001 and the Criminal Law Act 1977 (see **11.4.2**).
- Section 125 creates the offence of dishonestly obtaining an electronic communications service with intent to avoid the applicable payment.
- Possession or control of apparatus which may be used dishonestly to obtain an electronic communications service, or in connection with obtaining such a service is also an offence under s 126.
- A PND may be issued by a police officer, PCSO, or other accredited person for an offence under s 127(2) (see **7.1.1**).

| Summary | 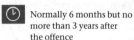 Normally 6 months but no more than 3 years after the offence |

 6 months' imprisonment and/or a fine

7.12.3 **Giving/cause to be given false alarm of fire**

Section 49 of the Fire and Rescue Services Act 2004 creates an offence of giving or causing to be given a false alarm of fire.

> **Offences**
>
> A person commits an offence if he **knowingly** gives or causes to be given a false alarm of fire to a person acting on behalf of a **fire and rescue authority**.
>
> Fire and Rescue Services Act 2004, s 49(1)

Points to prove

✓ knowingly
✓ gave/caused to be given
✓ a false alarm of fire
✓ to a person acting on behalf of a fire and rescue authority

---

Meanings

Knowingly (see **9.1.3**)

PND Penalty notice for disorder offences   **PCSO** Police community support officers

Fire and rescue authority

A fire and rescue authority for the county/county borough/area or the London Fire and Emergency Planning Authority.

Practical considerations

- The prosecutor may apply to the court for an **injunction** (see **7.13.1**) or a **criminal behaviour order** (see **7.13.2**).
- PND can be issued by a police officer/PCSO (see **7.1.1**).

 Summary 6 months

3 months' imprisonment and/or a level 4 fine

Links to alternative subjects and offences

7.13 Anti-Social Behaviour

Anti-social behaviour is dealt with in this chapter under the Anti-social Behaviour, Crime and Policing Act 2014, the Criminal Justice and Immigration Act 2008, and the Police Reform Act 2002.

7.13.1 Injunctions—application/breach

Section 1 of the Anti-social Behaviour, Crime and Policing Act 2014 allows a court to grant an injunction against a person involved in anti-social behaviour for the purpose of preventing further behaviour, and if there is a risk of violence, s 4 allows a court to attach a power of arrest to the injunction.

Power to grant injunctions

(1) A court may grant an injunction under this section against a person aged 10 or over ("the respondent") if two conditions are met.
(2) The **first condition** is that the court is satisfied, on the balance of probabilities, that the respondent has engaged or threatens to engage in **anti-social behaviour**.
(3) The **second condition** is that the court considers it just and convenient to grant the injunction for the purpose of preventing the respondent from engaging in anti-social behaviour.
(4) An injunction under this section may for the purpose of preventing the respondent from engaging in anti-social behaviour—
  (a) prohibit the respondent from doing anything described in the injunction;
  (b) require the respondent to do anything described in the injunction.

Anti-social Behaviour, Crime and Policing Act 2014, s 1

Meanings

Anti-social behaviour

Means conduct—
- that has caused, or is likely to cause, harassment, alarm or distress to any person;
- capable of causing nuisance or annoyance to a person in relation to that person's occupation of residential premises; or
- capable of causing **housing-related** nuisance or annoyance to any person.

Housing related

Means directly or indirectly relating to the housing management functions of a housing provider or a local authority.

Explanatory notes

- This civil injunction could be used to deal with anti-social nuisance or annoyance across a wide range of behaviours. This can include vandalism, public drunkenness, drug issues, aggressive begging, irresponsible dog owners, noisy or abusive behaviour or bullying against neighbours or others.
- If the county court, High Court (youth court if under 18) issues an injunction, this will prohibit the person from doing and require them to do what is described in the injunction, with the intention of addressing their anti-social behaviour.
- The injunction can provide protection for victims and communities and set a clear standard of behaviour in order to prevent escalation.
- If an injunction includes a requirement, it must specify the person responsible for ensuring compliance with the requirement. The person may be an individual or an organisation.
- Before including a requirement, the court must receive evidence about its suitability and enforceability. If two or more requirements are included, the court must consider their compatibility with each other.
- A respondent subject to a requirement must keep in touch with the person responsible for ensuring compliance, regarding any instructions given by that person, and notify that person of any change of address. These obligations are requirements of the injunction.
- These are civil proceedings, but the standard of proof is to the criminal standard.
- An injunction may be granted only on the application of: a local authority; a housing provider; the chief officer of police for a police area; the chief constable of the BT police; Transport for London; the Environment Agency; the Natural Resources Body for Wales; the Secretary of State; a Special Health Authority; or the Welsh Ministers.
- The court may vary or discharge an injunction under the application of the person who applied for the injunction, or the respondent.
- Under s 4 a court granting an injunction may attach a power of arrest to a prohibition or **requirement** of the injunction if the court thinks that—
  + the respondent has engaged or threatened to engage in violence against other persons, or
  + there is a significant risk of **harm** to other persons from the respondent.
- **Requirement** does not include the respondent participating in activities. **Harm** includes serious ill-treatment or abuse, whether physical or not.

Arrest without warrant—breach of injunction

Where a power of arrest is attached to a provision of an injunction under section 1, a constable may arrest the respondent without warrant if he or she has reasonable cause to suspect that the respondent is in breach of the provision.

Anti-social Behaviour, Crime and Policing Act 2014, s 9(1)

Practical considerations

- A person arrested under s 9(1) must, within 24 hours from the time of the arrest, be brought before the appropriate judge of the High Court or county court. Christmas Day, Good Friday, and any Sunday are to be disregarded when calculating the 24 hours.
- Examples of injunction requirements could be attending dog training or alcohol awareness classes, or mediation sessions with neighbours or victims.
- Prohibitions or requirements in the injunction can be for a fixed or indefinite period, but must have a specified time limit to a maximum of 12 months if the respondent is under 18.
- Although breach of an injunction is not a criminal offence, the breach procedure is to the criminal standard of proof. Breach is treated as contempt of court, and sanctions could be up to 2 years' imprisonment and/or unlimited fine or, if under 18, supervision, detention, curfew, or activity requirement.
- An injunction may have the effect of excluding the respondent from the place where they normally live ('the premises') only if the—
  + respondent is aged 18 or over;
  + injunction is granted on the application of a local authority, the chief officer of police for the area where the premises are located, or if the premises are owned or managed by a housing provider, that housing provider, and
  + court thinks that the respondent has used or threatened to use violence against other persons, or there is a significant risk of harm to other persons from the respondent.
- An ASBO under s 1 or 1B of the Crime and Disorder Act 1998 and a DBO under s 3 or 4 of the Violent Crime Reduction Act 2006 continue to be effective for as long as the order is in force.

7.13.2 Criminal behaviour orders—application/breach

Section 22 of the Anti-social Behaviour Crime and Policing Act 2014 empowers any criminal court to make a criminal behaviour order (CBO) against a person convicted of a criminal offence, whose behaviour has caused or was likely to cause harassment, alarm, or distress. It is a criminal offence under s 30 to breach such an order.

> ### Offences
>
> A person who without reasonable excuse—
> (a) does anything he or she is prohibited from doing by a **criminal behaviour order**, or
> (b) fails to do anything he or she is required to do by a criminal behaviour order, commits an offence.
>
> Anti-social Behaviour, Crime and Policing Act 2014, s 30(**1**)

Points to prove

✓ without reasonable excuse
✓ did anything prohibited from doing **or**
✓ failed to do anything required to do
✓ by criminal behaviour order

Meanings

Criminal behaviour order

(1) This section applies where a person ('the offender') is convicted of an offence.

(2) The court may make a criminal behaviour order against the offender if two conditions are met.

(3) The first condition is that the court is satisfied, beyond reasonable doubt, that the offender has engaged in behaviour that caused or was likely to cause harassment, alarm, or distress to any person.

(4) The second condition is that the court considers that making the order will help in preventing the offender from engaging in such behaviour.

(5) A **criminal behaviour order** is an order which, for the purpose of preventing the offender from engaging in such behaviour—

    (a) prohibits the offender from doing anything described in the order;

    (b) requires the offender to do anything described in the order.

Anti-social Behaviour, Crime and Policing Act 2014, s 22

Explanatory notes

• The CBO can deal with a wide range of anti-social behaviours following conviction for a criminal offence, for example, threatening violence against others, being aggressive due to alcohol or drugs in public or causing or threatening criminal damage.

• The court may make a CBO only if it is in addition to a sentence imposed in respect of the offence or if the offender has been conditionally discharged, and on application by the prosecution (CPS or local authority).

• The CBO will include prohibitions to stop the behaviour, but can include requirements to get the offender to address the underlying cause of their behaviour.

• If the offender is under the age of 18 the prosecution must find out the views of the local youth offending team (YOT) before applying for a CBO.

• A CBO that includes a requirement must specify the person responsible for ensuring compliance with the requirement. The person may be an individual or an organisation.

• Before including a requirement, the court must receive evidence about its suitability and enforceability. If two or more requirements are included, the court must consider their compatibility with each other.

• A respondent subject to a requirement must keep in touch with the person responsible for ensuring compliance, regarding any

instructions given by that person, and notify that person of any change of address. These obligations are requirements of the order.
- It is the duty of the responsible person to promote compliance, and if the offender has complied with all or failed to comply with any relevant requirement to inform the police and prosecution.
- The court may vary or discharge a CBO on the application of the offender or the prosecution.

Practical considerations

- Requirements of the CBO should aim to tackle the underlying cause of the behaviour and be made to suit the needs of each offender. They could include—
  - attendance at an anger management course;
  - youth mentoring;
  - substance misuse awareness sessions; and
  - a job readiness course to help an offender get employment.
- The duration of a CBO is a minimum of 2 years up to an indefinite period, but must be between 1 to 3 years if the offender is under 18.
- Consider making the public aware of the offender and the terms of the CBO. Each case should be decided carefully, whether it is necessary and proportionate, being balanced to re-assure the victim and inform the community so they can report any breaches.
- An ASBO under the Crime and Disorder Act 1998, s 1 will still be in force for as long as the order remains in force.

 Either way None

 Summary: 6 months' imprisonment and/or a fine

Indictable: 5 years' imprisonment and/or a fine

7.13.3 **Act in anti-social manner—fail to give name/address**

Section 50 of the Police Reform Act 2002 empowers a police officer to request the name and address of a person behaving in an anti-social manner, and creates an offence of failing to comply with that request.

Offences

Any person who—
(a) fails to give his name and address when **required** to do so **under subsection (1)**, or
(b) gives a false or inaccurate name or address in response to a requirement under that subsection,

is guilty of an offence.

Police Reform Act 2002, s 50(2)

Points to prove

✓ being a person whom a constable had reason to believe
✓ had been/was acting in anti-social manner
✓ failed or gave false/inaccurate details
✓ when required by the constable to provide their name and address

Meanings

Required under subsection (1)

If a constable in uniform has reason to believe that a person has been acting, or is acting, in an **anti-social manner**, he may require that person to give his name and address to the constable.

Anti-social manner (behaviour) (see **7.13.1**)

Explanatory notes

- A person who fails to give their name and address **or** provides a false or inaccurate name or address will commit an offence.
- This power also applies to a PCSO.

Practical considerations

A constable must be in uniform to make the request.

 Summary   6 months

 Level 3 fine

7.13.4 **Public nuisance**

Types of behaviour which used to be prosecuted as a 'public nuisance' are now covered by statute (eg food, noise, waste disposal, highways, animals, agriculture, medicines). However, 'public nuisance' is still an offence at common law.

Offences

A person is guilty of this offence if he—
(a) does an **act not warranted by law**, or
(b) omits to discharge a **legal duty**,
and the effect of the act or omission is to endanger the life, health, property, morals or comfort of the public, or to obstruct the public in the exercise or enjoyment of rights common to everyone.

Common Law

Points to prove

✓ by doing an act not warranted by law or omitting to discharge a legal duty
✓ caused
✓ a public nuisance

Meanings

Act not warranted by law

Means illegal conduct, but does not have to be a specific offence covered by legislation.

Legal duty

Means a duty under any enactment, instrument, or rule of law.

Explanatory notes

- This offence is described as 'a nuisance that is so widespread in its range or so indiscriminate in its effect that it would not be reasonable to expect any one person to take proceedings on their own responsibility to put a stop to it, but that it should be taken on the responsibility of the community at large'.
- The purpose that the defendant has in mind when they commit the act is immaterial if the probable result is to affect the public as described in the offence.
- Where some work is done by an employee in a manner that causes a nuisance it is no defence for the employer to claim that they did not personally supervise the work and had instructed that it be carried out in a different way.

Related cases

R v Rimmington, R v Goldstein [2005] UKHL 63, HL If a statutory offence was made out, with possible defences, mode of trial, and maximum penalty, then prosecution should be under statute and not common law where the potential penalty was unlimited.

R v Shorrock [1993] 3 All ER 917, CA Defendant leased a field at his farm for a weekend which was used for an acid house party/rave. S was away during the event and denied any knowledge that a public nuisance would be committed on his land. The farmer was held responsible for this nuisance which S knew or ought to have known about; because the means of knowledge were available, so was the consequences of what S did or omitted to do.

R v Johnson [1996] 2 Cr App R 434, CA Over a number of years, J used the public telephone system to cause nuisance annoyance, harassment, alarm, and distress to a number of women by making hundreds of obscene calls. The cumulative effect of all the calls was a public nuisance, as the number of individuals affected was sufficient for his actions to be public.

Practical considerations

- This common law offence is still important because of its flexibility in adapting to those areas not covered by specific legislation.
- For extreme acts of unpleasantness or lewdness consider offences under the Sexual Offences Act 2003 (see **Chapter 6**) or the common law offence of outraging public decency (see **6.7.2**).
- Conspiracy to commit this offence is contrary to s 1(1) of the Criminal Law Act 1977.

 Either way None

 Summary: 6 months' imprisonment and/or a fine
Indictment: Imprisonment and/or a fine

7.13.5 Closure of premises (nuisance/disorder)

Section 76 of the Anti-social Behaviour, Crime and Policing Act 2014 gives police powers to close premises by issuing a closure notice if satisfied that the use of the premises has resulted or is likely to result in nuisance to members of the public or disorder near those premises, and the notice will prevent the nuisance or disorder from continuing, recurring, or occurring. Section 86 deals with offences regarding a closure notice/order.

Offences

(1) A person who without reasonable excuse remains on or enters premises in contravention of a **closure notice** (including a **notice continued in force under section 81**) commits an offence.
(2) A person who without reasonable excuse remains on or enters premises in contravention of a **closure order** commits an offence.
(3) A person who without reasonable excuse obstructs a **person acting under section 79** or **85(1)** commits an offence.

Anti-social Behaviour, Crime and Policing Act 2014, s 86

Points to prove

Closure notice s 86(1)

✓ without reasonable excuse
✓ remained on/entered premises
✓ in contravention of a closure notice or s 81 continue notice

Closure order s 86(2)

✓ without reasonable excuse
✓ remained on/entered premises
✓ in contravention of a closure order

Obstruction s 86(3)

✓ without reasonable excuse
✓ obstructed person
✓ acting under
✓ s 79 (service notice)/s 85(1) (order enforcement)

Meanings

Premises

Includes any—
- land or other place (whether closed or not);
- outbuildings that are, or are used as, part of premises.

Closure notice (power to issue)

(1) A police officer of at least the rank of inspector, or the **local authority**, may issue a closure notice if satisfied on reasonable grounds—
    (a) that the use of particular premises has resulted, or (if the notice is not issued) is likely soon to result, in nuisance to members of the public, or
    (b) that there has been, or (if the notice is not issued) is likely soon to be, disorder near those premises associated with the use of those premises,

and that the notice is necessary to prevent the nuisance or disorder from continuing, recurring or occurring.

(2) A closure notice is a notice prohibiting access to the premises for a period specified in the notice.

For the **maximum period**, see section 77.

(3) A closure notice may prohibit access —
- (a) by all persons except those specified, or by all persons except those of a specified description;
- (b) at all times, or at all times except those specified;
- (c) in all circumstances, or in all circumstances except those specified.

(4) A closure notice may not prohibit access by—
- (a) people who habitually live on the premises, or
- (b) the owner of the premises,

and accordingly they must be specified under subsection (3)(a).

(5) A closure notice must—
- (a) identify the premises;
- (b) explain the effect of the notice;
- (c) state that failure to comply with the notice is an offence;
- (d) state that an application will be made under section 80 for a closure order;
- (e) specify when and where the application will be heard;
- (f) explain the effect of a closure order;
- (g) give information about the names of, and means of contacting, persons and organisations in the area that provide advice about housing and legal matters.

(6) A closure notice may be issued only if reasonable efforts have been made to inform—
- (a) people who live on the premises (whether habitually or not), and
- (b) any person who has control of or responsibility for the premises or who has an interest in them,

that the notice is going to be issued.

(7) Before issuing a closure notice the police officer or local authority must ensure that any body or individual the officer or authority thinks appropriate has been consulted.

Anti-social Behaviour, Crime and Policing Act 2014, s 76

Local authority

In England: district council, county council (for area with no district council), London borough council, Common Council of the City of London, or the Council of the Isles of Scilly.

In Wales: a county council or a county borough council.

Maximum period (s 77—Duration of closure notices)

- The maximum period that may be specified in a closure notice is 24 hours. An extension notice may extend this for up to a further 24 hours, by a superintendent (issued by police) or CEO of the authority (issued by local authority).

7.13.5 Closure of premises (nuisance/disorder)

- The maximum period of a notice issued by a superintendent or CEO is 48 hours. In calculating when the period of 48 hours ends, Christmas day is to be disregarded.

The local authority CEO means the head of the paid service of the authority designated under s 4 of the Local Government and Housing Act 1989.

Notice continued in force under s 81

Where application has been made to a magistrates' court under s 80 for a closure order. If the court does not make a closure order it may instead order that the closure notice shall continue for a specified further period (maximum 48 hours), if satisfied that conditions for making a s 76 notice are met, and that the continuation of the notice is necessary to prevent the nuisance or disorder from continuing, recurring or occurring.

Similarly the court may adjourn the application hearing for up to 14 days to enable: the occupier of the premises, the person in control of or responsible for the premises, or any other person with an interest in the premises, to show why a closure order should not be made. If adjourned, the closure notice will continue in force until the end of the adjournment period.

Closure order (power of court to make order)

(1) Whenever a closure notice is issued an application must be made to a magistrates' court for a closure order (unless the notice has been cancelled under section 78).

(2) An application for a closure order must be made—
   (a) by a constable, if the closure notice was issued by a police officer;
   (b) by the authority that issued the closure notice, if the notice was issued by a local authority.

(3) The application must be heard by the magistrates' court not later than 48 hours after service of the closure notice.

(4) In calculating when the period of 48 hours ends, Christmas Day is to be disregarded.

(5) The court may make a closure order if it is satisfied—
   (a) that a person has engaged, or (if the order is not made) is likely to engage, in disorderly, offensive or criminal behaviour on the premises, or
   (b) that the use of the premises has resulted, or (if the order is not made) is likely to result, in serious nuisance to members of the public, or
   (c) that there has been, or (if the order is not made) is likely to be, disorder near those premises associated with the use of those premises,
   and that the order is necessary to prevent the behaviour, nuisance, or disorder from continuing, recurring, or occurring.

(6) A closure order is an order prohibiting access to the premises for a period specified in the order. The period may not exceed 3 months.

(7) A closure order may prohibit access—
   (a) by all persons, or by all persons except those specified, or by all persons except those of a specified description;

    (b) at all times, or at all times except those specified;

    (c) in all circumstances, or in all circumstances except those specified.

(8) A closure order—

    (a) may be made in respect of the whole or any part of the premises;

    (b) may include provision about access to a part of the building or structure of which the premises form part.

(9) The court must notify the relevant licensing authority if it makes a closure order in relation to premises in respect of which a **premises licence** is in force.

Anti-social Behaviour, Crime and Policing Act 2014, s 80

Premises licence

Means a licence granted under Part 3 of the Licensing Act 2003, in respect of any premises, which authorises the premises to be used for one or more licensable activities.

Person acting under s 79 (service of notice)

(1) A closure notice, an extension notice, a cancellation notice, or a variation notice must be served by—

    (a) a constable, in the case of a notice issued by a police officer;

    (b) a representative of the authority that issued the notice, in the case of a notice issued by a local authority.

(2) The constable or local authority representative must if possible—

    (a) fix a copy of the notice to at least one prominent place on the premises,

    (b) fix a copy of the notice to each normal means of access to the premises,

    (c) fix a copy of the notice to any outbuildings that appear to the constable or representative to be used with or as part of the premises,

    (d) give a copy of the notice to at least one person who appears to the constable or representative to have control of or responsibility for the premises, and

    (e) give a copy of the notice to the people who live on the premises and to any person who does not live there but was informed (under section 76(6)) that the notice was going to be issued.

(3) If the constable or **local authority representative** reasonably believes, at the time of serving the notice, that there are persons occupying another part of the building or other structure in which the premises are situated whose access to that part will be impeded if a closure order is made under section 80, the constable or representative must also if possible serve the notice on those persons.

(4) The constable or local authority representative may enter any premises, using reasonable force if necessary, for the purposes of complying with subsection (2)(a).

Anti-social Behaviour, Crime and Policing Act 2014, s 79

7.13.5 Closure of premises (nuisance/disorder)

Local authority representative

Means an employee of the authority, or a person, or employee of a person, acting on behalf of the authority.

Person acting under s 85(1) (enforcement of closure orders)

An **authorised person** may—
(a) enter premises in respect of which a closure order is in force;
(b) do anything necessary to secure the premises against entry.

Anti-social Behaviour, Crime and Policing Act 2014, s 85(1)

Authorised person

In relation to a closure order made on the application of—
- a constable, means a constable or a person authorised by the chief officer of police for the area in which the premises are situated;
- a local authority, means a person authorised by that authority.

Explanatory notes

- The closure notice is a fast, flexible power that allows the police or council to protect victims and communities by quickly closing premises that are causing, or likely to cause nuisance or disorder.
- A closure notice is issued by the police/council in the first instance, then if required a closure order can be applied for through the courts.
- The closure notice can close premises for up to 48 hours, but cannot stop the owner or those who habitually live there accessing the premises. Whereas an order can close the premises for up to six months and can restrict all access.
- Both the notice and order can cover any land or any other place, whether enclosed or not including residential, business, non-business and licensed premises.
- Under s 78, where a closure notice is in force and the police/authority decide to cancel the notice, they can issue a cancellation notice (all the premises) or variation notice (if part of the premises). The court should then be informed prior to the hearing for the closure order.

Defences

Having a reasonable excuse for remaining on or entering premises in contravention of a closure notice/order or obstructing a person under s 79 or 85(1) (as the case may be).

Anti-social Behaviour, Crime and Policing Act 2014, s 86

Practical considerations

- Consultation is required as part of the closure notice process. This should include the victim, others that may be affected, community representatives, other organisations and bodies, the police or local council (if not the issuing body), or others using the premises. Consider those who use the premises to access other premises, not subject to the closure notice.

- The method of consultation will depend on the situation and urgency. A record must be kept of those consulted if the case is challenged in court.
- Include in the closure notice the following information—
  + identify the premises;
  + explain the effect of the notice;
  + state that failure to comply with the notice is an offence;
  + state that an application will be made for a closure order;
  + specify when and where the application will be heard;
  + explain the effect of the closure order; and
  + contact details of providers giving advice about housing and legal matters.
- A criminal offence is committed when a person, without reasonable excuse—
  + remains on or enters premises in contravention of a closure notice/ order;
  + obstructs a police officer or local council employee who is: serving a closure notice, cancellation notice or variation notice; entering the premises; or securing the premises.
- A closure notice cannot be appealed. Although a closure order can be appealed to the Crown Court within 21 days from the date of the decision to which the appeal relates.
- Notices under s 1 and s 11A of the Anti-social Behaviour Act 2003; orders under ss 2, 11B, and 40 of the 2003 Act; orders under s 161 and s 165(2)(b), (c), or (d) of the Licensing Act 2003, will continue to be effective for as long as the notice or order is in force.

PCSO

 Summary   6 months

 s 86(2)—6 months' imprisonment and/or a fine

s 86(1) or (3)—3 months' imprisonment and/or a fine

7.13.6 **Causing nuisance/disturbance on NHS premises**

Sections 119 and 120 of the Criminal Justice and Immigration Act 2008 create both the offence of causing a nuisance or disturbance to NHS staff

7.13.6 Causing nuisance/disturbance on NHS premises

on NHS premises, and power to remove a person suspected of committing or having committed the offence.

Offences

(1) A person commits an offence if—
   (a) the person causes, without reasonable excuse and while on **NHS premises**, a nuisance or disturbance to an **NHS staff member** who is working there or is otherwise there in connection with work,
   (b) the person refuses, without reasonable excuse, to leave the NHS premises when asked to do so by a constable or an NHS staff member, and
   (c) the person is not on the NHS premises for the purpose of obtaining medical advice, treatment or care for himself or herself.

Criminal Justice and Immigration Act 2008, s 119

Power to remove

(1) If a constable reasonably suspects that a person is committing or has committed an offence under section 119, the constable may remove the person from the NHS premises concerned.
(2) If an authorised officer reasonably suspects that a person is committing or has committed an offence under section 119, the authorised officer may—
   (a) remove the person from the NHS premises concerned, or
   (b) authorise an appropriate NHS staff member to do so.
(3) Any person removing another person from NHS premises under this section may use reasonable force (if necessary).
(4) An **authorised officer** cannot remove a person under this section or authorise another person to do so if the authorised officer has reason to believe that—
   (a) the person to be removed requires medical advice, treatment or care for himself or herself, or
   (b) the removal of the person would endanger the person's physical or mental health.

Criminal Justice and Immigration Act 2008, s 120

Points to prove

✓ while on NHS premises
✓ other than for the purpose of obtaining medical advice or treatment/care for yourself
✓ caused without reasonable excuse while on those premises
✓ a nuisance **or**
✓ a disturbance to an NHS staff member who is working there **or**

✓ was otherwise there in connection with work
✓ refused without reasonable excuse to leave the premises
✓ when asked to do so by a constable/NHS staff member

Meanings

NHS premises

Means—
• any hospital vested in, or managed by, a **relevant NHS body**;
• any building or other structure, or **vehicle**, associated with the hospital and situated on **hospital grounds** (whether or not vested in, or managed by, a relevant NHS body), and
• the hospital grounds.

Relevant NHS body

Means—
• a National Health Service trust (see National Health Service Act 2006), all or most of whose hospitals, establishments, and facilities are situated in England;
• a NHS foundation trust (England).

Vehicle

Includes an air ambulance.

Hospital grounds

Means land in the vicinity of a hospital and associated with it.

NHS staff member

Means a person employed by a relevant English body, or otherwise working for such a body (whether as or on behalf of a contractor, as a volunteer, or otherwise).

Authorised officer

Means any NHS staff member authorised by a relevant NHS body to exercise the powers which are conferred by this section on an authorised officer in respect of NHS premises.

Explanatory notes

• For the purposes of s 119, a person ceases to be on NHS premises for the purpose of obtaining medical advice, treatment, or care for him/herself, once the person has received the advice, treatment, or care, or if the person has been refused the advice, treatment, or care during the last 8 hours.
• This offence addresses behaviour which disrupts NHS staff in the performance of their duties. There is no requirement that the delivery of healthcare is impeded.
• This offence is quite restricted, as it does not apply to a person who is on the premises for the purpose of obtaining medical advice, treatment, or care, patients, and those attending for consultations, to collect medication or test results, or convalescing after treatment.

7.13.6 Causing nuisance/disturbance on NHS premises

Practical considerations

- Although the offence/power relates to England and Wales, it is currently (March 2015) only in force for England.
- A nuisance or disturbance can include any form of non-physical behaviour which breaches the peace, such as verbal aggression or intimidating gestures towards NHS staff.
- A person will not commit the offence if s/he has a reasonable excuse. Behaviour consequential to the receipt of upsetting news or bereavement may, for example, constitute a reasonable excuse.
- The nuisance or disturbance must be towards a NHS staff member, rather than any other person. The NHS staff member must either be working at the premises or be there for some other purpose relating to their work, such as walking between buildings or taking a break.
- Where NHS bodies wish to have the option to exercise the power of removal without recourse to police, they will need to authorise a member of staff (known as the '**authorised officer**') to exercise the powers of removal. Any person exercising the power of removal may use reasonable force if necessary.

 Summary   6 months

 Level 3 fine

Links to alternative subjects and offences

7.14 Vehicles Causing Annoyance

Section 59 of the Police Reform Act 2002 empowers police officers to seize motor vehicles used in a way as to cause alarm, distress, or annoyance to members of the public. The Police (Retention and Disposal of Motor Vehicles) Regulations 2002 govern how such seized vehicles should be retained and disposed of.

7.14.1 Vehicles used in a manner causing alarm, distress, or annoyance

Section 59 of the Police Reform Act 2002 concerns the use of vehicles in a manner that causes alarm, distress, or annoyance to members of the public.

Police powers

(1) Where a constable in uniform has reasonable grounds for believing that a **motor vehicle** is being used on any occasion in a manner which—
   (a) contravenes section 3 or 34 of the Road Traffic Act 1988 (careless and inconsiderate **driving** and prohibition of off-road driving), **and**
   (b) is causing, or is likely to cause, alarm, distress or annoyance to members of the public,
   he shall have the powers set out in subsection (3).

(2) A constable in uniform shall also have the powers set out in subsection (3) where he has reasonable grounds for believing that a motor vehicle has been used on any occasion in a manner falling within subsection (1).

(3) Those powers are—
   (a) power, if the motor vehicle is moving, to order the person driving it to stop the vehicle;
   (b) power to seize and remove the motor vehicle;
   (c) power, for the purposes of exercising a power falling within paragraph (a) or (b), to enter any **premises** on which he has reasonable grounds for believing the motor vehicle to be;
   (d) power to use reasonable force, if necessary, in the exercise of any power conferred by any of paragraphs (a) to (c).

(4) A constable shall not seize a motor vehicle in the exercise of the powers conferred on him by this section unless—
   (a) he has warned the person appearing to him to be the person whose use falls within subsection (1) that he will seize it, if that use continues or is repeated; and
   (b) it appears to him that the use has continued or been repeated after the warning.

(5) Subsection (4) does not require a warning to be given by a constable on any occasion on which he would otherwise have the power to seize a motor vehicle under this section if—

  (a) the circumstances make it impracticable for him to give the warning;

  (b) the constable has already on that occasion given a warning under that subsection in respect of any use of that motor vehicle or of another motor vehicle by that person or any other person;

  (c) the constable has reasonable grounds for believing that such a warning has been given on that occasion otherwise than by him; or

  (d) the constable has reasonable grounds for believing that the person whose use of that motor vehicle on that occasion would justify the seizure is a person to whom a warning under that subsection has been given (whether or not by that constable or in respect of the same vehicle or the same or a similar use) on a previous occasion in the previous twelve months.

(7) Subsection (3)(c) does not authorise entry into a **private dwelling house**.

Police Reform Act 2002, s 59

Offences

A person who fails to comply with an order under subsection (3)(a) is guilty of an offence.

Police Reform Act 2002, s 59(6)

Points to prove

✓ failed to stop
✓ a moving vehicle
✓ on the order of a police constable in uniform
✓ having reasonable grounds for believing
✓ that the vehicle was being used in a manner given in s 59(1)

Meanings

Motor vehicle

Any mechanically propelled vehicle, whether or not it is intended or adapted for use on roads (see **10.1.3**).

Driving (see **10.1.4**)

Private dwelling house

Does not include any garage or other structure occupied with the dwelling house, or any land appurtenant to the dwelling house.

Explanatory notes

- An offence is committed if the driver of the moving motor vehicle fails to stop the vehicle when ordered to do so by a constable in uniform.
- A constable in uniform has the power to seize the vehicle but only after warning the person. If, after the warning has been given, the driving continues or is repeated then the vehicle can be seized.
- The requirement to give the warning does not apply where it is impracticable to do so or where it has been given on a previous occasion in the previous 12 months.
- The powers under this section cannot be exercised unless the driver is **both** using the vehicle anti-socially **and** is driving contrary to s 3 (careless and inconsiderate driving, see **10.6.1**) or s 34 (prohibition of off-road driving, see **10.23**) of the Road Traffic Act 1988.

Practical considerations

- The warning under s 59(4) **must** be given and ignored before the vehicle can be seized (see **7.14.2**). Therefore it is important that the warning is both heard and understood.
- A warning given within the last 12 months does not have to have been given in respect of the same vehicle.
- Where a motor vehicle is seized a seizure notice must be given to the person who appears to be the owner of the vehicle.
- A previous warning given on the same occasion need not have been given by the same constable nor does it have to have been given to the same person **or** in respect of the same vehicle. It could have been given to the same person using another vehicle or to a different person using the same vehicle. This covers situations where people use their vehicles anti-socially and swap them around.
- Consider the dispersal powers or powers under a PSPO (see **7.15**) or the public nuisance offence (see **7.13.4**).

 Summary   6 months

 Level 3 fine

7.14.2 **Retention/disposal of seized motor vehicle**

The Police (Retention and Disposal of Motor Vehicles) Regulations 2002 relate to vehicles seized under s 59 of the Police Reform Act 2002 (see **7.14.1**).

Power

A **relevant motor vehicle** shall be passed into and remain in the custody of a constable or other person authorised under this regulation by the chief officer of the police force for the area in which the vehicle was seized ('the authority') until—

(a) **the authority** permit it to be removed from their custody by a person appearing to them to be the owner of the vehicle; or

(b) it has been disposed of under these Regulations.

Police (Retention and Disposal of Motor Vehicles) Regulations 2002, reg 3(1)

Meanings

Relevant motor vehicle

As seized and removed under s 59(3)(b) of the Police Reform Act 2002 (see **7.14.1**).

The authority

Means a constable or other person authorised by the chief officer.

Explanatory notes

- A relevant motor vehicle will pass into and remain in the custody of a constable or other person authorised under this regulation by the chief officer of police in the area in which it was seized, until the authority permits a person appearing to them to be the owner of it to remove it, or it has been disposed of under these regulations.
- While the vehicle is in the custody of the authority, they must take any necessary steps for its safe keeping.
- As soon as reasonably practicable after taking a vehicle into their custody the authority must take reasonable steps to serve a seizure notice on the person who is, or appears to be, the owner, except where the vehicle has been released from their custody.
- If a person satisfies the authority that they are the owner of the vehicle and pays the charges accrued concerning its removal and retention, the authority shall permit them to remove it from custody.
- A person otherwise liable to pay charges concerning the removal and retention of the vehicle will not be liable if they were not the user when it was seized under s 59 and they did not know of its use leading to the seizure, had not consented to such use, and could not, by reasonable steps, have prevented such use.

- Where it has not been possible to serve a seizure notice on the relevant person, or such a notice has been served and the vehicle has not been released from their custody under these regulations, they may dispose of the vehicle in accordance with reg 7.
- The authority may not dispose of the vehicle under reg 7—
  (a) during the period of 14 days, starting with the date of seizure;
  (b) if the 14 day period has expired, until after the deadline specified in the seizure notice;
  (c) if (a) or (b) does not apply, during the period of 7 working days starting with the date on which the vehicle is claimed.
- Where the authority disposes of the vehicle by way of selling, it must pay the net proceeds of the sale to any person who, within a year of the sale, satisfies them that they were the vehicle owner at the time of the sale.

Practical considerations

- A seizure notice may be served by personal delivery to the person addressed in it, by leaving it at their usual or last known address or by registered delivery to their last known address.
- If the owner is a body corporate (eg a company) the notice must be served or sent to the company secretary or clerk at its registered office.
- The seizure notice must inform the owner that they have 7 working days to collect the vehicle and that charges are payable from when the vehicle is claimed by the owner under reg 5.

Links to alternative subjects and offences

7.15 Dispersal Powers/Public Spaces Protection Orders

7.15.1 Dispersal powers

Sections 34 and 35 of the Anti-social Behaviour, Crime and Policing Act 2014 provide, if the proper authority is in place, police powers to direct a person in a public place, to leave the area for up to 48 hours, and return persons under the age of 16 to their place of residence or a place of safety. Failure to comply is an offence under s 39.

Authorisation

(1) A police officer of at least the rank of inspector may authorise the use in a **specified** locality, during a specified period of not more than 48 hours, of the powers given by section 35.
Specified means specified in the authorisation.

(2) An officer may give such an authorisation only if satisfied on reasonable grounds that the use of those powers in the locality during that period may be necessary for the purpose of removing or reducing the likelihood of—
   (a) members of the public in the locality being harassed, alarmed or distressed, or
   (b) the occurrence in the locality of crime or disorder.

(3) In deciding whether to give such an authorisation an officer must have particular regard to the rights of freedom of expression and freedom of assembly set out in articles 10 and 11 of the **Convention**.

(4) An authorisation under this section—
   (a) must be in writing,
   (b) must be signed by the officer giving it, and
   (c) must specify the grounds on which it is given.

Anti-social Behaviour, Crime and Policing Act 2014, s 34

Directions to exclude person

(1) If the **conditions** in subsections (2) and (3) are met and an authorisation is in force under section 34, a constable in uniform may direct a person who is in a **public place** in the locality specified in the authorisation—
   (a) to leave the locality (or part of the locality), and
   (b) not to return to the locality (or part of the locality) for the period specified in the direction ('**the exclusion period**').

(2) The **first condition** is that the constable has reasonable grounds to suspect that the behaviour of the person in the locality has contributed or is likely to contribute to—

(a) members of the public in the locality being harassed, alarmed or distressed, or

(b) the occurrence in the locality of crime or disorder.

(3) The **second condition** is that the constable considers that giving a **direction** to the person is necessary for the purpose of removing or reducing the likelihood of the events mentioned in subsection (2)(a) or (b).

(4) The **exclusion period** may not exceed 48 hours.

The period may expire after (as long as it begins during) the period specified in the authorisation under section 34.

(5) A **direction** under this section—

(a) must be given in writing, unless that is not reasonably practicable;

(b) must specify the area to which it relates;

(c) may impose requirements as to the time by which the person must leave the area and the manner in which the person must do so (including the route).

(6) The constable must (unless it is not reasonably practicable) tell the person to whom the direction is given that failing without reasonable excuse to comply with the direction is an offence.

(7) If the constable reasonably believes that the person to whom the direction is given is under the age of 16, the constable may remove the person to a place where the person lives or a place of safety.

(8) Any constable may withdraw or vary a direction under this section; but a variation must not extend the duration of a direction beyond 48 hours from when it was first given.

(9) Notice of a withdrawal or variation of a direction—

(a) must be given to the person to whom the direction was given, unless that is not reasonably practicable, and

(b) if given, must be given in writing unless that is not reasonably practicable.

Anti-social Behaviour, Crime and Policing Act 2014, s 35

Directions to surrender property

(1) A constable who gives a person a direction under section 35 may also direct the person to surrender to the constable any item in the person's possession or control that the constable reasonably believes has been used or is likely to be used in behaviour that harasses, alarms or distresses members of the public.

(2) A direction under this section must be given in writing, unless that is not reasonably practicable.

(3) A constable who gives a person a direction under this section must (unless it is not reasonably practicable)—

(a) tell the person that failing without reasonable excuse to comply with the direction is an offence, and

(b) give the person information in writing about when and how the person may recover the surrendered item.

(4) The surrendered item must not be returned to the person before the end of the **exclusion period**.

(5) If after the end of that period the person asks for the item to be returned, it must be returned (unless there is power to retain it under another enactment).

(6) But if it appears to a constable that the person is under the age of 16 and is not accompanied by a parent or other responsible adult, the item may be retained until the person is so accompanied.

(7) If the person has not asked for the return of the item before the end of the period of 28 days beginning with the day on which the direction was given, the item may be destroyed or otherwise disposed of.

Anti-social Behaviour, Crime and Policing Act 2014, s 37

Offences

(1) A person given a direction under section 35 who fails without reasonable excuse to comply with it commits an offence.

(3) A person given a direction under section 37 who fails without reasonable excuse to comply with it commits an offence.

Anti-social Behaviour, Crime and Policing Act 2014, s 39

Points to prove
✓ failed
✓ without reasonable excuse
✓ to comply with a direction given under s 35 or s 37

Meanings

Convention (see 1.1)

Public place

Means a place to which at the material time the public or a section of the public has access, on payment or otherwise, as of right or by virtue of express or implied permission.

Exclusion period (see s 35(1)(b) 'Directions to exclude person' above)

Explanatory notes

- If there is likely to be anti-social behaviour, crime, or disorder in an area and it may be necessary to use the dispersal power, an inspector can authorise officers to use the power for a period of up to 48 hours.
- If a person's behaviour is causing or likely to cause harassment, alarm or distress, or crime or disorder in the public place specified in the authorisation, then under s 35 a police officer or suitable designated PCSO (see 11.1) can issue a direction for that person to leave the area.
- A direction can be issued to anyone over the age of 10, and if they are under 16 can be taken home or to a place of safety.

- The direction must be given in writing, unless impracticable to do so. A written notice must specify the relevant area, when they must leave the area, and the route they must take. Any item possessed/under control of that person can be confiscated under s 37. The person must also be told that failure to comply with the direction (excluded from area and/or surrender of such item), without reasonable excuse, is an offence.
- The information provided in the direction should be as clear as possible, ensuring that the person has understood it. If the direction is given verbally a written record of it must be kept in order to enforce it in the event that it is breached, and to be able to monitor use of the power. The written notice can be admitted in evidence in breach proceedings.

Defences

Having a reasonable excuse for failing to comply with a direction given under s 35 (exclude from area) or s 37 (surrender property).

Anti-social Behaviour, Crime and Policing Act 2014, s 39

Practical considerations

- When authorising the dispersal power, the inspector (or above) must have regard to Arts 10 and 11 of the ECHR which provides for the right for freedom of expression and freedom of assembly. Ensure that this power is used proportionately and reasonably so it is compatible with the Human Rights Act 1998 (see **1.1**).
- When pre-authorising or authorising an area, the locality should be clearly defined as a specific geographic location, for example by listing the streets to which it applies or the streets which form the boundary of the area. The authorisation should not cover an area larger than necessary.
- This power can only be used in the specific location authorised, so if the behaviour occurs outside the authorised area, the inspector (or above) will have to increase the area or the officer cannot issue the dispersal.
- The exclusion period may not exceed 48 hours, and it may be that this period expires after (as long as it begins during) the period specified in the authorisation under s 34.
- The police officer or PCSO can require the person given the direction to hand over items causing or likely to cause anti-social behaviour under s 37. These items could be alcohol, fireworks, offensive material, noisy equipment, eggs or spray paint, for example.
- An officer/PCSO can confiscate an item handed over to them, but there is no power to seize the item, although they will commit an offence under s 39 if they do not hand over the item when directed to do so.
- Surrendered items can be collected at the expiry of the direction period, but if the item is not collected within 28 days it can be

destroyed or disposed of. A person under the age of 16 can be required to be accompanied by a parent/responsible adult to collect the item; thus ensuring that the adult is made aware of the incident to encourage parental responsibility.

- Section 36 places restrictions, so that a direction cannot be given to someone engaged in lawful conduct: peaceful picketing (Trade Union and Labour Relations (Consolidation) Act 1992, s 220) or taking part in a public procession (Public Order Act 1986, s 11). In addition, the direction cannot restrict access to where they live or work, or prevent them from attending court/tribunal or education/training, or for receiving medical treatment during the direction time period.

- A person who is given a direction and feels they have been incorrectly dealt with should speak to the duty inspector at the local police station. Details should be given to the person on the written notice.

- This dispersal power is a more flexible tool for officers/PCSOs to deal with anti-social behaviour, crime, and disorder. This is not only when they have occurred or are occurring, but when they are likely to occur and in any locality, thus extending the capability of the police/PCSOs to prevent incidents before they happen.

- Dispersal powers under s 27 of the Violent Crime Reduction Act 2006 and s 30 of the Anti-social Behaviour Act 2003 will continue to have effect for as long as they are in force.

- Helpful features of this power under the 2014 Act are that—
  + There is no requirement to pre-designate a 'dispersal zone', it can now be used in any locality forthwith;
  + Publicity is no longer required to highlight an authorisation;
  + An individual can be dispersed rather than requiring two or more people to be engaged in the offending behaviour;
  + The power can be used across a broader spectrum of anti-social behaviour, crime, and disorder;
  + There is an additional power to confiscate items associated with the behaviour;
  + The exclusion period has been extended to a maximum of 48 hours;
  + There is no need to establish the person's age as the power applies to a person who appears to be aged 10 or over;
  + The requirement to keep a written record of when the power is used enables effective enforcement of any breach and will be evidentially important for prosecution of breaches.

 Summary 6 months

s 39(1)—3 months' imprisonment or a level 4 fine

s 39(3)—Level 2 fine

7.15.2 **Public spaces protection orders (PSPOs)**

Section 59 of the Anti-social Behaviour, Crime and Policing Act 2014 provides the local authority (LA) with power to make a public spaces protection order (PSPO) with regard to activities in a public place that has a detrimental effect on the quality of life of those in the locality. It is an offence to fail to comply with a PSPO, breach can also be dealt with by a fixed penalty notice (FPN) under s 68.

Power to make orders

(1) A **local authority** may make a public spaces protection order if satisfied on reasonable grounds that two conditions are met.

(2) The **first condition** is that—
 (a) activities carried on in a **public place** within the authority's area have had a detrimental effect on the quality of life of those in the locality, or
 (b) it is likely that activities will be carried on in a public place within that area and that they will have such an effect.

(3) The **second condition** is that the effect, or likely effect, of the activities—
 (a) is, or is likely to be, of a persistent or continuing nature,
 (b) is, or is likely to be, such as to make the activities unreasonable, and
 (c) justifies the restrictions imposed by the notice.

(4) A **public spaces protection order** is an order that identifies the public place referred to in subsection (2) ('the **restricted area**') and—
 (a) prohibits specified things being done in the restricted area,
 (b) requires specified things to be done by persons carrying on specified activities in that area, or
 (c) does both of those things.

(5) The only prohibitions or requirements that may be imposed are ones that are reasonable to impose in order—
 (a) to prevent the detrimental effect referred to in subsection (2) from continuing, occurring or recurring, or
 (b) to reduce that detrimental effect or to reduce the risk of its continuance, occurrence or recurrence.

(6) A prohibition or requirement may be framed—
 (a) so as to apply to all persons, or only to persons in specified categories, or to all persons except those in specified categories;
 (b) so as to apply at all times, or only at specified times, or at all times except those specified;
 (c) so as to apply in all circumstances, or only in specified circumstances, or in all circumstances except those specified.

(7) A public spaces protection order must—
 (a) identify the activities referred to in subsection (2);
 (b) explain the effect of **section 63** (where it applies) and **section 67**;
 (c) specify the period for which the order has effect.

(8) A public spaces protection order must be published in accordance with regulations made by the Secretary of State.

Anti-social Behaviour, Crime and Policing Act 2014, s 59

7.15.2 Public spaces protection orders (PSPOs)

Offences

(1) It is an offence for a person without reasonable excuse—
   (a) to do anything that the person is prohibited from doing by a **public spaces protection order**, or
   (b) to fail to comply with a requirement to which the person is subject under a public spaces protection order.

Anti-social Behaviour, Crime and Policing Act 2014, s 67

Points to prove

✓ in a public place subject to a PSPO
✓ without reasonable excuse
✓ did anything prohibited from doing by
or
✓ failed to comply with a requirement to which subject under
✓ a public spaces protection order (PSPO)

Meanings

Local authority (LA) (see **7.13.4**)

Public place (see **7.15.1**)

Public spaces protection order (PSPO) (see **s 59(4)** above)

Section 63 (see **9.4**)

Section 67 (see '**Offences**' box section above)

Explanatory notes

- A PSPO can deal with a nuisance/problem in a public area being detrimental to the local community's qualify of life, by imposing conditions on using the specified area which apply to everyone. Intending that the law-abiding majority can use and enjoy public spaces, safe from anti-social behaviour.
- Local authorities (LA) are responsible for making the PSPO, although enforcement of the order will be broader, involving LA officials, police officers, PCSOs, designated groups, and officers accredited under the community safety accreditation scheme.
- Before a PSPO can be made, the LA has to be satisfied, on reasonable grounds, that activities in a public space: have had or will be likely to have a detrimental effect on the quality of life of those in the locality; it is/likely to be, persistent or continuing in nature, so making the activities unreasonable; and the order justifies the restrictions imposed.
- The meaning of a public space is wide and includes any place to which the public or any section of the public has access, on payment or otherwise, as of right or by virtue of express or implied permission, for example a shopping centre.

- Prior to making a PSPO, the LA must consult with the police, the land owner or occupier, together with appropriate community representatives (eg residents association). It could include an individual or group of individuals, for instance, regular users of a park or specific activities such as busking or other types of street entertainment.

Defences

(1) Having a reasonable excuse for failing to comply with a public spaces protection order.

(3) A person does not commit an offence under this section by failing to comply with a prohibition or requirement that the local authority did not have power to include in the public spaces protection order.

Anti-social Behaviour, Crime and Policing Act 2014, s 67

Practical considerations

- The maximum duration of a PSPO is three years, but this can be for a shorter period if required. If considered necessary, the LA can extend a PSPO before its expiry by up to three years, and if appropriate further consultation should again take place.
- If required a PSPO can be varied, such as changing the size of the restricted area or the specific requirements or restrictions. For example, a PSPO deals with controlling dogs in a park, but a year later, groups now congregate in the park drinking alcohol, so the LA could vary the PSPO to deal with both issues. The LA can also discharge a PSPO at any time.
- Section 63 can restrict the consumption of alcohol in a public space subject of a PSPO, and s 62 provides details of premises and places where a PSPO cannot apply. For details of restrictions and enforcing the order see **9.4** for further details.
- In relation to dogs and their owners, a PSPO could, for example: exclude dogs from designated areas (eg a children's play area in a park); require dog faeces to be picked up by owners; require dogs to be kept on leads; and restrict the number of dogs that can be walked by one person at any one time.
- A PSPO must be published in accordance with regulations (SI 2591/2014), identifying the activities subject of the order, sanctions for breach, and the duration of the PSPO. The LA should publish details of making, extending, varying, or discharging a PSPO on its website and display notices with details of the PSPO at the public place to which the order relates.
- The PSPO or variation can be challenged in the High Court by an interested person (person who lives or regularly works in or visits the area) within six weeks of it being made/varied. Grounds could be that the LA did not have power to make the order, or include certain

7.15.2 Public spaces protection orders (PSPOs)

prohibitions or requirements, or that proper consultation had not taken place. The High Court can uphold the PSPO, quash it, or vary it.

- A person who fails to comply with a PSPO, without reasonable excuse, will commit an offence; except breach of a PSPO by consuming alcohol which is an offence under s 63 (see **9.4**). Both the s 63 and s 67 offences can be dealt with by a FPN (up to £100) under s 68.
- Section 64A(1B)(ca) of PACE provides the power to photograph person(s) who are given a direction by a constable under s 35.
- Current designated public place orders, gating orders, and dog control orders could remain in force for three years from the commencement day of PSPOs (20 October 2014).
- A PSPO takes precedence over a byelaw in the restricted area, if the byelaw prohibits the same activity that is now covered by the PSPO.

PCSO

 Summary   6 months

 Level 3 fine

Links to alternative subjects and offences

7.16 Community/Environmental Protection

The Anti-social Behaviour Act 2014 deals with issuing a community protection notice (CPN) for environmental nuisances; other matters such as litter, abandoned vehicles, and refuse are dealt with by the Environmental Protection Act 1990, the Litter Act 1983, and the Refuse Disposal (Amenity) Act 1978.

7.16.1 Community protection notices (CPN)

Section 43 of the Anti-social Behaviour, Crime and Policing Act 2014 gives an authorised person power to issue a CPN to a person or body if their conduct is unreasonable and it has a detrimental effect on the quality of life of those in the locality. Failure to comply with a CPN is an offence under s 48, and breach can be dealt with by a fixed penalty notice (FPN) under s 52.

Power to issue notices

(1) An **authorised person** may issue a **community protection notice** to an individual aged 16 or over, or a body, if satisfied on reasonable grounds that—

    (a) the **conduct** of the individual or body is having a detrimental effect, of a persistent or continuing nature, on the quality of life of those in the locality, and

    (b) the conduct is unreasonable.

(3) A **community protection notice** is a notice that imposes any of the following requirements on the individual or body issued with it—

    (a) a requirement to stop doing specified things;

    (b) a requirement to do specified things;

    (c) a requirement to take reasonable steps to achieve specified results.

(4) The only requirements that may be imposed are ones that are reasonable to impose in order—

    (a) to prevent the detrimental effect referred to in subsection (1) from continuing or recurring, or

    (b) to reduce that detrimental effect or to reduce the risk of its continuance or recurrence.

(5) A person (A) may issue a community protection notice to an individual or body (B) only if—

    (a) B has been given a written warning that the notice will be issued unless B's conduct ceases to have the detrimental effect referred to in subsection (1), and

---

(b) A is satisfied that, despite B having had enough time to deal with the matter, B's conduct is still having that effect.

(6) A person issuing a community protection notice must before doing so inform any body or individual the person thinks appropriate.

(7) A community protection notice must—
   (a) identify the conduct referred to in subsection (1);
   (b) explain the effect of **sections 46 to 51**.

(8) A community protection notice may specify periods within which, or times by which, requirements within subsection (3)(b) or (c) are to be complied with.

Anti-social Behaviour, Crime and Policing Act 2014, s 43

Offences

A person issued with a **community protection notice** who fails to comply with it commits an offence.

Anti-social Behaviour, Crime and Policing Act 2014, s 48(1)

Points to prove

✓ being a person/body having been issued with a CPN
✓ failed to comply with a requirement in the CPN
✓ by doing or did not stop doing or achieve things/results as specified in the CPN

Meanings

Authorised person

Means a constable, PCSO or person designated by the relevant **local authority**.

Local authority (LA) (see 7.13.4)

Community Protection Notice (CPN) (see s 43(3) above)

Conduct

This includes a failure to act.

Sections 46 to 51

These sections relate to the following—
• s 46 Appeals against notices;
• s 47 Remedial action by local authority;
• s 48 Offence of failing to comply with notice;
• s 49 Remedial orders;
• s 50 Forfeiture of item used in offence; and
• s 51 Seizure of item used in offence.

Explanatory notes

- A CPN cannot be issued until a written warning has been given to the person/body; this must make it clear that if they do not stop the anti-social behaviour, a CPN could be issued. Identify in the written warning the behaviour that has to be changed, and give a time period for it to be achieved, advising them of potential sanctions on breaching a CPN if a notice is then issued.
- When a written warning has been issued, enough time should be given to allow the person or body to deal with the matter, before issuing a CPN. This will be on a case-by-case basis, for example where an area is to be cleared several days or weeks may be required, but in a case of playing loud music this could require the behaviour to stop immediately.
- A CPN can be issued by a LA enforcement officer, social landlord (designated by LA), constable, or PCSO against a person aged 16 or over, business, or organisation, if satisfied on reasonable grounds that their conduct: is having a detrimental effect on the quality of life of those in the locality; is persistent or continuing in nature; and is unreasonable.
- A CPN requirement should be appropriate to the situation, it could be to stop doing or to do specified things, or to take reasonable steps to achieve specified results. This means that not only can the officer stop someone being anti-social, they can also put steps in place to ensure the behaviour does not recur.
- If a body, the CPN should be given to the most appropriate person, such as the shop owner or a store manager. The issuing officer has to be satisfied that the person can be reasonably expected to control, affect, or deal with the behaviour. The notice can be given directly to the person in question, posted to them, or posted on the premises (if the owner or occupier is not known).

Defences

A person does not commit an offence under this section if—
(a) the person took all reasonable steps to comply with the notice, or
(b) there is some other reasonable excuse for the failure to comply with it.

Anti-social Behaviour, Crime and Policing Act 2014, s 48(3)

Practical considerations

- Consider if a requirement or timescale is reasonable and achievable before issuing the notice. Furthermore, a CPN is designed to deal with short or medium-term issues, and while restrictions and requirements may be similar to those in civil injunctions (see **7.13.1**), more serious conditions, such as attending a drug rehabilitation course, should be dealt with by a court order.

7.16.1 Community protection notices (CPN)

- Failing to comply with a CPN is an offence under s 48(1). If appropriate, a police officer, PCSO, or LA officer could issue a FPN (up to £100) under s 52(1) for failing to comply with a CPN. Other options to consider could be remedial action or a court remedial, forfeiture, or seizure order.
- Remedial action could be the LA or their agent clearing a garden on the perpetrator's behalf, and when completed charging the perpetrator with the cost for the clearance, which could include officer time, equipment, labour, and administration costs. Work undertaken on land 'open to the air' can be done without the consent of the owner or occupier, but any indoor work will require the permission of the owner or occupier.
- Issuing a CPN does not discharge the LA from its duty to issue an Abatement Notice if it is a statutory nuisance as listed in s 79(1) of the Environmental Protection Act 1990.
- On conviction for failing to comply with a CPN, the prosecutor may ask the court to impose a remedial and/or a forfeiture order as—
  - ◆ it is a serious matter that requires a court order;
  - ◆ remedial work is in an area that requires consent from the owner/occupier and this is not forthcoming; or
  - ◆ forfeiture or seizure of items may be required as a result of the behaviour (eg sound-making equipment).
- The court can order the forfeiture of items used in committing the s 48 CPN offence, this may be spray paints, sound equipment, or dog (owner unable to control the dog). Forfeited items can be destroyed or disposed of appropriately (including re-homing a dog). A warrant issued under s 51 can authorise seizure of such items, and an officer may use reasonable force, if necessary, to do this.
- Failure to comply with any of the requirements in the court order constitutes contempt of court and could lead to a custodial sentence.
- Anyone issued with a CPN can appeal to a magistrates' court, but this must be within 21 days of issue of the notice. Appeal could be that the behaviour: did not take place; was not persistent or continuing; was not unreasonable; or did not have a detrimental effect on the quality of life of those in the locality. Other grounds for appeal may be: unreasonable CPN requirements; was issued to the wrong person; or the individual cannot reasonably be expected to control or affect the behaviour.

PCSO

 Summary

 6 months

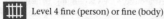 Level 4 fine (person) or fine (body)

7.16.2 **Leaving litter/removing or interfering with litter bins**

Section 87 of the Environmental Protection Act 1990 creates an offence of defacing a place by the leaving of litter.

Offences

A person is guilty of an offence if he throws down, drops or otherwise **deposits** any **litter** in any **place** to which this section applies, and leaves it.

Environmental Protection Act 1990, s 87(1)

Points to prove

✓ threw down/dropped/deposited litter
✓ in a place to which this section applies
✓ and left it there

Meanings

Deposits

Means no more than places or puts (*Felix v DPP* [1998] Crim LR 657).

Litter

Includes the discarded ends of cigarettes, cigars, and like products, chewing gum, and the remains of other products designed for chewing.

Place

- Any place in the area of a **principal litter authority** that is open to the air. Land shall be treated as 'open to the air' notwithstanding that it is covered, providing it is open to the air on at least one side.
- This section does not apply to a place which is 'open to the air' if the public does not have access to it, with or without payment.

Principal litter authority

Means a county council; county borough council; district council; London borough council; Common Council of the City of London; and the Council of the Isles of Scilly.

Explanatory notes

- It is immaterial whether the litter is deposited on land or in water, so the offence extends to dropping or depositing litter in bodies of water such as rivers and lakes.
- Under s 88 an authorised officer of a litter authority or a suitably designated constable may, if they have reason to believe that a person has committed an offence under s 87, issue a fixed penalty notice to that person.

7.16.2 Leaving litter/removing or interfering with litter bins

Defences

No offence is committed under subsection (1) above where the depositing of the litter is—
(a) authorised by law, or
(b) done with the consent of the owner, occupier or other person having control of the place where it is deposited.

Environmental Protection Act 1990, s 87(4A)

Defence notes

A person may only give consent under s 87(4A)(b) in relation to the depositing of litter in a lake, pond, or watercourse if they are the owner, occupier, or other person having control of all the land adjoining that lake, pond, or watercourse and all the land through or into which water in that lake, pond, or watercourse directly or indirectly discharges, otherwise than by means of a public sewer.

Practical considerations

- The area of a local authority which is on the coast extends down to the low-water mark (s 72 of the Local Government Act 1972). Therefore, it is an offence to deposit litter on the beach.
- Consider issuing a PND (see **7.1**) for this litter offence (applies to constable only).
- If a **fixed penalty notice** is issued under s 88 by an authorised officer (suitably designated constable or PCSO) a copy of it must be sent to the relevant litter authority within 24 hours.

Removing or interfering with litter bins

It is a summary offence under s 5(9) of the Litter Act 1983 for any person to wilfully remove or otherwise interfere with any litter bin or noticeboard provided or erected under this section or s 185 of the Highways Act 1980.

 Summary 6 months

 Level 4 fine

7.16.3 **Unauthorised dumping/abandoned vehicles/fly tipping**

Section 2 of the Refuse Disposal (Amenity) Act 1978 creates an offence of abandoning motor vehicles or any other thing on land in the open (fly tipping).

Offences

Any person who, without lawful authority—
(a) abandons on any land in the open air, or on any other land forming part of a highway, **a motor vehicle** or any thing which formed part of a motor vehicle and was removed from it in the course of dismantling the vehicle on the land; or
(b) **abandons** on any such land any thing other than a motor vehicle, being a thing which he has brought to the land for the purpose of abandoning it there,
shall be guilty of an offence.

Refuse Disposal (Amenity) Act 1978, s 2(1)

Points to prove

✓ without lawful authority
✓ abandoned on land
✓ in the open air/forming part of a highway
✓ a motor vehicle/part of a motor vehicle **or**
✓ an item brought to the land
✓ for the purpose of abandoning it there

Meanings

Motor vehicle

Means a mechanically propelled vehicle intended or adapted for use on roads, whether or not it is in a fit state for such use, and includes any trailer intended or adapted for use as an attachment to such a vehicle, any chassis or body, with or without wheels, appearing to have formed part of such a vehicle or trailer and anything attached to such a vehicle or trailer.

Abandoned

A person who leaves any thing on any land in such circumstances or for such a period that they may reasonably be assumed to have abandoned it or to have brought it to the land for the purpose of abandoning it there shall be deemed to have abandoned it there or, as the case may be, to have brought it to the land for that purpose unless the contrary is shown.

7.16.3 Unauthorised dumping/abandoned vehicles/fly tipping

Explanatory notes

In addition to any penalty, the court may order the defendant to pay any costs involved in the removal and disposal of the offending article.

Practical considerations

- Removal and disposal of items under this section is the responsibility of the local authority.
- Section 2A of the Refuse Disposal (Amenity) Act 1978 gives an authorised officer of a local authority the power to issue a fixed penalty in respect of the offence of abandoning a vehicle.
- Before contacting the local authority, consider checking the motor vehicle to ascertain whether it is stolen or used for involvement in crime.

 Summary   6 months

 3 months' imprisonment and/or a level 4 fine

Links to alternative subjects and offences

7.17 Trespassing on Premises/Land

Section 144 of the Legal Aid, Sentencing and Punishment of Offenders Act 2012 relates to squatting in a residential building. Sections 61 to 62C of the Criminal Justice and Public Order Act 1994 deal with trespassers residing on land who fail to leave, whereas s 6 and s 7 of the Criminal Law Act 1977 concern the use or threat of violence to secure entry into premises and unauthorised entry or remaining on premises.

7.17.1 Trespassers (squatting) in residential building/residing on land (failing to leave)

Section 144 of the Legal Aid, Sentencing and Punishment of Offenders Act 2012 creates the offence of squatting in a residential building.

Offences

A person commits an offence if —
(a) the person is in a **residential building** as a **trespasser** having entered it as a trespasser,
(b) the person knows or ought to know that he or she is a trespasser, and
(c) the person is living in the **building** or intends to live there for any period.

Legal Aid, Sentencing and Punishment of Offenders Act 2012, s 144(1)

Points to prove

✓ being in a residential building
✓ having entered it as a trespasser
✓ lived/intended to live in the building

Meanings

Residential building

A building is residential if it is designed or adapted, before the time of entry, for use as a place to live.

Building

Includes any structure or part of a structure (including a temporary or moveable structure).

Trespasser (see **7.17.2**)

Explanatory notes

- The fact that a person derives title from a trespasser, or has permission from a trespasser, does not prevent the person from being a trespasser.
- For the purposes of s 144(1)(a) (above), it is irrelevant whether the person entered the building as a trespasser before or after this section came into force.

Practical considerations

- A MOJ Circular 4/2012 provides further details regarding this squatting offence, which requires that the trespasser 'is living' or 'intends to live' in the building for any period.
- Section 17(1)(c)(vi) of PACE provides a power of entry to arrest a person for the offence of squatting in a residential building (see **12.3.2**).
- Section 6 of the Criminal Law Act 1977 provides the offence of using or threatening violence to secure entry to premises (see **7.17.2**), but the police still have lawful authority to enter the property to arrest for the s 144 squatting offence.
- Section 7 of the 1977 Act concerns the offence of failing to leave residential premises once the lawful occupiers have gained legitimate entry (see **7.17.3**).

Trespassers residing on land—failing to leave

- The Criminal Justice and Public Order Act 1994 gives the police powers for dealing with people, vehicles and caravans trespassing on land.
- Section 61 gives the police power to direct two or more people trespassing on land, intending to reside there for a period of time, to leave that land and to remove any vehicles or other property they have with them on the land. This is providing that reasonable steps have been taken by or on behalf of the occupier to ask them to leave, and they have—
  - caused damage to the land or to property on the land or
  - used threatening, abusive or insulting words or behaviour towards the occupier or family member/employee/agent of the occupier, or
  - six or more vehicles on the land between them.
- It is a summary offence under s 61(4) if a person knowing that a direction has been given which applies to them, and either—
  - fails to leave the land as soon as is reasonably practicable, or
  - having left, again enters the land as a trespasser within the period of 3 months beginning with the day on which the direction was given.
- Section 62 provides that a constable may seize and remove a vehicle if a direction has been given under s 61 and they reasonably suspect that a person to whom it applies has, without reasonable excuse, failed to

remove a vehicle which appears to belong to them, or to be in their possession or under their control; or they have entered the land as a trespasser with a vehicle within 3 months of the direction being given.
• Sections 62A to 62C provide for the directing of trespassers to leave land and remove their vehicles/caravans, when there is a relevant caravan site in the local authority area, and it is managed by a relevant site manager.

 Summary   6 months

 6 months' imprisonment and/or a fine

7.17.2 **Violent entry to premises**

Section 6 creates the offences of using or threatening violence to secure entry to premises.

> ### Offences
>
> Subject to the following **provisions of this section**, any person who, without lawful authority, uses or threatens violence for the purpose of securing entry into any **premises** for himself or for any other person is guilty of an offence, provided that—
> (a) there is someone present on those premises at the time who is opposed to the entry which the violence is intended to secure; **and**
> (b) the person using or threatening the violence knows that that is the case.
>
> Criminal Law Act 1977, s 6(1)

Points to prove
✓ without lawful authority
✓ used/threatened violence
✓ to secure entry to premises
✓ knowing someone present on the premises opposed entry

Meanings

Premises

Any building, part of a building under separate occupation (eg flat), land ancillary to a building, and the site comprising any building(s) together with any land ancillary thereto.

7.17.2 Violent entry to premises

Provisions of this section

Section 6(1) does not apply to a **displaced residential occupier** or a **protected intending occupier** of the relevant premises or a person acting on behalf of such an occupier. If the defendant produces sufficient evidence that they are, or were acting on behalf of, such an occupier they will be presumed to be so unless the prosecution prove the contrary.

Displaced residential occupier

Subject to the following **exception**, any person who was occupying any premises as a residence immediately before being excluded from occupation by anyone who entered those premises, or any **access** to those premises, as a **trespasser** is a displaced residential occupier of the premises so long as they continue to be excluded from occupation of the premises by the original trespasser or by any subsequent trespasser.

Exception

A person who was occupying the relevant premises as a trespasser immediately before being excluded from occupation shall not be a displaced residential occupier of the premises.

Access

Means, in relation to any premises, any part of any site or building within which those premises are situated that constitutes an ordinary means of access to those premises (whether or not that is its sole or primary use).

Trespasser

Someone who wrongfully enters onto someone else's premises.

Protected intending occupier

This is extensively defined in s 12A, but, in brief, means someone who has made a formal declaration to a commissioner of oaths that they were due to move into the affected premises.

Explanatory notes

- Anyone who enters, or is on or in occupation of, any premises under a title derived from a trespasser or by a licence or consent given by a trespasser or by a person deriving title from a trespasser will themselves be treated as a trespasser (whether or not they would be a trespasser apart from this provision).
- The fact that a person has an interest in, or right to possession or occupation of, the premises does not, for s 6(1) constitute lawful authority for the use or threat of violence by them or anyone else to secure entry into those premises.

Related cases

Wakolo v DPP [2012] EWHC 611 (Admin), QBD There was no s 6(1A) defence to a co-owner of a matrimonial home, even though not excluded by an occupation order, when he knew that his entry was opposed by the occupier (his estranged wife). After entry was refused he used violence to gain entry by using a bar to force open the front door. In these circumstances W was not a 'protected intending occupier' under s 12A.

Practical considerations

- It is immaterial whether the violence is directed against a person or property and whether the violent entry is to acquire possession of the premises.
- A person who, by virtue of the definition of 'displaced residential occupier', is a displaced residential occupier of any premises is also deemed a displaced residential occupier of any access to those premises.
- A person on premises as a trespasser does not cease to be a trespasser under this legislation by being allowed time to leave there, nor does a person cease to be a displaced residential occupier of any premises because of any such allowance of time to a trespasser.
- Proceed with care where squatting appears to have lasted for a long time. It is possible for a squatter (someone who possesses premises without the lawful consent of the owner) to gain legal title if they have held the property for 12 years adversely but without disturbance or legal attempts to repossess it.

 Summary   6 months

 6 months' imprisonment and/or a fine

7.17.3 **Adverse occupation of residential premises**

Section 7 creates an offence of failing to leave residential premises once the lawful occupiers have gained legitimate entry.

Offences

Subject to the provisions of this section and s 12A(9), any person who is on any **premises** as a **trespasser** after having entered as such is guilty of an offence if he fails to leave those premises on being required to do so by or on behalf of—

(a) a **displaced residential occupier** of the premises; or

(b) an individual who is a **protected intending occupier** of the premises.

Criminal Law Act 1977, s 7(1)

7.17.3 Adverse occupation of residential premises

> **Points to prove**
> - ✓ on premises
> - ✓ as a trespasser
> - ✓ having entered as such
> - ✓ failed to leave when required
> - ✓ by/on behalf of a displaced residential occupier/protected intending occupier

Meanings

Premises (see **7.17.2**)

Trespasser (see **7.17.2**)

Displaced residential occupier (see **7.17.2**)

Protected intending occupier (see **7.17.2**)

Explanatory notes

A reference to any premises includes a reference to any access to them, whether or not the access itself constitutes premises.

> **Defences**
>
> 7(2)   It is a defence for the accused to prove that he believed that the person requiring him to leave the premises was not a displaced residential occupier or protected intending occupier of the premises or a person acting on their behalf.
>
> 7(3)   It is a defence for the accused to prove that—
> (a) the premises in question are, or form part of, premises used mainly for non-residential purposes; and
> (b) he was not on any part of the premises used wholly or mainly for residential purposes.
>
> 12A(9) Where the accused was requested to leave the premises by a person claiming to be or to act on behalf of a protected intending occupier of the premises—
> (a) it shall be a defence for the accused to prove that, although asked to do so by the accused at the time the accused was requested to leave, that person failed at that time to produce to the accused such a statement as is referred to in s 12A(2)(d) or s 12A(4)(d) or such a certificate as is referred to in s 12A(6)(d); and
> (b) any document purporting to be a document under 12A(6)(d) will be received in evidence and, unless the contrary is proved, will be determined to have been issued by or on behalf of the authority stated in the certificate.
>
> Criminal Law Act 1977, ss 7 and 12A

Practical considerations

- Officers wishing to apply these provisions in an operational situation should make themselves conversant with the terms—displaced residential occupier, squatters, and protected intending occupier (see **7.17.2**).
- A displaced residential occupier or a protected intending occupier (once they have completed the formalities) can use force (either personally or by others on their behalf) to break into the premises to regain possession. They can also demand that the premises be vacated and s 7 makes it an offence (subject to any defences) for the trespassers to remain.
- If the squatter is being evicted by a protected intending occupier (this does not apply to an eviction by a displaced residential occupier) then they are entitled to see a copy of the statement or certificate which must be held by the person making the eviction. They have a statutory defence if the certificate is not produced.

E&S

 Summary   6 months

 6 months' imprisonment and/or a fine

Links to alternative subjects and offences

7.18 **Football/Sporting Event Offences/Banning Orders**

At designated sporting events and grounds, the Sporting Events (Control of Alcohol) Act 1985 deals with police powers and offences in connection with alcohol, articles capable of causing injury, flares and other articles; whereas at designated football matches, the Football (Offences) Act 1991 deals with offences such as throwing missiles, indecent/racist chanting or going onto the pitch, and the Football Spectators Act 1989 controls admission through football banning orders.

7.18.1 **Possess alcohol/article or drunk at sporting event**

Offences

(1) A person who has **alcohol** or an **article to which this section applies** in his possession—
  (a) at any time during the **period** of a **designated sporting event** when he is in any area of a designated sports ground from which the event may be directly viewed, or
  (b) while entering or trying to enter a **designated sports ground** at any time during the period of a designated sporting event at that ground,
  is guilty of an offence.
(2) A person who is **drunk** in a designated sports ground at any time during the period of a designated sporting event at that ground or is drunk while entering or trying to enter such a ground at any time during the period of a designated sporting event at that ground is guilty of an offence.

Sporting Events (Control of Alcohol) Act 1985, s 2

Points to prove

s 2(1)(a) offence

✓ possessed
✓ alcohol/article to which s 2 applies
✓ during period of designated sporting event
✓ in area of designated sports ground
✓ with a direct view of the event

---

s 2(1)(b) offence

✓ possessed
✓ alcohol/article to which s 2 applies
✓ while entering/trying to enter
✓ a designated sports ground
✓ during period of designated sporting event

s 2(2) offence

✓ drunk
✓ in/while entering/trying to enter
✓ a designated sports ground
✓ during period of a designated sporting event

Section 7 of the Sporting Events (Control of Alcohol) Act 1985 provides the police with powers of entry, stop and search in connection with the Act.

Powers

(1) A constable may, at any time during the **period** of a **designated sporting event** at any **designated sports ground**, enter any part of the ground for the purpose of enforcing the provisions of this Act.

(2) A constable may search a person he has reasonable grounds to suspect is committing or has committed an **offence under this Act**.

(3) A constable may stop a **public service vehicle** (within the meaning of section 1 of this Act) or a **motor vehicle** to which section 1A of this Act applies and may search such a vehicle or a railway passenger vehicle if he has reasonable grounds to suspect that an offence under that section is being or has been committed in respect of the vehicle.

Sporting Events (Control of Alcohol) Act 1985, s 7

Meanings

Alcohol (see **9.1.1**)

Article to which s 2 applies

Applies to any article capable of causing injury to a person struck by it, being—

- a bottle, can or other portable container (including such an article when crushed or broken) which is for holding any drink, and when empty, is normally discarded or returned/recovered by, the supplier, or
- part of any of the above articles;
- but does not apply to anything that holds medicinal/veterinary products.

7.18.1 Possess alcohol/article or drunk at sporting event

Designated sporting event

Is a sporting event or proposed sporting event for the time being designated, or of a class designated, by order made by the Secretary of State, and the order may apply to events or proposed events outside GB as well as those in England and Wales.

Period of a designated sporting event

This is the period beginning 2 hours before the start of the event or (if earlier) 2 hours before the time at which it is advertised to start and ending 1 hour after the end of the event.

Designated sports ground

Means any place used (wholly or partly) for sporting events where accommodation is provided for spectators, and for the time being designated, or of a class designated, by order made by the Secretary of State. Such an order may include the outer limit of any designated sports ground.

Drunk (see 7.2.1)

Offence under this Act (see 'Practical considerations')

Public service vehicle (PSV)

Means a motor vehicle (other than a tramcar), used for carrying passengers for hire or reward, and either adapted to carry more than 8 passengers; or not so adapted, which in the course of business carries passengers at separate fares.

Motor vehicle

Means a mechanically propelled vehicle intended or adapted for use on roads.

Explanatory notes

- Article 2 of the Sports Grounds and Sporting Events (Designation) Order 2005 designates the classes of sports grounds in sch1 and sporting events in sch 2 with regards to offences under the 1985 Act.
  - ◆ Sch 1 refers to any sports ground in England and Wales.
  - ◆ Sch 2 lists sporting events—FA matches at sports grounds, being within or outside England and Wales, in which one or both of the participating teams represents a club which is for the time being a member (whether a full or associate member) of the—
    - Football League,
    - Football Association Premier League,
    - Football Conference National Division,
    - Scottish Professional Football League or
    - Welsh Premier League, or
    - represents a country or territory.

    FA matches in competition for the FA Cup (other than in a preliminary or qualifying round).
- Whilst this Act was aimed primarily at football matches, it can also apply to other sporting events.

Practical considerations

- **Offences under this Act**: are s 2 (above), and—
  - ◆ s 1 Where a vehicle, being a PSV or train, is mainly used for carrying passengers for the whole or part of a journey to or from a designated sporting event; then if the operator/hirer or their servant/agent, knowingly causes/permits alcohol to be carried on the vehicle they will commit an offence. An offence is also committed if a person is drunk or in possession of alcohol on the vehicle.
  - ◆ s 1A Where a motor vehicle, which is not a PSV but is adapted to carry more than 8 passengers, is mainly used for carrying 2 or more passengers for the whole or part of a journey to or from a designated sporting event; then a person who knowingly causes/permits alcohol to be carried on the motor vehicle is guilty of an offence if they are the driver, if not the driver but is the keeper or their servant/agent or a person to whom it is made available (by hire, loan or otherwise) by its keeper or their servant/agent. An offence is also committed if a person is drunk or in possession of alcohol on the motor vehicle.
  - ◆ s 2A This offence replicates the s 2(1) offence, but instead of alcohol or connected receptacle, it applies to flares, fireworks or an article/substance that emits smoke or visible gas (eg, distress flares, fog signals or pellets/capsules used for testing pipes or as fumigators).
- Consider CPS charging standards and guidance for these offences.
- A constable may, at any time during the period of a designated sporting event at any designated sports ground, enter any part of the ground for the purpose of enforcing the provisions of this Act.
- A constable may search a person he has reasonable grounds to suspect is committing or has committed an offence under this Act, all of which are summary offences.

 Summary   6 months

 s 2(1) offence

    3 month's imprisonment and/or level 3 fine

    s 2(2) offence

    Level 2 fine

7.18.2 **Throw object—designated football match/football banning orders**

Offences

It is an offence for a person at a **designated football match** to throw anything at or towards—

(a) the playing area, or any area adjacent to the playing area to which spectators are not generally admitted, or
(b) any area in which spectators or other persons are or may be present,

without lawful authority or lawful excuse (which shall be for him to prove).

Football (Offences) Act 1991, s 2

Points to prove

✓ while at a designated football match
✓ without lawful authority/excuse
✓ threw missile/object
✓ at/towards

s 2(a) offence

✓ first four 'Points to Prove' (above)
✓ the playing area/area adjacent to playing area
✓ where spectators not generally admitted

s 2(b) offence

✓ first four 'Points to Prove' (above)
✓ an area where spectators/other persons
✓ were/may be present

Meaning of designated football match

Means an association football match designated, or of a description designated, for the purposes of this Act by order of the Secretary of State.

Explanatory notes

- Article 3 of the Football (Offences) (Designation of Football Matches) Order 2004 provides the definition of a designated match, which is an FA match—
  - in which one or both of the participating teams represents a club which is for the time being a member (whether a full or associate member) of the Football League, the Football Association Premier League, the Football Conference or the Scottish Football League or the Welsh Premier League, or whose home ground is for the time being situated outside England and Wales, or represents a country or territory.
  - in competition for the FA Cup (other than in a preliminary or qualifying round).
- Offences under this Act can only be committed in England and Wales. The Act covers acts done within a period of 2 hours before the start of the match (or 2 hours before the advertised start, if earlier) and ending 1 hour after the end of the match. Offences could also apply where the match is cancelled, if it has been advertised to start at a particular time on a particular day, in which case it will apply, within

a period beginning 2 hours before and 1 hour after the advertised starting times.

Related cases

DPP v Stoke on Trent MC [2003] 3 All ER 1086, QBD Using the term 'Paki' within the context of a chant at other supporters, is racialist in nature and is an offence under s 3 of the 1991 Act.

Practical considerations

- Offences under this Act: are s 2 (above), and—
  + s 3 It is an offence to engage or take part in **chanting** of an indecent or **racialist nature** at a designated football match. For this purpose—
    - **chanting**: means the repeated uttering of any words or sounds (whether alone or in concert with one or more others); and
    - **racialist nature**: means consisting of or including matter which is threatening, abusive or insulting to a person by reason of his colour, race, nationality (including citizenship) or ethnic or national origins.
  + s 4 It is an offence for a person at a designated football match to go onto the playing area, or any area adjacent to the playing area to which spectators are not generally admitted, without lawful authority or lawful excuse (which shall be for him to prove).
- The act of throwing the missile/object constitutes the s 2 offence. There is no need to prove that it was directed at anyone, or that anyone was likely to be alarmed or distressed by it.
- Be aware of 'ticket touting' offences under s 166 of the Criminal Justice and Public Order Act 1994, where it is an offence for an unauthorised person to sell a ticket for a designated football match, or otherwise to dispose of such a ticket to another person.

Football banning orders

- The Football Spectators Act 1989 controls the admission of spectators to designated football matches by means of a national membership scheme. For the purpose of preventing violence or disorder at or in connection with both designated and regulated football matches, it empowers the courts to make a 'banning order'. A banning order prohibits the person who is subject to the order from entering any premises for the purpose of attending regulated football matches in the UK, and in relation to regulated football matches outside the UK, can require that person to report at a police station as directed by the court.
- Section 14A of the 1989 Act applies where a person (the offender) is convicted of a **relevant offence**. Then if the court is satisfied that there are reasonable grounds to believe that making a banning order would help to prevent violence or disorder at or in connection with any regulated football matches, it must make such an order in respect of the offender.
- Schedule 1 to the 1989 Act provides the list of **relevant offences** in relation to applications for banning orders—

7.18.2 Throw object—designated football match

- breaches/offences regarding banning orders under this Act;
- s 2 or 2A offence under the 1985 Act (see **7.18.1**);
- any offence under the 1991 Act (see above);
- any offence under s 166 of the Criminal Justice and Public Order Act 1994 (sale of tickets by unauthorised persons) which relates to tickets for a football match.
- the following offences committed during a period relevant to a designated football match while the accused was at any premises, or was entering/leaving or trying to enter/leave, the premises—
  - under s 4A (see **7.7**) or s 5 (see **7.8**) of the Public Order Act 1986 (harassment, alarm or distress) or ss 17 to 29 (see **7.9**) of that Act (racial hatred);
  - the use or threat of violence by the accused towards another person (see **2.1**) or property (see **4.4**);
  - the use, carrying or possession of an offensive weapon (see **8.9**) or a firearm (see **8.1**);
- the following offences committed while the accused was on a journey to or from a designated football match, being an offence which the court declares related to football matches—
  - under s 12 of the Licensing Act 1872 (drunk in highway or public place) (see **7.2.2**);
  - under s 91(1) of the Criminal Justice Act 1967 (drunk and disorderly in a public place) (see **7.2.1**);
  - under s 1 of the 1985 Act (see **7.18.1**);
  - under s 4A (see **7.7**) or s 5 (see **7.8**) of the Public Order Act 1986 (harassment, alarm or distress) or ss 17 to 29 (see **7.9**) of that Act (racial hatred);
  - under s 4 (see **10.10.1**), s 5 (see **10.11.1**) or s 5A (see **10.11.2**) of the Road Traffic Act 1988 (drive while unfit through drink or drugs, while over the alcohol prescribed limit, or above the drugs specified limit) (see **7.2.1**);
  - the use or threat of violence by the accused towards another person (see **2.1**) or property (see **4.4**);
  - the use, carrying or possession of an offensive weapon (see **8.9**) or a firearm (see **8.1**);
- the following offences, which do not apply to any of the above circumstances, but was committed during a period relevant to a designated football match, and the court declares that the offence related to that match or to that match and any other football match which took place during that period—
  - under s 4A (see **7.7**) or s 5 (see **7.8**) of the Public Order Act 1986 (harassment, alarm or distress) or ss 17 to 29 (see **7.9**) of that Act (racial hatred);
  - the use or threat of violence by the accused towards another person (see **2.1**) or property (see **4.4**);
  - the use, carrying or possession of an offensive weapon (see **8.9**) or a firearm (see **8.1**).

Summary

 6 months

 Level 3 fine

Links to alternative subjects and offences

Chapter 8

Firearms, Fireworks, and Weapons

8.1 'Section 1 Firearms' Offences

The Firearms Act 1968 provides various offences connected with fire arms, air weapons, shotguns, and associated ammunition.

8.1.1 Possessing s 1 firearm/ammunition without certificate

This offence involves being in possession of a firearm/ammunition with out a valid firearm certificate. Any weapon or ammunition applicable to s 1 is commonly known as a 'section 1 firearm/ammunition'.

Offences

Subject to any **exemption** under this Act, it is an offence for a person—
(a) to have in his **possession**, or to **purchase** or **acquire**, a **firearm to which this section applies** without holding a **firearm certificate** in force at the time, or otherwise than as authorised by such a certificate;
(b) to have in his possession, or to purchase or acquire, any **ammunition to which this section applies** without holding a firearm certificate in force at the time, or otherwise than as authorised by such a certificate, or in quantities in excess of those so authorised.

Firearms Act 1968, s 1(1)

Points to prove

✓ possessed/purchased/acquired
✓ s 1 firearm/ammunition
✓ without/not authorised by/in quantities exceeding those authorised by
✓ a firearms certificate

Meanings

Exemptions

This includes: antique firearms; rifles loaned on private land; carriers, auctioneers, and warehousemen; Crown servants; police; BTP; Civil Nuclear Constabulary; armed forces; athletics and other approved activities; museums; police permits; registered firearms dealers; rifle and pistol clubs; ship and aircraft equipment; licensed slaughterers; theatres and cinemas; Northern Ireland firearms certificate holder; visiting forces; visitors' permits.

Possession

This has a wide meaning. The term has two distinct elements—

* The mental element: whereby the defendant must know of the existence of the firearm, but cannot claim ignorance that it was technically 'a firearm'.
* The practical element: this term is broader than actual physical possession; a person can 'possess' a firearm in a house or premises under their control, even though they are not at the premises. Similarly, the same firearm could be 'possessed' by two people at the same time, such as the firearm's lawful owner and also its custodian who keeps the firearm at his home (see **5.2.1** notes on '**constructive possession**' of drugs).

Purchase

This is not defined and should be given its natural meaning.

Acquire

Means hire, accept as a gift, or borrow.

Firearm to which s 1 applies

This section applies to every **firearm** except—

* normal shotguns (see **8.2.1** for description);
* normal air weapons (see **8.7.2** for description).

Firearm

Means a **lethal barrelled weapon** of any description from which any **shot, bullet, or other missile** can be discharged and includes—

* any **prohibited weapon**, whether it is such a lethal weapon as aforesaid or not; **and**
* any **component part** of such a lethal or prohibited weapon; and
* any **accessory** to any such weapon designed or adapted to diminish the noise or flash caused by firing the weapon;

but excludes component parts of, and accessories for, a shotgun or air weapon (being firearms excluded by s 1).

Lethal barrelled weapon

This is not defined although the courts have determined that the weapon must be capable of causing injury from which death may result. This also includes a weapon not designed to kill or inflict injury but capable of doing so if misused (such as a signal pistol or a flare launcher).

8.1.1 Possessing s 1 firearm/ammunition without certificate

Shot, bullet, or other missile

These terms are not defined and should be given their natural meaning—
- 'shot' usually means round pellets;
- 'bullet' is normally discharged from a weapon with a rifled barrel;
- 'missile' is a more general term—darts and pellets have been held to be missiles.

Prohibited weapons

- Prohibited weapons require an authority from the Secretary of State and are listed under s 5, being weapons such as: machine gun; self-loading or pump-action rifled gun (other than a 0.22 rifle); rocket launcher; CS spray; electric stun gun (applying contacts/probes directly to the body to achieve incapacitation) or conducted energy device (CED); air weapon with self-contained gas cartridge system; grenade; any weapon of whatever description designed or adapted for the discharge of any noxious liquid, gas, or other thing.
- This written authority will have conditions imposed so as not to endanger the public safety or the peace.
- A person commits an offence under s 5 if, without an authority from the Secretary of State, they possess, purchase, acquire, manufacture, sell, or transfer any prohibited weapon.
- Failure to comply with any condition imposed by this authority is an offence under s 5(5).
- The Secretary of State may revoke an authority by notice in writing. Failure to return the authority within 21 days is an offence under s 5(6)
- The Anti-social Behaviour, Crime and Policing Act 2014, s 108, inserted s 5(2A) so that an offence will be committed if, without authority a person manufactures; sells or transfers; possesses, purchases or acquires for sale or transfer, any prohibited weapon or prohibited ammunition. This offence carries a sentence of life imprisonment if a person manufactures, distributes or possesses for distribution any prohibited weapons or ammunition. HOC 9/2014 provides further details.

Component part

Means any working part of the mechanism of a lethal weapon. This will include the trigger but not the trigger guard, for example.

Accessory

This is given its natural meaning, and includes such accessories as silencer or flash eliminator.

Firearm certificate

Means a certificate granted by a chief officer of police in respect of any firearm or ammunition to which s 1 applies.

Ammunition to which s 1 applies

This section applies to any **ammunition** for a firearm, except the following articles, namely—
- cartridges containing 5 or more shot, none of which exceeds 0.36 inch in diameter;
- ammunition for an air gun, air rifle, or air pistol; and
- blank cartridges not more than one inch in diameter.

Ammunition

Means ammunition [*being any shot, bullet, or other missile*] for any firearm and includes grenades, bombs, and other like missiles, whether capable of use with a firearm or not, and also includes prohibited ammunition.

Explanatory notes

- This is an offence of strict liability (*R v Gregory* [2011] EWCA Crim 3276, CA).
- A telescopic laser/night sight is **not** a component part or accessory that requires a firearm certificate.
- Whether a silencer or flash eliminator can be an accessory will be a question of fact to be determined in all the circumstances; whether it could be used with that firearm and did the defendant have it with them for that purpose. It is the accessory that must be 'so designed or adapted' not the weapon.
- Blank cartridges are cases with primer (small explosive charge at the end of the cartridge) and gunpowder; or primed cartridges (as blank but without the gunpowder) both able to be used in a firearm and producing an explosive effect when fired.
- It is a summary offence under s 35 of the Violent Crime Reduction Act 2006 for a person to sell or purchase a cap-type primer designed for use in metallic ammunition for a firearm being either—
  + a primer to which this section applies;
  + an empty cartridge case incorporating such a primer
  unless that person: is a registered firearms dealer; it is their trade or business; produces a certificate authorising possession; is in Her Majesty's Services entitled to do so; or shows that they are entitled by virtue of any enactment.
- Blank cartridges greater than one inch in diameter are s 1 ammunition.
- The diameter of a cartridge is obtained by measuring immediately in front of the cannelure or rim of its base.

Defences

There is no statutory defence as it is an offence of strict liability (*R v Gregory* [2011] EWCA Crim 3276, CA).

Related cases

Flack v Baldry [1988] 1 All ER 673, HL A hand-held 'stun gun' with two prongs and designed to discharge 46,000 volts of electricity into a victim's body was held to be a prohibited weapon under s 5(1)(b) being 'a weapon designed or adapted for the discharge of any noxious liquid, gas or other thing'. Emission of electricity from the device to stun a victim was a 'discharge of other thing'.

R v Deyemi and Edwards [2007] All ER 369, CA Defendants were in possession of an electrical stun gun which discharged electricity through electrodes. In it were a lens and a bulb. The defendants believed that it was a torch, but it was a s 5(1)(b) prohibited weapon. Held: This is an absolute offence. Prosecution to prove possession of a s 5 prohibited firearm.

Moore v Gooderham [1960] 3 All ER 575, QBD A lethal barrelled weapon must be capable of causing injury from which death may result.

Read v Donovan [1947] 1 All ER 37 A lethal barrelled weapon includes a weapon not designed to kill or inflict injury, but is capable of doing so if misused (signal pistol or flare launcher).

Grace v DPP [1989] Crim LR 365, QBD Evidence that the firearm can be fired is required to prove that it is a lethal barrelled weapon.

Price v DPP [1996] 7 CL 49 The defendant had someone else's rucksack containing s 1 ammunition. Although unaware of the contents of the rucksack, the offence was still committed.

Sullivan v Earl of Caithness [1976] 1 All ER 844, QBD Possession does not have to be physical possession.

R v Stubbings [1990] Crim LR 811, CA Primer cartridges are ammunition.

Watson v Herman [1952] 2 All ER 70 A telescopic laser/night sight is not a component part or accessory.

R v Buckfield [1998] Crim LR 673 A silencer designed for a different weapon does not prevent it from being an accessory to a firearm if it could be used as such and the defendant had it for that purpose.

Practical considerations

- The prosecution need only prove knowledge of the existence of the item, as opposed to its nature. Similarly, there is no onus to prove that the defendant knew that the article was a firearm.
- In practice, forensic testing will determine whether weapons are lethal or not. The main characteristic that is measured is the muzzle velocity (the speed at which the projectile leaves the barrel).
- Certain imitation or replica firearms may be a s 1 firearm (see **8.1.4**).
- A s 1 firearm can only be possessed by a firearms certificate holder or some other lawful authority such as a registered firearms dealer, member of the armed forces, or police officer.
- If someone had a silencer in their possession with no evidence linking it to a suitable weapon, possession alone is unlikely to be an offence.
- All repeating shotguns holding more than two cartridges (eg pump-action and revolver shotguns) are 'section 1 firearms'.

 Either way   None

 Summary: 6 months' imprisonment and/or a fine
Indictment: 5 years' imprisonment and/or a fine

8.1.2 **Aggravated s 1 offences/registered firearms dealers**

The offences of possessing, purchasing, or acquiring a s 1 firearm carry a greater punishment if they are aggravated by the shotgun barrel being less than 24 inches (creating a 'sawn-off' shotgun) or illegally converting anything having the appearance of a firearm into a s 1 firearm.

Offences

(1) Subject to this section [see '**Defences**'], it is an offence to shorten the barrel of a shotgun to a length less than 24 inches.

(3) It is an offence for a person other than **a registered firearms dealer** to convert into a firearm anything, which though having the appearance of being a firearm, is so constructed as to be incapable of discharging any missile through its barrel.

(4) A person who commits an offence under section 1 of this Act by having in his possession, or purchasing or acquiring, a shotgun which has been shortened contrary to subsection (1) above or a firearm which has been converted as mentioned in subsection (3) above (whether by a registered firearms dealer or not), without holding a firearm certificate authorising him to have it in his possession, or to purchase or acquire it, shall be treated for the purposes of provisions of this Act relating to the punishment of offences as committing that offence in an aggravated form.

Firearms Act 1968, s 4

Points to prove

✓ possessed/purchased/acquired
✓ a shortened shotgun barrel (to length less than 24 inches) or a thing converted into a firearm
✓ without holding/not authorised by
✓ a firearm certificate

Meanings

Registered

means registered, as a **firearms dealer**, under s 33 of this Act; and references to 'the register', 'registration', and a 'certificate of registration' shall be construed accordingly, except in s 40.

Firearms dealer

means a person who, by way of trade or business—

8.1.2 Aggravated s 1 offences/registered firearms dealers

- manufactures, sells, transfers, repairs, tests, or proves firearms, or ammunition to which s 1 of this Act applies, or shotguns; or
- sells or transfers air weapons.

Explanatory notes

- This offence could apply to weapons such as starting pistols or imitation firearms which have been converted to s 1 firearms. For example, the Olympic. 38 is manufactured as a non-lethal blank firing pistol for use in sports or drama, but has been classified as readily convertible into a lethal barrelled firearm.
- A shotgun which has a barrel shortened to less than 24 inches becomes a s 1 firearm. The length of the barrel is determined by measuring from the muzzle to the point at which the charge is exploded on firing the cartridge.

Defences

It is not an offence under subsection (1) above for a **registered firearms dealer** to shorten the barrel of a shotgun for the sole purpose of replacing a defective part of the barrel so as to produce a barrel not less than 24 inches in length.

Firearms Act 1968, s 4(2)

Practical considerations

- Section 3(1) makes it an offence, if by way of trade or business, a person—
  + manufactures, sells, transfers, repairs, tests, or proves any firearm or ammunition to which s 1 of this Act applies, or a shotgun;
  + exposes for sale or transfer, or has in his possession for sale, transfer repair, test, or proof any such firearm or ammunition, or a shotgun or
  + sells or transfers an air weapon, exposes such a weapon for sale or transfer, or has such a weapon in his possession for sale or transfer; without being registered under this Act as a firearms dealer.
- Consider confiscation of cash and property for the s 3(1) offence (above), as this is given as a 'criminal lifestyle' offence under Sch 2 to the Proceeds of Crime Act 2002 (see **5.5** for details).
- Section 32 of the Violent Crime Reduction Act 2006 makes it a summary offence to sell air weapons by way of trade or business othe than face-to-face to an individual who is not a registered firearms dealer. This allows an air weapon to be sent from one registered firearms dealer to another to make the final transfer in person to the buyer. Guidance is given on ss 31 and 32 in HOC 31/2007.

Either way · None

Summary: 6 months' imprisonment and/or a fine

Indictment: 7 years' imprisonment and/or a fine

8.1.3 Restrictions on s 1 firearms/ammunition to under 14 years

Sections 22(2) and 24(2) of the Firearms Act 1968 place tight restrictions on persons under the age of 14 years from possessing, receiving as gifts or on loan any s 1 firearm/ammunition.

Offences

Possession by under 14

It is an offence for a person under the age of 14 to have in his **possession** any firearm or ammunition to which **section 1** of this Act or **section 15** of the Firearms (Amendment) Act 1988 applies, except where under section 11(1) or (4) of this Act he is entitled to have possession of it without holding a firearm certificate.

Firearms Act 1968, s 22(2)

Make gift, lend, or part with possession to under 14

It is an offence—

(a) to make a gift of or lend any firearm or ammunition to which section 1 of this Act applies to a person under the age of 14; or

(b) to part with the possession of any such firearm or ammunition to a person under that age, except in circumstances where that person is entitled under **section 11(1) or (4)** of this Act or section 15 of the Firearms (Amendment) Act 1988 to have possession thereof without holding a firearm certificate.

Firearms Act 1968, s 24(2)

Points to prove

Possess

✓ being a person under the age of 14 years
✓ possessed
✓ any s 1 firearm or ammunition

8.1.3 Restrictions on s 1 firearms/ammunition to under 14 years

> *Make gift/lend/part possession*
> ✓ make a gift/lend/part with possession
> ✓ a s 1 firearm or ammunition
> ✓ to a person under the age of 14 years

Meanings

Possession

This has a wide meaning (see **8.1.1**).

Section 1 firearm or ammunition (see **8.1.1**)

Section 15 of the Firearms (Amendment) Act 1988

This provides the mechanism for the creation of approved rifle and **muzzle loading pistol** clubs where members can, if they wish, use such weapons without being the holder of a firearm certificate.

Muzzle loading pistol

Means a pistol designed to be loaded at the muzzle end of the barrel or chambered with a loose charge (such as gun powder) and a separate ball (or other missile).

Explanatory notes

- These restrictions are in addition to those imposed on persons under 18 and 15 years of age.
- Both offences can be committed anywhere and not just in a public place.
- The 1968 Act **s 11 exceptions**, applicable to both offences are—
  + carrying a firearm or ammunition belonging to a certificate holder (18 or over) under instructions from, and for the use of, that person for sporting purposes only;
  + a person conducting or carrying on a miniature rifle range (whether for a rifle club or otherwise) or shooting gallery at which no firearms are used other than air weapons or miniature rifles not exceeding .23 inch calibre, may possess, purchase, or acquire, such miniature rifles and ammunition suitable for that purpose; and any person using such rifles/ammunition at such a range or gallery.
- Any firearm or ammunition found on a person for these offences may be confiscated by the court.

> ## Defences
> **Both offences**—the s 11 exceptions (see 'Explanatory notes' above) may apply.
> **Section 24(2) offence**—under s 24(5) having reasonable grounds to believe that the person was 14 years of age or over (see **8.7.1**).

Related cases

Morton v Chaney [1960] 3 All ER 632 Shooting rats has been held not to be for sporting purposes.

 Summary   48 months (consent of DPP
required after 6 months)

6 months' imprisonment and/or a fine

8.1.4 **Imitation/replica firearm—convertible to s 1 firearm**

Section 1 of the Firearms Act 1982 controls imitation firearms that can be readily converted to become a working s 1 firearm.

Offences

This Act applies to an **imitation firearm** if it—
(a) has the appearance of being a **firearm** to which **section 1** of the 1968 Act (firearms requiring a **certificate**) applies; and
(b) is so constructed or adapted as to be **readily convertible into a firearm** to which that section applies.

Firearms Act 1982, s 1(1)

Points to prove

✓ possessed/purchased/acquired
✓ an imitation firearm
✓ having the appearance of a section 1 firearm **and**
✓ is constructed/adapted so as to be readily converted into a s 1 firearm
✓ without holding a firearms certificate

Meanings

Imitation firearm (see 8.3.3)
Section 1 firearm (see 8.1.1)
Certificate (see 8.1.1)

8.1.4 Imitation/replica firearm—convertible to s 1 firearm

Readily convertible into a firearm

Section 1(6) states that an imitation firearm shall be regarded as readily convertible into a firearm to which s 1 of the 1968 Act applies if—

(a) it can be so converted without any special skill on the part of the person converting it in the construction or adaptation of firearms of any description; and

(b) the work involved in converting it does not require equipment or tools other than such as are in common use by persons carrying out works of construction and maintenance in their own homes.

Explanatory notes

- A readily convertible imitation firearm that can be turned into a s 1 firearm will require a firearms certificate.
- The Firearms Act 1982, s 1 was enacted because some 'replica' weapons could be converted into s 1 working firearms with no specialist skill/tools.
- Excepting s 4(3) and (4), ss 16 to 20 and s 47 of the 1968 Act shall apply in relation to an imitation firearm to which this Act applies as it applies to a 's 1 firearm'.
- Apart from excepted air weapons, component parts, and accessories, any expression given a meaning for the purposes of the 1968 Act has the same meaning in this Act.

> #### Defences
>
> It shall be a defence for the accused to show that he did not know and had no reason to suspect that the imitation firearm was so constructed or adapted as to be readily convertible into a firearm to which s 1 of that Act applies.
>
> Firearms Act 1982, s 1(5)

Related cases

R v Howells [1977] 3 All ER 417, CA The defendant believed he had an antique gun (thereby falling within an agreed Home Office exemption) but it was in fact a replica, so was a s 1 firearm. The offence is one of strict liability.

Cafferata v Wilson [1936] 3 All ER 149, KBD A solid barrel that can be readily converted/adapted to fire missiles by boring the barrel may be a component part of a firearm.

 Either way

 None

Summary: 6 months' imprisonment and/or a fine
Indictment: 5 years' imprisonment and/or a fine
Aggravated offence (see **8.1.2**): 7 years' imprisonment and/or a fine

8.1.5 Failing to comply with firearm certificate conditions

Offences

It is an offence for a person to fail to comply with a condition subject to which a **firearm certificate** is held by him.

Firearms Act 1968, s 1(2)

Points to prove

✓ failed to comply with condition
✓ subject to which firearm certificate is held

Meaning of firearm certificate (see **8.1.1**)

Explanatory notes

Section 27(2) of the 1968 Act stipulates that a firearm certificate shall be in the prescribed form and shall specify the **conditions** subject to which it is held. Those conditions are set out in the Firearms Rules 1998 (SI 1941/1998) and HOC 41/1998; with prescribed forms under HOC 16/2013.

A statutory **condition** under the Firearms (Amendment) Act 1988, s 14 also imposes a duty on auctioneers, carriers, or warehousemen to take reasonable care of the custody of firearms and/or ammunition which they have in their possession without holding a certificate; being an offence if they fail to keep them in safe custody or fail to notify any loss or theft forthwith to the police.

Related cases

Hall v Cotton [1976] 3 WLR 681, QBD The owner/certificate holder is in possession' of the firearms even though they do not have physical control. Similarly, a custodial keeper of the guns has possession requiring certificate.

R v Chelmsford Crown Court, ex parte Farrer [2000] 1 WLR 1468, QBD Family members had knowledge of where the key to the gun cabinet

8.1.5 Failing to comply with firearm certificate conditions

was kept and so could gain access to the weapons. The Chief Constable was right to refuse certificate renewal on the grounds of a breach of the condition to prevent, as far as is reasonably practicable, access to the guns by an unauthorised person.

DPP v Houghton-Brown [2010] EWHC 3527, QBD Leaving a loaded .22 rifle under a pile of clothing on the back seat of a parked secure car was considered to be safe custody of the firearm.

 Summary 48 months

 6 months' imprisonment and/or a fine

Links to alternative subjects and offences

8.2 **Shotgun Offences**

The Firearms Act 1968 provides various offences connected with firearms, associated ammunition, air weapons, and shotguns.

8.2.1 **Shotgun without a certificate**

Section 2 of the Firearms Act 1968 creates the offence of possess, purchase, or acquire a shotgun when not being the holder of a relevant certificate.

Offences

Subject to any **exemption** under this Act, it is an offence for a person to have in his **possession** or to **purchase** or **acquire** a shotgun without holding a **certificate** under this Act authorising him to possess shotguns.

Firearms Act 1968, s 2(1)

Points to prove

✓ possessed/purchased/acquired
✓ a shotgun
✓ without a certificate

Meanings

Exemptions (see **8.1.1**)

Possession (see **8.1.1**)

Purchase (see **8.1.1**)

Acquire (see **8.1.1**)

Shotgun

means a smooth-bore gun (not being an air gun), which—
has a barrel not less than 24 inches in length and does not have any barrel with a bore exceeding 2 inches in diameter;
either has no magazine or has a non-detachable magazine incapable of holding more than 2 cartridges; **and**
is not a **revolver** gun.

Revolver

in relation to a smooth-bore gun, means a gun containing a series of chambers which revolve when the gun is fired.

Shotgun certificate

means a certificate granted by a chief officer of police under this Act authorising a person to possess shotguns.

8.2.1 Shotgun without a certificate

Explanatory notes

- The length of the barrel of a firearm is measured from the muzzle to the point at which the charge is exploded on firing and, in the case of a shotgun that length must not be less than 24 inches, otherwise it becomes a s 1 firearm (see **8.1.2**).
- Some antique shotguns may be classed as an 'antique firearm' and thus be exempt from shotgun offences. However, if 'modern' cartridges can be bought and fired using an antique shotgun it cannot be exempt. This exemption does not cover a modern replica of an antique weapon.
- An auctioneer cannot sell shotguns without either being a registered firearms dealer or obtaining a police permit.
- A person may, without holding a shotgun certificate, borrow a shotgun from the occupier of private premises and use it on that land in the occupier's presence; but where the person borrowing the shotgun is under the age of 18, this subsection applies only if the occupier is of or over the age of 18 (s 11(5)).
- A person may, without holding a shotgun certificate, use a shotgun at a time and place approved for shooting at artificial targets by the chief officer of police for the area in which the place is situated (s 11(6)).

Related cases

Watts v Seymour [1967] 1 All ER 1044, QBD The test as to when a purchase/sale was complete was if the purchaser could validly sell and transfer title to the weapon to another person.

R v Howells [1977] 3 All ER 417 A modern reproduction is not an antique

Richards v Curwen [1977] 3 All ER 426, QBD Whether a firearm is an 'antique' is a matter of fact for the justices to decide in each case.

Hall v Cotton [1976] 3 WLR 681, QBD The owner/certificate holder remained in possession of their shotguns despite having no physical control. Similarly, the custodial keeper of the shotguns also has possession and therefore requires a certificate.

Practical considerations

- All repeating shotguns holding more than two cartridges (eg pump-action and revolver shotguns) are s 1 firearms.
- Offences may be committed in relation to persons under 15 years where they have an assembled shotgun with them or for a person to give them a shotgun/ammunition as a gift (see **8.2.2**).
- Any offence involving a shotgun that has an illegally shortened barrel (less than 24 inches), thus creating a 'sawn-off' shotgun, will be an 'aggravated offence' (see 8.1.2) carrying a greater penalty. It will also make the shotgun a s 1 firearm.
- A shotgun is deemed to be loaded if there is a cartridge in the barrel or approved magazine that can feed the cartridge into the barrel by manual or automatic means.
- A shotgun adapted to have a magazine must bear a mark on the magazine showing approval by the Secretary of State.

• 'Shotgun' includes any component part and any accessory for a shotgun designed or adapted to diminish the noise or flash caused by firing the gun.

 Either way   None

Summary: 6 months' imprisonment and/or a fine
Indictment: 5 years' imprisonment and/or a fine

8.2.2 Shotgun restrictions to under 15 years

Sections 22 and 24 of the Firearms Act 1968 impose shotgun restrictions relating to persons under 15.

Offences

Under 15 have with them

It is an offence for a person under the age of 15 to have **with him** an assembled **shotgun**, except while under the supervision of a person of or over the age of 21, or while the shotgun is so covered with a securely fastened gun cover that it cannot be fired.

Firearms Act 1968, s 22(3)

Make gift to under 15

It is an offence to make a gift of a shotgun or ammunition for a shotgun to a person under the age of 15.

Firearms Act 1968, s 24(3)

Points to prove

Have with them

✓ person under 15
✓ had with them
✓ assembled shotgun

Make gift

✓ made a gift of
✓ shotgun/ammunition for a shotgun
✓ to a person under 15

8.2.3 Fail to comply with shotgun certificate conditions

Meanings

With him (see 8.3.6)

Shotgun (see 8.2.1)

> **Defence for person making gift** (see s 24(5) 8.7.1)

Practical considerations

- Unless exempted, or s 11(5) and (6) applies (see 8.2.1) the person concerned must also be the holder of a shotgun certificate before they can possess, purchase, or acquire a shotgun.
- Offences in relation to air weapons/firearms are imposed on persons under 18 years (see 8.7.1 and 8.7.2).
- Both ss 22(3) and 24(3) offences can be committed anywhere and not just in a public place.
- A court can order the destruction of any shotgun and ammunition to which this offence relates.
- Restrictions also apply to persons under 14 years in relation to s 1 firearms (see 8.1.3).

 SSS

 Summary   6 months

 Level 3 fine

8.2.3 **Fail to comply with shotgun certificate conditions**

Section 2 of the Firearms Act 1968 creates an offence of failing to comply with a condition imposed by a shotgun certificate.

> **Offences**
>
> It is an offence for a person to fail to comply with a condition subject to which a **shotgun certificate** is held by him.
>
> Firearms Act 1968, s 2(2)

Points to prove

✓ failed to comply with condition
✓ subject to which shotgun certificate is held

Meaning of shotgun certificate (see **8.2.1**)

Practical considerations

Regarding public safety, the two main **conditions** applying to shotgun certificate holders are the failure to keep the shotgun(s) and/or cartridges in safe custody or in failing to notify any loss forthwith to the police.
Under s 28(1) a chief officer of police has to be satisfied that the applicant can be permitted to possess a shotgun without danger to the public safety or to the peace.
Section 28(1A) states that no certificate shall be granted or renewed if the chief officer of police has reason to believe that the applicant is prohibited from possessing a shotgun; **or** does not have a good reason for possessing, purchasing, or acquiring one.
It is an offence, under s 28A(7), to knowingly or recklessly make a false statement for the purpose of procuring the grant or renewal of a certificate.
There is a presumption in favour of granting unless the police can prove any of the exemptions.
The certificate must contain a description of the weapon including any identity numbers.

 Summary   48 months

 6 months' imprisonment and/or a fine

Links to alternative subjects and offences

8.3 **Criminal Use of Firearms**

There is a raft of legislation which has been put in place to try and cur[b] possession of firearms by criminals: some of these measures are discusse[d] below.

8.3.1 **Ban on possession by convicted perso[n]**

Section 21 of the Firearms Act 1968 creates an offence for the possessio[n] of any firearm or ammunition by convicted criminals. The section fir[st] provides three types of ban: total; 5 years from date of release; whi[le] under a licence, order, or binding over condition.

Lengths of ban

Total ban

Anyone sentenced to custody for life or preventive detention, imprison-
ment or corrective training for a term of 3 years or more, or to yout[h] custody, or detention in a young offender institution for such a ter[m] shall not **at any time** have a firearm or ammunition in his possession—
s 21(1).

5 years

- A person who has been sentenced to imprisonment for a term of
  3 months or more but less than 3 years, or to youth custody, or
  detention in a young offender institution for such a term, or who ha[s] been subject to a secure training order, or a detention and training
  order, shall not at any time before the expiration of the period of
  5 years from **the date of release** have a **firearm** or **ammunition** in
  their **possession**—s 21(2).
- A person who has been sentenced to imprisonment for a term of
  3 months or more, and the sentence is suspended under s 189 of
  the CJA 2003, shall not have a firearm or ammunition in his
  possession at any time during the period of 5 years beginning
  with the second day after the date on which the sentence is
  passed—s 21(2C).

Other bans

- A person while—
  - (a) discharged on licence, being holder of licence, issued for
    detention of children and young persons convicted of serious
    crime;
  - (b) subject of recognizance to keep peace or be of good behaviour, o[r] community order with a condition not to possess, use, or carry a
    firearm;

  shall not have a firearm or ammunition in their possession—s 21(3).

Offences

Possess whilst banned

It is an offence for a person to contravene any of the foregoing provisions of this section [*contravene above bans*].

Firearms Act 1968, s 21(4)

Sell/transfer/repair/test/prove for banned person

It is an offence for a person to sell or transfer a firearm or ammunition to, or to repair, test or prove a firearm or ammunition for, a person whom he knows or has reasonable ground for believing to be prohibited by this section from having a **firearm or ammunition** in his **possession**.

Firearms Act 1968, s 21(5)

Points to prove

Possess whilst banned

✓ being person sentenced to
✓ imprisonment/youth custody/detention in YOI/detention and training order/secure training order/suspended sentence or other sentence subject to s 21(3)
✓ for a term of [period]
✓ possessed a firearm and/or ammunition namely [description]
✓ while banned/before the expiration of ban

Sell/transfer/repair/test/prove for banned person

✓ sell/transfer **or** repair/test/prove
✓ firearm or ammunition for
✓ a person
✓ prohibited by s 21 from possessing

Meanings

Date of release

Details vary and are as follows—

• Normal sentence—actual date a prisoner leaves prison.
• Part imprisonment and part suspended sentence—date of release from prison.
• A 'secure training order' or 'detention and training order' whichever is the latest of the following—
  ✦ actual date of release;
  ✦ date the person was released from the order because of a breach;
  ✦ date halfway through the total period of the order.

Possession (see **8.1.1**)

Firearm or ammunition (see **8.1.1**)

8.3.2 Possession with intent to endanger life

Practical considerations

- A person given a suspended sentence of 3 months or more imprisonment will be subject to a 5 year ban under s 21(2C).
- Where there are several short sentences, it is the total sentence that counts.
- Anyone who is banned by these provisions can apply to the Crown Court under s 21(6) for removal of the ban.
- Do not confuse the terms firearm or ammunition with s 1 firearms or ammunition. This section includes **all** firearms including air weapons and shotguns.
- If it is an air weapon, it must be proved that it can discharge a shot or missile and that it is a lethal barrelled weapon, capable of causing injury from which death could result.

 Either way   None

 Summary: 6 months' imprisonment and/or a fine
Indictment: 5 years' imprisonment and/or a fine

8.3.2 **Possession with intent to endanger life**

Section 16 of the Firearms Act 1968 creates the offence of possession of a firearm or ammunition with intent to endanger life.

Offences

It is an offence for a person to have in his **possession** any **firearm or ammunition** with **intent** by means thereof to **endanger life** or to enable another person by means thereof to endanger life, whether any injury has been caused or not.

Firearms Act 1968, s 16

Points to prove

✓ possessed firearm/ammunition
✓ with intent
✓ to endanger life/enable another to endanger life thereby

Meanings

Possession (see **8.1.1**)

Firearm or ammunition

Includes all firearms and ammunition (see **8.1.1**).

Intent (see **4.1.2**)

Endanger life

Life need not actually be endangered, although if there is danger to life this may assist in proving intent. There is no need to prove any harm or injury to the victim.

Explanatory notes

The intention to endanger life need not be immediate, but it must result from the firearm/ammunition (eg if the defendant possesses the firearm or ammunition but intends to endanger life some other way, say by arson, this offence is **not** committed).

Related cases

R v Salih [2007] EWCA Crim 2750, CA If a person is in fear of an imminent attack and is carrying a firearm or offensive weapon for self-protection against an explicit and specific threat then self-defence may apply; it is a matter for the jury to decide.

R v Bentham [1972] 3 All ER 271, CA Possession is a continuing state and the intention to endanger life might last as long as the possession. The intent may not be limited to an immediate intention.

R v El-hakkaoui [1975] 2 All ER 146, CA It is an offence for a person to have in his possession a firearm/ammunition with intent to endanger the life of people outside the UK.

R v Jones [1997] 2 WLR 792, CA Possession for another to endanger life requires the firearm to be held for that reason, not just for someone involved in crime.

Practical considerations

Intention to endanger life in another country is also an offence under this section.

The offence of possession for another to endanger life requires the firearm to be specifically held intending that the other should endanger life with it. If the firearm/ammunition is simply held for someone known to be involved in crime, that will be insufficient for this offence. Consider the alternative offences of possession—

+ with intent to cause fear of violence (which covers a wider set of circumstances) (see **8.3.3**);
+ at the time of committing/being arrested for a relevant offence (see **8.3.5**).

Indictable

None

Life imprisonment and/or a fine

8.3.3 **Possession with intent to cause fear of violence**

Section 16A of the Firearms Act 1968 creates an offence of possessing firearm (or imitation firearm) with intent to cause others to fear unlawfu violence being used against them.

Offences

It is an offence for a person to have in his **possession** any **firearm** or **imitation firearm** with **intent**—
(a) by means thereof to cause; or
(b) to enable another person by means thereof to cause
any person to believe that **unlawful violence** will be used against him or another person.

Firearms Act 1968, s 16A

Points to prove

✓ had in your possession
✓ a firearm/imitation firearm
✓ with intent
✓ to cause/enable another to cause
✓ any person
✓ to believe unlawful violence will be used
✓ against them or another person

Meanings

Possession (see **8.1.1**)

Firearm

Means all firearms, not just s 1 firearms (see **8.1.1**).

Imitation firearm

Means any thing that has the appearance of being a firearm (other tha appearance of prohibited weapon under s 5(1)(b) for discharge of ar noxious liquid, gas, or other thing) whether or not it is capable of discharging any shot, bullet, or other missile.

Intent (see **4.1.2**)

Unlawful violence

Means the unlawful exercise of physical force so as to cause injury or damage to property.

Practical considerations

* The offence can be committed anywhere and does not require intent to commit any specific criminal offence.
* It does not matter if the weapon is an imitation, inoperative, or unloaded.

 Indictable None

 10 years' imprisonment and/or a fine

8.3.4 Using a firearm to resist or prevent a lawful arrest

Section 17(1) of the Firearms Act 1968 creates the offence of using a firearm or imitation firearm to resist or prevent a lawful arrest.

Offences

It is an offence for a person to make or attempt to make any use whatsoever of a **firearm** or **imitation firearm** with **intent** to resist or prevent the lawful arrest or detention of himself or another person.

Firearms Act 1968, s 17(1)

Points to prove

✓ made/attempted to make use
✓ of a firearm/an imitation firearm
✓ with intent
✓ to resist/prevent lawful arrest/detention
✓ of self/another

8.3.5 Possession at time of committing/being arrested

Meanings

Firearm

Means all firearms, not just s 1 firearms (see **8.1.1**). Although it does not include component parts and accessories designed or adapted to diminish the noise or flash caused by firing the weapon.

Imitation firearm (see **8.3.3**)

Intent (see **4.1.2**)

Explanatory notes

It has to be proved that the firearm was being used intentionally to resist/prevent the lawful arrest of the offender or another person.

 Indictable None

Life imprisonment and/or a fine

8.3.5 **Possession at time of committing/being arrested**

Section 17(2) of the Firearms Act 1968 makes it an offence to be in possession of a firearm or imitation firearm at the time of arrest for certain specified offences.

> ### Offences
>
> If a person at the time of his committing or being arrested for an **offence** specified in **schedule 1** to this Act, has in his **possession** a **firearm** or **imitation firearm** he shall be guilty of an offence under this subsection unless he shows that he had it in his possession for a **lawful object**.
>
> Firearms Act 1968, s 17(2)

Points to prove
✓ at the time of being arrested for/committing
✓ a Sch 1 offence
✓ possessed firearm/imitation firearm

Meanings

Schedule 1 offences

- Criminal Damage Act 1971, s 1—damage; damage with intent endanger life; arson.
- Offences Against the Person Act 1861—
  - ◆ s 20—wounding/GBH;
  - ◆ s 21—criminal intent choke/strangle;
  - ◆ s 22—criminal use of stupefying drugs;
  - ◆ s 30—laying explosive to building etc;
  - ◆ s 32—endangering persons by tampering with railway;
  - ◆ s 38—assault with intent to resist lawful arrest;
  - ◆ s 47—assault occasioning actual bodily harm.
- Child Abduction Act 1984, Pt 1—abduction of children.
- Theft Act 1968—burglary; blackmail; theft: robbery; taking of motor vehicles.
- Police Act 1996—assaulting/impeding a police officer.
- Criminal Justice Act 1991—assault prisoner custody officer.
- Criminal Justice and Public Order Act 1994—assault secure training centre custody officer.
- Criminal Justice and Courts Act 2015—assault secure college custody officer.
- Sexual Offences Act 2003—
  - ◆ rape;
  - ◆ assault by penetration;
  - ◆ cause person to engage in sexual activity involving penetration;
  - ◆ rape of a child under 13;
  - ◆ assault of a child under 13 by penetration;
  - ◆ cause/incite child under 13 to engage in sexual activity involving penetration;
  - ◆ sexual activity with a mentally disordered person involving penetration;
  - ◆ cause/incite mentally disordered person to engage in penetrative sexual activity.

Aiding and abetting any of the Sch 1 offences.

Attempting to commit any of the Sch 1 offences.

Possession (see **8.1.1**)

Firearm (see **8.3.4**)

Imitation firearm (see **8.3.3**)

Defences

Proving possession of the firearm or imitation firearm for a lawful reason or purpose.

Explanatory notes

In this section, 'firearm' means a complete weapon and does not include component parts, and such items as silencers and flash eliminators.

8.3.6 Carrying firearm—criminal intent/resist arrest

- There is no need to prove any use or intended use of the firearm. Possession of it may be completely unconnected with the other offence committed by the person or for which they are arrested.

Related cases

R v Guy (1991) 93 Cr App R 108, CA Schedule 1 applies to any offence where theft is an element.

R v Nelson [2000] 2 Cr App R 160, CA When the defendant is arrested for a 'relevant' Sch 1 offence there is no need to prove the Sch 1 offence itself.

R v Bentham [2005] UKHL 18, HL The defendant carried out a robbery with his finger in his jacket pocket pointing towards the victim. Held: That as the fingers were part of the person, and not separate and distinct then they could never be possessed as a 'thing' having the appearance of a firearm.

 Indictable

 None

 Life imprisonment and/or a fine

8.3.6 **Carrying firearm—criminal intent/ resist arrest**

Section 18 of the Firearms Act 1968 makes it an offence to carry a firearm or imitation firearm with criminal intent or to resist/prevent arrest.

> **Offences**
>
> It is an offence for a person to **have with him** a **firearm** or **imitation firearm** with **intent** to commit an **indictable offence**, or to resist arrest or prevent the arrest of another, in either case while he has the firearm or imitation firearm with him.
>
> Firearms Act 1968, s 18 (1)

Points to prove

✓ had with you
✓ a firearm/imitation firearm
✓ with intent
✓ to commit an indictable offence/resist arrest/prevent the arrest of another

Meanings

Has with him

This is a narrower definition than 'possession' (see **8.1.1**). Here there is a need to prove—

- a knowledge of the existence of the article;
- that the article was 'to hand and ready for use' (eg, it may be hidden a few feet away: it does not have to be physically on the defendant's person).

Firearm (see **8.3.3**)

Imitation firearm (see **8.3.3**)

Intent (see **4.1.2**)

Indictable offence

This includes either way offences.

Related cases

R v Duhaney, R v Stoddart (1998) 2 Cr App R 25, CA Whether or not the firearm is used, or intended to be used, to further that particular offence, is irrelevant.

R v Pawlicki and Swindell [1992] 3 All ER 903, CA Accessibility, not distance, is the test for 'have with him'.

Practical considerations

- Proof that the defendant had a firearm or imitation firearm with them and intended to commit the offence, or to resist or prevent arrest, is evidence that they intended to have it with them while doing so.
- Consider 'possess firearm with intent to cause the fear of unlawful violence' (see **8.3.3**) which has a much wider scope.

 Indictable   None

 Life imprisonment and/or a fine

8.3.7 **Using person to mind a firearm/ weapon**

Section 28 of the Violent Crime Reduction Act 2006 makes it an offence to use another person to look after, hide, or transport a dangerous weapon, subject to an agreement that it would be available when required for an unlawful purpose.

Offences

(1) A person is guilty of an offence if—
  (a) he uses another to look after, hide or transport a **dangerous weapon** for him; and
  (b) he does so under arrangements or in circumstances that facilitate, or are intended to facilitate, the weapon's being **available** to him for an unlawful purpose.

Violent Crime Reduction Act 2006, s 28

Points to prove

✓ uses another person to
✓ look after/hide/transport
✓ dangerous weapon and
✓ under arrangements made or facilitation agreed/intended
✓ the weapon is made available
✓ for an unlawful purpose

Meanings

Dangerous weapon (s 28(3))

In this section 'dangerous weapon' means—
(a) a firearm (see **8.1.1**) **other than** an air weapon or a component part of, or accessory to, an air weapon (see **8.1.2**); or
(b) a weapon to which s 141 (see **8.9.2**) or s 141A (see **8.10.2**) of the Criminal Justice Act 1988 applies (specified offensive weapons, knives, and bladed weapons).

Available for an unlawful purpose (s 28(2))

For the purposes of this section the cases in which a dangerous weapon is to be regarded as available to a person for an unlawful purpose include any case where—
(a) the weapon is available for him to take possession of it at a time and place; **and**
(b) his possession of the weapon at that time and place would constitute, or be likely to involve or to lead to, the commission by him of an offence.

Indictable None

 4 to 10 years' imprisonment and/or a fine (details given in s 29)

Links to alternative subjects and offences

8.4 **Trespassing with Firearms**

The Firearms Act 1968 provides various offences connected with firearms, air weapons, shotguns, and associated ammunition. Some such offences involve trespassing.

8.4.1 **Trespass with any firearm in a building**

Section 20 of the Firearms Act 1968 creates two offences of trespassing with firearms, one of which is concerned with trespass in buildings.

Offences

A person commits an offence if, while he **has a firearm** or **imitation firearm with him**, he enters or is in any building or part of a building as a trespasser and without reasonable excuse (the proof whereof lies on him).

Firearms Act 1968, s 20(1)

Points to prove
- ✓ had with you
- ✓ firearm/imitation firearm
- ✓ entered or was in
- ✓ building/part of building
- ✓ as a trespasser
- ✓ without reasonable excuse

Meanings

Firearm (see **8.3.3**)

Imitation firearm (see **8.3.3**)

Has with him (see **8.3.6**)

Explanatory notes
- A firearm in these circumstances means any firearm—shotgun, air weapon, prohibited weapon, and s 1 firearm.
- The terms 'enters', 'building', 'part of a building', and 'trespasser' should be interpreted as terms used in legislation/case law relating to burglary (see **3.3.1**).

Defence

Reasonable excuse (the burden of proof lies with the defendant). This defence could include saving life/property or self-defence (eg the police carrying out a planned firearms operation).

Practical considerations

- It is important to note that although this is an either way offence, if the weapon is an air weapon or imitation firearm it is triable summarily only.
- The burden of proof lies with the defendant if they claim to have a reasonable excuse. Whether an excuse is reasonable would be for the court to decide having considered all the circumstances.
- Unless it is an imitation, there needs to be some evidence that the weapon is a firearm.
- Consider the offences of aggravated burglary (see **3.3.2**) or attempt aggravated burglary (see **4.1.1**) (especially if an imitation or air weapon is used—greater penalty).

 SSS   E&S

 Either way   None

 Summary: 6 months' imprisonment and/or a fine
Indictment: 7 years' imprisonment and/or a fine

Air weapons/imitation firearms

 Summary   48 months

 6 months' imprisonment and/or a fine

8.4.2 Trespass with firearm on land

Section 20(2) of the Firearms Act 1968 creates an offence of trespass with a firearm on land.

8.4.2 Trespass with firearm on land

Offences

A person commits an offence if, while he **has** a **firearm** or **imitation firearm with him**, he enters or is on any **land** as a **trespasser** and without reasonable excuse (the proof whereof lies on him).

Firearms Act 1968, s 20(2)

Points to prove

✓ had with you
✓ firearm/imitation firearm
✓ entered/was on land
✓ as a trespasser
✓ without reasonable excuse

Meanings

Firearm (see **8.3.3**)

Imitation firearm (see **8.3.3**)

Has with him (see **8.3.6**)

Land

This includes land covered with water.

Trespass (see **3.3.1**)

Explanatory notes

A firearm in these circumstances means any firearm—shotgun, air weapon, prohibited weapon, and s 1 firearm.

Defences

Reasonable excuse (see **8.4.1**)

Practical considerations

- In order to prove a trespass it must be shown that the defendant knew that they were a trespasser or was reckless as to whether the facts existed which made them a trespasser.
- If a defence of reasonable excuse is claimed, the burden of proof lies with the defendant.
- Unless it is an imitation firearm, there needs to be some evidence that the weapon is 'a firearm'.

ername

 Summary 48 months

3 months' imprisonment and/or a level 4 fine

Links to alternative subjects and offences

8.5 Possess Firearm or Imitation Firearm in a Public Place

Section 19 of the Firearms Act 1968 provides various offences relating to the possession of shotguns, air weapons, firearms, and imitation firearms in a public place.

Offences

A person commits an offence if, without lawful authority or reasonable excuse (the proof whereof lies on him) he **has with him** in a **public place**—
(a) a **loaded shotgun**,
(b) an **air weapon** (whether loaded or not),
(c) any **other firearm** (whether loaded or not) together with ammunition suitable for use in that firearm, or
(d) an **imitation firearm**.

Firearms Act 1968, s 19

Points to prove

✓ without lawful authority/reasonable excuse
✓ had with you in a public place
✓ firearm (together with suitable ammunition) **or**
✓ loaded shotgun **or**
✓ loaded/unloaded air weapon **or**
✓ an imitation firearm

Meanings

Has with him (see **8.3.6**)

Public place

This includes any highway and any other premises or place to which at the material time the public have or are permitted to have access, whether on payment or otherwise.

Loaded

Means if there is a cartridge in the barrel or approved magazine that can feed the cartridge into the barrel by manual or automatic means.

Shotgun (see **8.2.1**)

Air weapon (see **8.7.2**)

Other firearm (see **8.1.1**)

Imitation firearm (see **8.3.3**)

Explanatory notes

In this offence the requirement for the weapons to be loaded or not varies—

- the requirement for a loaded weapon only applies to shotguns;
- for air weapons, there is no need to have ammunition for it;
- for other firearms, the defendant must have ammunition suitable for use with that firearm.

Defences

Having lawful authority or reasonable excuse (the burden of proof lies with the defendant). This defence could include saving life/property or self-defence (eg the police carrying out a planned firearms operation). Whether an excuse is reasonable would be for the court to decide having considered all the circumstances.

Related cases

R v Harrison [1996] Crim LR 200 During a robbery one of the robbers had a loaded sawn-off shotgun which the other knew nothing about. On police arrival the other offender took possession of the gun and although not knowing it was loaded still commits the offence.

Bates v DPP (1993) 157 JP 1004, QBD Inside a vehicle may be a public place.

Anderson v Miller [1976] Crim LR 743 The space behind a counter in a shop was held to be a public place.

Ross v Collins [1982] Crim LR 368, QBD A shotgun certificate gives no lawful authority for a loaded shotgun in a public place.

R v Jones [1995] 2 WLR 64, CA A firearms certificate does not give the holder a defence of 'lawful authority' against a charge under s 19. The certificate is granted for a specific purpose with conditions attached.

R v Morris & King (1984) 149 JP 60, 79 Cr App Rep 104, CA The test for an imitation firearm is whether the 'thing' looked like a firearm at the time when the accused actually had it with him.

Practical considerations

- Section 161 of the Highways Act 1980 deals with the offence of discharging any firearm within 50 feet from the centre of a highway (see **8.8.6**).
- Section 28 of the Town Police Clauses Act 1847 deals with the offence of reckless discharge of a firearm in the street to the annoyance or danger of residents or passengers (see **8.8.6**).
- The 'guilty knowledge' that the prosecution must prove is knowledge of existence of the firearm, not the nature and quality of the weapon.
- The prosecution must prove that the firearm is 'to hand and able to be used'.
- With an imitation firearm, the key issue is whether it looked like a firearm at the time of the offence. It is for the jury to decide on the circumstances of each case.

8.5 Possess Firearm or Imitation Firearm in a Public Place

- Offences involving imitation firearms are of having or possessing an imitation firearm not of falsely pretending to have one (*R v Bentham* [2005] UKHL 18—see **8.3.5**).
- Imitation or replica weapons that can be converted into working firearms will be classed as s 1 firearms (see **8.1.4**).
- Unless it is an imitation firearm, there needs to be some evidence that the weapon is a firearm (see **8.1.1**).

 Either way None

 Summary: 6 months' imprisonment and/or a fine
Indictment: 7 years' imprisonment and/or a fine
Imitation firearm: 12 months' imprisonment and/or a fine

Air weapons

 Summary 48 months

 6 months' imprisonment and/or a fine

Links to alternative subjects and offences

SSS Stop, search and seize powers   **E&S** Entry and search powers

8.6 Police Powers—Firearms

The Firearms Act 1968 provides various offences and powers connected with firearms, air weapons, shotguns, and associated ammunition.

8.6.1 Requirement to hand over firearm/ ammunition

Section 47 of the Firearms Act 1968 deals with police powers to stop and search for firearms and provides an offence for failure to do so.

Police stop and search powers

A constable may require any person whom he has **reasonable cause to suspect—**
(a) of having a **firearm**, with or without **ammunition, with him** in a **public place**; or
(b) to be committing or about to commit, elsewhere than in a public place, an **offence relevant** for the purposes of this section,
to hand over the firearm or any ammunition for examination by the constable.

Firearms Act 1968, s 47(1)

Meanings

Reasonable cause to suspect
There must be objective grounds for the suspicion based on facts, information, or intelligence that are relevant to the likelihood of finding the article(s) (see **12.1.1**).

Firearm/ammunition (see **8.1.1**)

Has with him (see **8.3.6**)

Public place (see **8.5**)

Relevant offence
This refers to s 18 and s 20 offences, being either having a firearm or imitation firearm—
• with intent to commit an indictable offence, or to resist arrest, or prevent the arrest of another (see **8.3.6**);
• with them and enters either a building, or part of a building, or land as a trespasser (see **8.4**).

8.6.1 Requirement to hand over firearm/ammunition

Offences

It is an offence for a person having a firearm or ammunition with him to fail to hand it over when required to do so by a constable under subsection (1) above.

Firearms Act 1968, s 47(2)

Points to prove

✓ failed to hand over
✓ a firearm/ammunition for a firearm
✓ in your possession
✓ when required to do so
✓ by a constable

Section 47 of the Firearms Act 1968 also provides qualified powers to search for firearms in respect of both people and vehicles and detain them for that purpose.

Police search and detain powers

Person

If a constable has reasonable cause to suspect a person of having a firearm with him in a public place, **or** to be committing or about to commit **elsewhere** than in a public place an offence relevant for the purposes of this section, the constable may search that person and may detain him for the purpose of doing so.

Firearms Act 1968, s 47(3)

Vehicle

If a constable has reasonable cause to suspect that there is a firearm in a vehicle in a public place, **or** that a vehicle is being or is about to be used in connection with the commission of an offence relevant for the purposes of this section elsewhere than in a public place, he may search the vehicle and for that purpose require the person driving or in control of it to stop it.

Firearms Act 1968, s 47(4)

Explanatory notes

- In exercising these powers, s 47(5) also gives a constable power to enter any place.
- The police also have the power to demand the production of shotgun or firearm certificates (see **8.6.2**).
- The power to stop the vehicle is not restricted to a constable in uniform.
- Officers should ensure that the stop and search procedures comply with PACE and the relevant Code (see **12.1.2**).
- With regard to premises a search warrant will have to be obtained under s 46 (see **8.6.3**).

Summary 48 months

 3 months' imprisonment and/or a level 4 fine

8.6.2 **Police powers—firearms/shotgun certificates**

Section 48 of the Firearms Act 1968 gives a constable power to demand from a person they believe to be in possession of a s 1 firearm/ammunition or shotgun the production of a valid certificate or European pass or to show that they are exempt.

> **Production of certificate**
>
> A constable may **demand**, from any person whom he **believes** to be in **possession** of a **firearm** or **ammunition** to which **section 1** of this Act applies, or of a **shotgun**, the **production** of his **firearm certificate** or, as the case may be, his **shotgun certificate**.
>
> Firearms Act 1968, s 48(1)

Meanings

Demand production

Where a person upon whom a demand has been made by a constable under subsection (1) and whom the constable believes to be in possession of a firearm fails—

(a) to produce a firearm certificate or, as the case may be, a shotgun certificate;

(b) to show that he is a person who, by reason of his place of residence or any other circumstances, is not entitled to be issued with a document identifying that firearm under any of the provisions which in the other member States correspond to the provisions of this Act for the issue of European firearms passes; or

(c) to show that he is in possession of the firearm exclusively in connection with the carrying on of activities in respect of which, he or the person on whose behalf he has possession of the firearm, is recognised, for the purposes of the law of another member State relating to firearms, as a collector of firearms or a body concerned in the cultural or historical aspects of weapons, the constable may demand from that person the production of a document which has been issued to that person in another member State under any such corresponding provisions, identifies that firearm as a firearm to which it relates and is for the time being valid.

Firearms Act 1968, s 48(1A)

Believes

This is a more stringent requirement than 'suspects' and requires stronger grounds.

Section 1 firearm/ammunition (see **8.1.1**)

Firearm certificate (see **8.1.1**)

Shotgun (see **8.2.1**)

Shotgun certificate (see **8.2.1**)

Offences

It is an offence for a person who is in possession of a firearm to fail to comply with a demand under subsection (1A) above.

Firearms Act 1968, s 48(4)

Points to prove

✓ being in possession
✓ of a firearm/shotgun
✓ failed
✓ to comply with a demand
✓ by constable
✓ to produce a valid certificate/document or show exemption

Seize/detain weapon and require details

If a person upon whom a demand is made fails to produce the certificate or document, or to permit the constable to read it, or to show that he is entitled by virtue of this Act to have the firearm, ammunition or shotgun in his possession without holding a certificate, the constable may seize and detain the firearm, ammunition or shotgun and may require the person to declare to him immediately his name and address.

Firearms Act 1968, s 48(2)

Offences

If under this section a person is required to declare to a constable his name and address, it is an offence for him to refuse to declare it or to fail to give his true name and address.

Firearms Act 1968, s 48(3)

Points to prove

✓ having possession
✓ of a firearm/shotgun
✓ failed/refused
✓ to divulge
✓ when required by a constable
✓ their name and address

Explanatory notes

- A firearm certificate also includes a Northern Ireland Certificate.
- As the requirement is to declare 'immediately' their name and address, it is taken that the demand to produce a valid certificate/document or show exemption and (if applicable) the subsequent seizure of the firearm, ammunition, or shotgun will also follow the same immediacy.

 Summary   6 months

Level 3 fine

8.6.3 Premises search warrant

Section 46 of the Firearms Act 1968 deals with the issue of premises search warrants for firearms and authorities attached thereto.

Granting of warrant

If a justice of the peace is satisfied by information on oath that there is reasonable ground for suspecting—

(a) that an **offence relevant** for the purposes of this section has been, is being, or is about to be committed; or

(b) that, in connection with a firearm or ammunition, there is a danger to the public safety or to the peace,

he may grant a warrant for any of the **purposes** mentioned in subsection (2) below.

Firearms Act 1968, s 46(1)

8.6.3 Premises search warrant

Meanings

Relevant offences

All offences under this Act except an offence under s 22(3) [unsupervised 15-year-old possess shotgun—see **8.2.3**] or an offence relating specifically to air weapons.

Purposes of warrant

A warrant under this section may authorise a constable or civilian officer—

(a) to enter at any time any premises or place named in the warrant, if necessary by force, and to search the premises or place and every person found there;

(b) to seize and detain anything which he may find on the premises or place, or on any such person, in respect of which or in connection with which he has reasonable ground for suspecting—

    (i) that an offence **relevant** for the purposes of this section has been, is being or is about to be committed; or

    (ii) that in connection with a firearm, imitation firearm, or ammunition, there is a danger to the public safety or to the peace.

Firearms Act 1968, s 46(2)

Offences

It is an offence for any person intentionally to obstruct a constable or civilian officer in the exercise of his powers under this section.

Firearms Act 1968, s 46(5)

Points to prove

✓ intentionally obstruct
✓ constable/civilian officer
✓ whilst exercising their powers under s 46

Meaning of civilian officer

Means a person employed by a police authority or the Corporation of the City of London who is under the direction and control of a chief officer of police.

Explanatory notes

- Ensure that the application and execution of the warrant complies with PACE and the COP (see **12.4**).
- In some forces inspections of gun clubs and other routine firearms enquiries are performed by civilian staff rather than police officers.

Summary 48 months

6 months' imprisonment and/or a fine

Links to alternative subjects and offences

8.7 Firearms, Air Weapons, Imitation Firearms—Age Restrictions

The Firearms Act 1968 provides various offences connected with firearms, imitation firearms, air weapons, shotguns, and associated ammunition. Invariably restrictions are in place as to the age of the person involved.

8.7.1 Purchase/hire or supply by/to under 18

Sections 22(1) and 24(1) of the Firearms Act 1968 prohibit purchase/hire or supply (sell or let on hire) of any firearm or ammunition by or to a person under 18 years of age.

Offences

Purchase/hire by under 18

It is an offence for a person under the age of 18 to purchase or hire **any firearm or ammunition**.

Firearms Act 1968, s 22(1)

Supplier (sell/hire) to under 18

It is an offence to sell or let on hire **any firearm or ammunition** to a person under the age of 18.

Firearms Act 1968, s 24(1)

Points to prove

Purchase/hire

✓ being a person under the age of 18
✓ purchased/hired
✓ any firearm/ammunition

Supplier (sell/hire)

✓ sold/let on hire, **either**
✓ any firearm/ammunition
✓ to a person under the age of 18

Meanings of firearm/ammunition

- Air weapons and air pellets/darts (see **8.7.2**).
- Shotguns and cartridges (see **8.2.1**).
- Section 1/other firearms or ammunition (see **8.1.1**).

Defence for supplier under s 24

In proceedings for an offence under any provision of this section it is a defence to prove that the person charged with the offence believed the other person to be of or over the age mentioned in that provision and had reasonable ground for the belief.

Firearms Act 1968, s 24(5)

Practical considerations

- The Firearms (Amendment) Regulations 2010 (SI 1759/2010) increased the age to 18 for lawfully purchasing or hiring all firearms and ammunition under ss 22(1), 24(1) (above), and for s 11 exemptions (see **8.1.3, 8.2.1**). Details are given in HOC 12/2010.
- Further prohibition on minors possessing, acquiring, or being supplied with firearms and/or ammunition is given in other s 22 and s 24 offences—
  - **'Section 1' firearms/ammunition (under 14)**—possessing, making a gift of, lending, or part with possession (see **8.1.3**).
  - **Shotgun/cartridges (under 15)**—having an assembled shotgun without being supervised (by a person aged 21 years or over) or securely fastened in a gun cover or making a gift of a shotgun or cartridges to such person (see **8.2.2**).
  - **Air weapons/ammunition (under 18)**—having, making a gift of, or part with possession (see **8.7.2**).
- It is an offence under s 24A for a person under 18 to purchase or to be sold an imitation firearm (see **8.7.5**).

 Summary   48 months (6 months if air weapon/ammunition)

 If firearm/ammunition by/to a person aged 17—3 months' imprisonment and/or a fine. If air weapon/ammunition or any other case—6 months' imprisonment and/or a fine

8.7.2 Air weapons—further offences (others)/under 18 restrictions

The Firearms Act 1968 provides exceptions for young people to possess air weapons, but generally it is an offence for a person under 18 to have with them or be given, an air weapon, or ammunition for an air weapon.

Possess, make gift, or part possession

Offences

Under 18 have with them

Subject to **section 23**, it is an offence for a person under the age of 18 to **have with him** an air weapon or ammunition for an **air weapon**.

Firearms Act 1968, s 22(4)

Make gift/part with possession to under 18

It is an offence—

(a) to make a gift of an **air weapon** or ammunition for an air weapon to a person under the age of 18; or

(b) to part with the possession of an air weapon or ammunition for an air weapon to a person under the age of 18 except where by virtue of **section 23** of this Act the person is not prohibited from having it with him.

Firearms Act 1968, s 24(4)

Points to prove

Have with them

✓ being under 18 years of age
✓ had with you
✓ an air weapon or ammunition for an air weapon

Make a gift

✓ made a gift
✓ of an air weapon/ammunition for an air weapon
✓ to a person under the age of 18

Part possession (not s 23 excepted)

✓ parted with possession
✓ of an air weapon/ammunition for an air weapon
✓ to a person under the age of 18
✓ being prohibited from having possession

Meanings

Section 23 (see **'Fire missile beyond premises'** below)

Has with him (see 8.3.6)

Air weapon

In reality, most air weapons are firearms, but not s 1 firearms (see **8.1.1**). Part of the definition of a s 1 firearm (s 1(3)(b) of the Firearms Act 1968) relates to every firearm, except air weapons: 'an air weapon that is to say an air rifle, air gun or air pistol which does not fall within s 5(1) [*being a* *prohibited weapon—having compressed gas cartridge system*] and which is not of a type declared by rules [*sets the power levels at which an air weapon becomes a s 1 firearm*] made by the Secretary of State under s 53 of this Act to be specially dangerous'.

Defences

Sections 22(4) and 24(4)(b)

Consider s 23 (see 'Fire missile beyond premises' section).

Section 24

Consider s 24(5) (see **8.7.1**).

Fire missile beyond premises

Offences

Fire missile beyond premises (any age)

A person commits an offence if—

(a) he **has with him** an air weapon on any premises; and

(b) he uses it for firing a missile beyond those premises.

Firearms Act 1968, s 21A(1)

Section 23 exceptions and supervisor offence

(1) It is **not** an offence under section 22(4) of this Act for a person to have with him an air weapon or ammunition while he is under the supervision of a person of or over the age of 21; **but** where a person has with him an air weapon on any premises in circumstances where he would be prohibited from having it with him but for this subsection, it is an **offence** for the person under whose supervision he is to allow him to use it for firing any missile beyond those premises.

(2) It is **not** an offence under section 22(4) of this Act for a person to have with him an air weapon or ammunition at the time when—

(a) being a member of a rifle club or miniature rifle club for the time being approved by the Secretary of State for the purposes of this section or section 15 of the Firearms (Amendment) Act 1988, he is engaged as such a member in or in connection with target shooting; or

(b) he is using the weapon or ammunition at a shooting gallery where the only firearms used are either air weapons or miniature rifles not exceeding .23 inch calibre.

(3) It is **not** an offence under section 22(4) of this Act for a person of or over the age of 14 to have with him an air weapon or ammunition on private premises with the consent of the occupier.

Firearms Act 1968, s 23

Points to prove

s 21A(1) offence (anyone)

✓ had with you on premises
✓ an air weapon
✓ which you used for firing missile(s)
✓ beyond those premises

s 23(1) offence (supervisor)

✓ being person 21 or over
✓ supervising person under 18 who had an air weapon
✓ on premises (specify)
✓ allowed them to fire a missile beyond those premises

Defences

Offences under s 23(1) or s 21A(1)

It shall be a defence for him to show that the only premises into or across which the missile was fired were premises the occupier of which had consented to the firing of the missile (whether specifically or by way of a general consent).

Firearms Act 1968, ss 23(1A) and 21A(2)

Fail to prevent under 18 from having air weapon

Offences

It is an offence for a person in possession of an air weapon to fail to take reasonable precautions to prevent any person under the age of 18 from having the weapon with him.

Firearms Act 1968, s 24ZA(1)

Points to prove

✓ having possession of air weapon
✓ failed to take reasonable precautions
✓ to prevent person under 18
✓ from having air weapon

Defences

(2) Subsection (1) does not apply where by virtue of **section 23** [*above*] of this Act the person under the age of 18 is not prohibited from having the weapon with him.

(3) In proceedings for an offence under subsection (1) it is a defence to show that the person charged with the offence—

    (a) believed the other person to be aged eighteen or over; and

    (b) had reasonable ground for that belief.

(4) For the purposes of this section a person shall be taken to have shown the matters specified in subsection (3) if—

    (a) sufficient evidence of those matters is adduced to raise an issue with respect to them; and

    (b) the contrary is not proved beyond a reasonable doubt.

Firearms Act 1968, s 24ZA

Explanatory notes

- Section 46 of the Crime and Security Act 2010 inserted s 24ZA, this makes it an offence for the person in possession of the air weapon to fail to take reasonable precautions to prevent a person under the age of 18 from gaining unauthorised access to it. HOC 4/2011 provides guidance and further details on this offence.
- HOC 31/2007 provides guidance in relation to air weapons as to: raising the age limits to 18; firing air weapons beyond premises; sales or transfer to be only through a registered firearms dealer by 'face-to-face' transactions (see **8.1.2**).
- As 'air gun', 'air rifle', and 'air pistol' are not defined in the Firearms Act 1968, each case will have to be considered on its own facts and the article in question. Whether a weapon falls into these categories, the court will have to be aware of the following—
  - ✦ an 'air gun' is generally a weapon that has an unrifled barrel;
  - ✦ an 'air rifle' is a weapon that does have a rifled barrel; and
  - ✦ an 'air pistol' is a weapon designed to be fired by using one hand and having the appearance of a pistol;
  - ✦ air weapons using or designed/adapted for use with a self-contained compressed gas cartridge system will be prohibited weapons (see **8.7.3**).
- An air weapon is deemed to be loaded if there is ammunition in the chamber or barrel.

Related cases

Moore v Gooderham [1960] 3 All ER 575, QBD As an airgun is capable of causing injury from which death could result it is a lethal barrelled weapon.

Grace v DPP [1989] Crim LR 365, QBD Evidence that the weapon in question can be fired is required. The prosecution needs to prove that the rifle was a lethal barrelled weapon capable of discharging a shot or missile.

Practical considerations

- The prosecution have to prove that the air weapon was a lethal barrelled weapon capable of discharging a shot or missile.
- In practice, forensic testing will determine whether weapons are lethal or not. The main characteristic which is measured is the muzzle velocity (the speed at which the projectile leaves the barrel).
- An air weapon normally fires a projectile by compressed air/gases and is a firearm, namely 'a lethal barrelled weapon of any description from which any shot, bullet, or other missile can be discharged' (do not confuse a 'firearm' with the narrower definition of a s 1 firearm).
- Certain air weapons can be subject to the prohibition under rules denoting them as especially dangerous.
- Air weapons using, or designed/adapted for use with, a self-contained compressed gas cartridge system will be prohibited weapons (**8.7.3**).
- Application may be made to the court for a confiscation order in relation to a seized air weapon or ammunition.
- For police powers relating to firearms/ammunition see **8.6**.
- Normally it is an offence for a person under 18 years to have an air weapon and/or ammunition anywhere. However, a young person may possess one if accompanied by someone of or over 21 years of age.
- On premises the person under 18 years old is allowed to fire the weapon, but the missiles must not go beyond those premises—otherwise an offence is committed by the supervisor (subject to defence). Furthermore, the user (who must be at least 14 years old) may have with them an air weapon or ammunition on private premises with permission of the occupier.
- Section 21A(1) (above), makes it an offence for **any person** to use an air weapon on premises which fires a missile beyond those premises. Although it is a defence if the occupier of the premises into or across which the missile was fired had consented.
- Under s 19 it is an offence for a person to have with them in a public place an air weapon (loaded or not) or imitation firearm without lawful authority or reasonable excuse (see **8.5**).

 Summary 6 months

 Level 3 fine

8.7.3 **Air weapons deemed prohibited weapons**

Any person who has with him any air rifle, air gun, or air pistol that uses, or is designed, or adapted for use with, a self-contained compressed gas cartridge system (SCGC) will be in possession of a prohibited weapon under s 5(1)(af) of the Firearms Act 1968 (see **8.1.1**).

Explanatory notes

- Weapons that use a CO_2 bulb system are not affected because CO_2 bulbs do not contain a projectile and are not therefore self-contained.
- A CO_2 bulb system that gives a pressure less than 12 ft/lbs on air rifles or 6 ft/lbs on air pistols is not restricted, but over that pressure they become s 1 firearms.
- If the air weapon contains a brass cartridge system and uses a self-contained gas cartridge system that can be converted to fire conventional ammunition, say, then this would make it a prohibited weapon under s 5(1)(af).
- If the weapon comes under s 5(1)(af), then it cannot be possessed, purchased, acquired, manufactured, sold, or transferred without a written authority from the Secretary of State. Although under special arrangements, a person may have been granted permission to possess such a weapon under the terms of a firearms certificate.
- Further details on this matter are given in HOC 1/2004.

8.7.4 **'BB guns'**

BB guns derived their name from guns that fired ball bearings by different methods such as compressed air or an electrical system, some even fire 4.5 mm lead shot. Such weapons would almost certainly be firearms for the purposes of s 1(3) (see **8.1.1**).

If the method of propulsion is a self-contained compressed gas cartridge, the BB gun may be a prohibited weapon (see **8.7.3**). However, most gas BB guns do not have cartridges: the built-in gas container is recharged by an external aerosol, which is not the same thing.

A more common and readily available BB gun is designed to fire plastic or aluminium pellets which may be too powerful to be officially classed as a toy.

These are unlikely to be lethal barrelled weapons (see **8.1.1**) because they are usually too low powered to be 'lethal'.

This type of BB gun will normally have a power rating of about 0.06 ft/lbs.

Compare this to a BSA Airsporter. 22 air rifle that has a power rating of 10.07 ft/lbs (150 times more powerful).

If required, forensic testing of the BB gun can ascertain its power rating, categorise the gun, and say whether or not it is lethal.

As some BB guns closely resemble other firearms, if one is being used in a public place, consider the offence of possession of an imitation firearm in a public place (see **8.5.1**).

8.7.5 **Under 18—sell/buy an imitation firearm**

Section 24A of the Firearms Act 1968 makes it an offence to sell an imitation firearm to a person under the age of 18, or for a young person under the age of 18 to purchase one.

Offences

(1) It is an offence for a person under the age of 18 to purchase an imitation firearm.
(2) It is an offence to sell an imitation firearm to a person under the age of 18.

Firearms Act 1968, s 24A

Points to prove

s 24A(1) under 18 purchase

✓ being a person under 18 years of age
✓ purchased an imitation firearm

s 24A(2) sell to under 18

✓ sold an imitation firearm
✓ to a person under 18 years of age

Meaning of imitation firearm

Means any thing which has the appearance of being a firearm whether or not it is capable of discharging any shot, bullet, or other missile.

Explanatory notes

Imitation firearms have been increasingly misused to threaten and intimidate others. Although offences and controls exist relating to imitation firearms, s 24A seeks to tackle the problem at source by restricting the sale of imitation firearms.

Defence for seller

In proceedings for an offence under subsection (2) it is a defence to show that the person charged with the offence—

(a) believed the other person to be aged eighteen or over; and

(b) had reasonable ground for that belief.

Firearms Act 1968, s 24A(3)

Practical considerations

- The onus is on the prosecution to show that the seller did not take sufficient steps (eg producing ID) to establish that the purchaser was 18 or over.
- Under the Violent Crime Reduction Act 2006—
  - ◆ s 36 makes it an offence to manufacture, import, or sell a realistic imitation firearm;
  - ◆ s 37 provides a defence to s 36 if it is shown that the only purpose of making the imitation firearm was for:
    - a museum or gallery;
    - theatrical performances and rehearsals;
    - production of films or television programmes;
    - an organisation for holding historical re-enactments;
    - Crown servants;
  - ◆ s 38 defines realistic imitation firearm (for ss 36 and 37) as an imitation firearm which appears so realistic that it can only be distinguished from a real firearm by:
    - an expert or on close examination; or
    - attempting to load or fire it; and
    - it is not a de-activated firearm or an antique;

The Violent Crime Reduction Act 2006 (Realistic Imitation Firearms) Regulations 2007 (SI 2606/2007) provide defences, burden of proof, details on historical re-enactments, size, and colours of imitation firearms. HOC 31/2007 gives guidance on ss 36–41 (realistic imitation firearms and supplying to under 18).

 Summary   48 months

 6 months' imprisonment and/or a fine

8.7.5 Under 18—sell/buy an imitation firearm

Links to alternative subjects and offences

8.8 **Fireworks**

The Fireworks Regulations 2004, and the Pyrotechnic Articles (Safety) Regulations 2010 give firework prohibitions that are enforced by the Fireworks Act 2003 and Consumer Protection Act 1987 respectively. The Highways Act 1980 and Town Police Clauses Act 1847 also deal with offences involving fireworks in a street or highway.

8.8.1 **Categories of fireworks**

There are different categories of fireworks in relation to supply or possession offences. Category 1, 2, and 3 fireworks are considered suitable for use by the general public: whereas a Category 4 firework is only for use by people with specialist knowledge.

Category 1 fireworks present very low hazard, negligible noise level, which are intended for use in confined areas: including fireworks which are intended for use inside domestic buildings (Indoor Fireworks). These are pretty innocuous fireworks (eg cap, cracker snap, novelty match, party popper, serpent, sparkler, or throwdown).

Category 2 fireworks present a low hazard and low noise level, which are intended for outdoor use in confined areas (Garden Fireworks). They normally require a minimum spectator distance of 5 metres.

Category 3 fireworks present a medium hazard, which are intended for outdoor use in large open areas and the noise level is not considered harmful to human health (Display Fireworks). They normally require a minimum spectator distance of 25 metres.

Category 4 fireworks present a high hazard, which are intended for use only by people with specialist knowledge and whose noise level is not considered harmful to human health (Fireworks for professional use). The general public is prohibited from possessing these fireworks.

Firework means a **pyrotechnic article** intended for entertainment purposes.

Pyrotechnic article means any article containing explosive substances or an explosive mixture of substances designed to produce heat, light, sound, gas, or smoke or a combination of such effects through self-sustained exothermic chemical reactions.

8.8.2 **Under 18 years—possess 'adult' fireworks**

Offences

Any person who contravenes a **prohibition** imposed by fireworks regulations is guilty of an offence.

Fireworks Act 2003, s 11(1)

8.8.2 Under 18 years—possess 'adult' fireworks

Points to prove

✓ breached a reg 4 prohibition, namely
✓ being a person under the age of 18
✓ possessed in a public place
✓ an adult firework

Prohibition

Subject to **regulation 6** below, no person under the age of eighteen years shall possess an **adult firework** in a **public place**.

Fireworks Regulations 2004, reg 4(1)

Meanings

Regulation 6

- Regulations 4 and 5 shall not prohibit the possession of any firework by any person who is employed by/in trade or business as—
  ♦ professional organiser or operator of firework displays;
  ♦ manufacture of fireworks or assemblies;
  ♦ supply of fireworks or assemblies;
  ♦ local authority/government department/forces of the Crown for use at a firework display or national public celebration/commemorative event;
  ♦ special effects in the theatre, on film, or on television;
  ♦ acting on behalf of and for purposes of exercising enforcement powers of local authority or enforcement body;
  ♦ government department use for research or investigations;
  ♦ supplier of goods designed and intended for use in conjunction with fireworks or assemblies for testing and safety purposes.

Adult firework

Means any firework, except Category 1 Indoor Fireworks (see **8.8.1**).

Public place

Includes any place to which at the material time the public have or are permitted access, whether on payment or otherwise.

Explanatory notes

- This offence prohibits any person under the age of 18 years, from possessing any firework in a public place (except Category 1 Indoor Fireworks) (see **8.8.1**).
- Those people listed in reg 6 (above) are exempted from liability for this offence and are not prohibited from possession.

Practical considerations

- Any breach of the prohibitions in the Fireworks Regulations 2004 is a criminal offence under the Fireworks Act 2003, s 11(1).

Consider stop, search, and seizure powers under s 1 (8B) of PACE (see **12.1.1**).

 Summary   12 months

6 months' imprisonment and/or a fine

8.8.3 **Ban on possession of Category 4 fireworks**

Offences

Any person who contravenes a **prohibition imposed** by fireworks regulations is guilty of an offence.

Fireworks Act 2003, s 11(1)

Points to prove

✓ breached a reg 5 prohibition, namely
✓ possessed a Category 4 firework
✓ when not exempt from such possession

Prohibition

Subject to **regulation 6**, no person shall possess a **Category 4 firework**.

Fireworks Regulations 2004, reg 5

Explanatory notes

Those people listed in reg 6 (see **8.8.2**) are exempted from liability for this offence and are not prohibited from possession.
Unless exempted by reg 6, this prohibits a person of any age from possessing **anywhere** a Category 4 firework and an offence will be committed by that person if they breach that regulation.

Practical considerations

Any breach of the prohibitions in the Fireworks Regulations 2004 is a criminal offence under s 11(1) of the Fireworks Act 2003.
Consider issuing a PND for this offence (see **7.1.1**).

8.8.4 **Use firework after 11 p.m.**

- Consider stop, search, and seizure powers under s 1 (8B) of PACE (see **12.1.1**).
- Category 4 fireworks are for specialist use only (see **8.8.1**).
- Consider the offence of supplying a Category 4 firework (see **8.8.5**).

 Summary 12 months

 6 months' imprisonment and/or a fine

8.8.4 **Use firework after 11 p.m.**

Offences

Any person who contravenes a **prohibition** imposed by fireworks regulations is guilty of an offence.

Fireworks Act 2003, s 11(1)

Points to prove

✓ breached a reg 7(1) prohibition, namely
✓ use an adult firework
✓ during night hours

Prohibition

Subject to **paragraph (2)** [*exception*] below, no person shall use **an adult firework during night hours.**

Fireworks Regulations 2004, reg 7(1)

Meanings

Exception (reg 7(2))

Regulation 7(1) above shall not prohibit the use of a firework—
(a) during **a permitted fireworks night;** or
(b) by any person who is employed by a local authority and who uses the firework in question:
    (i) for the purposes of putting on a firework display by that local authority; or

    (ii) at a national public celebration or a national commemorative
        event.

Adult firework (see **8.8.2**)

Night hours

Means the period beginning at 11 p.m. and ending at 7 a.m. the following
day.

Permitted fireworks night

Means a period beginning at 11 p.m.—

- on the first day of the Chinese New Year and ending at 1 a.m. the
following day;
- and ending at midnight on 5 November;
- on the day of Diwali and ending at 1 a.m. the following day;
- on 31 December and ending at 1 a.m. the following day.

Explanatory notes

- This prohibits the use of a firework (except Category 1 Indoor
Fireworks) (see **8.8.1**) after 11 p.m. at night and an offence being
committed by that person if they breach that regulation.
- Exceptions are New Year's Eve, Diwali, Chinese New Year (extended
11 p.m.–1 a.m.); Bonfire Night (extended 11 p.m.–midnight) or the
local authority putting on a firework display.
- This offence is not restricted to a public place and will be committed
if a person breaches this prohibition in their own private garden/land.

Practical considerations

- A breach of this prohibition is a criminal offence under s 11(1) of the
Fireworks Act 2003, for which a PND can be issued (see **7.1.1**).
- Consider stop, search, and seizure powers under s 1(8B) of PACE (see
12.1.1).

 Summary   12 months

 6 months' imprisonment and/or a fine

8.8.5 **Supply of fireworks offences**

The Pyrotechnic Articles (Safety) Regulations 2010 prohibit the supply
of fireworks to people under the age of 12, 16, or 18 years, and the supply
of Category 4 fireworks, except to a person with specialist knowledge.

8.8.5 Supply of fireworks offences

Offences (Category 1, 2, or 3 fireworks)

Where **safety regulations prohibit** a person from supplying or offering or agreeing to supply any goods or from exposing or possessing any goods for supply, that person shall be guilty of an offence if he contravenes the **prohibition**.

Consumer Protection Act 1987, s 12(1)

Points to prove

✓ breached safety regulations prohibition, namely
✓ supply Category 1, 2, or 3 firework
✓ to person prohibited from being supplied
✓ by reason of age

Safety regulations prohibitions

15(1) No person shall supply
    (a) a **Christmas cracker** to any person under the age of twelve years;
    (b) any other **Category 1 firework** to any person under the age of sixteen years.
15(2) No person shall supply a **Category 2 or 3 firework** to any person under the age of eighteen years.

Pyrotechnic Articles (Safety) Regulations 2010, reg 15

Meanings

Christmas cracker

Means a paper or foil tube, crimped at each end, enclosing novelties and with one or more **snaps** running along the length of the tube.

Snap

Means two overlapping strips of cardboard or paper, or two strings, with a friction-sensitive pyrotechnic composition in sliding contact with an abrasive surface and designed to be held in the hand.

Category 1, 2 or 3 firework (see 8.8.1)

Defences (Category 1, 2 or 3 fireworks)

Section 39(1) of the Consumer Protection Act 1987 states that it shall be a defence for that person to show that he took all reasonable steps and exercised all due diligence to avoid committing the offence under the Act.

Practical considerations

- A breach of these prohibitions (except Category 4) is a criminal offence under s 12(1) of the Consumer Protection Act 1987.

- Regulation 15 prohibits the supply of a Christmas cracker to a person under 12, Category 1 firework to a person under 16, and Category 2 or 3 fireworks to a person under 18.
- Supply includes offering or agreeing to supply, and exposing or possessing for supply: it is not limited to sale.
- Prosecution will be more likely where fireworks have been supplied in the course of a business, rather than a 'casual supply' between friends or family.
- None of the supply offences is subject to the PND procedure.

Category 4 fireworks

- The 2010 Regulations, reg 33 prohibits the supply of a Category 4 firework (see **8.8.1**), except to a person under reg 42. It is an either way offence under reg 39 (not a safety provision under the 1987 Act). The enforcement authorities are the HSE and Trading Standards.
- The **reg 42 exemption** relates to a person with specialist knowledge, and has undergone specialist training (recognised in the fireworks business) in using Category 4 fireworks.

 Category 1, 2, or 3 offences: Summary   12 months

Category 4 offence: Either way

 Category 1, 2, or 3 offences:
6 months' imprisonment and/or a fine

Category 4 offence
Summary: 3 months' imprisonment or a fine
Indictment: 2 years' imprisonment and/or a fine

8.8.6 **Other fireworks/firearms offences (in a highway/street)**

Explosives Act

Section 80 of the Explosives Act 1875 creates various offences relating to throw, cast, or fire any fireworks in the highway or public place.

8.8.6 Other fireworks/firearms offences (in a highway/street)

Offences

If any person throw, cast, or fire any fireworks in or into any highway, street, thoroughfare, or public place, he shall be guilty of an offence.

Explosives Act 1875, s 80

Points to prove

✓ throw/cast/fire
✓ a firework
✓ in/into a highway/street/thoroughfare/public place

Practical considerations

Consider issuing a PND for this offence—'Throwing fireworks in a thoroughfare' (see **7.1.1**).

 Summary   6 months

 Fine

Highways Act

Section 161 of the Highways Act 1980 creates various offences relating to causing danger on the highway.

Offences

If a person without lawful authority or excuse—
(a) lights any fire on or over a **highway** which consists of or comprises a **carriageway**; or
(b) discharges any firearm or firework within 50 feet of the centre of such a highway,
and in consequence a user of the highway is injured, interrupted or endangered, that person is guilty of an offence.

Highways Act 1980, s 161(2)

Points to prove

✓ without lawful authority/excuse
✓ discharged a firework or firearm

  SSS Stop, search and seize powers   **PND** Penalty notice for disorder offences   **PCSO** Police community support officers

---

✓ within 50 ft of centre of highway
✓ comprising a carriageway
✓ as a result user injured/interrupted/endangered

Meanings

Highway (see **10.22.1**)

Carriageway

Means a way constituting or comprised in a highway, being a way (other than a cycle track) over which the public have a right of way for the passage of vehicles.

 Summary   6 months

 Level 3 fine

Town Police Clauses Act

Section 28 of the Town Police Clauses Act 1847 creates numerous offences.

Offences

Every person who wantonly (without lawful motive and thoughtless as to possible consequences) throws or sets fire to a firework in the **street** to the obstruction, annoyance, or danger of residents or passengers will commit an offence.

Town Police Clauses Act 1847, s 28

Points to prove

✓ in street
✓ wantonly
✓ threw/set fire to a firework
✓ to the obstruction/annoyance/danger of residents/passengers

Meaning of street

Street includes any road, square, court, alley, thoroughfare, public passage, carriageway, and footways at the sides.

8.8.6 Other fireworks/firearms offences (in a highway/street)

Explanatory notes

- Section 28 of the Town Police Clauses Act 1847 also states that every person who wantonly (recklessly, without regard for consequences) discharges a **firearm** in the street to the obstruction, annoyance, or danger of residents or passengers will commit an offence.
- None of the Town Police Clauses Act offences are complete unless it can be proved that they would obstruct, annoy, or cause danger to any residents or passengers.

Related cases

Mantle v Jordan [1897] 1 QB 248 The Town Police Clauses Act offences can only be committed in the street, but the annoyance may be to 'residents', meaning the occupiers of houses in the street, although they may not be in the street at the time.

 Summary   6 months

 14 days' imprisonment or a level 3 fine

Links to alternative subjects and offences

8.9 **Offensive Weapons and Crossbows**

Possession of or threatening with offensive weapons in a public place, the manufacture and sale of offensive weapons, trespassing with a weapon of offence, and offences involving crossbows form a key part of operational policing.

8.9.1 **Offensive weapons in public place— possess/threaten**

The Prevention of Crime Act 1953 deals with offences regarding possession of or threatening with offensive weapons in a public place.

Offences

Possess

1(1) Any person who without lawful authority or reasonable excuse, the proof whereof shall lie on him, **has with him** in any **public place** any **offensive weapon** shall be guilty of an offence.

Threaten

1A(1) A person is guilty of an offence if that person -
    (a) has an offensive weapon with him or her in a public place,
    (b) unlawfully and **intentionally** threatens another person with the weapon, and
    (c) does so in such a way that there is an immediate risk of **serious physical harm** to that other person.

Prevention of Crime Act 1953, ss 1(1) and 1A(1)

Points to prove

Possess (s 1(1))

✓ without lawful authority/reasonable excuse
✓ had with you
✓ in a public place
✓ an offensive weapon

Threaten (s 1A(1))

✓ had with you an offensive weapon in a public place
✓ unlawfully and intentionally threaten another person with the weapon

---

✓ in a way that there was immediate risk of serious physical harm
✓ to that other person

Meanings

Has with him (see 8.3.6)

Public place

Includes any highway and any other premises or place to which at the material time the public have or are permitted to have access, whether on payment or otherwise.

Offensive weapon

Means any article **made** or **adapted** for use for causing injury to the person, or **intended** by the person having it with them for such use by them, or by some other person.

Intentionally (see 4.1.2)

Serious physical harm

Serious harm amounting to grievous bodily harm (see 2.3.1).

Explanatory notes

- Within the meaning of offensive weapon particular terms used and case law has provided meanings to those terms as follows—
  + 'made' includes articles that have been specifically created for the purpose of causing injury, and includes knuckledusters, flick knives, butterfly knives, sword sticks, truncheons, daggers, bayonets, and rice flails. All of these items are generally classed as offensive weapons per se ('by themselves');
  + 'adapted' consists of articles that have generally been altered in some way with the intention of causing injury, such as smashing a bottle to make the broken end into a weapon for causing injury;
  + 'intended' these can be otherwise inoffensive articles that the defendant proposes to use to cause injury to a person, such as a bunch of keys held in the fist with the keys projecting through the fingers (making it an impromptu knuckleduster).
- The primary aim of the s 1 possession offence is the **carrying** of such weapons rather than their **use** in the heat of the moment.
- The s 1A offence involves a person having the weapon and unlawfully and intentionally threatening another person with it in such a way that there is an immediate risk of grievous bodily harm to that other person.

Defences

Possess (s1)

Lawful authority

This extends to people such as an on-duty police officer with a baton.

Reasonable excuse

Whether an excuse is reasonable is for the court to decide having heard all the circumstances. These could include—

* people carrying the tools of their trade (eg hammer/saw by a carpenter or filleting knife by a fishmonger);
* self-defence—if there is an imminent threat, this defence may be available.

Threaten (s1A)

The use of the weapon must be unlawful; this allows the person to raise relevant defences such as self-defence, defence of others or of property, and prevention of crime.

Related cases

Evans v Hughes [1972] 3 All ER 412, QBD Before a defence of reasonable excuse can be successful, an imminent threat (in this instance self-defence) has to be shown as to why the weapon was carried.

R v Cugullere [1961] 2 All ER 343, CA The defendant must knowingly have article with them in a public place.

Davis v Alexander [1971] Crim LR 595, QBD No need for intention to use if offensive weapon per se.

Ohlson v Hylton [1975] 2 All ER 490, QBD and **R v Veasey [1999] Crim LR 158, CA** If the defendant seized a weapon for 'instant use' on the victim or grabbed something innocuous (like a hammer or snooker cue) in the heat of the moment, then the 'weapon' was not carried unlawfully with prior intent.

R v Allamby and R v Medford [1974] 3 All ER 126, CA Kitchen knives were not offensive weapons per se and so intent to use must be proved.

Practical considerations

* For further information regarding this offence see MOJ Circular 8/2012.
* If a person is found not guilty of the s 1A (threaten) offence (whether on indictment or not), but it is proved that the person committed the s 1 (possess) offence, then they may be convicted of the s 1 offence.
* Consider stop, search, and seizure powers under s 1 of PACE (see **12.1.1**).
* For the s 1 possession offence, where an article is 'made' or 'adapted' to cause injury (offensive per se), the prosecution do not need to prove intent to cause injury as merely having it with them is sufficient.
* The 'intended' use requires an element of intent to use the article to cause injury, which must be proved. An instant use of an innocent article will need proof of a prior intent otherwise no offence is committed, either by possessing or threatening with the weapon.
* Upon conviction the court may make an order for the forfeiture or disposal of any weapon in respect of which the offence was committed.

8.9.2 Offensive weapons—provide/trade/manufacture

- If appropriate, consider the offence of possession of a blade/pointed article in a public place (see **8.10**).
- There is a need to prove a knowledge of the existence of the article and that the article is 'to hand and ready for use' (eg it may be hidden a few feet away, it does not have to be physically on the defendant's person).
- The burden of proof for lawful authority or reasonable excuse lies with the accused and it is for the prosecution to disprove it (*R v Archbold* [2007] EWCA Crim 2137, CA).

 Either way   None

Summary: 6 months' imprisonment and/or a fine
Indictment: 4 years' imprisonment and/or a fine

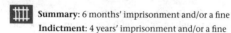

8.9.2 Offensive weapons—provide/trade/ manufacture

Transferring ownership, trading in, importing, or manufacturing certain offensive weapons is an offence.

Offences

Any person who manufactures, sells or hires or offers for sale or hire, exposes or has in his possession for the purpose of sale or hire, or lends or gives to any other person, a **weapon to which this section applies** shall be guilty of an offence.

Criminal Justice Act 1988, s 141(1)

Points to prove

✓ manufactured/sold/hired/lent/gave

or

✓ possess/exposed/offered
✓ for sale/hire
✓ an offensive weapon

Meaning of weapon to which section 141 applies

The Criminal Justice Act 1988 (Offensive Weapons) Order 1988 specifies weapons to which s 141 applies (see **8.9.3**).

Explanatory notes

- The importation of weapons to which s 141 applies is prohibited.
- Some will also fall into the category of being a bladed/pointed article (see **8.10**).
- See also a warrant to search for and a power to stop/search/seize these weapons (see **8.11**).
- It is an offence to lend, give or trade in flick or gravity knives (see **8.10.2**).
- This section does not apply to any weapons subject to the Firearms Act 1968 (see **8.1**) or crossbows (see **8.9.5**).
- Consider the offence of using another person to look after, hide, or transport a firearm, offensive/bladed weapon or knife, so that it would be available when required for an unlawful purpose (see **8.3.7**).

Defences

This applies to an offence under s 141(1) or s 50(2) or (3) of the Customs and Excise Management Act 1979 (improper importation) if it can be shown that their conduct was only for the purposes of—
- functions carried out on behalf of the Crown or of a visiting force;
- making the weapon available to a museum or gallery;
- making the weapon available for the purposes specified in s 141(11B).

Defence notes

- A person acting on behalf of a **museum or gallery** can use the above defence if they had reasonable grounds to believe that the person to whom they lent or hired it would use it only for cultural, artistic, or educational purposes. The defence will only apply if the **museum or gallery** does not distribute profits.
- **Museum or gallery** includes any institution which has as its purpose, or one of its purposes, the preservation, display, and interpretation of material of historical, artistic, or scientific interest; and gives the public access to it.
- The purposes under s 141(11B) are for theatrical performances and rehearsals for such performances or for the production of films or television programmes.
- An antique weapon is exempt (more than 100 years old).

Summary 6 months

 6 months' imprisonment and/or a fine

8.9.3 The Criminal Justice Act 1988 (Offensive Weapons) Order 1988

This order provides a list of weapons where their sale, hire, offering for sale/hire, exposing, or importation is prohibited. The order excludes antique weapons and provides that a weapon is an antique if it was manufactured more than 100 years before the date of any offence alleged to have been committed in respect of that weapon.

This list only applies to s 141 offences (see **8.9.2**) and is not a list of all offensive weapons per se: knuckleduster; swordstick; butterfly knife; death star; belt buckle knife; hollow kubotan (cylinder holding sharp spikes); push dagger; kusari (rope, cord, wire, or chain with hooked knife, sickle, hard weight or hand grip fastened at one end); foot or hand claw; blowpipe; telescopic truncheon; disguised knife; baton; stealth knife (non-metallic); disguised knife (blade or sharp point concealed within an everyday object such as a comb, brush, writing instrument, cigarette lighter, key, lipstick, or telephone); and sword with a curved blade.

Explanatory notes

- There are exceptions even if the weapon is on this list.
- The list given above is not an exhaustive or descriptive list, it just gives an idea of the type of weapons included in this Order.
- Stealth knives are non-metallic hunting or stiletto knives, made of a range of materials, such as nylon zytel or high impact plastic. Although they look like conventional knives, they are difficult to detect by security apparatus. Their design and construction means that their possession in public may be an offence under—
  - ◆ s 1(1) of the Prevention of Crime Act 1953 (**8.9.1**); or
  - ◆ s 139(1) of the Criminal Justice Act 1988 (**8.10**).
- The 2008 Weapons Amendment Order (SI 973/2008) added a sword with a curved blade of 50 cms or over in length to the list, the length of the blade being measured in a straight line from the top of the handle to the tip of the blade. It is a defence if a person can show that—
  - ◆ the sword was made in Japan before 1954 or at any other time using traditional Japanese methods of forging swords; and

✦ an organisation requires the use of the weapon for a permitted activity (historical re-enactment or a sporting activity), and that public liability insurance was in force which indemnified those taking part in the activity.

8.9.4 **Trespassing with weapon of offence**

Section 8 of the Criminal Law Act 1977 creates the offence of 'trespassing with a weapon of offence'.

Offences

A person who is on any **premises** as a **trespasser**, after having entered as such, is guilty of an offence if, without lawful authority or reasonable excuse, he **has with him** on the premises any **weapon of offence**.

Criminal Law Act 1977, s 8(1)

Points to prove

✓ on premises as trespasser
✓ having entered as such
✓ had weapon of offence
✓ without lawful authority or reasonable excuse

Meanings

Premises

This consists of any—
- building/part of a building (under separate occupation);
- land adjacent to and used/intended for use in connection with a building;
- site comprising any building(s) together with ancillary land;
- fixed structure; and
- movable structure, vehicle, or vessel designed, or adapted for residential purposes.

Trespasser (see **3.3.1**)

Has with him (see **8.3.6**)

Weapon of offence (see **3.3.2**)

Practical considerations

- This offence is worth bearing in mind if the carrying of offensive weapons in a public place/school premises or aggravated burglary does not apply.
- Consider stop, search and seizure powers under s 1 of PACE (see **12.1.1**).
- Entry must have been as a trespasser—it does not extend to a person who has entered lawfully and later becomes a trespasser (eg being asked to leave by the occupier).

 Summary   6 months

 3 months' imprisonment and/or a fine

8.9.5 Crossbows

Crossbows are extremely accurate weapons and potentially as lethal as a firearm. This legislation creates offences in relation to persons under 18 years possessing, hiring, or purchasing crossbows.

Sell, purchase, or hire crossbow

> **Offences**
>
> *Sell/hire to under 18*
>
> A person who sells or lets on hire a **crossbow** or part of a crossbow to a person under the age of 18 is guilty of an offence unless he believes him to be 18 years of age or older and has reasonable grounds for that belief.
>
> Crossbows Act 1987, s 1
>
> *Purchase/hire by under 18*
>
> A person under the age of 18 who buys or hires a crossbow or a part of a crossbow is guilty of an offence.
>
> Crossbows Act 1987, s 2

Points to prove

Sell/hire (s 1)

✓ sold/let on hire or sold/let on hire part(s) of
✓ a crossbow
✓ to person under 18 years of age

Purchase/hire (s 2)

✓ person under 18 years of age
✓ hired/purchased or purchased/hired part(s) of
✓ a crossbow

Meaning of crossbow

Does not apply to crossbows with a draw weight of less than 1.4 kg.

Defences (sell/hire)

Reasonable grounds to believe that the person is 18 years or older.

Practical considerations

- Proof required of age (eg ID card or birth certificate).
- Only applies to crossbows of a certain strength, having a draw weight of 1.4kg or over.
- The draw weight limit is very low and can be determined by the forensic testing; only toys will be excluded by this definition.

 Summary   6 months

 Sell/hire (s 1) 6 months' imprisonment and/or a fine

Purchase/hire (s 2) Level 3 fine

Under 18—possess a crossbow

Offences

A person under the age of 18 who **has with him**—
(a) a **crossbow** which is capable of discharging a missile, or
(b) parts of a crossbow which together (and without any other parts) can be assembled to form a crossbow capable of discharging a missile,
is guilty of an offence, unless he is under the supervision of a person who is 21 years of age or older.

Crossbows Act 1987, s 3

8.9.5 Crossbows

Points to prove

✓ being under the age of 18
✓ had with you
✓ a crossbow/crossbow parts (able to form a crossbow)
✓ capable of discharging a missile

Meanings

Has with him (see 8.3.6)

Crossbow (see s 1 above)

Explanatory notes

- This offence can be committed anywhere and not just in public.
- No offence will be committed if under supervision of person age 21 or over.

Practical considerations (see also s 1 and s 2 above)

Although the Act may allow a person of 18 or over to possess a crossbow in public, it may be an offence under s 139 of the Criminal Justice Act 1988 (pointed article/blades, see **8.10.1**) due to the crossbow bolts.

 Summary

 6 months

 Level 3 fine

Crossbows—search and seizure powers

Section 4 of the Crossbows Act 1987 gives police officers quite wide powers of search, detain, seizure, and entry onto land if a person under 18 years is unsupervised and is in possession of a crossbow/parts.

Powers

(1) If a constable suspects with reasonable cause that a person is committing or has committed an offence under section 3, the constable may—
  (a) search that person for a crossbow or part of a crossbow;
  (b) search any vehicle, or anything in or on a vehicle, in or on which the constable suspects with reasonable cause there is a crossbow, or part of a crossbow, connected with the offence.

(2) A constable may detain a person or vehicle for the purpose of a search under subsection (1).

(3) A constable may seize and retain for the purpose of proceedings for an offence under this Act anything discovered by him in the course of a search under subsection (1) which appears to him to be a crossbow or part of a crossbow.

(4) For the purpose of exercising the powers conferred by this section a constable may enter any land other than a dwelling-house.

Crossbows Act 1987, s 4

Explanatory notes

* A constable may detain a person or vehicle for the search.
* A constable may seize and retain anything found during the search which appears to be a crossbow or part of a crossbow.
* In exercising this power a constable may enter on any land **other than** a dwelling house.

Practical considerations (see also **ss 1, 2,** and **3** above)

Consider powers under s 1 of PACE and ensure compliance with the PACE Codes procedures relating to stop and searches (see **12.1**).

Links to alternative subjects and offences

8.10 Bladed Articles/ Knives Offences

The Criminal Justice Act 1988 deals with offences of having knives/ bladed articles in a public place or on school premises, and sale to persons under 18 years.

8.10.1 Possession of bladed/pointed article in public place

Section 139 of the Criminal Justice Act 1988 creates an offence of having a bladed or pointed article in a public place.

Offences

Subject to subsections (4) and (5) [Defences] below, any person who has an **article** to which this section applies **with him** in a **public place** shall be guilty of an offence.

Criminal Justice Act 1988, s 139(1)

Points to prove

✓ had with them
✓ without good reason/lawful authority
✓ an article being bladed/sharply pointed
✓ in a public place

Meanings

Article

Applies to any article which has a **blade** or is sharply pointed, including a folding pocket knife if the cutting edge of the blade exceeds 3 inches (7.62 cm).

Blade

Examples of this will be the blade of a knife, sword.

Has with him (see 8.3.6)

Public place

Includes any place to which at the material time the public have or are permitted access, whether on payment or otherwise.

Explanatory notes

- A folding pocket knife does not include a lock knife, regardless of the blade length (*Harris v DPP* [1993] 1 WLR 82, QBD).
- Possession of a multi-tool incorporating a prohibited blade/pointed article is capable of being an offence under this section, even if there are other tools on the instrument that may be of practical use (such as a bottle-opener). It is for the defendant to show that s/he had good reason for possession (*R v Giles* [2003] EWCA Crim 1287, CA).

Defences

(4) It shall be a defence for a person charged with an offence under this section to prove that he had good reason or lawful authority for having the article with him in a public place.

(5) Without prejudice to the generality of subsection (4) above, it shall be a defence for a person charged with an offence under this section to prove that he had the article with him—
   (a) for use at work;
   (b) for religious reasons; or
   (c) as part of any national costume.

Criminal Justice Act 1988, s 139

Defence notes

The burden of proof is with the defendant to show good reason or lawful authority for having the blade/pointed article with them. Examples of s 139(5) could be—

- **for use at work**—fishmonger, carpet fitter, chef;
- **for religious reasons**—members of the Sikh religion having a kirpan;
- **as part of a national costume**—the skean dhu in Highland dress.

Related cases

R v Clancy [2012] EWCA Crim 8, CA A fear of attack can constitute good reason. The defendant's state of mind was relevant and 'good reason' should be allowed a natural meaning.

Chahal v DPP [2010] EWHC 439 (Admin), QBD C had a lock knife in his jacket. This was used for casual work, but C had forgotten about it. The lapse of time since using the knife had been short. C had good reason for possession.

R v McAuley [2009] EWCA Crim 2130, CA Carrying a knife for protection from an imminent attack could be a good reason. It was for the jury to decide how imminent, likely, and serious any possible attack might be.

Harriott v DPP [2005] EWHC 965 (Admin), QBD The unrestricted front area of private premises is not a public place, unless it is shown that the general public have a right of access.

R v Davis [1998] Crim LR 564, CA A screwdriver is not a 'bladed article'. A blade needs to fall within the same category as a sharply pointed item or the blade on a folding pocket knife having a cutting edge.

R v Daubney (2000) 164 JP 519, CA The prosecution must prove that the defendant had the article with them and their actual knowledge of the article.

R v Cheong Wang [2003] EWCA Crim 3228, CA A Buddhist practising the martial art of Shaolin had a sword and Gurkha-type knife with him in public, but had failed to provide sufficient religious reason for possession.

Practical considerations

- Consider stop, search, and seizure powers under s 1(8A) of PACE (see **12.1.1**).
- Consider s 139AA if offences relate to threats made when in possession of articles/offensive weapons in public or on school premises (see **8.10.3**).
- Sections 52 to 55A of the Courts Act 2003 give a court security officer powers to search, exclude, remove, or restrain person(s) in a court building with regard to an article/knife in their possession; including seizing any article or knife found by that officer.

 Either way   6 months

 Summary: 6 months' imprisonment and/or a fine
Indictment: 4 years' imprisonment and/or a fine

8.10.2 **Sale of knives/blades to persons under 18**

Section 141A of the Criminal Justice Act 1988 creates the offence of selling knives or certain articles with a blade or point to people under the age of 18.

Offences

Any person who sells to a person under the age of 18 years an **article to which this section applies** shall be guilty of an offence.

Criminal Justice Act 1988, s 141A(1)

Points to prove

✓ sold to person under 18 years
✓ knife/axe/knife blade/razor blade or
✓ bladed sharply pointed article being made/adapted for use for causing injury

Meanings

Article to which this section applies

Subject to **subsection (3)** below, this section applies to—

(a) any knife, knife blade, or razor blade,
(b) any axe, and
(c) any other article which has a blade or which is sharply pointed and which is made or adapted for use for causing injury to the person.

Subsection (3)

This section does not apply to any article described in—

(a) section 1 of the Restriction of Offensive Weapons Act 1959,
(b) an order made under s 141(2) of this Act, or
(c) an order made by the Secretary of State under this section.

Explanatory notes

- Section 1 of the Restriction of Offensive Weapons Act 1959 makes it a summary offence regarding lending, giving, or trading of flick or gravity knives.
- An order made under s 141(2) of this Act (see **8.9.2**) relates to weapons given in the Criminal Justice Act 1988 (Offensive Weapons) Order 1988 such as knuckledusters, swordsticks, belt daggers (see **8.9.3**).
- The Criminal Justice Act 1988 (Offensive Weapons) (Exemption) Order 1996, states that this section does not apply to—
  + folding pocket knives if the cutting edge of the blade does not exceed 7.62 cms (3 inches);
  + razor blades permanently enclosed in a cartridge or housing where less than 2 mm of any blade is protruding.

Defences

To prove that they took all reasonable precautions and exercised all due diligence to avoid the commission of the offence.

Criminal Justice Act 1988, s 141A(4)

Practical considerations

- The above defence goes beyond appearance or enquiring about the age of the purchaser, such as proving age by ID card.

- Consider the offence of using another person to look after, hide, or transport a firearm, offensive/bladed weapon, or knife, so that it would be available when required for an unlawful purpose (see **8.3.7**).

Summary 6 months

6 months' imprisonment and/or a fine

8.10.3 **Threaten with article in public place/ school premises**

Section 139AA of the Criminal Justice Act 1988 creates the offence of threatening another person with an article in a public place or on school premises, if there is immediate risk of serious physical harm to that other person.

Offences

A person is guilty of an offence if that person—
(a) has an **article to which this section applies** with him or her in a **public place** or on **school premises**
(b) unlawfully and **intentionally** threatens another person with the article, and
(c) does so in such a way that there is an immediate risk of **serious physical harm** to that other person.

Criminal Justice Act 1988, s 139AA(1)

Points to prove

✓ had with you
✓ a bladed/sharp pointed article
✓ in a public place/on school premises
✓ unlawfully and intentionally threatened another person with it
✓ in a way that there was an immediate risk of
✓ serious physical harm to that person

Meanings

Article to which this section applies

- In a public place: means an article to which s 139 applies (see **8.10.1**)
- On school premises means –
    + an article to which s 139 applies (see **8.10.1**);
    + an offensive weapon (see **8.9.1**).

Public place (see **8.10.1**)

School premises (see **8.10.4**)

Intentionally (see **4.1.2**)

Serious physical harm

Means harm amounting to grievous bodily harm (see **2.3.1**).

Explanatory notes

- The meaning of an article will depend on if it occurs in a public place or on school premises (see above).
- If a person is found not guilty of an offence under this section (whether on indictment or not), but it is proved that the person committed an offence under s 139 (see **8.10.1**) or s 139A (see **8.10.4**), then the person may be convicted of that offence.

Defences

The use of the weapon must be unlawful, so this allows the person to raise relevant defences such as self-defence, defence of others or of property, and prevention of crime.

Practical considerations

- For further information regarding this offence see MOJ Circular 8/2012.
- Consider the offence of possess article/weapon on school premises (see **8.10.4**) and causing/permitting a nuisance/disturbance on school premises (see **8.10.5**).
- There is a specific police power under s 139B to enter and search school premises regarding s 139A and s 139AA offences (see **8.11.2**).
- Consider stop, search, and seizure powers under s 1(8A) of PACE (see **12.1.1**).

SSS **E&S**

 Either way   None

 Summary: 6 months' imprisonment and/or a fine
Indictment: 4 years' imprisonment and/or a fine

8.10.4 **Possess weapon/blade/sharp point on school premises**

Section 139A of the Criminal Justice Act 1988 creates the offence of possessing an article with a blade or sharp point, or an offensive weapon on school premises.

Offences

(1) Any person who has an **article** to which section 139 of this Act applies **with him** on **school premises** shall be guilty of an offence.
(2) Any person who has an **offensive weapon** within the meaning of section 1 of the Prevention of Crime Act 1953 with him on school premises shall be guilty of an offence.

Criminal Justice Act 1988, s 139A

Points to prove

✓ without good reason/lawful authority
✓ had with you
✓ on school premises
✓ an offensive weapon/article being a blade/sharply pointed

Meanings

Has with him (see **8.3.6**)

School premises

Means land used for the purposes of a **school**, excluding any land occupied solely as a dwelling by a person employed at the school.

School (Education Act 1996, s 4)

Means an educational institution which is outside the further or higher education sector and is an institution for providing—
(a) primary education,
(b) secondary education, or
(c) both primary and secondary education
whether or not the institution also provides further education.

Article (see **8.10.1**)

Offensive weapon (see **8.9.1**)

Explanatory notes

• School premises can include open land, such as playing fields or schoolyards. However, dwellings occupied within the premises by

employees, such as caretakers' or wardens' houses, are outside the
scope of this section.
• The offence applies to both publicly maintained and independent
schools.
• This offence can be committed at any time of the day or night, during
term time or holidays; it does not have to be during school hours.
• Many schools do not allow access to the general public outside or
even during, school hours: so these offences cover the situation where
such weapons are carried on school premises that are not public
places.

Defences

(3) It shall be a defence for a person charged with an offence under
subsection (1) or (2) above to prove that he had good reason or lawful
authority for having the article or weapon with him on the premises in
question.

(4) Without prejudice to the generality of subsection (3) above, it shall be
a defence for a person charged with an offence under subsection (1)
or (2) above to prove that he had the article or weapon in question
with him—
  (a) for use at work,
  (b) for educational purposes,
  (c) for religious reasons, or
  (d) as part of any national costume.

Criminal Justice Act 1988, s 139A

Practical considerations

• If threats are used, when in possession of the article or offensive
weapon, then consider the s 139AA offence (see **8.10.3**).
• Consider the offence of causing/permitting a nuisance/disturbance
on school premises and power to remove offenders (see **8.10.5**).
• Section 139B gives the police power to enter and search school premises
in connection with the s 139A and s 139AA offences (see **8.11.2**).
• Consider powers given to teachers at schools, and members of staff at
higher education establishments (see **8.10.5**).

 Either way

 None

 Summary: 6 months' imprisonment and/or a fine
Indictment: 4 years' imprisonment and/or a fine

SSS Stop, search
and seize powers   E&S Entry and
search powers   **489**

8.10.5 **Nuisance/disturbance/powers at school premises**

Section 547 of the Education Act 1996 creates the offence of causing a nuisance or disturbance on school premises and provides the police with a power to remove offenders. A number of education acts also give school staff members various powers.

Offences

Any person who without lawful authority is present on premises to which this section applies and causes or permits nuisance or disturbance to the annoyance of persons who lawfully use those premises (whether or not any such persons are present at the time) is guilty of an offence.

Education Act 1996, s 547(1)

Points to prove

✓ without lawful authority
✓ was present on
✓ premises of local authority maintained/grant-maintained school
✓ and permitted/caused
✓ a nuisance/disturbance
✓ to the annoyance of persons lawfully using those premises

Power to remove offenders

If a police constable, or an authorised person (of appropriate authority) has reasonable cause to suspect that any person is committing or has committed an offence under this section, he may remove him from the premises in question.

Education Act 1996, s 547(3)

Explanatory notes

- Section 139B gives the police a power (see **8.11.2**) to enter school premises and search people on those premises in relation to offences under s 139A (see **8.10.4**) or s 139AA (see **8.10.3**).
- **Premises** includes playgrounds, playing fields, and other premises for outdoor recreation of any—
  + school maintained by a local authority;
  + special school not so maintained;
  + independent school; and
  + an Academy (not independent school).

- **Premises** also applies to those provided by the local education authority and used wholly or mainly in connection with instruction or leadership in sporting, recreational, or outdoor activities.

School staff members' powers

- Education acts give school teachers and members of staff at higher education premises various powers.
- Section 93 of the Education and Inspections Act 2006 gives members of staff powers to restrain pupils to prevent the pupil from: committing an offence; causing personal injury/damage to another pupil or personal property; or engaging in any behaviour prejudicial to the maintenance of good order and discipline at the school.
- In England ss 550ZA and 550ZB of the Education Act 1996 allow the head teacher or authorised member of staff to use reasonable force to search a pupil if they have reasonable grounds to suspect that the pupil has a prohibited item in their possession. A prohibited item is a bladed article/knife (see **8.10.1**); offensive weapon (see **8.9.1**); alcohol (see **9.1.1**); controlled drugs (see **5.2.1**); stolen goods (see **3.5**); an article likely to be used to commit an offence or cause personal injury or damage to property; an article as specified in regulations (see below); any item which the school rules identify as an item for which a search may be made.
- The Schools (Specification and Disposal of Articles) Regulations 2012 (SI 951/2012) list further items that are prohibited under ss 550ZA. They are: tobacco and cigarette papers, firework and a pornographic image.
- The above regulations and s 550ZC give power to seize and retain, and give directions as to disposal of, any prohibited items found.
- In Wales s 550AA of the 1996 Act applies and only allows a search of pupils for a bladed article/knife or an offensive weapon. It also provides conditions for such a search, together with powers to seize, retain, and directions as to dispose of any such items found.
- Similar powers exist under the Further and Higher Education Act 1992—
  - under s 85A a person who is causing a nuisance or disturbance on higher educational premises will commit an offence. The Act also gives a constable or authorised person power to remove such a person from those premises;
  - in England ss 85AA to 85AB gives the principal or authorised member of staff in a further education institution, the same powers to search further education students and their possessions for the same prohibited items as given in ss 550ZA–550ZB (above). Section 85AC gives power to seize, retain and dispose of any prohibited items found;
  - in Wales s 85B of the 1992 Act applies and only allows staff to search for weapons as given in s 550AA above. Section 85B also gives power to seize, retain, and dispose of such items found.

8.10.5 Nuisance/disturbance/powers at school premises

 Summary

 6 months

 Level 2 fine

Links to alternative subjects and offences

8.11 **Stop and Search Powers—Knives and Weapons**

The Criminal Justice Act 1988 deals with premises search warrants and stop and search powers for school premises.

8.11.1 **Search warrant for premises**

Section 142 of the Criminal Justice Act 1988 creates a search power in respect of premises.

Grounds for issue of warrant

If on an application made by a constable a justice of the peace is satisfied that there are reasonable grounds for believing—
(a) that there are on premises specified in the application—
   (i) knives such as are mentioned in section 1(1) of the Restriction of Offensive Weapons Act 1959; **or**
   (ii) weapons to which section 141 applies; **and**
(b) that an offence under section 1 of the Restriction of Offensive Weapons Act 1959 **or** section 141 above has been or is being committed in relation to them; **and**
(c) that any of the **conditions** specified in subsection (3) below applies, he may issue a warrant authorising a constable to enter and search the premises.

Criminal Justice Act 1988, s 142(1)

Meaning of conditions

The conditions relate to any of the following, in that—

- it is not practicable to communicate with any person entitled to grant entry to the premises or grant access to the knives or weapons to which the application relates;
- entry to the premises will not be granted unless a warrant is produced;
- the purpose of a search may be frustrated or seriously prejudiced unless a constable arriving at the premises can secure immediate entry to them.

Explanatory notes

- Restriction of Offensive Weapons Act 1959 refers to any flick knife, flick gun, or gravity knife (see **8.10.2**).
- Weapons under s 141 are listed in the Offensive Weapons Order 1988 (see **8.9.2** and **8.9.3**).

- A constable may seize and retain anything for which a search has been authorised under s 142(1) above.

8.11.2 Powers for article/weapon on school premises

Section 139B of the Criminal Justice Act 1988 provides a power of entry to school premises to search for offensive weapons or articles with a blade or sharp point, and to seize/retain any weapon/article found.

Enter and search

A constable may enter school premises and search those premises and any person on those premises for—
(a) any article to which section 139 of this Act applies, or
(b) any offensive weapon within the meaning of section 1 of the Prevention of Crime Act 1953,
if he has reasonable grounds for suspecting that an offence under section 139A or 139AA of this Act is being, or has been, committed.

Criminal Justice Act 1988, s 139B(1)

Seize and retain

If, in the course of a search under this section, a constable discovers an article or weapon which he has reasonable grounds for suspecting to be an article or weapon of a kind described in subsection (1) above, he may seize and retain it.

Criminal Justice Act 1988, s 139B(2)

Explanatory notes

- A constable may use reasonable force, if necessary, in the exercise of the power of entry conferred by this section.
- For the offence under s 139A see **8.10.4** and s 139AA see **8.10.3**.
- An article under s 139 is a bladed/sharply pointed article (see **8.10.1**).
- For offensive weapon under the Prevention of Crime Act 1953, s 1 see **8.9.1**.

Practical considerations

- Powers under s 139B are additional to entry and search powers under s 17 of PACE (see **12.3.2**).
- If a large number of people are involved, causing fear of a serious public order situation, then consider stop and search powers under the Criminal Justice and Public Order Act 1994, s 60 (see **8.11.3**).
- Consider the offence and power to remove a person who causes or permits a nuisance or disturbance on school premises (see **8.10.5**).

8.11.3 **Stop and search—serious violence/ offensive weapon**

Section 60 of the Criminal Justice and Public Order Act 1994 allows senior police officers to authorise constables to stop and search people or vehicles in a specific area, either where a serious public order problem is likely to arise, has taken place or people are carrying offensive weapons or sharp pointed blades. An offence will be committed if that person fails to comply with a constable's requirements.

Authorisation

If a police officer of or above the rank of inspector reasonably believes—
(a) that incidents involving serious violence **may take place** in any locality in his police area, and that it is expedient to give an authorisation under this section to prevent their occurrence,
(aa) that
   (i) an incident involving serious violence **has taken place** in England and Wales in his police area;
   (ii) a dangerous instrument or offensive weapon used in the incident is being carried in any locality in his police area by a person; and
   (iii) it is expedient to give an authorisation under this section to find the instrument or weapon; or
(b) that persons are carrying dangerous instruments or offensive weapons in any locality in his police area without good reason,
he may give an authorisation that the powers conferred by this section are to be exercisable at any place within that locality for a specified period not exceeding 24 hours.

Criminal Justice and Public Order Act 1994, s 60(1)

Explanatory notes

- Where a serious violent incident has occurred, and the weapon used in the incident is believed to still be in the locality; this power assists in locating the weapon used, and in apprehending the offender before they leave the area or disperse.
- If an authorisation has been given orally under s 60(1)(aa) it needs to be in writing as soon as practicable. Authorisations made under s 60(1)(a) or (b) will still need to be made in writing.
- The inspector giving an authorisation must, as soon as practicable, inform an officer of or above the rank of superintendent.
- If it appears to an officer of or above the rank of superintendent that it is expedient to do so, they may direct that the authorisation shall continue being in force for a further 24 hours. This shall be recorded in writing as soon as practicable.
- Any authorisation shall be in writing signed by the officer giving it, and shall specify the grounds, locality, and the period during which the powers are exercisable.

8.11.3 Stop and search—serious violence/offensive weapon

Power to stop and search pedestrian/vehicle

(4) This section confers on any constable in uniform power—
  (a) to stop any pedestrian and search him or anything carried by him for **offensive weapons** or **dangerous instruments**;
  (b) to stop any **vehicle** and search the vehicle, its driver and any passenger for offensive weapons or dangerous instruments.
(5) A constable may, in the exercise of the powers conferred by subsection (4) above, stop any person or vehicle and make any search he thinks fit whether or not he has any grounds for suspecting that the person or vehicle is carrying weapons or articles of that kind.

Criminal Justice and Public Order Act 1994, s 60

Power to seize

If in the course of such a search under this section a constable discovers a dangerous instrument or an article which he has reasonable grounds for suspecting to be an offensive weapon, he may seize it.

Criminal Justice and Public Order Act 1994, s 60(6)

Offences

A person who fails to stop, or to stop a vehicle, when required to do so by a constable in the exercise of his powers under this section commits an offence.

Criminal Justice and Public Order Act 1994, s 60(8)

Points to prove

✓ failed to stop (person) or vehicle
✓ when required to do so
✓ by a constable in uniform
✓ in exercising powers of stop/search

Meanings

Offensive weapon (see 8.9.1)

However, for incidents involving serious violence under s 60(1)(aa)(i)—means any article used in the incident to cause or threaten injury to any person or otherwise to intimidate.

Dangerous instrument

Means instruments which have a blade or are sharply pointed.

Vehicle

This is its natural meaning (see 12.1.1) and includes a caravan.

Explanatory notes

- Once a written authority has been given for searches, under s 60(5) a constable can stop any person/vehicle or make any search that they think fit, whether or not there are grounds for suspecting that the person or vehicle is carrying weapons or articles.
- Ensure compliance with paras 2.12 to 2.14B of Code A in relation to searches of persons and vehicles under s 60. Persons involved are entitled to a written statement as to being stopped and/or searched under s 60, if they apply within 12 months.
- A person carries a dangerous instrument or an offensive weapon if they have it in their physical possession.

Related cases

Roberts v Commissioner of Police for the Metropolis [2014] EWCA Civ 69, CA The Criminal Justice and Public Order Act 1994, s 60 did not provide an arbitrary power of stop and search; it was circumscribed by specific requirements and therefore in accordance with the law.

R (on the application of Laporte) v CC of Gloucestershire [2006] UKHL 55, HL This case involved three coaches stopped and searched under a s 60 authority (see **'Related cases'** under **7.3** for further details).

Practical considerations

- Apart from BT police, only inspectors and superintendents from Home Office forces may authorise these powers to be exercised, although officers from other police forces (RMP, Civil Nuclear Constabulary) may be involved in such searches.
- With the necessary modifications, s 60 also applies to ships, aircraft, and hovercraft as it applies to vehicles.
- Powers conferred by s 60 are in addition to and do not derogate from any other statutory powers.
- Where a s 60 authority is in force, then s 60AA can be utilised, whereby any items, masks, or disguises which are used in order to conceal identity can be removed and seized. An offence will be committed if a person fails to remove an item worn by them when required to do so by a constable under s 60AA(7).

 SSS

 Summary   6 months

 1 month's imprisonment and/or a level 3 fine

Links to alternative subjects and offences

Chapter 9

Alcohol and Licensing

9.1 Alcohol Restrictions on Persons under 16/18

The sale and supply of alcohol is regulated by the Licensing Act 2003 which creates a number of offences relating to children, young people, alcohol, drunkenness, and disorderly conduct.

The following offences protect children both on and off licensed premises; some of them apply anywhere and are not restricted to licensed premises.

9.1.1 Unaccompanied children prohibited from certain premises

It is an offence to admit children under 16 to certain categories of relevant premises if they are not accompanied by an adult or allow them to be on these premises between midnight and 5 a.m., and those premises are open for the supply of alcohol for consumption therein.

Offences

A **person to whom subsection (3) applies** commits an offence if—

(a) knowing that **relevant premises** are **within subsection (4)**, he allows an **unaccompanied child** to be on the premises at a time when they are open for the purposes of being used for the **supply of alcohol** for consumption there, **or**

(b) he allows an **unaccompanied child** to be on relevant premises at a time between the hours of midnight and 5 a.m. when the premises are open for the purposes of being used for the supply of alcohol for consumption there.

Licensing Act 2003, s 145(1)

9.1.1 Unaccompanied children prohibited from certain premises

> **Points to prove**
> ✓ being a person to whom subsection (3) applies
> ✓ knowing they were relevant premises
> ✓ allowed an unaccompanied child to be on premises
> ✓ when open **or** open between midnight and 5 a.m.
> ✓ when used for supplying alcohol for consumption therein

Meanings

Person to whom subsection (3) applies

Any person who—
- works at the premises in a capacity, whether paid or unpaid, which authorises them to request the unaccompanied child to leave the premises;
- in the case of licensed premises, to the holder of a premises licence in respect of the premises, and the designated premises supervisor (if any) under such a licence;
- in the case of premises in respect of which a club premises certificate has effect, to any member or officer of the club which holds the certificate who is present on the premises in a capacity which enables him to make such a request;
- in the case of premises which may be used for a permitted temporary activity by virtue of Pt 5, to the premises user in relation to the temporary event notice in question.

Relevant premises

Means premises that—
- are licensed; or
- have a club premises certificate in force; **or**
- may be used for a permitted temporary activity (under Pt 5).

Relevant premises within subsection 4

Relevant premises are within this subsection if they are—
- exclusively or primarily used for the supply of alcohol for consumption on the premises; or
- open for the purposes of the supply of alcohol for consumption on the premises by virtue of Pt 5 (permitted temporary activities) and, at the time the temporary event notice has effect, they are exclusively or primarily used for such supplies.

Child

Means an individual aged under 16.

Alcohol (s 191)

Means spirits, wine, beer, cider, or any other fermented, distilled, or spirituous liquor, but does **not** include—
- alcohol which is of a strength not exceeding 0.5 per cent at the time of the sale or supply in question;

- perfume;
- flavouring essences recognised by HMRC as not being intended for consumption as or with dutiable alcoholic liquor;
- aromatic flavouring essence commonly known as Angostura bitters;
- alcohol which is, or is included in, a medicinal product, or a veterinary medicinal product;
- denatured alcohol;
- methyl alcohol;
- naphtha; or
- alcohol contained in liqueur confectionery.

Unaccompanied

Means not in the company of an individual aged 18 or over.

Supply of alcohol

Means the sale by retail of alcohol, or the supply of alcohol by or on behalf of a club to, or to the order of, a member of the club.

Explanatory notes

No offence is committed if the unaccompanied child is on the premises solely for the purpose of passing to or from some other place to or from which there is no other convenient means of access or exit.

Defences—s 145(6) to (8)

- That the conduct was by act or default of some other person and the defendant exercised all due diligence to avoid committing it.
- Where the defendant by reason of their own conduct—
  - believed that the unaccompanied child was aged 16 or over or that an individual accompanying the child was aged 18 or over; and
  - either:
    - had taken all reasonable steps to establish the individual's age; or
    - nobody could reasonably have suspected from the individual's appearance that they were aged under 16 or, as the case may be, under 18.

Defence notes

A person is treated as having 'taken all reasonable steps' to establish an individual's age if—

- they asked the individual for evidence of their age; and
- the evidence would have convinced a reasonable person.

This defence will fail if the prosecution prove that the evidence of age was such that no reasonable person would have been convinced by it—for example, if the proof of age was either an obvious forgery or clearly belonged to another person (see **11.3.1**).

- The defence also applies in situations where the child looks exceptionally old for his or her age.

Practical considerations

Age to be confirmed by ID card, driving licence, or similar document.

 Summary 12 months

 Level 3 fine

9.1.2 **Sale of alcohol to person under 18**

The sale of alcohol to a person under 18 anywhere is an offence.

Offences

A person commits an offence if he sells **alcohol** to an individual aged under 18.

Licensing Act 2003, s 146(1)

Points to prove

✓ sold alcohol
✓ to person under the age of 18

Meaning of alcohol (see 9.1.1)

Explanatory notes

- Similar offences apply where a club supplies alcohol to under 18 by it or on its behalf (s 146(2)) or where a person supplies to under 18 on behalf of the club (s 146(3)).
- The sale of alcohol to children is not only an offence if it occurs on relevant licensed premises, but **anywhere**.

Defences—s 146(4) to (6)

- Where a defendant by reason of their own conduct—
    + believed that the individual was aged 18 or over, and either:
        - they had taken all reasonable steps to establish the individual's age; or
        - nobody could reasonably have suspected from the individual's appearance that they were aged under 18.
- That the offence was committed by act or default of some other person and that the defendant exercised all **due diligence** to avoid committing it.

Defence notes

- For 'having taken all reasonable steps' (see **9.1.1 'Defence notes'**).
- The second part of the defence could be where the actual sale was made by a barman and the manager had exercised all due diligence to avoid this offence being committed.

Practical considerations

- Age to be confirmed by ID card, driving licence, or similar document.
- This offence can be dealt with by PND (see **7.1.1**).

PND	Issue for s 146(1), (3) offences only (**not** s 146(2) club offences)
PCSO	Applies to s 146(1) offences only (no powers in relation to clubs)

 Summary   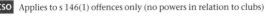 12 months

 Fine

9.1.3 Allowing sale/persistently sell alcohol to person under 18

It is also an offence to allow alcohol to be sold to a person under 18.

Offences

A **person to whom subsection (2) applies** commits an offence if he **knowingly** allows the sale of **alcohol** on **relevant premises** to an individual aged under 18.

Licensing Act 2003, s 147(1)

9.1.3 Allowing sale/persistently sell alcohol to person under 18

Points to prove

✓ being person to whom subsection (2) applies
✓ on relevant premises
✓ knowingly allowed the sale of alcohol
✓ to a person under the age of 18

Meanings

Person to whom subsection (2) applies

Any person who works at the premises in a capacity, whether paid or unpaid, which authorises them to prevent the sale.

Knowingly

Means having knowledge (see '**Related cases**' below), an awareness, informed, consciously, intentionally, or an understanding.

Alcohol (see **9.1.1**)

Relevant premises (see **9.1.1**)

Explanatory notes

- There are no statutory defences to this offence. The mental element 'knowingly' applies only to allowing the sale; it does not require knowledge that the individual was under 18. The prosecution need only prove that the individual was under 18.
- Similar offences apply under s 147(3) where an employee or member/officer of a club fail to prevent supply on relevant premises by or on behalf of the club to a member/individual who is aged under 18.

Related cases

Ross v Moss and Others [1965] 3 All ER 145, QBD If the licensee or other appropriate person is on the premises and looks the other way to a particular unlawful practice they cannot then say that they had no personal knowledge. 'Knowledge' not only means actual knowledge, but it also includes 'shutting one's eyes' to what is going on and the intention that what is happening should happen but deliberately looking the other way.

Practical considerations

- Age to be confirmed by ID card, driving licence, or similar document.
- **Persistently selling alcohol to children (under 18):** A summary offence will be committed under s 147A if on two or more different occasions, within a period of three consecutive months, alcohol is unlawfully sold on the same premises to an individual aged under 18.
- The following procedural requirements under s 147A also apply—
  + The premises must be either licensed premises or authorised premises for a permitted temporary activity by virtue of Pt 5, and

the offender must hold the premises licence or be the named premises user for a temporary event notice.

♦ The same sale may not be counted as different offences for this purpose.

♦ The following shall be admissible as evidence that there has been an unlawful sale of alcohol to an individual aged under 18 on any premises on any occasion:

- a conviction for a s 146 offence in respect of a sale to that individual on those premises on that occasion;
- a caution in respect of such an offence; or
- PND issue/payment in respect of such a sale.

Section 147B provides that if the holder of a premises licence is convicted of a s 147A offence for sales on those premises, the court may order that the premises licence is suspended for a period not exceeding 3 months.

A closure notice for persistently selling alcohol to children under 18 can be issued (see **9.3.4**).

 Summary   12 months

 Fine

9.1.4 Purchase of alcohol by or on behalf of person under 18

Offences are committed by a person under 18, or person on behalf of the under 18, who purchases or attempts to purchase alcohol anywhere. Similarly it is an offence for a person to buy or attempt to buy alcohol for consumption by a person who is under 18 on licensed premises.

Offences

(1) (a) An individual aged under 18 commits an offence if he buys or attempts to buy **alcohol**.

(3) (a) A person commits an offence if he buys or attempts to buy **alcohol** on behalf of an individual aged under 18.

(4) (a) A person commits an offence if he buys or attempts to buy alcohol for consumption on **relevant premises** by an individual aged under 18.

Licensing Act 2003, s 149

9.1.4 Purchase of alcohol by or on behalf of person under 18

Points to prove

s 149(1)(a) offence

✓ being a person under the age of 18
✓ bought **or** attempted to buy alcohol

s 149(3)(a) offence

✓ bought **or** attempted to buy alcohol
✓ on behalf of individual under the age of 18

s 149(4)(a) offence

✓ bought **or** attempted to buy alcohol
✓ for consumption on relevant premises
✓ by an individual under the age of 18

Meanings

Alcohol (see **9.1.1**)

Relevant premises (see **9.1.1**)

Explanatory notes

- Offences in s 149(1)(a) and s 149(3)(a) may be committed **anywhere**.
- **'On behalf of'** does not mean that the purchase must be instigated by the child; the alcohol need only be bought for a child.
- Section 149(2) states that the s 149(1) offence does not apply to an individual aged under 18 who buys or attempts to buy the alcohol at the request of a constable, or a weights and measures inspector who are acting in the course of their duty. This exception allows test-purchasing operations to take place (see **9.3.1**).
- Similarly s 149(5) states that a s 149(4) offence does not apply if—
  + the relevant person is aged 18 or over;
  + the individual is aged 16 or 17;
  + the alcohol is beer, wine, or cider;
  + its purchase or supply is for consumption at a **table meal** on **relevant premises**, and
  + the individual is accompanied at the meal by an individual aged 18 or over.
- **Table meal** means a meal eaten by a person seated at a table, or at a counter or other structure which serves the purpose of a table and is not used for the service of refreshments for consumption by persons not seated at a table or structure serving the purpose of a table.
- Bar snacks do not amount to a table meal.
- Similar offences apply to clubs, under s 149(1)(b), (3)(b), and (4)(b) respectively, where a member of a club is supplied with alcohol by or on behalf of that club for—

+ that member (being under 18), as a result of his act, default or attempts to do so;
+ an individual aged under 18 as a result of his making, attempting to make such arrangements; and
+ consumption on relevant premises by an individual aged under 18, by his act, default or attempts to do so.

Defences—s 149(6)

Section 149(3) and (4) offences only

The defendant had no reason to suspect that the individual was aged under 18.

Related cases (on test purchases see **9.3.1**)

Practical considerations

Consider issuing a PND for the s 149(3)(a) and (4) offences (see **7.1.1**), but not the s 149(1) offence, as PND's can no longer be issued to a person under 18.

 PND s 149(3)(a) and (4) only   **PCSO** (Except clubs)

 Summary   12 months

 s 149(1) offence
Level 3 fine

   s 149(3) and s 149(4) offences
   Fine

9.1.5 Consumption of alcohol by person under 18

Persons aged under 18 are not allowed to consume alcohol on relevant premises.

Offences

(1) An individual under 18 commits an offence if he **knowingly** consumes alcohol on **relevant premises**.

9.1.5 Consumption of alcohol by person under 18

(2) A **person to whom subsection (3) applies** commits an offence if he knowingly allows the consumption of alcohol on relevant premises by an individual aged under 18.

Licensing Act 2003, s 150

Points to prove

s 150(1) offence

✓ being a person under the age of 18
✓ knowingly consumed alcohol on relevant premises

s 150(2) offence

✓ being a person to whom subsection (3) applies
✓ knowingly allowed
✓ an individual under the age of 18
✓ to consume alcohol on relevant premises

Meanings

Knowingly (see **9.1.3**)

Alcohol (see **9.1.1**)

Relevant premises (see **9.1.1**)

Person to whom subsection (3) applies

This subsection applies—

(a) to a person who works at the premises in a capacity, whether paid or unpaid, which authorises him to prevent the consumption, and

(b) where the alcohol was supplied by a club to or to the order of a member of the club, to any member or officer of the club who is present at the premises at the time of the consumption in a capacity which enables him to prevent it.

Explanatory notes

- The s 150(1) knowingly consumed offence will not be committed if the individual inadvertently consumes alcohol, for example if the drink is spiked.
- Section 150(4) states the s 150(1) and (2) offences do not apply if—
  + the individual is aged 16 or 17;
  + the alcohol is beer, wine, or cider;
  + its consumption is at a **table meal** on relevant premises; and
  + the individual is accompanied at the meal by an individual aged 18 or over.
- Both offences under s 150(1) and (2) also apply to clubs.

Practical considerations

- Knowledge has to be proved for both offences, either to 'knowingly' consume or to 'knowingly' allow consumption of the alcohol.
- Age to be proved by ID card, driving licence, or similar documentation.
- Consider issuing a PND for the s 150(2) offence (see **7.1.1**), but not the s 150(1) offence as PND's can no longer be issued to a person under 18.

 PND s 150(2) only   **PCSO** (Except clubs)

 Summary   12 months

 s 150(1) offence
Level 3 fine

s 150(2) offence
Fine

9.1.6 Delivering alcohol to person under 18

It is an offence for certain people to deliver or allow delivery of alcohol to a person under 18.

Offences

(1) A person who works on **relevant premises** in any capacity, whether paid or unpaid, commits an offence if he **knowingly** delivers to an individual aged under 18—
  (a) **alcohol** sold on the premises, or
  (b) alcohol supplied on the premises by or on behalf of a club to or to the order of a member of the club.
(2) A **person to whom subsection (3) applies** commits an offence if he knowingly allows anybody else to deliver to a person under 18 **alcohol** sold on **relevant premises**.

Licensing Act 2003, s 151

Points to prove

s 151(1) offence
✓ being a person who worked in a capacity, whether unpaid or paid
✓ on relevant premises

9.1.6 Delivering alcohol to person under 18

- ✓ knowingly delivered to an individual under the age of 18
- ✓ alcohol sold on those premises **or**
- ✓ supplied on those premises (by or on behalf of a club/order of member)

s 151(2) offence

- ✓ being a person to whom subsection (3) applies
- ✓ on relevant premises
- ✓ knowingly allowed another person to deliver
- ✓ to an individual under the age of 18
- ✓ alcohol sold on those premises

Meanings

Relevant premises (see **9.1.1**)

Knowingly (see **9.1.3**)

Alcohol (see **9.1.1**)

Person to whom subsection (3) applies

Any person who works on the premises in a capacity, whether paid or unpaid, which authorises him to prevent the delivery of the alcohol.

Explanatory notes

- Offences in this section cover various situations, for example under s 151(1)(a) a child takes delivery of a consignment of alcohol bought by a parent from an off-licence (unless the defence applies); or a person authorises a delivery of that sort, under s 151(2).
- A similar offence to s 151(2), is to knowingly allow somebody else to deliver alcohol supplied by a club under s 151(4).

Defences—s 151(6)

Subsections (1), (2), and (4) do not apply where—
- (a) the alcohol is delivered at a place where the buyer or, as the case may be, person supplied lives or works, or
- (b) the individual aged under 18 works on the relevant premises in a capacity, whether paid or unpaid, which involves the delivery of alcohol, or
- (c) the alcohol is sold or supplied for consumption on the relevant premises.

Defence notes

This covers cases where, for example, a child answers the door and signs for the delivery of an order for the house, or where a 16-year-old office worker is sent to collect an order for their employer.

Practical considerations

Knowledge has to be proved for all the offences, either to 'knowingly' (see **9.1.3**) deliver or to 'knowingly' allow anybody else to deliver the alcohol.

Age to be proved by ID card, driving licence, or similar document.

Consider issuing a PND for these offences (see **7.1.1**).

 Summary   12 months

 Fine

9.1.7 Sending person under 18 to obtain alcohol

A person under 18 must not be sent to obtain alcohol.

Offences

A person commits an offence if he **knowingly** sends an individual aged under 18 to obtain—

(a) **alcohol** sold or to be sold on **relevant premises** for consumption off the premises, or

(b) **alcohol** supplied or to be supplied by or on behalf of a club to or to the order of a member of the club for such consumption.

Licensing Act 2003, s 152(1)

Points to prove

✓ knowingly sent an individual under the age of 18
✓ to obtain alcohol
✓ sold/to be sold on relevant premises or
✓ supplied/to be supplied (by/on behalf of club/order of member)
✓ for consumption off those premises

Meanings

Knowingly (see **9.1.3**)

9.1.7 Sending person under 18 to obtain alcohol

Alcohol (see **9.1.1**)

Relevant premises (see **9.1.1**)

Explanatory notes

- Section 152(3) allows an individual under 18 who works on the relevant premises in a capacity (whether paid or unpaid) that involve delivery of alcohol.
- Similarly s 152(4) states that no offence will be committed if an individual aged under 18 is sent by a constable, or a weights and measures inspector, who are acting in the course of their duty. This exception allows test-purchasing operations to take place (see **9.3.1**).

Related cases (on test purchases see **9.3.1**)

Practical considerations

- This offence covers, for example, circumstances where a parent sends their child (being under 18) to an off-licence to buy and collect alcohol for them.
- Knowledge has to be proved as to 'knowingly' send an individual aged under 18 to obtain alcohol sold or supplied from the relevant premises
- It is an offence under s 153 to knowingly allow a person under 18 to sell or, in the case of a club to supply alcohol, unless each sale or supply is approved by a responsible person.
- It is no longer an offence under s 148 to sell liquor confectionery (chocolate liqueurs) to children under 16 as it has been repealed by the Deregulation Act 2015, s 70.

 Summary   12 months

 Fine

Links to alternative subjects and offences

Drunkenness on Licensed Premises

The Licensing Act 2003 creates a number of offences relating to alcohol and offences concerning drunkenness and disorderly conduct.

9.2.1 Sale of alcohol to person who is drunk

It is an offence to sell or attempt to sell alcohol to a person who is drunk, or to allow alcohol to be sold to such a person, on relevant premises.

Offences

A **person to whom subsection (2) applies** commits an offence if, on **relevant premises**, he **knowingly**—
(a) sells or attempts to sell **alcohol** to a person who is **drunk,** or
(b) allows alcohol to be sold to such a person.

Licensing Act 2003, s 141(1)

Points to prove

✓ person to whom subsection (2) applies
✓ knowingly sold/attempted to sell/allowed sale of alcohol
✓ on relevant premises to a person who was drunk

Meanings

Person to whom subsection (2) applies

Any person who works at the premises in a capacity, whether paid or unpaid, which gives him authority to sell the alcohol concerned.
In licensed premises, clubs, or permitted temporary activity premises, the same persons as given in s 145(3) (see **9.1.1**).

Relevant premises (see 9.1.1)

Knowingly (see 9.1.3)

Alcohol (see 9.1.1)

Drunk (see 7.2.1)

Explanatory notes

In each case, drunkenness will be a question of fact for the court to decide.

- It is also an offence, under s 141(3), to supply alcohol by or on behalf of a club or to the order of a member of the club to a person who is drunk.

Practical considerations

- If the person is under 18 consider offences under s 145 (see **9.1.1**).
- Knowledge has to be proved as to 'knowingly' sell, attempt to sell, or allow to be sold alcohol to a person who is drunk.
- This offence can be dealt with by PND (see **7.1.1**).
- Details of the licence holder and/or the designated premises supervisor should be clearly displayed in the premises.
- Under s 142 it is also an offence to knowingly obtain or attempt to obtain alcohol on relevant premises for consumption on those premises by a person who is drunk.

  (Except clubs)

 Summary 12 months

 Level 3 fine

9.2.2 **Failure to leave licensed premises**

People who are drunk or disorderly may be requested to leave certain premises and commit an offence if they fail to do so.

Offences

A person who is **drunk** or **disorderly** commits an offence if, without reasonable excuse—

(a) he fails to leave **relevant premises** when requested to do so by a constable or by a **person to whom subsection (2) applies**, or

(b) he enters or attempts to enter relevant premises after a constable or a person to whom subsection (2) applies has requested him not to enter.

Licensing Act 2003, s 143(1)

Points to prove

✓ without reasonable excuse while drunk or disorderly
✓ failed to comply with request
✓ by a constable or a person to whom subsection (2) applies
✓ to leave **or** not to enter/attempt to enter relevant premises

Meanings

Drunk (see **7.2.1**)

Disorderly (see **7.2.1**)

Relevant premises (see **9.1.1**)

Person to whom subsection (2) applies

* Any person who works at the premises in a capacity, whether paid or unpaid, which authorises them to make such a request.
* In licensed premises, clubs, or permitted temporary activity, the same persons as given in s 145(3) (see **9.1.1**).

Explanatory notes

* An offence may not be committed if the person has a reasonable excuse, for example if they are physically prevented by serious disability or injury from leaving the premises.
* Apart from licensed premises, this offence also applies to clubs and premises being used for a permitted temporary activity.
* Whether a person is drunk and/or disorderly will be a question of fact for the court to decide.

Practical considerations

On being requested to do so by the appropriate person, a constable must help to expel from relevant premises a person who is drunk/disorderly or help to prevent such a person from entering relevant premises.
Consider either drunk and disorderly in a public place (see **7.2.1**) or drunk on licensed premises/public place (see **7.2.2**)—both can be dealt with by PND (see **7.1.1**).

 Summary   12 months

 Level 1 fine

9.2.3 Allowing disorderly conduct on licensed premises

It is also an offence to knowingly allow disorderly conduct on relevant premises.

Offences

A person to whom subsection (2) applies commits an offence if he knowingly allows disorderly conduct on relevant premises.

Licensing Act 2003, s 140(1)

9.2.3 Allowing disorderly conduct on licensed premises

Points to prove
- ✓ being a person to whom subsection (2) applies
- ✓ knowingly allowed disorderly conduct on relevant premises

Meanings

Person to whom subsection (2) applies
- Any person who works at the premises in a capacity, whether paid or unpaid, which authorises them to prevent the conduct.
- In licensed premises, clubs, or permitted temporary activity, the same persons as given in s 145(3) (see **9.1.1**).

Knowingly (see **9.1.3**)

Disorderly (see **7.2.1**)

Relevant premises (see **9.1.1**)

Explanatory notes
- Knowledge has to be proved as to 'knowingly' allow disorderly conduct on the relevant premises.
- Apart from licensed premises, this offence also applies to clubs and premises which may be used for a permitted temporary activity.

 Summary   12 months

 Level 3 fine

Links to alternative subjects and offences

9.3 **Powers to Enter/Close Licensed Premises and Test Purchases**

The Licensing Act 2003 provides a variety of offences relating to alcohol and powers to enter/close licensed premises/clubs and allows test purchases.

9.3.1 **Test purchases**

Sections 149 and 152 allow the police and trading standards officers to use individuals under 18 to make test purchases to ascertain if such individuals can buy or be supplied with alcohol from on/off licensed premises, certified club premises, or premises used for a permitted temporary activity without any offences being committed.

Authorities

149(2) But subsection (1) [see **9.1.4**] does not apply where the individual buys or attempts to buy the alcohol at the request of—
  (a) a constable, or
  (b) a weights and measures inspector,
  who is acting in the course of his duty.
152(4) Subsection (1) [see **9.1.7**] also does not apply where the individual aged under 18 is sent by—
  (a) a constable, or
  (b) a weights and measures inspector,
  who is acting in the course of his duty.

Licensing Act 2003, ss 149(2) and 152(4)

Explanatory notes

This statutory authority allows test-purchasing operations to establish whether licensees and staff working in relevant licensed premises are complying with the prohibition on the sale/supply of alcohol to individuals aged under 18.

Related cases

DPP v Marshall [1988] 3 All ER 683, QBD Police in plain clothes bought alcohol from a shop; it was argued that evidence should be excluded under s 78 of PACE, as the officers had not revealed the fact that they were policemen at the time of the purchase and this was unfair. On appeal it was held that evidence of police officers had been wrongly excluded; it had not been shown that the evidence would have had an adverse effect on the proceedings.

R v Loosely/A-G's Reference (No 3 of 2000) [2001] UKHL 53, HL This was a case on entrapment; police officers must not instigate the commission of an offence. But if police do what an ordinary customer would do, whether lawful or unlawful, this will not normally be regarded as objectionable.

Practical considerations
- Consider the protection of children engaged in such operations.
- Assess the reliability of their evidence.

9.3.2 **Powers to enter licensed premises and clubs**

The Licensing Act 2003 contains provisions dealing with powers of entry to investigate licensable activities and offences, namely:

- Section 179(1) gives power to a constable or an authorised person to enter premises, if they have reason to believe that they are being, or are about to be, used for a licensable activity, in order to see whether the activity is being carried on in accordance with the authorisation. However, this does not apply to clubs, unless there is other authorisation apart from a club premises licence.
- Similarly under s 180(1) a constable may enter and search any premises in respect of which they have reason to believe that an offence under the Licensing Act has been, is being, or is about to be committed.
- PCSOs can enter and search premises (other than clubs), in the relevant police area, providing they are in the company and under the supervision of a constable, unless they are 'off-licence' premises (see **11.1.2**).
- Section 97(1) allows a constable to enter and search club premises if they have reasonable cause to believe that certain offences relating to the supply of drugs have been, are being, or are about to be committed or that there is likely to be a breach of the peace.

Explanatory notes
- In exercising these powers a constable may, if necessary, use reasonable force.
- It is not necessary to obtain a warrant.
- Police have lawful authority to require production of a premises licence, club premises certificate, or temporary event notice.
- The police may lawfully enter premises in order to inspect them before a licence or certificate is granted.

9.3.3 **Police powers—closure notice**

Where an offence of persistently selling alcohol to children (under 18) has been committed under s 147A (see **9.1.3**) then a closure notice can be issued by a superintendent (or above) to close the premises.

Closure notice

A **relevant officer** may give a notice under this section (a **'closure notice'**) applying to any premises if—
(a) there is evidence that a person ('the offender') has committed an offence under section 147A in relation to those premises;
(b) the relevant officer considers that the evidence is such that, if the offender were prosecuted for the offence, there would be a realistic prospect of his being convicted; and
(c) the offender is still, at the time when the notice is given, the holder of a premises licence in respect of those premises, or one of the holders of such a licence.

Licensing Act 2003, s 169A(1)

Meaning of relevant officer

Means a police officer of the rank of superintendent or above; or an appointed inspector of weights and measures.

Explanatory notes

- The **closure notice** will—
  + prohibit sale of alcohol on the premises, for at least 48 hours but no more than 336 hours; and
  + if accepted will discharge all criminal liability in respect of the s 147A offence (see **9.1.3**).
- A closure notice must—
  + be in the form as prescribed by regulations;
  + specify the premises and circumstances surrounding the offence;
  + specify the period when sales of alcohol are prohibited;
  + explain the consequences/penalties of any sale of alcohol on the premises during that period; the rights of that person; and how those rights may be exercised.

Practical considerations

The period specified must be 48 to 336 hours; and the time specifying when that period begins must be not less than 14 days after the date of the service of the closure notice.

9.3.3 Police powers—closure notice

- Service of the closure notice may be served on the premises by a
  constable, PCSO, or trading standards officer to a person having
  control/responsibility for the premises; and only when licensable
  activities are being carried on there. A copy must be served on the
  licence holder of the premises.
- A closure notice must not be given more than 3 months after the
  s 147A offence.
- No more than one closure notice may be given in respect of offences
  relating to the same sales; nor may such a notice be given in respect of
  an offence in respect of which a prosecution has already been
  brought.
- Section 169B prescribes other matters when a closure notice has
  been issued—
  - No proceedings may be brought for the s 147A offence or any
    related offence at any time before the time when the prohibition
    proposed by the notice would take effect.
  - If the premises' licence holder accepts the proposed prohibition
    in the manner specified in the notice then that prohibition
    takes effect (as specified) and no proceedings may be
    brought against that person for the alleged offence or any
    related offence.
  - 'Related offence' means an offence under s 146 (see **9.1.2**) or s 147
    (see **9.1.3**) in respect of any of the sales to which the alleged offence
    relates.

PCSO

Links to alternative subjects and offences

9.4 Public Spaces Protection Order—Alcohol Restrictions

Section 63 of the Anti-social Behaviour, Crime and Policing Act 2014 empowers the police/PCSO to prohibit consumption of alcohol in the restricted area of a public place covered by a **public spaces protection order** (PSPO). A police officer/PCSO can require a person to cease drinking alcohol in the restricted area in breach of the PSPO, with powers to confiscate and dispose, and failure to comply is an offence.

9.4.1 Power to require person to cease drinking alcohol

Powers

(1) This section applies where a constable or an **authorised person** reasonably believes that a person (P) —
  (a) is or has been consuming **alcohol** in breach of a prohibition in a **public spaces protection order**, or
  (b) intends to consume alcohol in circumstances in which doing so would be a breach of such a prohibition.
(2) The constable or authorised person may **require** P—
  (a) not to consume, in breach of the order, alcohol or anything which the constable or authorised person reasonably believes to be alcohol;
  (b) to surrender anything in P's possession which is, or which the constable or authorised person reasonably believes to be, alcohol or a container for alcohol.

Anti-social Behaviour, Crime and Policing Act 2014, s 63

Meanings

Authorised person
Means a PCSO (see **11.1.2**) or authorised LA enforcement officer.

Alcohol (see **9.1.1**)

Public spaces protection order (PSPO) (see **7.15.2**)

Explanatory notes

- A requirement imposed by a constable/PCSO/LA authorised enforcement officer is not valid if they are asked by P to show evidence of their authorisation, and they fail to do so.
- Local authorities are responsible for making a PSPO and will have to be satisfied, on reasonable grounds, that activities in a public space: have had or will be likely to have a detrimental effect on the quality

of life of those in the locality; it is, or is likely to be, persistent or continuing in nature, such as to make the activities unreasonable; and the order justifies the restrictions imposed (see **7.15.2**).

- The person must be informed that failure to comply with the officer's request, without reasonable excuse, is an offence (see **9.4.2**).
- A prohibition in a PSPO on consuming alcohol does not apply to—
  + premises (other than council-operated) which have a premises licence or club premises certificate for the supply of alcohol; or
  + a place within the curtilage of those premises;
  + a place where the sale of alcohol is for the time being authorised by a temporary event notice or was so authorised within the last 30 minutes;
  + a place where facilities/activities relating to the sale/consumption of alcohol are permitted by a permission granted under s 115E of the Highways Act 1980.
- A constable/PCSO or authorised LA enforcement officer may dispose of anything surrendered to them under s 63(2)(b) in such manner as they consider appropriate.
- Consider using the power to confiscate alcohol from people under 18 years of age (see **9.5**).

9.4.2 Failure to comply with alcohol requirements

Example of constable's requirement

'This is a restricted area in a public place and I have reason to believe that you are/have been consuming or intend to consume alcohol in breach of a prohibition in a public spaces protection order. I require you to stop drinking and give me the container from which you are/have been drinking and any other containers (sealed or unsealed). I must inform you that failure to comply with my request, without reasonable excuse, is an offence.'

Offences

A person who fails without reasonable excuse to comply with a **requirement** imposed on him or her under subsection 63(2) [see **9.4.1**] commits an offence.

Anti-social Behaviour Crime and Policing Act 2014, s 63(6)

Points to prove

Surrender alcohol

✓ without reasonable excuse
✓ failed to surrender
✓ something that was or reasonably believed to be

✓ alcohol or container for such
✓ in their possession
✓ in a restricted area subject of a PSPO
✓ when required by a constable/PCSO/LA officer

Consume alcohol

✓ without reasonable excuse
✓ failed to comply with requirement
✓ imposed by constable/PCSO/LA officer
✓ not to consume in a restricted area of a PSPO
✓ something that was or reasonably believed to be alcohol

Practical considerations

- A constable/PCSO/LA officer who imposes the requirement shall inform the person concerned that failing without reasonable excuse to comply with the requirement is an offence.
- The seizure and disposal of alcohol in both sealed and unsealed containers is allowed, although officers should follow their own force orders or LA procedure in relation to disposal.
- Consider issuing a FPN under s 68 for this offence (see **7.15.2**).
- A PND (see **7.1.1**) for the offence of consuming alcohol in a designated public place under the Criminal Justice and Police Act 2001, s 12 can still be issued if the order is still in force.

 Summary   6 months

 Level 2 fine

Links to alternative subjects and offences

9.4.2 Failure to comply with alcohol requirements

9.5 Alcohol in Public Place (under 18)—Offences/Confiscation

The Confiscation of Alcohol (Young Persons) Act 1997 allows the police to confiscate alcohol from people under 18 years in certain public places, with a failure to comply offence. Whereas s 30 of the Policing and Crime Act 2009 makes it an offence for a person under 18 to persistently possess alcohol in a public place.

9.5.1 Offences/confiscation of alcohol (under 18)

Power

(1) Where a constable reasonably suspects that a person in a **relevant place** is in **possession** of **alcohol** and that either—

    (a) he is under the age of 18; or

    (b) he intends that any of the alcohol should be consumed by a person under the age of 18 in that or any other relevant place; or

    (c) a person under the age of 18 who is, or has **recently** been, with him has recently consumed alcohol in that or any other relevant place,

the constable may require him to surrender anything in his possession which is, or which the constable reasonably believes to be, alcohol or a container for alcohol.

(1AA) A constable who imposes a requirement on a person under subsection (1) shall also require him to state his name and address.

Offences

(3) A person who fails without reasonable excuse to comply with a requirement imposed on him under subsection (1) or (1AA) commits an offence.

Confiscation of Alcohol (Young Persons) Act 1997, s 1

Points to prove

✓ without reasonable excuse
✓ failed to comply with requirement
✓ imposed by constable
✓ to surrender

9.5.1 Offences/confiscation of alcohol (under 18)

> ✓ alcohol/suspected alcohol **or** a container for such
> ✓ in their possession
> ✓ and/or state their name and address

Meanings

Relevant place

Means any **public place**, other than **licensed premises**; or any place, other than a public place, to which the person has unlawfully gained access.

Licensed premises

Means premises which may by virtue of Pt 3 or Pt 5 of the Licensing Act 2003 (premises licence; permitted temporary activity) be used for the **supply of alcohol**.

Supply of alcohol (see **9.1.1**)

Public place

For this purpose a place is a public place if at the material time the public or any section of the public has access to it, on payment or otherwise, as of right, or by virtue of express, or implied permission.

Possession

At common law possession is defined as: **actual** or **potential** physical control and an intention to possess. In practice visible or external signs of possession, which can be demonstrated to a court, must support the two conditions above (*Jowetts Dictionary of English Law*).

Alcohol (see **9.1.1**)

Recently

Defined by the *Oxford English Dictionary* as 'lately' or 'comparatively near to the present time'.

Explanatory notes

- Officers can seize sealed and open containers, as well as the alcohol they hold, and dispose of both in an appropriate manner. Where a young person has, for example, a sealed six-pack under his arm, officers should still consider who sold it, and whether there are any child welfare issues, and take action as appropriate.
- A constable may dispose of anything surrendered in such manner as s/he considers appropriate.
- When imposing a requirement to surrender a constable must inform the person of the suspicion and that failing without reasonable excuse to comply with the requirement as to surrender of alcohol and/or to state their name and address is an offence.

Example of officer's requirement:

'I have reason to suspect that you are in possession of alcohol and that either you are under 18 years of age or you intend that any of the alcohol will be consumed or it has recently been consumed by a person under 18 in this or any other relevant place. (If applicable) You must stop drinking immediately. I require you to give me that can/bottle/plastic cup etc. and to give me your name and address. I must warn you that failure to comply with my requirements is an offence.'

Practical considerations

- A constable imposing a requirement under s 1(1) may, if the constable reasonably suspects that person to be under the age of 16, remove that person to their place of residence or a place of safety.
- Officers should follow their own force orders in relation to disposal.
- A PCSO has the same powers as a police constable under this section (other than the arrest power) (see **11.1.2**).

 Summary

 6 months

 Level 2 fine

9.5.2 **Persistently possess alcohol in public (under 18)**

Offences

A person under the age of 18 is guilty of an offence if, without reasonable excuse, the person is in **possession** of **alcohol** in any **relevant place** on 3 or more occasions within a period of 12 consecutive months.

Policing and Crime Act 2009, s 30(1)

Points to prove

✓ person under 18
✓ without reasonable excuse
✓ in **possession** of **alcohol**
✓ in any **relevant place**
✓ on 3 or more occasions
✓ within a 12-month (consecutive) period

9.5.2 Persistently possess alcohol in public (under 18)

Meanings

Possession (see 9.5.1)

Alcohol (see 9.1.1)

Relevant place

Means any public place, other than **excluded premises**; or any place, other than a **public place**, to which the person has unlawfully gained access.

Excluded premises

Means premises which may by virtue of the Licensing Act 2003—

- Pt 3 or 5 (premises licence or permitted temporary activity) be used for the supply of alcohol;
- Pt 4 (club premises certificate) be used for the supply of alcohol to members or guests.

Public place (see 9.5.1)

Explanatory notes

This offence only applies to people under the age of 18 if they possess alcohol in a relevant public place; and this has occurred on 3 or more occasions within a 12-month period.

PCSO

 Summary   6 months

 Level 2 fine

Links to alternative subjects and offences

Chapter 10
Road Traffic

10.1 Meanings: Roads, Public Places, Vehicles, and Drives

10.1.1 Roads

The term 'road' has many meanings within various pieces of legislation.

Meaning of road

'Road' is defined in several Acts. The two most commonly used meanings of a road are—
- any highway and any other road to which the public has access, and includes bridges over which a road passes (Road Traffic Act 1988, s 192(1));
- any length of highway and any other road to which the public has access, and includes bridges over which a road passes (Road Traffic Regulation Act 1984, s 142(1)).

Explanatory notes

- 'Road' includes public highways, footpaths, and bridleways maintained by government agencies or local authorities.
- The term 'public road' in the Vehicle Excise and Registration Act 1994 means a road repairable at public expense.
- The physical nature of a road provides a defined or definable route, or way to which the general public has legal access, being a route allowing travel between two places.
- A field used for parking at an agricultural show was held not to be a road, as it had no definable way.
- A privately owned hotel forecourt used as a shortcut between two streets is a road.
- Walking or driving must take place on the road and such walking or driving must be lawful.
- Case decisions regarding roads need to be considered very carefully. As questions of 'fact', usually taken by lower courts, these

decisions are heavily dependent on the individual circumstances of the case.

Related cases

Hallett v DPP [2011] EWHC 488 (Admin), QBD A 'service road' ran alongside another road, with 20 houses leading off this 'service road'. It was open at both ends and had 'give way' road markings at the entrance/exit. Residents were responsible, by covenant, to maintain this 'service road', but it had no barriers or 'private road' signs in place. Actual use of the road by the public must be evidenced in order for it to be a public road.

Cutter v Eagle Star Insurance Company Ltd [1998] 4 All ER 417, HL and **Clarke v Kato and others [1998] 4 All ER 417, HL** A part of a car park may be a road but the whole of the car park will not necessarily be (ie properly designated parking bays will not be a road, but a definable route (direction arrows, lane markings, etc) may make the rest of the car park a road).

Sadiku v DPP [2000] RTR 155, QBD A paved area used as a thoroughfare by pedestrians can be a road.

McGurk and another v Coster [1995] CLY 2912, CC Access to a temporary car park on a beach by driving over part of the beach between the sea and sand dunes was held not to be a road.

Practical considerations

- What are the physical characteristics, function, and public access of the place involved?
- Public access alone is not sufficient to make a place a road; similarly, some form of private use will not necessarily prevent it from being a road.
- Most important road traffic legislation relates to 'public places' as well—this is a wider and different definition that should be considered in each case (see **10.1.2**).
- The footway, lay-by, or verge is normally part of the road.
- The mode of transport is not relevant and such travellers may be on foot, riding on animals, or in a vehicle.
- In instances of real doubt the courts have to decide on a case-by-case basis.

10.1.2 **Public place**

Meaning of public place

The term 'public place' has, for the purposes of the Road Traffic Act 1988, been defined as: 'Any place to which the public have open access is a public place, even if payment must be made to gain entry.'

Explanatory notes

- Whether a place to which the public have limited or restricted access is a public place is a question of fact and degree in each case.
- The time at which the place was being used is important in dealing with 'public place' considerations. A car park of a public house may be a public place during licensing hours but may not be so outside those hours.
- An off-road parking bay adjacent to a highway with no physical impediment between the bay and the road is a public place.
- Lanes at a ferry port could be a public place or road as the public have access to them.

Related cases

Cowan v DPP [2013] EWHC 192 (Admin) QBD No evidence was provided for the court to conclude that a university campus was a public place, so it was unable to convict for an offence of driving a motor vehicle while OPL.

R v Spence [1999] Crim LR 975, CA A company car park in an industrial estate, used by employees, customers, and visitors on business was held not to be a public place.

Practical considerations

- The test for whether or not it is a public place is to consider: 'Do the people gaining access there have a special characteristic or personal reason which is not possessed by the general public?'
- Public use of the area must be shown evidentially.

10.1.3 **Vehicles/motor vehicles/mechanically propelled vehicles**

Meaning of vehicles

General

The *Oxford English Dictionary* defines a 'vehicle' as a conveyance, usually with wheels, for transporting people, goods, etc; a car, cart, truck, carriage, sledge, etc; any means of carriage or transport; a receptacle in which something is placed in order to be moved.

For vehicle excise duty purposes

In the following provisions of this Act 'vehicle' means:

(a) a mechanically propelled vehicle, or
(b) any thing (whether or not it is a vehicle) that has been, but has ceased to be, a mechanically propelled vehicle.

Vehicle Excise and Registration Act 1994, s 1(1B)

10.1.3 Vehicles/motor vehicles/mechanically propelled vehicles

Explanatory notes

- The above definitions of 'vehicle' should not be confused with the meaning of 'motor vehicle' or 'mechanically propelled vehicle'.
- **Motor vehicle** means as follows—
  - ✦ Subject to s 20 of the Chronically Sick and Disabled Persons Act 1970 (which makes special provision about invalid carriages, within the meaning of that Act), a **mechanically propelled vehicle** intended or adapted for use on roads (Road Traffic Act 1988, s 185);
  - ✦ any mechanically propelled vehicle, whether or not it is intended or **adapted for use on a road** (Police Reform Act 2002, s 59);
- **Mechanically propelled vehicle**—this is not legally defined but, it has a wider meaning than 'motor vehicle' as a mechanically propelled vehicle does not have to be 'intended or adapted for use on a road'. It means a vehicle which can be propelled by mechanical means and would include electric or steam powered vehicles. Whether it is a mechanically propelled vehicle will have to be determined by the court.
- **Adapted for use on a road** means fit and apt for use on a road.
- A sidecar is part of a motor vehicle when attached to a motorbike and is not a trailer (Road Traffic Act 1988, s 186(1)).
- Conversely, a semi-trailer of an articulated vehicle is a trailer and not part of the towing vehicle (Road Traffic Act 1988, s 187(1)).
- An articulated bus ('bendy bus') should be treated as one vehicle (Road Traffic Act 1988, s 187(2)).
- A hovercraft is a motor vehicle (Road Traffic Act 1988, s 188).
- Certain specialised vehicles may be used as invalid carriages on pavements without being classified as motor vehicles.

Related cases

DPP v King [2008] EWHC 447 (Admin), QBD A 'City Mantis' electric scooter that looked like a bicycle, except that it did not have any pedals or other means of manual propulsion and was capable of speeds up to 10 mph, was held to be a motor vehicle.

CC of North Yorkshire Police v Saddington [2001] Crim LR 41, QBD A 'Go-Ped' (which resembles a child's scooter with an engine) has been held to be a motor vehicle. Despite a warning on it that it was not intended for use on a road, the correct test would be whether a reasonable person would say that one of its uses would be some general use on a road.

Thomas v Hooper [1986] RTR 1, QBD A vehicle may no longer be a motor vehicle if it has none of the normal vehicular controls operative.

Reader v Bunyard [1987] RTR 406, QBD A motor vehicle remains a mechanically propelled vehicle unless there was evidence that there was no likelihood of it being so used again. The onus is on the prosecution to prove that the vehicle is capable of being repaired or used.

Burns v Currell [1963] 2 All ER 297, QBD When deciding whether one of the uses of a vehicle would be on a road a 'reasonable person' test should be applied to the vehicle and not the intentions of the specific user at the time it was stopped.

Practical considerations

- What was the vehicle intended for and to what use is it currently being put?
- The onus of proving that a motor vehicle remained a mechanically propelled vehicle lies with the prosecution.
- Pedestrian-controlled mowing machines, other pedestrian-controlled vehicles and electrically assisted pedal cycles approved by the Secretary of State are **not** motor vehicles (Road Traffic Act 1988, s 189).
- It is a matter of fact and degree for the court to decide whether or not a vehicle is a motor vehicle or mechanically propelled vehicle at the time of a specific incident.
- In such cases, include evidence of the characteristics of the vehicle, which may be a photograph if appropriate.

10.1.4 **Drives/driving**

Meaning of drives/driving

- The statutory definition of a 'driver' is—Where a separate person acts as a steersman of a motor vehicle, includes (except for the purposes of s 1 of this Act) that person as well as any other person engaged in the driving of the vehicle, and 'drive' is to be interpreted accordingly (Road Traffic Act 1988, s 192(1)).
- This means that a driver is any person who is engaged in the driving of the vehicle including, where a separate person acts as a steersman of a motor vehicle, that person.
- Case law provides matters to consider but the principal test is—
  - ◆ 'the essence of driving is the use of the driver's controls for the purpose of directing the movement of the car however the movement is produced' (*R v McDonagh* [1974] 2 All ER 257, CA).
- Whether or not a person was driving is ultimately a matter of fact and degree. It is for the court or jury to decide on the facts in each case (*Edkins v Knowles* [1973] 2 All ER 503, QBD).

Explanatory notes

- The vehicle does not have to be moving. A driver is still driving until he has completed the normal operations, such as applying the handbrake, that occur at the end of a journey.
- A vehicle may halt temporarily such as at traffic lights, so consider—
  - ◆ what was the purpose of the stop?
  - ◆ how long was the vehicle stopped?
  - ◆ did the driver get out of the vehicle?
- It is also possible for two people to be driving the same vehicle.

Related cases

Avery v CPS [2011] EWHC 2388 (Admin), DC A car driven on a private driveway collided with a parked car on the adjacent road, with the collision being caused by the protruding boot of the car. Held: Although the tyres of the car remained on private land and only part of the car (the boot) encroached onto the road, the driver was still found to have driven the vehicle 'on' a road.

Cawthorn v DPP [2000] RTR 45, QBD Driver left vehicle for a few minutes. C set the handbrake and switched on the hazard warning lights, but the passenger released the handbrake, the vehicle rolled down a hill and hit a brick wall. This intervening act did not make that person the driver, as the passenger did not have sufficient control to fulfil the definition of driving. C still remained the driver until the journey was complete or someone else had taken over the driving. Whether someone was a driver at any particular time was a question of fact for the court or jury to decide.

DPP v Hastings (1993) 158 JP 118, QBD A passenger snatching the wheel momentarily is not a 'driver' because this action does not constitute the act of driving. H had interfered with the driving of the car, but was not the driver.

Burgoyne v Phillips [1982] RTR 49, QBD B had set the car in motion, was sitting in the driving seat, and was trying to control the car; the fact that the steering was momentarily locked did not prevent B from 'driving' the car.

McQuaid v Anderton [1980] 3 All ER 540, QBD Steering a car being towed can be 'driving'. The essence of 'driving' was the use of the driver's controls in order to direct the movement of the car, the method of propulsion being irrelevant.

Tyler v Whatmore [1975] RTR 83, QBD Two people can be driving a vehicle at the same time. T was sitting in the front passenger seat and was leaning across steering the car, whilst the other driver manipulated the controls. In this case neither person had full control of both the brakes and the steering and although T could not control the propulsion, there was some control over the handbrake and ignition system. T was therefore driving the vehicle.

Practical considerations

- If there is some doubt as to whether a person is driving or not, the circumstances must be looked at individually.
- As a general rule there are three elements to driving—
  - ✦ control of the steering; *and*
  - ✦ control of the propulsion; *and*
  - ✦ the actions of the person must fall within the everyday meaning of driving.

Links to alternative subjects and offences

10.2 Powers to Stop/Direct Vehicles and Pedestrians

The Road Traffic Act 1988 provides various powers to stop vehicles; these are given, in varying degrees, to police officers, traffic wardens, authorised vehicle examiners, and PCSOs.

10.2.1 Drivers to comply with traffic directions

Section 35 of the Road Traffic Act 1988 provides for drivers who refuse or neglect to comply with traffic directions given by a police constable.

Offences

(1) Where a constable or **traffic officer** is for the time being engaged in the regulation of traffic in a **road**, a person **driving** or propelling a **vehicle** who neglects or refuses—
   (a) to stop the **vehicle**; or
   (b) to make it proceed in, or keep to, a particular line of traffic,
   when directed to do so by the constable in the exercise of his duty or the traffic officer (as the case may be) is guilty of an offence.

(2) Where—
   (a) a traffic survey of any description is being carried out on or in the vicinity of a road, and
   (b) a constable or traffic officer gives a person driving or propelling a vehicle a direction—
      (i) to stop the vehicle,
      (ii) to make it proceed in, or keep to, a particular line of traffic, or
      (iii) to proceed to a particular point on or near the road on which the vehicle is being driven or propelled,
   being a direction given for the purposes of the survey (but not a direction requiring any person to provide any information for the purposes of a traffic survey),
the person is guilty of an offence if he refuses or neglects to comply with the direction.

Road Traffic Act 1988, s 35

Points to prove

s 35(1) offence

✓ constable/traffic warden/PCSO/traffic officer
✓ engaged in the regulation of traffic in a road

- ✓ driver/rider of vehicle neglected/refused
- ✓ to stop vehicle/proceed/keep to particular line of traffic
- ✓ as directed

s 35(2) offence

- ✓ traffic survey on/in vicinity of a road
- ✓ driver/rider of vehicle
- ✓ refused/failed/neglected to comply
- ✓ with directions given by constable/TW/PCSO/traffic officer
- ✓ for purposes of the survey

Meanings

Traffic officer

Person designated under the Traffic Management Act 2004, s 2.

Road (see 10.1.1)

Driving (see 10.1.4)

Vehicle (see 10.1.3)

Explanatory notes

- The constable/traffic officer must be engaged in the regulation of traffic and acting in the execution of their duty.
- A constable may direct a person to disobey a traffic sign if it is reasonably necessary for the protection of life.
- A suitably designated PCSO has the same powers as a constable under s 35. Including the issue of a TFPN (see 10.4.1) if offence committed by a cyclist.
- Reference to a constable includes a traffic warden.
- The prosecution needs to show that the given signal was obvious and should have been evident to the motorist, not that the motorist saw it.
- Although a constable/traffic officer can direct a driver/rider to a specific point for a traffic survey, they cannot direct any person to supply information for the survey.
- Any direction in connection with a traffic survey must not cause undue delay to a person who indicates that they are unwilling to give information for the survey.

Practical considerations

- Offences under s 35 are not confined to mechanically propelled vehicles.
- Stop does not automatically mean the driver must remain stationary until signalled to proceed, unless the direction was to remain stationary.
- Notice of intended prosecution (NIP) to be issued (see 10.5).
- Consider issuing a TFPN (see 10.4.1).

Summary 6 months

 Level 3 fine

Discretionary disqualification and obligatory endorsement of 3 penalty points—if committed in a motor vehicle

10.2.2 **Directions to pedestrians**

Section 37 of the Road Traffic Act 1988 empowers a constable in uniform or traffic officer engaged in the direction of vehicular traffic on a road, to also direct a pedestrian walking along or across the carriageway, to stop.

Offences

Where a constable in uniform or **traffic officer** is for the time being engaged in the regulation of vehicular traffic in a **road**, a person on foot who proceeds across or along the carriageway in contravention of a direction to stop given by the constable in the execution of his duty or the traffic officer (as the case may be), either to persons on foot or to persons on foot and other traffic, is guilty of an offence.

Road Traffic Act 1988, s 37

Points to prove

✓ being a pedestrian proceeded along/across carriageway
✓ contravened direction of constable/traffic officer/PCSO/TW
✓ engaged in direction of vehicular traffic on a road

Meanings

Traffic officer (see 10.2.1)

Road (see 10.1)

Explanatory notes

- Reference to a constable includes reference to a traffic warden.
- A suitably designated PCSO has the same powers as a constable under s 37.

Practical considerations

- A pedestrian breaching s 37 may be required to give their name and address.
- The constable must be in uniform—include details in evidence.

 Summary   6 months

 Level 3 fine

10.2.3 Testing the condition of vehicles on a road

Section 67 of the Road Traffic Act 1988 empowers authorised vehicle examiners to test motor vehicles on the road, but any vehicle stopped for a test must be stopped by a constable in uniform, or suitably designated PCSO or 'stopping officer'.

Offences

If a person obstructs an **authorised examiner** acting under this section, or fails to comply with a requirement of this section or Schedule 2 (deferred **tests** of conditions of **vehicles**) to this Act, he is guilty of an offence.

Road Traffic Act 1988, s 67(9)

Meanings

Authorised vehicle examiner

Includes a constable authorised by or on behalf of the chief officer of police.

Test

Includes inspect or inspection.

Vehicle (see **10.1.3**)

Includes a trailer drawn by it.

Explanatory notes

- Vehicle examiners may test all motor vehicles that are on the road.

10.2.4 Police powers to stop a vehicle on a road

- A vehicle shall not be required to stop for a test except by a constable in uniform, a suitably designated PCSO, or a 'stopping officer'. The Road Vehicles (Powers to Stop) Regulations 2011 (SI 996/2011) provides for appointment of 'stopping officers' under s 66B, with powers to stop certain commercial vehicles for specific checks by vehicle examiners and other authorised persons.

Related cases

Sadiku v DPP [2000] RTR 155, QBD A constable requiring the test to be carried out may ask for the keys while awaiting the arrival of the examiner.

Practical considerations

- An authorised examiner may test a motor vehicle on a road to ascertain whether it meets construction and use requirements, and its condition does not involve a danger of injury to any person.
- For the purpose of testing a vehicle the examiner may require the driver to comply with reasonable instructions, and to drive the vehicle.
- The driver may elect for the test to be deferred to a time and place in accordance with Sch 2. However, if the vehicle has been involved in an accident on a road or is so defective that it ought not to be allowed to proceed, the constable may require that the vehicle shall not be taken away until the test has been carried out.
- A constable who is not an authorised examiner cannot use s 67 to carry out this test. However, a constable can still enforce regulations concerning construction and use where the driver is co-operative.
- This section applies to vehicles registered outside Great Britain.

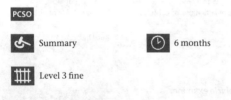

PCSO	
♿ Summary	🕐 6 months
▥ Level 3 fine	

10.2.4 **Police powers to stop a vehicle on a road**

Section 163 of the Road Traffic Act 1988 empowers a police constable in uniform or a traffic officer to stop a mechanically propelled vehicle on a road.

Offences

(1) A person **driving a mechanically propelled vehicle** on a **road** must stop the vehicle on being required to do so by a constable in uniform or a **traffic officer**.

(2) A person riding a cycle on a road must stop the cycle on being required to do so by a constable in uniform or a traffic officer.

(3) If a person fails to comply with this section he is guilty of an offence.

Road Traffic Act 1988, s 163

Points to prove

✓ drove mechanically propelled vehicle/rode cycle
✓ on a road
✓ required by constable/TW/traffic officer/PCSO
✓ to stop the vehicle/cycle
✓ failed to do so

Meanings

Driving (see **10.1.4**)

Mechanically propelled vehicle (see **10.1.3**)

Road (see **10.1.1**)

Traffic officer (see **10.2.1**)

Explanatory notes

- 'Mechanically propelled vehicle' is not defined in the Act and is a matter of fact and degree to be decided by the court (see **10.1.3**).
- Reference to a constable includes traffic warden.
- A suitably designated PCSO has powers to stop a cycle and issue a TFPN, but only for listed TFPN offences (see **11.1.2**).
- Plain clothed police officers can use the common law to stop vehicles they reasonably believe to be involved in crime, eg a stolen car (*R (on the application of Rutherford) v IPCC* [2010] EWHC 2881).

Practical considerations

Consider issuing a traffic fixed penalty notice (see **10.4.1**).

 Summary   6 months

 Fine (Level 3 fine if a cycle)

Links to alternative subjects and offences

10.3 **Fail to Comply with Traffic Signs**

Section 36 of the Road Traffic Act 1988 creates an offence of failing to comply with certain traffic signs.

Offences

Where a **traffic sign**, being a sign—
(a) of the prescribed size, colour and type, or
(b) of another character authorised by the Secretary of State under the provisions in that behalf of the Road Traffic Regulation Act 1984,
has been **lawfully placed** on or near a **road**, a person **driving** or propelling a **vehicle** who fails to comply with the indication given by the sign is guilty of an offence.

Road Traffic Act 1988, s 36(1)

Points to prove

✓ authorised traffic sign lawfully placed
✓ on or near a road
✓ driver/rider of vehicle on that road
✓ failed to comply with the direction of that sign

Meanings

Traffic sign

As given in the Traffic Signs and General Directions Regulations 2002.

Lawfully placed

A sign will not be lawfully placed unless it indicates a statutory prohibition, restriction, or requirement, or a provision of the Traffic Acts specifically states that it is a sign to which this section applies.

Road (see **10.1.1**)

Driving (see **10.1.4**)

Vehicle (see **10.1.3**)

Explanatory notes

• Some of the traffic signs to which this section applies are: double white line markings; box junction markings; traffic lights (including temporary traffic lights at roadworks); 'stop' sign (including manually operated at roadworks); flashing red 'stop' lights on motorways or

automatic tram/railway crossing; no entry sign; give way sign; directional arrow; keep left/right sign; bus/cycle/tramcar route sign; no U turn sign; weight/height restriction sign.
- This section applies to traffic survey signs and emergency traffic signs put out by police (eg football matches, processions).
- A single dotted white line in the centre of the road separating two carriageways does not fall into this section.
- For contravention of a 'stop' sign or red traffic light signal it is necessary to prove that the vehicle did not stop at the stop line or, if the stop line is not visible, before entering the major road or beyond the mounting of the primary signal respectively.
- Emergency vehicles may be exempted from the requirement to conform to a red traffic light, but must proceed so as not to cause danger to the driver of another vehicle or to cause such driver to change their speed or direction to avoid an accident, or cause danger to non-vehicular traffic.
- Failure by the driver to see the traffic sign is not a defence, except in very limited situations (see *Coombes v DPP* [2006] below), and will generally be evidence to support an offence of driving without due care and attention (see **10.6**).

Defences

This section creates absolute offences except for the possible defences of mechanical defect, automatism, or not seen due to badly located signage.

Defence notes

- 'Automatism' has been defined as 'the involuntary movement of a person's body or limbs' and its source or cause must be something of which the driver was unaware or something that they could not reasonably be expected to foresee.
- Falling asleep whilst driving a vehicle does not amount to automatism.
- In very limited situations where a driver fails to see the sign (see *Coombes v DPP* [2006]).

Related cases

Peake v DPP [2010] EWHC 286 (Admin), QBD If the prosecution establish the route taken by the driver, it would only have to show that compliant signs provided adequate guidance, at the point of enforcement, for someone taking that route. Otherwise, they would have to show that there were compliant signs on all routes which the driver might have taken.

McKenzie v DPP [1997] Crim LR 232, QBD A vehicle can stop on a road where double white lines are present to drop/pick up passengers, load/unload goods, to carry out road/building work, or to remove obstructions.

Coombes v DPP [2006] EWHC 3263, QBD Signs must indicate the relevant speed limit. This requires, at the very least, speed limit signs to be properly located so that an approaching motorist has sufficient time to reduce their speed from the previous lawful limit to a speed within the new limit.

Watmore v Jenkins [1961] 2 All ER 868, QBD A driver took the correct dosage of insulin prior to driving and drove normally most of the day, but drove erratically for 5 miles before being stopped. The driver was dazed when stopped, but recovered after treatment. The defence of automatism was not accepted as there had been an element of conscious control in the driving.

A-G's Reference (No 2 of 1992) [1993] 4 All ER 683, CA Driving without awareness (such as falling asleep) is not a case where automatism could be used as a defence.

Practical considerations

- Traffic signs placed on or near a road are deemed to be of the correct specification and to have been lawfully placed unless the contrary is proved.
- A stop sign at a junction indicates that a vehicle must at least momentarily stop at the stop line and not merely slow down.
- Section 87 of the Road Traffic Regulation Act 1984 exempts fire, ambulance, responding to an emergency for NHS ambulance service, and police vehicles from speed limits if observance would hinder the use of the vehicle for the purpose it was being used for on that occasion. The Deregulation Act 2015 amended s 87 to include providing a response to an emergency at the request of an NHS ambulance service.
- The Motor Vehicles (Variation of Speed Limits) Regulations 2014 (SI 3552/2014) increased the speed limit for HGVs exceeding 7.5 tonnes on national speed limit roads. This is from 50mph to 60mph on dual carriageways and from 40mph to 50mph on single carriageways. HGV speed limits on other roads remain the same.
- A suitably designated PCSO may stop a cycle and issue a TFPN for failing to comply with a red traffic light (see **11.1.6** and **11.1.1**).
- Consider issuing a TFPN (see **10.4.1**).
- Is the traffic sign one that is specified for this section?
- Is the contravention evidence of a more serious offence (eg dangerous driving, driving without due care and attention)?
- An NIP must be served for offences of failing to comply with some types of traffic signs (see **10.5**).

 Summary   6 months

10.3 Fail to Comply with Traffic Signs

Level 3 fine

Discretionary disqualification, obligatory endorsement—3 penalty points

Links to alternative subjects and offences

10.4 **Traffic Fixed Penalty Notices**

Traffic Fixed Penalty Notices (TFPNs) and procedures with regard to road traffic offences are covered by s 51 to s 90 of the Road Traffic Offenders Act 1988.

10.4.1 **Traffic fixed penalty notices**

Section 54 of the Act allows a constable in uniform who has reason to believe that a person is committing or has committed a traffic penalty offence to then issue a TFPN in respect of that offence.

Offences

A person is guilty of an offence if he removes or interferes with any **notice** fixed to a vehicle under this section, unless he does so by or under the authority of the driver or person in charge of the vehicle or the person liable for the fixed penalty offence in question.

Road Traffic Offenders Act 1988, s 62(2)

A person who, in a response to a notice to owner, provides a statement which is false in a material particular and does so recklessly or knowing it to be false in that particular is guilty of that offence.

Road Traffic Offenders Act 1988, s 67

Points to prove

s 62(2) offence

✓ without authority of driver/person in charge or liable for TFPN
✓ removed/interfered with TFPN fixed to vehicle

s 67 offence

✓ in response to notice to owner
✓ provided false statement
✓ recklessly/knowing it to be false

Meaning of 'Traffic Fixed Penalty Notice'

Means a notice offering the opportunity of the discharge of any liability to conviction of the offence to which the notice relates by payment of a fixed penalty in accordance with Pt 3 of this Act.

10.4.1 Traffic fixed penalty notices

Explanatory notes

- TFPNs apply where a constable in uniform believes that a person is committing or has committed a **relevant offence** (see below), and may be issued either at the time of the offence or at a police station.
- If the offence involves obligatory endorsement the constable may only issue a TFPN if the offender produces and surrenders their driving licence to the constable and is not liable to disqualification under s 35—the 'totting up' procedure.
- Where the offender has no licence with them, the constable may issue a notice requiring its production within 7 days at a specified police station and, if certain requirements are met, can then be issued with a TFPN.
- References to constable include a traffic warden.
- A suitably designated PCSO may issue a TFPN for the offences of: cycling on a footway; contravening a prohibition or restriction relating to stopping, waiting or parking at or near a school entrance, one-way traffic on a road, lanes/routes for use only by cycles and/or buses; more than one person on a one-person bicycle; cycle rider failing to comply with traffic directions; cycle rider failing to comply with red traffic light; contravening or failing to comply with a construction or use requirement relating to lighting equipment or reflectors for cycles, using a motor vehicle on a road in a way that causes excessive noise, stopping the action of a stationary vehicle's machinery, using a vehicle's horn on a road while stationary or on a restricted road at night, or opening a vehicle's door on a road so injuring or endangering a person; failing to stop vehicle or cycle when required to do so by constable or traffic office.
- A TFPN must give details of the offence, **suspended enforcement period**, penalty payable, and how it should be paid.
- '**Suspended enforcement period**' means the period following the date of the offence during which no proceedings will be brought against the offender.
- Where the penalty has not been paid or a hearing elected during the suspended enforcement period, the penalty plus 50 per cent may be registered against them.
- If the offence involves obligatory endorsement, the person receiving the surrendered licence must issue a receipt and forward the surrendered licence on to the fixed-penalty clerk.
- If the licence holder is liable to disqualification under the 'totting up' (see **10.13**) system, the fixed-penalty clerk must forward the licence on to the chief officer of police who may commence proceedings. Where such proceedings are commenced any action already taken (eg registration as a fine) is void.
- At the end of the suspended enforcement period, if the penalty has not been paid or a hearing requested by the driver at the relevant time, a notice to owner may be served on the owner.
- A notice to owner must include particulars as to the offence, TFPN issued, response time allowed (minimum 21 days), penalty if it is not paid, requesting a hearing.
- If the person on whom the notice to owner was served was not the owner of the vehicle at the time of the offence and provides a

statutory statement of ownership to that effect, they are not liable for the fine registered against them.

If a notice to owner has been served, proceedings may not be brought against anybody else in relation to that offence unless they are identified as the driver at the relevant time in a statutory statement of facts.

Relevant offences

Schedule 3 to this Act lists the TFPN offences—

Highways Act 1835

72—driving/cycling on footway.

Transport Act 1968

96(11)—contravened drivers' hours.
96(11A)—contravened periods of driving.
97(1)—contravened recording equipment regs.
98(4)—contravened drivers' hours written records regs.
99(4)—fail to produce records/obstruction.
99ZD(1)—fail to comply with requirements/obstruction.
99C—fail to comply with prohibition/direction.

Road Traffic (Foreign Vehicles) Act 1972

3(1)—drive foreign GV or PSV in contravention of prohibition.

Greater London Council (General Powers) Act 1974

15—parking vehicles on footways, verges, other related offences.

Highways Act 1980

137—obstruction of highway committed in respect of a vehicle.

Public Passenger Vehicles Act 1981

12(5)—use PSV on road without PSV operator's licence.

Road Traffic Regulation Act 1984

5(1)—traffic regulation order outside Greater London.
8(1)—traffic regulation order in Greater London.
11—experimental traffic order.
13—breach of experimental traffic scheme.
16(1)—temporary prohibition or restriction.
17(4)—wrongful use of special road.
18(3)—one-way traffic order on trunk road.
20(5)—prohibition/restriction of driving on certain classes of road.
25(5)—breach of pedestrian crossing regulations, except offence in respect of moving motor vehicle, other than contravention of regs 23, 24, 25, and 26 of the Zebra, Pelican and Puffin Pedestrian Crossings Regulations and General Directions 1997.
29(3)—street playground order.
35A(1)—local authority parking place on a road.
37(1)—parking place designation order.
53(5)—parking place designation order under s 53(1)(a).
53(6)—designation order authorised parking on road without charge.

10.4.1 Traffic fixed penalty notices

s 88(7)—minimum speed limit.
s 89(1)—speeding.

Road Transport (International Passenger Services) Regulations 1984

reg 19(1)—use vehicle for carriage of passengers without authorisation/certificate.
reg 19(2)—use vehicle for carriage of passengers without passenger waybill

Road Traffic Act 1988

s 3—driving mechanically propelled vehicle on a road/public place without due care and attention, or reasonable consideration.
s 14—seat belt regulations.
s 15(2)—restriction re children in front of vehicles.
s 15(4)—restriction re children in rear of vehicles.
s 16—crash helmet regulations re motorcycle rider/passenger.
s 18(3)—breach use of eye protector regulations on motorcycles.
s 19—parking heavy commercial vehicle on verge/footway.
s 22—leave vehicle in dangerous position.
s 23—unlawfully carry passenger on motorcycle.
s 24—carry more than one person on pedal cycle.
s 34—drive mechanically propelled vehicle elsewhere than on road.
s 35—fail to comply with traffic directions.
s 36—fail to comply with prescribed traffic signs (see **10.3**).
s 40A—use vehicle where condition; purpose used; passengers carried; load involves danger of injury.
s 41A—breach of requirements re brakes, steering-gear, or tyres.
s 41B—breach of weight requirement re goods and passenger vehicles.
s 41D—breach of requirements re control, view of road, or use hand-held device.
s 42—breach of other construction and use regulations.
s 47—using vehicle without a test certificate.
s 71(1)—contravened prohibition order or fail comply order.
s 87(1)—drive vehicle otherwise than in accordance with licence.
s 143—using a motor vehicle without insurance.
s 163—fail to stop vehicle when required by officer in uniform.
s 172—failed to give information re driver of motor vehicle.

Road Traffic Offenders Act 1988

s 90D(6)—drive in contravention of prohibition or fail to comp direction.

Goods Vehicles (Community Authorisations) Regulations 1992

reg 3—use goods vehicle without community authorisation.
reg 7—use vehicle contravening regulations under community authorisation.

Vehicle Excise and Registration Act 1994

s 34—use trade licence for unauthorised purposes/circumstances.
s 42—driving/keeping vehicle without required registration mark.

s 43—drive/keep vehicle with registration mark obscured.

s 43C—offence of using an incorrectly registered vehicle.

s 59—fail to affix prescribed registration mark to vehicle.

Goods Vehicles (Licensing of Operators) Act 1995

s 2(5)—use GV on road for carriage of goods—no operator's licence.

Public Service Vehicles (Community Licences) Regulations 1999

reg 3—use PSV on road without community licence.

reg 7—use PSV under community licence—contravened licence conditions.

Road Transport (Passenger Vehicles Cabotage) Regulations 1999

reg 3—using vehicle on road for UK cabotage operations—no EC licence.

reg 4—using vehicle on road for UK cabotage operations—no control document.

reg 7(1)—fail to produce EC licence when requested.

reg 7(3)—failed to produce control document when requested.

Vehicle Drivers (Certificates of Professional Competence) Regulations 2007

reg 11(7)—driver of relevant vehicle failed to produce evidence/document.

HGV Road User Levy Act 2013

s 11—using/keeping HGV if HGV road user levy not paid.

Practical considerations

- Consider the seriousness of the offence. There is no obligation to issue a TFPN—it is at the discretion of the constable, TW, or PCSO.
- Is the fixed penalty scheme appropriate?
- Is the offence endorsable—if so, is the offender with the vehicle?
- Only a non-endorsable TFPN may be attached to a vehicle.
- Is the offender liable to disqualification under the totting up system?

 TFPN   PCSO

 Summary   **s 62 offence:** 6 months

 s 67 offence: If statutory declaration is made, 6 months from date of declaration, up to a maximum of 12 months from the original offence. In all other cases—6 months.

 s 62 offence
Level 2 fine

s 67 offence
Fine

10.4.2 **Control of vehicle and use of hand-held device**

Offences

A person who contravenes or fails to comply with a **construction and use requirement**—

(a) as to not driving a motor vehicle in a position which does not give proper control or a full view of the road and traffic ahead, or not causing or permitting the driving of a motor vehicle by another person in such a position, or

(b) as to not driving or supervising the driving of a motor vehicle while using a hand-held mobile telephone or other hand-held interactive communication device, or not causing or permitting the driving of a motor vehicle by another person using such a telephone or other device

is guilty of an offence.

Road Traffic Act 1988, s 41D

Points to prove

s 41D(a) offence

✓ contravened/failed to comply with requirement
✓ by driving a motor vehicle on a road
✓ without proper control of vehicle or full view **or**
✓ caused/permitted the above offences

s 41D(b) offence

✓ contravened/failed to comply with requirement
✓ being the driver/driving supervisor
✓ of a motor vehicle on a road
✓ driver **used hand-held** mobile/similar device **or**
✓ caused/permitted above offence

Meaning of 'construction and use requirement'

Means requirement imposed by regulations made under s 41 of the Road Traffic Act 1988, being mainly the Road Vehicles (Construction and Use) Regulations 1986.

Explanatory notes

- Not being in a position to have proper control of the vehicle or a full view of the road and traffic ahead comes under reg 104 of the Road Vehicles (Construction and Use) Regulations 1986.
- Using a hand-held mobile telephone or similar device comes under reg 110 of the Road Vehicles (Construction and Use) Regulations 1986.

Practical considerations

- These offences provide for obligatory endorsement and disqualification (at the court's discretion).
- A two-way radio, which performs an interactive communication function by transmitting and receiving data is not a device under reg 110.
- Regulation 110(5) states that a person does not contravene reg 110 if—
  + they are using the telephone or device to call the police, fire, ambulance, or other emergency service on 112 or 999;
  + they are acting in response to a genuine emergency; and
  + it is unsafe or impracticable for them to cease driving in order to make the call.
- A mobile telephone or other device is to be treated as hand-held if it is, or must be, held at some point during the course of making or receiving a call or performing any other interactive communication function.
- A person supervises the holder of a provisional licence if they do so pursuant to a condition imposed on that licence holder.

TFPN

 Summary   6 months

 Level 4 fine for goods vehicle or vehicle carrying more than eight passengers

Level 3 fine in any other case

Discretionary disqualification. Obligatory endorsement—3 penalty points

10.4.3 Graduated fixed penalties, penalty deposits, and immobilisation

The Road Safety Act 2006 introduced the graduated fixed penalty scheme, roadside deposits, and vehicle immobilisation.

Schedule 2 to the Fixed Penalty Order 2000 lists the graduated fixed penalties and graduates the level of specified fixed penalties based on the seriousness of the offending. It increases the level of fine for some offences to above the default amount (£100 endorsable and £50 non-endorsable). Initially these graduated fixed penalties only apply to specific offences relating to commercial and PSV vehicles.

10.4.3 Graduated fixed penalties, penalty deposits, immobilisation

Any officer appointed by their force or a DVSA officer will have responsibility for dealing with graduated fixed penalties.

Roadside deposits

The Road Traffic Offenders Act 1988, ss 90A to 90D provide enforcement powers under what is termed the 'roadside deposit scheme'.

Offences

A person who—
(a) drives a vehicle in contravention of a **prohibition** under this section,
(b) causes or permits a vehicle to be driven in contravention of such a prohibition, or
(c) fails to comply within a reasonable time with a **direction** under subsection (5) above,
is guilty of an offence.

Road Traffic Offenders Act 1988, s 90D(6)

Points to prove

✓ drives a vehicle or causes/permits vehicle to be driven
✓ in contravention of a prohibition or
✓ fails to comply within a reasonable time with a direction under s 90D(5)

Meanings

Prohibition

(1) This section applies where a person on whom a financial penalty deposit requirement is imposed does not make an immediate payment of the appropriate amount in accordance with section 90B(1) of this Act (and any order made under it).
(2) The constable or vehicle examiner by whom the requirement was imposed may prohibit the driving on a road of any vehicle of which the person was in charge at the time of the offence by giving to the person notice in writing of the prohibition.
(3) The prohibition—
   (a) shall come into force as soon as the notice is given, and
   (b) shall continue in force until the happening of whichever of the events in subsection (4) below occurs first.
(4) Those events are—
   (a) the person making a payment of the appropriate amount in accordance with section 90B(1) of this Act (and any order made under it) at any time during the relevant period,
   (b) (where a fixed penalty notice was given, or a conditional offer handed, to the person in respect of the offence) payment of the fixed penalty,

(c) the person being convicted or acquitted of the offence,
(d) the person being informed that he is not to be prosecuted for the offence, and
(e) the coming to an end of the prosecution period.

Direction

5) A constable or vehicle examiner may by direction in writing require the person to remove the vehicle to which the prohibition relates (and, if it is a motor vehicle drawing a trailer, also to remove the trailer) to such place and subject to such conditions as are specified in the direction; and the prohibition does not apply to the removal of the vehicle (or trailer) in accordance with the direction.

Road Traffic Offenders Act 1988, s 90D

Explanatory notes

Section 90A gives a constable in uniform or vehicle examiner power to require the payment of a deposit from a person, whom they believe is committing or has committed an offence in relation to a motor vehicle and is unable to provide a satisfactory address in the UK at which they can be found. Furthermore, the police officer or vehicle examiner must also believe that the person, the offence, and the circumstances in which the offence is committed are of a description specified by order made by the Secretary of State.

Under s 90B a financial penalty deposit, of an amount specified by order, can be paid to the constable or examiner. That person must then be given either a fixed penalty notice or written notice as to proposed court proceedings for the offence.

The specified amounts are—

♦ when it is a TFPN, the amount of that fixed penalty;
♦ in other cases it is a maximum of £500 per offence, to a maximum of £1,500 per vehicle stoppage.

Once payment is made, s 90C stipulates that the person must be issued with a written receipt and notice outlining the process that applies through the various provisions of s 90C.

If the driver does not contest the roadside deposit within 28 days, then the deposit is paid into court and that is the end of the matter. Alternatively should the driver contest and the court decide in their favour or if the case did not go to court within a year (or less than this if a shorter prosecution period applies), then the deposit would be refunded with the relevant interest. Similarly, if the court decided against them, the deposit would be retained to be offset against all, or part, of the fine imposed.

Under s 90D, if a person does not make an immediate roadside deposit payment of the appropriate amount, the constable or vehicle examiner may then give the person a prohibition notice which prohibits the moving of the vehicle, though the vehicle/trailer may be moved to a specified place by way of a written direction.

This prohibition will remain in force until one of the following occurs—

10.4.3 Graduated fixed penalties, penalty deposits, immobilisation

- ◆ payment of the appropriate amount, during the relevant period;
- ◆ payment of the fixed penalty notice;
- ◆ conviction or acquittal of the offence;
- ◆ driver informed that they will not be prosecuted; or
- ◆ the prosecution period has expired.

Practical considerations

- This legislation provides enforcement powers against both UK and non-UK drivers who do not have a satisfactory UK address and were previously able to avoid payment of fixed penalties and prosecution as a result. It applies to both fixed penalty offences and other traffic offences.
- Enforcement of this scheme is through prohibition notices and vehicle immobilisation, removal, and disposal powers.
- Under the Road Safety (Immobilisation, Removal and Disposal of Vehicles) Regulations 2009 a vehicle may be immobilised when the vehicle was being driven—
  - ◆ whilst unfit for service or overloaded;
  - ◆ in contravention of the drivers' hours rules;
  - ◆ in contravention of international transport requirements;
  - ◆ by a person who has failed to pay the financial penalty deposit.
- Immobilisation will physically prevent a prohibition being disregarded, but the vehicle cannot be immobilised simply because it appears that the driver is likely to abscond.
- Therefore, where a driver does not make a payment under the roadside deposit scheme, the prohibition and immobilisation powers can be applied by the enforcement officer until such time as the prohibition requirements are satisfied or, in cases of offenders who do not have a reliable UK address, until such time as a deposit is paid or the case is settled in court.
- Prior to this scheme, prohibitions were usually imposed for breaches of drivers' hours or when the vehicle was not roadworthy.
- Payment will normally be made by cash or debit cards, as payment by credit cards can be cancelled prior to the transfer taking place.

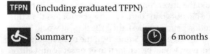

TFPN (including graduated TFPN)

♿ Summary   🕐 6 months

▦ Fine
Discretionary disqualification

Links to alternative subjects and offences

10.5 **Notice of Intended Prosecution**

Section 1 of the Road Traffic Offenders Act 1988 requires a notice of intended prosecution to be given to a defendant for certain offences.

Requirement

Subject to section 2 of this Act, a person shall not be convicted of an offence to which this section applies unless—

(a) he was warned at this time the offence was committed that the question of prosecuting him for one or other of the offences to which this section applies would be taken into consideration, or

(b) **within 14 days** of the commission of the offence a summons for the offence was served on him, or

(c) within 14 days of the commission of the offence a notice of the intended prosecution specifying the nature of the alleged offence and the time and place where it is alleged to have been committed, was—

   (i) in the case of an offence under section 28 or 29 of the Road Traffic Act 1988 (cycling offences) [see **10.12**], served on him, or

   (ii) in the case of any other offence, served on him or on the person, if any, registered as the keeper of the vehicle at the time of the commission of the offence.

Road Traffic Offenders Act 1988, s 1(1)

Meanings

Subject to section 2

This section will not apply if—

- At the time of the offence or immediately after it, the vehicle concerned was involved in an accident.
- A fixed penalty notice or a notice under the fixed penalty scheme requiring production of the defendant's licence and counterpart at a police station is issued (see **10.4**).

Within 14 days

Means the notice must be posted to reach the defendant within 14 day of the offence.

Explanatory notes

- NIPs may be served personally, or by registered post, recorded delivery, or first class post to their last known address.
- A notice of intended prosecution sent by registered post or recorded delivery is deemed served if addressed to them at their last known

address even if it is returned undelivered or not received by them for some other reason.

Requirements of s 1 are met unless the contrary is proved or if the defendant is charged and given a copy of the charge within 14 days of the commission of the offence.

A notice of intended prosecution posted the day after the offence, which failed to arrive within the 14 days, was good service; whereas one sent by recorded delivery on the 14th day was deemed not 'served'.

Failure to comply with s 1 is not a bar to conviction if the name and address of the defendant or the registered keeper could not be ascertained with due diligence in time to comply, or that the accused's conduct contributed to the failure.

If an alternative verdict is returned by the court and the alternative offence requires NIP this is not a bar to conviction, providing the original offence did not require NIP.

Related cases

Shield v Crighton [1974] Crim LR 605, DC 'At the time the offence was committed' is not limited to the exact time of the offence. It has to be construed sensibly, not literally.

v Myers [2007] EWCA Crim 599, CA There has to be a causal link between a traffic offence and the accident, otherwise the driver requires serving with NIP.

Relevant offences

Schedule 1 to the Road Traffic Offenders Act 1988 lists the offences for which NIP is required under s 1, being—

Road Traffic Regulation Act 1984

16—contravene speed restriction at road works.
17(4)—contravene motorway speed limit.
88(7)—contravene minimum speed limit.
89(1)—exceeding speed limit.

Road Traffic Act 1988

2—dangerous driving.
3—careless, and inconsiderate, driving.
22—leaving vehicles in dangerous position.
28—dangerous cycling.
29—careless, and inconsiderate, cycling.
35—failing to comply with traffic directions.
36—failing to comply with traffic signs prescribed under s 36 (see **10.3**).

Practical considerations

If the offence arises out of an accident of which the driver may not be aware NIP required (*Bentley v Dickinson* [1983] RTR 356).

10.5 Notice of Intended Prosecution

- No NIP required if a TFPN (see **10.4**) is issued, or notice that one will be issued on production and surrender of driving licence, and counterpart at a police station is issued.
- There is no need to quote exact Act and section of the offence—keep it simple.

Links to alternative subjects and offences

10.6 **Driving without Due Care and Attention**

Section 3 of the Road Traffic Act 1988 relates to the offence of driving without due care and attention or without reasonable consideration for other users of the road or public place. Section 168 requires a person alleged to have committed this offence to give their details to any person having reasonable grounds for obtaining them.

10.6.1 **Driving without due care and attention**

Offences

If a person **drives** a **mechanically propelled vehicle** on a **road** or other **public place** without **due care and attention**, or without **reasonable consideration** for other persons using the road or public place, he is guilty of an offence.

Road Traffic Act 1988, s 3

Points to prove

✓ drove mechanically propelled vehicle
✓ on road/other public place
✓ without due care and attention/reasonable consideration for other road users

Meanings

Drives (see **10.1.4**)

Mechanically propelled vehicle (see **10.1.3**)

Road (s192) (see **10.1.1**)

Public place (see **10.1.2**)

Driving without due care and attention or reasonable consideration

1) This section has effect for the purposes of sections 2B, 3, and 3A.
2) A person is to be regarded as driving **without due care and attention** if (and only if) the way he drives falls below what would be expected of a competent and careful driver.

10.6.1 Driving without due care and attention

(3) In determining for the purposes of subsection (2) above what would be expected of a careful and competent driver in a particular case, regard shall be had not only to the circumstances of which he could be expected to be aware but also to any circumstances shown to have been within the knowledge of the accused.

(4) A person is to be regarded as driving **without reasonable consideration** for other persons only if those persons are inconvenienced by his driving.

Road Traffic Act 1988, s 3ZA

Explanatory notes

- Breaching certain road traffic regulations (eg crossing central white lines without explanation) can be enough to prove this offence.
- Section 168 of the Road Traffic Act 1988 empowers the obtaining of the defendant's name and address (see **10.6.2**).
- Riding a pedal cycle without due care and attention is an offence under s 29 (see **10.12.2**).

Defences

The defences of automatism, unconsciousness and sudden illness, duress, sudden mechanical defect, assisting in the arrest of offenders and taking part in an authorised motoring event may be used.

Defence notes

- 'Automatism' means an affliction which overcomes the driver and causes them to lose control of the vehicle. It must be sudden and something that they were unaware of and could not reasonably be expected to foresee.
- 'Unconsciousness and sudden illness' applies if a driver is rendered unconscious and unable to control the vehicle. For example a blow to the head or sudden and unforeseen epileptic fit may cause this.
- The defence of duress may be split into two parts—duress by threat or duress of necessity (of circumstances).
- For duress by threat to apply a person cannot deliberately put themselves in a position where they are likely to be subject to threats and, if they can escape the duress by escaping the threats, they must do so.
- Sudden mechanical defect applies if a sudden and unexpected defect in the motor vehicle causes the driver to totally lose control. It does not apply to a defect already known to the driver or one that could be easily discovered with reasonable prudence.
- The defence of assisting in the arrest of offenders may be available to a driver if their driving, though careless or inconsiderate, amounted to reasonable force assisting in the arrest of an offender (see **1.2.1**).
- Section 13A(1) states that a person shall not be guilty of an offence under s 1, s 1A, s 2, s 2B, or s 3 of this Act by virtue of driving a vehicle

in a public place other than a road if they show that they were driving in accordance with an authorisation for a motoring event given under regulations made by the Secretary of State (currently the Motor Vehicles (Off Road Events) Regulations 1995 (SI 1371/1995)).

Related cases

Agnew v DPP [1991] RTR 144, QBD A police officer driving an unmarked surveillance vehicle in a training exercise on a public road crossed a red traffic signal and collided with another vehicle. 'Special reasons' for not endorsing licence refused as public safety is paramount and must always take priority over police training.

DPP v Harris [1994] 158 JP 896, QBD A detective constable driving an unmarked police car was covertly following a vehicle carrying suspects planning to commit an armed robbery when H went through a red traffic light and collided with another vehicle. Care due in these circumstances would involve edging slowly forwards, being prepared to stop if required. For defence of 'necessity' it would be necessary to show that actions were reasonable and proportionate in the light of a threat of death or serious injury.

McCrone v Riding [1938] 1 All ER 157, KBD The standard of driving required from a driver is an objective one, fixed in relation to the safety of other users of the highway. It does not relate to the degree of proficiency or experience attained by the individual driver.

Kay v Butterworth (1945) 110 JP 75, CA If a driver falls asleep whilst driving, they are guilty of at least driving without due care and attention.

Watts v Carter The Times, 22 October 1959, QBD A car leaving the road and mounting the footpath can be driving without due care and attention.

Practical considerations

- This offence requires NIP to be served (see **10.5**).
- This offence can be dealt with by TFPN (see **10.4.1**).
- Although there is no special standard for emergency vehicles, the courts have made it clear that public safety must be paramount (see '**Related cases**' above).
- This section creates two offences and it is bad for duplicity to charge both of them as alternatives.
- Other persons using the road includes other drivers, passengers, pedestrians, or cyclists.
- Section 38(7) of the Road Traffic Act 1988 states that failure to observe a provision of the Highway Code shall not render that person liable to criminal proceedings, but any such failure may be relied upon by any party to any proceedings (civil or criminal) as tending to establish or negate any liability which is in question in those proceedings.
- Consider CPS guidance on prosecuting cases of bad driving.
- The s 3ZA statutory meaning of driving without due or reasonable consideration for others also applies to s 3A (death by careless driving when under influence) (see **10.8.2**) and s 2B (death by careless driving) (see **10.8.3**).

Summary 6 months

 Fine

Discretionary disqualification, obligatory endorsement—3 to 9 penalty points

10.6.2 Request details after reckless, careless, or inconsiderate driving or cycling

Offences

Any of the following persons—

(a) the **driver** of a **mechanically propelled vehicle** who is alleged to have committed an offence under section 2 or 3 of this Act, or

(b) the rider of a cycle who is alleged to have committed an offence under section 28 or 29 of this Act,

who refuses, on being so required by any person having reasonable ground for so requiring, to give his name and address, or gives a false name and address, is guilty of an offence.

Road Traffic Act 1988, s 168

Points to prove

✓ driver of mechanically propelled vehicle/rider of cycle
✓ commits offence under ss 2/3 or 28/29 of RTA 1988
✓ when required by person having reasonable grounds
✓ refused to give name and address/gave false details

Meanings

Mechanically propelled vehicle (see **10.1.3**)

Driver (see **10.1.4**)

Explanatory notes

Above offences applicable to this section are—
• Dangerous driving, s 2 (see **10.7.1**).

Request details after reckless, careless, driving or cycling 10.6.2

- Driving without due care and attention/without reasonable consideration, s 3 (see **10.6.1**).
- ss 28 and 29 involve similar offences to above, but riding pedal cycles (see **10.12**).

 Summary   6 months

 Level 3 fine

Links to alternative subjects and offences

10.7 Dangerous Driving/Cause Serious Injury

10.7.1 Dangerous driving

Section 2 of the Road Traffic Act 1988 relates to dangerous driving.

Offences

A person who **drives a mechanically propelled vehicle dangerously** on a **road** or other **public place** is guilty of an offence.

Road Traffic Act 1988, s 2

Points to prove

✓ being driver of a mechanically propelled vehicle
✓ drove dangerously
✓ on a road/other public place

Meanings

Drives (see **10.1.4**)

Mechanically propelled vehicle (see **10.1.3**)

Driving dangerously (s 2A)

For the purposes of ss 1, 1A, and 2 a person is regarded as driving dangerously if the driving falls far below what would be expected of a competent and careful driver, and it would be obvious to a competent and careful driver that driving in that way and/or driving the vehicle in its current state would be dangerous.

Road (s 192) (see **10.1.1**)

Public place (see **10.1.2**)

Explanatory notes

- In considering the state of the vehicle, anything attached to or carried in or on it, and the manner of it being so attached or carried are also relevant.
- Dangerous refers to either danger of injury to any person or serious damage to property.
- Consideration will be taken not only of the circumstances which a competent and careful driver could be expected to be aware of, but also any circumstances shown to be within the defendant's knowledge.

* There is an offence of dangerous cycling under s 28 (see **10.12.1**).
* Section 168 empowers obtaining of driver's name and address (see **10.6.2**).

Defences (see **10.6.1**)

Defence notes (see **10.6.1**)

Related cases

R v Spurge [1961] 2 All ER 688, CA A driver aware of a mechanical defect, which caused the vehicle to be dangerous, could not use this defence.

R v Strong [1995] Crim LR 428, CA The danger is 'obvious' only if it can be seen or realised at first glance, or is evident to the competent or careful driver, or the defendant knew of it.

R v Roberts and George [1997] RTR 462, CA Where the driver was an employee it was important to consider the instructions he had from his employer concerning checks to be made on the vehicle. If they were reasonable it would be wrong to expect the driver to do more than instructed.

R v Woodward [1995] 3 All ER 79, CA Evidence of consumption of alcohol is admissible only where it is to the effect that the defendant had drunk so much of it as would adversely affect a driver.

R v Pleydell [2005] EWCA Crim 1447, CA Evidence that a driver had taken cocaine was, by itself, admissible as P had driven dangerously as a result of being adversely affected by drugs.

DPP v Milton [2006] EWHC 242 (Admin), QBD Excessive speed alone is insufficient for dangerous driving; the driving has to be considered with all the circumstances.

R v Bannister [2009] EWCA Crim 1571, CA Taking into account specialist driving skills is inconsistent with the objective test when considering whether driving was dangerous.

Practical considerations

This offence requires NIP to be served (see **10.5**).
Consider CPS guidance on prosecuting cases of bad driving.
A court may convict of an alternative offence under s 3 (see **10.6.1**).
Consider any CCTV evidence that may be available.
Forfeiture of the vehicle used may also be ordered.

E&S

 Either way

 None

10.7.2 Cause serious injury by dangerous driving

 Summary: 6 months' imprisonment and/or a fine

Indictment: 2 years' imprisonment and/or a fine. Obligatory disqualification until test passed

Obligatory endorsement—3 to 11 penalty points (unless special reasons apply)

10.7.2 **Cause serious injury by dangerous driving**

Section 1A of the Road Traffic Act 1988 relates to causing serious injury by dangerous driving.

Offences

A person who causes **serious injury** to another person by **driving a mechanically propelled vehicle dangerously** on a **road** or other **public place** is guilty of an offence.

Road Traffic Act 1988, s 1A

Points to prove
- ✓ being driver of a mechanically propelled vehicle
- ✓ caused serious injury to another person
- ✓ by driving dangerously
- ✓ on a road/other public place

Meanings

Serious injury

Physical harm which amounts to grievous bodily harm (see **2.3.1**).

Drives (see **10.1.4**)

Mechanically propelled vehicle (see **10.1.3**)

Driving dangerously (see **10.7.1**)

Road (s 192) (see **10.1.1**)

Public place (see **10.1.2**)

Explanatory notes (see 10.7.1)

This offence was created by the Legal Aid, Sentencing and Punishment of Offenders Act 2012. It came into force on 3rd December 2012, and only applies to s 1A driving after that date.

Defences (see **10.6.1**)

Defence notes (see **10.6.1**)

Related cases (see **10.7.1**)

Practical considerations (see **10.7.1**)

- A court may convict of an alternative offence under s 2 (see **10.7.1**) or s 3 (see **10.6.1**).
- For further information see MOJ Circular 8/2012.

 Either way   None

Summary: 6 months' imprisonment and/or a fine

Indictment: 5 years' imprisonment and/or a fine.
Obligatory disqualification until test passed

Obligatory endorsement—3 to 11 penalty points (unless special reasons apply)

10.7.3 **Wanton or furious driving**

Section 35 of the Offences Against the Person Act 1861 provides for the offence of wanton or furious driving.

Offences

Whosoever, having the charge of any carriage or **vehicle**, shall by **wanton** or furious **driving** or racing, or other wilful misconduct, or by wilful neglect, do or cause to be done any **bodily harm** to any person whatsoever, shall be guilty of an offence.

Offences Against the Person Act 1861, s 35

Points to prove

✓ in charge of a carriage/vehicle
✓ by wanton/furious driving/racing or other wilful misconduct/neglect
✓ did/caused bodily harm to be done to another

10.7.3 Wanton or furious driving

Meanings

Vehicle (see **10.1.3**)

Wanton

Means without any lawful motive and being thoughtless as to the possible consequences.

Driving (see **10.1.4**)

Bodily harm (see **2.1.2**)

Explanatory notes

A person riding a pedal cycle in a wanton or furious manner resulting in injuries to another person may be convicted under this section.

Practical considerations

- This offence can be committed anywhere.
- Consider CPS guidance on prosecuting cases of bad driving.

 Indictment   None

 2 years' imprisonment

If a mechanically propelled vehicle—discretionary disqualification and obligatory endorsement of 3 to 9 penalty points

Links to alternative subjects and offences

10.8 **Fatal Road Traffic Collision Incidents**

A driver involved in a fatal road traffic incident has the same obligations as a driver involved in any other reportable road traffic collisions (RTC) (see **10.9**). Offences connected with deaths caused by road traffic incidents are found in s 1 (dangerous driving); s 2B (due care); s 3A (careless driving when under influence of drink or drugs); s 3ZB (no licence/insurance) and s 3ZC (disqualified).

10.8.1 **Causing death by dangerous driving**

Causing death by dangerous driving is an offence created by s 1 of the Road Traffic Act 1988.

Offences

A person who causes the death of **another person** by **driving** a **mechanically propelled vehicle dangerously** on a **road** or other **public place** is guilty of an offence.

Road Traffic Act 1988, s 1

Points to prove

✓ caused the death of another person
✓ by driving a mechanically propelled vehicle dangerously
✓ on a road/public place

Meanings

Another person

Means anybody, other than the defendant. It has been held to include a foetus in utero (still in the uterus) and subsequently born alive, but who later dies of their injuries.

Driving (see **10.1.4**)

Mechanically propelled vehicle (see **10.1.3**)

Driven dangerously (see **10.7.1**)

Road (s 192) (see **10.1.1**)

Public place (see **10.1.2**)

10.8.1 Causing death by dangerous driving

Explanatory notes

- The death of the person concerned must be shown to have been caused in some way by the incident to which the charge relates.
- The cause of death does not need to be a substantial cause, but neither should it be a slight or trifling link. It will suffice if the driving was a cause of the death even though it was not the sole or even a substantial cause.
- A person charged with this offence may be convicted of the alternative offences of dangerous driving (see **10.7**); death by driving without due care (see **10.8.3**); or careless, and inconsiderate, driving (see **10.6**).

Defences (see 10.6.1).

Defence notes (see 10.6.1)

Related cases (see also 'Dangerous driving' cases **10.7.1**)

R v Hennigan [1971] 3 All ER 133, CA A vehicle on the main road was travelling at an excessive speed, and collided with a vehicle emerging from the side road, killing the driver. The other driver was convicted of s 1, even though the deceased was mainly to blame, excessive speed and dangerous driving by the defendant was partly to blame.

R v Buono [2005] EWCA Crim 1313, CA A fatal collision had been caused by the defendant taking a bend in the middle of the road at excessive speed. Similar fact evidence was admitted to show the manner in which the car had been driven earlier—swerving across the road and driving at excessive speed. Such evidence had considerable probative force which undoubtedly outweighed any prejudice to the defendant.

Practical considerations

- This section applies to tramcars and trolley vehicles operating under a statutory power.
- If appropriate consider manslaughter (see **2.7**) for this offence.
- Theoretically, two different drivers could cause the same death.
- *R v Beckford* (1994) 159 JP 305, CA (see **10.8.2**) also applies to this offence.
- Consider CPS guidance on prosecuting cases of bad driving.
- When dealing with the incident follow **force policy**, preserve the scene, involve supervision, scenes of crime, CID, and other agencies.
- Check for CCTV evidence that may be available.
- Consider seizing the vehicle as it may be forfeited. This will also ensure that the vehicle can be examined for any mechanical defect defences before eventual disposal.

Indictment   None

 14 years' imprisonment

Obligatory disqualification until extended test passed

Obligatory endorsement—3 to 11 penalty points (only if special reasons apply)

10.8.2 Causing death by careless driving when under influence

Section 3A of the Road Traffic Act 1988 provides an offence of causing the death of another by careless driving when under the influence of drink or drugs, or failing to provide or give permission for a specimen.

Offences

If a person causes the death of **another person** by **driving a mechanically propelled vehicle** on a **road** or other **public place without due care and attention**, or without **reasonable consideration** for other persons using the road or place, and—

(a) he is, at the time when he is driving, **unfit to drive through drink or drugs**, or

(b) he has consumed so much **alcohol** that the proportion of it in his breath, blood or urine at that time **exceeds the prescribed limit**, or

(ba) he has in his body a specified controlled drug and the proportion of it in his blood or urine at that time **exceeds the specified limit** for that **drug**, or

(c) he is, within 18 hours after that time, required to provide a specimen in pursuance of section 7 of this Act [see **10.11.2**], but without reasonable excuse fails to provide it, or

(d) he is required by a constable to give his permission for a laboratory test of a specimen of blood taken from him under section 7A of this Act [see **10.11.2**], but without reasonable excuse fails to do so,

he is guilty of an offence.

Road Traffic Act 1988, s 3A(1)

Points to prove

✓ caused the death of another person

✓ by driving a motor vehicle

✓ on a road/public place

10.8.2 Causing death by careless driving when under influence

✓ without due care or reasonable consideration for other road users and
✓ at the time of driving was unfit through drink/drugs **or**
✓ was over the prescribed (alcohol) or specified (drugs) limit
✓ within 18 hours of incident failed to provide specimen **or**
✓ on being required failed to give permission to take specimen of blood

Meanings

Another person (see 10.8.1)

Driving (see 10.1.4)

Mechanically propelled vehicle (see 10.1.3)

Road (s 192) (see 10.1.1)

Public place (see 10.1.2)

Without due care and attention or reasonable consideration (see 10.6.1)

Unfit to drive

When the ability to drive properly is impaired.

Through drink or drugs (see 10.10)

Exceeds the prescribed limit (alcohol) (see 10.11.1)

Exceeds the specified limit (drugs) (see 10.11.2)

Explanatory notes

- The careless or inconsiderate driving (see 10.6) must be a cause of the death of another person, as must being under the influence of drink/drugs, or failing to provide or give permission for a specimen.
- Section 3A(3) states that s 3A(1)(b), (ba), (c), and (d) do not apply to a mechanically propelled vehicle. They only apply to a motor vehicle.
- It is not necessary for the intoxication to be a direct cause of the careless/inconsiderate driving.
- A person charged with this offence may be convicted of the alternative driving offences of careless and inconsiderate (see 10.6); unfit through drink/drugs (see 10.10); excess alcohol in breath/blood/urine (see 10.11.1); while over the specified (drugs) limit in blood/urine (see 10.11.2); or failing to provide a specimen (see 10.11.3).

Defences (see 10.6.1)

Defence notes (see 10.6.1)

Related cases

R v Coe [2009] EWCA Crim 1452, CA C refused to provide breath/blood samples after a fatal RTC. The police obtained a court order so the medical blood sample could be analysed for s 3A evidence. At trial, C applied to exclude this evidence, but it was admitted and C's conviction was upheld.

R v Ash [1999] RTR 347, QBD Where only one blood sample is taken, the analysis result can still be used under s 3A. The requirement to take two samples under s 15 of the Road Traffic Offenders Act 1988 does not apply to s 3A.

R v Beckford (1994) 159 JP 305, CA A vehicle was scrapped shortly after being involved in a fatal RTC. Defendant relied upon defence of 'mechanical defect' where the steering had locked. Court stated that police 'procedures' should ensure that cars are not scrapped unless the police give permission; this will not be given where serious criminal charges are to be brought which may involve a mechanical defect in the car.

Practical considerations

- Consider CPS driving offences charging standards.
- As with all fatal RTCs, protect and prevent contamination of the scene. Seize the vehicle as it may be forfeited.
- Consider CCTV evidence, if available.

 Indictment   None

 14 years' imprisonment

Obligatory disqualification until extended test passed

Obligatory endorsement—3 to 11 penalty points (only if special reasons apply)

10.8.3 Causing death by driving: disqualified driver

Section 3ZC of the Road Traffic Act 1988 provides for the offence of causing the death of another person by driving a motor vehicle on a road and at the time was disqualified from driving.

10.8.3 Causing death by driving: disqualified driver

Offences

A person is guilty of an offence under this section if he or she—
(a) causes the death of **another person** by **driving** a **motor vehicle** on a **road**, and
(b) at that time, is committing an offence under section 103(1)(b) of this Act (driving while disqualified).

Road Traffic Act 1988, s 3ZC

Points to prove

✓ caused the death of another person
✓ by driving a motor vehicle
✓ on a road
✓ whilst disqualified

Meanings

Another person (see **10.8.1**)

Driving (see **10.1.4**)

Motor vehicle (see **10.1.3**)

Road (s 192) (see **10.1.1**)

Explanatory notes

This offence is subject to a fatal RTC and committing an offence under s 103(1)(b) driving whilst disqualified (see **10.13.1**). It has effect only in relation to driving which occurs on or after 13 April 2015.

Practical considerations

- Consider CPS driving offences charging standards.
- Protect and prevent contamination of the scene. Consider CCTV, if available.
- This offence requires some element of fault by the driver that they caused the death of another person (*R v Hughes* [2013] UKSC 56, see **10.8.5**), not just driving a motor vehicle whilst disqualified.
- Annex A of MOJ Circular 1/2015 provides guidance on this matter.

 Indictment   None

---

10 years' imprisonment and/or a fine
Obligatory disqualification until extended test passed
Obligatory endorsement—3 to 11 penalty points

10.8.4 **Causing death by driving without due care**

Section 2B of the Road Traffic Act 1988 provides for the offence of causing death by driving without due care and attention or reasonable consideration for others.

Offences

A person who causes the death of **another person** by **driving** a **mechanically propelled vehicle** on a **road** or other **public place** **without due care and attention,** or without **reasonable consideration** for other persons using the road or place is guilty of an offence.

Road Traffic Act 1988, s 2B

Points to prove

✓ caused the death of another person
✓ by driving a mechanically propelled vehicle
✓ on a road/public place
✓ without due care and attention/reasonable consideration for others

Meanings

Another person (see 10.8.1)

Driving (see 10.1.4)

Mechanically propelled vehicle (see 10.1.3)

Road (s 192) (see 10.1.1)

Public place (see 10.1.2)

Without due care and attention or reasonable consideration (see 10.6.1)

Explanatory notes (see 10.6.1)

Defences (see 10.6.1)

10.8.5 Causing death by driving: no insurance or licence

Practical considerations (see also **10.6.1** and **10.8.2**)

- This section may be an alternative verdict to an offence under—
  - ✦ s 1 (causing death by dangerous driving—see **10.8.1**);
  - ✦ s 3A (causing death by driving without due care when under the influence—see **10.8.2**).
- Ensure compliance with the law in relation to reporting RTCs (see **10.9**).

 Either way   None

▥ **Summary**: 12 months' imprisonment and/or a fine

Indictment: 5 years' imprisonment and/or a fine. Obligatory disqualification and obligatory endorsement with 3 to 11 penalty points

10.8.5 Causing death by driving: no insurance or licence

Section 3ZB of the Road Traffic Act 1988 provides for the offence of causing the death of another person by driving a motor vehicle on a road otherwise than in accordance with a licence, or without insurance.

Offences

A person is guilty of an offence under this section if he causes the death of **another person** by **driving** a **motor vehicle** on a **road** and, at the time when he is driving, the circumstances are such that he is committing an offence under—

(a) section 87(1) of this Act (driving otherwise than in accordance with a licence),

(b) *omitted*, or

(c) section 143 of this Act (using motor vehicle while uninsured or unsecured against third party risks).

Road Traffic Act 1988, s 3ZB

Points to prove

✓ caused the death of another person
✓ by driving a motor vehicle
✓ on a road
✓ without driving licence/insurance

Meanings

Another person (see **10.8.1**)

Driving (see **10.1.4**)

Motor vehicle (see **10.1.3**)

Road (s 192) (see **10.1.1**)

Explanatory notes

This offence is subject to a fatal RTC by **causing** the death by their driving and committing an offence under—

- s 87(1) driving otherwise than in accordance with a licence (see **10.14.1**); or
- s 143 using motor vehicle without insurance (see **10.16.1**).

Related cases

R v Hughes [2013] UKSC 56, SC The s 3ZB offence requires at least some act or omission in respect of the control of the car. The act/omission must involve some element of fault, whether amounting to s 3 driving or not, and must contribute in more than a minimal way to the death, but does not necessarily have to be the principal cause of death.

Practical considerations

- Consider CPS driving offences charging standards.
- Protect and prevent contamination of the scene.
- Consider powers of seizure and removal under s 165A (see **10.16.6**).
- This offence requires some element of fault by the driver (*R v Hughes* [2013] UKSC 56) of causing the death.
- Consider CCTV evidence, if available.

 E&S

  Either way   None

Summary: 12 months' imprisonment and/or a fine

Indictment: 2 years' imprisonment and/or a fine. Obligatory disqualification and obligatory endorsement with 3 to 11 penalty points

---

Links to alternative subjects and offences

10.9 **Road Traffic Collisions**

Section 170 of the Road Traffic Act 1988 imposes duties on the driver of a mechanically propelled vehicle involved in certain RTCs on a road or other public place.

10.9.1 **Incidents to which applicable**

Collisions which apply

If owing to the presence of a **mechanically propelled vehicle** on a **road** or other **public place**, an **accident** occurs by which—

(a) personal **injury** is caused to a person other than the **driver** of that mechanically propelled vehicle, or

(b) damage is caused—

   (i) to a vehicle other than that mechanically propelled vehicle or a trailer drawn by that mechanically propelled vehicle, or

   (ii) to an **animal** other than an animal in or on that mechanically propelled vehicle or a trailer drawn by that mechanically propelled vehicle, or

   (iii) to any other property constructed on, fixed to, growing in or otherwise forming part of the land on which the road or place in question is situated or land adjacent to such land.

Road Traffic Act 1988, s 170(1)

Meanings

Mechanically propelled vehicle (see **10.1.3**)

Road (s 192) (see **10.1.1**)

Public place (see **10.1.2**)

Accident

This is an unintended occurrence having an adverse physical result.

Injury

Includes any actual bodily harm and may well include nervous shock.

Driver (see **10.1.4**)

Animal

Means horse, cattle, ass, mule, sheep, pig, goat, or dog.

Practical considerations

- There must be some link between the presence of the vehicle and the occurrence of the accident.

- 'Vehicle', in respect of the other vehicle damaged, may include a pedal cycle.
- If attending a potential fatal RTC (see **10.8**).

10.9.2 **Duties of driver after accident**

Offences

(2) The **driver** of the **mechanically propelled vehicle** must stop and, if required to do so by any person having reasonable grounds for so requiring, give his name and address and also the name and address of the owner and the identification marks of the vehicle.

(3) If for any reason the driver of the mechanically propelled vehicle does not give his name and address under subsection (2) above, he must report the **accident**.

(4) A person who fails to comply with subsection (2) or (3) above is guilty of an offence.

Road Traffic Act 1988, s 170

Points to prove

✓ being the driver of a mechanically propelled vehicle
✓ involved in a road traffic accident
✓ failed to stop **and**
✓ on being requested by a person having grounds to do so
✓ failed to provide details, as required

Meanings

Driver (see **10.1.4**)

Mechanically propelled vehicle (see **10.1.3**)

Accident (see **10.9.1**)

Explanatory notes

- If the driver does not stop immediately they must do so as soon as it is safe and convenient to do so.
- If personal injury is involved and the vehicle is a motor vehicle, and the driver does not, at the time of the collision, produce evidence of insurance to a constable or some person having reasonable grounds for requiring them to do so, they must report the collision and produce such evidence (see **10.9.3**).
- After stopping, the driver must remain there long enough to enable them, if required, to furnish the relevant information.

Related cases

DPP v Hay [2005] EWHC 1395 (Admin), QBD H was driving a vehicle involved in an accident and was taken to hospital without exchanging details or reporting the RTC to the police, and subsequently failed to report the accident after being discharged from hospital. H failed to comply with s 170, even though the police observed the RTC and had made no request for information.

DPP v McCarthy [1999] RTR 323, DC The requirement to give a name and address has a wider meaning than just the driver's home address. An address needs to be somewhere where a person can be contacted.

McDermott v DPP [1997] RTR 474, QBD The driver of a horsebox collided with the side of a car causing damage, and drove on to some stables 80 yards away. Although returning, the driver had left the scene, and could have stopped at the time of the RTC.

Practical considerations

- The driver does not commit this offence if they are unaware that the RTC has occurred.
- These two subsections create two separate offences (failing to stop and give information **and** failing to report). Therefore the driver may be charged with either one or both of them. A further offence may be committed in a s 170(1)(a) injury accident and the driver fails to comply with s 170(5) (see **10.9.3**).
- The scene of the RTC is the place in the road or public place where the collision occurs. Remember the vehicles themselves may also be 'scenes'.

 Summary   6 months

 6 months' imprisonment and/or a fine
Discretionary disqualification obligatory endorsement—5 to 10 penalty points

10.9.3 **Duty of driver to report the incident**

Section 170 provides for the obligation and a subsequent offence where a reportable RTC occurs.

10.9.3 Duty of driver to report the incident

Offences

(5) If, in a case where this section applies by virtue of subsection (1)(a) above [*injury, see* 10.9.1], the **driver** of a **motor vehicle** does not at the time of the **accident** produce such a certificate of **insurance** or **security**, or other evidence, as is mentioned in **section 165(2)(a)** of this Act—
   (a) to a constable, or
   (b) to some person who, having reasonable grounds for so doing, has required him to produce it,
   the driver must report the accident and produce such a certificate or other evidence.

(7) A person who fails to comply with a duty under subsection (5) above is guilty of an offence.

Road Traffic Act 1988, s 170

Points to prove

✓ being driver of a motor vehicle
✓ involved in a relevant road traffic accident
✓ did not at the time of the accident
✓ produce to a constable/person with grounds for requiring
✓ relevant evidence of insurance **or**
✓ failed to report the accident and produce relevant insurance

Meanings

Driver (see **10.1.4**)

Motor vehicle (see **10.1.3**)

Accident (see **10.9.1**)

Insurance/security (see **10.16.1**)

Section 165(2)(a) (see **10.16.5**)

Explanatory notes

- To comply with the requirement to produce the relevant proof of insurance, s 170(6) states that the driver must do so at a police station or to a constable, which must be done as soon as is reasonably practicable and, in any case, within 24 hours of it occurring.
- A person will not be convicted of this offence only because they failed to produce the relevant insurance document if, within 7 days following the accident it is produced at a police station specified by them at the time they reported the accident.
- The obligation to report the accident includes where there is nobody else about to whom the driver can give the details (eg damage to street furnishings).

Practical considerations

- Note that whereas s 170(2) and s 170(3) create offences in relation to a mechanically propelled vehicle, this offence is in relation to the use of a motor vehicle.
- This requirement does not apply to an invalid carriage.
- 'At a police station' means the motorist should report it in person at a police station or to a constable; a report by telephone will not suffice.

 Summary   6 months

 6 months' imprisonment and/or a fine
Discretionary disqualification, obligatory endorsement—5 to 10 penalty points

Links to alternative subjects and offences

10.10 Drive/Attempt to Drive/in Charge of Vehicle While Unfit through Drink/Drugs

10.10.1 Drive while unfit drink/drugs

Section 4 of the Road Traffic Act 1988 provides for the offences of driving, attempting to drive, and being in charge of a mechanically propelled vehicle on a road or public place while unfit through drink or drugs.

Offences

(1) A person who, when **driving** or attempting to drive a **mechanically propelled vehicle** on a **road** or other **public place**, is unfit to drive through drink or drugs is guilty of an offence.

(2) Without prejudice to subsection (1) above, a person who, when **in charge** of a mechanically propelled vehicle which is on a road or other public place, is unfit to drive through drink or drugs is guilty of an offence.

Road Traffic Act 1988, s 4

Points to prove

s 4(1) offence

✓ drove/attempted to drive
✓ a mechanically propelled vehicle
✓ on a road/other public place
✓ when unfit to drive through drink/drugs

s 4(2) offence

✓ in charge of a mechanically propelled vehicle
✓ on a road/public place
✓ being unfit to drive through drink/drugs

Meanings

Driving (see **10.1.4**)

Mechanically propelled vehicle (see **10.1.3**)

Road (s 192) (see **10.1.1**)

Public place (see **10.1.2**)

In charge

There is no legislation or test for what constitutes 'in charge' for the purposes of being in charge of a vehicle under s 4, s 5, or s 5A (see **10.11**), but a close connection between the defendant and control of the vehicle is required.

Explanatory notes

- A person is **unfit to drive** properly if their ability is for the time being impaired. The prosecution must give evidence of unfitness.
- It needs to be ascertained whether the person is in charge of the vehicle by virtue of being the owner, lawful possessor, or recent driver. Are they still in charge or have they relinquished charge at the relevant time; have they assumed charge?
- Factors that need to be considered in establishing whether the person was in charge include—
  - Who is the registered keeper of the vehicle; who is insured to drive it; where were the other insured drivers (if any)?
  - What were their immediate and future intended movements?
  - If away from their home/accommodation, how did they propose to return without driving?
  - How had the vehicle got to where it was; when did they last drive it; are they in possession of a key which fits the ignition?
  - What was their position in relation to the car; were they in the vehicle; if not how far away were they?
  - Was anyone else in or around the vehicle; what were they doing at the relevant time?
  - Is there evidence of an intention to take control of the vehicle?
  - When and where had they been drinking; time of last drink; what had they been doing since then?
- The evidence of a doctor who examines the defendant at the request of the police is admissible even if they had to persuade the defendant to allow the examination.

Defences

For the purposes of subsection (2) above, a person shall be deemed not to have been in charge of a mechanically propelled vehicle if he proves that at the material time the circumstances were such that there was no likelihood of his driving it so long as he remained unfit to drive through drink or drugs.

Road Traffic Act 1988, s 4(3)

Defence notes

- In the case of *Sheldrake v DPP (A-G's Reference No 4 of 2002)* [2005] 1 Cr App R 28 it was held that the burden of proof should remain on the defendant, to be decided on the balance of probabilities. This imposition did not contravene the presumption of innocence and was compatible with the ECHR.

10.10.1 Drive while unfit drink/drugs

- The court, in determining whether there was a likelihood of a person driving whilst still unfit through drink or drugs, should disregard any injury to them and any damage to the vehicle (ie it is not the practical possibility of the person being able to drive the vehicle that is relevant here, but rather the possibility of that person driving at all while still impaired).

Related cases

R v Ealing, ex parte Woodman (1994) 158 JP 997, QBD If there was sufficient proof that they had taken more than their normal dose of insulin and failed to counterbalance it with food intake, insulin would be treated by the court as a drug under this section.

Smith v Mellors & Another [1987] RTR 210, QBD If the driver cannot be identified and each occupant of the car is over the prescribed limit, each one can be charged with the relevant drink driving offence and alternatively with aiding and abetting the other(s) to commit the drink driving offence. However, evidence of the aiding must be put to the court.

Practical considerations

- A charge under this section, which uses both the alternatives of 'drink or drugs', is not bad for duplicity.
- The CPS are unlikely to take the case forward unless there is evidence that the suspect was likely to drive whilst under the influence of drink/drugs. Similarly if in charge, ensure that the s 4(3) defence can be countered if raised.
- This section applies to trolley vehicles operated under statutory powers, but not to tramcars.
- An indictment containing a charge under s 1 of the Road Traffic Act 1988 (see **10.8**) should not include a charge under this section, as this section is triable summarily only.
- A non-expert witness may give evidence of the defendant's condition, but not of their fitness to drive.

 E&S

 Summary   6 months

 s 4(1) offence

    6 months' imprisonment and/or a fine

    Obligatory disqualification for a minimum of 12 months

    Obligatory endorsement—3 to 11 penalty points

    s 4(2) offence

    3 months' imprisonment and/or a level 4 fine

    Discretionary disqualification, obligatory endorsement—10 penalty points

10.10.2 **Preliminary test powers**

Section 6 of the Road Traffic Act 1988 provides for the requiring of preliminary tests for alcohol, impairment, or drugs to drivers of motor vehicles. Sections 6A to 6C relate to the specific tests, whilst s 6D provides a power of arrest and s 6E a power of entry.

Offences

A person commits an offence if without reasonable excuse he **fails** to co-operate with a **preliminary test** in pursuance of a **requirement** imposed under this section.

Road Traffic Act 1988, s 6(6)

Points to prove

✓ without reasonable excuse
✓ failed to cooperate with a preliminary test
✓ when required under this section

Meanings

Fails

Fail includes refuse.

Preliminary test

This refers to any of the tests described in sections 6A to 6C and means a preliminary test—of breath/impairment or for drugs.

Requirements

Under s 6(1)–(5) a constable may require a person to cooperate with any one or more preliminary tests administered to them by that constable or another constable, if the constable reasonably suspects that—

- they are driving, attempting to drive, or are in charge of a motor vehicle on a road or other public place, and have alcohol or a drug in their body or are under the influence of a drug; **or**
- they had been driving, attempting to drive, or in charge of a motor vehicle on a road or other public place while having alcohol or a drug in their body, or while unfit to drive because of a drug, and still have alcohol or a drug in their body, or are still under the influence of a drug; **or**
- they are or have been driving, attempting to drive, or in charge of a motor vehicle on a road or other public place, and have committed a **traffic offence** while the vehicle was in motion; or
- an accident has occurred owing to the presence of a motor vehicle on a road or other public place, and a constable reasonably believes that they were driving, attempting to drive, or in charge of the vehicle at the time of the accident.

10.10.2 Preliminary test powers

Traffic offence

Means an offence under the Public Passenger Vehicles Act 1981, Pt 2 (ss 6–29); Road Traffic Regulation Act 1984; Road Traffic Offenders Act 1988 (except Pt 3—fixed penalties); or Road Traffic Act 1988 (except Pt 5—driving instruction).

Explanatory notes

- Only a constable in uniform may administer a preliminary test, except if it relates to an accident under s 6(5).
- A preliminary breath test (s 6A) is a procedure by which the person taking the test provides a specimen of breath to ascertain, using a device approved by the Secretary of State, whether the proportion of alcohol in their breath or blood is likely to exceed the prescribed limit.
- For a preliminary impairment test (s 6B) the constable requesting it observes the person taking it performing tasks specified by the constable and makes any observations of the person's physical state as they think is expedient. The constable shall have regard to the code of practice issued by the Secretary of State which governs preliminary impairment tests.
- For a preliminary drug test (s 6C) a specimen of sweat or saliva is obtained (using a device approved by the Secretary of State) to ascertain whether the person tested has a drug in their body; if so, whether it is a specified controlled drug; if it is, whether the proportion of it in their blood or urine is likely to exceed the specified limit for that drug. Up to three preliminary drug tests may be administered at or near the place where the test requirement is imposed or if expedient at a specified police station.
- A person will not be required at random to provide a specimen of breath for a breath test.
- An asthma sufferer who is incapable of providing a sample has a duty to inform the officer requiring it.
- A person who refuses (without good cause) to take a test is deemed to have failed to take it.
- While in hospital, no person will be requested to supply a breath sample or laboratory specimen without the knowledge and permission of the doctor in charge of their case.

Power of arrest

(1) A constable may arrest a person without warrant if as a result of a preliminary breath test or preliminary drug test the constable reasonably suspects that—

    (a) the proportion of alcohol in that person's breath or blood exceeds the prescribed limit, or

    (b) the person has a specified controlled drug in his body and the proportion of it in the person's blood or urine exceeds the specified limit for that drug.

(2) A constable may arrest a person without warrant if—
  (a) the person fails to co-operate with a preliminary test in pursuance of a requirement imposed under s 6, and
  (b) the constable reasonably suspects that the person has alcohol or a drug in his body or is under the influence of a drug.

Road Traffic Act 1988, s 6D

Power of entry (after injury accident)

A constable may enter any place (using reasonable force if necessary) for the purpose of—
(a) imposing a requirement by virtue of section 6(5) following an accident in a case where the constable reasonably suspects that the accident involved injury of any person, or
(b) arresting a person under section 6D following an accident in a case where the constable reasonably suspects that the accident involved injury of any person.

Road Traffic Act 1988, s 6E(1)

Related cases

DPP v Wilson [2009] EWHC 1988 (Admin), QBD W was breathalysed at hospital following a RTC; it showed a positive result and W was arrested. The doctor consented to blood being taken, the result confirmed that W was OPL. Argued that as arrest was unlawful per s 6D(3), then the blood result could not be used as evidence. Held: The fact that an arrest is prohibited does not prevent the blood and breath test procedures; provided they are taken in accordance with statutory requirements, they remain valid.

Gearing v DPP [2008] EWHC 1695 (Admin), QBD There is clear conflict between s 58 of PACE as to consulting a solicitor and requirements under the 1988 Act. What is important is the public interest of evidential testing as soon as possible. Safeguards accompany the procedure itself. G had been drinking, failed the roadside test, and had no medical or physical reason for not taking the further evidential breath test.

Whelehan v DPP [1995] RTR 177, QBD A constable does not need to administer a caution prior to asking a person who had obviously been drinking whether they had driven the motor car in which they were sitting because the constable would have no grounds for suspecting an offence under s 5 until after they had obtained a positive breath test.

R v Beckford [1995] RTR 251, CA A constable questioned, without a caution, a driver who had been involved in a fatal accident as to how much drink he had consumed. The man replied '3 pints' which then gave rise to a requirement that a caution be given before any further questions were put.

Practical considerations

- A constable can arrest a person under s 6D(1A) if specimens of breath have been provided under s 7 (see **10.11.3**) and the constable

10.10.2 Preliminary test powers

imposing the requirement has reasonable cause to believe that the approved device used for analysis did not produce a reliable result.

- A preliminary breath test requested because a constable suspects that a person has alcohol or a drug in their body or is under the influence of a drug may only be given at or near the place where it is requested.
- Following a RTC a preliminary impairment test or preliminary drugs test may be given at or near the place where it is requested or, if the constable requesting it thinks it expedient, at a police station specified by them.
- Only a constable approved by their chief officer may give a preliminary impairment test, which must satisfy the COP.
- A person arrested under the above powers may, instead of being taken to a police station, be detained at or near the place where the preliminary test was, or would have been, administered, to impose a requirement there under s 7 on them (see **10.11.3**).
- A person may not be arrested under s 6D(3) while at a hospital as a patient.
- A constable may enter any place (by reasonable force if necessary) to impose a requirement by virtue of a RTC having occurred, or to arrest a person under s 6D following a RTC, where they reasonably suspect that such RTC involved injury to a person.
- If a motorist supplies enough breath for the device to give a reading they cannot be said to have failed to cooperate.
- Evidential specimens can be obtained at the roadside.

E&S

 Summary   6 months

 Level 3 fine

Discretionary disqualification, obligatory endorsement—4 penalty points

Links to alternative subjects and offences

10.11 Drive/Attempt to Drive/in Charge While over the Prescribed/Specified Limit

10.11.1 Drive motor vehicle while over the prescribed (alcohol) limit

Section 5 of the Road Traffic Act 1988 provides the offences of driving, attempting to drive, and being in charge of a motor vehicle on a road or public place while over the prescribed limit of alcohol in blood, breath, or urine.

Offences

If a person—
(a) **drives** or attempts to drive a **motor vehicle** on a **road** or other public place, or
(b) is **in charge** of a motor vehicle on a road or other public place,

after **consuming** so much alcohol that the proportion of it in his breath, blood or urine exceeds the **prescribed limit** he is guilty of an offence.

Road Traffic Act 1988, s 5(1)

Points to prove

✓ drove/attempted to drive/in charge of motor vehicle
✓ on a road/public place
✓ proportion of alcohol in blood/breath/urine exceeded prescribed limit

Meanings

Drive (see 10.1.4)

Motor vehicle (see 10.1.3)

Road (s 192) (see 10.1.1)

Public place (see 10.1.2)

In charge (see 10.10.1)

Consuming

With regard to alcohol primarily means by mouth, but can include other means of ingesting it into the blood, breath, or urine.

Prescribed limit

For driving offences the limits are—
- 35 microgrammes of alcohol in 100 millilitres of breath;
- 80 milligrammes of alcohol in 100 millilitres of blood;
- 107 milligrammes of alcohol in 100 millilitres of urine.

Explanatory notes

- Be aware of the powers to administer a preliminary breath test (see **10.10.2**).
- Being so hopelessly drunk that they are incapable of driving a motor vehicle is not a defence to this offence.
- If the offence is under s 5(1)(b) then it needs to be ascertained whether the person is in charge of the vehicle (see '**Explanatory notes**' **10.10.1**).
- Evidence of the proportion of alcohol at the time of driving other than that provided by the specimen is admissible.
- Where it is established that the defendant was driving and has given a positive sample, it is assumed that the amount of alcohol at the time of the alleged offence is not less than the specimen provided.

Power of arrest (see 10.10.2)

Defence—being in charge

It is a defence for a person charged with an offence under subsection (1)(b) above to prove that at the time he is alleged to have committed the offence the circumstances were such that there was no likelihood of his driving the vehicle whilst the proportion of alcohol in his breath, blood or urine remained likely to exceed the prescribed limit.

Road Traffic Act 1988, s 5(2)

Defence notes (see also 10.10.1)

- The burden of proof is on the defendant.
- In determining whether there was any likelihood of them driving, the court may ignore any injury to them or damage to the vehicle.

Related cases (see also 10.1.4 and 10.10 cases)

CPS v Thompson [2007] EWHC 1841 (Admin), QBD The court should consider whether the defendant has shown that there is no likelihood of their driving the vehicle whilst the alcohol in their body remains likely to be above the prescribed limit.

DPP v Mullally [2006] EWHC 3448 (Admin), QBD Once a defence of duress is raised the burden of proof rests upon the prosecution to dispel the evidence. The court must consider—

10.11.1 Drive motor vehicle while over the prescribed (alcohol) limit

- Was s/he forced to act as they did because of a genuine belief that death or serious injury would result if they had not acted in that manner?
- Would a sober person of reasonable firmness have been forced into acting in the same way?

DPP v Wilson [1991] Crim LR 441, QBD An officer is entitled to form an opinion that a driver has been drinking from information from an anonymous caller.

DPP v Johnson (1994) 158 JP 891, QBD The 'consumption' of alcohol may be by injection.

Sharpe v DPP (1994) JP 595, QBD If an officer is a trespasser at the time of the screening test it may invalidate the procedure.

Drake v DPP [1994] Crim LR 855, QBD A clamped vehicle may allow the 'being in charge' defence to be used.

DPP v H [1997] 1 WLR 1406, QBD Insanity cannot be used as a defence against a s 5 offence as there is no requirement for any intent; the offence is one of strict liability.

Lafferty v DPP [1995] Crim LR 430, QBD In a claim that the intoximeter reading was inaccurate, the court may consider evidence of the road-side breath test.

Practical considerations

- The CPS are unlikely to take the case forward unless there is evidence of a likelihood of driving whilst under the influence of drink or drugs. Similarly if in charge, ensure that the s 5(2) defence can be countered if raised.
- A person acting as a supervisor of a provisional licence holder is 'in charge' of the vehicle and can commit that offence under this section.
- 'Lacing' a person's drink without their knowledge may constitute an offence of aiding and abetting the commission of an offence under this section, if there is proof that the intent was to bring about the offence.
- Be aware of the 'Hip Flask Defence' (where the suspect claims to have had an alcoholic drink since driving but before providing a specimen). Ascertain amount drunk and inform the laboratory so the appropriate calculations can be made.
- A power of entry is available for the provision of a preliminary test in cases which involve an injury accident. Reasonable force may be used to effect entry under s 6E, or carry out a preliminary test and arrest a person under s 6D (see **10.10.2**).

 Summary   6 months

s 5(1)(a) offence

6 months' imprisonment and/or a fine

Obligatory disqualification, obligatory endorsement—3 to 11 penalty points (if special reasons apply)

s 5(1)(b) offence

3 months' imprisonment and/or a level 4 fine

Discretionary disqualification, obligatory endorsement—10 penalty points

10.11.2 Drive motor vehicle while over the specified (drugs) limit

Section 5A of the Road Traffic Act 1988 provides the offences of driving, attempting to drive, and being in charge of a motor vehicle on a road or public place while over the specified limit of a specified controlled drug in blood or urine.

Offences

(1) This section applies where a person ('D')—
   (a) **drives** or attempts to drive a **motor vehicle** on a **road** or other **public place**, or
   (b) is **in charge** of a motor vehicle on a road or other public place,
and there is in D's body a **specified controlled drug**.
(2) D is guilty of an offence if the proportion of the drug in D's blood or urine exceeds the **specified limit** for that drug.

Road Traffic Act 1988, s 5A

Points to prove

✓ drove/attempted to drive/in charge of motor vehicle
✓ on a road/public place
✓ proportion of specified controlled drug in blood/urine
✓ exceeded specified limit for that drug

Meanings

Drive (see **10.1.4**)

Motor vehicle (see **10.1.3**)

Road (s 192) (see **10.1.1**)

10.11.2 Drive motor vehicle while over the specified (drugs) limit

Public place (see 10.1.2)

In charge (see 10.10.1)

Specified
Means specified in regulations made by the Secretary of State.

Controlled drug (see 5.1.1)

Specified controlled drug/limit
The Drug Driving (Specified Limits) Regulations 2014, reg 2 (SI 2868/2014) specifies the controlled drugs and specified limits (microgrammes per litre of blood) that apply to the s 5A offence: Amphetamine (250); Benzoylecgonine (50); Clonazepam (50); Cocaine (10); Delta-9-Tetrahydrocannabinol (2); Diazepam (550); Flunitrazepam (300); Ketamine (20); Lorazepam (100); Lysergic Acid Diethylamide (1); Methadone (500); Methylamphetamine (10); Methylenedioxymethamphetamine (10); 6-Monoacetylmorphine (5); Morphine (80); Oxazepam (300); and Temazepam (1000).

Explanatory notes

- Officers can screen for specified drugs at the roadside by using an approved device under s 6C (see 10.10.2).
- If the offence is under s 5A(1)(b) then it needs to be ascertained whether the person is in charge of the vehicle (see 'Explanatory notes' 10.10.1).
- The s 5A offence makes it easier for police to detect and prosecute drug-drivers, being an offence to drive/attempt to drive or being in charge while over the limit for drugs (as specified), as it is for drink driving over the prescribed limit (see 10.11.1).
- There is no requirement to provide proof of impairment for this offence.

Power of arrest (see 10.10.2)

Defences

(3) It is a defence for a person ('D') charged with an offence under this section to show that—
  (a) the specified controlled drug had been prescribed or supplied to D for medical or dental purposes,
  (b) D took the drug in accordance with any directions given by the person by whom the drug was prescribed or supplied, and with any accompanying instructions (so far as consistent with any such directions) given by the manufacturer or distributor of the drug, and
  (c) D's possession of the drug immediately before taking it was not unlawful under section 5(1) of the Misuse of Drugs Act 1971 (restriction of possession of controlled drugs) because of an exemption in regulations made under section 7 of that Act (authorisation of activities otherwise unlawful under foregoing provisions).
(4) The defence in subsection (3) is not available if D's actions were—
  (a) contrary to any advice, given by the person by whom the drug was prescribed or supplied, about the amount of time that should elapse between taking the drug and driving a motor vehicle, or

(b) contrary to any accompanying instructions about that matter (so far as consistent with any such advice) given by the manufacturer or distributor of the drug.

(5) If evidence is adduced that is sufficient to raise an issue with respect to the defence in subsection (3), the court must assume that the defence is satisfied unless the prosecution proves beyond reasonable doubt that it is not.

(6) It is a defence for a person ('D') charged with an offence by virtue of subsection (1)(b) to prove that at the time D is alleged to have committed the offence the circumstances were such that there was no likelihood of D driving the vehicle whilst the proportion of the specified controlled drug in D's blood or urine remained likely to exceed the specified limit for that drug.

(7) The court may, in determining whether there was such a likelihood, disregard any injury to D and any damage to the vehicle.

Road Traffic Act 1988, s 5A

Defence notes (see also **10.10.1**)

- The burden of proof is on the defendant to show that the drug had been prescribed or supplied to them for medical or dental purposes, was taken as directed, and they complied with the accompanying instructions; but this defence is not available if their actions were contrary to the advice or instructions given.
- If there is sufficient evidence to show a valid defence under s 5A(3), then the prosecution would have to prove beyond reasonable doubt that this is not the case.
- It is a defence for a person charged with the s 5A(1)(b) offence that the circumstances were such that there was no likelihood of them driving the vehicle whilst over the specified limit for that drug. In determining whether there was any likelihood of them driving, the court may ignore any injury to them or damage to the vehicle.

Related cases (see **10.1.4**, **10.10**, and **10.11** cases)

Practical considerations

- The CPS are unlikely to take the case forward unless there is evidence of a likelihood of driving whilst under the influence of drink or drugs. Similarly, ensure that the s 5A(3)–(7) defences are considered and can be countered if raised.
- A person acting as a supervisor of a provisional licence holder is 'in charge' of the vehicle and can commit that offence under this section.
- The s 5A offence will work alongside the existing s 4 offence (see **10.10.1**) of being unfit through drink or drugs, which will continue to be used for drugs which are not specified controlled or prescribed drugs, including 'legal highs'.
- Limits are set at very low levels for the illegal drugs including cocaine, cannabis, ecstacy, and ketamine; while some legally prescribed drugs,

including diazepam and methadone, are included, as certain strong
medication can affect people's ability to drive safely.

- As s 5A sets limits for specified legal drugs, it's vital that anyone taking
prescribed medication reads the instructions carefully and keeps to
the prescribed dosage. If anyone is unsure as to whether their
medication affects their ability to drive they should obtain advice
from a doctor or pharmacist.

- The medication specified in s 5A is usually prescribed for the
following treatments: clonazepam (epilepsy); diazepam, lorazepam
(anxiety/insomnia); oxazepam (anxiety); flunitrazepam, temazepam
(insomnia); morphine (severe pain); methadone (severe pain/heroin
substitute).

- A power of entry is available for the provision of a preliminary test in
cases involving an injury accident. Reasonable force may be used to
effect entry under s 6E, or carry out a preliminary test and arrest a
person under s 6D (see **10.10.2**).

 Summary   6 months

 s 5A(1)(a) and (2) offence

6 months' imprisonment and/or a fine

Obligatory disqualification, obligatory endorsement—3 to 11
penalty points

s 5A(1)(b) and (2) offence

3 months' imprisonment and/or a level 4 fine

Discretionary disqualification, obligatory endorsement—10 penalty points

10.11.3 **Provision of specimens for analysis**

Section 7 of the Road Traffic Act 1988 relates to the offences of failing to
provide specimens for analysis and s 7A the offence of failing to give
permission to submit the blood sample for a laboratory test.

Offences

A person who, without reasonable excuse, **fails** to provide a **specimen**
when required to do so in pursuance of this section is guilty of an offence.

Road Traffic Act 1988, s 7(6)

Points to prove

✓ without reasonable excuse
✓ failed/refused to provide specimen
✓ when lawfully required to do so

Meanings

Fails (see **10.10.2**)

Specimen

Specimens taken under s 7 may consist of two specimens of breath for analysis by an approved device (alcohol) or a specimen of blood or urine for laboratory analysis (alcohol or drugs).

Explanatory notes

Specimens may be required from a person suspected of having committed an offence under—

- s 3A causing death by careless driving when under influence of drink or drugs (see **10.8.2**);
- s 4 driving, or being in charge, when under influence of drink or drugs (see **10.10.1**);
- s 5 driving or being in charge of a motor vehicle with alcohol concentration above prescribed limit (see **10.11.1**).
- s 5A driving or being in charge of a motor vehicle with specified controlled drug being over specified limit (see **10.11.2**).

Related cases

Chalupa v CPS [2009] EWHC 3082 (Admin), QBD Only in exceptional circumstances (where a solicitor is readily available) could a breath test be delayed to allow an individual to take legal advice as there is a public interest requirement that a test be undertaken promptly.

DPP v Smith The Times, 1 June 1994, QBD A defendant cannot insist that blood should be taken by their own GP.

Wade v DPP [1996] RTR 177, QBD A defendant on medication may have a medical reason for not providing a specimen of blood.

DPP v Nesbitt and Duffy [1995] 1 Cr App R 38, QBD Where a request for blood or urine is made at a hospital the required warnings must explain the procedures in full, with reasons, and state the consequences of failing to comply.

DPP v Coyle [1996] RTR 287, CA It is not necessary to wait for the intoximeter machine to 'time out' before a suspect's refusal or failure to give a sample of breath will be complete.

DPP v Garrett [1995] RTR 302, QBD Where the blood sample procedure was flawed, but the sample was not taken and used, it did not affect the request for a urine sample.

10.11.3 Provision of specimens for analysis

Hague v DPP [1997] RTR 146, QBD Breath samples were taken on an intoximeter machine. The officer believed the machine to be faulty and requested blood or urine, which was refused. The machine was examined and found to be working correctly so the readings were still admissible.

Francis v DPP [1997] RTR 113, QBD A request can be legitimately made of a mentally unstable person if they understand what is happening.

DPP v Wythe [1996] RTR 137, QBD If a medical reason is put forward by the suspect, the final decision as to whether or not blood can be taken is the doctor's.

DPP v Furby [2000] RTR 181, QBD A medical condition of which they are unaware cannot later be used as an excuse for failing to provide the required sample.

DPP v Baldwin [2000] RTR 314, QBD The purpose of the requirement to provide a specimen of urine one hour after the first specimen is to give the motorist a finite time. If this period is extended, that extension does not make any findings inadmissible.

Practical considerations

- On requiring a person to provide a specimen under this section, a constable **must** warn them that failure to provide it may render them liable to prosecution.
- A requirement for a specimen of breath can only be made at a police station, a hospital, or at or near a place where a relevant breath test has been given to the person concerned or would have been so given but for their failure to cooperate.
- The constable requiring the breath sample must be in uniform, or have imposed a requirement on the defendant to cooperate with a breath test as a result of an accident.
- Where a requirement has been imposed for a person to cooperate with a relevant breath test at any place, the constable may remain at or near there to impose a requirement under this section.
- If a requirement is made for two samples of breath for analysis by an approved device at a place other than a police station, it may revert to being made at a police station if a device or reliable device is not available there, or it is not practicable to use one there, or the constable making the previous requirement believes that the device has not produced a reliable result.
- Under this section, a requirement for a specimen of blood or urine can only be made at a police station or a hospital.
- A requirement for a sample of blood or urine can be made at a police station unless the constable requiring it believes that for medical reasons it cannot or should not be made, specimens of breath have not been provided elsewhere and an approved device is not available there, an approved device has been used but the constable believes the result to be unreliable, the constable believes, following a preliminary drugs test, that the defendant has a drug in their body or, if the offence is under s 3A, s 4 or s 5A of the Act, the constable has

been informed by a medical practitioner that the person's condition may be because of a drug.

- The above requirement may be made even if the defendant has been required to supply two specimens of breath.
- If a specimen other than breath is required, the question as to whether it is blood or urine (and, if it is blood, who will take it) will be decided by the constable making the requirement.
- If a medical or health care practitioner thinks that, for medical reasons, blood cannot or should not be taken the requirement will not be made. A urine sample may then be required instead.
- A specimen of urine must be provided within an hour of its being required and after the provision of a previous such specimen.
- In cases involving a failure to provide breath, consider retaining the mouthpiece as a possible exhibit.
- If a person is involved in a traffic accident and their medical condition prevents them from giving consent, then s 7A(1) allows taking a blood specimen from that person—providing blood could have been requested under s 7.
- If blood has been taken by a 'police medical or health care practitioner' under s 7A(1), then under s 7A(5) a constable must require the person to give permission for a laboratory test of the blood specimen taken, and warn that failure to give this permission may render them liable to prosecution under s 7A(6).
- **Section 7A(6) offence**—A person who, without reasonable excuse, fails to give his permission for a laboratory test of a specimen of blood taken from him under this section is guilty of a summary offence.

 Summary   6 months

 Driving or attempting to drive

    6 months' imprisonment and/or a fine

    Obligatory disqualification for 12 months, obligatory endorsement—3 to 11 penalty points (if special conditions apply)

In all other cases

    3 months' imprisonment and/or a level 4 fine

    Discretionary disqualification, obligatory endorsement—10 penalty points

.inks to alternative subjects and offences

10.11.3 Provision of specimens for analysis

10.12 **Pedal Cycle Offences**

Sections 28, 29, and 30 of the Road Traffic Act 1988 provide similar offences for cyclists to those contained in ss 1, 2, and 3 for motorists. Additionally, there is the offence of driving or cycling on a footpath under s 72 of the Highways Act 1835.

10.12.1 **Dangerous cycling**

Section 28 creates an offence of dangerous cycling on a road.

Offences

A person who rides a **cycle** on a **road dangerously** is guilty of an offence.

Road Traffic Act 1988, s 28(1)

Points to prove

✓ rode a cycle
✓ on a road
✓ dangerously

Meanings

Cycle

Means a bicycle, a tricycle, or a cycle having four or more wheels, not being in any case a motor vehicle.

Road (s 192) (see **10.1.1**)

Dangerously

A person is to be regarded as riding dangerously if and only if—
• the way that they ride falls far below what would be expected of a competent and careful cyclist; **and**
• it would be obvious to a competent and careful cyclist that riding in that way would be dangerous.

Explanatory notes

• The term 'danger' refers to danger either of injury to any person or of serious damage to property.
• To determine what would be obvious to a competent and careful cyclist in a particular case regard shall be had not only to the circumstances of which s/he could be expected to be aware, but also to any shown to have been within their knowledge.

10.12.2 Careless, and inconsiderate, cycling

• A person may be convicted of the alternative offence of careless, and inconsiderate, cycling (see **10.12.2**).

Practical considerations

• NIP to be issued (see **10.5**).
• This offence must be on a road—it does not extend to a public place.
• Section 168 empowers obtaining of cyclist's name and address (see **10.6.2**).
• Section 163 of the Road Traffic Act 1988 empowers a police constable in uniform to stop a cycle on a road. A person who fails to stop the cycle will be guilty of an offence (see **10.2.4**).

 Summary   6 months

 Level 4 fine

10.12.2 Careless, and inconsiderate, cycling

Section 29 creates an offence of cycling on a road without due care and attention or without reasonable consideration for other road users.

Offences

If a person rides a **cycle** on a **road** without **due care and attention**, or **without reasonable consideration** for other persons using the road, he is guilty of an offence.

Road Traffic Act 1988, s 29

Points to prove

✓ rode a cycle
✓ on a road
✓ without due care and attention/reasonable consideration for other road users

Meanings

Cycle (see 10.12.1)

Road (s 192) (see 10.1.1)

Without due care and attention

Means that their cycling falls below the level of care, skill, and attention that would have been exercised by a competent and careful cyclist.

Without reasonable consideration

Requires other persons to be inconvenienced by the defendant's cycling.

Explanatory notes

- Cycling on a road without due care and attention is a question of fact for the court to decide on the evidence as to whether or not the cycling is careless. The standard of care and attention is an objective one.
- Cycling on a road without reasonable consideration for other road users is a subjective test that has to be decided by the court on the evidence before it. The other persons using the road can include drivers or passengers in vehicles, pedestrians, or other cyclists. It can include giving a misleading signal, cutting across a car, or causing a pedestrian to stop.

Practical considerations (see 10.12.1)

 Summary   6 months

 Level 3 fine

10.12.3 Cycling when under the influence of drink or drugs

Section 30 creates an offence of cycling on a road or public place while unfit through drink or drugs.

Offences

A person who, when riding a cycle on a **road** or other **public place**, is unfit to ride through drink or drugs (that is to say, is under the influence of drink or a drug to such an extent as to be incapable of having proper control of the cycle) is guilty of an offence.

Road Traffic Act 1988, s 30(1)

Points to prove

✓ rode a cycle
✓ on a road/other public place
✓ while unfit to ride through drink/drugs

Meanings

Road (s 192) (see **10.1.1**)

Public place (see **10.1.2**)

Practical considerations

- As there is no power to require a specimen of breath, blood, or urine, other methods of calculating the extent to which the defendant is under the influence of drink or drugs need to be used.
- Section 163 of the Road Traffic Act 1988 empowers a police constable in uniform to stop a cycle on a road. A person who fails to stop the cycle will be guilty of an offence (see **10.12.1**).
- This offence does not extend to being in charge of a cycle as it would with other forms of transport.
- A bicycle or tricycle is a carriage under the Licensing Act 1872. Therefore consider the offence of being drunk in charge of a carriage on any highway or other public place under s 12 of that Act (see **7.2.2**)

 Summary   6 months

 Level 3 fine

10.12.4 **Riding or driving on the footpath**

Section 72 of the Highways Act 1835 creates an offence of wilfully ridin or driving on the footpath.

Offences

If any person shall **wilfully** ride upon any **footpath** or causeway by the side of any road, made or set apart for the use or accommodation of foot passengers; or shall wilfully lead or drive any horse, ass, sheep, mule, swine, cattle or **carriage of any description**, or any truck or sledge, upon any such footpath or causeway or tether any horse, ass, mule, swine or cattle on any highway so as to suffer or permit the tethered animal to be thereon, he shall be guilty of an offence.

Highways Act 1835, s 72

Points to prove

✓ wilfully rode/drove/led/tethered
✓ carriage of any description, truck, sledge, or animal (as described)
✓ upon a footpath/causeway
✓ by the side of a road
✓ made/set apart
✓ for the use/accommodation of foot passengers

Meanings

Wilfully

'Wilful' under this section means 'purposely'.

Footpath

A footpath is part of a highway, if it is beside a road.

Carriage of any description

This includes bicycles, tricycles, motor vehicles, and trailers.

Explanatory notes

- Section 72 applies not only to the riding of bicycles or tricycles on the footpath/causeway, but also to the riding/driving of motor vehicles/ trailers/truck/sledge and leading/tethering any animals as described.
- A Segway is a 'carriage' for the purposes of s 72 (*Coates v CPS* [2011] EWHC 2032 (Admin)).
- This offence requires proof of wilfully riding, driving a carriage or leading/tethering animals as specified.
- Proceedings may be instituted by anyone.
- Consider issuing a TFPN for driving or cycling on the footway (see **10.4.1**). A PCSO can stop a cyclist and issue a TFPN for cycling on a footway.

TFPN   PCSO

 Summary   6 months

 Level 2 fine. Discretionary disqualification, not endorsable

Links to alternative subjects and offences

FPN Traffic Fixed
Penalty Notices

PCSO Police community
support officers

10.13 Driving While Disqualified/ Cause Serious Injury

10.13.1 Obtain licence/drive on a road— while disqualified

Section 103 of the Road Traffic Act 1988 creates the offences of obtaining a driving licence while disqualified from driving and driving a motor vehicle on a road while so disqualified.

Offences

A person is guilty of an offence if, while **disqualified** for holding or obtaining a **licence**, he—
(a) obtains a licence, or
(b) **drives a motor vehicle** on a **road**.

Road Traffic Act 1988, s 103(1)

Points to prove

✓ while disqualified for holding/obtaining a licence
✓ obtained a licence/drove a motor vehicle on a road

Meanings

Disqualified

Means disqualified for holding or obtaining a licence and, where the disqualification relates only to vehicles of a particular class, a licence to drive vehicles of that particular class.

Licence (see 10.14.1)

Drives (see 10.1.4)

Motor vehicle

This is defined by s 185 (see 10.1.3).

Road (s 192) (see 10.1.1)

Explanatory notes

- An underage driver (unless disqualified by the court) should be charged with the offence of 'driving otherwise than in accordance with a licence' (see 10.14.1).

- Subsection (1)(b) does not apply to a person disqualified for obtaining a licence authorising them to drive a motor vehicle of a specific class while they hold another licence to drive that class of vehicle.
- Such a person is disqualified for obtaining such a licence, even if the licence held is suspended (s 102).
- Disqualification given in England and Wales applies to all of Great Britain, even if they hold a foreign or international driving licence or permit or service driving licence.
- A driver disqualified in a foreign country would not be guilty of this offence, but may be guilty of driving without a licence.
- Disqualification by a court is usually for a specified period as punishment for a road traffic offence.
- If penalty points imposed by the court, together with any to be taken into account on that occasion, total 12 or more (the 'totting up' system) the court must, other than in exceptional circumstances, disqualify the defendant for at least a **minimum period** (Road Traffic Offenders Act 1988, s 35).
- **Minimum period** is 6 months if no previous disqualification, one year if one such period is to be taken into account and 2 years if two or more such periods are taken into account.
- The court may order a driver to be disqualified until they pass a driving test. Such driver may not drive during the disqualification period; after this period they can only drive on a provisional licence. Thereafter, if they fail to comply with the provisional licence conditions they may be guilty of driving whilst disqualified. Disqualification will only come to an end after they have passed the driving test.

Related cases (see also **10.1.4** cases)

Pattison v DPP [2005] EWHC 2938 (Admin), QBD Prosecution must prove that the defendant was a disqualified driver. Identification of the defendant as the person convicted in court may be established by admission, fingerprints, or by a person in court at time of conviction.

DPP v Barker [2004] EWHC 2502 (Admin), QBD If a person was disqualified until they had passed a driving test, the burden of proof was on the driver to show that they had a provisional licence and were driving in accordance with the licence conditions.

Practical considerations

This offence is committed only if the defendant drives a motor vehicle of a class that is subject of the disqualification, although a disqualification by order of the court will not normally be limited to a particular class of vehicle.

A licence obtained by a disqualified person is not valid.

Proving beyond reasonable doubt that the person named on the certified court extract is the accused is an essential element of the prosecution case, although there is no prescribed way in which identity must be proved.

10.13.2 Causing serious injury by driving: disqualified driver

- Proof that the defendant knew of the disqualification is not necessary.
- A person is disqualified for holding or obtaining a licence to drive a certain class of motor vehicle if they are under the age stipulated for that class (s 101), but the offence would be contrary to s 87(1) (see **10.14.1**).
- Minimum ages for driving specified classes of motor vehicles are shown in **10.14.2**.

 Summary

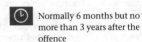 Normally 6 months but no more than 3 years after the offence

 s 103(1)(a) offence

Level 3 fine

s 103(1)(b) offence

6 months' imprisonment and/or a fine

Discretionary disqualification, obligatory endorsement—6 penalty points

10.13.2 Causing serious injury by driving: disqualified driver

Section 3ZD of the Road Traffic Act 1988 provides for the offence of causing the serious injury of another person by driving a motor vehicle on a road and at the time was disqualified from driving.

Offences

(1) A person is guilty of an offence under this section if he or she—

    (a) causes **serious injury** to **another person** by **driving** a **motor vehicle** on a **road** and,

    (b) at that time, is committing an offence under section 103(1)(b) of this Act (driving while disqualified).

Road Traffic Act 1988, s 3ZD

Points to prove

✓ caused the serious injury of another person
✓ by driving a motor vehicle
✓ on a road
✓ whilst disqualified

Meanings

Serious injury
Physical harm which amounts to grievous bodily harm (see **2.3.1**).

Another person (see **10.8.1**)

Driving (see **10.1.4**)

Motor vehicle (see **10.13**)

Road (s 192) (see **10.1.1**)

Explanatory notes

- This offence is subject to driving a motor vehicle on a road and **causing** serious injury to another person whilst disqualified from driving under s 103(1)(b) (see **10.13.1**). It has effect only in relation to driving which occurs on or after 13 April 2015.

Practical considerations

- Consider CPS driving offences charging standards.
- Consider drive disqualification offence matters (see **10.13.1**).
- This offence requires some element of fault by the driver that they caused the death of another person (*R v Hughes* [2013] UKSC 56 see **10.8.5**), not just driving a motor vehicle whilst disqualified.
- Annex A of MOJ Circular 1/2015 provides further guidance on this offence.

 Either way

 None

Summary: 6 months' imprisonment and/or a fine

Indictment: 4 years' imprisonment and/or a fine.
Obligatory disqualification until test passed
Obligatory endorsement—3 to 11 penalty points

Links to alternative subjects and offences

10.13.2 Causing serious injury by driving: disqualified driver

10.14 Driving Not in Accordance with a Driving Licence

Section 87 of the Road Traffic Act 1988 requires all people driving a motor vehicle on a road to hold a driving licence for that class of vehicle and to comply with any conditions attached to it.

10.14.1 Drive motor vehicle of a class not authorised

Offences

(1) It is an offence for a person to **drive** on a **road** a **motor vehicle** of any **class** otherwise than in accordance with a **licence** authorising him to drive a motor vehicle of that **class**.

(2) It is an offence for a person to **cause** or **permit** another person to drive on a road a motor vehicle of any class otherwise than in accordance with a **licence** authorising that other person to drive a motor vehicle of that class.

Road Traffic Act 1988, s 87

Points to prove

s 87(1) offence

✓ drove motor vehicle
✓ on a road
✓ otherwise than in accordance with licence
✓ authorising driving of that class of vehicle

s 87(2) offence

✓ caused/permitted
✓ another person to commit s 87(1) offence

Meanings

Drive (see **10.1.4**)

Road (s 192) (see **10.1.1**)

Motor vehicle (see **10.1.3**)

Class (see **10.14.2** and **Appendix 2**)

Cause

Means involving some degree of control or dominance by or some express mandate from the causer. It also requires some positive action and knowledge by the defendant (*Price v Cromack* [1975] 1 WLR 988).

10.14.1 Drive motor vehicle of a class not authorised

Permit

Is less direct or explicit than causing and involves leave or licence to do something. Permission can be express or inferred. A person cannot permit a vehicle to be used unless they are in a position to forbid and no one can permit what he cannot control.

Licence

Means a licence to drive a motor vehicle under Pt 3 of the Road Traffic Act 1988 or a **community licence**.

Community licence

Means a document issued by an EEA state (other than the UK) by authority of the EEA state authorising the holder to drive a motor vehicle.

Full licence

Means a licence other than a **provisional licence**.

Provisional licence

Means a licence issued to enable an applicant to drive motor vehicles with a view to passing a test of competence to drive.

Explanatory notes

- The holder of a convention driving permit, a domestic driving licence/permit issued by a country outside the UK, or a British Forces driving permit who is resident outside the UK may drive any class of vehicle specified in the permit or licence for 12 months.
- A person who is an EU citizen and holds a driving licence or permit issued in another EU country may drive on that licence or permit in this country in accordance with that licence or permit. They would not need to exchange the licence or permit for a UK licence no matter how long they stayed here.
- Under s 88 a person who has held a driver's licence, a community licence, a Northern Ireland licence, a British external licence, a British Forces licence, or an exchangeable licence may, in certain circumstances, still drive a relevant vehicle even if the licence and its counterpart have been surrendered or revoked. This includes where a qualifying application has been received at DVLA or their licence to drive that class of vehicle and its counterpart has been revoked, or surrendered for renewal, it was granted in or contains an error, or for amendment of a requirement or the holder's name and address.

Practical considerations

- Where a person is charged with driving without a licence, the burden of proving that they have a licence is with that person (*John v Humphreys* [1955] 1 All ER 793, QBD).
- The police have powers to seize and remove a motor vehicle if the driver has no driving licence or there is no insurance in force for the vehicle (see **10.16.6**).

- It is an offence for a person not to produce their driving licence (see **10.16.4**).
- A TFPN can be issued for the s 87(1) offence (see **10.4**).
- This offence includes circumstances where the driver is driving under age.
- The classes of vehicles which a licence holder is authorised by it to drive are stated on the licence itself.
- A licence is valid only when it is used in accordance with its conditions of use.

 Summary   6 months

 s 87(1) offence

Level 3 fine. Discretionary disqualification, obligatory endorsement—3 to 8 penalty points

s 87(2) offence

Level 3 fine
Obligatory endorsement—minimum 3 penalty points

10.14.2 **Minimum ages for holding/ obtaining driving licences**

Section 101 of the Road Traffic Act 1988 provides that a person is disqualified from holding or obtaining a licence to drive a motor vehicle of a class specified if he is under the age specified. The class of motor vehicle and minimum ages are as follows—

- Invalid carriage—16 years.
- Moped—16 years.
- Motor bicycle—17 years.
  - ✦ Where the motor bicycle is a large motor bicycle that age becomes 21 years (see **Appendix 2**), unless it is used for military purposes.
- Agricultural or forestry tractor—17 years.
  - ✦ However, that age will be 16 years, if it is a wheeled tractor (not tracked) and is not more than 2.45 metres wide or has a trailer which is either 2-wheeled or close-coupled 4-wheeled (maximum 840mm gap) and both have a maximum width of 2.45 metres **and** the person has passed, is going to, taking or returning from a test for a category F vehicle.
- Small vehicles (cars)—17 years.
  - ✦ This age may become 16 years if driven by a person in receipt of the higher rate component of the disability living allowance without a trailer.

10.14.2 Minimum ages for holding/obtaining driving licences

- Medium-sized goods vehicles—18 years, except—
  - where vehicle is towing a trailer and the maximum authorised mass of the combination exceeds 7.5 tonnes that age will be 21 years; or
  - if the vehicle is being used for military purposes the minimum age will be 17 years.
- Other motor vehicles—21 years.

This age will be 18 years for—

- a vehicle which carries over 8 passengers if the driver holds a full licence for that category **and** is carrying passengers on a regular 50 kilometre route or driving a vehicle in category D1;
- a passenger-carrying vehicle if the driver has a provisional licence for that category and there are no passengers;
- a vehicle which is a category D1 vehicle AND is an ambulance;
- a vehicle in category *C1 + E* with a maximum mass not exceeding 7.5 tonnes;
- a person who is part of a training scheme for large goods vehicle drivers either with their employer or an authorised school.

This age will be 17 years if—

- the vehicle is being used for military purposes or the vehicle is a road roller propelled otherwise than by steam, has no wheel fitted with pneumatic, soft, or elastic tyres, does not exceed 11.69 tonnes unladen, and only carries tools and equipment for its own use.

Explanatory notes

- If a person under the minimum age for driving a particular class of motor vehicle drives that vehicle without such a licence he commits the offence of driving without a licence for that class under s 87(1) (see **10.14.1**).
- The Motor Vehicles (Driving Licences) (Amendment) Regulations 2012 (SI 977/2012) amended the principal 1999 Regulations, in particular regarding driving mopeds and motorcycles, these came into effect from 19th January 2013.
- **Appendix 2** contains two tables and provides further information on—
  - comparing old groups/class with new categories;
  - vehicle categories and minimum driving age.

Links to alternative subjects and offences

10.15 Drive with Defective Eyesight

Section 96 of the Road Traffic Act 1988 creates an offence of driving with defective eyesight.

Offences

Drive with uncorrected defective eyesight

(1) If a person **drives** a **motor vehicle** on a **road** while his eyesight is such (whether through a defect which cannot be or one which is not for the time being sufficiently corrected) that he cannot comply with any **requirement** as to **eyesight prescribed** under this Part of this Act for the purposes of tests of competence to drive, he is guilty of an offence.

Refuse to submit to eyesight test

(2) A constable having reason to suspect that a person driving a motor vehicle may be guilty of an offence under subsection (1) above may require him to submit to a test for the purpose of ascertaining whether, using no other means of correction than he used at the time of driving, he can comply with the requirement concerned.

(3) If that person refuses to submit to the test he is guilty of an offence.

Road Traffic Act 1988, s 96

Points to prove

s 96(1) offence

✓ drove a motor vehicle
✓ on a road
✓ while unable to meet eyesight requirements

s 96(3) offence

✓ being the driver of a motor vehicle
✓ on a road
✓ and being required to take eyesight test
✓ by a constable under s 96(2)
✓ refused to take such test

Meanings

Drives (see **10.1.4**)

Motor vehicle (see **10.1.3**)

Road (s 192) (see **10.1.1**)

10.15 Drive with Defective Eyesight

Explanatory notes

- This section creates two offences—
  + driving with defective eyesight;
  + refusing to submit to an eyesight test.
- The **requirement** as to **eyesight prescribed** can be found in reg 72 of the Motor Vehicles (Driving Licences) Regulations 1999. This requires a person to be able to read, in good light (with visual aids if used) a number plate on a vehicle containing characters of the **prescribed size**.
- **Prescribed size** means characters which are 79 mm high and 50 mm wide.
- The distance from which the number plate should be read is 20 metres, but for a category K vehicle (eg mowing machine and pedestrian-controlled vehicle) it is 12 metres.
- Spectacles or contact lenses may be used for the test if they were wearing them while driving.
- For the purposes of this offence it does not matter whether the defect is one that can be corrected or not. The important matter is the state of their eyesight at the time they were driving.
- Knowledge of the defect by the defendant is not necessary, although this may be used in mitigation if the defendant has suffered a gradual and unnoticed deterioration in their eyesight.
- However, under s 92(1) any person holding or applying for a licence has a duty to inform the DVLA of any prescribed disability likely to cause the driving of a vehicle by them in accordance with the licence to be a source of danger to the public. This includes a 'prospective' disability such as a condition that does not at the time amount to a relevant disability, but which is likely to deteriorate to that level in the course of time.

Practical considerations

- The degree by which the defendant's eyesight fails to meet the requirement is particularly relevant as this will reflect the degree of risk taken or danger created by them.
- The more severe the defect the more difficult it will be for the defendant to mitigate the offence.
- An inability to read the characters in the test will amount to a prescribed disability and the person will have to inform the DVLA under s 92(1).

 Summary   6 months

 Level 3 fine
Discretionary disqualification, obligatory endorsement—3 penalty points

Links to alternative subjects and offences

10.16 **Vehicle Document Offences and Seizure of Vehicles**

10.16.1 **No insurance (use, cause, or permit)**

Section 143 of the Road Traffic Act 1988 requires the user of a motor vehicle to be insured or secured against third party risks.

Offences

(1) Subject to the provisions of this Part of this Act—
   (a) a person must not **use a motor vehicle** on a **road** or other **public place** unless there is in force in relation to the use of the vehicle by that person such a **policy of insurance** or such a **security** in respect of third party risks as complies with the requirements of this Part of this Act, and
   (b) a person must not **cause** or **permit** any other person to use a motor vehicle on a road or other public place unless there is in force in relation to the use of the vehicle by that other person such a policy of insurance or such a security in respect of third party risks as complies with the requirements of this Part of this Act.
(2) If a person acts in contravention of subsection (1) above he is guilty of an offence.

Road Traffic Act 1988, s 143

Points to prove

✓ used/caused/permitted another to use
✓ motor vehicle
✓ on a road/public place
✓ without insurance/security for third party risks

Meanings

Use

Means the driver of a vehicle, the driver's employer while it is being used for their business, the vehicle owner if they are in it while somebody else is driving it, or the steersman of a broken down vehicle which is being towed.

Motor vehicle (see **10.1.3**)

Road (s 192) (see **10.1.1**)

Public place (see **10.1.2**)

Policy of insurance

This includes a cover note.

Security

This section does not apply to a vehicle owned by a person who has deposited and keeps deposited with the Accountant General of the Senior Courts the sum of £500,000, at a time when the vehicle is being driven under the owner's control.

Cause (see **10.14.1**)

Permit (see **10.14.1**)

Explanatory notes

- This section does not apply to invalid carriages.
- Section 144 states that s 143 does not apply to—
  - a vehicle owned by: a county or county district council, Broads Authority, City of London Common/Borough Council, National Park Authority, Inner London Education Authority, London Fire and Emergency Planning Authority, joint (local government) waste authorities, or a joint authority, or a joint board or committee which includes member representatives of such council—at a time when the vehicle is being driven under the owner's control;
  - a vehicle owned by a local policing body when it is being driven under the owner's control or a vehicle being driven for police purposes by or under the direction of a constable, by civilian staff of a police force or member of staff of the police and crime commissioner's/Mayor's office (within the meaning of Part 1 of the Police Reform and Social Responsibility Act 2011);
  - a vehicle being driven to or from a place for the purposes of salvage under the Merchant Shipping Act 1995;
  - a vehicle owned by a health service body, or Local Health Board—at a time when the vehicle is being driven under the owner's control;
  - an ambulance owned by an NHS Trust or Foundation Trust at a time when the vehicle is being driven under the owner's control;
  - a vehicle made available to a person, body, or local authority under s 12 or s 80 of the National Health Service Act 2006 (s 10 or s 38 of the National Health Service (Wales) Act 2006) while being used in accordance with the terms under which it was made available;
  - a vehicle owned by the Care Quality Commission, at a time when the vehicle is being driven under the owner's control.
- Section 144(2)(b), on its plain and ordinary meaning, exempts a police officer on duty using his own vehicle for police purposes, from the requirement for third party insurance (*Jones v Chief Constable of Bedfordshire* [1987] RTR 332).

10.16.1 No insurance (use, cause, or permit)

Defences

A person charged with using a motor vehicle in contravention of this section shall not be convicted if he proves—

(a) that the vehicle did not belong to him and was not in his possession under a contract of hiring or of loan,

(b) that he was using the vehicle in the course of his employment, and

(c) that he neither knew nor had reason to believe that there was not in force in relation to the vehicle such a policy of insurance or security as is mentioned in subsection (1) above.

Road Traffic Act 1988, s 143(3)

Related cases

Plumbien v Vines [1996] Crim LR 124, QBD A vehicle left on a road for several months such that it could not be moved, is still at the disposal of the owner and so requires insurance.

Dodson v Peter H Dodson Insurance Services [2001] 1 WLR 1012, CA In the absence of a condition in the policy of insurance making it clear that the policyholder would only be covered while they were the owner of the relevant vehicle, the policy is valid until expiry.

DPP v Hay [2005] EWHC 1395 (Admin), QBD It is for the defendant to show that there was in force a policy of insurance, once it has been proved that they used the motor vehicle on a road or public place.

Practical considerations

- Read the conditions on the insurance very carefully as they may, for example cover a person who is not a current driving licence holder. Similarly, a valid insurance certificate may not cover that person for the vehicle being used or for that particular purpose.
- A TFPN for the s 143(1)(a) 'using' offence can be issued (see **10.4**).
- The policy must be issued by an authorised insurer (eg a member of the Motor Insurers' Bureau).
- It is an offence to fail to produce insurance (see **10.16.5**).
- The motor vehicle can be seized if no insurance is in force for the vehicle (see **10.16.6**).

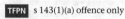 **TFPN** s 143(1)(a) offence only

 Summary

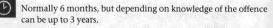 Normally 6 months, but depending on knowledge of the offence can be up to 3 years.

Fine

Discretionary disqualification, obligatory endorsement—6 to 8 penalty points

10.16.2 **No insurance (registered keeper)**

Section 144A makes it an offence to keep a registered vehicle which is not insured or secured against third party risks.

> **Offences**
>
> If a **motor vehicle registered** under the Vehicle Excise and Registration Act 1994 does not meet the **insurance requirements,** the person in whose name the vehicle is registered is guilty of an offence.
>
> Road Traffic Act 1988, s 144A(1)

> **Points to prove**
>
> ✓ person in whose name a motor vehicle is registered
> ✓ failed to ensure
> ✓ insurance requirements met for vehicle

Meanings

Motor vehicle (see **10.1.3**)

Registered

Means a vehicle registered with the Secretary of State under s 21 of the Vehicle Excise and Registration Act 1994.

Insurance requirements

A vehicle meets the insurance requirements if—

- Covered by a **policy of insurance** or **security** in respect of third party risks as complies with the requirements of Pt 6 of this Act **and**
- **Either** of the following **conditions** is satisfied.
  - **First condition** is that the policy or certificate of insurance or security identifies the vehicle by its registration mark as a vehicle covered by the policy or security.
  - **Second condition** is that the vehicle is covered by the policy or security, which covers any vehicle, or vehicle of a particular description; the owner being named in that policy or certificate of insurance or security, and the vehicle is owned by that person.

Policy of insurance (see **10.16.1**)

Security (see **10.16.1**)

10.16.2 No insurance (registered keeper)

Explanatory notes

- For the purposes of this section a vehicle is covered by a policy of insurance or security if the policy of insurance or security is in force in relation to the use of the vehicle.
- Section 144B provides exceptions for either the registered keeper or owner of the vehicle regarding the s 144A offence under the following conditions—
  - owns vehicle and a security is in force or most of the exceptions to s 144 apply (see **10.16.1 'Explanatory notes'**);
  - owns vehicle with the intention that it should be used for the purposes of salvage under the Merchant Shipping Act 1995 or for NHS or social care purposes;
  - not keeping vehicle, required details provided;
  - keeping vehicle, but not used on a road/public place, required details provided;
  - vehicle stolen before relevant time, not recovered, and theft reported as required;
  - keeping vehicle, no VEL in force on or since 31 January 1998 and not used or kept on a road after that date.

Practical considerations

- The Motor Vehicles (Insurance Requirements) (Immobilisation, Removal and Disposal) Regulations 2011 (SI 1120/2011) provide for the immobilisation and/or removal of uninsured vehicles found stationary on roads and other public places.
- Sections 144A to 144D of this Act give DVLA and the MIB, who administer the Motor Insurance Database, powers to deal with registered keepers of vehicles that are taxed but not insured, through the introduction of Continuous Insurance Enforcement (CIE).
- Where a vehicle is taxed, but uninsured, the MIB will issue an 'Insurance Advisory Letter' to the registered keeper advising them as follows—
  - If not insured, insure immediately.
  - If insured, contact insurance provider immediately to check that the Motor Insurance Database has been correctly updated.
  - Send a SORN to DVLA so the vehicle is not included in CIE.
  - If they no longer have the vehicle, notify DVLA in writing.
- If the keeper fails to act and the vehicle remains taxed but not insured, DVLA will issue a £100 Fixed Penalty Notice to the keeper (reduced to £50 if paid in 21 days).
- These sections only apply to GB (vehicles registered in Northern Ireland, Channel Islands, and Isle of Man are excluded as they have their own registration authorities).

 Summary   6 months

 Level 3 fine

10.16.3 **No test certificate**

Section 47 creates an offence relating to motor vehicles over three years old being on a road without a valid test certificate in force, and s 53 creates a similar offence for goods vehicles over 12 months old.

Offences

Motor vehicle

A person who **uses** on a **road** at any time, or **causes** or **permits** to be so used, a **motor vehicle** to which **this section applies**, and as respects which no test certificate has been issued within the **appropriate period** before that time, is guilty of an offence.

Road Traffic Act 1988, s 47(1)

Goods vehicle

If any person at any time on or after the relevant date—
(a) uses on a road a **goods vehicle** of a class required by regulations under s 49 to have been submitted for a goods vehicle test, or
(b) causes or permits to be used on a road a goods vehicle of such a class, and at that time there is no goods vehicle test certificate in force for the vehicle, he is guilty of an offence.

Road Traffic Act 1988, s 53(2)

Points to prove

s 47(1) offence

✓ used/caused to use/permitted to use
✓ a motor vehicle to which s 47 applies
✓ on a road
✓ without a valid test certificate

s 53(2) offence

✓ used/caused to use/permitted to use
✓ a goods vehicle as specified by regulations under s 49
✓ on a road
✓ without a valid goods vehicle test certificate

Meanings

Uses (see **10.16.1**)

Road (see **10.1.1**)

Causes (see **10.14.1**)

Permits (see **10.14.1**)

10.16.3 No test certificate

Motor vehicles to which section 47 applies

Motor vehicles (see **10.1.3**) (not being goods vehicles) which have been registered under the Vehicles Excise and Registration Act 1994 for not less than three years or were manufactured at least three years ago and have been used on roads (whether in GB or elsewhere) before being so registered.

Appropriate period

Means a period of 12 months or shorter as may be prescribed.

Related cases

Plumbien v Vines [1996] Crim LR 124, QBD A vehicle left on a road for several months in such condition that it could not be moved, is still at the disposal of the owner and still requires a test certificate for its use.

Explanatory notes

Motor vehicles

- Types of motor vehicles to which s 47 applies are—
  + passenger vehicles with not more 8 seats (excluding the driver's seat);
  + rigid goods motor cars—unladen weight does not exceed 1525 kg;
  + dual-purpose vehicles, motor cycles (including 3 wheelers, mopeds), and motor caravans.

These vehicles (unless exempt) must obtain a test certificate annually, after the first test certificate.

- Similarly a motor vehicle used to carry passengers and having more than 8 seats excluding the driver's seat, a taxi licensed to ply for hire or an **ambulance**, is required to be submitted for an annual test from the first anniversary of its registration or manufacture.
- 'Ambulance' means a motor vehicle that is constructed or adapted, and primarily used, for the carriage of persons to a place where they will receive, or from a place where they have received, medical or dental treatment, and which, by reason of design, marking, or equipment is readily identifiable as a vehicle so constructed or adapted.

Goods vehicles

- Heavy motor cars, motor cars constructed or adapted to form part of an articulated vehicle, other heavy motor cars that exceed 3500 kg design weight, semi-trailers, converter dollies manufactured on or after 1.1.1979 and trailers exceeding 1020 kg unladen weight **all require a goods vehicle test certificate.**
- All vehicles requiring a goods vehicle test certificate must be submitted for their first test, in the case of a motor vehicle, before the last day of the calendar month in which falls the first anniversary of its date of registration, and in relation to trailers, before the last day of the calendar month in which falls the first anniversary of the date on which it was first sold or supplied by retail.

Practical considerations

• Vehicles exempted from a s 47 test certificate are vehicles—
  ✦ being driven to a pre-arranged test;
  ✦ being tested by an authorised examiner;
  ✦ where a test certificate is refused, vehicles:
    ▪ being driven from the test;
    ▪ being delivered by pre-arranged delivery to or from a place where work is to be or has been done to remedy the defects;
    ▪ delivering or towing to a place to be scrapped;
  ✦ being removed under a statutory power;
  ✦ being tested by a motor trader under a trade licence;
  ✦ that are imported and which are being driven from entry port to the owner's residence;
  ✦ detained/seized by police and HMRC;
  ✦ exempt from testing by order under s 44 (see below).
• Vehicles exempted by s 44 are described in reg 6(1) of the Motor Vehicles (Tests) Regulations 1981, being vehicles that are: temporarily in GB (not exceeding 12 months); manufactured before 1 January 1960; proceeding to a port for export; used on a public road only to travel between land in occupation of the vehicle keeper n/e aggregate of 6 miles per calendar week; provided for police purposes by a police authority and maintained in approved workshops; provided for NCA; heavy locomotive; light locomotive; motor tractor; track laying vehicle; goods vehicle exceeding 3500 kg design gross weight (subject to goods vehicle testing); articulated vehicle not being an articulated bus; works truck; pedestrian-controlled vehicle; invalid carriage n/e 306 kg u/w (510kg u/w if supplied by NHS), visiting forces' or imported Armed Forces' vehicles; current Northern Ireland test certificate; electrically propelled goods vehicle n/e 3500 kg design gross weight; licensed hackney carriage or private hire car which undergo testing by the local authority; agricultural motor vehicle; street cleansing, refuse, and gully cleaning vehicle constructed and not merely adapted being either—3-wheeled vehicle, or maximum design speed of 20 mph or inside track width less than 810 mm; tramcar and trolley vehicles.
• Vehicles exempt from goods vehicle testing are given in Sch 2 to the Goods Vehicle (Plating and Testing) Regulations 1988. Nearly 40 categories of vehicles are listed and in some instances they are similar to those given in s 44 exemptions list—above.
• It is an offence to fail to produce (if required) the test certificate, plating certificate, or goods vehicle test certificate (see **10.16.5**).
• The date of manufacture is taken to be the last day of the year in which its final assembly is completed.
• Consider issuing a TFPN for a motor vehicle s 47 offence (see **10.4**).
• A TFPN **cannot** be issued for a goods vehicle s 53 offence.
• Authorised examiners may carry out roadside tests on vehicles under s 67 (see **10.2.3**).
• Under s 68(4) a vehicle examiner or police officer in uniform, may direct a goods vehicle or PSV to proceed to a suitable place for inspection, provided it is within 5 miles from where the requirement

10.16.4 Fail to produce driving licence

has been made. It is a summary offence to obstruct the examiner under s 68(3) or refuse/fail to comply with request under s 68(5).

 TFPN s 47(1) offence

 Summary   6 months

 s 47(1) offence

Level 3 fine. Level 4 if vehicle adapted to carry more than 8 passengers

s 53(2) offence

Level 4 fine

10.16.4 Fail to produce driving licence

Section 164 empowers a constable or vehicle examiner to require production of a driving licence and a certificate of completion of a motorcycle course.

Offences

If a person **required** under the preceding provisions of this section to **produce** a licence or **state his date of birth** or to produce his certificate of completion of a training course for motorcyclists fails to do so he is, subject to subsections (7) to (8A) *[defences]*, guilty of an offence.

Road Traffic Act 1988, s 164(6)

Points to prove

✓ when required by a constable/vehicle examiner
✓ failed to state date of birth or produce driving licence, motorcycle training certificate

Meanings

Required to produce (s 164(1))

Any of the following persons—
(a) driving a motor vehicle on a road,
(b) whom a police constable or vehicle examiner has reasonable cause to believe to have been the driver of a motor vehicle at a time when an accident occurred owing to its presence on a road,

(c) whom a constable or vehicle examiner has reasonable cause to believe to have committed an offence in relation to the use of a motor vehicle on a road, or

(d) a person—

   (i) who supervises the holder of a **provisional licence** while the holder is driving a motor vehicle on a road, or

   (ii) whom a constable or vehicle examiner has reasonable cause to believe was supervising the holder of a provisional licence while driving, at a time when an accident occurred owing to the presence of the vehicle on a road or at a time when an offence is suspected of having been committed by the holder of the provisional licence in relation to the use of the vehicle on a road,

must, on being so required by a constable or vehicle examiner, produce his licence for examination, so as to enable the constable or vehicle examiner to ascertain the name and address of the holder of the licence, the date of issue, and the authority by which they were issued.

State date of birth (s 164(2))

A person required by a constable under s 164(1) to produce their licence must in **prescribed circumstances**, on being required by the constable, state his date of birth.

Prescribed circumstances

The circumstances in which a constable may require a person's date of birth are given in reg 83(1) of the Motor Vehicles (Driving Licences) Regulations 1999. Where the person—

- fails to produce their licence for immediate examination;
- produces a licence which the constable suspects was not granted to that person, was granted to them in error, or contains an alteration in particulars entered on the licence made with intent to deceive or where the driver number has been altered, removed, or defaced; or
- is a supervisor under s 164(1)(d) and the constable suspects they are under 21 years of age.

Provisional licence (see 10.14)

Explanatory notes

Other preceding provisions for fail to produce offences under s 164(6) are—

- s 164(3): where a licence has been revoked by the Secretary of State, a constable may require its production, and, if it is produced, may seize it and deliver it to the Secretary of State;
- s 164(4): if a constable reasonably believes that a licence holder, or any other person, has knowingly made a false statement to obtain a licence he may require the holder to produce it to them;
- s 164(4A): where a provisional licence is produced by a motorcyclist and a constable reasonably believes that the holder was not riding it as part of an approved training course, the constable may require production of his certificate of completion of a training course for motorcyclists;

10.16.4 Fail to produce driving licence

- s 164(5): if a person has been required to produce his licence to a court and fails to do so, a constable may require him to produce it and, when it is produced, may seize it and deliver to the court.

Defences

(7) Subsection (6) [*offences*] above does not apply where a person required on any occasion under the proceeding provisions of this section to produce a licence—
  - (a) produces on that occasion a current receipt for the licence issued under section 56 of the Road Traffic Offenders Act 1988 and, if required to do so, produces the licence in person immediately on its return at a police station that was specified on that occasion, or
  - (b) within 7 days after that occasion produces such a receipt in person at a police station that was specified by him on that occasion and, if required to do so, produces the licence in person immediately on its return at a police station.

(8) In proceedings against any person for the offence of failing to produce a licence it shall be a defence for him to show that—
  - (a) within 7 days after the production of his licence was required he produced it in person at a police station that was specified by him at the time its production was required, or
  - (b) he produced it in person there as soon as was reasonably practicable, or
  - (c) it was not reasonably practicable for him to produce it there before the day on which the proceedings were commenced.

(8A) Subsection (8) above shall apply in relation to a certificate of completion of a training course for motorcyclists as it applies in relation to a licence.

Road Traffic Act 1988, s 164

Practical considerations

- As from 8 June 2015 the driving licence paper counterpart will no longer be issued with driving licences. Endorsements will no longer be entered onto counterparts, as they will be entered onto a person's electronic driving record, maintained by the DVLA. GB licence holders will no longer be required to retain or produce the paper counterpart.
- In certain circumstances reference to a constable includes reference to a TW.

 Summary   ⏱ 6 months

 Level 3 fine

10.16.5 **Fail to provide details or produce vehicle documents**

Section 165 empowers a constable or vehicle examiner to require production of insurance and vehicle test documents.

Requirements

Any of the following persons—

(a) driving a motor vehicle (other than an invalid carriage) on a road, or

(b) whom a constable or vehicle examiner has reasonable cause to believe to have been the driver of a motor vehicle (other than an invalid carriage) at a time when an accident occurred owing to its presence on a road or other public place, or

(c) whom a constable or vehicle examiner has reasonable cause to believe to have committed an offence in relation to the use on a road of a motor vehicle (other than an invalid carriage),

must, on being so required by a constable or vehicle examiner, give his name and address and the name and address of the **owner** of the vehicle and produce the following **documents** for examination.

Road Traffic Act 1988, s 165(1)

Offences

Subject to subsection (4) *[defences]*, a person who fails to comply with a requirement under subsection (1) is guilty of an offence.

Road Traffic Act 1988, s 165(3)

Points to prove

✓ being a person falling under s 165(1)

✓ failed when required by a constable/vehicle examiner

✓ to give name and address or name and address of vehicle owner **and/or**

✓ produce for inspection a test certificate or goods vehicle test certificate or certificate of insurance, or certificate of security

Meanings

Owner

In relation to a vehicle which is the subject of a hiring agreement this includes each party to the agreement.

Documents (s 165(2))

The documents specified in subsection (1) are—

10.16.5 Fail to provide details or produce vehicle documents

- a relevant certificate of insurance or certificate of security;
- a test certificate required by s 47; and
- a plating certificate or goods vehicle test certificate required by s 53.

Explanatory notes

- Under s 165(5) a supervisor of a provisional licence holder must, on being required by a constable/vehicle examiner, give their name and address, and the name and address of the owner of the vehicle.
- This supervisor's requirement applies when the provisional driver was driving a motor vehicle (except invalid carriage) on a road; or whom a constable/vehicle examiner believes was supervising when an accident occurred owing to presence of that vehicle on a road or suspecting that the provisional licence holder committed an offence by using the vehicle on a road.
- If the supervisor fails to comply with the name and address requirements, then under s 165(6) they will commit an offence.

Defences

A person shall not be convicted of an offence under subsection (3) by reason only of failure to produce any certificate or other evidence in proceedings against him for the offence if he shows that—
(a) within 7 days after the date on which the production of the certificate or other evidence was required it was produced at a police station that was specified by him at the time when its production was required, or
(b) it was produced there as soon as was reasonably practicable, or
(c) it was not reasonably practicable for it to be produced there before the day on which the proceedings were commenced,
and for the purposes of this subsection the laying of the information shall be treated as the commencement of the proceedings.

Road Traffic Act 1988, s 165(4)

Practical considerations

- In the above defence, the question of whether a defendant produced documents 'as soon as was reasonably practicable' will be a question of fact for the court to decide in each case.
- Reference to a constable includes, in certain circumstances, a TW.

 Summary   6 months

Level 3 fine

10.16.6 Seize and remove motor vehicle (no insurance/driving licence)

Section 165A empowers a constable to seize and remove a motor vehicle, which they believe is being used without a driving licence or insurance.

Powers

Seizure conditions

Under s 165A a constable may seize a motor vehicle under this section if any of the following sections apply—

- s 164, by a constable in uniform to produce their licence for examination (see **10.16.3**), a person fails to do so, and the constable reasonably believes that they are or were driving without a licence (see **10.14**);
- s 165, by a constable in uniform to produce evidence of insurance, a person fails to do so (see **10.16.4**), and the constable reasonably believes that the vehicle was being driven without such insurance (see **10.16.1**);
- s 163, by a constable in uniform to stop a vehicle, the driver fails to do so (see **10.2.4**), or fails to do so long enough for the constable to make appropriate enquiries, and the constable reasonably believes that they are or were driving without a licence or insurance.

Removal

The Road Traffic Act 1988 (Retention and Disposal of Seized Motor Vehicles) Regulations 2005, made under s 165B, specifically provide for the retention, safe keeping, and disposal by the police or persons authorised by them, of vehicles seized under s 165A.

Explanatory notes

- Before seizing the motor vehicle the driver or person appearing to be the driver must be warned of the consequences of failure to immediately produce their driving licence, or provide evidence of insurance, unless circumstances make it impracticable to give the warning.
- If the vehicle fails to stop or drives off, and cannot be seized immediately, it may be seized at any time within 24 hours of the original incident.
- In order to seize the vehicle a constable may enter any premises (except a private **dwelling house**) on which they reasonably believe the vehicle to be. If necessary, reasonable force may be used in the exercise of this power.
- A **dwelling house** does not include a garage or other structure occupied with the dwelling house or land belonging to it.

Related cases

Pryor v CC of Greater Manchester Police [2011] EWCA Civ 749, CA P lent his recently acquired motor vehicle to B with written authority and B was stopped by the police. Although B's insurance policy allowed him to drive a car not owned by him (with consent of the owner), the police still seized the car under s 165A for no insurance, as PNC showed no current keeper and no insurance in force. P was awarded damages for wrongful interference with his car, as the police had failed to establish grounds for seizure.

Practical considerations

- In this section motor vehicle does not include an invalid carriage.
- A constable must be in uniform and may use reasonable force, if necessary, to exercise these powers.
- The police are under a duty to ensure the retention and safe keeping of a seized vehicle until it is released to the owner or otherwise disposed of under the 2005 Regulations (see '**Removal**' above).
- Regulation 4 of the 2005 Regulations states that when the vehicle is seized, a seizure notice shall be given to the driver of the seized vehicle, unless the circumstances make it impracticable to do so. It also gives the procedure to follow in respect of seized vehicles.
- Where practicable a seizure notice must be given to the registered keeper and the owner.

Links to alternative subjects and offences

10.17 **Seat Belts**

Section 14 of the Road Traffic Act 1988 relates to the wearing of seat belts in motor vehicles by adults and s 15 by children.

10.17.1 **Seat belts—adults**

Section 14 empowers the Secretary of State to make regulations concerning the wearing of seat belts in motor vehicles by adults, and creates an offence of failing to comply with such regulations.

Offences

A person who **drives** or rides in a **motor vehicle** in contravention of **regulations** under this section is guilty of an offence; but notwithstanding any enactment or rule of law, no person other than the person actually committing the contravention is guilty of an offence by reason of the contravention.

Road Traffic Act 1988, s 14(3)

Points to prove

✓ drove/rode in a motor vehicle
✓ contravened regulations made under s 14

Meanings

Drives (see **10.1.4**)

Motor vehicle

Defined by s 185 (see **10.1.3**), **but** for s 14 or s 15(1) **does not include** a motorcycle (with or without a sidecar).

Regulations

(1) Subject to the following provisions of these regulations, every person—
    (a) driving a motor vehicle; or
    (b) riding in a front or rear seat of a motor vehicle;
    shall wear an adult belt.

(2) Paragraph (1) **does not apply** to a person under the age of 14 years.
    Motor Vehicles (Wearing of Seat Belts) Regulations 1993, reg 5

Exemptions

Regulation 6 of the above regulations gives exemptions to reg 5 requirements—
• person holding a medical certificate;

10.17.1 Seat belts—adults

- driver/passenger in a motor vehicle constructed or adapted for carrying goods, being on a journey which does not exceed 50 metres used for delivery or collection;
- driver of a vehicle performing a manoeuvre including reversing;
- qualified driver supervising provisional licence holder who is performing a manoeuvre including reversing;
- driving test examiner conducting a test of competence to drive and wearing a seat belt would endanger the examiner or any other person;
- person driving or riding in a vehicle being used for fire and rescue authority, police, or NCA purposes or for carrying a person in lawful custody;
- person riding in a motor ambulance while they are providing medical attention or treatment to a patient which cannot be delayed;
- driver of a licensed taxi used for seeking hire, or answering a call for hire, or carrying a passenger for hire, or driver of a private hire vehicle used to carry a passenger for hire;
- person riding in a vehicle, used on trade plates to investigate or remedy a fault in the vehicle;
- disabled person wearing a disabled person's belt;
- person riding in a vehicle taking part in a procession organised by or on behalf of the Crown;
- person driving a vehicle if the driver's seat is not provided with an adult belt;
- person riding in the front/rear of a vehicle if no adult belt is available for them;
- person riding in a small or large bus which is—
  - ◆ being used to provide a local service in a built-up area; or
  - ◆ constructed or adapted for the carriage of standing passengers and on which the operator permits standing.

Explanatory notes

- Regulation 47(1) of the Road Vehicles (Construction and Use) Regulations 1986 stipulates that seatbelts are required to be fitted to a motor vehicle to which reg 46 applies—seat belt anchorage points to be fitted to motor vehicles.
- Regulation 46 applies to a motor vehicle, which is not an **excepted vehicle** and is a—
  - ◆ bus first used on or after 1 April 1982;
  - ◆ wheeled motor car first used on or after 1 January 1965;
  - ◆ 3-wheeled motorcycle having an u/w exceeding 255 kg, first used on or after 1 September 1970; or
  - ◆ heavy motor car first used on or after 1 October 1988.
- **Excepted vehicles** are listed in reg 46(2) being a: goods vehicle (except a dual-purpose vehicle) being first used before 1 April 1967 or 1 April 1980–1 October 1988 (exceeding 3500 kg max gross wt) or u/w exceeding 1525 kg before 1 April 1980 (but if manufactured before 1 October 1979 then first used before 1 April 1982); motor tractor; works truck; goods vehicle (electrically propelled—first used before 1 October 1988); pedestrian controlled vehicle; vehicle used on roads outside GB (being driven from port of entry place of residence of owner or driver, or

to pre-arranged place for fitting of anchorage points and seat belts as required by regs 46 and 47); vehicle having max speed n/e 16 mph; locomotive or agricultural motor vehicle.

- The holder of a medical certificate cannot rely on the reg 5 exception unless they produce the certificate to the constable at the time of being reported for summons, or produce it within 7 days or as soon as practicable after being reported at a police station specified by them, or where it is not so produced it is not reasonably practicable to produce it there before the commencement of proceedings.

Practical considerations

- Consider issuing a TFPN for this offence (see **10.4**).
- Each passenger is responsible for wearing a seatbelt and liable for the s 14(3) offence, except passengers under the age of 14 years (see **10.17.2**) where the responsibility is then with the driver.
- Regulation 5 above does not apply where there is no adult seat belt available in that part of the vehicle.

 Summary 6 months

 Level 2 fine

10.17.2 **Seat belts—children**

Section 15 creates offences concerning the wearing of seat belts by children in motor vehicles.

Offences

Seated in front

(1) Except as provided by **regulations**, where a child under the age of 14 years is in the front of a **motor vehicle**, a person must not without reasonable excuse drive the vehicle on **a road** unless the child is wearing a **seat belt** in conformity with regulations.

(1A) Where—
  (a) a **child** is in the front of a motor vehicle other than a **bus**,
  (b) the child is in a rear-facing child restraining device, and
  (c) the passenger seat where the child is placed is protected by a front air bag,

a person must not without reasonable excuse drive the vehicle on a road unless the air bag is deactivated.

(2) It is an **offence** for a person to drive a motor vehicle in contravention of subsection (1) or (1A) above.

Seated in rear

(3) Except as provided by regulations, where—

(a) a child under the age of three years is in the rear of a motor vehicle, or

(b) a child of or over that age but under the age of fourteen years is in the rear of a motor vehicle and any seat belt is fitted in the rear of that vehicle,

a person must not without reasonable excuse drive the vehicle on a road unless the child is wearing a seat belt in conformity with regulations.

(3A) Except as provided by **regulations**, where—

(a) a child who is under the age of 12 years and less than 150 cms in height is in the rear of a **passenger car**,

(b) no seat belt is fitted in the rear of the **passenger car**, and

(c) a seat in the front of the passenger car is provided with a seat belt but is not occupied by any person,

a person must not without reasonable excuse drive the passenger car on a road.

(4) It is an offence for a person to drive a motor vehicle in contravention of subsection (3) or (3A) above.

Road Traffic Act 1988, s 15

Points to prove

s 15(2) offence (front seated)

- ✓ without reasonable excuse
- ✓ drove a motor vehicle
- ✓ on a road
- ✓ child under 14 years
- ✓ in the front of the vehicle
- ✓ not wearing a seat belt or
- ✓ in a rear-facing restraining device and front air bag not deactivated

s 15(4) offence (rear seated)

- ✓ per first four points of s 15(2)
- ✓ in the rear of the vehicle
- ✓ a child under the age of 3 years **or** aged 3 years to 13 years
- ✓ not wearing a fitted seat belt
  or
- ✓ motor vehicle was a passenger car
- ✓ child under 12 years and less than 150 cms tall
- ✓ with no rear seat belt fitted and
- ✓ a front seat (with belt) was available

Meanings

Motor vehicle (see **10.17.1**)

Road (see **10.1.1**)

Seat belt

This includes any description of restraining device for a child.

Bus

Means a motor vehicle that—
- has at least four wheels;
- is constructed or adapted for the carriage of passengers;
- has more than 8 seats in addition to the driver's seat; and
- has a maximum design speed exceeding 25 kilometres per hour.

Passenger car

Means a motor vehicle which—
- is constructed or adapted for use for the carriage of passengers and is not a goods vehicle;
- has no more than 8 seats in addition to the driver's seat;
- has four or more wheels;
- has a maximum design speed exceeding 25 kilometres per hour; and
- has a **maximum laden weight** not exceeding 3.5 tonnes.

Maximum laden weight

In relation to a vehicle or combination of vehicles means—
- in respect of which a gross weight not to be exceeded in GB is specified in construction and use requirements, **that weight**;
- in respect of which **no such weight is specified** in construction and use requirements, the weight which the vehicle, or combination of vehicles, is designed or adapted not to exceed when in normal use and travelling on a road laden.

Regulations (seated in front)

Motor Vehicles (Wearing of Seat Belts by Children in Front Seats) Regulations 1993. Regulation 5 describes the belt or restraint to be worn.

Regulations (seated in rear)

Motor Vehicles (Wearing of Seat Belts) Regulations 1993.

Small child

Is a child under the age of 12 years and under 135 cm in height.

Large child

Is a child who is not a small child.

Explanatory notes

- The concept of a small child and a large child has been added by the above regulations, this has resulted in the lowering of the height from 150 cms down to 135 cms for a small child. This only affects the type of restraint that a small child should wear.

10.17.2 Seat belts—children

- Sections 15(3) and 15(3A) rear seat prohibitions do not apply to a—
    - child for whom there is a medical certificate;
    - small child aged **under 3 years** who is riding in a licensed taxi or licensed hire car, if no appropriate seat belt is available for them in the front or rear of the vehicle;
    - small child aged **3 years or more** who is riding in a licensed taxi, a licensed hire car, or a small bus and wearing an adult belt if an appropriate seat belt is not available for them in the front or rear of the vehicle;
    - small child aged 3 years or more who is wearing an adult belt and riding in a passenger car or light goods vehicle where the use of child restraints by the child occupants of two seats in the rear of the vehicle prevents the use of an appropriate seat belt for that child and no appropriate seat belt is available for them in the front of the vehicle;
    - small child riding in a vehicle being used for the purposes of the police, security, or emergency services to enable the proper performance of their duty;
    - small child aged 3 years or more who is wearing an adult belt and who, because of an unexpected necessity, is travelling a short distance in a passenger car or light goods vehicle in which no appropriate seat belt is available for them; or
    - disabled child who is wearing a disabled person's belt or whose disability makes it impracticable to wear a seat belt where a disabled person's belt is unavailable to them.
- Prohibitions in s 15(1) do not apply to a—
    - small child aged 3 years or more who is riding in a bus and is wearing an adult belt if an appropriate seat belt is not available for them in the front or rear of the vehicle;
    - child for whom there is a medical certificate;
    - disabled child who is wearing a disabled person's belt;
    - child riding in a bus which is being used to provide a local service in a built-up area, or which is constructed/adapted for the carriage of standing passengers and on which the operator permits standing; or
    - large child if no appropriate seat belt is available for them in the front of the vehicle.
- The driver of a motor vehicle has the same opportunity to produce a medical certificate for a child not wearing a seat belt as an adult (see **10.17.1**).

Practical considerations

- Consider issuing a TFPN for this offence (see **10.4**).
- The seat belt must be appropriate for a child of a particular weight and height travelling in a particular vehicle.
- A seat is regarded as provided with child restraint if the child restraint is—
    - fixed in such a position that it can be worn by an occupier of that seat, or

♦ elsewhere in or on the vehicle but—could readily be fixed in such a position without the aid of tools, and is not being worn by a child for whom it is appropriate and who is occupying another seat.

- A seat belt is considered appropriate in relation to a—
  ♦ **small child**, if it is a child restraint of a description prescribed for their height and weight by reg 5;
  ♦ **large child**, if it is a child restraint of a description prescribed for their height and weight by reg 5 or an adult belt; or
  ♦ person aged 14 years or more, if it is an adult belt.
- In relation to ages and height, subject to exceptions/requirements—
  ♦ aged under 3 must travel in front or rear in an appropriate baby/child seat:
    ■ EU-approved and selected according to weight;
    ■ where a rear facing baby seat is in the front seat, the air bag has to be deactivated;
  ♦ aged 3 to 11 and under 135 cms in rear using appropriate child seat, booster seat, or booster cushion;
  ♦ aged 12 to 13 or under 12 but over 135 cm, front or rear using adult seat belt, if no suitable child restraint is available;
  ♦ aged 14 and over adult regulations apply (see **10.17.1**).

 Summary

 6 months

 s 15(2) offence
Level 2 fine

s 15(4) offence
Level 1 fine

Links to alternative subjects and offences

10.18 Motorcycle—No Crash Helmet/Eye Protectors

Section 16 of the Road Traffic Act 1988 empowers the Secretary of State to make regulations concerning the wearing of crash helmets by motorcyclists and an offence of breaching such regulations.

Offences

A person who **drives** or rides on a **motor cycle** in contravention of **regulations** under this section is guilty of an offence; but not withstanding any enactment or rule of law no person other than the person actually committing the contravention is guilty of an offence by reason of the contravention unless the person actually committing the contravention is a child under the age of 16 years.

Road Traffic Act 1988, s 16(4)

Points to prove
✓ drove/rode on motorcycle
✓ contravened regulations under s 16

Meanings

Drives (see 10.1.4)

Motorcycle

Means a **mechanically propelled vehicle**, not being an invalid carriage, having less than 4 wheels and the unladen weight does not exceed 410 kg.

Mechanically propelled vehicle (see 10.1.3)

Regulations

Every person driving or riding (otherwise than in a sidecar) on a **motor bicycle** when on a **road** shall wear protective headgear (Motor Cycles (Protective Helmets) Regulations 1998, reg 4).

Road (see 10.1.1)

Explanatory notes

- 'Motor bicycle' means a **2-wheeled motorcycle**, whether or not having a sidecar attached, although where the distance measured between the centre of the area of contact with the road surface of any 2 wheels of a motorcycle is less than 460 mm, those wheels are counted as one wheel.

- This section does not include people riding in a sidecar or of the Sikh religion while wearing a turban.
- A British/EU standards mark must be on the helmet.
- Regulation 4 does not apply to a mowing machine or if propelled by a person on foot.
- If the vehicle is being propelled by 'scooter' style (eg the rider sat astride the machine and propelling it by pushing on the ground with their foot/feet) then a helmet should be worn.
- **Eye protectors offence**—Motor Cycles (Eye Protectors) Regulations 1999, reg 4 creates an offence under s 18(3) of not wearing approved eye protectors. Each person driving or riding (otherwise than in a sidecar) on a motor bicycle is required to wear eye protectors of a prescribed type.

Related cases

DPP v Parker [2005] RTR 1616, QBD A motorcycle fitted with enhanced safety features (eg a roof) does not negate the requirement to wear protective headgear.

Practical considerations

- In general, the rider of a quad bike would not be required to wear a crash helmet.
- Consider issuing a TFPN for these offences (see **10.4**).
- Any helmet worn must be securely fastened using straps or other means of fastening provided.
- If the helmet has a chin cup it must have an additional strap to fit under the jaw.
- Eye protectors/visors marked 'Daytime Use' or bearing a symbol of the same meaning should only be used in daytime.
- Visors that transmit less than 50 per cent of visible light cannot be legally used on the road.

 Summary 6 months

 Level 2 fine

Links to alternative subjects and offences

10.19 **Improper Use of Trade Plates**

The Vehicle Excise and Registration Act 1994 provides for the registration and excise duty payable in respect of motor vehicles. Section 34 relates to offences committed in relation to trade licences.

Offences

A person holding a trade licence or **trade licences** is guilty of an offence if he—
(a) **uses** at any one time on a **public road** a greater number of vehicles (not being vehicles for which vehicle licences are for the time being in force) than he is authorised to use by virtue of the trade licence or licences,
(b) uses a **vehicle** (not being a vehicle for which a vehicle licence is for the time being in force) on a public road for any purpose other than a purpose which has been prescribed under **section 12(2)(b)**, or
(c) uses the trade licence, or any of the trade licences, for the purposes of keeping on a public road in any circumstances other than circumstances which have been prescribed under **section 12(1)(c)** a vehicle which is not being used on that road.

Vehicle Excise and Registration Act 1994, s 34(1)

Points to prove

s 34(1)(a) offence

✓ being the holder of trade licence(s)
✓ used on a public road
✓ by virtue of that licence
✓ more vehicles than authorised by the licence

s 34(1)(b) offence

✓ being the holder of trade licence(s)
✓ used a vehicle on a public road
✓ by virtue of that licence
✓ for purposes other than as prescribed in the licence

s 34(1)(c) offence

✓ being the holder of trade licence(s)
✓ kept a vehicle on a public road
✓ by virtue of that licence
✓ when the vehicle was not being used on that road

Meanings

Trade licence

Is a licence issued under s 11.

Uses (see **10.16.1**)

Public road (s 62)

Means a road repairable at public expense.

Road (s 192) (see **10.1.1**)

Vehicle (s 1(1B))

Means a mechanically propelled vehicle, or anything (whether or not it is a vehicle) that has been, but has ceased to be, a mechanically propelled vehicle.

Section 12(2)(b)

Regulations giving purposes for which the holder of a trade licence may use a vehicle under that licence.

Section 12(1)(c)

Holder of a trade licence is not entitled to keep any vehicle on a road if it is not being used on the road for the purposes prescribed by regulations.

Regulations

Currently these are the Road Vehicles (Registration and Licensing) Regulations 2002 (SI 2742/2002).

Explanatory notes

- A trade licence will only be issued to a motor trader (including a vehicle manufacturer), vehicle tester, or person intending to start a business as a motor trader or vehicle tester.
- Where the conviction is for a continuing offence the offence will be taken as committed on the latest date to which the conviction relates.
- The trade licence holder who changes their name or the name and/or address of their business must notify the Secretary of State and submit the licence for amendment.
- It is an offence under s 44 for a person to forge, fraudulently alter or use, or fraudulently lend or allow to be used by another person any trade plate.
- Nothing that can be mistaken for a trade plate should be displayed on a vehicle.

Practical considerations

- Consider issuing a TFPN (see **10.4.1**) for offences under s 34.
- A trade licence is valid only for vehicles temporarily in the possession of a motor trader (including a vehicle manufacturer) or vehicle tester in the course of their business.
- A trade licence only authorises the use of one vehicle at any one time under s 12(1)(a), but a person may hold more than one licence.
- A vehicle and semi-trailer superimposed thereon counts as only one vehicle.

10.19 Improper Use of Trade Plates

- If a question arises as to the number of vehicles used, their character, weight, or cc rating, the seating capacity or the purpose for which they were being used, s 53 places the burden of proof on the defendant.
- Section 29 creates the offence of using/keeping an unlicensed vehicle (including trade licence) on a public road (see **10.20.1**).

TFPN

 Summary   36 months

 Level 3 fine or 5 times VEL duty amount

Links to alternative subjects and offences

10.20 Vehicle Excise/Trade Licences, HGV Levy, and Registration Marks/Documents

The Vehicle Excise and Registration Act 1994 offences include failing to fix a registration mark to a vehicle, produce a registration document; and using or keeping an unlicensed vehicle on a road or a vehicle bearing an obscured/misrepresented registration mark.

10.20.1 Using/keeping unlicensed vehicle/ HGV levy not paid

Section 29 creates the offence of using or keeping an unlicensed vehicle on a public road.

Offences

If a person **uses**, or **keeps**, a **vehicle** which is **unlicensed** he is guilty of an offence.

Vehicle Excise and Registration Act 1994, s 29(1)

Points to prove

✓ used/kept a vehicle
✓ without VEL or trade licence being in force

Meanings

Uses (see **10.16.1**)

Vehicle (see **10.19**)

Unlicensed

If there is no vehicle licence or trade licence in force for vehicle.

Exempt vehicles (exempt from vehicle excise duty)

Applies to the following vehicles listed under Sch 2—

- certain vehicles first constructed before 1 January 1973;
- electrically assisted pedal cycles;
- vehicles not used or adapted for carrying a driver or passenger;
- emergency vehicles;
- disabled persons' vehicles;
- a vehicle on test;
- a vehicle travelling between parts of private land;

10.20.1 Using/keeping unlicensed vehicle/HGV levy not paid

- a vehicle for export or imported by members of foreign armed forces;
- an off-road vehicle after notifying DVLA (SORN);
- tractor, light agricultural vehicle, agricultural engine;
- mowing machine;
- steam powered vehicles;
- electrically propelled vehicle, trams, and snow ploughs.

Explanatory notes

- Various people can 'use' a vehicle being the driver, employer if the vehicle is being used for the employer's business, owner being driven by another person while owner is in the vehicle, or steersman where a broken down vehicle is being towed.
- Where a vehicle licence has expired, and the vehicle is not to be used/kept on a road, the vehicle keeper must send a SORN to the Secretary of State.

Practical considerations

- All exempt vehicles require a nil licence except trams; electrically assisted pedal cycles; vehicles that do not carry a driver or passenger; vehicles going to, from, or taking a test of road worthiness or pollution; or vehicles which are zero rated whilst awaiting export. It is an offence under s 43A to use/keep a vehicle that requires a nil licence without such licence.
- The Finance Act 2014, sch 19 omitted s 10 and s 33 from 1 October 2014. This means that when a vehicle changes ownership the VEL cannot be transferred onto the new owner anymore, so the buyer will have to get a new VEL, and the seller can obtain a VEL refund once they notify DVLA. It also means it is no longer an offence to fail to display a VEL or trade licence—as a result these paper licences have stopped being issued.
- The burden of proof that the defendant was the keeper of the vehicle on the relevant day is on the prosecutor, but it is on the defendant to prove that a VEL was in force for the vehicle.
- Under s 53 the burden of proof is on the defendant if a question arises as to the character, weight, cubic capacity (cc) rating, or seating capacity of the vehicle; or the purpose for which it was being used.
- If offences involve misuse of trade plates under s 34 see **10.19**.

HGV road user levy not paid

- The HGV Road User Levy Act 2013 ensures that a duty of excise, called HGV road use levy, is charged to any HGV that is used/kept on a public road (see **10.19**) in the UK.
- It applies to all UK and non-UK HGVs, 12 tonnes or more; with the UK registered keeper or holder of a Community licence (non-UK), and any person by whom the HGV is kept, being liable for the levy.
- The levy rates are given in sch 1 of the Act, and vary according to the time used, weight, and axle configuration. It has 7 levy bands which align with existing VED bands.

- DVLA will collect the levy from UK registered HGVs at the same time as the VED, when the VED will be reduced accordingly—thus ensuring that most UK HGV operators will not experience a rise in the excise duty paid.
- Non-UK registered HGVs must pay the levy prior to entering the UK. Payment can be made online, by telephone, or at point of sale terminals on ferries and truck stops.
- Payment of the levy will be recorded on a database using the vehicle registration as the unique identifier. There will be no physical sign of payment through the display of a paper disc, sticker or similar item.
- It is a summary offence, under s 11 of the 2013 Act, if a person uses/keeps such an HGV on a public road without paying the road user levy.
- Failure to pay the levy will be a criminal offence, attracting a £300 **TFPN** (see **10.4.1**), or in the case of foreign HGVs a deposit taken at the roadside—'roadside deposit scheme' (see **10.4.3**). The HGV road user levy scheme will be primarily enforced by the DVSA.

 Summary   6 months

 A level 3 fine or 5 times VEL duty payable. A greater penalty can be imposed if the keeper commits the offence or if a SORN declaration has been made

10.20.2 **No registration mark on vehicle/fail to produce registration document**

Section 42 relates to the fixing of the registration mark to a vehicle and creates an offence of failure to do so.

Offences

If a **registration mark** is not fixed on a **vehicle** as **required** by virtue of **section 23**, the **relevant person** is guilty of an offence.

Vehicle Excise and Registration Act 1994, s 42(1)

Points to prove

✓ drove/kept
✓ vehicle on a road
✓ registration mark not fixed to front/rear of vehicle as required

10.20.2 No registration mark on vehicle

Meanings

Registration mark required by section 23(1)

A vehicle registered under s 21(1) shall be assigned a registration mark indicating the registered number of that vehicle.

Vehicle (see 10.19)

Relevant person

Driver of vehicle or, if not being driven, the keeper.

Explanatory notes

- The Road Vehicles (Display of Registration Marks) Regulations 2001 govern how such marks must be displayed on vehicles first registered on or after 1 October 1938; such as the size, shape, and character of the lettering and the manner by which the registration marks are to be displayed and rendered easily distinguishable (whether by day or by night) (see 10.20.3).
- The above regulations apply to all vehicles except works trucks, road rollers, and agricultural machines.
- A registration plate must be fixed to the rear of the vehicle or, if towing a trailer or trailers, the rear of the rearmost trailer, in a vertical position or, if that is not practicable, as close to vertical as possible, and in such position that, in normal daylight, the characters are easily distinguishable.
- Similarly, except a motorcycle, a registration plate must be fixed to the front of the vehicle in a vertical position or, if that is not practicable, as close to vertical as possible, and in such position that, in normal daylight, the characters are easily distinguishable.

Defences

(4) It is a defence for a person charged with an offence under subsection (1) to prove that—
   (a) he had no reasonable opportunity to register the vehicle under this Act, and
   (b) the vehicle was being driven for the purpose of being so registered.
(5) It is a defence for a person charged with an offence under subsection (1) in relation to a vehicle to which s 47 of the Road Traffic Act 1988 applies by virtue of subsection (2)(b) of that section (vehicles manufactured before the prescribed period and used before registration) to prove that he had no reasonable opportunity to register the vehicle under this Act and that the vehicle was being driven in accordance with subsection (6).

Vehicle Excise and Registration Act 1994, s 42

Defence notes

A vehicle is driven under s 42(6) if it is being driven for, or in connection with, examination under s 45 of the Road Traffic Act 1988 (MOT tests) in circumstances in which its use is exempted from s 47(1) of that Act by regulations.

Practical considerations

- Consider issuing a TFPN (see **10.4**).
- The Regulations concerning the displaying of registration marks do not apply to invalid vehicles or pedestrian controlled vehicles.
- A motorcycle first registered on or after 1 September 2001 **must not** have a registration plate fixed to the front, and one first registered before that date does not need to have a front registration plate fixed to it.
- If an agricultural machine is towing a trailer the registration plate on the rear of the trailer may show the registration mark of any similar machine owned by the keeper.

Produce registration document

- Section 28A of the Act makes it a summary offence if, when using (eg driver or keeper) a vehicle, they fail to produce the registration document for inspection on being so required by a constable or authorised person (authorised by the Secretary of State).
- Like other document production offences, s 28A does not apply if the registration document is produced at a police station specified by the person required to produce, within 7 days of the request or as soon as reasonably practicable.

 TFPN

 Summary 6 months

 Level 3 fine

10.20.3 **Obscured/misrepresented registration marks**

Section 43 requires a registration plate fixed to a vehicle to be unobscured, easily distinguishable, and not be misrepresented.

10.20.3 Obscured/misrepresented registration marks

Points to prove

✓ drove/kept
✓ vehicle on a road
✓ registration mark obscured/rendered/allowed to become indistinguishable

Meanings

Registration mark required by section 23 (see 10.20.2)

The Road Vehicles (Display of Registration Marks) Regulations 2001 have been made under s 23.

Vehicle (see 10.19)

Relevant person (see 10.20.2)

Practical considerations

- Examples of this offence could be where the registration plate is obscured by the tow bar/ball, or covered by a pedal cycle rack, or is covered by dirt/mud and is allowed to remain there.
- Officers should use their discretion when dealing with this type of offence.
- The Vehicles (Crime) Act 2001 concerns the control of registration plate suppliers. It is an offence under s 28 of that Act to sell a plate where the registration mark is misrepresented. Prosecution to show that the supplier knew of the defective plate or was reckless as to the nature of the plate.
- DVLA has issued guidelines for tackling misrepresented number plates. Action should be considered where the number plate: may be

unreadable by ANPR, uses bolts/screws to change appearance of characters, has illegal font, looks foreign (on GB vehicle), is patterned or textured, has incorrectly spaced/sized characters, does not show plate supplier, displays illegal graphics, or appears offensive.

Where s 43 offences are dealt with by TFPN (see **10.4**) or report for summons, photographic evidence should be obtained (where possible) and the driver issued with a DVLA form V796. Send an offence notification report form to DVLA, accompanied by photograph and details of plate supplier. DVLA will then take follow-up action, including revocation of registration mark for repeat offences or repeat use of misrepresented plates; but DVLA will take no action if it is dealt with by VDRS.

The BS for number plates states that characters must be a 'Shade of Black', 3D characters meet this description and are acceptable, but patterns, such as stripes, are not allowed. Plates with 3D characters must comply with other BS requirements.

If a vehicle is liable for vehicle excise duty or is an exempt vehicle that requires a nil licence to be in force (see **10.20.1**), s 43C makes it a summary offence to use such a vehicle on a public road/place if the keeper details are incorrect or not recorded in the DVLA vehicle register. A TFPN can be issued for this offence (see **10.4.1**).

 Summary 6 months

 Level 3 fine

inks to alternative subjects and offences

10.21 Using Vehicle without an Operator's Licence

The Goods Vehicles (Licensing of Operators) Act 1995 provides for the licensing of certain goods vehicles. If a person uses a goods vehicle on a road for carrying goods for hire or reward or in connection with their business, then s 2 requires them to have an operator's licence.

Offences

(1) Subject to **subsection (2)** and **section 4**, no person shall use a **goods vehicle** on a **road** for the carriage of **goods**—
  (a) for **hire or reward**, or
  (b) for or in connection with any trade or business carried on by him,
  except under a licence issued under this Act; and in this Act such a licence is referred to as an **'operator's licence'**.
(5) A person who uses a vehicle in contravention of this section is guilty of an offence.

Goods Vehicles (Licensing of Operators) Act 1995, s 2

Points to prove

✓ used a goods vehicle for the carriage of goods
✓ for hire/reward/in connection with a business
✓ on a road
✓ without an operator's licence

Meanings

Subsection (2)

Subsection (1) does not apply to—
- the use of a goods vehicle for international carriage by a haulier established in a member State other than the UK and not established in the UK;
- the use of a goods vehicle for international carriage by a haulier established in Northern Ireland and not established in GB; or
- the use of a vehicle of any class specified in **regulations**.

Regulations

Means the Goods Vehicles (Licensing of Operators) Regulations 1995 (SI 2869/1995).

Section 4

Allows for the Traffic Commissioners to issue a temporary exemption (a standard licence) in an emergency, or some other special need.

Goods vehicle

Means a motor vehicle constructed or adapted for use for the carriage/haulage of goods, or a trailer so constructed or adapted, but does not include a tramcar or trolley vehicle.

Road

Means any highway or any other road to which the public has access, and includes bridges over which a road passes.

Goods

This includes goods or burden of any description.

Hire or reward

Means a systematic carrying of passengers for reward that went beyond the bounds of mere social kindness (*Albert v Motor Insurance Bureau* [1972] AC 301).

Explanatory notes

• The performance by a local or public authority of their functions constitutes the carrying on of a **business**.
• Different types of **operator's licence** are denoted by the colour of the identity disc—
  ✦ Restricted (orange)—own goods nationally and internationally;
  ✦ Standard National (blue)—hire and reward transportation nationally only;
  ✦ Standard International (green)—as blue, plus international as well;
  ✦ Interim/temporary (yellow).
The licence may specify the maximum number of vehicles that may be used under it, or may specify the maximum number of vehicles exceeding a certain weight (specified therein), for which it authorises the use.
The Traffic Commissioner for an area issues an operator's licence.
An operator may hold a licence in more than one area, but cannot hold more than one licence in the same area.

Related cases

Gout v Swallow Hotels Ltd [1993] RTR 80, QBD Swallow Hotels Group operated courtesy coaches. No fares were charged but the coaches were driven by company employees and were exclusively for use of hotel guests. Held to be for hire or reward. No binding contract was necessary and the customers obviously paid for this service in their hotel bills.

VOSA v Greenfarms Ltd [2005] EWHC 3156 (Admin), CA An articulated tractor unit had been adapted to allow it to draw a trailer tank carrying liquid fertilizer. G had borne the burden of proof and failed to show purpose and evidence of reinstatement. Despite the modification the vehicle remained a heavy goods vehicle and not an agricultural tractor, and so required an operator's licence.

10.21 Using Vehicle without an Operator's Licence

Practical considerations

- If the defendant has previously held an operator's licence specify the date on which it expired.
- Vehicles must only be used from a centre specified in the licence as the operating centre.
- This section extends to foreign vehicles by virtue of the Road Traffic (Foreign Vehicles) Act 1972.
- A standard licence may authorise transport operations both nationally and internationally.
- An operator's licence authorises the use of any vehicle in the lawful possession of the licence holder and any trailer so possessed.
- An authorised person, believing that an offence under s 2 is being or has been committed, may detain the vehicle and its contents.
- Where a vehicle is seized, the authorised person may immobilise that vehicle there or may remove it, or cause it to be removed, to a more convenient place for it to be immobilised.
- A power of entry exists under s 40 where an **officer**/constable may, at any reasonable time having regard to the circumstances of the case, enter any premises of the applicant or holder of an Operator's licence and inspect any facilities there for the maintenance of vehicles used under that licence. An offence will be committed if that officer/constable is obstructed.
- **Officer** means an examiner appointed under s 66A of the Road Traffic Act 1988 or person authorised by the Traffic Commissioner.
- A power of seizure also exists under ss 41 and 42 where if an officer/constable has reason to believe that a document or article carried on or by the driver of a vehicle, or a document produced may be subject to s 38 (forge/alter with intent to deceive) or s 39 (false statement to obtain a licence) offences, then they may seize that document or article.
- Consider issuing a TFPN for this s 2(5) offence (see **10.4.1**).

TFPN

 Summary   6 months

 Fine

Links to alternative subjects and offences

10.22 Obstruction of the Road/ Footpath

Obstruction of a road is catered for by the Highways Act 1980, and the Road Vehicles (Construction and Use) Regulations 1986.

10.22.1 Wilful obstruction of the highway

Section 137 of the Highways Act 1980 provides an offence of wilful obstruction of the highway.

Offences

If a **person**, without lawful authority or excuse, in any way **wilfully** obstructs the free passage along a **highway** he is guilty of an offence.

Highways Act 1980, s 137(1)

Points to prove

✓ without lawful authority/excuse
✓ wilfully obstructed
✓ free passage of the highway

Meanings

Person

includes a body corporate.

Wilfully

means purposefully, deliberately.

Highway

means the whole or part of a highway other than a ferry or waterway. Where a highway passes over a bridge or through a tunnel, that bridge or tunnel is taken to be part of the highway.

Explanatory notes

Stopping someone from using the highway by fear alone is insufficient to commit obstruction: there should be some physical obstruction.

The highway does not need to be completely blocked, only made less convenient or roomy.

10.22.2 Builders' skips on the highway

- If a person is convicted under s 137 and the obstruction is continuing, the court may, instead of or in addition to imposing any punishment, order them to remove it within a fixed period under s 137ZA. Failure to comply with this order, without reasonable excuse, will be an offence.

Related cases

Birch v DPP [2000] Crim LR 301, QBD People at a demonstration sat in the road blocking traffic. The defendant admitted obstructing the traffic but claimed to have a lawful excuse. Held: Lawful excuse included activities that were lawful in themselves. Only the evidence of the purpose of this action (obstruct the traffic) was relevant.

Torbay Borough Council v Cross (1995) 159 JP 882, QBD Although the *de minimis* principle (eg court is not concerned with trifles) applies to obstruction cases, it is reserved for cases of fractional obstructions.

Nagy v Weston [1965] 1 All ER 78, QBD The test for determining whether a particular use of the highway amounts to an obstruction is if in the particular circumstances, such use is unreasonable. Circumstances would include duration, position of the obstruction, its purpose, and whether it caused an actual or potential obstruction.

Practical considerations

- Consider whether the obstruction is wilful or deliberate (as opposed to accidental) or without lawful excuse.
- If a motor vehicle is involved consider issuing a TFPN (see **10.4**).
- If it can be proved the obstruction was with the consent or connivance of an officer of a body corporate, then they may have committed the offence as well as the body corporate.
- Duration and extent of the obstruction are important considerations.
- The Town Police Clauses Act 1847, s 28 obstruction offences have been repealed by the Deregulation Act 2015, sch 23.

 6 months

10.22.2 **Builders' skips on the highway**

Section 139 of the Highways Act 1980 controls the use of builders' ski deposited on the highway.

Offences

(3) If a **builder's skip** is deposited on a **highway** without a permission granted under this section, the **owner** of the skip is, subject to subsection (6) below, guilty of an offence.

(4) Where a builder's skip has been deposited on a highway in accordance with a permission granted under this section, the owner of the skip shall secure—

   (a) that the skip is properly lighted during the **hours of darkness** and, where regulations made by the Secretary of State under this section require it to be marked in accordance with the regulations (whether with reflecting or fluorescent material or otherwise), that it is so marked;

   (b) that the skip is clearly and indelibly marked with the owner's name and with his telephone number or address;

   (c) that the skip is removed as soon as practicable after it has been filled;

   (d) that each of the conditions subject to which that permission was granted is complied with;

and, if he fails to do so, he is, subject to subsection (6) below, guilty of an offence.

Highways Act 1980, s 139

Points to prove

s 139(3) offence

✓ deposited builder's skip on a highway
✓ without permission under s 139

s 139(4) offence

✓ owner of a builder's skip
✓ deposited skip on a highway
✓ with a permission granted under s 139
✓ failed to secure that the skip was
✓ properly lighted during the hours of darkness; **or**
✓ clearly and indelibly marked with owner's details; **or**
✓ removed as soon as practicable after being filled; **or**
✓ not complying with each of the conditions

Meanings

Builder's skip

Means a container designed to be carried on a road vehicle and to be placed on a highway or other land for the storage of builders' materials, or for the removal and disposal of builders' rubble, household waste, and other rubbish or earth.

10.22.2 Builders' skips on the highway

Highway (see 10.22.1)

Owner

In relation to a builder's skip, subject of a hiring agreement, being an agreement for a hiring of not less than one month, or a hire purchase agreement means the person in possession of the skip under that agreement.

Hours of darkness

Half an hour after sunset and half an hour before sunrise.

Power to move skip

Under s 140, the highways authority or a constable in uniform may require the owner of a skip to remove or reposition it; or cause it to be so removed or repositioned themselves. This applies even though it has been deposited with a permission granted under s 139.

Explanatory notes

- A permission under s 139 authorises a person to whom it is granted to deposit, or cause to be deposited, a skip on a highway specified therein
- Such permission may be granted unconditionally or with specified conditions such as: siting of skip; its dimensions; manner in which it must be marked to be visible to oncoming traffic; care and disposal of contents; way in which it must be lighted or guarded; and its removal at the expiry of the permission.
- Permission must be in writing and blanket permission is not allowed (*York City Council v Poller* [1976] RTR 37).
- Nothing in this section authorises the creation of a nuisance or a danger to users of the highway or imposes on a highway authority granting permission any liability for any injury caused, damage, or loss resulting from the presence on a highway of a skip to which the permission relates.

Defences

(6) In any proceedings for an offence under this section it is a defence, subject to subsection (7) below, for the person charged to prove that the commission of the offence was due to the act or default of another person and that he took all reasonable precautions and exercised all due diligence to avoid the commission of such an offence by himself or any person under his control.

(7) A person charged with an offence under this section is not, without leave of the court, entitled to rely on the defence provided by subsection (6) above unless, within a period ending 7 clear days before the hearing, he has served on the prosecutor a notice in writing giving such information identifying or assisting in the identification of that other person as was then in his possession.

---

(8) Where any person is charged with an offence under any other enactment for failing to secure that a builder's skip which has been deposited on a highway in accordance with a permission granted under this section was properly lighted during the hours of darkness, it is a defence for the person charged to prove that the commission of the offence was due to the act or default of another person and that he took all reasonable precautions and exercised all due diligence to avoid the commission of such an offence by himself or any person under his control.

(9) Where a person is charged with obstructing, or interrupting any user of, a highway by depositing a builder's skip on it, it is a defence for the person charged to prove that the skip was deposited on it in accordance with a permission granted under this section and either—

    (a) that each of the requirements of subsection (4) above had been complied with; or

    (b) that the commission of any offence under that subsection was due to the act or default of another person and that he took all reasonable precautions and exercised all due diligence to avoid the commission of such an offence by himself or any person under his control.

Highways Act 1980, s 139

Practical considerations

- If a person commits an offence under s 139 because of an act or default of another person, that other person is guilty of the offence, and may be charged with and convicted of the offence whether or not proceedings are taken against the first-mentioned person.
- Requirement for a skip to be moved must be made face to face (*R v Worthing Justices, ex parte Waste Management Ltd* (1988) 152 JP 362, DC).

 Summary   6 months

 Level 3 fine

10.22.3 Cause injury/danger/annoyance on the highway

Section 161 of the Highways Act 1980 creates various offences that relate to causing danger on a highway, including annoyance by playing games on the highway.

10.22.3 Cause injury/danger/annoyance on the highway

Offences

(1) If a person, without lawful authority or excuse, deposits any thing whatsoever on a **highway** in consequence of which a user of the **highway** is injured or endangered, that person is guilty of an offence.

(2) *[See 8.8.6]*

(3) If a person plays at football or any other game on a highway to the annoyance of a user of the highway he is guilty of an offence.

(4) If a person, without lawful authority or excuse, allows any filth, dirt, lime or other offensive matter or thing to run or flow on to a highway from any adjoining premises, he is guilty of an offence.

Highways Act 1980, s 161

Points to prove

s 161(1) offence

✓ without lawful authority/excuse
✓ deposits any thing whatsoever on a highway
✓ thus injuring/endangering user of the highway

s 161(3) offence

✓ played football/a game on a highway
✓ thus annoying a user of the highway

s 161(4) offence

✓ without lawful authority/excuse
✓ allowed any filth, dirt, lime or other offensive matter or thing
✓ to run or flow on to a highway
✓ from any adjoining premises

Meaning of highway (see 10.22.1)

Explanatory notes

- The s 161(2) offences relate to lighting any fire on/over a highway or discharging any firearm or firework within 50 feet of the centre of a highway and are dealt with in **8.5** and **8.8.6**.
- Section 161A creates another offence of lighting a fire on any land (not part of a highway/carriageway) and as a result the user of any highway is injured, interrupted, or endangered by smoke from that fire.
- Any rope, wire, or other apparatus placed across a highway so as to cause danger to users of the highway is an offence under s 162, unless adequate warning has been given of this danger.
- The s 161(3) offence is very wide and covers all types of 'game'. For example, a mock hunt with a man dressed as a stag being chased by people in fancy dress and with trumpets has been held to be a game (*Pappin v Maynard* (1863) 27 JP 745).

Summary 6 months

 s 161(1) offence
Level 3 fine

s 161(3) and (4) offences
Level 1 fine

10.22.4 **Unnecessary obstruction**

Regulation 103 of the Road Vehicles (Construction and Use) Regulations 1986 creates an offence of causing an unnecessary obstruction.

Offences

No person in charge of **a motor vehicle** or **trailer** shall cause or permit the vehicle to stand on a **road** so as to cause any unnecessary obstruction of the road.

Road Vehicles (Construction and Use) Regulations 1986, reg 103

Points to prove

✓ in charge of a motor vehicle/trailer
✓ caused/permitted vehicle
✓ to stand on a road
✓ so causing an unnecessary obstruction on road

Meanings

Motor vehicle (see **10.1.3**)

Mechanically propelled vehicle intended or adapted for use on roads.

Trailer

Vehicle drawn by a motor vehicle, but does not apply to any part of an articulated bus.

Road

Includes the footpath.

10.22.4 Unnecessary obstruction

Explanatory notes

- A motor vehicle left on a road for an unreasonable time may be unreasonable obstruction.
- Consider the use to which the highway was being put by the vehicle causing the obstruction. The highway is intended as a means of transit, not a store (*Nelmes v Rhys Howells Transport Ltd* [1977] RTR 266).
- Where a motorist parks their vehicle on one side of the road and the subsequent parking of vehicles on the opposite side of the road causes an obstruction, no offence under this regulation was committed by the parking of the original vehicle (*Langham v Crisp* [1975] Crim LR 652).

Related cases

Carey v CC of Avon and Somerset [1995] RTR 405, CA The purpose of the Removal and Disposal of Vehicles Regulations 1986 is to clear the road of an 'obstruction' as a matter of urgency even if no one is really at fault. They do not apply to s 137 of the Highways Act 1980 and reg 103 of the Road Vehicles (Construction and Use) Regulations 1986 which relate to obstruction of the highway without a lawful excuse and constitute an unreasonable use of the highway.

Practical considerations

Consider the offence of wilfully obstructing the free passage of the highway, without lawful authority or excuse, under s 137(1) of the Highways Act 1980 (see **10.22.1**). A TFPN can be issued for this offence (see **10.4.1**).

 Summary   6 months

 Level 4 fine if goods vehicle or a vehicle adapted to carry more than 8 passengers. Level 3 fine in any other case

Links to alternative subjects and offences

10.23 **Off-Road Driving/Immobilise Vehicles on Land**

Section 34 of the Road Traffic Act 1988 prohibits the driving of motor vehicles elsewhere than on a road.

Offences

Subject to the provisions of this section, if without lawful authority a person **drives a mechanically propelled vehicle**—

(a) on to or upon any **common land**, moorland or land of any other description, not being land forming part of a **road**, or

(b) on any road being a **footpath, bridleway** or **restricted byway**,

he is guilty of an offence.

Road Traffic Act 1988, s 34(1)

Points to prove

✓ without lawful authority
✓ drove a mechanically propelled vehicle
✓ on to/upon common land/moorland/land
✓ not being land forming part of a road or
✓ on a road being a footpath/bridleway/restricted byway

Meanings

Drives (see 10.1.4)

Mechanically propelled vehicle (see 10.1.3)

Excluding a pedestrian-controlled vehicle, a pedestrian-controlled mowing machine, or an electrically assisted pedal cycle.

Common land

Land that is—

• subject to '**rights of common**' whether those rights are exercisable at all times or only during limited periods; and

• waste land of a manor not subject to 'rights of common'.

Rights of common

This includes—

• rights of sole or several vesture, or herbage (rights to take vegetation or flowers from the land);

• rights of sole or several pasture (allowing animals to be put out to pasture on the land);

- cattlegates and beastgates (a particular right, mainly existing in northern England, to graze an animal on common land).

They do not include rights held for a term of years or from year to year.

Road (see 10.1.1)

Footpath

Means a highway over which the public have a right of way on foot only, not being a footway.

Bridleway

A way over which the public have the following, but no other, rights of way: a right of way on foot and a right of way on horseback, or leading a horse, with or without a right to drive animals of any description along the way.

Restricted byway

A way over which the public have restricted byway rights within the meaning of Pt 2 of the Countryside and Rights of Way Act 2000, with or without a right to drive animals of any description along the way, but no other rights of way.

Explanatory notes

- A way shown in a definitive map and statement as a footpath, bridleway, or restricted byway is taken to be so, unless the contrary is shown.
- Nothing in s 34 prejudices the rights of the public over: commons and waste lands, or any by-laws applying to any land, or affects the law of trespass to land, or any right or remedy to which a person may by law be entitled in respect of any such trespass, or in particular confers a right to park a vehicle on any land.
- It is not an offence under s 34 to drive on any land within 15 yards of a road, for purpose only of parking the vehicle on that land (s 34(3)).
- Police powers concerning the stopping, seizure, and removal of a motor vehicle that is used in contravention of s 34, which is causing, or likely to cause, alarm, distress, or annoyance to members of the public can be used under s 59 of the Police Reform Act 2002 (see 7.14).

Defences

(2A) It is not an offence under this section for a person with an **interest in land**, or a visitor to any land, to drive a mechanically propelled vehicle on a road if, immediately before the commencement of section 47(2) of the Countryside and Rights of Way Act 2000, the road was—

    (a) shown in a definitive map and statement as a road used as a public path, and

    (b) in use for obtaining access to the land by the driving of mechanically propelled vehicles by a person with an interest in the land or by visitors to the land.

(3) It is not an offence under this section to drive a mechanically propelled vehicle on land within 15 yards of a road, being a road on which a motor vehicle may legally be driven, for the purpose only of parking the vehicle on that land.

(4) A person shall not be convicted of an offence under this section with respect to a vehicle if he proves to the satisfaction of the court that it was driven in contravention of this section for the purpose of saving life or extinguishing fire or meeting any other like emergency.

Road Traffic Act 1988, s 34

Practical considerations

- **Interest in land**—includes any estate in land and any right over land (whether exercisable by virtue of the ownership of an estate or interest in the land or by virtue of a licence or agreement) and, in particular, includes rights of common and sporting rights.
- Consider issuing a TFPN (see **10.4**).
- A power of entry to premises to exercise the powers of seizure and removal of the motor vehicle is granted by s 59 of the Police Reform Act 2002. Reasonable force may be used, if necessary, to stop, seize, remove the motor vehicle, or for the power of entry (see **7.14**).
- **Immobilise vehicles left on land**: Section 54 of the Protection of Freedoms Act 2012 provides that a person commits an offence, if without lawful authority they immobilise a motor vehicle by attaching an immobilising device (eg wheel clamp), or move or restrict the movement of, such a vehicle by any means, intending to prevent or inhibit the removal of the vehicle by a person otherwise entitled to remove it.
- The restriction of movement of the vehicle offence does not apply to a lawfully erected fixed barrier in place at the time of parking. In this section motor vehicle means a mechanically propelled vehicle or a vehicle designed or adapted for towing by a mechanically propelled vehicle.

 Summary   6 months

 Level 3 fine

Links to alternative subjects and offences

Chapter 11

General: Patrol

11.1 Police Community Support Officers (PCSOs)

Section 38 of the Police Reform Act 2002 enables the chief officer of police to designate suitably skilled and trained police staff under their direction and control as Police Community Support Officers (PCSOs) in order to exercise powers and undertake duties as described in Sch 4 to the Police Reform Act 2002.

Under s 38A a number of discretionary powers have been designated within Sch 4 as standard powers, thus ensuring that PCSOs have sufficient powers to support NPT's and deal with low level anti-social behaviour and disorder.

These powers are listed in the Police Reform Act 2002 (Standard Powers and Duties of Community Support Officers) Order 2007 and apply to every PCSO designated under s 38.

HOC 33/2007 provides guidance on the standard powers, duties, and training of PCSOs and lists: standard powers that apply to all PCSOs; discretionary powers and issue of PNDs that can be designated by chief officers. Although they may be given the *powers* of a constable under certain circumstances, PCSOs do not have the common law *duties* of a constable.

The Anti-social Behaviour, Crime and Policing Act 2014 provided further discretionary powers to PCSOs with regard to issuing TFPN: seizure under PACE 1984, ss 19, 21, and 22; obtain details of charity collectors; power to stop cycles for listed TFPN offences; and enforcement of CPN or PSPO, together with issuing fixed penalties for breaching a CPN or PSPO. It is an offence to assault, resist, or wilfully obstruct a designated person (PCSO) in the execution of their duty under the Police Reform Act 2002, s 46 (see 2.2.5).

11.1.1 **General powers**

Enter premises

- Where a power allows for the use of reasonable force when exercised by a constable, a PCSO has the same entitlement to use reasonable force when exercising a designated power.
- If a PCSO has been granted the power to force entry to premises, **it will be limited** to when they are both under the direct supervision of a constable and accompanied by them. The only exception to this is when the purpose of forcing entry is to save life or limb or to prevent serious damage to premises.

Entry to save life or limb, or prevent serious damage to property

Standard power

Powers of a constable under s 17 of PACE (see **12.3**), to enter and search any premises in the relevant police area for the purpose of saving life or limb, or preventing serious damage to property.

Reasonable force

Where a PCSO has a power to detain they can use reasonable force in respect of—
- relevant penalty notice offences;
- relevant licensing offences; (note conditions—see **11.1.2**);
- anti-social behaviour;
- searches for alcohol/tobacco;
- power to give directions under the Anti-social Behaviour, Crime and Policing Act 2014—s 35 to leave area or s 37 to surrender property (see **7.15.1**);
- preventing the person making off when subject to the requirement to provide details or accompany the PCSO to the police station;
- power to remove truants or excluded pupils, and return them to school or designated premises;
- offences connected with begging or a relevant by-law.

Issue traffic fixed penalty notices (TFPN)

Power of a constable in uniform to give a person a **TFPN** (see **10.4.1**) under s 54 of the Road Traffic Offenders Act 1988 for the offences of: cycling on a footway (see **10.12.4**); contravening a prohibition or restriction relating to: stopping, waiting or parking at or near a school entrance, one-way traffic on a road, lanes/routes for use only by cycles and/or buses; more than one person on a one-person bicycle; cycle rider failing to comply with traffic directions (see **10.2.1**); cycle rider failing to comply with red traffic light (see **10.3**); contravening or failing to comply with a construction or use requirement relating to: lighting equipment or reflectors for cycles, using a motor vehicle on a road in a way that causes excessive noise, stopping the action of a stationary vehicle's machinery, using a vehicle's horn on a road while stationary or on a restricted road at night, or opening a vehicle's door on a road so injuring or endangering a person; failing to stop vehicle or cycle when required to do so by constable or traffic officer (see **10.2.4**).

Issue fixed penalty notices

Standard power—Issue **fixed penalty notices** for litter offences, and offences against certain by-laws under s 237A of the Local Government Act 1972.

Discretionary power—Issue **fixed penalty notices** for failure to attend school, an excluded pupil found in a public place, graffiti, fly-posting, failing to comply with **CPN** (see **7.16.1**), and failing to comply with **PSPO** (see **7.15.2** and **9.4.1**).

Issue community protection notices (CPN)

Discretionary power—**CPN** can be issued under the Anti-social Behaviour, Crime and Policing Act 2014, s 43 (see **7.16.1**) if the conduct specified in the notice has been taking place within the **relevant police area**, including issuing a fixed penalty notice under s 52.

Issue penalty notices for disorder (PND)

Discretionary power—In addition, **PND** can be issued in respect of a range of anti-social behaviour and disorder offences under the Criminal Justice and Police Act 2001 (**except** the **theft and litter** listed offences). These offences are shown in 'Penalty Notices for Disorder' (see **7.1.1**).

Require name and address

Standard power
- Can be given this power without also being given the power to detain.
- Can require the name and address of a person who has committed the following offence—
  + **relevant offence** in the relevant police area; or
  + **relevant licensing offence within or outside the relevant police area**;
  + failure to provide name and address is in itself an offence.

Discretionary power
May enforce a relevant by-law only within the place to which the by-law relates. Where a PCSO has this power they also have the power of a constable under a relevant by-law to remove a person from a place.

Detain a person

Discretionary power
- Can only be given the power to detain a person if they have also been given the power to request the person's name and address (but note the licensing exceptions to detention—see **11.1.2**).

11.1.1 General powers

- Where there is non-compliance with the request, or the PCSO has reason to believe the information is false or inaccurate, they can require the other person to wait with them for up to 30 minutes, pending the arrival of a constable.
- The individual may choose, if asked, to accompany the PCSO to a police station rather than wait.
- A refusal of the requirement to wait or making off while subject to a requirement pending the arrival of a constable; or making off while accompanying the PCSO to the police station, is an offence.
- See also '**Reasonable force**' (above).

Search of detained person

Discretionary power

- Where a person has been required to wait (detained for up to 30 minutes, pending the arrival of a constable), the PCSO has a limited power to search that person for any item that could be used to injure themselves or others if the PCSO believes the person may present a danger to themselves or others.
- A PCSO also has a power to search that person for anything that could be used to assist them to escape.
- Anything found while exercising these search powers can be seized and retained. They must comply with the instructions of a constable about what to do with any seized item and inform the person from whom it has been seized where enquiries may be made about its recovery.

PACE (premises)—search, seize, and retain

Where a designation applies, the PCSO shall when lawfully on any premises in the **relevant police area** have the same powers as a constable—
- under s 19 of PACE (see **12.3.4**) (general powers of seizure) to seize things, including protection for legally privileged material from seizure under s 19(6);
- to impose a requirement by virtue of s 19(4) of PACE in relation to information accessible from such premises;
- under s 21(1) and (2) of PACE (see **12.3.4**) (provision of record of seizure) in relation to the seizure of anything by that PCSO in exercising the s 19 power, as if the references to a constable included references to a PCSO;
- under s 21(3) to (8) and s 22 of PACE (see **12.3.4**) (access, copying and retention) in relation to anything seized by that PCSO in exercising that power or taken away by him following the requirement imposed by s 19(4), as if the references to a constable included references to a PCSO.

Meanings

Relevant offence

This means—
- a relevant fixed penalty offence (see above and **7.1**);

- an offence under the Anti-social Behaviour, Crime and Policing Act 2014, s 39 (fail to comply with direction to leave—s 35—or surrender property—s 37) (see **7.15.1**);
- an offence under a by-law for which a fixed penalty notice can be issued under s 237A of the Local Government Act 1972;
- an offence that appears to have caused alarm, injury, or distress to any other person, or loss of, or damage to any other person's property;
- an offence under the Parks Regulation Act 1872 (contravention of park regulations/assaulting park-keeper);
- begging (Vagrancy Act 1824, s 3);
- where a person has been convicted of begging and sleeps in certain unoccupied premises or in the open air without being able to give a valid reason for doing so;
- showing wounds or deformities to aid begging and to collect money for charitable purposes under false pretence (Vagrancy Act 1824, s 4);
- an offence under a relevant by-law.

Relevant licensing offences (see **11.1.2**)

Relevant police area (see **11.1.2**)

11.1.2 Powers relating to licensing/alcohol

Entry to investigate licensing offences

Discretionary power

- Limited powers to enter and search licensed premises, other than clubs, under s 180 of the Licensing Act 2003 if they believe that one of the **relevant licensing offences** (see below) has been, or is being, committed in relation to alcohol.
- These licensing offences are all connected with the sale and consumption of alcohol by and to young people, or persons who are drunk.
- Can enter any premises, other than clubs, for the purposes of investigating a relevant licensing offence with a constable.
- Can only enter premises alone where they reasonably believe that a premises licence authorises the sale of alcohol for consumption off the premises.
- This limited power of entry and search adds to a PCSO's powers to deal with alcohol-related anti-social behaviour and those who supply alcohol to young people.

Power to require name and address

Standard power

- Can require the name and address of a person who has committed a **relevant licensing offence** within or outside the **relevant police area**. Failure to provide details is an offence.

11.1.2 Powers relating to licensing/alcohol

- Although they have the power to require name and address, the power to detain does **not** apply to licensing offences in relation to the sale of alcohol to a drunk, to under 18 (or knowingly allow such sale), if the offence is believed to have been committed on relevant licensed premises in any police area.
- Powers to enter and search premises other than clubs in relation to a relevant licensing offence are restricted to the relevant police area in the company and under the supervision of a constable, **unless** the PCSO has reason to believe the premises are off-licence premises.

Meanings

Relevant licensing offences

These offences relate to alcohol and are as follows—
- sale (or attempt) to a person who is drunk (see **9.2.1**);
- allow sale to drunken person (see **9.2.1**);
- obtaining for a person who is drunk (see **9.2.1**);
- sale to children under 18 (see **9.1**);
- purchase (or attempt) by a child under 18 (see **9.1.4**);
- purchase (or attempt) on behalf of person under 18 (see **9.1.4**);
- purchase (or attempt) for consumption on relevant premises by person under 18 (see **9.1.4**);
- knowingly consume on relevant premises by person under 18 (see **9.1.5**);
- knowingly allow consumption on relevant premises by person under 18 (see **9.1.5**);
- knowingly send person under 18 to obtain alcohol on relevant premises (see **9.1.7**).

Relevant police area

This is the police area in which a PCSO's powers apply.

Power to serve closure notice

Discretionary power

Where the s 147A offence of persistently selling alcohol to children under 18 has been committed on licensed premises (see **9.1.3**) then a PCSO can enter those premises to serve a closure notice under s 169A on a responsible person during licensing hours (see **9.3.3**).

Alcohol consumption in designated public places

Standard power

- Powers of a constable under s 63 of the Anti-social Behaviour, Crime and Policing Act 2014 (see **9.4.1**) to—
  + require a person to cease drinking alcohol (or anything reasonably believed to be alcohol) in a public place in breach of a prohibition under a **PSPO**, and
  + surrender the alcohol/container. The PCSO may dispose of the surrendered alcohol/container.

- Surrender/disposal applies to both sealed and unsealed containers.
- The person **must** be informed that failure to comply with the PCSO's request, without reasonable excuse, is an offence under s 63(6). A PCSO may issue a fixed penalty notice under s 68 for failing to comply with a **PSPO** (see **7.15.2**).

Confiscation of alcohol from young persons

Standard power

- Same powers (except for arrest) as a constable under s 1 of the Confiscation of Alcohol (Young Persons) Act 1997 (see **9.5.1**).
- Confiscate and dispose of the alcohol, and its container.
- Seizure can apply to both sealed and unsealed containers.
- The person **must** be informed that failure to comply with the PCSO's request, without reasonable excuse, is an offence.

Search and seizure powers (alcohol)

Discretionary power

- In association with the power to confiscate alcohol, PCSOs have the power to search the person if they reasonably believe the person has either alcohol or its container in their possession.
- Search is limited to what is reasonably required for the purpose and does not authorise the PCSO to require a person to remove any of their clothing in public other than an outer coat, jacket, or gloves.
- A person who refuses to be searched can be required to give their name and address.
- If a person refuses to give their name and address, or gives an answer that a PCSO has reasonable grounds for suspecting to be false or inaccurate, PCSOs can then invoke their detention powers.
- If on searching the person the PCSO discovers what they are searching for, they may seize and dispose of it.

11.1.3 **Powers relating to tobacco**

Confiscation of tobacco

Standard power

- Power of a constable or a uniformed park-keeper under s 7(3) of the Children and Young Persons Act 1933 to 'seize tobacco or cigarette papers from any person who appears to be under 16 years old who they find smoking in any street or public place' (see **11.5.2**).
- May then dispose of any seized material in such manner as the relevant police authority provides.

Search and seizure powers: tobacco

Discretionary power

- In addition the power to search the person if they reasonably believe the person has either tobacco or cigarette papers in their possession.
- Search is limited to what is reasonably required for the purpose and does not authorise the PCSO to require a person to remove any of their clothing in public other than an outer coat, jacket, or gloves.
- A person who refuses to be searched can be required to give their name and address.
- If a person refuses to give their name and address, or gives an answer that a PCSO has reasonable grounds for suspecting to be false or inaccurate, PCSOs can then invoke their detention powers.

11.1.4 **Powers relating to drugs**

Seize and detain controlled drugs

Standard power

- Can seize and retain controlled drugs when found in a person's unlawful possession (see **5.2.1**).
- Must comply with a constable's instructions about disposal of any controlled drugs seized. If a person maintains that they are lawfully in possession of the drug then the PCSO must inform the person about where enquiries can be made about recovery.
- If a PCSO finds a controlled drug in a person's unlawful possession or reasonably believes that a person is in unlawful possession of a controlled drug then the PCSO may require the person's name and address.
- If a person refuses to give their name and address, or gives an answer that a PCSO has reasonable grounds for suspecting to be false or inaccurate, the PCSO can then invoke their detention powers.

11.1.5 **Powers relating to truancy**

Discretionary power

- Power of a constable, to remove a child or young person to **designated premises**, or to the school from which they are absent, if they have reasonable cause to believe that the child or young person found by the PCSO in a public place in a **specified area** during a **specified period**—
  + is of compulsory school age; **and**
  + is absent from a school without lawful authority.

Notes: *In England only this power also applies to excluded pupils.*

- **Designated premises** are those premises notified to the police by the relevant Local Authority.
- **Specified area** and 'specified period' are to be determined by a police officer of at least the rank of superintendent.

11.1.6 **Powers relating to traffic matters**

Power to require name and address

Standard power

- Powers to direct traffic and to require the name and address of a person who fails to comply with these directions. This is based on those of constables under ss 35 and 37 of the Road Traffic Act 1988 (see **10.2**) and allows PCSOs to direct a person driving a vehicle to stop or follow a line of traffic, and to direct pedestrians and traffic for the purposes of conducting a traffic survey.
- Can require a driver or pedestrian to give their name and address for failure to follow the directions of a PCSO or a police officer.
- If a person refuses to give their name and address, or gives an answer that a PCSO has reasonable grounds for suspecting to be false or inaccurate, then PCSOs can invoke their detention powers.
- Can only exercise these traffic powers within their own police force area.

Vehicles causing obstruction/danger

Standard power

Same powers as a constable in uniform, within the relevant police area, under s 99 of the Road Traffic Regulation Act 1984—to require the removal of vehicles that are causing an obstruction or likely to cause a danger to other road users, or are parked in contravention of a prohibition or restriction.

Power to stop vehicles for testing

Discretionary power

- Powers of a constable in uniform, within the relevant police area, to stop a vehicle under s 67(3) of the Road Traffic Act 1988 (see **10.2**), for the purposes of a test under s 67(1).
- These powers would enable PCSOs to help agencies such as the Vehicle Inspectorate, the Vehicle and Operator Services Agency (VOSA), and local authorities to conduct roadworthiness and emissions tests and also to facilitate the escorting of abnormal loads.

11.1.6 Powers relating to traffic matters

Power to control traffic

Standard power

- Power to control traffic for the purposes of escorting a load other than of exceptional dimensions (either to or from the relevant police area). **Discretionary power** if it is an exceptional dimension load.
- Can also direct traffic in other situations, based on the powers constables have under ss 35 and 37 of the Road Traffic Act 1988 (see **10.2**). This will allow PCSOs to direct a person driving a vehicle to stop or follow a line of traffic and to direct pedestrians.
- HOC 2/2009 states that traffic wardens who are also designated PCSOs under s 38 of the Police Reform Act 2002, should wear the local PCSO uniform without differentiation.
- PCSOs have the power to direct traffic for the purposes of conducting a traffic survey.
- A PCSO can require a driver or pedestrian to give their name and address for failure to follow the directions of a PCSO or a police officer.
- If a person refuses to give their name and address, or gives an answer that a PCSO has reasonable grounds for suspecting to be false or inaccurate, then the PCSOs can invoke their detention powers.
- Can only exercise these traffic powers within their own police force area (except for escorting a load of exceptional dimensions).
- These powers will enable PCSOs to assist with traffic management at public events, road traffic accidents, and other incidents where traffic diversions are necessary.

Power to stop cycles

Power of a constable in uniform under s 163(2) of the Road Traffic Act 1988 to stop a cycle (see **10.2.4**). But this power may only be exercised by the PCSO on reasonable belief that the cyclist has committed a TFPN offence listed in the '**Issue traffic fixed penalty notices (TFPN)**' section at **11.1.1**.

Carrying out of road checks

Standard power

- Power of a police officer to carry out an authorised road check under s 4 of PACE (see **10.2** for details). This enables a road check (authorised by a police superintendent or above) to be established for the purposes of ascertaining—
  - whether a vehicle is carrying a person who has committed an offence (other than a road traffic offence or a vehicle excise offence);
  - a person who is witness to such an offence;
  - a person intending to commit such an offence; or
  - a person who is unlawfully at large.
- It also includes the powers of a constable conferred under s 163 of the Road Traffic Act 1984 (see **10.2.4**) to enable him to require a vehicle to stop for the purpose of a road check.

Power to place traffic signs

Standard power

- Power as a constable (under s 67 of the Road Traffic Regulation Act 1984) (see **10.3** for details) to place temporary traffic signs on a road in extraordinary circumstances.
- A driver who fails to comply with a traffic sign placed by a PCSO commits an offence.
- This power helps a PCSO provide assistance with road traffic accidents and other road incidents.

Seizure of vehicles used to cause alarm

Standard power

- Powers of a constable under s 59 of the Police Reform Act 2002 (see **7.14.1**) regarding vehicles used in a manner causing alarm, distress, or annoyance.
- These include powers to stop and to seize, and to remove motor vehicles where they are being driven—
  - ✦ off-road, contrary to s 34 of the Road Traffic Act 1988 (see **10.23**); or
  - ✦ on the public road or other public place without due care and attention or reasonable consideration for other road users, contrary to s 3 of the 1988 Act (see **10.6**).
- A police officer may enter premises, other than a private dwelling house, for the purpose of exercising these powers. However, the powers, insofar as they include power to enter premises, **are only exercisable by a PCSO** when in the company of and under the supervision of a constable.
- It is an offence for a person to fail to stop a vehicle when required to do so by a police officer (or a PCSO) acting in accordance with this section.
- The officer (or PCSO) must warn the person before seizing the vehicle, to enable its anti-social use to be stopped. But the requirement to give prior warning does not apply where it is impracticable to do so or where a warning has previously been given.

11.1.7 **Power relating to anti-social behaviour**

Require name and address

Standard power

- Powers of a constable under s 50 of the Police Reform Act 2002 (see **7.13.3**) to require the name and address of a person who is, or is

believed to have been, acting in an anti-social manner (as defined in s 2 of the Anti-social Behaviour, Crime and Policing Act 2014—see **7.13.1**).
- Can then invoke the power of detention in relation to a person who fails to comply with the requirement or appears to have given a false or inaccurate name or address.

11.1.8 **Power relating to terrorism**

Cordon areas

Standard power

- Powers of a constable in uniform under s 36 of the Terrorism Act 2000, in respect of cordoned areas established under the Act.
- This includes the power to give orders, make arrangements, or impose prohibitions or restrictions.

Stop and search vehicles in specified areas

Standard power

- Certain powers of a constable in 'authorised areas' under s 47A of the Terrorism Act 2000 (see **12.1.2** '**Terrorism stop and search powers**'), regarding stop and search vehicles; search anything carried by the driver, passenger, or a pedestrian. Also seizure and retention of any article discovered in the course of such a search, on reasonable suspicion that it is intended to be used in connection with terrorism.
- **However**, these powers cannot be exercised by PCSOs unless they are in the company of and under the supervision of a constable, which must be in accordance with the Terrorism Act 2000 Code relating to ss 43, 43A and 47A.

11.1.9 **Power relating to illegal trading**

Park trading offences

Discretionary power

- Where a PCSO reasonably suspects a person to have committed illegal trading in a Royal Park (or other specified place) and has required a person to await the arrival of a constable, the PCSO may take possession of anything of a non-perishable nature that the person has under their control and the PCSO reasonably believes to have been used in the commission of the offence.
- A PCSO can retain the thing for a period not exceeding 30 minutes until able to transfer control of it to a constable.

11.1.10 **Power relating to charity collectors**

Where a designation applies, the PCSO shall, in the **relevant police area**, have the powers of a constable—
- under s 6 of the House to House Collections Act 1939 to require a person to give his name and address and to sign his name; and
- under regs under s 4 of that Act to require a person to produce his certificate of authority.

11.1.11 **Power relating to photographing persons**

Persons arrested, detained, or given fixed penalty notices

Standard power

A PCSO has the power to photograph a person who has been arrested, detained, or given fixed penalty notices elsewhere than at a police station.

Links to alternative subjects and offences

11.2 Mentally Disordered People in Public Places

The Mental Health Act 1983 makes provisions in relation to people with a suspected mental disorder found in public places, in order to ensure their safety and that of the public.

Powers

(1) If a constable finds in a **place** to which the **public** have access a person who appears to him to be suffering from **mental disorder** and to be in immediate need of care or control, the constable may, if he thinks it necessary to do so in the interests of that person or for the protection of other persons, remove that person to a **place of safety** within the meaning of s 135.

(2) A person removed to a place of safety under this section may be detained there for a period not exceeding 72 hours for the purpose of enabling him to be examined by a registered medical practitioner and to be interviewed by an **approved mental health professional** and of making any necessary arrangements for his treatment or care.

(3) A constable, an approved mental health professional or a person authorised by either of them for the purposes of this subsection may, before the end of the period of 72 hours mentioned in subsection (2) above, take a person detained in a place of safety under that subsection to one or more other places of safety.

(4) A person taken to a place of a safety under subsection (3) above may be detained there for a purpose mentioned in subsection (2) above for a period ending no later than the end of the period of 72 hours mentioned in that subsection.

Mental Health Act 1983, s 136

Meanings

Public place

This does not include a place adjacent to areas to which the public have access (*R v Roberts* [2003] EWCA Crim 2753, CA).

Mental disorder

Means any disorder or disability of the mind, and mentally disordered shall be construed accordingly.

Place of safety

Means residential accommodation provided by a local social services authority, a hospital as defined by this Act, a police station, an **independent hospital** or **care home** for mentally disordered persons, or any other suitable place the occupier of which is willing temporarily to receive the patient.

Approved mental health professional

Means a person approved under s 114(1) by any local social services authority.

Care home/independent hospital

These have the same meaning as in the Care Standards Act 2000.

Related cases

Francis v DPP [1997] RTR 113, QBD Police officers were not precluded from administering a breath test to a drink-drive suspect detained under s 136. Although they had formed an opinion about the suspect's mental state justifying detention under s 136, they could still conclude that the suspect understood both the request and knew what was happening. On that basis they had the right to breath test that person.

Practical considerations

- An ambulance must be requested to transport a person detained under s 136. If the person is considered to present a high risk of violence, the police will transport them, accompanied by an ambulance crew member. If the risk is low, the police will follow the ambulance, but if medium risk a joint decision will be made as to mode of transport.
- A person suspected of having a mental disorder who is removed under s 136(1) can only be taken from a place to which the public have access.
- Section 135 deals with an application for a warrant on suspicion that a person is suffering from a mental disorder and has been, or is being, ill-treated, neglected, or kept otherwise than under proper control, in any place or being unable to care for him/herself, is living alone in any such place. The warrant may authorise any constable to enter the place, if need be by force in order to take that person to a place of safety.
- A person cannot be deemed to be suffering from mental disorder by reason only of their promiscuity, immoral conduct, sexual deviancy, dependence on alcohol or drugs.
- If an offence has also been committed, the appropriate power of arrest could be considered.
- The power under s 136 is a **power of removal** for the purposes of getting the person out of a public place until they can be examined by an approved mental health professional.
- As the Mental Health Act 2007 has simplified the meaning of mental disorder and allowed transfer between different places of safety within the 72-hour period, it has removed conflict between the police, medical practitioners, psychiatrists, and mental health professionals as to: the meaning of 'mental disorder', how long the police could 'hold' a person detained under s 136, and whether a police station was an appropriate place for detaining such a person for 72 hours.

11.2 Mentally Disordered People in Public Places

- Problems may arise where a person although 'confused' is assessed as not suitable for further compulsory detention under the Act and is released without any treatment or care.
- Forming inter-agency agreements with NHS agencies is encouraged by HOC 66/1990 and 12/1995. Similarly HOC 17/2004 provides guidance and best practice regarding local protocols between the police and health services on handling potentially violent individuals detained under s 136.
- The 2014 Mental Health COP issued by the Department of Health provides guidance to professionals, clarifying their roles and responsibilities under the Act. It deals with the CJ system, the Victims Code (see **13.4**), policies to reduce the use of ss 135 and 136, police removing people from public/private places, transfer to places of safety.
- HOC 7/2008 guidance states that a police station should only be used as a place of safety in exceptional circumstances; although it may be necessary to do so if the person's behaviour poses an unmanageably high risk to other patients, staff, or users in a healthcare setting.
- Where possible, the detainee's general medical practitioner should be involved, their role will be important in deciding whether or not there is to be a medical admission.
- Legality of detention issues—
  + People removed from public places under s 136 should be assessed as soon as possible. If that assessment is to take place in a police station, an approved mental health professional and registered medical practitioner **must** be called to carry out the interview and examination (PACE Code C 3.16). Once interviewed, examined, and suitable arrangements made for their treatment or care they can no longer be lawfully detained under s 136;
  + The person should not be released until they have been assessed by an approved mental health professional and the registered medical practitioner;
  + If the decision has been made that the person is not 'mentally disordered', admittance for treatment can only be given by that person's consent.

Links to alternative subjects and offences

11.3 **Illegal Entry into the UK/ Identity Documents**

Legislation relating to immigration is vast. However, three major aspects potentially affect everyday policing and include: illegal entry into the UK, illegal entry by deception, and assisting and harbouring an illegal immigrant.

11.3.1 **Illegal entry into the UK/identity documents/powers relating to passports**

Section 24 of the Immigration Act 1971 creates offences in relation to illegal entry.

Offences

A person who is not a British citizen shall be guilty of an offence in any of the following cases—

(a) if contrary to this Act he knowingly enters the UK in breach of a deportation order or without leave;

(b) if, having only a limited leave to enter or remain in the UK, he knowingly either—
   (i) remains beyond the time limited by the leave; or
   (ii) fails to observe a condition of the leave;

(c) if, having lawfully entered the UK without leave by virtue of section 8(1), he remains without leave beyond the time allowed by section 8(1);

(d) if, without reasonable excuse, he fails to comply with any requirement imposed on him under Schedule 2 to this Act to report to a medical officer of health, or to attend, or submit to a test or examination, as required by such an officer;

(e) if, without reasonable excuse, he fails to observe any restriction imposed on him under Schedule 2 or 3 to this Act as to residence, as to his employment or occupation or as to reporting to the police to an immigration officer or to the Secretary of State;

(f) if he disembarks in the UK from a ship or aircraft after being placed on board under Schedule 2 or 3 to this Act with a view to his removal from the UK;

(g) if he embarks in contravention of a restriction imposed by or under an Order in Council under section 3(7) of this Act.

Immigration Act 1971, s 24(1)

11.3.1 Illegal entry into the UK/identity documents

Points to prove

✓ not being a British citizen
✓ committed one or more of the acts in s 24(1)

Explanatory notes

- European Union nationals and those exercising EU rights do not need leave to enter or remain in the UK.
- A person commits an offence under s 24(1)(b)(i) on the day when they first knew that the time limited by the leave had expired and continues to commit it throughout any period during which they remain in the UK; but that person shall not be prosecuted more than once in respect of the same limited leave.

Related cases

R v Uxbridge Magistrates' Court, ex parte Sorani, Adimi and Kaziu [1999] 4 All ER 529, QBD Provides guidance on the prosecution of asylum seekers as illegal immigrants (see below).

Practical considerations

- Illegal entrants should not be prosecuted for offences of illegal entry or travelling on false documents if they are claiming political asylum, arriving directly from a place where they were in danger, present themselves immediately and show good reason for their entry. This is in line with the UN Convention relating to refugee status and was followed in the case of *R v Uxbridge Magistrates' Court, ex parte Sorani, Adimi and Kaziu* [1999] 4 All ER 529, QBD. This only applies to offences relating to asylum seekers who face charges relating to illegal entry and the use of false travel documents; they are still subject to prosecution for other offences in the usual way.
- Section 25D provides that where a person has been arrested for assisting in illegal entry (see **11.3.3**) or any of the following offences—
  - ♦ s 25 Assist in unlawful immigration to Member State/does act in breach of immigration law;
  - ♦ s 25A For gain—help asylum seeker gain entry into UK;
  - ♦ s 25B Assist arrival/entry/remain in UK in breach of deportation/exclusion order;

  then any vehicle, ship, or aircraft used when committing these offences may be seized and detained by a police constable or senior immigration officer, pending a court order for their forfeiture.
- Consider confiscation of cash and property for the s 25, s 25A, or s 25B Immigration Act 1971 (assisting unlawful immigration) offences. These and other people trafficking offences are given as 'criminal lifestyle' offences under Sch 2 to the Proceeds of Crime Act 2002 (see **5.5** for details).

Identity documents

- Section 4 of the Identity Documents Act 2010 makes it an indictable offence for a person with an improper intention to have in their possession or control an **identity document** that is false, improperly obtained, or relates to someone else.
- Section 6 of the Identity Documents Act 2010 makes it an 'either way' offence for a person, without reasonable excuse, to have in their possession or control an **identity document** that is false, improperly obtained, relates to someone else, or any apparatus/article which is specially designed or adapted for the making of false identity documents.
- An **identity document** means any document that is or purports to be an immigration document, UK passport, passport for a country or territory outside the UK, a document that can be used instead of a passport, UK driving licence or driving licence for a country or territory outside the UK.
- HOC 4/2010 provides guidance on the entry, search and seizure powers, relating to nationality or identity documents, which are available to a constable or the UKBA under ss 44 to 47 of the UK Borders Act 2007.

Powers relating to passports

- Schedule 8 of the Anti-social Behaviour, Crime and Policing Act 2014, provides search powers in relation to passports and if required to seize and retain the passport/travel document.
- HOC 4/2014 provides guidance for the police, immigration and customs officials in applying these powers at ports; and for the police to seize/retain passports that have been cancelled by the Secretary of State where a person is suspected of involvement in activities contrary to the public interest.

Powers of search and seizure at ports (para 2)

- An **examining officer** may exercise any of the following powers in the case of a person at a **port** whom the officer believes to be there in connection with entering or leaving GB or Northern Ireland, or travelling by air within GB or Northern Ireland. The powers are to—
  - ◆ require the person to hand over all travel documents in their possession for inspection by the officer;
  - ◆ search for travel documents, and take possession to inspect any found by the officer;
  - ◆ (subject to para 4) retain any **travel document** taken from the person, while its validity is checked or which the examining officer believes to be **invalid**.
- In order to search for travel documents, the officer has a power to search—
  - ◆ the person;
  - ◆ anything that the person has with them;
  - ◆ any vehicle in which the examining officer believes the person to have been travelling or to be about to travel.
- An examining officer may—
  - ◆ stop a person or vehicle and if necessary use reasonable force for the purposes of exercising the above powers;
  - ◆ authorise a person to carry out a search on behalf of the officer.

11.3.1 Illegal entry into the UK/identity documents

- An examining officer, other than a constable, in exercising the above powers has the same powers of arrest (without warrant) as a constable in relation to the below offences or for the offences under s 4 or s 6 of the Identity Documents Act 2010 (above).

Meanings

Examining officer

Means: a constable, immigration officer, or a general customs official.

Port

Means—
- an airport, sea port, hoverport, heliport;
- a railway station where passenger trains go to/from places outside the UK; or
- any other place at which a person is able, or attempting, to get on or off any craft, vessel or vehicle in connection with entering or leaving GB or Northern Ireland.

Travel document

Means anything that is, or appears to be, a passport or other document which has been issued by or for HM Government, or the government of another state, and enables or facilitates travel from one state to another.

Invalid travel document

A travel document is invalid if: it has been cancelled or expired; it was not issued by the government or authority by which it purports to have been issued; or it has undergone an unauthorised alteration.

Constables search and seizure powers (para 3)

- A constable may exercise any of the below powers, at a place that is not a port, if the constable reasonably believes that a person is in possession of a passport which—
  - ◆ was issued by or for Her Majesty's Government;
  - ◆ has been cancelled by the Secretary of State on the basis that the person to whom it was issued has or may have been, or will or may become, involved in activities so undesirable that it is contrary to the public interest for the person to have access to passport facilities; and
  - ◆ is specified in an authorisation issued by the Secretary of State for the use of the powers under this paragraph.
- The powers are to—
  - ◆ require the person to hand over all travel documents in their possession for inspection by the constable;
  - ◆ search for travel documents and to take possession of any that the constable finds;
  - ◆ inspect any travel document taken from the person and to retain it while its validity is checked;
  - ◆ (subject to para 4) retain any travel document taken that the constable believes to be invalid.
- The power to search for travel documents, is a power to search—
  - ◆ the person;
  - ◆ anything that the person has with them;

+ any vehicle in which the constable believes the person has travelled in or is about to travel in;
+ any premises on which the constable is lawfully present.
- A constable may—
  + if necessary use reasonable force for the purpose of exercising the above powers;
  + authorise a person to carry out the above search powers on the constable's behalf.

Retention or return of documents seized (para 4)

- If a travel document is retained under para 2 or 3 while its validity is checked, the checking must be carried out as soon as possible.
- If such a travel document is valid, or is invalid only because it has expired, it must be returned to the person straight away.
- A travel document taken under para 2 or 3 must be returned to the person before the end of the period of 7 days beginning with the day on which it was taken, unless during that period it is established that the document is invalid for some reason other than expiry.
- A requirement to return an expired travel document does not apply where the officer concerned reasonably believes that the person from whom they took the document, or some other person, intends to use it for purposes for which it is no longer valid.
- A requirement to return a travel document has effect subject to any provision not in this Sch under which the document may be lawfully retained.

Schedule 8 offences (para 5)

- A person who is required under para 2 or 3 to hand over all travel documents in their possession commits an offence if they fail without reasonable excuse to do so.
- A person who intentionally obstructs, or seeks to frustrate, a search under para 2 or 3 commits an offence.

Illegal entry/Passports

 Summary 6 months

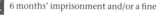 6 months' imprisonment and/or a fine

Identity documents

E&S

 s 4 Indictable; s 6 Either way   None

11.3.2 Illegal entry by deception

 s 4 offence
Indictment: 10 years' imprisonment and/or a fine

 s 6 offence
Summary: 6 months' imprisonment and/or a fine
Indictment: 2 years' imprisonment and/or a fine

11.3.2 **Illegal entry by deception**

Offences

A person who is not a British citizen is guilty of an offence if, by means which include deception by him—

(a) he obtains or seeks to obtain leave to enter or remain in the UK; or
(b) he secures or seeks to secure the avoidance, postponement or revocation of **enforcement action** against him.

Immigration Act 1971, s 24A(1)

Points to prove

✓ not being a British citizen
✓ by any means including deception
✓ obtained/sought to obtain leave to enter/remain in UK
or
✓ secured/sought to secure the avoidance/postponement/ revocation of enforcement action

Meaning of enforcement action

Enforcement action in relation to a person means—
• giving of directions for removal from the UK;
• making of a deportation order under s 5; or
• removal from UK from directions or deportation order.

E&S

 Either way

 None

 Summary: 6 months' imprisonment and/or a fine
Indictment: 2 years' imprisonment and/or a fine

11.3.3 **Assisting illegal entry**

Section 25 of the Immigration Act 1971 deals with assisting unlawful immigration to a Member State.

Offences

A person commits an offence if he—
(a) does an act which facilitates the commission of a breach of **immigration law** by an individual who is not a **citizen of the European Union**,
(b) knows or has reasonable cause for believing that the act facilitates the commission of a breach of immigration law by the individual, and
(c) knows or has reasonable cause for believing that the individual is not a citizen of the European Union.

Immigration Act 1971, s 25(1)

Points to prove

✓ did an act
✓ which facilitated breach of immigration law
✓ by a person
✓ who was not a citizen of the EU
✓ knowing/having reasonable cause for believing
✓ that the act facilitated breach of immigration law
✓ by that person
✓ knowing/having reasonable cause for believing
✓ that person was not a citizen of the EU

Meanings

Immigration law (s 25(2))

Means a law which has effect in a **Member State** and which controls, in respect of some or all persons who are not nationals of the State, entitlement to enter, transit across, or be in the State.

Member State

Apart from an EC Member State, it also includes a State named on a list known as the 'Section 25 List of Schengen Acquis States'.

Citizen of the European Union

Includes reference to a national of a State on the s 25 list.

Practical considerations

Section 25(4), states that s 25(1) applies to things done whether inside or outside the UK.

11.3.3 Assisting illegal entry

- The 'Section 25 List of Schengen Acquis States' are regarded as member states for the purposes of s 25, and they are Norway and Iceland.
- Section 25A of the Immigration Act 1971 creates an offence of knowingly and for gain facilitating the arrival/entry into the UK of an individual, and knowing/having reasonable cause to believe that the individual is an asylum seeker.
- Section 25D gives a power to seize the means of transport used for this offence and s 25C provides the court with a power to order forfeiture of this transport (see **11.3.1**).
- Consider confiscation of cash and property for the s 25 offences of assisting unlawful immigration/entry. This and other people trafficking offences are given as 'criminal lifestyle' offences under Sch 2 to the Proceeds of Crime Act 2002 (see **5.5** for details).

E&S

 Either way   None

 Summary: 6 months' imprisonment and/or a fine
Indictment: 14 years' imprisonment and/or a fine

Links to alternative subjects and offences

11.4 **Wasting Police Time**

This section considers two aspects of taking up police resources on false pretences, that of wasting police time and of carrying out a bomb hoax.

11.4.1 **Wasting police time**

Section 5(2) of the Criminal Law Act 1967 creates the offence of the wasteful employment of the police by making false reports.

Offences

Where a person causes any wasteful employment of the police by knowingly making to any person a false report tending to show that an offence has been committed or to give rise to apprehension for the safety of any persons or property, or tending to show that he has information material to any police inquiry, he commits an offence.

Criminal Law Act 1967, s 5(2)

Points to prove

✓ knowingly caused
✓ wasteful employment of police
✓ by false report
✓ that offence committed **or**
✓ gives apprehension for safety of persons/property **or**
✓ had information material to police enquiry

Explanatory notes

Giving rise to apprehension for safety of any persons or property could apply where a person falsely reports a house fire in order to commit a burglary or a mother falsely reports that her child is missing in an attempt to get her estranged husband back.

Practical considerations

- Consent of DPP is required before commencing a prosecution.
- If suitable, consider issuing a PND (see **7.1.1**).
- Decisions to prosecute are often inconsistent and may bear no relation to the number of hours wasted on the investigation.
- Consider other similar offences such as hoax bomb calls (see **11.4.2**) or false messages (see **7.12**).

Summary 6 Months

 6 months' imprisonment and/or a level 4 fine

11.4.2 **Bomb and terrorist-type hoaxes**

Bomb hoaxes

Section 51 of the Criminal Law Act 1977 concerns bomb hoaxes.

> ### Offences
>
> (1) A person who—
>   (a) places any **article** in any place whatever; or
>   (b) dispatches any article by post, rail or any other means whatever of
>   sending things from one place to another,
>   with the **intention** (in either case) of inducing in some other **person** a
>   belief that it is likely to explode or ignite and thereby cause personal
>   injury or damage to property is guilty of an offence.
> (2) A person who communicates any information which he knows or
>   believes to be false to another **person** with the intention of inducing
>   in him or any other person a false belief that a bomb or other thing
>   liable to explode or ignite is present in any place or location whatever
>   is guilty of an offence.
>
> Criminal Law Act 1977, s 51

> ### Points to prove
>
> #### s 51(1) offence
> ✓ placed in any place **or** dispatched by post/rail/other means of
>   sending things
> ✓ an article
> ✓ with intent
> ✓ to induce in another the belief
> ✓ that the article
> ✓ was likely to explode/ignite
> ✓ and cause personal injury/damage to property

---

s 51(2) offence

✓ communicated
✓ information to another person
✓ knew/believed to be false
✓ with intent
✓ of inducing a false belief in that person/any other person
✓ that bomb/thing was in place or location and
✓ was liable to explode/ignite at that place/location

Meanings

Article

This includes substance.

Intention (see **4.1.2**)

Person

It is not necessary to have any particular person in mind as the person in whom they intend to induce the belief in question.

Explanatory notes

- Section 51(1) concerns the placing or dispatching of articles with the intention that people believe that they are bombs or explosive devices; whereas s 51(2) concerns people who communicate false information intending others to believe there is a bomb or explosive device likely to explode.
- This section does not require a specific place or location to be given.

Related cases

R v Webb [1995] 27 LS Gaz R 31, CA The hoax message does not have to give a specific place or location.

Terrorist-type hoaxes

Section 114 of the Anti-terrorism, Crime and Security Act 2001 has created a similar offence for biological, chemical, and nuclear hoaxes. These include actions such as sending powders or liquids through the post and claiming that they are harmful.

Offences

(1) A person is guilty of an offence if he—
    (a) places any **substance** or other thing in any place; or
    (b) sends any substance or other thing from one place to another (by post, rail or any other means whatever);

---

with the **intention** of inducing in a **person** anywhere in the world a belief that it is likely to be (or contain) a noxious substance or other noxious thing and thereby endanger human life or create a serious risk to human health.

(2) A person is guilty of an offence if he communicates any information which he knows or believes to be false with the intention of inducing in a person anywhere in the world a belief that a noxious substance or other noxious thing is likely to be present (whether at the time the information is communicated or later) in any place and thereby endanger human life or create a serious risk to human health.

Anti-terrorism, Crime and Security Act 2001, s 114

Points to prove

s 114(1) offence

- ✓ placed **or** sent
- ✓ a substance/thing
- ✓ intending
- ✓ to induce in a person
- ✓ a belief that it is likely to be/contain a noxious substance/thing
- ✓ and thereby endanger human life/create a serious risk to human health

s 114(2) offence

- ✓ communicated information
- ✓ knew/believed to be false
- ✓ intending
- ✓ to induce in a person
- ✓ anywhere in the world
- ✓ a belief that a noxious substance/thing
- ✓ was likely to be present in any place
- ✓ thereby endanger human life/create a serious risk to human health

Meanings

Substance

Includes any biological agent and any other natural or artificial substance (whatever its form, origin, or method of production).

Intention (see 4.1.2)

Person (see 'Bomb hoaxes' above)

Practical considerations

- A related offence is food contamination contrary to s 38 of the Public Order Act 1986. It is an offence under s 38(1) to intend to cause alarm, injury, or loss by contamination or interference with **goods** or by making it appear that goods have been contaminated or interfered with in a place where goods of that description are consumed, used, sold, or otherwise supplied. It is also an offence under s 38(2) to make threats or claims relating to s 38(1) or to possess materials under s 38(3) with a view to committing a s 38(1) offence.

- Section 38 concerns 'consumer terrorism' which could involve animal rights activists or an individual trying to blackmail a manufacturer or supermarket chain. **Goods** includes substances whether natural or manufactured and whether or not incorporated in or mixed with other goods.
- The court should be made aware of the disruptions and anxiety caused by the hoax.
- How much time and expense were wasted by the hoax?

 Either way   None

 Summary: 6 months' imprisonment and/or a fine
Indictment: 7 years' imprisonment and/or a fine

Links to alternative subjects and offences

SSS Stop, search and seize powers   **E&S** Entry and search powers

11.5 Supplying Intoxicating Substances / Tobacco

This subject is presented in two parts: first, the supplying of intoxicating substances and second, the supplying of butane lighter refills and tobacco.

11.5.1 Supplying intoxicating substances

Section 1 of the Intoxicating Substances (Supply) Act 1985 creates offences, and a defence, in relation to the supply of 'inhalants' other than controlled drugs to people under 18 years of age.

Offences

It is an offence for a person to **supply** or offer to supply a substance other than a **controlled drug**—
(a) to a person under the age of 18 whom he knows or has reasonable cause to believe, to be under that age; or
(b) to a person—
    (i) who is acting on behalf of a person under that age; and
    (ii) whom he knows or has reasonable cause to believe, to be so acting,
if he knows or has reasonable cause to believe that the substance is, or its fumes are, likely to be inhaled by the person under the age of 18 for the purpose of causing intoxication.

Intoxicating Substances (Supply) Act 1985, s 1(1)

Points to prove

✓ supplied/offered to supply a substance other than a controlled drug

s 1(1)(a) offence

✓ to a person under 18
✓ that you knew/had reasonable cause to believe was under that age

s 1(1)(b) offence

✓ person acting on behalf of person under 18 and
✓ whom you knew/had reasonable cause to believe was so acting
✓ knowing/having reasonable cause to believe substance/fumes were likely to be inhaled
✓ by person under 18 to cause intoxication

Meanings

Supply

Provide or make available (something needed or wanted); furnish for use or consumption.

Controlled drug (see **5.1.1**)

Explanatory notes

- This legislation was introduced to try and curb 'glue sniffing' or getting high on the fumes from solvents.
- The offence does not require that the substance must actually cause intoxication or even have the potential to do so; just that the person under 18 is likely to inhale it for that purpose.
- There may be a case against a shopkeeper who has the appropriate intentions and beliefs about the substance, believing that the person under 18 was going to be intoxicated on the substance supplied.

Defences

In proceedings against any person for an offence under subsection 1(1) it is a defence for him to show that at the time he made the supply or offer they were under the age of 18 and were acting otherwise than in the course or furtherance of business.

Intoxicating Substances (Supply) Act 1985, s 1(2)

Practical considerations

- If you are unsure about a substance's likely effect, it may be possible to contact the manufacturers who may be willing to give expert advice.
- There is no definitive list of substances and more or less any chemical substance could be involved (eg, young people inhaling laughing gas (nitrous oxide) as a party drug for its hallucinatory properties).
- The substance could even include products considered harmful such as aerosols for air fresheners, pain relief, and antiperspirants/deodorants. This is because it is the propellant and not the liquid in aerosols, which is inhaled, and the majority of aerosol products use butane as the main propellant.

 Summary   6 months

 6 months' imprisonment and/or a fine

11.5.2 **Supplying butane lighter refills and tobacco**

The Cigarette Lighter Refill (Safety) Regulations 1999 (SI 1844/1999) make it an offence to supply butane lighter refills to people under 18. The Children and Young Persons Act 1933 makes it an offence to sell tobacco or cigarette papers to a person under 18, with a power to search and seize from people under 16 found smoking in a street or public place.

Offences

No person shall **supply** any cigarette lighter refill canister containing butane or a substance with butane as a constituent part to any person under the age of 18 years.

Cigarette Lighter Refill (Safety) Regulations 1999, reg 2

Points to prove

✓ supplied
✓ cigarette lighter refill canister containing butane
✓ to person aged under 18 years

Meaning of supply (see 11.5.1)

Explanatory notes

- These Regulations prohibit the supply of cigarette lighter refill canisters containing butane to persons under the age of 18.
- Contravention of these Regulations is an offence under s 12 of the Consumer Protection Act 1987.

Defences

It shall be a defence for that person to show that he took all reasonable steps and exercised all due diligence to avoid committing the offence.

Consumer Protection Act 1987, s 39(1)

Possession of tobacco or cigarette papers

- Section 7 of the Children and Young Persons Act 1933 makes it an offence to sell to a person under the age of 18 any tobacco or cigarette papers, whether for their own use or not. It is a defence for the seller to prove that they took all reasonable precautions and exercised all due diligence to avoid committing the offence.

- A power of seizure exists, but there is an anomaly in that it only applies to a person who appears to be under 16. A constable in uniform can seize any tobacco or cigarette papers from a person who appears to be under 16, whom they find smoking in any street or public place, and can dispose of any seized tobacco or cigarette papers as directed by the police authority.
- PCSO's have the same powers as a constable to seize tobacco or cigarette papers from any person, who appears to be under 16, whom they find smoking in any street or public place. A PCSO may have an additional power to search, beyond a constable's power, if they reasonably believe the person has tobacco/cigarette papers in their possession. The PCSO must be designated with this 'discretionary' power (see **11.1.3**).

PCSO

 Summary   6 months

 Butane refills: 6 months' imprisonment and/or a fine
Tobacco: Level 4 fine

Links to alternative subjects and offences

11.6 Animal Welfare and Control of Dogs

The Animal Welfare Act 2006 is discussed in the first subject area, and the remaining topics deal with dangerous dogs; orders for their control; and guard dogs.

11.6.1 Animal welfare offences

The Animal Welfare Act 2006 has introduced a large number of offences that are intended to prevent harm and distress to animals. The offence of unnecessary suffering under s 4 is dealt with, but other offences within the Act are given in a bullet point/précis form so that the reader is at least aware of them.

Unnecessary suffering

Offences

(1) A person commits an offence if—
   (a) an act of his, or a failure of his to act, causes an **animal** to suffer,
   (b) he knew, or ought reasonably to have known, that the act, or failure to act, would have that effect or be likely to do so,
   (c) the animal is a **protected animal**, and
   (d) the **suffering** is unnecessary.
(2) A person commits an offence if—
   (a) he is **responsible** for an animal,
   (b) an act, or failure to act, of another person causes the animal to suffer,
   (c) he permitted that to happen or failed to take such steps (whether by way of supervising the other person or otherwise) as were reasonable in all the circumstances to prevent that happening, and
   (d) the suffering is unnecessary.

Animal Welfare Act 2006, s 4

Points to prove

s 4(1) offence

✓ did an act/failed to act
✓ that caused a protected animal to suffer
✓ knowing/ought to have known by this act/failure to act
✓ caused/was likely to cause this suffering and
✓ the suffering is unnecessary

---

s 4(2) offence
- ✓ being responsible for an animal where
- ✓ another person did an act/failed to act
- ✓ that caused the animal to suffer
- ✓ permitted/failed to prevent this suffering happening
- ✓ it caused/was likely to cause this suffering and
- ✓ the suffering is unnecessary

Meanings

Animal

Means a vertebrate other than man. It does not apply to an animal while in a foetal or embryonic form.

Protected animal

An animal if it is—
- of a kind which is commonly domesticated in the British Islands;
- under the control of man whether permanent or temporary; or
- not living in a wild state.

Suffering

Means physical or mental suffering.

Responsible

A person is responsible for an animal—
- whether on a permanent or temporary basis;
- when they are in charge of it;
- when they own it;
- when they have actual care and control of a person under the age of 16 who is responsible for it.

Explanatory notes

- Matters to consider whether suffering is unnecessary include—
  - could it have been avoided or reduced?;
  - complying with legislation/licence/code of practice;
  - was it for a legitimate purpose, such as benefiting the animal, or protecting a person, property, or another animal?;
  - was it proportionate to the purpose of the conduct concerned?;
  - was the conduct that of a reasonably competent and humane person?

This section does not apply to the destruction of an animal in an appropriate and humane manner.

Other animal welfare offences

Section 5—Mutilation

It is an offence if a person carries out/causes to be carried out a prohibited procedure on a protected animal.

11.6.1 Animal welfare offences

- Similarly the person responsible for the animal will commit an offence if they carry out the procedure or permit/fail to prevent this happening.
- The procedure involves interference with the sensitive tissues or bone structure of the animal, otherwise than for the purpose of its medical treatment.

Section 6—Docking of dogs' tails

- With certain exceptions it is an offence if a person removes/causes to be removed all/part of a dog's tail.
- Similarly the person responsible for the dog is liable if the dog's tail is docked or permits/fails to prevent this happening.

Section 7—Administration of poisons or injurious drug/substance

- It is an offence if a person, without lawful authority or reasonable excuse administers or causes to be taken any poisonous or injurious drug or substance to/by a protected animal, knowing it to be poisonous or injurious.
- Similarly a person responsible for an animal, commits an offence if—
  + without lawful authority or reasonable excuse, another person administers a poisonous or injurious drug or substance to the animal or causes the animal to take such a drug or substance; **and**
  + they permitted that to happen or, knowing the drug or substance to be poisonous or injurious, they failed to take such steps (whether by way of supervising the other person or otherwise) as were reasonable in all the circumstances to prevent that happening.
- A poisonous or injurious drug or substance includes a drug or substance which, by virtue of the quantity or manner in which it is administered or taken, has the effect of a poisonous or injurious drug or substance.

Section 8—Offences involving animals fighting

- A person commits an offence if they—
  + cause an **animal fight** to take place, or attempt to do so;
  + knowingly receive money for admission to an animal fight;
  + knowingly publicise a proposed animal fight;
  + provide information about an animal fight to another with the intention of enabling or encouraging attendance at the fight;
  + make or accept a bet on the outcome of an animal fight, or on the likelihood of anything occurring or not occurring in the course of an animal fight;
  + take part in an animal fight;
  + have in their possession anything designed or adapted for use in connection with an animal fight with the intention of its being so used;
  + keep or train an animal for use for or in connection with an animal fight;
  + keep any premises for use for an animal fight.
- A person commits an offence if, without lawful authority or reasonable excuse, they are present at an animal fight.

- **Animal fight**—means an occasion on which a protected animal is placed with an animal, or with a human, for the purpose of fighting, wrestling, or baiting.
- Section 22(1) gives a constable power to seize any animal that appears to have been involved in fighting, where an offence under s 8 has been committed.

Section 11—Transfer animals by sale/transaction/prize to under 16

- A person commits an offence if they sell an animal to a person having reasonable cause to believe to be under the age of 16 years—
  - ✦ selling includes transferring ownership in consideration of entering into another transaction.
- It is an offence to enter into an arrangement with a person having reasonable cause to believe to be under the age of 16 years, where the 16-year-old has the chance to win an animal as a prize, unless it is—
  - ✦ in the presence of and they are accompanied by a person over 16 years; or
  - ✦ in the belief that the person who has care and control has consented; or
  - ✦ arranged in a family environment.

Practical considerations

- Section 18 gives a constable powers to take such steps as appear to be immediately necessary to alleviate a protected animal's suffering. It is an offence to intentionally obstruct a person exercising the s 18 powers.
- Section 19 allows a constable to enter premises (except a part which is used as a private dwelling) to search for a protected animal in order to exercise their s 18 power, having reasonable belief that the animal is on the premises, and is suffering or likely to suffer. A constable may use reasonable force to gain entry, but only if it appears that entry is required before a warrant can be obtained (under s 23) and executed.
- Section 54 states that a constable in uniform may stop and detain a vehicle for the purpose of entering and searching it in the exercise of a search power conferred under—
  - ✦ s 19 for a protected animal believed to be suffering; or
  - ✦ s 22 for an animal, believed involved in fighting under s 8.
- A vehicle may be detained for as long as is reasonably required to permit a search or inspection to be carried out (including the exercise of any related power under this Act) either at the place where the vehicle was first detained or nearby.
- Section 17(1)(c)(v) of PACE (see **12.3.2**) gives further power to a constable in order to enter and search premises for the purpose of arresting a person for offences under ss 4, 5, 6(1) and (2), 7, and 8(1) and (2) of this Act.

11.6.2 Dangerous dogs not under control

Applies to s 4, s 5, s 6, s 7, and s 8 offences

 Summary

 Maximum of three years from date of offence, **but** six months from date of having sufficient evidence to justify proceedings

6 months' imprisonment and/or a fine

11.6.2 **Dangerous dogs not under control**

The Dangerous Dogs Act 1991 imposes restrictions on keeping dogs which are a danger to the public and creates offences relating to a dog being dangerously out of control.

> ### Offences
>
> If a dog is **dangerously out of control** in any place in England or Wales (whether or not a **public place**)—
> (a) the **owner**; and
> (b) if different, the person for the time being in charge of the dog,
> is guilty of an offence, or, if the dog while so out of control injures any person or **assistance dog**, an aggravated offence, under this subsection.
>
> Dangerous Dogs Act 1991, s 3(1)

Points to prove
Standard offence
✓ owner/person in charge of dog
✓ dangerously out of control
✓ in any place

Aggravated offence
✓ while out of control caused injury to any person or assistance dog

Meanings

Dangerously out of control

Means when there are grounds for reasonable apprehension that the dog will injure any person or **assistance dog**, whether or not it actually does so.

Public place

Means any street, road, or other place (whether or not it is enclosed) to which the public have or are permitted to have access, whether for payment or otherwise, including the common parts of a building containing two or more separate dwellings.

Owner

Where a dog is owned by a person who is under 16, any reference to its owner shall include a reference to the head of the household, if any, of which that person is a member.

Assistance dog

Means a dog which has been trained—

- to guide a blind person;
- to assist a deaf person;
- by a prescribed charity to assist a disabled person with a disability that consists of epilepsy or otherwise affects their mobility, manual dexterity, physical co-ordination or ability to lift, carry or otherwise move everyday objects;
- to assist a disabled person who has a disability of a prescribed kind (not given above), and the dog is of a prescribed category.

Explanatory notes

- The Anti-social Behaviour, Crime and Policing Act 2014, s 106 extended the s 3 offence to not just be a public place, or a private place where the dog is not permitted to be, but to all places including private property.
- The exemptions given in ss 3(1A) and (1B) (see 'Defences') cover cases where a dog becomes dangerously out of control when a trespasser is inside, or is in the process of entering, a building that is a place where a person lives. It does not matter whether the person actually was a trespasser; if the owner is in the building when the dog becomes out of control and believes that the person is a trespasser that is sufficient.
- People who live in buildings which serve a dual purpose as a place of residence and a place of work (for example, a shopkeeper and his or her family who live above the shop), can rely on the defence of self-defence given in s 76(8B) of the Criminal Justice and Immigration Act 2008 (see **1.2.1**) regardless of which part of the building they were in when they were confronted by an intruder, providing that there is internal means of access between the two parts of the building.

Defences

(1A) A person ('D') is not guilty of an offence under subsection (1) in a case which is a **householder case**.

(1B) For the purposes of subsection (1A) 'a **householder case**' is a case where—

(a) the dog is dangerously out of control while in or partly in a building, or part of a building, that is a dwelling or is forces accommodation (or is both), and

(b) at that time—

(i) the person in relation to whom the dog is dangerously out of control ('V') is in, or is entering, the building or part as a trespasser, or

(ii) D (if present at that time) believed V to be in, or entering, the building or part as a trespasser.

Section 76(8B) to (8F) of the Criminal Justice and Immigration Act 2008 (use of force at place of residence) *[see 1.2.1]* apply for the purposes of this subsection as they apply for the purposes of subsection (8A) of that section (and for those purposes the reference in section 76(8D) to subsection (8A)(d) is to be read as if it were a reference to paragraph (b)(ii) of this subsection).

(2) In proceedings for an offence under subsection (1) above against a person who is the owner of a dog, but was not at the material time in charge of it, it shall be a defence for the accused to prove that the dog was, at the material time, in the charge of a person whom he reasonably believed to be a fit and proper person to be in charge of it.

Dangerous Dogs Act 1991, s 3

Destruction and disqualification orders

(1) Where a person is convicted of an offence under section 1 or 3(1) above the court—

(a) may order the destruction of any dog in respect of which the offence was committed and, subject to subsection (1A) below, shall do so in the case of an offence under section 1 or an aggravated offence under section 3(1) above; and

(b) may order the offender to be disqualified, for such period as the court thinks fit, for having custody of a dog.

(1A) Nothing in subsection (1)(a) above shall require the court to order the destruction of a dog if the court is satisfied that the dog would not constitute a danger to public safety.

(1B) For the purposes of subsection (1A)(a), when deciding whether a dog would constitute a danger to public safety, the court—

(a) must consider—

(i) the temperament of the dog and its past behaviour, and

(ii) whether the owner of the dog, or the person for the time being in charge of it, is a fit and proper person to be in charge of the dog, and

(b) may consider any other relevant circumstances.

Dangerous Dogs Act 1991, s

Related cases (see **11.6.4** for further cases)

L v CPS [2010] EWHC 341, DC L took a dog into a public place and asked co-defendant G to take the lead. G released the dog and shouted 'Get him', so the dog attacked and injured V. Although G took physical control, L remained 'in charge' as the dog obeyed L's commands.

R v Gedminintaite [2008] EWCA Crim 814, CA The behaviour of the dog and the fact that the handler had no proper control over it was sufficient evidence that a dog is dangerously out of control in a public place.

R v Bezzina; R v Codling; R v Elvin [1994] 3 All ER 964, CA Court stated that the s 3(1) offence imposes strict liability, as no 'mens rea' is required on the part of the owner or handler of dogs.

Practical considerations

- In considering whether a dog is dangerously out of control, references to a dog injuring a person or assistance dog or there being grounds for reasonable apprehension that it will do so, do not include references to any case in which the dog is being used for a lawful purpose by a constable or a person in the service of the Crown.
- An order under s 2 of the Dogs Act 1871 (order on complaint that dog is dangerous and not kept under proper control) (see **11.6.3**) may be made whether or not the dog is shown to have injured any person; and may specify measures for keeping the dog under proper control, whether by muzzling, keeping on a lead, excluding it from specified places, requiring it to be neutered or otherwise.
- If animals are injured, apart from an assistance dog, consider using powers under s 2 of the 1871 Act (see **11.6.3**).
- Section 1 of the Dogs (Protection of Livestock) Act 1953 provides an offence for the owner (person in charge) of a dog that has worried livestock on agricultural land. This could be attacking or chasing livestock, or being at large in a field or enclosure in which there are sheep. Any dog found under such circumstances (without an owner/ person in charge on any land) may be seized and detained by a police officer under s 2 of that Act.

Standard offence

🏃 Summary　　🕐 6 months

⧵⧵⧵ 6 months' imprisonment and/or a fine

Aggravated offence

🏃 Either way　　🕐 None

 Entry and search powers　　711

11.6.3 Dog control orders

 Summary: 6 months' imprisonment and/or a fine

Indictment: If a person dies as a result of being injured: 14 years imprisonment and/or a fine

Where a person is injured: 5 years' imprisonment and/or a fine

Where an assistance dog is injured/dies: 3 years' imprisonmen and/or a fine

11.6.3 **Dog control orders**

Section 2 of the Dogs Act 1871 allows magistrates' courts to make order in respect of dangerous dogs.

> ### Complaint
>
> Any magistrates' court may hear a complaint that a dog is **dangerous** and not kept under **proper control**, and if satisfied that it is dangerous, may order that it be kept under proper control by the owner, or destroyed.
>
> Dogs Act 1871, s 2

Meanings

Dangerous

Is not limited to meaning dangerous to people. It could include othe animals.

Proper control

Is also a question of fact for the court. If a dog is kept under proper control, an order cannot be made in respect of it.

Explanatory notes

The expression '**dangerous**' will be a question of fact for the courts determine, it includes—

- being dangerous to livestock, birds, and other dogs (*Briscoe v Shattock* [1999] 1 WLR 432, QBD);
- however, a dog that killed two pet rabbits on only one occasion was held not to be dangerous, as it was in the nature of dogs to chase and kill other small animals;
- a dog could be dangerous on private property to which people have right of access.

Practical considerations

- Where a court orders a dog to be destroyed, it may appoint a person to undertake the seizure and destruction, and require any person with custody to deliver it up, and in addition may disqualify the owner from having custody of a dog, under s 1 of the Dangerous Dogs Act 1989, or under s 4(1)(b) of the 1991 Act (see **11.6.2**).
- In a statement of complaint, the victim must identify the dog. It is usually necessary for the victim to then identify the dog in the presence of the owner and the investigating officer. Any injuries should be examined by the officer and described in both their statement and that of the victim. This is a complaint rather than an offence, but it is advisable to interview the owner under the provisions of PACE.
- If there has been a genuine transfer of ownership of the dog, an order could only be made against the new owner.

11.6.4 **Restrictions on dangerous dog breeds**

The Dangerous Dogs Act 1991 imposed restrictions on keeping dogs that are a danger to the public. Section 1 created offences relating to dogs bred or fighting.

Offences

(2) No person shall—
  (a) breed, or breed from, a **dog to which this section applies**;
  (b) sell or exchange such a dog or offer, **advertise** or expose such a dog for sale or exchange;
  (c) make or offer to make a gift of such a dog or advertise or expose such a dog as a gift;
  (d) allow such a dog of which he is the owner or for the time being in charge, to be in a **public place** without being muzzled and kept on a lead; or
  (e) abandon such a dog of which he is the owner or, being the owner or for the time being in charge of such a dog, allow it to stray.

(3) No person shall have any dog to which this section applies in his possession or custody except—
  (a) in pursuance of the power of seizure; or
  (b) in accordance with an order for its destruction under the subsequent provisions of this Act.

(7) Any person who contravenes this section is guilty of an offence.

Dangerous Dogs Act 1991, s 1

11.6.4 Restrictions on dangerous dog breeds

Points to prove

s 1(2) offence

✓ breed from/sell/exchange/offer/advertise/make a gift of **or**
✓ allow in public place without muzzle and kept on lead **or**
✓ abandon/allow to stray
✓ a fighting dog (as defined in s 1(1))

s 1(3) offence

✓ had in possession/custody
✓ a fighting dog (as defined in s 1(1))

Meanings

Dog to which this section applies

- Any dog of—
  (a) the type known as the **Pit Bull Terrier;**
  (b) the type known as the **Japanese Tosa;** and
  (c) any dog of any type designated for the purposes of this section by an order of the Secretary of State, being a type appearing to him to be bred for fighting or to have the characteristics of a type bred for that purpose.

  Dangerous Dogs Act 1991, s 1(1)

- SI 1743/1991 added two more dogs to s 1(1) above—
  ✦ the type known as the **Dogo Argentino;** and
  ✦ the type known as the **Fila Braziliero.**

Advertise

This includes any means of bringing a matter to the attention of the public.

Public place (see **11.6.2**)

Defences

The above does not apply to dogs being used for lawful purposes by a constable or any other person in the service of the Crown, such as dogs being used by the Police, Prison Service, Military Police, and Customs & Excise.

Related cases (see **11.6.2** for further cases)

R v Haringey Magistrates' Court, ex parte Cragg (1996) 161 JP 61, QBD and **R v Trafford Magistrates' Court, ex parte Riley (1996) 160 JP 418, QBD** The offender may not be the owner, in which case the owner must be identified and be made party to, or informed of, a destruction hearing

DPP v Kellet (1994) 158 JP 1138, QBD A dangerous dog wandered into a public place because the defendant was drunk and had left their front door open. Held: Voluntary intoxication is not a defence.

Bates v DPP (1993) 157 JP 1004, QBD An unmuzzled pit bull terrier was found loose in the back of a car and B was convicted under s 1(2)(d). Held: A dog in a vehicle may be deemed to be in a public place, if the vehicle itself is in a public place.

Cummings v DPP The Times, 26 March 1999, QBD Common areas located around council housing held to be a public place.

Practical considerations

- The Dangerous Dogs Exemption Schemes (England and Wales) Order 2015 (SI 138/2015) states that the prohibition in s 1(3) of the Act shall not apply if the Agency (DEFRA) has issued a certificate of exemption in respect of a dog.
- A certificate of exemption can be issued by DEFRA (see **Appendix 1**) if it is satisfied that a court has determined that: the dog is not a danger to public safety, the person is a fit and proper person to be in charge of the dog, and made the dog subject to a contingent destruction order under s 4A. Also that the dog has been neutered, microchipped, and third-party insurance is in force regarding death or bodily injury to any person caused by the dog.
- For further guidance on this Act see HOC 29/1997.
  The word '**type**' has a wider meaning than '**breed**' in that behavioural characteristics can also be taken into account: *Brock v DPP* [1993] 4 All ER 491, QBD.
  If it is alleged that a dog is of a type to which this section applies, it is presumed to be so until the owner proves to the contrary. If there is any doubt, the dog may be seized and taken to kennels where the owner may have it examined at his own expense.
  DEFRA (see **Appendix 1**) have guidance on their website to help police and local authorities enforce dangerous dog laws more effectively and crack down on irresponsible dog owners. It provides—
  - an outline and explanation of current law;
  - best practice for the main enforcement authorities;
  - guidance on identifying pit bull terrier-type dogs; and
  - local initiatives.

 Summary   6 months

 6 months' imprisonment and/or a fine

1.6.5 **Guard dogs**

The Guard Dogs Act 1975 was introduced to regulate the use of guard dogs.

11.6.5 Guard dogs

Offences

1(1) A person shall not use or permit the use of a **guard dog** at any **premises** unless a person ('the handler') who is capable of controlling the dog is present on the premises, and the dog is under the control of the handler at all times while being so used, except while it is secured so that it is not at liberty to go freely about the premises.

1(2) The handler of a guard dog shall keep the dog under his control at all times while it is being used as a guard dog at any premises, except—
(a) while another handler has control over the dog; or
(b) while the dog is secured so that it is not at liberty to go freely about the premises.

1(3) A person shall not use or permit the use of a guard dog at any premises unless a notice containing a warning that a guard dog is present is clearly exhibited at each entrance to the premises.

5(1) A person who contravenes **section 1 or 2** of this Act shall be guilty of an offence.

Guard Dogs Act 1975, ss 1 and 5

Points to prove

s 1(1) offence

✓ use/permit the use of
✓ a guard dog(s)
✓ on premises without a capable controller present and not under control
✓ of handler at all times

s 1(2) offence

✓ handler of guard dogs(s) fail
✓ to keep dogs
✓ under control at all times
✓ on premises

s 1(3) offence

✓ use/permit the use of
✓ a guard dog(s)
✓ on premises
✓ when warning notice(s) that a guard dog was present
✓ was/were not clearly exhibited at each entrance

Meanings

Guard dog

Means a dog which is being used to protect: premises; or property kept on the premises; or a person guarding the premises or such property.

Premises

Means land **other than agricultural land** and land within the curtilage of a dwelling house; and buildings, including parts of buildings, other than dwelling houses.

Agricultural land (see **11.6.2**)

Section 2

This states that a person shall not keep a dog at guard dog kennels unless a licence under s 3 is held in respect of the kennels.

Related cases

Hobson v Gledhill [1978] 1 All ER 945, QBD The handler is not required to be on the premises whilst the dog is properly secured. Whether a dog is secured so that it is not at liberty to go freely about the premises, will depend on the facts of each case.

 Summary   6 months

 Fine

Links to alternative subjects and offences

Chapter 12

Powers and Procedures

12.1 Stop and Search Powers

The Police and Criminal Evidence Act 1984 (PACE) creates the generic stop and search powers for a constable in places to which the public has access.

12.1.1 Search and detain

Section 1 of PACE creates the power for a constable to stop and search people and vehicles for stolen property, offensive weapons, bladed, pointed articles, or prohibited fireworks.

Power—search and detain

(1) A constable may exercise any power conferred by this section—
    (a) in any place to which at the time when he proposes to exercise the power the public or any section of the public has access, on payment or otherwise, as of right or by virtue of express or implied permission; or
    (b) in any other place to which people have ready access at the time when he proposes to exercise the power but which is not a dwelling.
(2) Subject to **subsection (3)** to (5) below, a constable—
    (a) may **search**—
        (i) any person or **vehicle**;
        (ii) anything which is in or on a vehicle;
    for **stolen** or **prohibited articles**, any **article** to which subsection **(8A)** below applies or any **firework** to which subsection **(8B)** below applies; and
    (b) may **detain** a person or vehicle for the purpose of such a search.

Police and Criminal Evidence Act 1984, s 1

Meanings

Vehicle

This is not defined. In the *Oxford English Dictionary* it means 'a conveyance, usually with wheels, for transporting people, animals, goods or other objects and includes (amongst others) a car, cart, truck, bus, train carriage or sledge'. Although, the Act states that vessels (including any ship, boat, raft, or other apparatus constructed or adapted for floating on water), aircraft, and hovercraft, also fall within the meaning of vehicles.

Stolen article (see **3.1**)

Prohibited articles

Prohibited articles given under s 1(7) and (8) means—
- an offensive weapon (see **8.9.1**)—this includes firearms (see **8.1.1**);
- an article made or adapted for use in the course of or in connection with the following offences **or** intended by the person having it with them for such use by them or by some other person—
  + burglary (see **3.3.1**);
  + theft (see **3.1**);
  + taking a conveyance without consent (see **4.3**);
  + fraud (see **3.8**);
  + criminal damage (see **4.5**).

Article (s 1(8A) applies)

Any pointed or bladed article, in which a person has committed, or is committing or is going to commit, an offence under s 139 (see **8.10.1**) or s 139AA (see **8.10.3**) of the Criminal Justice Act 1988.

Firework (s 1(8B) applies)

Any firework possessed in breach of prohibition imposed by fireworks regulations (see **8.8**).

Reasonable grounds for suspicion (subsection (3))

This section **does not** give a constable power to search a person or vehicle or anything in or on a vehicle **unless** he has **reasonable grounds for suspecting** that he will find stolen or prohibited articles, any article to which subsection (8A) applies or any firework to which subsection (8B) applies.

Meaning of reasonable grounds

PACE Code A (updated March 2015) governs the exercise by police officers of statutory powers of stop and search. Paragraphs 2.2 to 2.11 provide an explanation of what are considered to be reasonable grounds for suspicion when conducting a search.

PACE Code of Practice A

Reasonable grounds for suspicion depend on the circumstances in each case—

12.1.1 Search and detain

- The officer must have formed a genuine suspicion in their own mind that they will find the object for which the search power being exercised allows them to search. This must be a reasonable suspicion, which means there must be an objective basis for that suspicion based on facts, information, and/or intelligence that are relevant to the likelihood of finding the object, or that the person is a terrorist (for a s 43 Terrorism Act 2000 search).
- Stop and search powers depend on the likelihood that the person searched is in possession of an item for which they may be searched, it does not depend on them being suspected of committing an offence.
- It can never be supported on the basis of personal factors alone without reliable supporting intelligence or information, or specific behaviour by the person concerned. For example, unless a suspect description is available, a person's physical appearance (including any of the 'protected characteristics' (see **13.6**) set out in the Equality Act 2010), or the fact that they have a previous conviction, cannot be used alone or in combination with each other, as the reason for stopping and searching that person.
- It cannot be based on generalisations, or stereotyping certain groups or categories of people as more likely to be involved in criminal activity.

Further points contained within this code are—
- Reasonable suspicion can be on the basis of behaviour of a person (eg an officer encountering someone on the street at night who is obviously trying to hide something). A hunch or instinct which cannot be explained or justified to an objective observer can never amount to reasonable grounds.
- On reliable information or intelligence that members of a group or gang habitually carry knives unlawfully, or weapons, or controlled drugs, and they wear a distinctive item of clothing or denote their membership by other means, if that distinctive means of identification is displayed that may provide the reasonable grounds to stop and search a person. A similar approach could be applied to organised protest groups.
- An officer who has reasonable grounds for suspicion may detain that person in order to carry out a search.
- Before carrying out a search the officer may ask questions relating to the circumstances giving rise to the suspicion; as a result the grounds for suspicion may be confirmed or, because of a satisfactory explanation, be eliminated.
- Reasonable grounds for suspicion cannot be provided retrospectively by such questioning during a person's detention or by refusal to answer any questions put.
- Once reasonable grounds to suspect that an article is being carried cease to exist, no search may take place. In the absence of any other lawful power to detain, the person is free to leave and must be so informed.
- There is no power to stop or detain a person in order to find grounds for a search.
- A brief introductory conversation or exchange is desirable to: avoid unsuccessful searches, explain the grounds for the stop/search, gain cooperation, and so reduce any possible tension.

- If a person is lawfully detained for the purpose of a search, but no search takes place, the detention will not subsequently be rendered unlawful.
- Paragraph 5 requires supervisors to monitor stop and search powers used by officers to ensure they are being applied appropriately and lawfully; this can be by observation, asking the officer to give reasons for the search, and examining search records. Misuse of stop and search powers may lead to formal performance or disciplinary proceedings.

Restrictions in a garden/yard (subsections (4) and (5))

If a person or vehicle is in a garden or yard occupied with and used for the purposes of a dwelling or on other land so occupied and used, a constable may not search that person or vehicle, in exercising the power under s 1, unless the constable has reasonable grounds for believing that the suspect or—

- person in charge of the vehicle does not reside in the dwelling; **and**
- the vehicle is not in the place in question with the express or implied permission of a person who resides in the dwelling.

Power to seize

If in the course of such a search a constable discovers an article which he has reasonable grounds for suspecting to be a stolen or prohibited article, an article to which subsection (8A) applies or a firework to which subsection (8B) applies, he may seize it.

Police and Criminal Evidence Act 1984, s 1(6)

12.1.2 **Conduct of a search**

Section 2 of PACE provides safeguards for when a constable detains a person or **vehicle** under s 1 or in the exercise of **any search powers prior to arrest**. They are—

- A search can be abandoned if it is no longer required or it is impracticable to conduct one.
- The time for which a person or vehicle may be detained for a search is as reasonably required to permit the search to be carried out, either at the place detained or nearby.
- A search and detain power does not authorise a constable to—
  - require a person to remove any of his clothing in public other than an outer coat, jacket, or gloves; or
  - stop a vehicle, if not in uniform.
- Before commencing a search (excepting an unattended vehicle), a constable shall take reasonable steps to bring to the attention of the detainee or person in charge of the vehicle the following matters and provide the following details—
  - name of constable and police station (where based), plus identification if the constable is not in uniform;
  - object of the proposed search;

12.1.2 Conduct of a search

  + grounds for proposing the search;
  + entitlement to a copy of the written stop and search record, unless it appears to the constable that it will not be practicable to make/provide the record at the time of the search (see **12.1.3**).
- Where an unattended vehicle is searched, a constable shall leave a notice inside the vehicle (unless it would damage the vehicle) stating: they have searched it; name of police station where based; that an application for compensation for any damage caused by the search may be made to that police station; the procedure as to the entitlement of a copy of the written stop and search record (see **12.1.3**).

Meaning of vehicle (see **12.1.1**)

Terrorism stop and search powers

- A police officer may stop and search a person under s 43 of the Terrorism Act 2000, if they reasonably suspect that person to be a terrorist, to discover whether that person has in their possession anything which may constitute evidence that they are a terrorist. In exercising this power, if a constable stops a vehicle, they may search the vehicle and anything in or on it to discover evidence that the person is a terrorist and may seize and retain any such evidence found. This power can be exercised at any time and in any location.
- Section 43A of the Terrorism Act 2000 provides that a constable on reasonable suspicion that a vehicle is being used for the purposes of terrorism; may stop and search the vehicle and driver, passenger or anything in or on the vehicle or carried by the driver or a passenger to discover evidence that the vehicle is being used for the purposes of terrorism. A constable may seize and retain anything discovered in the course of such a search.
- If a senior officer reasonably suspects that an act of terrorism will take place and considers that the stop and search powers are **necessary** to prevent such an act of terrorism, then under s 47A of the 2000 Act the senior officer may authorise the use of those powers in an area within the officer's police force area no larger than necessary and for a period no longer than necessary for that purpose. This empowers uniformed police officers to stop and search vehicles/people in the 'authorised area' for the purposes of discovering evidence that the vehicle is being used for terrorism or that the person is or has been concerned in the commission, preparation, or instigation of acts of terrorism.
- Ensure compliance with the Code of Practice relating to the above stop and search powers under ss 43, 43A and 47A.
- Section 4.13 of this Code deals with photography/film matters, as concerns had been raised among photographers and journalists about the use of stop and search powers in relation to photography. It is important to note that members of the public and media do not generally need any form of permit or express authority to take photographs nor is it an offence to take photographs/film in a public

place or of a public building (unless there are any specific, advertised restrictions such as those applying to various Ministry of Defence buildings). Similarly, the police do not have any general power to stop people taking photographs.

- Police officers can stop and search someone taking photographs/film within an authorised area under s 47A, just as they can stop and search any other member of the public in the proper exercise of their powers under the 2000 Act, but an authorisation itself does not prohibit the taking of photographs or digital images.
- Digital images can be viewed as part of a search under s 43, s 43A, or s 47 to discover whether the person has in their possession anything which may constitute evidence that they are a terrorist, or to determine whether the images are of a kind which could be used in connection with terrorism.
- Film and memory cards may be seized as part of such a search if the police officer reasonably suspects they are evidence that the person is a terrorist, or a vehicle is being used for the purposes of terrorism, but officers do not have a power to delete images, destroy film or to require the person to do so.

12.1.3 **Written records of stop and search**

Section 3 of PACE details the following procedures to be adhered to when making written records of stop searches carried out by a constable, while exercising **any of their stop and search powers**, relating to a person or **vehicle**—

- If an arrest has been made as a result of a 'stop and search', a written record of the search must be included as part of the custody record. In any other case, if it is not practicable to make a record 'on the spot', then it shall be made as soon as practicable after the completion of the search.
- A record of the search of a person or vehicle shall include—
  - ♦ object of the search;
  - ♦ grounds for making it;
  - ♦ date and time made;
  - ♦ place where it was made;
  - ♦ except in the search of an unattended vehicle, the ethnic origins of the person searched or the person in charge of the vehicle searched (*ethnic origin is as described by that person, and if different as perceived by the constable*); and
  - ♦ shall identify the constable who carried out the search.
- Apart from the above mandatory fields, some forces continue to record all fields including name, outcome, and damage/injury caused.
- A person searched, or the owner/person in charge of a searched vehicle, are entitled to a copy of the record. This can be requested up to 3 months from the date when the search was made.

12.1.3 Written records of stop and search

Meaning of vehicle (see 12.1.1)

Explanatory notes

- Fireworks possessed in breach of prohibitions imposed by the Fireworks Regulations 2004 would give grounds for invoking the 'stop and search' powers (see **8.8** for details).
- Articles that are made, adapted, or intended for use for one of the listed offences could include—
  - ✦ crowbar/screwdriver (burglary);
  - ✦ car keys (for taking a vehicle without owner's consent);
  - ✦ stolen credit card (fraud); or
  - ✦ spray paint can/pens intending to cause graffiti (damage).
- This section does not give a constable power to search a person or vehicle, or anything in or on a vehicle unless they have reasonable grounds for suspecting that they will find stolen property, prohibited articles or fireworks.

Related cases (see also **5.4.1** cases)

Howarth v Commissioner of the Metropolitan Police [2011] EWHC 2818, QBD Searching protestors travelling to a demonstration had been justified by intelligence that the protestors were carrying items which had been used to cause criminal damage at previous demonstrations.

B v DPP [2008] EWHC 1655 (Admin), QBD Failure by a constable in plain clothes to produce their warrant card was a breach of s 2(2) of PACE and para 3.8 of Code A. As a result the drugs search was deemed unlawful.

R v Bristol [2007] EWCA Crim 3214, CA If a person is searched for drugs under s 23 of the Misuse of Drugs Act 1971 (see **5.4**) then s 2 of PACE applies. As the officer had failed to state his name and police station, then s 2 was breached, the search was unlawful and the conviction was set aside (following *Osman v DPP* (1999) 163 JP 725, QBD).

R v Park (1994) 158 JP 144, CA PACE and COP procedures have to be followed as far as practicable. Any breach of these procedures could justify exclusion of evidence and render the search unlawful.

R v Fennelley [1989] Crim LR 142, CC F had not been properly informed of the reasons for a street search. Held that the evidence obtained was unfair and so was excluded under s 78 of PACE.

O'Hara v CC of the RUC [1997] 1 All ER 129, HL Reasonable grounds for suspicion can arise from information/intelligence passed to an officer by a colleague, an informant, or anonymously.

Practical considerations

- Paragraph 4.12 of Code A states that there is no longer a national requirement for an officer to make any record of a 'stop and account' incident or to give the person a receipt. Although after consulting with local communities, forces can continue to record self-defined ethnicity if it is considered necessary to monitor any local 'disproportionality'.

- All COPs are legally binding; failure to comply with them could result in the CPS declining to institute or continue proceedings. A court case may be lost through evidence being disallowed and the police officer could be subject to severe penalties.
- The COPs are not confined to police officers, they apply to all people involved in criminal investigations: HMRC, DSS, private investigators, and security staff in industry.
- Code A provides assistance and guidance to police officers in the exercise of their powers to stop and search people and vehicles.
- Searches based on up-to-date and accurate intelligence are likely to be effective and lawful, thus securing public confidence. Ensure that all stop and search powers are used objectively, fairly, and without any bias against ethnic or other groups within the community.
- Officers must be fully aware and ready to take account of the special needs of juveniles and other vulnerable groups.

Links to alternative subjects and offences

12.2 Powers of Arrest

Sections 24, 24A, and 28 to 31 of PACE deal with arrests made by a constable or other people and other related matters.

12.2.1 Arrest without warrant: constables

Arrest without warrant

Section 24 of PACE provides the power of arrest for a constable without a warrant and the conditions that must apply before the arrest power can be used.

Powers of arrest

Arrest

(1) A constable may arrest without a warrant—
  (a) anyone who is about to commit an offence;
  (b) anyone who is in the act of committing an offence;
  (c) anyone whom he has reasonable grounds for suspecting to be about to commit an offence;
  (d) anyone whom he has reasonable grounds for suspecting to be committing an offence.

(2) If a constable has reasonable grounds for suspecting that an offence has been committed, he may arrest without a warrant anyone whom he has reasonable grounds to suspect of being guilty of it.

(3) If an offence has been committed, a constable may arrest without a warrant—
  (a) anyone who is guilty of the offence;
  (b) anyone whom he has reasonable grounds for suspecting to be guilty of it.

Necessity criteria

(4) But the power of summary arrest conferred by subsection (1), (2) or (3) is exercisable only if the constable has reasonable grounds for believing that for any of the reasons mentioned in subsection (5) it is necessary to arrest the person in question.

Reasons

(5) The reasons are—
  (a) to enable the name of the person in question to be ascertained (in the case where the constable does not know, and cannot readily ascertain, the person's name, or has reasonable grounds for doubting whether a name given by the person as his name is his real name);
  (b) correspondingly as regards the person's address;

(c) to prevent the person in question—
  (i) causing physical injury to himself or any other person;
  (ii) suffering physical injury;
  (iii) causing loss of or damage to property;
  (iv) committing an offence against public decency (subject to subsection (6)); or
  (v) causing an unlawful obstruction of the highway; or
(d) to protect a child or other vulnerable person from the person in question;
(e) to allow the prompt and effective investigation of the offence or of the conduct of the person in question;
(f) to prevent any prosecution for the offence from being hindered by the disappearance of the person in question.

(6) Subsection (5)(c)(iv) applies only where members of the public going about their normal business cannot reasonably be expected to avoid the person in question.

Police and Criminal Evidence Act 1984, s 24

Explanatory notes

- The use of this arrest power is governed by PACE Code G.
- If a person is arrested on suspicion of being a terrorist, then Code H would apply in connection with the detention, treatment, and questioning for persons arrested under s 41 and Sch 8 of the Terrorism Act 2000.
- The Director General of NCA may confer some or all of the s 24 powers on NCA staff, and nominate them as 'designated persons' (role of constable, officer of HMRC, or immigration officer).
- The s 24 power means that a constable/designated person may only arrest a person without a warrant under this general power where—
  ✦ they are about to commit/in the act of committing an offence;
  ✦ there are reasonable grounds to suspect they are about to commit/ to be committing an offence;
  ✦ there are reasonable grounds to suspect that an offence has been committed, has reasonable grounds to suspect they are guilty of it;
  ✦ an offence has been committed: they are guilty of the offence; reasonable grounds to suspect they are guilty of it;
  and the constable has reasonable grounds to believe (more than 'suspect') that it is **necessary** to arrest that person for any of the reasons listed.
- A lawful arrest requires both elements of—
  ✦ a person's involvement or suspected involvement, or attempted involvement in the commission of a criminal offence; **and**
  ✦ reasonable grounds to believe that the arrest is necessary.
- The requirement for reasonable grounds makes this an **objective test**—that is, it requires some verifiable material fact other than the belief of the arresting officer.

12.2.1 Arrest without warrant: constables

- The exercise of these arrest powers will be subject to a test of necessity, based on the nature and circumstances of the offence, and the interests of the criminal justice system.
- An arrest will only be justified if the constable believes it is necessary for any of the reasons set out, **and** they had reasonable grounds on which that belief was based.
- Criteria for what may constitute necessity remain an operational decision at the discretion of the arresting officer.
- Paragraph 4 of Code G deals with 'Records of Arrest' in that—
  - ✦ The arresting officer is required to record in his pocketbook or other methods used for recording information
    - ▪ the nature and circumstances of the offence leading to arrest;
    - ▪ the reason or reasons why arrest was necessary;
    - ▪ the giving of the caution;
    - ▪ anything said by the person at the time of arrest;
  - ✦ Such record should be made at the time of arrest unless impracticable to do so, in which case to be completed as soon as possible thereafter.
- Some of the reasons to consider under s 24(5)(e), as to a prompt and effective investigation, are given in para 2.9 of Code G; this may be where there are reasonable grounds to believe that the person—
  - ✦ has made false statements;
  - ✦ has made statements which cannot be readily verified;
  - ✦ has presented false evidence;
  - ✦ may steal or destroy evidence;
  - ✦ may make contact with co-suspects or conspirators;
  - ✦ may intimidate or threaten, or make contact with witnesses; or
  - ✦ where it is necessary to obtain evidence by questioning
    - ▪ it is thought unlikely that the person would attend the police station voluntarily to be interviewed;
    - ▪ arrest would enable 'special warnings' to be given per Code C paras 10.10 and 10.11.
- If an arrest is for an indictable offence, there could be other reasons under s 24(5)(e) to consider such as a need to—
  - ✦ enter and search any premises occupied or controlled by a person;
  - ✦ search the person;
  - ✦ prevent contact with others;
  - ✦ take fingerprints, footwear impressions, samples or photographs; or
  - ✦ ensure compliance with statutory drug testing requirements.
- Apart from arrest, other options such as—
  - ✦ report for summons;
  - ✦ grant street bail;
  - ✦ issue a fixed penalty notice, PND; or
  - ✦ other methods of disposal

  will have to be considered and excluded before arrest is decided upon.
- This statutory power of arrest for a constable applies to all offences except offences under s 4(1) (assisting offenders) and s 5(1) (concealing information on relevant offences of the Criminal Law Act 1967), which require that the offences to which they relate carry a

sentence fixed by law or one in which a first-time offender aged 18 or over could be sentenced to 5 years' or more imprisonment.
- Also some preserved powers of arrest under Sch 2 have been retained.
- Arrest (without warrant) by other people is subject to s 24A of PACE (see **12.2.4**).
- Use of reasonable force—see '**Use of force resolution**' subject at **1.2**.

12.2.2 **Information to be given on arrest**

Cautions

Code of Practice C deals with when a caution must be given.

PACE Code of Practice C

Police officers and other persons subject to observing PACE should be aware of the following paragraphs in this code of practice—
- A person whom there are grounds to suspect of an offence must be cautioned before any questions about an offence or further questions (if the answers provide the grounds for suspicion) are put to them; if either the suspect's answers or silence, may be given in evidence to a court in a prosecution (para 10.1).
- A person need not be cautioned if questioned in order to—
  - ✦ solely establish identity or ownership of vehicle;
  - ✦ obtain information to comply with a statutory requirement;
  - ✦ conduct a proper and effective search;
  - ✦ seek clarification for a written record.
- A person who is arrested or further arrested, must also be cautioned unless—
  - ✦ it is impracticable to do so by reason of their condition or behaviour at the time;
  - ✦ they have already been cautioned immediately prior to arrest (para 10.4).
- The **caution** that must be given on—
  - ✦ arrest;
  - ✦ before a person is charged or informed they may be prosecuted; **should** (unless the restriction on drawing adverse inferences from silence applies) **be in the following terms**:
  'You do not have to say anything. But it may harm your defence if you do not mention when questioned something which you later rely on in Court. Anything you do say may be given in evidence.' (Code C para 10.5; for terrorism Code H para 10.4.)

Explanatory notes

- Whenever a person **not under arrest**, including voluntary attendees at a police station, are interviewed under caution they must be told that they are not under arrest, are not obliged to remain at the station or other location but if they agree to remain they can be given free and independent legal advice (Code C para 3.21).

12.2.2 Information to be given on arrest

- Minor deviations from the words of any caution given in accordance with this code do not constitute a breach of this code, provided the sense of the relevant caution is preserved.
- After any break in questioning under caution the person being questioned must be made aware they remain under caution. If there is any doubt, the relevant caution shall be given again in full when the interview resumes.
- Failure to comply with cautioning procedures will allow the accused to claim a breach of this code at any subsequent court proceedings. By virtue of s 76 or s 78 of PACE, the court may then exclude the evidence of confession so obtained.

Statutory requirements

Section 28 of PACE determines the information that must be given to a person when arrested.

Information to be given on arrest

(1) Subject to subsection (5) below, where a person is arrested, otherwise than by being informed that he is under arrest, the arrest is not lawful unless the person arrested is informed that he is under arrest as soon as is practicable after his arrest.

(2) Where a person is arrested by a constable, subsection (1) above applies regardless of whether the fact of the arrest is obvious.

(3) Subject to subsection (5) below, no arrest is lawful unless the person arrested is informed of the ground for the arrest at the time of, or as soon as practicable after, the arrest.

(4) Where a person is arrested by a constable, subsection (3) above applies regardless of whether the ground for the arrest is obvious.

(5) Nothing in this section is to be taken to require a person to be informed—

    (a) that he is under arrest; **or**

    (b) of the ground for the arrest,

if it was not reasonably practicable for him to be so informed by reason of his having escaped from arrest before the information could be given.

Police and Criminal Evidence Act 1984, s 28

Explanatory notes

- A person who is arrested, or further arrested, must be informed at the time, or as soon as practicable thereafter, in a language they understand (see COP and ECHR), that they are under arrest and the grounds for their arrest.
- When arresting using the power under s 24, the officer must tell the person, not only the offence/suspected offence involved, but also the reason why the officer believes that arrest is necessary. The necessity criteria (see **12.2.1**) must also be recorded by the officer.
- If it becomes apparent that a more serious offence may have been committed the suspect must be made aware of these facts

immediately (eg originally arrested and interviewed for sexual assault, which now transpires is rape).
- It would be manifestly unfair if the defendant did not know the true extent of the situation they were in and any interviews could be excluded at trial.

Related cases

R v Iqbal [2011] EWCA Crim 273, CA The common law indictable offence of escape from lawful custody does not cover those who escape from police restraint or control before they have been arrested.

Hayes v CC of Merseyside Police [2011] EWCA Civ 911, CA The arresting officer must actually believe that the arrest is necessary under s 24(4) for a s 24(5) reason and this belief must be objectively reasonable.

Richardson v CC of West Midlands Police [2011] EWHC 773, QBD Arrest unlawful as the police had failed to satisfy the s 24(4) necessity requirement. Sufficient grounds for making the arrest necessary had not been established under any of the s 24(5) reasons.

Buckley v CC of Thames Valley Police [2009] EWCA 356, CA Under s 24 the 'reasonable grounds for suspicion' threshold was low. Do not separate each element of suspicion to study them individually; they need to be looked at together as a whole to establish 'reasonable grounds for suspicion'.

Sneyd v DPP [2006] EWHC 560 (Admin), QBD Once a positive breath test had been provided under s 6(1) of the Road Traffic Act 1988, then the officer had grounds to suspect that an offence had been committed and was only then required to caution S.

Dhesi v CC of West Midlands Police The Times, 9 May 2000, CA The officer informing the offender that they were under arrest and giving the grounds does not have to be the same officer as the one who is physically detaining that person.

12.2.3 **Arrest procedures**

Arrest at police station—voluntary attendance

Where for the purpose of assisting with an investigation a person attends voluntarily at a police station or at any other place where a constable is present, or accompanies a constable to a police station or any such other place without having been arrested—
(a) he shall be entitled to leave at will unless he is placed under arrest;
(b) he shall be informed at once that he is under arrest if a decision is taken by a constable to prevent him from leaving at will.

Police and Criminal Evidence Act, s 29

12.2.3 Arrest procedures

Explanatory notes

- Confusion sometimes arises about the status of a suspect who has attended at a police station voluntarily. If the investigating officer concludes that the suspect should not be allowed to leave and an arrest is **necessary**, then the officer should caution the suspect (unless recently cautioned) and inform the suspect that they are under arrest and take them before the custody officer.
- Ensure that the **necessity test** is satisfied (see **12.2.1**). Simply giving the grounds for the arrest as 'for the prompt and effective investigation' is not a good enough reason, without further explanation.
- Under s 29 a person is free to leave the station interview at any time. If they do, then it may be lawful to arrest and the necessity criteria may be met. This is because, under para 2.9(e)(i) of Code G (see **12.2.1**), it may be 'necessary to obtain evidence by questioning', and here the person has refused or failed to comply with arrangements for voluntary attendance/interview.

Arrest—not at a police station

Section 30 of PACE provides the procedure to be applied when a constable either makes an arrest or takes a person into custody after arrest by a person other than a constable (at any place other than a police station), the relevant points are—

- The arrested person must be taken to a police station as soon as practicable after arrest.
- This must be a police station designated for dealing with 'PACE' prisoners, unless—
  - it is anticipated that the arrested person will be dealt with in less than six hours at any police station;
  - the arrest/taken into custody is without the assistance of any other constable(s) and none were available to assist;
  - it is considered that the arrested person cannot be conveyed to a designated police station without the arrested person injuring himself, the constable, or some other person.
- If the first police station to which an arrested person is taken after their arrest is not a designated police station, they shall be taken to a designated police station not more than six hours after their arrival at the first police station unless they are released previously.
- Prior to arrival at the police station, the arrested person must be released without bail if the constable is satisfied that there are no longer grounds for keeping them under arrest or releasing them on bail; if this occurs the constable shall record the fact that they have done so and shall make the record as soon as practicable after release. This requirement should be read in conjunction with the necessity criteria as, once the relevant criterion making the arrest necessary has ceased, arguably the person should be released.
- A constable can delay taking a person to a police station or releasing them on bail, if the presence of the arrested person at a place (other than a police station) is necessary in order to carry out such investigations as it is reasonable to carry out immediately; if such delay

occurs the reason(s) for the delay must be recorded when the person first arrives at a police station or (as the case may be) is released on bail.

Explanatory notes

- There is no requirement that a person must be taken to the nearest police station: s 30(1A) states 'The person must be taken by a constable to a police station as soon as practicable after the arrest'—there is no mention of the word 'nearest'.
- The type of record that has to be made, if the arrested person is 'de-arrested' prior to arrival at the police station, is not specified but could for example include completing a formal custody record, but is dependent on individual **force policies**.

Arrest—for further offences

Where—
(a) a person—
   (i) has been arrested for an offence; and
   (ii) is at a police station in consequence of that arrest; and
(b) it appears to a constable that, if he were released from that arrest, he would be liable to arrest for some other offence,
he shall be arrested for that other offence.

Police and Criminal Evidence Act 1984, s 31

Explanatory notes

Consider the necessity test under s 24(5) (see **12.2.1**).

12.2.4 **Arrest without warrant: other persons**

Section 24A of PACE gives the power of arrest (without warrant) which is available to other people.

Arrest power (other persons)

(1) A person other than a constable may arrest without a warrant—
   (a) anyone who is in the act of committing an **indictable offence**;
   (b) anyone whom he has reasonable grounds for suspecting to be committing an indictable offence.
(2) Where an indictable offence has been committed, a person other than a constable may arrest without a warrant—
   (a) anyone who is guilty of the offence;
   (b) anyone whom he has reasonable grounds for suspecting to be guilty of it.

12.2.4 Arrest without warrant: other persons

(3) But the power of summary arrest conferred by subsection (1) or (2) is exercisable only if—
  (a) the person making the arrest has reasonable grounds for believing that for any of the reasons mentioned in subsection (4) it is necessary to arrest the person in question; and
  (b) it appears to the person making the arrest that it is not reasonably practicable for a constable to make it instead.
(4) The reasons are to prevent the person in question—
  (a) causing physical injury to himself or any other person;
  (b) suffering physical injury;
  (c) causing loss of or damage to property; or
  (d) making off before a constable can assume responsibility for him.
(5) This section does not apply in relation to an offence under Part 3 or 3A of the Public Order Act 1986.

Police and Criminal Evidence Act 1984, s 24A

Meaning of indictable offence

- An indictable offence includes triable 'either way offences'.
- The Anti-social Behaviour, Crime and Policing Act 2014, s 176(6) states—
  ✦ Any reference in PACE 1984 to an **indictable offence** has effect as if it included a reference to **low-value shoplifting**.
- The Magistrates' Courts Act 1980, s 22A states—
  ✦ **Low-value shoplifting** is triable only summarily—unless a person aged 18 or over elects trial at Crown Court before the summary trial begins;
  ✦ **Low-value shoplifting** means an offence under the Theft Act 1968, s 1 where—
    ■ the value of the stolen goods does not exceed £200,
    ■ the goods were being offered for sale in a shop or any other premises, stall, vehicle or place from which there is carried on a trade or business, and
    ■ at the time of the offence, the person accused was, or was purporting to be, a customer or potential customer of the person offering the goods for sale.
- The value of the stolen goods is the price at which they were being offered for sale at the time of the offence, and if the accused is charged (on the same occasion) with two or more offences of low-value shoplifting, the value will be an aggregate of the values involved.

Explanatory notes

- This power of arrest does not apply to offences under ss 17 to 29N of the Public Order Act 1986 (see **7.9**).
- A person (other than a constable) may only arrest a person without a warrant where—
  ✦ they are in the act of committing an indictable offence;
  ✦ there are reasonable grounds to suspect that they are committing an indictable offence;

- an indictable offence has been committed and
  - they are guilty of the offence; **or**
  - there are reasonable grounds to suspect they are guilty of it.
- However, this arrest power is only exercisable if the person making the arrest—
  - has reasonable grounds to believe that it is **necessary** to arrest that person for any of the reasons listed in s 24A(4); **and**
  - decides that it is not reasonably practicable for a constable to make the arrest instead.

Practical considerations

- Searches, arrests, and any other statutory duties, including taking fingerprints and samples, are all subject to the use of reasonable force.
- Consideration should be given to lawful authorities for using reasonable force and use of force resolution (see **1.2**).
- All the COPs are legally binding, failure to comply with them could result in evidence being disallowed and the police officer could be subject to disciplinary proceedings.
- Code C deals with the detention, treatment, and questioning of persons.
- Code G deals with the statutory power of arrest by police officers.
- Search upon arrest is subject to s 32 of PACE (see **12.3.1**).
- Arrest powers under ss 24 and 24A of PACE have effect in relation to any offence/indictable offence whenever committed.

Links to alternative offences or subjects

12.3 Entry, Search, and Seizure Powers

Sections 32 and 17 to 22 of PACE deal with matters relating to searching people/premises, seizure and retention of property, plus entry and access for copying of seized items. These powers, without warrant, apply either upon or after arrest.

12.3.1 Search upon arrest

Section 32 of PACE creates powers of search relating to arrested persons before they are conveyed to a police station. **The relevant points are—**

Person

A constable may search any person arrested at a place other than at a police station on reasonable grounds to believe that—
- the person may present a danger to themselves or others;
- concealed on the arrested person is anything which might be:
  + used to assist escape from lawful custody;
  + evidence relating to an offence.

Premises

- If a person is arrested for an **indictable offence**, at a place other than at a police station, a constable can enter and search any **premises** in which that person was—
  + when arrested;
  + immediately before they were arrested;
  for evidence relating to the indictable offence for which arrested, providing reasonable grounds exist to believe that the evidence is on the premises.
- If the premises consist of two or more separate dwellings, the power to search is limited to any—
  + dwelling in which the arrest took place or in which the person arrested was immediately before their arrest; **and**
  + parts of the premises which the occupier of any such dwelling uses in common with the occupiers of any other dwellings comprised in the premises.

Seizure from person

A constable searching a person in the exercise of this power may seize and retain anything found on that person on reasonable grounds to believe that—

- the person might use it to cause physical injury to that person or to any other person;
- the person might use it to assist him/her to escape from lawful custody;
- it is evidence of an offence or has been obtained in consequence of the commission of an offence (other than an item subject to **legal privilege**).

Seizure from premises

Section 19 of PACE applies (see **12.3.4**).

Meanings

Indictable offence (see **12.2.4**)

Premises

Premises includes any place, and in particular, includes—
- any vehicle, vessel, aircraft, or hovercraft;
- any offshore installation;
- any renewable energy installation; and
- a tent or movable structure.

Legal privilege

- Items subject to legal privilege relate to communications between the client and—
  + a professional legal adviser;
  + any person representing them;
  + between such adviser/representative and any other person.
- This communication was made in connection with the—
  + giving of legal advice;
  + contemplation of legal proceedings for such purpose.
- It also includes items enclosed with or referred to in such communications, when they are in the possession of a person who is entitled to them.
- Items held with the intention of furthering a criminal purpose are not items subject to legal privilege.

Explanatory notes

- This power to search a person does not authorise a constable to require a person to remove any items of clothing in public other than an outer coat, jacket, or gloves.
- It does authorise a search of a person's mouth.
- The power to search premises is only to the extent that is reasonably required for the purpose of discovering any such thing or any such evidence.
- Any search of premises must comply with Code B.
- This power does not apply to an arrest which takes place at a police station.

- Unless an item is for furthering a criminal purpose, items held subject to legal privilege cannot be seized when discovered during a premises search or executing a search warrant for an indictable offence.
- Legal privilege does not extend to a conveyancing document, solicitor's time sheets, fee records, appointment books, and other similar documents.
- Generally, an expert working for the defence is covered by the same legal privilege as the rest of a defence team.
- If it is suspected that the person is a terrorist then stop and search powers given under the Terrorism Act 2000, s 43 will apply.
- For power to search other premises after arrest see **12.3.3** for details.
- For search warrants see **12.4** for details.

12.3.2 **Power of entry to arrest, save life, or prevent damage**

Section 17 of PACE creates a power to enter and search premises to effect an arrest or to save life/prevent damage.

Power to enter premises

(1) Subject to the following provisions of this section, and without prejudice to any other enactment, a constable may enter and search any premises for the purpose—

  (a) of executing—

    (i) a warrant of arrest issued in connection with or arising out of criminal proceedings; or

    (ii) a **warrant of commitment** issued under s 76 of the Magistrates' Courts Act 1980;

  (b) of arresting a person for an **indictable offence**;

  (c) of arresting a person for an offence under—

    (i) section 1 (prohibition of uniforms in connection with political objects) of the Public Order Act 1936;

    (ii) any enactment contained in sections 6, 7, 8 or 10 of the Criminal Law Act 1977 (offences relating to entering and remaining on property);

    (iii) section 4 of the Public Order Act 1986 (fear or provocation of violence);

    (iiia) section 4 (driving etc when under influence of drink or drugs) or 163 (failure to stop when required to do so by constable in uniform) of the Road Traffic Act 1988;

    (iiib) section 27 of the Transport and Works Act 1992 (which relates to offences involving drink or drugs);

    (iv) section 76 of the Criminal Justice and Public Order Act 1994 (failure to comply with interim possession order);

(v)   any of sections 4, 5, 6(1) and (2), 7 and 8(1) and (2) of the Animal Welfare Act 2006 (offences relating to the prevention of harm to animals);

(vi)   section 144 of the Legal Aid, Sentencing and Punishment of Offenders Act 2012 (squatting in a residential building);

(ca)   of arresting, in pursuance of s 32(1A) of the Children and Young Persons Act 1969, any child or young person who has been remanded to local authority or youth detention accommodation under s 91 of the Legal Aid, Sentencing and Punishment of Offenders Act 2012;

(caa)   of arresting a person for an offence to which s 61 of the Animal Health Act 1981 applies;

(cb)   of recapturing any person who is, or is deemed for any purpose to be, unlawfully at large while liable to be detained—

(i)   in a prison, remand centre, young offender institution or secure training centre, or

(ii)   in pursuance of s 92 of the Powers of Criminal Courts (Sentencing) Act 2000 (dealing with children and young persons guilty of grave crimes), in any other place;

(d)   of recapturing any person whatever who is unlawfully at large and whom he is pursuing; or

(e)   of saving life or limb or preventing serious damage to property.

(2) Except for the purpose specified in paragraph (e) of subsection (1) above, the powers of entry and search conferred by this section—

(a)   are only exercisable if the constable has reasonable grounds for believing that the person whom he is seeking is on the premises; and

(b)   are limited, in relation to premises consisting of two or more separate dwellings, to powers to enter and search—

(i)   any parts of the premises which the occupiers of any dwelling comprised in the premises use in common with the occupiers of any other such dwelling; and

(ii)   any such dwelling in which the constable has reasonable grounds for believing that the person whom he is seeking may be.

(3) The powers of entry and search conferred by this section are only exercisable for the purposes specified in subsection (1)(c)(ii), (iv) or (vi) above by a constable in uniform.

(4) The power of search conferred by this section is only a power to search to the extent that is reasonably required for the purpose for which the power of entry is exercised.

(5) Subject to subsection (6) below, all the rules of common law under which a constable has power to enter premises without a warrant are hereby abolished.

(6) Nothing in subsection (5) above affects any power of entry to deal with or prevent a breach of the peace.

Police and Criminal Evidence Act 1984, s 17

12.3.2 Power of entry to arrest, save life, or prevent damage

Conditions

- A concern for welfare may be too low a threshold for entry under s 17(1)(e) (see *Syed* case, below); as this power is for saving life or limb or preventing serious damage to property.
- Apart from entry under s 17(1)(e), to save life or limb or prevent serious damage to property, the s 17(1) powers are only exercisable if the constable has reasonable grounds for believing that the person whom they are seeking is on the premises.
- In relation to premises consisting of two or more separate dwellings, these powers are limited to—
  ✦ any parts of the premises which the occupiers of any dwelling comprised in the premises use in common with the occupiers of any other such dwelling; **and**
  ✦ any such dwelling in which the constable has reasonable grounds for believing that the person whom they are seeking may be.
- The power to search is only given to the extent that is reasonably required for the purpose for which the power of entry is exercised.

Explanatory notes

- Code B must be complied with when this power is exercised.
- A **warrant of commitment** is a commitment warrant to prison issued under the Magistrates' Courts Act 1980, s 76 for failing to pay fines. It does not include 'default warrants' where an offender has defaulted on their payment of a fine.
- An **indictable offence** includes triable 'either way offences' and low-value shoplifting (see **12.2.4**).
- Saving animals could be preventing serious damage to property.
- A designated PCSO has the same powers as a police constable to enter and search premises for the purpose of saving life or limb or preventing serious damage to property (see **11.1**).
- Nothing in this section affects any power of entry to deal with or prevent a breach of the peace at common law (see **7.3**).

Related cases

Syed v DPP [2010] EWHC 81 (Admin), QBD A neighbour reported screaming and shouting from S's house. On arrival the police found no sign of a disturbance. S came to the door, stating that there had been an argument between two brothers, but evaded further questions. Officers said they had a power of entry as there were concerns for a person's welfare. S refused entry and spat in the face of one officer and headbutted the other. Held: Police were not in the execution of their duty; there were no signs of injury, damage, or disturbance; and the occupants had no complaints. Concern for welfare was too low a threshold for entry under s 17(1)(e). The power is for saving life or limb or preventing serious damage to property.

Baker v CPS [2009] EWHC 299 (Admin), QBD On a report that B had 'gone berserk with a knife' inside her home, officers entered the property 'to save life or limb' under s 17(1)(e). B was sitting on the floor rocking to and fro, with blood on her head, pyjama bottoms, and arm, and a rolling pin between her legs. On asking B to stand up during the search for the knife, B punched the officer in the stomach and was arrested for police assault. Held: 'Saving life or limb' covered saving a person from causing serious harm to him/herself, or third parties. Police entry and search powers under s 17(1)(e) do not require consent of the occupier. Though it might be desirable to give reasons for search and entry, it may be impossible or impracticable to do so.

Blench v DPP [2004] EWHC 2717, QBD A call was received from a female that a drunken man was taking her baby; she then told the police not to attend. Held: Police were allowed to enter the property as they had reason to believe that a child was at risk and there had been, and was likely to be another breach of the peace. Therefore, their presence was lawful and they were not trespassers.

O'Loughlin v CC of Essex [1998] 1 WLR 374, CA When entry to premises is made in order to arrest a person for an offence, any occupier present should be informed of the reason for the entry, unless circumstances make it impossible, impracticable, or undesirable; otherwise the constable would be acting unlawfully.

D'Souza v DPP [1992] 4 All ER 545, HL Entry was forced to a dwelling by police officers to recapture a person unlawfully at large from a secure hospital (under the Mental Health Act). As the officers were not in 'immediate pursuit' they were acting unlawfully. **Notes:** This 'immediate pursuit' requirement does not apply to people unlawfully at large from prison/custody/remand/serving a sentence.

12.3.3 **Searching of premises after arrest**

Section 18 of PACE creates a power to enter and search premises after someone has been arrested for an **indictable offence** and provides a power to seize relevant items.

Power to enter/search after arrest

(1) Subject to the following provisions of this section, a constable may enter and search any premises **occupied** or **controlled** by a person who is under arrest for an **indictable offence**, if he has reasonable grounds for suspecting that there is on the premises evidence other than items subject to **legal privilege**, that relates—

    (a) to that offence; **or**

    (b) to some other indictable offence which is connected with or similar to that offence.

(2) A constable may seize and retain anything for which he may search under subsection (1) above.

(3) The power to search conferred by subsection (1) above is only a power to search to the extent that is reasonably required for the purpose of discovering such evidence.

12.3.3 Searching of premises after arrest

(4) Subject to subsection (5) below, the powers conferred by this section may not be exercised unless an officer of the rank of inspector or above has authorised them in writing.

(5) A constable may conduct a search under subsection (1)—
  (a) before the person is taken to police station or released on bail under section 30A; and
  (b) without obtaining an authorisation under subsection (4),
  if the condition in subsection (5A) is satisfied.

(5A) The condition is that the presence of the person at a place (other than a police station) is necessary for the effective investigation of the offence.

(6) If a constable conducts a search by virtue of subsection (5) above, he shall inform an officer of the rank of inspector or above that he has made the search as soon as practicable after he has made it.

(7) An officer who—
  (a) authorises a search; or
  (b) is informed of a search under subsection (6) above, shall make a record in writing—
    (i) of the grounds for the search; and
    (ii) of the nature of the evidence that was sought.

(8) If the person who was in occupation or control of the premises at the time of the search is in police detention at the time the record is to be made, the officer shall make the record as part of his custody record.

Police and Criminal Evidence Act 1984, s 18

Meanings

Occupied

This refers to premises where the arrested person resides or works, and may include occupancy as an owner, tenant, or 'squatter'.

Controlled

This includes premises in which the arrested person holds some interest, such as owning, renting, leasing, or has use of the premises.

Indictable (see 12.2.4)

Legal privilege (see 12.3.1)

Explanatory notes

- A search should only be conducted if the officer has reasonable grounds for suspecting that evidence of that or another connected or similar indictable offence is on the premises.
- The search must be conducted in accordance with Code B.
- In addition to making the written authority, it is a matter of good practice for the inspector (or above), who authorises the search, to endorse the custody record as well.
- A person does not have to be in police detention before a s 18 authority can be issued, as s 18(1) just requires them to be arrested for an indictable offence.

- Another power to search premises immediately after arrest is created by s 32 (see **12.3.1**).

Related cases

R v Commissioner of the Metropolitan Police and the Home Secretary ex parte Rottman [2002] UKHL 20, HL Common law powers of seizure still exist.

Cowan v Commissioner of the Metropolitan Police [2000] 1 WLR 254, CA Where a constable may seize 'anything' which is on premises, there is no reason why 'anything' could not mean 'everything' that was movable and it was practicable to remove. It does not matter that property itself could be considered to be premises, so the removal of a vehicle (being premises) is lawful and can be seized if necessary.

12.3.4 **Powers of seizure from premises**

Section 19 of PACE provides a constable who is lawfully on premises with a general power to seize property.

Power to seize

(1) The powers conferred by subsections (2), (3) and (4) below are exercisable by a constable who is **lawfully on any premises**.
(2) The constable may seize anything which is on the premises if he has reasonable grounds for believing—
   (a) that it has been obtained in consequence of the commission of an offence; **and**
   (b) that it is necessary to seize it in order to prevent it being concealed, lost, damaged, altered or destroyed.
(3) The constable may seize anything which is on the premises if he has reasonable grounds for believing—
   (a) that it is evidence in relation to an offence which he is investigating or any other offence; and
   (b) that it is necessary to seize it in order to prevent the evidence being concealed, lost, altered or destroyed.
(4) The constable may require any information which is stored in electronic form and is accessible from the premises to be produced in a form in which it can be taken away and in which it is visible and legible or from which it can readily be produced in a visible and legible form, if he has reasonable grounds for believing—
   (a) that—
      (i) it is evidence in relation to an offence which he is investigating or any other offence; or
      (ii) it has been obtained in consequence of the commission of an offence; **and**

12.3.4 Powers of seizure from premises

>   (b) that it is necessary to do so in order to prevent it being concealed,
>   lost, tampered with or destroyed.
>
> (5) The powers conferred by this section are in addition to any power
>   otherwise conferred.
>
> (6) No power of seizure conferred on a constable under any enactment
>   (including an enactment contained in an Act passed after this Act) is to
>   be taken to authorise the seizure of an item which the constable
>   exercising the power has reasonable grounds for believing to be
>   subject to **legal privilege**.
>
> Police and Criminal Evidence Act 1984, s 19

Explanatory notes

- Officers using this power can (at all times they are on the **premises lawfully**) seize any evidence whether it is owned by the defendant or by someone else, provided the seizure of it is necessary for the purpose(s) described. However, this Act does not provide a specific power for seizure of an innocent person's property when it is in a public place.
- As vehicles are deemed to be '**premises**' for the purposes of this Act, they can be seized under the same power (*Cowan v MPC* [2000] 1 WLR 254, CA).
- Motor vehicles, if owned by an innocent party and in a public place, may also be searched under authority of a s 8 warrant (see **12.4**) to search premises for evidence.
- A designated civilian investigating officer has the same seizure powers as a police constable.

Seizure of computerised information

Section 20 of the Police and Criminal Evidence Act 1984 relates to the seizure of computerised information from premises.

(1) Every power of seizure which is conferred by an enactment to which this section applies on a constable who has entered premises in the exercise of a power conferred by an enactment shall be construed as including a power to require any information stored in any electronic form and accessible from the premises to be produced in a form in which it can be taken away and in which it is visible and legible or from which it can readily be produced in a visible and legible form.

(2) This section applies—
    (a) to any enactment contained in an Act passed before this Act;
    (b) to sections 8 and 18 above;
    (c) to paragraph 13 of Schedule 1 to this Act; **and**
    (d) to any enactment contained in an Act passed after this Act.

Police and Criminal Evidence Act 1984, s 20

Seizure of bulk material

The Criminal Justice and Police Act 2001 allows seizure of bulk material in order to examine it elsewhere ('seize and sift').

Premises

Section 50 of the 2001 Act allows a person who is lawfully on premises to seize bulk material when using existing seizure powers, providing—
• there are reasonable grounds to believe that it is material which can be searched for and seized;
• in all the circumstances, it is not reasonably practicable for this to be ascertained whilst on the premises;
• it is necessary to remove it from the premises to enable this to be determined and the material to be separated;
• the existing seizure powers are listed in Pt 1 of Sch 1 to the Act—
  ✦ PACE, ss 8 to 33;
  ✦ any of the other 65 listed Acts with their named sections.

Person

Section 51 of the 2001 Act gives the police additional powers of seizure of bulk material from the person, where there is an existing power to search as shown in Pt 2 of Sch 1 to the Act—
• PACE, ss 24 to 33;
• any of the 8 named Acts and sections listed in the 2001 Act.

Explanatory notes

• Powers given under s 50 also includes any other authorised people such as HMRC or designated investigating officers.
• What is reasonably practicable will differ in each case. Factors to consider include the time to examine and separate the material, and the type and number of people involved. In addition, the need to reduce the risk of accidentally altering or damaging any of the material may be relevant.
• Where legally privileged material forms part of the 'whole thing' then this can be seized in order to separate from the bulk of the material.
• Section 51 (seizure from person) could apply for example where the person has a hand-held computer or computer disk which holds relevant electronic data, or a briefcase containing bulk correspondence which could not be examined in the street.
• Section 52 requires the occupier and/or some other person or persons from whom material has been seized to be given a notice specifying what has been seized and why, that they can apply to a judge for the return of the material or for access to and copying of the seized material.
• Section 21 of PACE provides a person, from whom material has been lawfully seized by the police, with certain rights to access to and/or copies of it.
• Section 22 of PACE provides powers to retain items that have been seized by the police.

12.3.4 Powers of seizure from premises

- A PCSO has the same seizure (and other related) powers as a constable in relation to ss 19, 21 and 22 of PACE (see **11.1.1**)—if they are designated with these powers and are lawfully on the premises in the first instance.

Links to alternative subjects and offences

12.4 **Enter and Search Warrants**

Procedures for premises search warrants, the application and execution process for warrants, and applying for access to excluded or special procedure material are all controlled by PACE.

There are several warrants provided under other legislation such as s 23 of the Misuse of Drugs Act 1971 and s 46 of the Firearms Act 1968. When executed they should be conducted in accordance with PACE and the COP, although they do retain individual powers peculiar to themselves.

12.4.1 **Premises search warrant**

Section 8 of the Police and Criminal Evidence Act 1984 provides the grounds and procedure to be followed when applying for a search warrant relating to an indictable offence. It also provides a power to seize certain incriminating items.

Search warrant-application and procedure

(1) If on an application made by a constable a justice of the peace is satisfied that there are reasonable grounds for believing—

    (a) that an **indictable offence** has been committed; and

    (b) that there is material on **premises** mentioned in subsection (1A) below which is likely to be of substantial value (whether by itself or together with other material) to the investigation of the offence; and

    (c) that the material is likely to be **relevant evidence**; and

    (d) that it does not consist of or include items subject to **legal privilege, excluded material or special procedure material**; and

    (e) that any of the following conditions specified in subsection (3) below applies in relation to each set of premises specified in the application,

he may issue a warrant authorising a constable to enter and search the premises.

(1A) The premises referred to in subsection (1)(b) above are—

    (a) one or more sets of premises specified in the application (in which case the application is for a '**specific premises warrant**'); or

    (b) any premises occupied or controlled by a person specified in the application, including such sets of premises as are so specified (in which case the application is for an '**all premises warrant**').

(1B) If the application is for an all premises warrant, the justice of the peace must also be satisfied—

    (a) that because of the particulars of the offence referred to in paragraph (a) of subsection (1) above, there are reasonable grounds for believing that it is necessary to search premises occupied or controlled by the person in question which are not

---

> specified in the application in order to find the material referred to in paragraph (b) of that subsection; and
>
> (b) that it is not reasonably practicable to specify in the application all the premises, which he occupies or controls and which might need to be searched.
>
> (1C) The warrant may authorise entry to and search of premises on more than one occasion if, on the application, the justice of the peace is satisfied that it is necessary to authorise multiple entries in order to achieve the purpose for which he issues the warrant.
>
> (1D) If it authorises multiple entries, the number of entries authorised may be unlimited, or limited to a maximum.
>
> (2) A constable may seize and retain anything for which a search has been authorised under subsection (1) above.
>
> (3) The conditions mentioned in subsection (1)(e) above are—
>
> (a) that it is not practicable to communicate with any person entitled to grant entry to the premises;
>
> (b) that it is practicable to communicate with a person entitled to grant entry to the premises but it is not practicable to communicate with any person entitled to grant access to the evidence;
>
> (c) that entry to the premises will not be granted unless a warrant is produced;
>
> (d) that the purpose of a search may be frustrated or seriously prejudiced unless a constable arriving at the premises can secure immediate entry to them.
>
> Police and Criminal Evidence Act 1984, s 8

Meanings

Indictable offence (see 12.2.4)

Premises (see 12.3.1)

Relevant evidence

In relation to an offence, means anything that would be admissible in evidence at a trial for the offence.

Legal privilege (see 12.3.1)

Excluded material (see 12.4.4)

Special procedure material (see 12.4.4)

Specific premises warrant

This consists of one or more sets of premises named/specified in the application.

All premises warrant

Being all premises occupied or controlled by an individual.

Explanatory notes

- Section 8(5) and HOC 88/1985 state that the power to issue a warrant under this section is in addition to any other powers to issue warrants.
- Warrants under s 8 only apply to indictable offences, and can be for entry to—
  + named/specific premises—'**Specific premises warrant**'; or
  + premises 'occupied or controlled by' an individual—'all premises warrant'.
- An '**All premises warrant**' will apply when it is necessary to search all premises occupied or controlled by an individual, but it is not reasonably practicable to specify all such premises at the time of application. The warrant will allow access to all premises occupied or controlled by that person, both those which are specified on the application, and those which are not.
- Section 16(3) states that a warrant for entry and search must be executed within three months from the date of its issue (see **12.4.3**).
- Where items falling outside those which may be seized under s 8(2) are found on the premises, consider the seizure provided by s 19 of PACE (see **12.3.4**).
- When applying for and executing warrants then s 15 (see **12.4.2**) and s 16 (see **12.4.3**) together with Code B must be complied with in relation to application, safeguards, and execution.
- In any application also consider the procedures for access to excluded material/special procedure material, if relevant, provided by s 9 of PACE (see **12.4.4**).
- Failure to comply with statutory requirements will make the entry and subsequent seizure of property unlawful (*R v CC of Lancashire, ex parte Parker* [1993] Crim LR 204, QBD).
- Officers should be aware of the extensive powers to search without a warrant on arrest under s 32 (see **12.3.1**) or after arrest under s 18 (see **12.3.3**).
- Warrants issued under the provision of s 8 only authorises searching of the premises not people who are in them.
- Such people may only be searched if arrested, but there can be a specific power to search people in warrants issued under s 23(2) of the Misuse of Drugs Act 1971 (see **5.5**) and s 46(2) of the Firearms Act 1968 (see **8.6.3**) (providing the application includes to search people in the premises).
- When applying for search warrants, 'reasonable grounds to believe' under s 8 PACE imposes a higher threshold test than 'reasonable grounds to suspect' under s 46(1) of the Firearms Act 1968 (*Eastenders Barking Limited v South Western MC* [2011] Cr App R 123).
- A designated investigating officer, can apply for this warrant for any premises in the relevant police area, as if they were a constable. Similarly they have the powers of seizure under s 8(2) above.
- In relation to seizure and examination of bulk material see **12.3.4** for details.

12.4.2 **Application procedures for a search warrant**

Section 15 of PACE sets out the procedure to be followed when applying for a search warrant. For quick reference s 15 is given in bulleted form as follows—

Application procedure

- This section (and s 16) relates to the issue of warrants (**under any enactment**) for constables to enter and search premises.
- Entering or searching of premises under a warrant is unlawful unless it complies with this section and s 16 (see **12.4.3**).
- Where a constable applies for such warrant the following details must be given—
  - grounds on which application made;
  - enactment under which the warrant would be issued;
  - identify (as far as practicable) the articles or persons sought.
- Furthermore, if the application is for—
  - a warrant authorising entry and search on more than one occasion
    - ground on which application made;
    - whether unlimited number of entries is sought;
    - otherwise the maximum number of entries desired;
  - a '**Specific premises warrant**' (see **12.4.1**)
    - each set of premises to be entered and searched;
  - an '**All premises warrant**' (see **12.4.1**)
    - specify (as far as reasonably practicable) the sets of premises to be entered and searched;
    - the person who is in occupation or control of those premises and any others which require entering and searching;
    - why it is necessary to search more premises than those specified and why it is not reasonably practicable to specify all the premises to be entered and searched.
- Such a warrant shall specify—
  - the name of the person who applied for it;
  - the date on which it is issued;
  - the enactment under which it is issued;
  - the articles or persons to be sought (identified as far as is practicable);
  - each set of premises to be searched;
  - in the case of an 'all premises warrant'
    - the person who is in occupation or control of premises to be searched, together with any premises under his occupation or control which can be specified and which are to be searched.
- The following points also have to be complied with—
  - applications shall be supported by an information in writing and made ex parte (subject does not have to be present);

+ the constable shall answer on oath any question that the justice of the peace or judge hearing the application puts to them;
+ a warrant shall authorise an entry on one occasion only—unless multiple entries are authorised, in which case it must specify whether the number of entries is unlimited, or limited to a specified maximum;
+ two copies shall be made of a specific premises warrant that specifies only one set of premises and does not authorise multiple entries. Otherwise, as many copies as are reasonably required may be made of any other kind of warrant;
+ copies shall be clearly certified as copies.

Explanatory notes

- Advice and guidance are given in Code B, under search warrants.
- Where premises are multiple occupancy (eg a single house converted into flats) the warrant must specify all the rooms required to be searched (including the common living areas), and not just give the main address.
- Section 15(1) states that entering or searching premises under authority of a warrant is unlawful, unless procedures given in s 15 and s 16 (see **12.4.3**) are complied with.

Related cases

AB and another v Huddersfield MC and another [2014] EWHC 1089 (Admin), QBD Where police had failed to inform the court that the occupants of premises were solicitors, a subsequent search warrant issued by a magistrates' court under s 8 of PACE was unlawful.

R (on the application of Lees) v Solihull MC [2013] EWHC 3779 (Admin), QBD Search warrants granted under s 8 to HMRC did not specify what material was sought. As a result the entry, search, and seizure were unlawful; because the warrants breached s 15(6)(b) by failing to identify the articles or persons sought.

R (on the application of Bhatti) v Croydon MC [2010] EWHC 522 (Admin), QBD In an 'all premises warrant' issued under s 8, all premises that can be identified at the time of application must be so identified. Premises identified at a later date must be added to the schedule attached to the warrant and signed by an inspector before attending the property. Failure to supply the occupier with a copy of the warrant/schedule at entry naming the premises or adding the address by hand as a warrant is executed breaches s 16(5), so entry, search, and seizure become unlawful under s 15(1).

R v CC of Lancashire Police, ex parte Parker and McGrath [1993] Crim LR 204, QBD The magistrate or judge who issues the warrant should make copies of the warrant and certify them with their signature.

12.4.3 **Execution of search warrants**

Section 16 of PACE sets out the procedure to be followed when executing a search warrant. For quick reference s 16 is given in bulleted form as follows—

Execution procedure

A warrant to enter and search **premises**—
- may be executed by any constable;
- it may authorise persons to accompany any constable who is executing it;
  + such a person has the same powers as the constable, but only whilst in the company and under the supervision of a constable;
    - such a person will then be able to execute the warrant, and seize anything to which the warrant relates;
- must be executed within three months from the date of its issue;
- must be executed at a reasonable hour unless it appears that the purpose of a search may be frustrated on an entry at a reasonable hour;
- will only authorise a search to the extent required for the purpose for which the warrant was issued.

Specifically, no premises may be entered or searched unless an inspector (or above) authorises, in writing, entry for—
- an '**All premises warrant**'—
  + premises which are not specified;
- a '**Multiple entries warrant**'—
  + for the second or subsequent entry and search.

Notification requirements exist: when a constable is seeking to execute a warrant to enter and search premises, the constable shall—
- where the occupier is present—
  + identify themselves to the occupier. If not in uniform documentary evidence produced to show that they are a constable;
  + produce the warrant and supply a copy of the warrant/schedule to the occupier;
- if the occupier is not present, but some other person is present who appears to the constable to be in charge of the premises—
  + the constable shall deal with that person as if they were the occupier and comply with the above requirements;
- if there is no person present (occupier or in charge)—
  + the constable shall leave a copy of the warrant in a prominent place on the premises.

Where a constable has executed a warrant they shall—
- endorse the warrant stating whether—
  + the articles or persons sought were found;
  + any articles were seized, other than articles which were sought;
- unless the warrant is for one set of premises only—
  + separately endorse each set of premises entered and searched providing the above details.

A warrant shall be returned to the **appropriate person**—
- when it has been executed;
- in the case of—
  + a '**Specific premises warrant**' (not been executed);
  + an 'all premises warrant';
  + any warrant authorising multiple entries;

upon the expiry of the 3 month period or sooner.

Meanings

Premises (see **12.3.1**)

All premises warrant (see **12.4.1**)

Multiple entries warrant (see **12.4.1**)

Appropriate person

If the warrant was issued by—
- a justice of the peace, it will be the designated officer for the local justice area in which the justice was acting when the warrant was issued;
- a judge, it will be the appropriate officer of the court from which the judge issued it.

Specific premises warrant (see **12.4.1**)

Explanatory notes

- A warrant returned to the appropriate person shall be retained by that person for 12 months from its return.
- An occupier of premises to which the warrant relates can inspect the warrant (and should be allowed to do so) during the 12-month retaining period.
- When executing a search warrant, advice and guidance should be obtained from Code B, under search warrants.
- A person authorised in the warrant to accompany the constable may be an expert in computing or financial matters. Such an expert will then be able to take a more active role in the search and in seizing material, rather than merely being present in an advisory or clerical capacity.
- In practical terms the supervising constable must identify any accompanying persons to the occupier of premises prior to the start of any search and explain that person's role in the process. The constable in charge will have overall supervisory responsibility and will be accountable for any action taken.

12.4.4 **Access to excluded and special procedure material**

Section 9 of PACE provides the procedures to be adopted in order to gain access to excluded material and special procedure material.

12.4.4 Access to excluded and special procedure material

Access procedure

(1) A constable may obtain access to **excluded material** or **special procedure material** for the purposes of a criminal investigation by making an application under **Schedule 1** and in accordance with that Schedule.

(2) Any Act (including a local Act) passed before this Act under which a search of **premises** for the purposes of a criminal investigation could be authorised by the issue of a warrant to a constable shall cease to have effect so far as it relates to the authorisation of searches—

   (a) for items subject to **legal privilege; or**

   (b) for excluded material; **or**

   (c) for special procedure material consisting of documents or records other than documents.

Police and Criminal Evidence Act 1984, s 9

Meanings

Excluded material

Means—

- **personal records** acquired or created in the course of any trade, business, profession, or other occupation or for the purposes of any paid or unpaid office;
- human tissue or tissue fluid taken for the purposes of diagnosis or medical treatment held in confidence;
- both sets of material held in confidence subject to—
  - ✦ an express or implied undertaking to do so;
  - ✦ a disclosure restriction or an obligation of secrecy contained in any legislation;

or

- **journalistic material** which consists of documents or records other than documents, being held or continuously held in confidence (by one or more persons), subject to an undertaking, restriction, or obligation of confidence since it was first acquired or created for the purposes of journalism.

Personal records

Means documentary and other records concerning an individual (whether living or dead) who can be identified from them and relates to—

- their physical or mental health;
- spiritual counselling or assistance given/to be given to them; or
- counselling or assistance given/to be given for their personal welfare, by any voluntary organisation or individual who by reason of—
  - ✦ their office or occupation has responsibilities for this; or
  - ✦ an order by a court has responsibilities for his supervision.

Journalistic material

- Is material acquired or created for the purposes of journalism.
- Providing it is in the possession of a person who acquired or created it for this purpose.

- It will be acquired if a person receives the material from someone who intends that the recipient uses it for that purpose.

Special procedure material

- Includes journalistic material, other than excluded material.
- Includes material, other than items subject to legal privilege and excluded material, in the possession of a person who acquired or created it in the course of any trade, business, profession, or for the purpose of any paid or unpaid office; and holds it in confidence subject to—
    + an express or implied undertaking to do so;
    + a disclosure restriction or an obligation of secrecy contained in any legislation.
- Where material is acquired by—
    + an employee from their employer in their course of employment;
    + a company from an associated company;
    it is only special procedure material if it was special procedure material immediately before the acquisition.
- Where material is created by—
    + an employee in the course of their employment;
    + a company on behalf of an associated company;
    it is only special procedure material if it would have been special procedure material had the employer/associated company created it.

Schedule 1

This gives full details of the procedure to be followed when making an application to a judge in order to gain access to excluded material or special procedure material.

Premises (see **12.3.1**)

Legal privilege (see **12.3.1**)

Explanatory notes

- Code B provides guidance regarding the conduct of searches and advice on Sch 1 searches.
- The CPS makes Sch 1 applications and advice should be sought from them in any application.
- A designated investigation officer can obtain the same access to excluded and special procedure material as a police constable.
- Case law has established that—
    + police cannot routinely examine hospital records;
    + search warrant not lawful without the proper paperwork;
    + a Sch 1 notice should specify the documents being sought.
- In relation to seizure and examination of bulk material see **12.3.4** for details.
- Officers should be mindful of the powers to search (without a warrant) on arrest (see **12.3.1**) or after arrest (see **12.3.3**).
- Special procedure and excluded material can be searched for and seized under PACE, ss 18 and 32, provided—
    + lawful arrest is made, in good faith; **and**
    + the search is carried out strictly within the terms of those sections.

12.4.4 Access to excluded and special procedure material

Related cases

R v Blackfriars CC and the Commissioner of Police of the Metropolis [2014] EWHC 1541 (Admin), QBD A warrant was the authority to go onto premises; if s 15(6)(b) was not complied with (e.g. by failing to specify in detail the article(s) sought), then the warrant—and therefore the entry—could be invalidated.

R (on application of Faisaltex Ltd) v Preston CC [2008] EWHC 2832 (Admin), QBD A computer and hard drive counted as a single item within 'material' under s 8(1) of PACE. This power was sufficient without using s 51 of the Criminal Justice and Police Act 2001 as well.

R v Leaf [2005] EWCA Crim 2152, CA Special procedure and excluded material can be searched for and seized under ss 18 and 32 provided a proper, good faith arrest is made; and that the search is within the terms of those sections.

R v Cardiff CC, ex parte Kellam The Times, 3 May 1993, QBD Hospital records relate to the health of an identifiable person; this means that they are 'excluded material' for which there was no power to gain access prior to PACE, so there is no power to gain access now.

R v Maidstone CC, ex parte Waitt [1988] Crim LR 384, QBD A hearing under Sch 1 should be with the knowledge and in the presence of both parties.

R v Leicester CC, ex parte DPP [1987] 3 All ER 654, QBD Normally parties to an application are the police and those with custody of the documents being sought.

R v Bristol CC, ex parte Bristol Press and Picture Agency (1986) 85 Cr App R 190, QBD Press photographs showing criminal acts. Access to them could identify the suspects. It was in the public interest to grant the order. Conditions were met.

Links to alternative subjects and offences

Chapter 13

Patrol Matters and Guidance

13.1 **Missing Persons**

Guidelines based on established 'best practice' are intended to provide guidance and assistance to police officers when taking a 'missing person' report. The report will be categorised to determine whether the person is either 'missing' or 'absent'.

Missing—Anyone whose whereabouts cannot be established and where the circumstances are out of character or the context suggests the person may be a subject of crime or at risk of harm to themselves or others.

Absent—A person not at a place where they are expected or required to be.

Individual **force policies** must always be complied with and acted upon.

Initial report

- The officer taking the report must thoroughly **investigate** why the person is missing, where they may have gone, gather and preserve evidence, as the report could turn into the investigation of a serious crime.
- The initiating officer must obtain the following details—
  - name, address, date of birth, sex, skin, marks, scars, tattoos, or peculiarities (eg walks with a limp, stutters);
  - description of height, build, hair style/colour, clothing (including shoes and outer clothing);
  - establish the circumstances of the disappearance—what was said, any clues as to where the missing person may be/may intend to go (keep accurate records of what is said and by whom);
  - time and date last seen, where and by whom (obtain full details of the people who had last seen/spoken to the missing person—including contact details);
  - a recent photograph (obtain permission to release this photograph, if required, to the press/television);
  - has the missing person left a note, taken any spare clothing, got a mobile phone (obtain number), passport, money, transport, access to savings/bank accounts, holder of credit/debit cards;

+ full details (contact numbers) of friends, relatives, work/school;
+ if this person has gone missing before—details/circumstances, where were they found;
+ suicidal, medical conditions, medication to be taken, details of doctor.
- Take details of the person reporting, relationship and contact details. Any support required for the family/person reporting.
- Make a risk assessment (see below) concerning the missing person and record the reasons for your decision.
- Gather relevant evidence for the investigation to continue. The higher the risk the more detailed the information required.
- In a high-risk case, notify a supervisor immediately; in a medium-risk case, notify a supervisor without undue delay; and in a low-risk case, notify a supervisor by the end of the tour of duty.
- Search the home and immediate vicinity. If appropriate, seize any items of investigatory/evidential value—diary, notes, correspondence, details of any medical treatment, and obtain a recent photograph.
- Carry out all relevant enquiries and make further searches to locate missing person.
- Circulate the person on PNC and any other relevant systems.

Making a risk assessment

When making the assessment, the officer attending the report must record in full all factors that lead to the decision whether missing/absent, and the risk category. An 'absent' person (low risk) will be: temporary (eg truants); unauthorised (eg local authority/foster care); or deliberate absence.

High risk

- Is in danger due to their own vulnerability.
- May have been the victim of a serious crime.
- May have been planning a serious crime.
- There are substantial grounds for believing that the public is in danger.

Action

- Immediate deployment of appropriate resources.
- Notify supervision immediately for involvement in the investigation.
- Notify a member of the senior management team.
- If the victim of/suspected in planning a serious crime an SIO should be informed.
- A press/media strategy should be implemented.
- Establish and maintain close contact with other relevant agencies.

Medium risk

The person is likely to be subject to danger and/or is a risk to themselves or others.

Action

- Notify supervision regarding the circumstances and concerns.
- Deployment of appropriate resources.

- Continue an active and measured response by police and other agencies.
- Involve the press/media.

Low risk

No apparent threat of danger to themselves or the public.

Action

- Carry out appropriate enquiries to locate the missing person.
- Notify supervision by the end of the tour of duty.
- Keep the report under regular review.

Risk assessment factors

- Is the person vulnerable, due to age or infirmity or any other factor?
- Is this type of behaviour out of character?
- Is the person suspected of being the victim of a serious crime in progress (eg abduction)?
- Are there any indications that the person is likely to commit suicide?
- Is there a reason for the person to go missing?
- Are there any indications that the person made preparations for their absence?
- What was the person intending to do when they were last seen (eg go out to the shops, see a friend), and did they carry out that intention?
- Are there family and/or relationship problems or recent history of family conflict?
- Is the person a victim or perpetrator of domestic violence?
- Does the missing person have any physical illness, disability, or mental health problems?
- Are they on the Child Protection Register?
- Do they need essential medical treatment that is not likely to be available to them?
- Is there a belief that the person may not have the physical ability to interact safely with others or in an unknown environment?
- Are there any ongoing bullying or harassment, sexual, racial, or homophobic or any other cultural or community concerns?
- Were they involved in a violent and/or racist incident immediately prior to their disappearance?
- Are they (or a relative) a witness to an offence or otherwise involved in proceedings (eg a juror)?
- Have they previously been missing and been exposed to or suffered harm?
- Any problems with work, school, college, university, or money?
- Are they drug or alcohol dependent?
- Any other problem which may affect the risk assessment not mentioned here?

ubsequent investigation

A multi-agency collaboration in sharing information is important. Forces utilise Multi-Agency Safeguarding Hubs (MASH) or similar structures to ensure that missing and absent incidents are properly managed.

- A detailed record must be kept of all enquiries carried out.
- Supervision must review the risk assessment/report and it should be reconsidered at every handover.
- The point of contact for the police must be kept up to date with all the progress.
- The Child Exploitation and Online Protection Centre (CEOP) (see **Appendix 1**) works with child protection partners both within and outside the UK, and should be notified about any missing or abducted children within 14 days.
- The NCA are the UK national and international point of contact for all missing person and unidentified body investigations, and maintain the national database of missing and unidentified records. The NCA run the UK Missing Persons Bureau website (see **Appendix 1**) to appeal to the public for help to identify currently unidentified people, both alive and dead.
- The Presumption of Death Act 2013 makes provision for the High Court to make a declaration that a person is deemed to have died if the Court is satisfied that the person has died or has not been known to be alive for a period of at least 7 years.
- Ensure access to specialists such as SIOs and Police Search Advisers (PoLSA) when needed.
- Could the person be in hospital, prison, or custody?
- Consider CCTV, taxi records, details of bank and phone records.
- Missing persons could vary between a person who is—
  + lost—temporarily disorientated, such as a young child or elderly person; or
  + under the influence of a third party—taken against their will (eg abduction or kidnap).
- An absent person has gone voluntarily, and has made a conscious decision to take this course of action (eg truant).
- It is always advisable to think the worst until the contrary is proved.

People in care

People in care are mostly, by their very nature, vulnerable and special consideration should be given to any person who goes missing from care.

Children in care

- Children in local authority care account for the largest number of absent person's reports, generally being a low risk category—unauthorised absence.
- Unauthorised absence is where the child has failed to return to the care home on time, is staying with a friend at a known location, or running away after a dispute with a member of staff.
- A risk assessment should still be carried out as normal. The situation should be kept under review and if the child has not returned, then the child should be reported missing.

- The children's home and foster carers are expected to act as any reasonable parent would and make the necessary enquiries into the whereabouts of the child, before making a report to the police.

Found safe and well

- When the missing person is located, if they are over 16 there is no obligation to inform the families of their whereabouts (only that they are safe and well), if it is against the person's wishes.
- If the missing person is under 16, then there **is** an obligation to return the child to their home or a **safe** location, if there are any doubts about the child's safety.
- The report must be completed with as much information gathering as possible as to the circumstances in which the person was found and where they had been.
- All computer systems must be updated and coordination with other agencies as to the return of the missing person and other relevant information.

Links to alternative subjects and offences

13.2 **Child Abuse**

Specialist departments will carry out most of the investigations into child abuse cases. However, patrol officers may well be the first point of contact with the victim and their families/carers; and it is important to recognise child abuse and what action to take.

The following information is based on guidelines established as 'best practice'. However, **force policy** must be adhered to and this section is intended as a guide to assist in following that policy.

Child abuse is—
- abuse involving any person under the age of 18;
- the abuse can be physical, emotional, or sexual;
- the abuse can also take the form of neglect, a persistent failure to meet a child's basic physical or psychological needs which is likely to result in serious impairment of the child's development or health.

Taking the initial report

The following is a suggested checklist regarding the relevant information to obtain when taking the initial report. All reports should be treated as serious no matter how minor they appear to be.

Checklist

- Details of the reporting person and relationship to the child.
- Nature and location of the incident or concern.
- Details of the child.
- Current location and identity of any suspect including relationship to child.
- If name not known, then a detailed description of the suspect.
- Whether there are any injuries. If so, details of injuries and whether any medical assistance is required.
- Details of any other children present and whether they are safe.
- Details and locations of any witnesses.
- Whether weapons were used.
- Whether any person present has taken alcohol or drugs.
- Whether there is any history of involvement by social services. If so, details of the social worker.
- Whether there are any relevant court orders in place.
- Whether there are any details of any special needs.
- Details of the behaviour of all parties, reporting person, victim, and suspect.
- A verbatim account of the caller's story.
- Details of the child's school and doctor, if known.
- The Child Protection/Child Abuse Unit and a supervisor must be notified as soon as possible.
- Check all computer systems both national (PNC) and local, including the Child Protection Register. This can be done through the Child Protection Unit or through Social Services.

Welfare of the child

In child abuse cases, the welfare of the child is paramount. As patrol officers you have a responsibility to check the welfare of the child.

- There is no legal requirement for a parent or guardian to be present for an officer to speak to a child.
- If that person is suspected of being involved in the abuse then **every** attempt should be made to speak to the child separately.
- Care should be taken when speaking to the child, to limit the conversation to the welfare of the child and obtaining the minimum amount of information about the incident (offence, suspect, and location), for fear of prejudicing any subsequent prosecutions.
- Officers should take into account the physical appearance, condition, and behaviour of the child.
- Officers should be mindful of the reasons behind a parent/guardian's decision not to allow the police to assess the welfare of a child.
- Further enquiries should be made to establish the welfare of the child, if cooperation with the police is refused.
- Officers should make a record of reasons for refusal of cooperation.
- Consider offences of child cruelty (see **2.4.1** for further details).

Police powers

Powers of entry

- Under **s 17(1)(b)** of **PACE** a constable may enter and search premises to arrest a person for an indictable offence (see **12.3.2**).
- Under **s 17(1)(e)** of **PACE** a constable may enter and search premises in order to save life or limb or prevent serious damage to property (see **12.3.2**).
- Under **common law** a constable has the power of entry to deal with or prevent a breach of the peace (see **7.3** and **12.3.2** for details).
- A **warrant** under the **Children Act 1989, s 48** to search for children who may be in need of emergency protection (see **2.4.2**).

Police protection (see **2.4.2** for further details)

- The **Children Act 1989, s 46**, allows a constable to remove a child if they have reasonable cause to believe is at risk of **significant harm** or to keep the child at a place of safety such as a hospital.
- 'Harm' is defined as 'ill treatment or the impairment of health or development' and could include 'impairment suffered from seeing or hearing ill treatment of another'.
- 'Significant' may be a traumatic event such as suffocating, poisoning, or other violence or a series of events, which together would constitute significant harm.
- Before exercising this power advice should be sought from the Child Protection Unit where possible.
- If this power is used the duty inspector must be informed as soon as possible.
- The child can only be removed under this section for a maximum of 72 hours (although it is unlikely to be for this length of time).

13.2 Child Abuse

+ This power should only be used in emergency situations. Wherever possible, child protection orders should be granted by the courts.
+ Where the power is exercised there will be an **investigating** officer (the officer who initially took the child into police protection) and a **designated** officer (an officer of at least the rank of inspector who is responsible for safeguarding and/or promoting the child's welfare).
+ The child should **not** be taken to a police station (only in exceptional circumstances). Where possible, early liaison with the local authority should be undertaken to find the child suitable accommodation.
+ Suitable accommodation would be a registered children's home, certified foster care, or, where necessary, with relatives, or other suitable carers (appropriate checks must be carried out, PNC, sex offenders register, child protection register, and any relevant local systems). The investigating officer must ensure that placement with relatives does not place the child at further risk.
+ If the local authority is not already aware of the situation, the investigating officer should inform them as soon as possible of the circumstances.
+ The investigating officer should also keep the child informed, at all stages, of what has and is going to happen. If appropriate take into account and act upon their views and wishes.

Links to alternative subjects and offences

13.3 **Domestic Violence**

Information in this chapter is based on guidelines established as 'best practice'.

HOC 3/2013 introduced government domestic violence and abuse definitions to encourage forces to review their guidance and policies in this area.

Domestic violence can be defined as: 'Any incident or pattern of incidents of **controlling, coercive**, threatening behaviour, violence or abuse between those aged 16 or over who are or have been intimate partners or family members regardless of gender or sexuality. The abuse can encompass, but is not limited to, psychological, physical, sexual, financial, and/or emotional abuse.'

Controlling behaviour is: a range of acts designed to make a person subordinate and/or dependent by isolating them from sources of support, exploiting their resources and capacities for personal gain, depriving them of the means needed for independence, resistance and escape and regulating their everyday behaviour.

Coercive behaviour is: an act or a pattern of acts of assault, threats, humiliation and intimidation or other abuse that is used to harm, punish, or frighten their victim.

This coercive behaviour definition includes so called 'honour' based violence, female genital mutilation (FGM) and forced marriage, (see **13.5**) and is clear that victims are not confined to one gender or ethnic group.

Parties involved

- It includes same sex partners and ex-partners irrespective of how long ago the relationship ended.
- Family members includes immediate family members (whether directly related or not), in-laws, and step relations.

Attending at the scene

- Prior to arrival at the scene, officers must be in possession of any previous history of domestic violence and any other relevant information, such as outstanding warrants, wanted markers, violence markers, child protection issues, and injunctions.
- The despatch/communications centre must ensure that all this information is passed to the officers prior to their arrival.
- The main duty of a police officer at a report of domestic violence is to protect the victims and children.

Initial report

A further risk assessment should be carried out in line with **force policy**, paying particular attention to weapons.

13.3 Domestic Violence

- Check details of suspect.
- Check if the suspect is still present at the scene and if not where they are.
- Circulate full description if suspect has left the scene.
- **Always separate** the parties involved if suspect still at the scene.
- Check the welfare of any person in the house, especially children and assess any needs they may have, ie medical assistance.
- **Do not** ask the victim in front of the defendant for details of the incident, and particularly not if they want to pursue a complaint.
- **Positive action** must always be taken when dealing with cases of domestic violence.
- It is advisable to take the decision about arresting the suspect away from the victim and tell both parties that it is **your** decision to arrest.
- Be prepared to justify your decision where you decide not to arrest, just as much as when you arrest.
- Record everything said by everyone at the scene and their behaviour.
- Evidence should be gathered at the scene of domestic violence as it would at the scene of any other incident.
- A victim statement should be taken in **all** cases even if it looks like the victim will not support any prosecution.

Responsibilities with regards to children

- A child is any person under 18.
- Police officers have a duty to protect a child from harm (see 2.4.2).
- If no children are present, establish whether any children reside there and their current whereabouts.
- Check the premises to establish the presence of children.
- Obtain details of all children at the scene—
  + name (all names presently or previously used);
  + date of birth;
  + sex;
  + address;
  + doctor;
  + details of school;
  + details of child's circumstances, clothing, behaviour, injuries, cleanliness;
  + details of all children normally resident at the address.

Subsequent investigation

- Always bear in mind the safety of the victim and any children.
- When considering bail and bail conditions keep the victim informed at all times.
- Inform the victim about bail and what the conditions are prior to the release of the suspect.
- Give details of local and national support groups to the victim (see **Appendix 1**).
- Follow **force policy** with regard to notifying the Domestic Violence Unit.

Police powers of entry

- PACE, s 17(1)(b)—enter premises for the purpose of arresting a person for an indictable offence (see **12.3.2**).
- PACE, s 17(1)(e)—enter premises for the purpose of saving life or limb or preventing serious damage to property (see **12.3.2**).
- Breach of the peace—enter premises to prevent or deal with a breach of the peace (see **7.3**).

Counter allegations

- These are often made in domestic violence cases, some in self-defence and some false allegations.
- The primary aggressor needs to be identified: note this is not necessarily the first person to use violence.
- Officers should establish the following when investigating counter allegations—
  + injuries of both parties need to be examined;
  + examine the version provided by both parties, to see if self-defence is a genuine issue for either party;
  + any previous reports of domestic violence and counter allegations;
  + any previous convictions/arrests for violence for either party.

Parental responsibility

- If the parents are married, both parents have parental responsibility.
- If the parents are not married the mother has parental responsibility but the father will only have it if he is named on the birth certificate or has obtained it through court proceedings.
- The police do not normally get involved in child custody disagreements unless there is a welfare concern for the child or the action constitutes a criminal offence (eg abduction).
- Any breach of a custody agreement is not a police matter and should be dealt with before a court.

Property

- The police will not get involved in the sharing of property between partners. If the parties involved cannot settle it between themselves then legal advice should be sought from a solicitor.
- If the parties are married all property is classed as joint regardless of whose name it is in or who bought it.
- Where the parties are unmarried it is more complicated and depends on who bought it and what contributions each party made.
- Each party has a right to collect property that belongs to them. The police will only get involved if there is a threat of violence to either party or a breach of the peace. The police will not get involved in resolving the property issues.

Restraining orders/injunctions

- Consider offences and powers available under the Protection from Harassment Act 1997 in relation to harassment or stalking (see **7.11**).

13.3 Domestic Violence

This Act also deals with restraining orders under s 5 and injunctions under s 3.

- The victim should be made aware that they have certain rights enforceable in a civil court but should be advised that civil action can be costly and also the consequence of this instead of involving the police.
- Victims should be told that if a civil injunction is obtained under s 3 (see **7.11.6**) with a power of arrest, then details would be recorded on police computer systems.
- Sections 24 to 30 of the Crime and Security Act 2010 deal with a Domestic Violence Protection Notice (DVPN) which can be issued by a superintendent (or above) to an alleged domestic abuse perpetrator (P), if they have reasonable grounds to believe the person has threatened or used violence against the victim. Under s 25(1)(b) a constable can arrest P for breach of the DVPN. Within 48 hours of the DVPN being served, the police must make an application for a Domestic Violence Protection Order (DVPO) to a magistrates' court for the area, when the MC can remand P.

Links to alternative subjects and offences

13.4 **Vulnerable Victim/Witness**

Police duties to all victims

All victims can expect support entitlements under the Code of Practice for Victims of Crime 2013.

A victim is defined as 'a person who has suffered harm, including physical, mental or emotional or economic loss which was directly caused by criminal conduct'. Under the Police Reform and Social Responsibility Act 2011 police and crime commissioners/Mayor's Office for Police and Crime must take account of the views of victims of crime in their planning.

Referrals to Victim Support

The police must ensure that all victims are provided with information and contact details of the appropriate local Victim Support Group.

- The information about support services must be provided as soon as possible after the allegation is made of the criminal conduct and no later than 5 working days. This may be done by handing the victim a current local copy of the 'Victims of Crime' leaflet. It should be explained to the victim that Victim Support is independent, offers support, practical help, and information by trained volunteers (eg about compensation and insurance), it is free and confidential, and can provide help in dealing with other organisations.
- It must be explained to the victim that the victim's contact details will be passed on to local support services unless the police are asked not to do so.
- These requirements could be met by officers using a standard form of words when recording details of the crime from the victim: 'Victim Support is an independent charity which can offer you help. We recommend their services, and it is our (force) policy to refer your details to them unless you ask us not to do so.'
- Notification of the victim should be recorded in order to demonstrate that any relevant details were only passed on to Victim Support with their knowledge.
- Contact details of **all** victims must be given to the local Victim Support Group within 2 days of the allegation of criminal conduct being made (or consent being given). Exceptions—
  + certain minor offences (theft of or from a motor vehicle, minor criminal damage, and tampering with motor vehicles, unless there are aggravating factors);
  + sexual offences or domestic violence/relatives of homicide victims: only with the explicit consent of the victim/relative;
  + where victims state they do not wish to be referred (this should be formally recorded); it should be explained that Victim Support can still be contacted at a later stage.

The initial needs assessment of the victim on the reverse of the MG11 statement form must always be completed.

- Similarly inform the victim/witness about Victim Support's witness service.
- Where the offender is under the age of 18 the victim's contact details must be passed on to the Youth Offending Team unless the victim asks the police not to do so.
- For further information see—
  + HOC 44/2001: Referral of victims' details to victim support, revised version of the 'Victims of Crime' leaflet;
  + ACPO—Victim Support: Victim Referral Agreement (2003).
- A Family Liaison Officer must be assigned to relatives where a victim has died as result of (suspected) criminal conduct.

Information for victims

- During the investigation the police must notify the victim at least monthly of the progress of the case and its conclusion. In cases of serious crime, where no person has been charged, information must be given about the review procedure.
- Certain information and reasons for decisions, court dates, etc must be given to the victim as soon as possible (generally within 5 working days at the latest, within 1 working day in the case of vulnerable and intimidated witnesses) if—
  + the police decide that there will be no investigation into that crime;
  + a suspect is arrested/released with no further action taken/released on police bail/bail altered/bail conditions;
  + a suspect is interviewed/reported for offence (within 3 working days);
  + summons issued by the court;
  + a decision to charge/not to prosecute/insufficient evidence to charge has been made;
  + a suspect is cautioned/reprimanded/given final warning/issued PND etc.
- The MOJ, Code of Practice for Victims of Crime, December 2013 has introduced a number of changes to the code—
  + victims of the most serious crimes and those persistently targeted will now receive an enhanced service in addition to vulnerable and intimidated victims. The defined most serious crimes are: domestic violence, hate crime, terrorism, sexual offences, human trafficking, attempted murder, kidnap, false imprisonment, arson with intent to endanger life, and wounding or causing GBH with intent;
  + all victims are entitled to make a victim personal statement (VPS), to be read at court;
  + businesses are now entitled to make an impact statement.
- Complainants in respect of sexual offences or domestic abuse and relatives of those who have died are also entitled to an enhanced service

Vulnerable and intimidated victims

The identification of a vulnerable or intimidated witness at an early stage is of paramount importance. It will assist the witness to give information to the investigating officer and later to the court, and also to the investigation, thus improving the process of evidence gathering. This process will lead to the likelihood of a more efficient and equitable trial. It will also help to ensure that the witness has been adequately supported throughout in order to give the best evidence. Consider witness anonymity orders (see **4.8.1**).

Vulnerable victims

- Children under the age of 18 at the time of the offence (in all cases).
- If the quality of the evidence given by the victim is likely to be diminished because the victim—
  - ♦ suffers from mental disorder within the meaning of the Mental Health Act 1983 (see **11.2**);
  - ♦ otherwise has a significant impairment of intelligence and social functioning; or
  - ♦ has a physical disability or is suffering from a physical disorder (Youth Justice and Criminal Evidence Act 1999, s 16).

Intimidated victims

- Are those where the police/court are satisfied that the quality of evidence given by the victim is likely to be diminished by reason of fear or distress on the part of the victim in connection with testifying in the proceedings. The following must be taken into account—
  - ♦ the nature and alleged circumstances of the offence;
  - ♦ the age of the victim;
  - ♦ where relevant: social and cultural background and ethnic origins of the victim; the domestic and employment circumstances of the victim; any religious beliefs or political opinions of the victim;
  - ♦ any behaviour towards the victim on the part of the accused, members of the family, or associates of the accused, or any other person who is likely to be an accused or a witness in the proceedings.
- Any views expressed by the victim should be taken into account when assessing whether a victim is intimidated (Youth Justice and Criminal Evidence Act 1999, s 17).
- Victims may feel intimidated for a variety of reasons such as fears of threats or reprisals, no confidence in the police, bad experience with the CJS, feeling vulnerable and at risk.
- Intimidated victims have three key needs: safety, information, and support. For advice on dealing with intimidated witnesses see: Office for Criminal Justice Reform, Working with intimidated witnesses, November 2006.
- All reasonable steps must be taken to identify vulnerable or intimidated victims using the above criteria. Where such a victim may be called as a witness in criminal proceedings, special measures under the Youth Justice and Criminal Evidence Act 1999 must be considered (see below). (See also **13.2 'Child abuse'**, **13.6 'Hate incidents/Equality'**, and **13.7 'People with disabilities'**.)
  - ♦ the police should consult the vulnerable victim/witness and those who know them best to seek advice on communicating with them;
  - ♦ a 'supporter' should be present while a vulnerable witness is being interviewed;
  - ♦ when deciding where interviews should take place, account should be taken of the needs and the wishes of the vulnerable witness.

Special measures for vulnerable/intimidated witnesses in court proceedings

Some witnesses are eligible for **special assistance** in criminal proceedings. The measures of the Youth Justice and Criminal Evidence Act 1999 are available to vulnerable and intimidated witnesses (see above for meanings).

Special assistance

- The **special measures** include screening the witness from the accused; evidence by live-link; evidence given in private; removal of wigs and gowns; video-recorded evidence in chief and cross/ re-examination; examination through an intermediary; and aids to communication (Youth Justice and Criminal Evidence Act 1999, ss 23–30). (For further information see HOC 39/2005.)
- A video interview will not be needed in all cases. When dealing with a victim/witness who is a child or a vulnerable adult advice should be sought from the appropriate department regarding children and from a supervisory officer for vulnerable adults.
- MOJ Circular 4/2011 deals with the Coroners and Justice Act 2009 changes to 'special measures' for vulnerable and intimidated witnesses.

Video interview of evidence

MOJ Circular 3/2011 provides details about Vulnerable and Intimidated Witnesses: A Police Service Guide (March 2011) (published online); ACPO guidance 'Advice on the Structure of Visually Recorded Witness Interviews' (2010) and ACPO 'National Investigative Interviewing Strategy' guidance (2009) all reinforce good practice with regard to **Achieving Best Evidence**.

When video recording vulnerable and intimidated witnesses the following steps should be taken—

- early identification of vulnerable and intimidated witnesses;
- ensure local CJ agencies work together and with other agencies develop effective networks and protocols for sharing information as well as comprehensive awareness-raising and training;
- decide on video interview or written statement;
- obtain authorisation to video interview;
- witnesses under 18: record reasons for obtaining or for **not** obtaining video interview on the appropriate form;
- decide if any other special measures are applicable;
- on the appropriate forms: provide explanation on how the quality of the evidence (coherence, completeness, accuracy) would be improved by video interview. Include views of victim/witness;
- arrange for trained video interviewer to conduct interview;
- ensure that room is booked and witness is attending;
- complete short descriptive note of video interview on the appropriate forms.

Explanatory notes

- For each vulnerable or intimidated witness an MG2 form must be filled in.
- The MOJ Circular 3/2011 communicates the online publication of the 3rd edition of 'Achieving Best Evidence: Guidance on Interviewing Victims and Witnesses and Guidance on Using Special Measures' (2011).

Links to alternative subjects and offences

13.5 Forced Marriages

The Anti-social Behaviour, Crime and Policing Act 2014 deals with the criminal offence of forced marriage. Whereas the Family Law Act 1996 provides civil remedies regarding forced marriage and the offence of breaching a forced marriage protection order.

13.5.1 Forced marriage offences

Section 121 of the Anti-social Behaviour, Crime and Policing Act 2014 gives various offences relating to forced marriage.

Offences

(1) A person commits an offence under the law of England and Wales if he or she—
  (a) uses violence, threats or any other form of coercion for the purpose of causing another person to enter into a **marriage**, and
  (b) believes, or ought reasonably to believe, that the conduct may cause the other person to enter into the marriage without free and full consent.
(3) A person commits an offence under the law of England and Wales if he or she—
  (a) practises any form of deception with the intention of causing another person to leave the United Kingdom, and
  (b) intends the other person to be subjected to conduct outside the United Kingdom that is an offence under subsection (1) or would be an offence under that subsection if the victim were in England or Wales.

Anti-social Behaviour, Crime and Policing Act 2014, s 121

Points to prove

s 121(1) offence
✓ used violence/threats/other form of coercion
✓ in order to cause a person to enter into marriage
✓ believed/ought to have believed
✓ this conduct would cause that person
✓ to marry without free and full consent

s 121(3) offence
✓ practised any form of deception
✓ with intent to cause a person to leave UK

> ✓ intending that person to be subject of s 121(1) offence outside UK or
> ✓ would be subject to s 121(1) offence if victim were in England and Wales

Meaning of marriage

This means any religious or civil ceremony of marriage (whether or not legally binding).

Explanatory notes

- If the intended victim lacks capacity (under the Mental Capacity Act 2005) to consent to marriage, the offence under s 121(1) is capable of being committed by any conduct carried out for the purpose of causing the victim to enter into a marriage (whether or not the conduct amounts to violence, threats or any other form coercion).
- It is irrelevant whether the conduct mentioned in s 121(1)(a) is directed at the victim or another person.

Practical considerations

- A person commits an offence under s 121(1) or (3) only if, at the time of the conduct or deception—
  - ✦ the person or the victim or both of them are in England or Wales,
  - ✦ neither the person nor the victim is in England or Wales but at least one of them is habitually resident in England and Wales, or
  - ✦ neither the person nor the victim is in the United Kingdom but at least one of them is a **UK national**.
- The term **UK national** means an individual who is—
  - ✦ a British citizen, a British overseas territories citizen, a British National (Overseas) or a British Overseas citizen;
  - ✦ a person who under the British Nationality Act 1981 is a British subject; or
  - ✦ a British protected person within the meaning of that Act.
- HOC 10/2014 provides guidance, further information for these offences.
- If a forced marriage protection order is breached, then this is an offence under s 63CA of the Family Law Act 1996 (see **13.5.2**).
- Obtain a certified copy of the religious or civil marriage certificate and whether or not it is a legally binding marriage.

 E&S

 Either way   None

Summary: 6 months' imprisonment and/or a fine
Indictment: 7 years' imprisonment

13.5.2 Forced marriage: protection orders/ guidance

Section 120 of the Anti-social Behaviour, Crime and Policing Act 2014 inserted the offence of breaching a forced marriage protection order under s 63CA of the Family Law Act 1996 (see below).

It is important that the difference between an arranged marriage and a forced marriage is recognised and understood.

An **arranged** marriage is **an agreement** between both parties (usually prompted by the parents) entered into freely and is a practice that has worked successfully in several cultures for many centuries.

A **forced** marriage is where one or both of the parties have **not agreed** to marry and have been forced to do so **against their own free will**. Although it is mostly women who are affected by this, there are cases of men who are also forced to marry and they should be treated in exactly the same way as a woman making the report.

Sections 63A to 63S of the Family Law Act 1996 makes provision for protecting individuals against being forced to enter into marriage without their free and full consent. It provides powers for the courts to issue protection orders, and deal with other associated matters, together with the offence of breaching a marriage protection order, as follows—

- s 63A Forced marriage protection orders;
- s 63B Contents of forced marriage protection orders;
- s 63C Applications and other occasions for making orders;
- s 63CA Offence of breaching order:
  - ✦ s 63CA(1) A person who without reasonable excuse does anything that the person is prohibited from doing by a forced marriage protection order is guilty of an offence;
  - ✦ s 63CA(2) Where an order is made under s 63D(1) a person is liable for the s 63CA offence only if that person was aware of the existence of the order;
  - ✦ s 63CA(3) If a person is convicted of the s 63CA offence, that conduct is not punishable as a contempt of court;
  - ✦ s 63CA(4) If any conduct has been punished as a contempt of court, a person cannot be convicted of the s 63CA offence;
  - ✦ s 63CA(5) This is an 'Either way' offence and is liable— **Indictment**: 5 years' imprisonment and/or a fine; **Summary**: 6 months' imprisonment and/or a fine;
- s 63D Ex parte orders;
- s 63E Undertakings instead of orders;
- s 63F Duration of orders;
- s 63G Variation of orders and their discharge;
- s 63J Arrest under warrant;
- s 63K Remand: General;
- s 63L Remand: medical examination and report;
- s 63M Jurisdiction of courts;
- s 63O Contempt proceedings;

- s 63P Appeals;
- s 63Q Guidance;
- s 63R Other protection or assistance against forced marriage;
- s 63S Interpretation of sections 63A to 63R.

Apart from the above powers, there are criminal offences that can be committed by the family and (potential) husband/wife of the person when forcing someone into marriage such as forced marriage (see **13.5.1**), assaults (see **2.1**), false imprisonment or kidnapping (see **2.6**), and sexual offences (see **Chapter 6**).

Information contained in this section is based on official guidelines. However, any **force policy** must be adhered to and the information below is intended as a guide to be read in conjunction with any such policy.

The initial report

The most important factors when dealing with cases of forced marriage are the safety of the person, assurance, and confidentiality.

- The victim must be seen in a secure place and **on their own**.
- The nominated officer who has responsibility for such matters must be contacted as soon as possible; otherwise duty supervision must be notified.
- Reassure the victim about the confidentiality of police involvement.
- It is important to establish a safe and discreet means of contact with the victim in the future.
- Obtain full details to pass on to the nominated officer.
- Treat the victim in a respectful and sensitive manner and take into account their feelings and concerns.
- If the victim is under 18 then contact the Child Protection Department.

If the nominated officer is not available to deal with the incident, then there are additional steps to take to ensure that information is gathered and the safety of the victim is ensured as far as possible.

- Ask the victim if they would prefer an officer of a certain gender, race, nationality, or religion to deal with the report.
- Obtain full details of the victim, including National Insurance number and a copy of their passport.
- Make a record of any birthmarks, distinguishing features.
- Obtain a recent photograph or take a photograph of the victim (with the victim's consent).
- Create a restricted entry on the local intelligence system.
- Make sure that the victim has the contact details for the nominated officer.
- Perform a risk assessment in every case.
- Consider the forced marriage offence (see **13.5.1**), identify any other criminal offences and if appropriate submit a crime report.
- Secure any evidence in case of any future prosecutions.
- Keep a full record of all decisions made and the explanations for those decisions (including decisions not to take action).

13.5.2 Forced marriage: protection orders/guidance

- With the victim's consent refer them to local and national support groups (eg Honour Network—see **Appendix 1**).
- Tell them of their right to seek legal advice and representation.

Apart from taking the above actions: **do not**—

- Send them back to the family home against their wishes.
- Approach the family without express consent of the victim.
- Inform anyone of the situation without express consent of the individual.
- Attempt to mediate and reconcile the family.

There are different types of situations where the issue of forced marriage can arise—

- Fear of being forced to marry in the UK or abroad.
- Already in a forced marriage.
- A third party report.
- A spouse brought from abroad.

It is likely that the nominated officer will take over enquiries; however, it is advisable to be aware of the action to be taken in these situations.

Fear of being forced to marry in the UK or abroad

Additional steps to be taken as well as those listed above are—

- Obtain as much detail as possible about the victim's family both here and abroad including the intended spouse's details.
- Consider the offence of forced marriage (see **13.5.1**).
- Discuss with the person if there is any way of avoiding going abroad and if they did not go what difficulties that could cause.
- Obtain exact details of where the victim would be staying abroad.
- Ascertain if there is a family history of forced marriage.
- Report details of the case to the Forced Marriage Unit (FMU) at the Foreign and Commonwealth Office and pass on contact details (see **Appendix 1**) to the victim. The FMU provides advice and assistance to potential and actual victims of forced marriage. It works with partnership agencies both in the UK and abroad to assist those affected by forced marriage.

If the victim does travel abroad ensure the following—

- That they have details of their passport in a safe place.
- That they can learn at least one telephone number and email address of a trusted person.
- Ensure that they contact you on their return **without fail** and ask for an approximate return date.
- Decide on a code word so that if contact is made, verification of identity can be made.
- Advise they take emergency cash and details of a trusted person in that country.
- Ask the victim for details of a trusted person in the UK with whom they will be keeping in touch and whom you can contact in case of problems, ie if they do not return on specified date. Contact that person prior to the departure of the victim and pass on your or the nominated officer's contact details.

- Ensure they have the details of the nearest Embassy/British High Commission in the country they are visiting.

Already in a forced marriage

Additional steps to be taken as well as those listed above are—
- The offence of forced marriage (see **13.5.1**) came into force on 16 June 2014.
- Obtain details of the marriage, where, when, who, etc.
- Ascertain if any other family members are at risk.
- Take a statement about adverse behaviour towards the victim, such as threats and harassment (if appropriate).
- Refer the victim with their consent to local and national support groups.
- Establish a safe way to contact the victim and maintain contact with them.
- Refer the matter to the FMU (see **Appendix 1** for contact details) who not only provide advice and assistance to victims of forced marriage, but also assist with concerns about visa issues for parties who are overseas.
- Make a referral to social services and Child Protection Department if the victim is, or has children under, 18.

A third party report

Additional steps to be taken as well as those listed above are—
- Obtain contact details of the informant and stay in contact with them and advise them against making their own enquiries as this may jeopardise the official investigation.
- Ascertain the relationship between the informant and the potential victim.
- Find out as many details as possible such as where the victim is being held and in what circumstances, and if there is any evidence available to corroborate the story.
- Check missing persons reports to see if the victim is reported missing.
- Obtain as much information as possible about the victim's family and the intended spouse's family, and extended family in the UK and overseas.
- Obtain a recent photograph of the victim.
- Obtain some details (about the victim) that only the victim would know (an aid for verification of identity).
- Prior to contacting the police overseas it is essential to establish if any reliable links exist within that police force (this can be done through other police forces, Interpol and the Foreign and Commonwealth Office). **Do not** contact the force directly without making these enquiries.

A spouse brought from abroad

Additional steps to be taken as well as those listed above—
- Ensure that an independent authorised interpreter is available if required.

13.5.2 Forced marriage: protection orders/guidance

- Ensure the victim is put at ease as they may be very frightened, vulnerable, and isolated.
- Refer the victim with their consent to the relevant agencies and support groups, such as solicitors, immigration, and counselling.
- Notify domestic violence vulnerable witness coordinator if applicable.
- Refer to social services and Child Protection Department if the victim is, or has children under, 18.

Support and assistance

A national charity called Karma Nirvana has launched a confidential helpline called the 'Honour Network' which provides support to victims of 'Honour' based violence and forced marriages. The helpline number is 0800 5999 247.

All operators on the helpline are survivors of honour based violence and/or forced marriages, and give both practical and emotional support as well as advocating for callers if they wish.

This helpline is endorsed by the Home Office, FMU (see **Appendix 1** for contact details) and NPCC.

Links to alternative subjects and offences

13.6 **Hate Incidents/Equality**

The information in this section is based on guidelines established as 'best practice'. However, **force policies** and procedure must be adhered to and this section is intended to assist when these policies are being acted upon.

Hate crime/incidents

- A **hate incident** is any incident, which may or may not constitute a criminal offence, which is perceived by the victim or any other person, as being motivated by prejudice or hate.
- A **hate crime** is any hate incident, which constitutes a criminal offence, perceived by the victim or any other person, as being motivated by prejudice or hate.
- Hate crimes and hate incidents have to be distinguished. All hate crimes are hate incidents, but some hate incidents may not constitute a criminal offence and will not be recorded as hate crime. The police are responsible for data collection in relation to hate incidents and hate crimes.
- A hate crime/incident is determined by the **perception of the victim or any other person**. It is not relevant if there is no apparent motivation as the cause of an incident.
- The prejudice or hate perceived can be based on a number of factors: disability, age, religion, faith, sexual orientation, gender identity, race, etc. A victim of a hate incident does not have to be a member of a minority group or someone who is generally considered to be vulnerable. Anyone can be a victim of hate crime.
- For data recording purposes, the police have to specifically record hate incidents where the prejudice is based upon race, religion, sexual orientation, gender identity or disability.
- Romany Gypsies and Irish Travellers are specific ethnic groups. They are entitled to the full protection of the Equality Act 2010 and associated legislation outlawing racially aggravated conduct.
- Hate incidents may be related to **race, homophobia/sexual orientation, religion/belief**, or **disability. Homophobia** is an irrational fear and dislike of people who identify themselves as lesbian, gay, or bisexual.
- An incident where the effectiveness of the police response is likely to have a significant impact on the confidence of the victim, their family and/or their community is defined as a **critical incident**.
- The aim of a hate crime investigation is to identify and prosecute offenders to the satisfaction of the victim and the community, and seek to reduce repeat victimisation.

Legislation

- A witness statement may be admitted in evidence instead of the witness having to give oral evidence in certain circumstances, if the witness has made a written statement to a police officer (or similar investigator) and is prevented from testifying either in person or through fear (CJA 2003, s 116).

- The Crime and Disorder Act 1998 creates **racially or religiously aggravated** provisions of the following offences: assault, criminal damage, public order offence, harassment, and stalking (see **7.10**).
- Similarly ss 17 to 29N of the Public Order Act 1986 relate to offences of racial or religious hatred or hatred on the ground of sexual orientation (see **7.9**).
- With other offences, the courts are required to consider racial or religious hostility as an aggravating factor when sentencing (CJA 2003, s 145).
- Hostility based on disability or sexual orientation must also be taken into account as an aggravating factor in sentencing (CJA 2003, s 146).

Equality Act 2010

- Under the Equality Act 2010 it is unlawful for employers and providers of certain services (viz public and transport authorities—including the police) to discriminate against people with 'protected characteristics'.
- Section 4 of the Equality Act 2010 lists the characteristics which are protected under the Act. The following characteristics are **protected characteristics—**
  + age;
  + disability;
  + gender reassignment;
  + marriage and civil partnership;
  + pregnancy and maternity;
  + race;
  + religion or belief;
  + sex;
  + sexual orientation.

Reporting and recording of hate crime

- Ignorance, prejudice, and hostility are largely the basis for hate crime rather than personal gain.
- It is important that all police personnel, when dealing with hate crime victims, are aware of their unique needs and vulnerability.
- Hate crime is significantly under-reported. The reasons include negative perception of and experience with the police (including with police abroad) and the sense that reporting will not change anything.
- One should consider issues such as language, religion, and cultural/ lifestyle backgrounds and should do the utmost to meet the diverse needs of each victim; consider also specialist officers.
- Understanding and respect must be shown to the victim. See also **13.4 'Vulnerable Victim/Witness'**.
- It is essential to be aware that hate crime may escalate into a critical incident. Failure to provide an appropriate and professional response

to such reports could cause irreparable damage to future community confidence in the police service.

- An officer should attend the scene in response to any hate crime incident reported to provide reassurance and immediate support to the victim. It is vital that the level of support offered to the victim or witness is appropriate to their needs.
- Hate crime victims face the added trauma of knowing that the perpetrator's motivation may be an impersonal group hatred, relating to some feature that they will share with others.
- A crime that may normally have a minor impact becomes, with the hate element, a very intimate and hurtful attack that is likely to undermine the victim's quality of life.
- It should be explained to the victim that the details of the incident are likely to be shared with other agencies.
- The report of a hate crime should not be taken over the phone unless the victim expresses the wish to report it that way.
- A supervising officer has to be informed and should attend the scene.
- An officer of at least the rank of inspector has to be informed of any hate crime incident that may develop into a critical incident.
- Victims of possible homophobia should not be questioned regarding their sexuality. If they want to volunteer this information this should be recorded in the report. Where such information is provided it is vital that it remains confidential, otherwise disclosure could seriously erode their confidence in the police.
- Friends/family of the victim or witness may not have been told of their sexuality. Inadvertent disclosure could seriously erode their confidence in the police and that of the community they represent.
- Evidence of an offence is **not** required when **recording a hate incident**. There is no evidential test as to what is or is not a hate incident. All that is required is that the incident is perceived by the victim or another person as being motivated by prejudice or hate.
- If it is not immediately apparent that there is a hate element the person reporting should be asked the reasons for their belief. This should be recorded in order to assist identifying possible lines of enquiry. Incidents may be recorded as hate incidents at a later stage, if the victim discloses such a perception or the original perception changes.
- Even where the victim does not regard the incident as a hate incident police officers may identify it as such. This should be recorded in the appropriate manner. Victims may be unwilling to reveal that they are being targeted because of skin colour, religion, or lifestyle or may not be aware that they are a victim of hate crime even if this is apparent to other people.
- Where a hate incident is reported it **must be recorded** regardless of who reported it, whether a crime has been committed, and whether there is any evidence to identify the hate element.
- Individual forces use different hate incident report forms and the computerised Crime Reporting System.
- For further information see Home Office Police Standards Unit/ACPO, Hate Crime: Delivering a Quality Service, Good Practice and Tactical Guidance (2005).

- For contact details regarding Hate crime (Stop Hate UK); Homophobic abuse (Galop, London); Stonewall (Lesbian, gay, and bisexual advice) see **Appendix 1**.
- **Appendix 4** contains a list of the dates of religious events and celebrations of the main religions.

Links to alternative subjects and offences

13.7 **People with Disabilities**

Definition of disabled person

A person (P) has a **disability** if P has a **physical or mental impairment** and the impairment has a **substantial** and **long-term adverse effect** on P's ability to carry out normal day-to-day activities.

Equality Act 2010, s 6

Meanings

Long-term (Sch 1)

Means that the effect has to have lasted, or be likely to last, for at least 12 months or it is likely to last for the rest of the life of the person affected.

Notes: The Equality Act 2010 (Disability) Regulations 2010 (SI 2128/2010), made under the authority of the Equality Act 2010, provide the following meanings—

Disability (reg 7)

A person is deemed to have a disability, and hence to be a disabled person, for the purposes of the Act where that person is certified as blind, severely sight impaired, sight impaired, or partially sighted by a consultant ophthalmologist.

Physical or mental impairment (regs 3 and 4)

The following conditions do not amount to an impairment—

- addiction/dependency to alcohol, nicotine, or any other substance (unless it is the result of administration of medically prescribed drugs or other medical treatment);
- tendency to: set fires, steal, physical or sexual abuse of other persons;
- exhibitionism and voyeurism; and
- seasonal allergic rhinitis (unless it aggravates the effect of any other condition).

Substantial adverse effect (reg 5)

A severe disfigurement is not to be treated as having a substantial adverse effect on the ability of the person concerned to carry out normal day-to-day activities if it consists of—

- a tattoo (which has not been removed); or
- a piercing of the body for decorative or other non-medical purposes, including any object attached through the piercing for such purposes.

Explanatory notes

- Under the Equality Act 2010 it is unlawful for employers and providers of certain services (viz public and transport authorities—including the police) to discriminate against people with 'protected characteristics' as given in s 4 (this includes disability) (see **13.6**).

13.7 People with Disabilities

- Certain words and phrases used may cause offence as preferences vary, so you should be prepared to ask the person. Terms such as 'the disabled' or 'the blind' should be avoided, and expressions like 'disabled people' or 'people with disabilities' used instead. Other terms to be used include 'mental health problems', 'learning difficulties', 'partially sighted', 'visually impaired', 'deaf and without speech', 'hard of hearing', 'a deaf person', 'short stature/restricted growth', 'a wheelchair user/physical disability'.
- Assumptions should not be made about what disabilities a person may have or what assistance they may require, always ask the individual and wait for any offer of assistance to be accepted before attempting to help.
- You should always speak directly to the disabled person, not through any companion, however severe the impairment may seem.

Visual impairments

- A white cane is often used by visually impaired people, a red and white one by deaf and blind people.
- When meeting visually impaired people you should introduce yourself clearly as well as other people present and indicate where they are located. The use of people's names makes clear who is being addressed.
- If you are using a personal radio tell the person about it as the noise may startle them.
- Use format as preferred by the disabled person, for example large print, Braille, audio cassettes. Typed or printed text is easier to read than handwritten.
- In unfamiliar areas you should describe the layout as well as any hazards. People should be guided to their seat and be told if someone wants to offer assistance. Also, they should be told if someone leaves a room, or if they will be left on their own.
- During the search of premises the person should be told what is being done. All items should be returned to their original position.

Deaf or hard of hearing

- There are various degrees of impairment of hearing. Therefore, communication has to be adapted to the wishes of the individual.
- Hearing loops or qualified British Sign Language interpreters may be used for interviews or meetings.
- Finger-spelling may be used as an alternative to sign language.
- Many people use lip-reading to reinforce what they hear, some, who have no hearing at all, use this alone. This is a demanding and tiring skill. To assist keep background noise low; make sure the deaf person is looking at the speaker before they begin to speak; the speaker should look directly at the person and make sure the speaker's face is clearly visible; the speaker should stop talking if they must turn away, and not speak with their back to the light source. You should speak clearly and at an even pace, but not exaggerate lip movement or gestures or block the mouth with hands, food, or cigarettes. Written

notes can help to present complicated information. Check regularly that everything has been understood.

- Also consider using RNID (Royal National Institute for Deaf People) Text Direct or Typetalk, a textphone service that enables deaf, deaf-blind, hard of hearing, or speech-impaired people to communicate with hearing people anywhere by telephone (see **Appendix 1**).

Speech impairment

- You should not assume that speech and language defects are caused by alcohol or drugs. Slow or impaired speech does not reflect a person's intelligence.
- You should not correct or speak for other persons, but wait while they speak and let them finish their sentence.
- It might help to break down questions, to deal with individual points, rather than with complex matters, so that short answers can be given.

Learning difficulties and disabilities

- People with such difficulties should be treated in a manner appropriate for their age.
- You should make sure that everything has been understood.
- It is helpful to repeat questions in plain, clear language if there are doubts.
- PACE Codes must be complied with when dealing with people who have a learning difficulty or mental illness. For example Code C, s 3, paras 3.12 to 3.20 deal with special groups such as the deaf, juveniles, mentally disordered, or otherwise mentally vulnerable when brought to a police station under arrest or if arrested at the police station (see **12.2.2**).

Wheelchair users

- You should use the term 'wheelchair user', not 'wheelchair bound'.
- When communicating with a wheelchair user, it is best to stand back far enough to maintain eye contact comfortably.
- Help with doors, steps, and kerbs should be offered, but you should not attempt to push the wheelchair without asking if help is required.
- Leaning on a wheelchair is often regarded as a major personal intrusion.

Links to alternative subjects and offences

Useful Contacts

ACPO (See **NPCC**)

Alcohol Concern
<http://www.alcoholconcern.org.uk> accessed 27 May 2015
Telephone: 020 7566 9800
Helpline (Drinkline): 0300 123 1110

Ask the police FAQ (see **PNLD**)

British Association of Women Police
<http://www.bawp.org> accessed 27 May 2015
Telephone: 07790 505204

CEOP (Child Exploitation and Online Protection Centre)
<http://www.ceop.police.uk> accessed 27 May 2015
Telephone: 0870 000 3344

Childline
<http://www.childline.org.uk> accessed 27 May 2015
Telephone: 0800 1111

Citizens Advice Bureau (provides local links)
<http://www.citizensadvice.org.uk> accessed 27 May 2015

CPS (Crown Prosecution Service)
<http://www.cps.gov.uk> accessed 27 May 2015
Telephone: 020 3357 0000

Crime Stoppers
<http://www.crimestoppers-uk.org> accessed 27 May 2015
Telephone: 0800 555 111

DEFRA (Department for Environment, Food and Rural Affairs)
<https://www.gov.uk/government/organisations/department-for-
environment-food-rural-affairs> accessed 15 April 2015
Telephone: 03459 33 55 77

Department for Transport (see **Transport**)

Disclosure and Barring Service (DBS)
<https://www.gov.uk/government/organisations/disclosure-and-barring-
service/> accessed 27 May 2015
Telephone: 03000 200 190

Appendix 1: Useful Contacts

Domestic Violence (see **National Domestic Violence Helpline**)

DVLA (Driver and Vehicle Licensing Agency)
<https://www.gov.uk/government/organisations/driver-and-vehicle-licensing-agency> accessed 27 May 2015
Provides links to service required

DVSA (Driver and Vehicle Standards Agency)
<https://www.gov.uk/government/organisations/driver-and-vehicle-standards-agency> accessed 27 May 2015
Provides links to service required

Equality and Human Rights Commission (EHRC)
<http://www.equalityhumanrights.com> accessed 27 May 2015
Telephone (Equality Advisory Support Service): 0808 800 0082

European Commission
<http://ec.europa.eu/index_en.htm> accessed 27 May 2015
Telephone: 00800 67891011

Forced Marriage Unit (see **Honour Network** for victim support)
<https://www.gov.uk/forced-marriage> accessed 27 May 2015
Telephone: 020 7008 0151 Outside office hours: 020 7008 1500

Foreign & Commonwealth Office
<http://www.gov.uk/government/organisations/foreign-commonwealth-office> accessed 27 May 2015
Telephone: 020 7008 1500

GMB (Union)
<http://www.gmb.org.uk> accessed 27 May 2015
Telephone: 020 7391 6700

GOV.UK (Government official information)
<https://www.gov.uk> accessed 27 May 2015

GOV.UK (Driving licence categories/ages/rules)
Categories <https://www.gov.uk/driving-licence-categories>
Ages <https://www.gov.uk/vehicles-can-drive> accessed 27 May 2015

Hate crime (Stop Hate UK)
<http://www.stophateuk.org> accessed 27 May 2015
Telephone: 0113 293 5100

Highways Agency
<http://www.highways.gov.uk> accessed 27 May 2015
Telephone: 0300 123 5000

HMCTS (Her Majesty's Courts & Tribunals Service)
<https://www.gov.uk/government/organisations/hm-courts-and-tribunals-service> accessed 27 May 2015
Provides links to courts/tribunals and other justice agencies

HMIC (HM Inspectorate of Constabulary)
<http://www.justiceinspectorates.gov.uk/hmic> accessed 27 May 2015
Telephone: 020 3513 0500

HM Prison Service
<https://www.gov.uk/government/organisations/hm-prison-service>
accessed 27 May 2015
Telephone: 0300 047 6325

HMRC (HM Revenue & Customs)
<https://www.gov.uk/government/organisations/hm-revenue-customs>
accessed 27 May 2015
Telephone: 0800 59 5000 (fraud)

Home Office
<http://www.gov.uk/government/organisations/home-office> accessed
27 May 2015
Telephone: 020 7035 4848

Homophobic abuse (London)
<http://www.galop.org.uk> accessed 27 May 2015
Telephone: 020 7704 2040

Honour Network (honour violence and forced marriages)
<http://www.karmanirvana.org.uk> accessed 17 March 2014
Telephone: 0800 5999 247

Hope for Justice (human trafficking and slavery)
<http://www.hopeforjustice.org.uk> accessed 27 May 2015
Telephone: 0845 519 7402

HSE (Health and Safety Executive)
<http://www.hse.gov.uk> accessed 27 May 2015
Incident Contact Centre: 0345 300 9923

Identity and Passport Service (Agency of the Home Office)
<https://www.gov.uk/government/organisations/hm-passport-office>
accessed 27 May 2015
Telephone: 0300 222 0000

Information Commissioner (data protection/freedom of information)
<http://www.ico.org.uk> accessed 27 May 2015
Telephone: 0303 123 1113

Intellectual Property Office
<http://www.gov.uk/government/organisations/intellectual-property-office> accessed 27 May 2015
Telephone: 0300 300 2000

International Police Association
<http://www.ipa-uk.org> accessed 27 May 2015
Telephone: 0115 981 3638

Appendix 1: Useful Contacts

IPCC (Independent Police Complaints Commission)
<http://www.ipcc.gov.uk> accessed 27 May 2015
Telephone: 030 0020 0096

Law Society
<http://www.lawsociety.org.uk> accessed 27 May 2015
Telephone: 020 7242 1222

Legislation
<http://www.legislation.gov.uk/> accessed 27 May 2015

Mental illness advice (SANE)
<http://www.sane.org.uk> accessed 27 May 2015
Telephone: 020 7375 1002 Helpline: 0300 304 7000

MIB (Motor Insurers' Bureau)
<http://www.mib.org.uk> accessed 27 May 2015

Ministry of Justice
<https://www.gov.uk/government/organisations/ministry-of-justice>
accessed 27 May 2015
Provides links to MOJ and other justice agencies
Telephone: 020 3334 3555

Missing persons (National Missing Persons Helpline)
<https://www.missingpeople.org.uk> accessed 28 May 2015
Telephone: 020 8392 4590 or Freefone: 116 000

National Black Police Association
<http://www.nbpa.co.uk> accessed 28 May 2015
Telephone: 07921 095262

National Domestic Violence Helpline (women and children)
<http://www.womensaid.org.uk> accessed 28 May 2015
Telephone: 0808 2000 247

National Domestic Violence Helpline (men)
<http://www.mankind.org.uk> accessed 28 May 2015
Telephone: 01823 334244

National Stalking Helpline
<http://www.stalkinghelpline.org> accessed 28 May 2015
Telephone(Support): 0808 802 0300

NCA (National Crime Agency)
<http://www.nationalcrimeagency.gov.uk> accessed 28 May 2015
Telephone: 0370 496 7622

NPCC (National Police Chiefs' Council—formerly **ACPO**)
<http://www.npcc.police.uk> accessed 27 May 2015
Telephone: 020 7084 8950

NSPCC (National Society for Prevention of Cruelty to Children)
<https://www.nspcc.org.uk> accessed 28 May 2015
Telephone: 0808 800 5000
ChildLine: 0800 1111

Parliament
<http://www.parliament.uk> accessed 28 May 2015

PNLD (Police National Legal Database)
<http://www.pnld.co.uk> accessed 28 May 2015
email: <pnld@westyorkshire.pnn.police.uk>
Telephone: 01924 294086

PNLD (**Ask the police FAQ** database)
<https://www.askthe.police.uk> accessed 28 May 2015

Police Federation
<http://www.polfed.org> accessed 28 May 2015
Telephone: 01372 352000

Rape (rape counselling and advice service)
<http://www.rapecrisis.org.uk> accessed 28 May 2015
Telephone: 0808 802 9999

Revenue & Customs (see **HMRC**)

RNID (Royal National Institute for Deaf People)
<http://www.actionhearingloss.org.uk> accessed 28 May 2015
Telephone: 0808 808 0123 Textphone: 0808 808 9000

RSPB (Royal Society for the Protection of Birds)
<https://www.rspb.org.uk> accessed 28 May 2015
Telephone: 01767 693 690

RSPCA (Royal Society for the Prevention of Cruelty to Animals)
<http://www.rspca.org.uk> accessed 28 May 2015
Telephone: 0300 1234 999

Samaritans (organisation)
<http://www.samaritans.org> accessed 28 May 2015
Telephone: 08457 90 90 90

Sentencing Council (Sentencing Guidelines)
<http://www.sentencingcouncil.org> accessed 28 May 2015
Telephone: 020 7071 5793

Stonewall (lesbian, gay, and bisexual charity)
<https://www.stonewall.org.uk> accessed 28 May 2015
Telephone: 0800 050 2020

Superintendents' Association
<http://www.policesupers.com> accessed 28 May 2015
Telephone: 0118 984 4005

Appendix 1: Useful Contacts

Trading Standards (Provides advice/contact details)
<http://www.tradingstandards.uk> accessed 28 May 2015

Transport (Department for Transport)
<https://www.gov.uk/government/organisations/department-for-transport> accessed 28 May 2015
Provides aviation, rail, roads, and shipping links
Telephone: 0300 330 3000

UK Intellectual Property Office
<https://www.gov.uk/government/organisations/intellectual-property-office> accessed 28 May 2015
Telephone: 0300 300 2000

UKMPB (UK Missing Persons Bureau)
<http://missingpersons.police.uk> accessed 28 May 2015
Telephone: 0845 000 5481

Unison (union)
<http://www.unison.org.uk> accessed 28 May 2015
Telephone: 0800 0 857 857

Victim Support
<https://www.victimsupport.org.uk> accessed 28 May 2015
Telephone: 0808 1689 111

VIPER® Video Identification Parade Electronic Recording
<http://www.viper.police.uk> accessed 28 May 2015
Telephone: 01274 373880

VOSA (see **DVSA**)

Youth Justice Board
<https://www.gov.uk/government/organisations/youth-justice-board-for-england-and-wales> accessed 28 May 2015
Telephone: 020 3334 5300

Appendix 2

Traffic Data—Vehicle Categories and Groups

This table is for guidance only as more details could apply than are given in this Appendix. In some instances a road traffic/policing officer should be consulted to confirm matters.

Some driving licence categories and minimum ages changed for new licence holders on 19/1/13, particularly new categories/ages for mopeds (AM, P and Q). For further details see GOV.UK in Appendix 1.

Vehicle description	Category	Minimum age
Mopeds[1]	P	16
Light motorcycles[2]	A1	17
Motorcycles[3]	A	17
Any sized motorcycle with or without sidecar	A	21[a]
3- or 4-wheeled light vehicles[4]	B1	17[b]
Cars[5]	B	17[c]
Automatic cars (with automatic transmission)	B Automatic	17[c]
Cars with trailers exceeding 750 kg[6]	B + E	17
Medium-sized Goods vehicles[7]	C1	18[d]
Medium-sized Goods vehicles combination[8]	C1 + E	21[d]

[1] Mopeds with an engine capacity not exceeding 50 cc and a maximum design speed not exceeding 50 km/hr.

[2] Light motorcycles not exceeding 125 cc and power output not exceeding 11 kW (14.6 bhp).

[3] Motorcycles up to 25 kW (33 bhp) with power to weight ratio not exceeding 0.16 kW/kg.

[4] Motor tricycles or quadricycles with design speed exceeding 50 km/hr and up to 550 kg unladen.

[5] Motor vehicles up to 3500 kg/not more than 8 passenger seats/trailer up to 750 kg; or vehicle and trailer up to 3500 kg **and** the trailer does not exceed unladen weight of towing vehicle.

[6] Where the combination does not come within category B.

[7] Lorries 3500–7500 kg, with a trailer **up to** 750 kg.

[8] Trailer exceeds 750 kg. Total weight up to 12000 kg and trailer is less than weight of towing lorry.

[a] Or two years after passing test on a standard motorcycle.[3] If owned or driven by armed forces—17 years.

[b] 16 if receiving disability living allowance at higher rate, providing no trailer is drawn.

[c] 16 if receiving disability living allowance at higher rate.

[d] 18 if combination weight is under 7500 kg.

Notes: If category B test was prior to 1/1/97 then some of the restrictions as to weight, passengers and trailers may not apply.

Appendix 2: Traffic Data—Vehicle Categories and Groups

Descriptions of Vehicle Categories and Minimum Ages

Vehicle description	Category	Minimum age
Large Goods vehicles[9] Large Goods vehicles[10]	C C + E	21[e] 21[e]
Minibuses[11] Minibuses[12]	D1 D1 + E	21[f] 21[f]
Buses[13] Buses[14]	D D + E	21[f] 21
Agricultural tractors	F	17[g]
Road rollers	G	21[h]
Tracked vehicles	H	21[i]
Mowing machines or pedestrian controlled vehicles	K	16

[9]   Vehicles over 3500 kg, with trailer **up to** 750 kg.

[10] Vehicles over 3500 kg, with trailer **over** 750 kg.

[11] With 9–16 passenger seats, and trailer **up to** 750 kg.

[12] With 9–16 passenger seats, and trailer **over** 750 kg. Provided total weight does not exceed 12000 kg and trailer does not exceed weight of towing lorry.

[13] More than 8 passenger seats, with trailer **up to** 750 kg.

[14] More than 8 passenger seats, with trailer **over** 750 kg.

[e]   17 if member of armed forces or 18 if member of young drivers scheme.

[f]   17 if member of armed forces or 18 while learning to drive or taking PCV test or CPC initial qualification.

[g]   16 if tractor less than 2.45 m wide. Trailer less than 2.45 m (2 wheel) or 4 wheels if close coupled.

[h]   17 for small road rollers with metal or hard rollers. Must not be steam powered, weigh more than 11.69 tonnes, or be made for carrying loads.

[i]   17 if the total weight of the tracked vehicle does not exceed 3500 kg.

B category exception

If the driver has held a car driving licence (category/group B) before 1 January 1997, then that person can (without taking separate tests) drive:

- a car and trailer exceeding 750 kg (B + E);
- motor vehicles 3500–7500 kg, with trailers up to a combined weight of 8250 kg (C1 + E);
- passenger vehicles with 9–16 passenger seats, not used for hire or reward (D1 and D1 + E).

These entitlements last for the duration of the licence, without being required to undergo a medical.

However, when the licence expires or is no longer in force, then that person will be required to pass the relevant test and medical examination (as required by new licence holders).

Comparison Guide—Original Groups to Current Categories

This table is for guidance only as more details could apply than are given in this Appendix. In some instances a road traffic/policing officer should be consulted to confirm matters.

Vehicle description	Current category	Original group/class
Moped	P	E
Motorcycles[15]	A	D
3- or 4-light wheeled vehicles[16]	B1	C
Invalid carriages	B1 Limited	J
Cars[17]	B	A
Cars—with trailers over 750 kg	B + E	A
Automatic cars	B Automatic	B
Medium-sized goods vehicles[18]	C1	A
Medium-sized goods vehicles[19]	C1 + E	A
Large goods vehicles[20]	C	HGV 2/3
Large goods vehicles[21]	C + E	HGV 2/3
Buses[22]	D1	A
Buses[23]	D	PSV 3
Buses[24]	D Limited	PSV 3
Buses[25]	D Limited	PSV 4

[15] With or without sidecar.

[16] Motor tricycles or quadricycles with design speed exceeding 50 km/hr and up to 550 kg unladen weight. If they exceed 550 kg they fall into a car category—B category.

[17] Includes cars or light vans up to 8 passenger seats and up to 3500 kg.

[18] Gross vehicle weight between 3500–7500 kg, with trailer up to 750 kg. The combined weight not to exceed 8250 kg.

[19] Gross vehicle weight between 3500–7500 kg, with trailer over 750 kg. The combined weight not to exceed 8250 kg.

[20] Gross weight of vehicle being over 3500 kg, with trailer up to 750 kg.

[21] Gross weight of vehicle being over 3500 kg, with trailer over 750 kg.

[22] Capacity between 9–16 passengers—not used for hire reward.

[23] Any bus with more than 8 passenger seats, with trailer up to 750 kg.

[24] Vehicles limited to 16 passenger seats.

[25] Vehicles with more than 8 passenger seats, but no longer than 5.5 m.

Firearms Offences Relating to Age

Under 18 offence

- Using a firearm for a purpose not authorised by the European weapons directive (despite lawful entitlement to possess—being the holder of a firearms/shotgun certificate).

Any firearm/ammunition

- Purchase or hire any firearm or ammunition of any other description (see **8.7.1**).
- Sell or let on hire any firearm or ammunition of any other description (see **8.7.1**).

'Section 1' firearm/ammunition

- Purchase or hire s 1 firearm/ammunition (see **8.7.1**).
- Sell or let on hire or hire s 1 firearm/ammunition (see **8.7.1**).

Shotgun/cartridges

- Purchase or hire shotgun/cartridges (see **8.7.1**).
- Sell or let on hire or hire shotgun/cartridges (see **8.7.1**).

Air weapon/ammunition

- Purchase or hire an air weapon or ammunition for an air weapon (see **8.7.1**).
- Sell or let on hire or hire an air weapon or ammunition for an air weapon (see **8.7.1**).
- Make a gift of an air weapon or ammunition for an air weapon (see **8.7.2**).
- Part with possession of an air weapon or ammunition for an air weapon *subject to exceptions below* (see **8.7.2**).
- Have an air weapon or ammunition for an air weapon (see **8.7.2**), *except if—*

  - that person is under the supervision of a person of or over the age of 21;
  - member of approved rifle clubs;
  - using at authorised shooting galleries (not exceeding .23 inch calibre);
  - that person has attained the age of 14 and is on private premises with the consent of the occupier, and is under the supervision of a person of or over the age of 21, but it is an offence for the

supervisor to allow him to fire any missiles beyond those premises (subject to defence—see **8.7.2**).

Imitation firearm

- Purchase an imitation firearm (see **8.7.5**).
- Sell an imitation firearm (see **8.7.5**).

Under 15 offences (shotgun/cartridges)

- Have an assembled shotgun except while under the supervision of a person of or over the age of 21, or while the shotgun is so covered with a securely fastened gun cover that it cannot be fired (see **8.2.2**).
- Make a gift of a shotgun or ammunition for a shotgun to a person under the age of 15 (see **8.2.2**).

Under 14 offences ('Section 1' firearm/ammunition)

- Possess s 1 firearm or ammunition (see **8.1.3**), except for—
  - ◆ use of a certificate holder, being under their instructions, and for sporting purposes only;
  - ◆ a member of an approved cadet corps when engaged as a member of the corps in or in connection with drill or target shooting;
  - ◆ a person conducting or carrying on a miniature rifle or shooting gallery for air weapons or miniature rifles not exceeding .23 inch calibre;
  - ◆ using such rifles/ammunition at such a range or gallery.
- Part with possession of a s 1 firearm or ammunition to a person under 14, subject to above exceptions (see **8.1.3**).
- Make a gift of or lend s 1 firearm or ammunition to a person under 14 (see **8.1.3**).

Religious Dates/Events

Advisory notes: These dates are provided for guidance purposes only. Some dates may vary as the festivals are guided by the lunar calendar and some local customs may also vary the date. The religions are listed alphabetically.

	2015	2016
Baha'l		
World Religion Day	18 January 2015	18 January 2016
Naw-Rúz (New Year)	21 March 2015	21 March 2016
First Day of Ridvan	21 April 2015	21 April 2016
Last Day of Ridvan	2 May 2015	2 May 2016
Declaration of the Báb	23 May 2015	24 May 2016
Ascension of Baha'u'llah	29 May 2015	29 May 2016
Martyrdom of the Báb	9 July 2015	10 July 2016
Birth of the Báb	20 October 2015	20 October 2016
Birth of Baha'u'llah	12 November 2015	12 November 2016
Day of the Covenant	26 November 2015	26 November 2016
Ascension of 'Abdu'l-Baha	28 November 2015	28 November 2016
Buddhist		
Mahayana Buddhist New Year	5–7 January 2015	24-27 January 2016
Paranirvana Day	8 February 2015	8 February 2016
Nirvana Day (alternative date)	15 February 2015	15 February 2016
Magha Puja Day	5 March 2015	23 March 2016
Therevadin Buddhist New Year	4 April 2015	22 April 2016
Wesak (Buddha Day)	3 May 2015	2 May 2016
Asalha (Puja Day)	2 July 2015	19 July 2016
Obon (Ulambana)	13–15 July 2015	13–15 July 2016
Bodhi Day (Rohatsu)	8 December 2015	8 December 2016

Appendix 4: Religious Dates/Events

	2015	2016
Catholic		
Mary Mother of God	1 January 2015	1 January 2016
Blessing of the Animals (Hispanic)	17 January 2015	17 January 2016
Corpus Christi	4 June 2015	26 May 2016
Sacred Heart of Jesus	19 June 2015	3 June 2016
St Benedict Day	11 July 2015	11 July 2016
Assumption of Blessed Virgin Mary	15 August 2015	15 August 2016
St Francis' Day	4 October 2015	4 October 2016
All Souls' Day	2 November 2015	2 November 2016
Immaculate Conception of Mary	8 December 2015	8 December 2016
Feast Day—Our Lady of Guadalupe	12 December 2015	12 December 2016
Feast of the Holy Family	27 December 2015	30 December 2016
Chinese		
Lunar New Year	18 February 2015	8 February 2016
Christian		
Twelfth Night	5 January 2015	5 January 2016
Epiphany	6 January 2015	6 January 2016
Shrove Tuesday	17 February 2015	9 February 2016
Ash Wednesday (Lent begins)	18 February 2015	10 February 2016
St David's Day	1 March 2015	1 March 2016
St Patrick's Day	17 March 2015	17 March 2016
Palm Sunday	29 March 2015	20 March 2016
Maundy Thursday	2 April 2015	24 March 2016
Good Friday	3 April 2015	25 March 2016
Easter Day	5 April 2015	27 March 2016
St George's Day	23 April 2015	23 April 2016
Ascension Day	2 May 2015	5 May 2016
Whit Sunday (Pentecost)	24 May 2015	15 May 2016
Trinity Sunday	31 May 2015	22 May 2016
Lammas	1 August 2015	1 August 2016
All Hallows Eve	31 October 2015	31 October 2016
Advent Sunday	29 November 2015	27 November 2016

Appendix 4: Religious Dates/Events

St Andrew's Day	30 November 2015	30 November 2016
Christmas Day	25 December 2015	25 December 2016

Hindu

Vasant Panchami (Saraswati's Day)	24 January 2015	12 February 2016
Maha Shivaratri	17 February 2015	8 March 2016
Holi	6 March 2015	23 March 2016
New Year	21 March 2015	8 April 2016
Ramayana Begins	21 March 2015	8 April 2016
Ramanavami	28 March 2015	15 April 2016
Hanuman Jayanti	4 April 2015	22 April 2016
Guru Purnima	31 July 2015	19 July 2016
Raksha Bandhan	29 August 2015	18 August 2016
Krishna Janmashtami	5 September 2015	25 August 2016
Ganesa Chaturthi	17 September 2015	5 September 2016
Navaratri first Day	13 October 2015	1 October 2016
Navaratri Ends	21 October 2015	10 October 2016
Dasera	22 October 2015	11 October 2016
Diwali (Deepavali)	11 November 2015	30 October 2016

Islam

Mawlid-al-Nabi (Birth of Prophet)	3 January 2015	12 December 2016
Lailat Al-Isra wa Al-Miraj (Ascension to Heaven)	16 May 2015	5 May 2016
Lailat al Bara'ah (Night of Emancipation)	2 June 2015	21 May 2016
Commencement of Ramadhan (Fasting)	18 June 2015	6 June 2016
Laylat el qadr	23 July 2014	1 July 2016
Eid Al-Fitr (Completion of Fasting)	29 July 2014	7 July 2016
Waqf al Arafa (Hajj—Pilgrimage Day)	22 September 2015	10 September 2016
Eid-al-Addha (Day of Sacrifice)	23 September 2015	11 September 2016
Muharram (Islamic New Year)	14 October 2015	2 October 2016
Day of Ashura	23 October 2015	12 October 2016

Jehovah's Witness

Lord's Evening Meal	15 April 2015	23 March 2016

	2015	2016
## Jewish		

Notes: All Jewish holidays commence/start on the evening before the actual day specified, as the Jewish day actually begins at sunset on the previous night.

	2015	2016
Rosh Chodesh Sh'vat	21 January 2015	11 January 2016
Tu B'Shvat	4 February 2015	25 January 2016
Shabbat Shekalim	14 February 2015	5 March 2016
Rosh Chodesh Adar	20 February 2015	9 February 2016
Ta'anit Esther	4 March 2015	23 March 2016
Shabbat Zachor	28 February 2015	19 February 2016
Purim	5 March 2015	24 March 2016
Shushan Purim	6 March 2015	25 March 2016
Shabbat Parah	14 March 2015	2 April 2016
Shabbat HaChodesh	21 March 2015	9 April 2016
Rosh Chodesh Nisan	21 March 2015	9 April 2016
Shabbat HaGadol	28 March 2015	16 April 2016
Ta'anit Bechorot	2 April 2015	22 April 2016
Pesach	4 April 2015	23 April 2016
Yom HaShoah	16 April 2015	5 May 2016
Rosh Chodesh Iyyar	19 April 2015	8 May 2016
Yom HaAtzma'ut	23 April 2015	12 May 2016
Yom HaZikaron	22 April 2015	11 May 2016
Lag B'Omer	7 May 2015	26 May 2016
Yom Yerushalayim	17 May 2015	5 June 2016
Rosh Chodesh Sivan	19 May 2015	7 June 2016
Shavuot	24–25 May 2015	12–13 June 2016
Rosh Chodesh Tamuz	17 June 2015	6 July 2016
Tzom Tammuz	5 July 2015	24 July 2016
Rosh Chodesh Av	28 July 2015	5 August 2016
Shabbat Hazon	25 July 2015	25 July 2016
Tish'a B'Av	26 July 2015	14 August 2016
Shabbat Nachamu	1 August 2015	20 August 2016
Rosh Chodesh Elul	15 August 2015	3 September 2016
Rosh Hashana	14–15 September 2015	14–15 September 2016
Tzom Gedaliah	16 September 2015	16 September 2016
Shabbat Shuva	19 September 2015	19 September 2016
Yom Kippur	23 September 2015	23 September 2016
Sukkot	28 September 2015	28 September 2016
Shmini Atzeret	5 October 2015	5 October 2016
Simchat Torah	6 October 2015	6 October 2016

Rosh Chodesh Cheshvan	13 October 2015	13 October 2016
Rosh Chodesh Kislev	12 November 2015	12 November 2016
Chanukah	5–14 December 2015	5–14 December 2016

Sikh

Birthday of Guru Gobind Singh Ji	5 January 2015	5 January 2016
Maghi	13 January 2015	13 January 2016
Hola Mohalla	6 March 2015	24 March 2016
Baisakhi (Vaisakhi)	14 April 2015	14 April 2016
Martyrdom of Guru Arjan Dev Ji	16 June 2015	16 June 2016
Installation of Scriptures as Guru Granth	20 October 2015	20 October 2016
Diwali (Deepavali)	11 November 2015	30 October 2016
Birthday of Guru Nanak Dev Ji	25 November 2015	14 November 2016
Martyrdom of Guru Tegh Bahadur Ji	24 November 2015	24 November 2016

Index

Index

Index

Index

Index

Index

Index

Index

Index

Index

Index

Index

Index

Index

Index

Index

Index

Index

Index

Index

Index

Index

Index

Index

Index

Index

Index